STUDIES IN EAST ASIAN BUDDHISM 24

Conceiving the Indian Buddhist Patriarchs in China

Stuart H. Young

A Kuroda Institute Book
University of Hawai'i Press
Honolulu

Printed in the United States of America

20 19 18 17 16 15   6 5 4 3 2 1

Library of Congress Cataloging-in-Publication Data

Young, Stuart H., author.
Conceiving the Indian Buddhist patriarchs in China / Stuart H. Young.
pages cm — (Studies in East Asian Buddhism ; 24)
"A Kuroda Institute book."
Includes bibliographical references and index.
ISBN 978-0-8248-4120-1
1. Buddhist hagiography—China—History. 2. Buddhist saints—Historiography. 3. Buddhism—China—History—To 581. 4. Buddhism—China—History—581-960. I. Title. II. Series: Studies in East Asian Buddhism ; no. 24.
BQ636.Y68 2015
294.3'610951—dc23
2014031133

The Kuroda Institute for the Study of Buddhism and Human Values is a nonprofit, educational corporation founded in 1976. One of its primary objectives is to promote scholarship on the historical, philosophical, and cultural ramifications of Buddhism. In association with the University of Hawai'i Press, the Institute also publishes Classics in East Asian Buddhism, a series devoted to the translation of significant texts in the East Asian Buddhist tradition.

University of Hawai'i Press books are printed on acid-free paper and meet the guidelines for permanence and durability of the Council on Library Resources.

Printed by Sheridan Books, Inc.

Contents

Acknowledgments

THANKS:

To my family—Mom, Dad, Jess, Ba, Nia, Evan, Chen Ayi, Meimei, and BB—without whom I would not be.

To James Benn, for reading everything I've written over the past fifteen years, including various incarnations of this book; for sage advice at every turn along my career path; and for being my very good mentor and friend.

To Stephen (Buzzy) Teiser and Jackie Stone, who artfully supervised my postgraduate education, who provide models of scholarship that I will always try to emulate, and whose support (and numerous letters of recommendation) helped pave my way to gainful employment.

To Chen Jinhua 陳金華, for scrutinizing all of my translations from Chinese, in this book and elsewhere; for inviting me to give research presentations at the University of British Columbia; and for supporting me through the early stages of my academic career.

To my great teachers of years past, Frederick Sontag and Tadeusz Skorupski, who inspired this once-young student to pursue his work with both rigor and imagination.

To Sue Naquin, Jeff Stout, and Lu Yang 陸揚, who showed me different dimensions of what it means to be a professional scholar and who helped shape this project during its early stages.

To Paul Copp, for showing me how good thinking and writing are done, for hosting my first visit to Princeton and later visits to Chicago, and for procuring some of the best baseball tickets I've ever had (both north side and south!).

To Kevin Osterloh, who exemplifies the ways of the wise warrior—of Roman Centurion-slash-Cincinnati Redleg ilk—with undying enthusiasm and positivity, and who through word and deed inspires me to be confident in what I am and what I can do.

To Mark Rowe, for teaching me how work and play are best conjoined, for authoring the most memorable email I have ever received (octopus themed; ca. 2004), and for agreeing to do what is necessary should I meet an untimely end.

To Asuka Sango, who once wrote a seven-page response to my dissertation prospectus, and who was otherwise the best cohort partner a doctoral candidate could ever hope for.

To my other Princeton colleagues, Micah Auerbach, Ian Chapman, Jessey Choo, Eduard Iricinschi, Ryan Bongseok Joo, Bryan Lowe, Levi McLaughlin, Mark Meulenbeld, Jesse Sloane, and Jimmy Yu, who helped form the *communitas* necessary for an excellent graduate-school education.

To Rob Campany and Pierce Salguero for reading late versions of this manuscript and offering valuable suggestions for improvement.

To the good folks who worked with the Kuroda Institute and the University of Hawai'i Press to help see this book through to completion: including Peter Gregory, Griff Foulk, Dan Stevenson, Pat Crosby, Stephanie Chun, Erika Stevens, and Molly Balikov.

To everyone in the Department of Religious Studies at Bucknell University—Maria Antonaccio, Brantley Gasaway, Paul MacDonald, Karline McLain, Rivka Ulmer, Kara Van Buskirk, and Carol White—who have made my time there most enjoyable and profitable, and whose engagement with my ideas has greatly improved this book.

To the Deans' and Provost's offices of Bucknell University for a subvention grant that contributed to the publication of this volume.

To the International College for Postgraduate Buddhist Studies (ICPBS; Kokusai Bukkyōgaku Daigakuin Daigaku 国際仏教学大学院大学), in Tokyo, for a research grant that allowed me to study Japanese manuscripts of the biographies of Aśvaghoṣa, Nāgārjuna, and Āryadeva in summer 2013.

To Ochiai Toshinori 落合俊典, for once agreeing to meet a fledgling American graduate student with little spoken Japanese at a coffee shop in Tokyo, then frequently mailing newly published research to that graduate student, and then years later helping to facilitate his visit to ICPBS.

To Yamano Chieko 山野智惠 for showing me around ICPBS and sharing her excellent work on Nāgārjuna.

To Fang Guangchang 方廣錩 and his graduate student Wang Meng 王孟, as well as Karashima Seishi 辛嶋靜志, for introducing me to recent research on the *Mahāyāna Awakening of Faith* (unfortunately too late to incorporate here).

To Maney Publishing and the Society for the Study of Chinese Religions for permission to republish parts of my article from the *Journal of Chinese Religions* (Young 2013), which appear in chapter 5 of this book.

To my Lewisburg friends, Mizuki, Yuki, Jon, and Eric, for introducing me to a whole new world of beer appreciation and for helping make central Pennsylvania a decent place to live.

To my South Pas friends, Dan and Norma, Ernest, Eric, Mike, Fran, and Brendan, who help make home still feel like home.

And to the Kisers—Terry, Roma, Lee, Kevin, Cory, Shawn, Rose, and baby Carter (born on my fortieth birthday!)—for being my second family.

Abbreviations and Conventions

BJ Numbered manuscripts from Dunhuang 敦煌 held in the National Library, Beijing

DZ *Daozang* (*Zhengtong Daozang* 正統道藏 [Daoist Canon of the Zhengtong Era]), 1445. 1,120 vols. Shanghai: Commercial Press, 1923–1926.

P Numbered manuscripts from Dunhuang in Fonds Pelliot chinois, Bibliothèque Nationale de France

S Numbered manuscripts from Dunhuang in the Aurel Stein collection, British Library, London

T *Taishō shinshū daizōkyō* 大正新修大藏經 (Buddhist Canon Newly Compiled in the Taishō Era). 85 vols. Eds. Takakusu Junjirō 高楠順次郎 and Watanabe Kaigyoku 渡邊海旭, 1924–1932. Tokyo: Taishō issaikyō kankōkai.

Z *Dainippon zokuzōkyō* 大日本續藏經 (Great Japanese Edition of the Buddhist Canon, Continued). 150 vols. Ed. Maeda Eun 前田慧雲 and Nakano Tatsue 中野達慧, 1905–1912. Kyoto: Zōkyō shoin.

Citations from the *Daozang* indicate text number (following Schipper and Verellen 2005), fascicle number, page, and register (a or b). For example, *Taishang ganying pian* 太上感應篇, DZ 1167, fasc. 836, 5a–6b. *Taishō shinshū daizōkyō* sources are cited by text number, volume number, page, and register (a through c). So, "*Zhiguan fuxing chuanhong jue* 止觀輔行傳弘決, T no. 1912, 46:445c" is a reference to *Taishō* text number 1912, volume 46, page 445, register "c." Citations from the *Dainippon zokuzōkyō* indicate series (*hen* 編) number, set (*tō* 套) number, volume (*satsu* 冊) number, leaf (*chō* 丁) number, and, where applicable, register (a through d). For example, *Maming pusa chengjiu xidi niansong* 馬鳴菩薩成就悉地念誦, Z 1:3:5:416b–d.

Unless otherwise indicated, all translations are my own.

Introduction

Sometime during the 660s, writing from Ximing monastery 西明寺 in the Tang-dynasty capital of Chang'an 長安, eminent Buddhist scholar-monk Daoshi 道世 (ca. 596–683) addressed a central problematic of his day. This problematic concerned the yawning gulf between medieval Chinese Buddhists and the ancient Indian origins of their religion. Many Chinese authors of the time lamented the derelict condition of Chinese Buddhism as a result of this gap, but Daoshi offered hope that the means to bridge it were well at hand:

> The Threefold Canon is vast and the seven groups [of Buddhist disciples] are multifarious. These establish the teaching fully in accord with circumstances, brilliantly understanding and explaining it. Hearing of suffering and its origin, compassion is ever nearer one's heart. Listening to the path toward [suffering's] end, one joyfully renounces [all attachments] and attains enlightenment. The pure harmony [of the Dharma] is luxuriant like ganoderma and epidendrum; as the lofty tones of the *shang* and *gong* [notes] it awakens the ears and eyes. Therefore Aśvaghoṣa expounded its subtle principles, Nāgārjuna restored its severed origins, Āryadeva analyzed its concepts and categories, and the arhats arranged its logical order. Together they supported the profound canon and subdued the non-Buddhists. A crossing was made at the ford of delusion; the long night [of *saṃsāra* finally] reached daybreak. Carrying forth the lofty paradigms of Śākyamuni's canon and exemplifying the art of instruction from master to disciple were among their [great accomplishments]. How truly magnificent! It is as if the Jetavana were present and the Deer Park could be seen. Indeed, those who have not yet reached enlightenment can thereby draw near to the Buddha!
>
> 惟夫三藏浩汗, 七眾紛綸. 設教備機, 煥然通解. 聞苦集, 則哀切追情; 聽滅道, 則喜捨啟寤. 清泠音韻, 鬱若芝蘭; 峻旨宮商, 開導耳目. 所以馬鳴迪其幽宗, 龍樹振其絕緒, 提婆折[1]

1. Here reading *xi* 析 for *zhe* 折, as in Xiao Ziliang's 蕭子良 (460–494) *Qi taizai jingling wenxuan wang faji lu xu* 齊太宰竟陵文宣王法集錄序 (preserved in the *Chu sanzang jiji* 出三藏記集, T no. 2145, 55: 85b), which Daoshi followed in part. I discuss Xiao Ziliang's account in chapter 2.

其名數, 羅漢總其條理. 並翊贊妙典, 俘剪外學. 迷津見衢, 長夜逢曉. 繼釋典之高範, 表師資之訓術, 屬于斯也. 可謂盛哉! 祇園若在, 鹿苑如瞻. 誠未證果, 趣佛邇也![2]

Here introducing the chapter on "skillful debate" (*jibian* 機辯) in his voluminous Buddhist encyclopedia *Grove of Pearls in a Dharma Garden* (*Fayuan zhulin* 法苑珠林), Daoshi began with a discourse of Buddhist embattlement allayed. Immediately following this brief introduction, Daoshi pieced together selections from earlier sources that illustrated the trials and triumphs (in debate and otherwise) of several Indian Buddhist saints. Daoshi explained how these Indian saints—identified here by both name and class—arose to save two worlds, and in the end to merge them together as one. Although he did not say so directly, Daoshi's Indian protagonists were those who upheld the Dharma in the generations after the death of the Buddha. With Śākyamuni long gone, evil deviants multiplied, suffering and delusion deepened, and the darkness of *saṃsāra* lingered on. With the appearance of these great Indian saints, the Dharma was restored and the lamp of truth relit. Having resurrected the teaching in ancient India, these masters also provided the means to salvation for the benighted masses of latter-day China. This latter kingdom was among those described in early Indian scriptures as severely hindered by their spatiotemporal distance from the epicenter of Buddhist enlightenment (see chapter 1). Removed by a continent and a millennium from the Buddha's original splendor, medieval China would seemingly have been doomed to darkness—that is, if not for the great Indian saints who arose in Śākyamuni's stead. These saints bequeathed the foremost models of Buddhist practice to their Dharma descendents in the east and thereby manifested in China the most sacred stations of original Indian Buddhism: the Deer Park where Śākyamuni first preached and the Jetavana monastery where he most often dwelt. Thereby these Indian saints bridged the gap between ancient India and latter-day China; they rendered China a Buddhist holy land where local devotees could likewise draw near to the Buddha.

Here Daoshi expressed a common concern among Buddhist authors in medieval China: to reconcile their Indian and Chinese heritages by defining models of Buddhist sainthood as best suited to the generations after the Buddha's nirvāṇa. This perceived distance from the origins of Buddhism incited widespread efforts by Chinese monastics to develop paradigms of Buddhist practice that would be both rooted in ancient India and tailor-made for a world without a Buddha. Through carefully crafted ritual and iconographic programs, standards of monastic comportment, ordination platforms, meditation guidelines, translation methodologies, modes of scriptural exegesis, and other methods, leaders of the Chinese sangha sought to demonstrate that the most authentic practices of Indian Buddhism were readily available in China. The true means to Buddhist enlightenment could therefore be pursued by local Chinese adepts, who could

2. *Fayuan zhulin* 法苑珠林, T no. 2122, 53:681b.

thus rise to the ranks of the most exalted Buddhist holy beings across the Sino-Indian divide.

At the same time that this divide was crossed by localizing ostensibly Indian models of Buddhist sainthood, Chinese authors also aimed to merge their own kingdom with the Buddhist heartland by demonstrating congruency between Indian and Chinese ideals of spiritual attainment. Just as Daoshi emphasized how the Indian Buddhist saints had transmitted paradigms of practice based on ancient scriptural canons, as well as models of master-disciple relations and skill in debate, many other Chinese authors similarly stressed that their ancient Indian forebears had instantiated repertoires of practice that were fully accordant with traditional Chinese norms. In this way, Chinese Buddhists could show that their avowedly foreign religion was in fact a most appropriate means to sainthood and salvation for latter-day China, and that by following the examples of the ancient Indian patriarchs, Chinese adepts could become great Buddhist saints in the generations after nirvāṇa.

This book is a study of how medieval Chinese Buddhists conceived their great Indian forebears as cornerstones of the pervasive effort to negotiate the gap between ancient India and latter-day China. As Daoshi intimated, Chinese Buddhists most famously used these Indian figures to bridge the Sino-Indian divide in genealogical fashion, forming long lines of master-disciple Dharma transmission that would ideally link local Chinese traditions with the Buddha himself. Such efforts on the part of seventh- and eighth-century Chan and Tiantai advocates in particular are well known. But these discourses were concerned with the Indian patriarchate as a whole rather than with individual Indian masters; only a corporate body of saints could connect China with India genealogically. And, in fact, the majority of Indian figures arranged within these lineages received little attention elsewhere, while the most celebrated Indian patriarchs in medieval China were not those known primarily as members of master-disciple genealogies.

Indeed, as Daoshi's brief introduction also indicates, one particular triad of Indian patriarchs was often singled out above the rest as having accomplished the most daunting task of propagating a Buddhist tradition that had *not* been transmitted directly to them. These Indian patriarchs were Aśvaghoṣa (Maming 馬鳴), Nāgārjuna (Longshu 龍樹), and Āryadeva (Tipo 提婆), who first appeared in Chinese sources as the next great world saviors after the Buddha himself, having single-handedly upheld the Dharma in the generations after his death, and who thereafter became the foremost Indian models of Buddhist sainthood for the Buddhaless realm of latter-day China. While Aśvaghoṣa, Nāgārjuna, and Āryadeva would also come to be placed within sectarian Dharma genealogies, these Indian masters initially and more frequently served to advance a variety of other projects aimed at developing avowedly Indian models of Buddhist sanctity that would integrate and supplant local Chinese religious traditions. In these contexts, the gap between India and China was both negated and exploited, as Chinese authors deliberately foregrounded the patriarchs' Indian identity in order to Buddhicize time-honored Chinese religious repertoires and thus demonstrate the fundamental unity between ancient India and latter-day China.

The history of Aśvaghoṣa, Nāgārjuna, and Āryadeva in China begins with the great Central Asian missionary and translator Kumārajīva (344–413 or 350–409), who arrived in Chang'an, the capital of the Later Qin 後秦 dynasty (ca. 384–417), at the beginning of 402 and shortly thereafter disseminated the earliest known tales about these ancient Indian masters. It was Kumārajīva who first promoted Aśvaghoṣa, Nāgārjuna, and Āryadeva in China as Buddhist exemplars par excellence. They became great bodhisattvas by resurrecting the Dharma in specific centuries after the Buddha's nirvāṇa. Kumārajīva himself was one of the most revered Western Buddhist masters in medieval China, having personally conveyed the foremost Indian sūtras, *śāstras* (treatises), Vinaya (monastic regulations), and meditation instructions, and so his endorsement of these three patriarchs soon precipitated their widespread acclaim across Chinese Buddhist exegetical circles. Kumārajīva and his associates translated into Chinese a number of seminal works attributed to Aśvaghoṣa, Nāgārjuna, and Āryadeva, which secured a central place for these patriarchs in subsequent Chinese discourses on all things Buddhist.

Over the next century, Aśvaghoṣa, Nāgārjuna, and Āryadeva became subsumed within the emerging Chinese concern with demonstrating a continuous lineal transmission of the Dharma, since they were first placed within Chinese Buddhist genealogies of Indian masters. With the subsequent application of this genealogical model to local Chinese traditions—each constructing its own lineage of Chinese and Indian patriarchs stretching back to the Buddha—Aśvaghoṣa, Nāgārjuna, and Āryadeva came to be counted among the founding fathers of almost all Chinese Buddhism. By the latter half of the Tang dynasty (618–907), these patriarchs found their way into many different genres of Chinese literature and the Chinese Buddhist visual arts. Their very personages became synecdoches for Mahāyāna Buddhism as a whole. At the same time, Aśvaghoṣa and Nāgārjuna were also transformed into local deities of some renown, who could be summoned within Chinese ritual arenas to personally provide a wide array of material boons and apotropaic services.

In the following chapters, I examine images of Aśvaghoṣa, Nāgārjuna, and Āryadeva in the context of medieval Chinese religion, culture, and society. I focus on the period from the beginning of the fifth century to the end of the tenth, which is when the most prominent representations of these Indian patriarchs first gained traction in Chinese Buddhist writings. I discuss how Aśvaghoṣa, Nāgārjuna, and Āryadeva were portrayed in a wide variety of Buddhist sources from this period—including translated and indigenous scriptures, exegetical writings, lineage histories, hagiographies, ritual manuals, and visual arts—and I show how Chinese Buddhists conceived these figures in ways that resonated with local soteriological and sociopolitical concerns. This study focuses primarily on the hagiographic imagery of these Indian patriarchs—the tales of their careers, travails, and triumphs along the bodhisattva path—as it shaped and was shaped by Chinese redactors' understanding of their own plight as Buddhists in latter-day China. I am not concerned with analyzing issues regarding Aśvaghoṣa's, Nāgārjuna's, or Āryadeva's influence on the development of Chinese Buddhist philosophy. I do not aim to engage discussions often found in modern scholarship; for example, on how Nāgārjuna's and Āryadeva's Madhyamaka doctrine was transposed into Chinese idiom by Kumārajīva's disciples Sengzhao 僧肇 (ca. 374–414) and Sengrui 僧叡 (ca. 352–436); how Jizang 吉藏 (549–623) molded it into the Chinese Three Treatise tradition (Sanlun 三論); or how it influenced the thought of later Huayan 華嚴, Tiantai 天台, or Chan 禪 Buddhist exponents. Such lines of inquiry have been well charted by previous scholars, on the one hand;[3] and on the other, their methodological presuppositions are somewhat different than my own. Instead, this study examines how the hagiographic images of Aśvaghoṣa, Nāgārjuna, and Āryadeva—as great Buddhist philosophers and exegetical authors, among other things—derived from and contributed to medieval Chinese ideals of Buddhist sainthood in a world without a Buddha.

By firmly situating Chinese representations of Aśvaghoṣa, Nāgārjuna, and Āryadeva in the context of medieval Chinese religion, this book stands in marked contrast to all previous studies of these ancient Indian figures. Because they are highly regarded in Western Buddhology as well as in premodern Asian Buddhist communities, Aśvaghoṣa, Nāgārjuna, and Āryadeva have received a great deal of attention in modern scholarship. Recognizing the centrality of these figures in the historical, mythic, and philosophical development of Buddhist traditions throughout Asia, the towering patriarchs of our own academic tradition—Samuel Beal (1883, 1886), Louis de La Vallée Poussin (1913), Sylvain Lévi (1896, 1908, 1928, 1929), Theodore Stcherbatsky (1923), and D. T. Suzuki (1900), among others—focused their efforts on elucidating the doctrinal systems and historicity of Aśvaghoṣa, Nāgārjuna, and Āryadeva. Succeeding generations of Buddhist studies scholars likewise emphasized the importance of these Indian patriarchs and tended to present them as erudite Mahāyāna philosophers on a par with the greatest minds of post-Enlightenment Europe.[4] However, because

3. See, e.g., Bocking 1995; Daoan 1978; Koseki 1977; Liebenthal 1968; Liu 1994; Robinson 1967; Swanson 1989; and Tucker 1984.

4. Nāgārjuna, as purported founder of the Madhyamaka school of Mahāyāna Buddhist philosophy, has received the lion's share of scholarly attention. Important expositions of this philosophical system are those of Lindtner 1982, 1986; Murti 1955; Ramanan 1966; Robinson 1967; Ruegg 1981; and Westerhoff 2009. Scholars who focus on his historicity include Jan 1970; Joshi 1965, 1977; Karambelkar 1952; Murty 1971; Tucci 1930; and Walleser (1923) 1979. See Mabbett 1998 and Walser 2002, 2005 for the most recent surveys of and attempts in the search for the historical Nāgārjuna. Following the late nineteenth- and early twentieth-century surge of interest in Aśvaghoṣa as author, poet, and philosopher—as exemplified in the works of Cowell 1893, 1894; Huber 1908; and Richard (1894) 1918, in addition to those

Aśvaghoṣa, Nāgārjuna, and Āryadeva all lived in first- to third-century Common Era (CE) India, almost every previous study of these figures has focused on locating them in the context of ancient Indian history, religion, or society. As part of this endeavor, scholars have utilized all available primary source materials—in Sanskrit, Tibetan, various Central Asian languages, and Chinese, produced all across the Asian continent over a time span of some fifteen hundred years—and viewed these sources as having bearing exclusively on ancient India. This method of examining pan-Asian Buddhist texts as reflective of originary Indian Buddhism illustrates a prevalent tendency in the field of Buddhist studies to look *through* rather than *at* the vast cultures and literary traditions in which Buddhism has flourished, in order to elucidate the traditionally conceived fountainhead of the religion.

By contrast, the present study focuses on the Chinese hagiographies of Aśvaghoṣa, Nāgārjuna, and Āryadeva, which are by far the earliest and most abundant in any body of Buddhist literature, precisely as a means of illuminating the beliefs and concerns of Chinese Buddhists themselves—quite apart from any Indic antecedents that one might imagine for these accounts. Through these hagiographies I explore broader questions of how Chinese Buddhists conceived Indian Buddhism as a whole, and how they thereby construed the problem of being Buddhist in latter-day China. I examine Chinese Buddhist appropriations of the ancient Indian patriarchs in order to elucidate medieval Chinese conceptions of Buddhist sanctity across the Sino-Indian divide. Based largely on evidence internal to these hagiographies—their evolving narrative structures, themes, and tropes—I argue that Buddhist authors propagated the life stories of their Indian forebears in order to secure patronage and prestige over rival Chinese religious traditions. In many cases we cannot prove definitively that these hagiographies were understood as advancing such sociopolitical agendas, and we cannot measure the degree to which these sources functioned effectively in this way. Nevertheless, while this is not a work of sociopolitical or institutional history per se, I aim to demonstrate that the Chinese hagiographic representations of Aśvaghoṣa, Nāgārjuna, and Āryadeva are indeed most compellingly interpreted as staking claims to the foremost means of salvation in a competitive religious environment.

In this study I focus on Aśvaghoṣa, Nāgārjuna, and Āryadeva not as ideal types of the "Indian patriarch" in Chinese Buddhism—if such a thing can be said to exist—but rather as the principal occupants of a specific niche that Chinese Buddhists carved for Indian exemplars of Buddhist sanctity during the generations after nirvāṇa. Without preempting the fuller categorical

cited previously—Western scholarship concerning his life and works has experienced a relative lull. Examples are Johnson 1932, (1936) 1984; de Jong 1978; Demiéville 1929; Girard 2004; Kanakura 1959; Khosla 1986; Salomon 1999; and Yamabe 2003. Relative to Nāgārjuna and Aśvaghoṣa, Āryadeva has been rather neglected in Western scholarship, particularly since his philosophy is often seen as derivative of Nāgārjuna's. For studies of his life and writings, see Bhattacharya 1931; Dutt 1934; Lang 1986; Mimaki 1987; Ruegg 1981; Sastri 1955; and Vaidya 1923.

discussion provided in chapter 6, suffice it to say here that Chinese Buddhists conceived Aśvaghoṣa, Nāgārjuna, and Āryadeva as unique sorts of Indian holy beings, distinct from the original arhat-disciples of the Buddha and the so-called celestial bodhisattvas of the Mahāyāna tradition.[5] One primary factor distinguishing these figures was time—their locus on at least two complementary timelines of Dharmic history. On the one hand, the history of the Dharma was seen to proceed on a cosmic scale, with Śākyamuni being only one Buddha among countless others who presided over the perpetual rise and decline of the Dharma, across eons and world systems as numerous as the sands of the Ganges. This was the timeline of great celestial bodhisattvas such as Avalokiteśvara, Kṣitigarbha, or Mañjuśrī, who often appeared throughout the present world-system in human form as expedient means (*upāya*) to liberate beings, but who had long ago freed themselves from the capricious winds of karma.

On the other hand, there was Dharmic history on a localized scale, with Śākyamuni being the progenitor of the religion in ancient India and the subsequent fate of the Dharma being measured as a function of this founder's rise and demise. The early arhat-disciples and later Indian patriarchs Aśvaghoṣa, Nāgārjuna, and Āryadeva were conceived primarily along this latter spatiotemporal axis. From both perspectives of Dharmic history, only the patriarchs who lived after the Buddha's *parinirvāṇa* (final extinction) were suitable objects of emulation for medieval Chinese Buddhists. Unlike the celestial bodhisattvas, Aśvaghoṣa, Nāgārjuna, and Āryadeva were largely seen to have perfected their qualities within the present world-system; and unlike the arhats, they did so long after the Buddha's death. So in terms of both cosmic and local histories of the Dharma, these Indian masters were proximal and familiar to the Chinese. Aśvaghoṣa, Nāgārjuna, and Āryadeva illustrated how soteriohistorical conditions similar to those of latter-day China were ripe for the creation of great bodhisattvas, and as a result their models of spiritual attainment were uniquely suited to the personal aspirations of medieval Chinese Buddhists.

However, it should be noted that there were no clear Chinese terminological distinctions between these Indian Buddhist holy beings. Throughout this study I refer to Aśvaghoṣa, Nāgārjuna, and Āryadeva primarily as "patriarchs," but not because they were always labeled as such with the corresponding Chinese term, *zu* 祖, while other Indian figures were not. Aśvaghoṣa, Nāgārjuna, and Āryadeva were also called "monks" (*biqiu* 比丘), "masters" (*shi* 師 or *shi* 士) or "saints" (*sheng* 聖), in addition to "patriarchs," and in fact Chinese authors most frequently designated them as "bodhisattvas" (*pusa* 菩薩). Perhaps the only term we never see applied to these figures is "arhat" (*luohan* 羅漢), though the arhats were also often called *zu*. In the contexts of institutional Buddhism, Daoism, and Confucianism, the term *zu* usually referred to those figures who stood in lineages of transmitted ordination precepts, ritual initiation procedures, scriptural canons, monastic

5. See the discussion in chapter 6 on the category "celestial bodhisattva."

properties, or other more abstract things such as Dharma (*fa* 法), the Way (*dao* 道), or simply "mind" (*xin* 心). Aśvaghoṣa, Nāgārjuna, and Āryadeva were likewise labeled *zu* (or *gaozu* 高祖 [high ancestor], *gaozushi* 高祖師 [high ancestral teacher], *shizu* 始祖 [first ancestor], *zushi* 祖師 [ancestral teacher], or in a similar way) in Chinese Buddhist lineage histories and other contexts where Dharma transmission was at issue. But in many other contexts they were not. As a result, I use the label "patriarch" in this study somewhat loosely. This term is not intended to demarcate a specific function or class of being; rather, it indicates more generally that medieval Chinese Buddhists conceived Aśvaghoṣa, Nāgārjuna, and Āryadeva as great forefathers who were worthy of veneration and emulation.

So why did these particular "patriarchs" achieve such widespread renown in medieval China, above and against other Indian masters who were seen to have lived in the generations after nirvāṇa? Aśvaghoṣa, Nāgārjuna, and Āryadeva alone enjoyed the wholehearted endorsement of Kumārajīva, who first promoted them as the foremost champions of Mahāyāna Buddhism as a whole. They authored some of the most seminal Indian treatises available in Chinese translation, which spoke directly to the doctrinal concerns of medieval Chinese Buddhists. They were depicted from the outset as the only post-*parinirvāṇa* Indian patriarchs capable of reviving the True Dharma when it was nearly lost to the world. These three patriarchs in particular were upheld as the greatest models of Buddhist sainthood for the generations after the Buddha, and this characterization afforded them a unique brand of authority and prestige among Indian figures in medieval China.

That said, it must be acknowledged at the outset that Aśvaghoṣa and Nāgārjuna achieved a much greater standing in China than did their ostensible understudy Āryadeva—in terms of their specific models of sainthood, their incorporation into broader realms of Chinese religion, and the general Chinese consensus that their personages encapsulated the entirety of Mahāyāna Buddhism. I have nonetheless included Āryadeva in this study because from the time of Kumārajīva and throughout subsequent Chinese Buddhist history he was joined with Aśvaghoṣa and Nāgārjuna to form a sort of patriarchal triad. These three patriarchs were grouped together as the foremost Indian Mahāyāna exegetes and exemplars of post-*parinirvāṇa* sainthood, and perhaps as a result they were also the only three among the multitude of ancient Indian figures in early Chinese sources to have their own widely circulating, independent hagiographies—at least until the sixth-century *Tradition of Dharma-Master Vasubandhu*, by Paramārtha (499–569).[6]

At the same time, however, Aśvaghoṣa, Nāgārjuna, and Āryadeva were not always grouped together as a discrete triad, separate from all the other Indian masters who propagated the Dharma after the Buddha. In Chinese doctrinal classification schemes, for example, Aśvaghoṣa was sometimes paired with the seventh-century Yogācāra master Sthiramati; in Chinese Pure Land writings, Nāgārjuna often appeared alongside Vasubandhu; and

6. *Poshupandou fashi zhuan* 婆藪槃豆法師傳, T no. 2049; trans. Dalia 2002.

Nāgārjuna and Āryadeva were occasionally juxtaposed with Asaṅga and Vasubandhu as propounding the most prevalent Mahāyāna traditions in post-*parinirvāṇa* India.[7] While it might therefore seem reasonable to include these and other Indian patriarchs in this study, I focus on Aśvaghoṣa, Nāgārjuna, and Āryadeva in particular because they exemplify a unique trajectory in the development of medieval Chinese conceptions of Buddhist sainthood. These three patriarchs illustrate how, from the time of Kumārajīva, Chinese Buddhists first conceived their post-*parinirvāṇa* Indian forebears as models of Buddhist practice for times when the Dharma was at death's door. Then, as new ideals of Dharma genealogy began to develop in China, Aśvaghoṣa, Nāgārjuna, and Āryadeva were repurposed to show how great Buddhist saints were forged within master-disciple transmission lineages, which upheld the teaching undimmed as when the Buddha walked the earth. Over the ensuing Sui-Tang period, when Chinese Buddhists were becoming less concerned with their distance from the origins of Buddhism and more confident in their own kingdom as a center of Buddhist civilization, this triad of patriarchs was again reconceived to demonstrate that the means and media of Indian sanctity were readily available in China. These media included Aśvaghoṣa and Nāgārjuna themselves, who came to be depicted as immanent deity-like figures who personally appeared before local Chinese adepts to convey the most powerful ritual magic of ancient India.

No other Indian patriarchs in medieval China were as famous as Aśvaghoṣa, Nāgārjuna, and Āryadeva, or were represented across a similarly broad range of Buddhist idioms and sources, or were made to follow a comparable developmental trajectory. For example, the one post-*parinirvāṇa* Indian master whose standing in medieval China might have approached that of Aśvaghoṣa, Nāgārjuna, and Āryadeva was the celebrated Mahāyāna convert Vasubandhu, who sometimes appeared together with these three patriarchs as the greatest world saviors after the Buddha.[8] A number of important doctrinal treatises were attributed to Vasubandhu in China, including most famously the *Abhidharmakośabhyāṣa* (Treatise on the Treasury of Further Dharma), *Triṃśikāvijñaptikārikā* (Thirty Verses on Consciousness-Only), *Daśabhūmikasūtraśāstra* (Treatise on the Ten Stages Scripture), and *Sukhāvativyūhopadeśa* (Commentary on the Scripture of Immeasurable Life), which made him a foundational figure in Chinese

---

7. On Aśvaghoṣa and Sthiramati, see, e.g., *Dasheng qixinlun yi ji* 大乘起信論義記, T no. 1846, 44:243c; and *Ru lengqie xin xuanyi* 入楞伽心玄義, T no. 1790, 39:426c. See chapter 3 for a discussion of Aśvaghoṣa's ostensive Yogācāra proclivities. On Nāgārjuna and Vasubandhu, see, e.g., *Anle ji* 安樂集, T no. 1958, 47:6b; and *Wuliangshou jing youpotishe yuansheng jie zhu* 無量壽經優婆提舍願生偈註, T no. 1819, 40:827a. On Nāgārjuna's (and Vasubandhu's) association with Pure Land devotionalism, see chapter 4. And, for an example of Nāgārjuna and Āryadeva juxtaposed with Asaṅga and Vasubandhu, see *Dafangguang fo huayan jing suishu yanyi chao* 大方廣佛華嚴經隨疏演義鈔, T no. 1736, 36:52c.

8. See, e.g., *Sanlun youyi yi* 三論遊意義, T no. 1855, 45:116c; and *Song gaoseng zhuan* 宋高僧傳, T no. 2061, 50:742b.

Abhidharma, Yogācāra, Dilun, and Pure Land exegetical circles, respectively.[9] Vasubandhu was ubiquitous in Chinese Buddhist doctrinal writings, especially during the Sui-Tang period, where he was commonly lauded as the foremost Mahāyāna philosopher (together with his brother Asaṅga) since Nāgārjuna and Āryadeva.

But unlike these latter patriarchs and their predecessor Aśvaghoṣa, Vasubandhu was not depicted as single-handedly reviving the Dharma at a time when it was dying out; he received only the most summary treatment in early Sino-Indian Dharma genealogies;[10] and he never became a significant object of ritual devotion in China.[11] It was more than a century after Kumārajīva first introduced Aśvaghoṣa, Nāgārjuna, and Āryadeva that Vasubandhu emerged on the Chinese scene. In his earliest full-blown hagiography, attributed to Paramārtha (and written sometime between 546 and 569), Vasubandhu was depicted primarily as a Buddhist doctrinal specialist, treatise author, and debate master who gained imperial support and served to demonstrate the superiority of Mahāyāna over Hīnayāna Buddhist teachings. In some respects this tale accorded with the early Chinese representations of Aśvaghoṣa, Nāgārjuna, and Āryadeva—in terms of the patriarchs' practical repertoires and concomitant themes advanced—but in subsequent Chinese Buddhist writings Vasubandhu remained relatively fixed to this initial characterization. The story of Vasubandhu in medieval China is one worth investigating, and would surely offer a range of novel perspectives on Chinese Buddhist conceptions of their Indian heritage, but it is a different story than that exemplified by Aśvaghoṣa, Nāgārjuna, and Āryadeva.

Here I examine how these three patriarchs were conceived in medieval China as models of Buddhist sainthood and divinity that could bridge the Sino-Indian divide and demonstrate the supremacy of Buddhism over competing religious traditions. In the writings of elite Chinese scholar-monks with imperial connections, Aśvaghoṣa, Nāgārjuna, and Āryadeva were shown to have achieved sainthood by perfecting paradigms of doctrinal exegesis, oral debate, meditation and eremitism, and master-disciple and state-sangha relations. As such, these Indian patriarchs served to demonstrate that Buddhist adepts had long since mastered the occupational priorities of Chinese religious and secular authorities. In other Chinese writings of less scholarly

9. *Apidamo jushe lun* 阿毘達磨俱舍論 (*Abhidharmakośabhyāṣa*), T nos. 1558, 1559; *Weishi sanshi lun song* 唯識三十論頌 (*Triṃśikāvijñaptikārikā*), T no. 1586; *Shidi jing lun* 十地經論 (*Daśabhūmikasūtraśāstra*), T no. 1522; and *Wuliangshou jing youpotishe* 無量壽經優波提舍 (*Sukhāvativyūhopadeśa*), T no. 1524.

10. Vasubandhu was introduced into China through a short notice in the *Fu fazang yinyuan zhuan* 付法藏因緣傳, T no. 2058, 50:321b. For a Chinese translation, see Li 1997a, 405–407 (discussed in chapter 2). Vasubandhu later appeared briefly in the lineages of the *Lidao fabao ji* 歷代法寶記 (trans. Adamek 2007, 308) and *Platform Sūtra* (trans. Yampolsky 1967, 179), and was given a much fuller account in the *Baolin zhuan* 寶林傳 (Japanese trans. Tanaka 2003, 212–228).

11. The only item of evidence I have seen to the contrary is a tale of a monk who painted images of Asaṅga and Vasubandhu and thereby attained rebirth in Tuṣita heaven. See *Sanbao ganying yaolüe lu* 三寶感應要略錄, T no. 2084, 51:856b–c.

persuasion and imperial aspiration, produced perhaps by local-level ritualists or lay devotees, Aśvaghoṣa and Nāgārjuna were represented in a manner akin to local Chinese gods, offering fantastic boons in exchange for ritual obeisance from Chinese religious practitioners across social, sectarian, and lay-monastic divisions. In these contexts, the Indian patriarchs were insinuated into broader fields of Chinese religiosity, functioning much the same as—and reportedly even better than—Chinese deities from all traditions. In these ways and others, Chinese Buddhists adduced their great Indian forebears as evidence that Buddhist masters from ancient times had instantiated the same ideals, practices, and powers expected of all holy beings in China, and that the expressly foreign religion of Buddhism was thus the best way to ensure prosperity in this world and ultimate salvation in the next. At each point along the arc of their conception in medieval China, the images of Aśvaghoṣa, Nāgārjuna, and Āryadeva reflected and contributed to shaping Chinese efforts to define Buddhism as an efficacious amalgam of ancient Indian and traditional Chinese ideals of religious practice.

Conceiving Repertoires of Indianness

One principal aim of this book is to examine, through the Chinese hagiographic representations of Aśvaghoṣa, Nāgārjuna, and Āryadeva, how Buddhist authors in medieval China broadly conceived Indian Buddhism as a touchstone for addressing local Chinese religious and sociopolitical concerns. How did medieval Chinese Buddhists understand the vicissitudes of Buddhism in India after the death of its founder, what did they think most important to emphasize about post-*parinirvāṇa* Indian Buddhism, and why? How did they characterize the Indian roots of their religion through the life stories of their great Indian forebears, and how did they understand this characterization as bearing on their own roles as representatives of an avowedly foreign religion in China? These and related questions have been largely overlooked in modern scholarship,[12] which has otherwise focused on the more panoptic question of how Buddhism changed through its transmission from India to China. That is, by hypostasizing the Sino-Indian divide as a site for documenting broad-scale religious transformation across sociocultural boundaries, scholars have neglected to consider their Chinese informants' active interest in shaping contemporary perspectives on the relationships between Indian and Chinese Buddhism. By contrast, this study investigates Chinese hagiographic representations of Aśvaghoṣa, Nāgārjuna, and Āryadeva as an index to how Chinese authors themselves addressed a question that has long preoccupied modern scholars: how to weigh the mutability and integrity of Buddhism across cultures, continents, and millennia.

One of the most salient features of these Indian patriarch hagiographies is that they vividly illustrate medieval Chinese efforts to redefine the categories of "Indian Buddhist" and "native Chinese." In these accounts

12. Partial exceptions include Jan 1966a, 1966b; Mather 1992; and Sen 2003, 6–12.

Aśvaghoṣa, Nāgārjuna, and Āryadeva were expressly allied with repertoires of religious practice that medieval Chinese audiences would have clearly recognized as the province of local deities and saints. In their guise as post-*parinirvāṇa* Dharma champions, the Indian patriarchs took on traits that, for Chinese readers, would have conjured images of spiritually inclined Chinese literati gentlemen living in the land of Buddhism's birth, engaged in public debate, philosophical authorship, meditation, and eremitism. In these contexts as well, Aśvaghoṣa, Nāgārjuna, and Āryadeva instantiated models of master-disciple relations and of sainthood at imperial court, much like Daoist and Confucian adepts, and the patriarchs also vividly demonstrated their capacity to match supernormal powers with the Chinese "transcendents" (*xian* 仙) of old. Aśvaghoṣa, Nāgārjuna, and Āryadeva thus served to illustrate how religious repertoires commonly associated with Chinese holy figures were actually of Indian provenance and were thus the rightful heritage of Buddhist adepts alone. Precisely because of their ancient Indian roots, then, Chinese Buddhists would ostensibly stand as the foremost exemplars of normative Chinese ideals and practices. And then when Aśvaghoṣa and Nāgārjuna came to be cast as immigrant deities of sorts, appearing personally to instruct Chinese devotees in the most efficacious ritual technologies of ancient India, these patriarchs instantiated models of divinity and ritual practice that Chinese audiences would likewise have recognized as fully accordant with traditional Chinese norms. Chinese sources advertising Aśvaghoṣa's and Nāgārjuna's divine incarnations and thaumaturgic prowess served to show that the most vaunted Chinese models of sanctity and salvation had in fact been perfected in ancient India, and that Buddhist ritual programs were thus the most powerful and suitable for religious devotees in latter-day China.

In these ways and others, the Indian identity of Aśvaghoṣa, Nāgārjuna, and Āryadeva was crucial to their various functions for medieval Chinese Buddhists. This identity was never fixed objectively according to specific sets of characteristic features (or lack thereof); rather, it was always in flux, continuously redefined in relation to other forms of identity and deployed to suit a variety of purposes. As a result, in this book I treat the category of Indianness in a manner accordant with recent studies of concepts like "otherness," "foreignness," or "alterity," which are more readily understood as constituted by relational valences.[13] Just as otherness can only be defined by sameness, foreignness finds its meaning in autochthony, and alterity is integrally intertwined with mimesis, Indianness is likewise shaped through juxtaposition with a host of opposing religious, sociocultural, geopolitical, and historical identities. Jonathan Smith, for one, notes that " 'Otherness' is not so much a matter of separation as it is a description of interaction," of "reciprocal relations," even though it might suggest "an ontological cleavage rather than an anthropological distinction" (Smith 2004, 241, 256). And in a similar vein, although the notion of Indianness has invited misconceptions

13. Saunders 2003 provides a useful exposition of recent approaches to these concepts.

concerning its objective determinacy—as a cultural or geographic identity sui generis—it is in fact a relational category that medieval Chinese Buddhists used to mold contemporary perspectives on things "indigenous" as well. Buddhist authors in medieval China conceived the hagiographic imagery of Aśvaghoṣa, Nāgārjuna, and Āryadeva as a means of reshaping the categories of native and foreign, redefining religious ideals as fundamentally Indian or Chinese; thereby, we might surmise, staking claims to authority, prestige, and patronage for local Buddhist institutions. For medieval Chinese Buddhists the category of Indianness, like alterity in Michael Taussig's formulation, was "every inch a relationship, not a thing in itself."[14]

Along similar lines, throughout this study I treat Indianness as a kind of "repertoire element" that was purposively affixed to Aśvaghoṣa, Nāgārjuna, and Āryadeva and that Chinese Buddhists themselves also instantiated to some degree. By this I mean that Indianness was part of the "toolkit" of cultural resources upon which Chinese authors could draw as they worked to define the patriarchs and themselves, particularly as juxtaposed with competing religious traditions. As Robert Campany explains, religious and cultural repertoires include vast arrays of "ideas, words, values, images, action patterns, stories, prototypes, persons, texts, strategies, goals, methods, collective memories," and so on, which are both fixed in meaning through past generations and readily adapted to suit the needs of present agents.[15] Individuals pick and choose from each of these repertoire elements as they negotiate their way through a wide variety of circumstances in life. In defining Indianness as one such repertoire element in medieval China, I emphasize that it was not a static, monolithic identity marker but was rather one of many "contestational fields" in which diverse groups of Chinese Buddhists tried to convince others of the authority of their traditions (Campany 2012a, 109).

As I will demonstrate in the following chapters, medieval Chinese authors associated the Indian patriarchs with many different repertoires of religious practice: centering on doctrinal authorship, public debate, eremitism, meditation, forming master-disciple lineages, counseling kings, spell-casting, alchemy, Pure Land devotionalism, Esoteric ritual, and so on. By portraying their greatest Indian forebears as masters of these repertoires, Chinese Buddhists could advance their own traditions as the foremost founts of religious sanctity in medieval China. And just as some Chinese sources emphasized the patriarchs' association with repertoires of doctrinal scholarship—thus perhaps claiming for the Buddhist institution a position of supremacy over competing Chinese literati groups—and other sources highlighted the patriarchs' expertise in liturgical repertoires above and against different classes of ritual masters, the Indian identity of Aśvaghoṣa,

14. Taussig 1993, 130. Huber 2008 adopts a similar approach in his study of Tibetan Buddhist representations of India.

15. Campany 2012b, 30. See also the recent, insightful discussions of cultural repertoires in Campany 2009, chap. 2; Campany 2012a; and McDaniel 2011, 9–14, 225–230. My thinking here is heavily indebted to Campany's work on the topic.

Nāgārjuna, and Āryadeva likewise functioned as a repertoire element that could be either foregrounded or muted depending on the agendas, authorships, and intended audiences of particular texts.

The concept of repertoires serves two interrelated purposes in this study. In addition to emphasizing the composite character of cultural identity and inciting inquiry into the processes by which Chinese Buddhists themselves worked to define the relationships between India and China, it also "has the double advantage of . . . allowing for a measure of individual meaning and agency in mobilizing and choosing a specific configuration of cultural resources, while also stressing the public, and publicly available nature of those resources."[16] In other words, Indian and Chinese identities were never wholly uncircumscribed in medieval China, such that any Chinese author could radically reinvent them in whatever way he saw fit. Cultural repertoires and their constituent elements are to some extent always already there, forged over time within a given community and thus publicly available for adoption by individual agents to suit particular needs. Through the process of this adoption the valence of each repertoire element is partially redefined within new relational configurations. In medieval China, Indianness had a predetermined range of meanings and relations, as defined over many generations, but then with each new application this identity category was reshaped anew. My shorthand for this dynamic is the notion of "conceiving," as in the book's title, which similarly indicates how individual Chinese agents at once passively received ("conceive" connoted as "perceive") and actively constructed ("conceive" as "create") the elements of available religiocultural repertoires—including the concept of Indianness—which they variously affixed to Aśvaghoṣa, Nāgārjuna, and Āryadeva. In these ways the Indian patriarchs themselves were "conceived" in medieval China, with Chinese authors simultaneously adopting and adapting the available hagiographic imagery of these figures as part of the broader Chinese effort to define models of Buddhist sanctity across the Sino-Indian divide.

Reading Indian Hagiography in China

Throughout this study I focus primarily on Indian hagiographic materials as they were conceived in medieval China, which is to say advanced by Chinese Buddhists as having originated in ancient India. We have no way of knowing whether or to what extent these Indian patriarch hagiographies are reflective of earlier accounts circulating in India, but that is beside the point. The aim of this book is not to parse out and compare Indic and Sinitic elements of the extant hagiographies of Aśvaghoṣa, Nāgārjuna, and Āryadeva but rather to examine how these accounts functioned in medieval China. There are three main corollaries to this approach. First, the history to be gleaned from these accounts is that of the medieval Chinese *imaginaire* of ancient Indian Buddhism, not of the Indian patriarchs as

16. McDaniel 2011, 10, quoting the sociologist Ilana Silber.

veritable personages.[17] In this regard I stand alongside recent scholars who argue convincingly that hagiography is best understood as a record of collective representations rather than of individual authors' attempts to construct didactic myth from prenarrative history. Secondly, and as a caveat to this position, I contend that Indian hagiographies in China must be approached somewhat differently than Chinese accounts of Chinese saints. Ostensibly derived from the Indian cradle of Buddhist civilization and thus entailing unique expectations of genre, these accounts manifest a certain rupture in the dialectic of collective representation evinced by tales of local holy figures. And lastly, as media through which the foremost Indian models of sainthood and divinity were transmitted to China, the sources examined in this book illustrate how hagiography was not always a discrete genre of holy vitae. In addition to conveying the life stories of the Indian patriarchs, these hagiographies also functioned in China to shape the contents and contexts of the doctrinal treatises and ritual manuals that the patriarchs had ostensibly bequeathed to posterity.

My efforts to examine Chinese accounts of Indian patriarchs as records of Chinese Buddhist history are informed by recent developments in the study of religious biography more broadly, according to which it is best employed as a window into the worlds of its authors rather than those of its subjects. Traditionally, scholars have tended to view hagiography as a composite genre of original historical events and subsequent mythic accretions. From this standpoint, hagiographers take the genuine facts of a saint's career and embellish them in order to advance religious ideals, thereby constructing literary fiction from natural fact in the hagiographic process of religious didacticism. Modern scholars who have adopted this understanding of religious biography have typically done so toward one of two ends. One common goal has been to recover the historical lives of famous religious personages by peeling back the layers of myth accreted within their hagiographies. The other goal has been to analyze the religious ideals prevalent within the hagiographers' own sociocultural contexts by focusing on the mythic tropes that they developed. However, these approaches represent two sides of the same coin; they rest upon a common set of problematic assumptions concerning the nature and function of hagiographic writing.

First of all, there are perhaps insurmountable difficulties with the initial attempt to differentiate between historical facts and mythic images in religious biography. While the miraculous feats depicted in hagiographic accounts have certainly strained the credulity of both modern and medieval audiences, the career arcs of religious adepts in these accounts cannot be said to have proceeded entirely without some gesture toward the ideal. Religious devotees who would become exemplary figures in later hagiographies themselves lived their lives according to certain models of

17. By *imaginaire* I simply mean the collective Chinese representations of ancient India, which were exemplified and advanced by the sources studied herein. For a helpful discussion of the concept, see Campany 2009, 30–31.

practice. Religious ideals and the hagiographies illustrating them guided actual lives, which in turn formed the basis for religious ideals presented in hagiographic accounts; facts and ideals, lives and literature, mutually generated in a perpetual dialectic. Hagiographic writing does not proceed in linear fashion from prenarrative history to literary myth, and idealized stories do not derive ultimately from veritable facts. As such, the quest for originary historical events at the core of religious biographies—distinct from and untainted by the mythic ideals of hagiographic storytelling—is doomed from the beginning.[18]

Secondly, because actual lives and religious ideals are mutually generative, hagiographic accounts cannot be said to arise ex nihilo from the drive to prescribe religious norms—from the sociocultural exigencies of a given community or from the imaginations of individual hagiographers. Religious biography does have empirical as well as injunctive bases, even if prenarrative historical events can never be neatly extracted from the whole. And along similar lines, the claim that hagiography originates ultimately in the imaginations or didactic aims of hagiographers ignores the fact that local communities themselves viewed the genre as empirically grounded. Producers and consumers of religious biography indeed understood it to represent the real world, at least to some extent. Otherwise, the injunctive purport of the medium would have had no force: "Precisely because hagiography intends to inspire belief, veneration, and perhaps emulation . . . it must give a recognizable model of life as readers know it, and cannot content itself only with giving models for the ideal religious life" (Campany 2002, 101).

Given that the empirical and injunctive aims of religious biography—as well as its factual and imaginative bases—cannot be conclusively demarcated, our goal in interpreting the genre should not be to pursue this schizophrenic segmentation. We cannot claim that hagiography is fact or fiction, that it originates ultimately in historical events or religious imaginations, or even that it is necessarily a composite of these polar opposites. Instead, I propose that hagiography is more profitably interpreted as a species of *exemplum,* a rhetorical figure first established as an explicit means of persuasive argumentation in Aristotle's *Rhetoric* and *Topics.* As explained most helpfully by John Lyons, *exemplum* in medieval Latin literally meant "a clearing in the woods" (Lyons 1989, 3). This meaning aptly illustrates the function of exemplum—and its loose English cognate *example*—to create order from an otherwise inchoate jumble of entities, ideas, events, and experiences: "Only the clearing gives form or boundary to the woods. Only the woods permit the existence of a clearing. Likewise, example depends on the larger mass of history and experience, yet without the 'clearings' provided by example that mass would be formless and difficult to integrate into any controlling systematic discourse. Most of all, the clearing, the *exemplum,* posits an inside and an outside—in fact, the clearing creates an outside by its existence" (ibid.).

18. A similar argument is made in Campany 2009, 11–13.

By constructing these "clearings" of exempla, then, the rhetorician expressly shapes the "outside" world in a manner conducive to the advancement of his or her own "internal" discourses: "Example is the figure that most clearly and explicitly attempts to shore up the 'inside' of discourse by gesturing toward its 'outside,' toward some commonly recognized basis in a reality shared by speaker and listener, reader and writer. In order to appeal to such an outside, example must in some way construct or reconstruct its reference, altering the perception of the world by selecting, framing, and regulating (that is, subordinating to a rule) some entity or event" (ibid., 3–4).

In similar fashion, hagiography-*cum*-exemplum can be understood as furnishing the "external" grounding for an author's own "internal" discourse—an ostensively empirical reality adduced to support that author's injunctive declarations. Hagiography, like example, "differs from simple authoritarian assertion by appealing to something that diverts the audience from a direct affirmation and says 'see for yourself'" (Lyons 1989, 28). Read like example as a form of rhetoric, hagiography is overtly injunctive or persuasive, but its avowedly empirical grounding is nonetheless integral to its intended function of authorizing discourses. The important question is not to what degree hagiography is actually empirical or injunctive, or whether it originates finally in prenarrative fact or didactic imagination; rather, the central issue becomes one of determining what sort of "internal" discourse the "external" exemplum of hagiography is intended to support. Simply put, "each hagiographic narrative is an artifact of an attempt to persuade an audience" (Campany 2009, 10), and so the aim here is to examine how medieval Chinese authors adduced tales of Aśvaghoṣa, Nāgārjuna, and Āryadeva in order to persuade their contemporaries of the truths of their traditions. I treat these accounts not as transparent windows into ancient Indian history, nor as products of a purely Chinese religious imagination, but rather as forms of exempla that help us delineate the contours of broader medieval Chinese discourses concerning Sino-Indian Buddhist sanctity.

One corollary to this understanding of hagiography as exemplum rather than myth-history amalgam is that it presupposes sets of expectations and aspirations of a collective whole, rather than of individual authors alone. The traditional approach to hagiography as an exercise in myth-making has also overemphasized the operative agency of its individual myth-makers. Surely hagiographies do, to some extent, reflect the interests of individual redactors; however, in their roles as exempla, such tales cannot but instantiate the norms and ideals of the broader communities that circulate them. As Campany argues, any given hagiographer "may not assert just anything about his subjects, or take whatever liberties or wield whatever narrative devices he might choose: he is constrained to some extent by what his audience will recognize and approve" (2009, 16). Without conforming to these social conventions, a hagiography would persuade no one and would quickly disappear from the record, having never been deemed worthy of public dissemination. As much as anything else, then, hagiographies are records of collective memories, mentalities, or representations that, like cultural repertoires, are both fixed in form over many generations and reconstituted within and through each subsequent instantiation. In this book I examine the Chinese hagiographies of Aśvaghoṣa, Nāgārjuna, and Āryadeva as indices to the broader medieval Chinese *imaginaire* of ancient Indian Buddhism. And just like hagiography as exemplum, which transcends the dichotomies of fact and fiction, prenarrative history and poetical injunction, this *imaginaire* was likewise neither invented ex nihilo nor fully reflective of some underlying objective reality. It was always both empirical and poetical all the way down, with individual Chinese authors adopting and adapting their society's visions of ancient India in order to persuade contemporary audiences of the primacy of Buddhism in a world without a Buddha.

At the same time, however, in their function of conveying ostensibly Indian models of Buddhist sanctity, the Chinese hagiographies of Aśvaghoṣa, Nāgārjuna, and Āryadeva differed markedly from other tales of local holy figures. Early medieval accounts of Chinese transcendents, for example, provide an excellent example of the dialectic of collective representation I have outlined. These accounts were often compiled from earlier Chinese sources, they adhered to formulaic structures inherent to the genre, and they reinscribed age-old Chinese cosmological, anthropological, and soteriological ideals.[19] In this way the hagiographies of Chinese transcendents represent an eminently collective process whereby narrative tales both reflected and affected the mentalities of the local communities that circulated them. Similarly, Campany explains that Chinese Buddhist miracle tales were "socially formed from the very beginning . . . fashioned in the context of social interactions involving multiple parties." The "intensely social nature of narrative formation and narrative exchange" exerted a "steady pressure of group expectation and precedent on the idiosyncratic," thus ensuring the "typedness" of these miracle tales. As such, Campany contends, "The types of stories people tell in any given place and time are shaped by collective expectations and cultural patterns, but they also shape these in turn" (2012b, 47). And it is in this regard, as conforming to collective expectations that were avowedly *foreign* to those of local Chinese communities, that the Indian patriarch accounts can be seen to manifest a certain rupture in the cycle of social reproduction evidenced in Chinese tales of transcendents or Chinese Buddhist saints.

First of all, because the hagiographies of Aśvaghoṣa, Nāgārjuna, and Āryadeva were seen to have originated in ancient India, they were not expected to have the same formal structures and methods of composition that defined biographical genres from ancient times in China. For example, the well-known *Traditions of Eminent Monks* (*Gaoseng zhuan* 高僧傳) collections, compiled in the sixth, seventh, and tenth centuries, were based upon locally produced source materials such as epitaphs and miracle tales, and followed the basic format of secular biographies as standardized from the turn of the Common Era: detailing their subjects' ancestral heritage, birth and

19. See Campany 2002; 2009, chap. 1.

death dates, official appointments and activities at court, posthumous honors, and significant career achievements that occasioned their placement in one of several categories according to which the collected biographies were arrayed.[20] In this way the Chinese *Traditions of Eminent Monks* and similar hagiographic compendia clearly display the sort of typedness that Campany articulates, though more in formal compositional terms. By contrast, the Indian patriarch accounts had no explicit connection with Chinese biographical conventions. As ostensibly Indian writings, these hagiographies had no clear basis in well-known source genres or structural heritage in the *liezhuan* 列傳 (arrayed traditions) of earlier dynastic histories, and as such they lacked the formal constraints of genre that marked Chinese accounts of Chinese Buddhist saints.

Moreover, the accounts of Aśvaghoṣa, Nāgārjuna, and Āryadeva that circulated in medieval China were not portrayed as reflecting local ideals and expectations; instead, they functioned expressly to convey the ostensive norms of ancient India. Along similar lines, Campany remarks that South Asian *avadāna* and *jātaka* literature differed from Chinese Buddhist miracle tales insofar as the latter endeavored to "situate events in the everyday world of relatively recent times familiar to their audience." It follows that, in these miracle tales it was "the very closeness between the assumed reader and the textually depicted world that work[ed] to legitimate the claims made in the texts" (Campany 2012b, 2–3). Although I argue that the Indian patriarchs were upheld as valuable resources in medieval China largely because of their perceived proximity and familiarity, their hagiographies were nonetheless situated in contexts that did *not* represent the everyday worlds of relatively recent times familiar to their Chinese audiences—at least as compared with Chinese Buddhist miracle tales, hagiographies of eminent Chinese monks, tales of transcendents, and the like. The Chinese hagiographies of Aśvaghoṣa, Nāgārjuna, and Āryadeva were not shaped by the same pressures of collective expectation and precedent that went into making these analogous Chinese hagiographic genres. We can still treat these Indian patriarch accounts as medieval Chinese exempla that served broader Chinese discourses about Sino-Indian Buddhist sainthood, but we should not thereby conflate them with Chinese tales that instantiated avowedly local collective representations. Only the Indian patriarch hagiographies functioned to integrate India into this Chinese dialectic of mutually generative lives and narratives, and as a result, they should be examined in terms of how they deployed Indianness as a repertoire element, merged ostensibly native and foreign models of religious sanctity, and thereby bridged the gap between ancient India and latter-day China.

Finally, as media through which avowedly Indian exemplars of Buddhist sainthood and divinity were conveyed to China, the hagiographies of

20. See Kieschnick 1997, introduction; Shinohara 1988; and Wright (1954) 1990. On the sources and structures of Chinese secular biography, see especially Twitchett 1961 and 1962.

Aśvaghoṣa, Nāgārjuna, and Āryadeva often functioned in tandem with various other classes of Buddhist literature. Hagiography was not always the discrete literary genre that scholars often take it to be, and it did not serve only to provide biographical accounts of saints.[21] Rather, as I show in the following chapters, the Indian patriarchs' Chinese hagiographies were seen to provide the necessary background for understanding the contents and contexts of the patriarchs' doctrinal treatises and ritual manuals. Why, for example, was Āryadeva's *Hundred Treatise* structured like a Socratic dialogue between Buddhist and non-Buddhist opponents? Because it was reportedly a verbatim record of his debates with non-Buddhists as described in his early hagiographies (see chapter 3). Why would medieval Chinese Buddhists have seen Aśvaghoṣa as the most appropriate author for the *Mahāyāna Awakening of Faith* (*Dasheng qixin lun* 大乘起信論)? Because of his relationship with Nāgārjuna, his proclivity for *dhyāna* practice, and his skill in writing for post-*parinirvāṇa* audiences—aspects of his career that were well established in his earliest hagiographic traditions (see chapter 3). Why did Nāgārjuna offer spells, talismans, and elixirs with which Chinese adepts could attain all sorts of spectacular boons? Because his hagiographies told how he was a master of all Buddhist and non-Buddhist arts and sciences, especially alchemy and spell-casting (see chapter 4). Why was Aśvaghoṣa capable of devising magical rites to help people raise healthy silkworms and produce quality silk? Because, as explained in his hagiographies, he once transformed his body into a silkworm and produced silk with which to clothe the destitute masses of his kingdom (see chapter 5). These examples illustrate how hagiography and other genres of Buddhist literature were often mutually reinforcing in medieval China. Consequently, a fuller understanding of Chinese Buddhist hagiographic, doctrinal, and ritual discourses can be gained by examining the ways in which these respective literary genres functioned interdependently for their Chinese authors and audiences.

Chapter Outline

In broad strokes, the following chapters illustrate a prominent historical trajectory in Chinese Buddhist discourses concerning the relationship between Buddhism in India and in latter-day China. This is a trajectory of localization, whereby ancient Indian founts of Buddhist sanctity were adduced initially as distant models of a True Dharma since diminished, before being increasingly portrayed as immanent presences within the newfound Buddhist heartland of imperial China. With the reunification of the empire under the Sui and Tang regimes, China came to be counted as a center of Buddhist civilization and cradle of Buddhist holy beings; before this time, however, the reigning rhetoric was of declining Dharma, and great Buddhist saints were largely confined to the ancient Indian past. This latter dynamic is exemplified first in the writings of Kumārajīva's Chinese associates,

21. See, for example, the definition of hagiography provided by Kleine 1998, 325–326.

examined in chapter 1, which include both the oldest extant images of Aśvaghoṣa, Nāgārjuna, and Āryadeva and the earliest accounts in China of what happened to Buddhism in India after the death of the Buddha. Within the works of Sengzhao, Sengrui, and their southern compatriot Huiyuan 慧遠 (ca. 334–416), one can observe a concerted effort to address the questions of how to be Buddhist in a world without a Buddha, and how Buddhist sainthood would be defined in the generations after nirvāṇa. Kumārajīva's associates advanced Aśvaghoṣa, Nāgārjuna, and Āryadeva as models of Buddhist revivalism in post-*parinirvāṇa* India, when the Dharma was reportedly on the verge of collapse. Here the Indian patriarchs were shown to have single-handedly resurrected the Buddha's teachings through specific repertoires of religious practice that closely accorded with the favored occupations of spiritually inclined Chinese literati gentlemen, with whom Buddhist scholar-monks competed for patronage and prestige. By promoting their great Indian forebears as having saved the world through traditional Chinese values, Sengzhao, Sengrui, and Huiyuan demonstrated that these values were fundamentally Indian and Buddhist and were thus the province of Chinese scholar-monks alone.

Chapter 2 illustrates a seismic shift in Chinese representations of post-*parinirvāṇa* Indian Buddhism and thus conceptions of Buddhist sainthood in a world without a Buddha. While Kumārajīva's associates initially advanced a cyclical model of Indian Buddhist history, with the Dharma waxing and waning in conjunction with the appearance and disappearance of great Buddhist holy beings, the sources examined in this chapter instead depicted Aśvaghoṣa, Nāgārjuna, and Āryadeva standing in long lines of Indian patriarchs who together perpetuated the Dharma undimmed over the generations after nirvāṇa. These sources include especially the fifth- or sixth-century *Tradition of the Causes and Conditions of the Dharma-Treasury Transmission* (*Fu fazang yinyuan zhuan* 付法藏因緣傳, hereinafter *Dharma-Treasury Transmission*) and the sixth-century Cave of Great Perduring Saints (Dazhusheng ku 大住聖窟) at Lingquan monastery 靈泉寺, near the modern city of Anyang 安陽 (Henan province). The former source served in large part to fill out the medieval Chinese *imaginaire* of post-*parinirvāṇa* Indian Buddhism, and in so doing it redefined Buddhist sainthood in terms of lineal master-disciple Dharma transmission. However, because this well-known Indian Buddhist lineage history depicted the patriarchate being cut off before ever having reached China, I argue that it promoted a soteriology of absence akin to the *Lotus Sūtra*. Precisely because the greatest saints of India were all long gone, Chinese Buddhists were exhorted to redouble their efforts at establishing local transmission lineages in order to preserve the Dharma in perpetuity. Then, in the Cave of Great Perduring Saints, which included a sculpted representation of the Indian lineage from the *Dharma-Treasury Transmission*, this message was both perpetuated and nullified. On the one hand, this cave depicted the Indian patriarchs as long-departed exemplars of Buddhist sainthood. And on the other hand, it rendered them as immanent presences that could be engaged directly in latter-day China.

This movement to localize the Indian patriarchs is further exemplified by the sources examined in chapter 3, which show how Sui-Tang Buddhist exegetes integrated Aśvaghoṣa, Nāgārjuna, and Āryadeva into broader efforts to redefine China as the epicenter of Buddhist enlightenment. Nearly all of the most famous Buddhist exegetes of this period had a hand in developing the imagery of this Indian patriarchal triad, and the Chinese authors discussed in this chapter worked to synthesize earlier sources concerning the patriarchs. Focusing on the writings of monastic luminaries like Guanding 灌頂 (561–632), Jizang, and Xuanzang 玄奘 (602–664)—as well as sources that ascribed the *Awakening of Faith* to Aśvaghoṣa—this chapter illustrates how the paradigms of Buddhist sainthood advanced by Kumārajīva's associates and in the *Dharma-Treasury Transmission* were amalgamated in a new idiom that focused especially on the importance of authoring doctrinal treatises. Aśvaghoṣa, Nāgārjuna, and Āryadeva have long been represented in modern scholarship primarily as doctrinal specialists, and this is largely because Chinese exegetes of the seventh to ninth centuries emphasized this aspect of their repertoires above all others. As such, scriptural exegesis became the central defining function of the Indian patriarchs in China, particularly as juxtaposed with other means of conveying the Dharma across the Sino-Indian divide. While the Sui-Tang period would later become well known for its burgeoning of sectarian Sino-Indian lineage histories, Aśvaghoṣa, Nāgārjuna, and Āryadeva were most often depicted transmitting the teaching not in genealogical fashion but through their doctrinal treatises and models of exegesis. In this way Chinese exegetes advanced a model of Buddhist sainthood through scholarship, but no longer in a benighted China marked by perpetually declining Dharma that paled in comparison to the brilliance of ancient India. Rather, this model was promoted as part of the broader process of relocating the means and media of Indian enlightenment within the new Buddhist heartland of latter-day China, its sacred mountains, glorious Buddhist monuments, and legions of Buddhist saints.

Among the most prominent Indian Buddhist media to be localized in medieval China were the Indian patriarchs themselves, particularly Aśvaghoṣa and Nāgārjuna, who came to be represented as immanent deities that could provide for Chinese devotees a wide variety of magical boons. While this transformation was indeed the most dramatic of the patriarchs' Chinese history, there is also a clear continuity between their early hagiographic and doctrinal characterizations and the ways in which they were later advertised as local Indian gods. Chapter 4 focuses on Chinese sources that depicted Nāgārjuna as a *dhāraṇī* master, alchemist, and Pure Land denizen, who personally appeared in Chinese oratories to provide his unique blend of ritual repertoires that reportedly derived from ancient India but were fully congruent with time-honored Chinese ritual traditions. These are sources of a less scholarly, exegetical bent—including especially *Nāgārjuna's Treatise on the Five Sciences* (*Longshu wuming lun* 龍樹五明論), the *Scripture on the Power and Virtue of Prince Kumbhīra* (*Jinpiluo tongzi weide jing* 金毘羅童子威德經), and several Chinese Pure Land writings—that potentially engaged a broad range of medieval Chinese audiences and thus insinuated Nāgārjuna into the religious practice of Chinese devotees across social and sectarian divisions. In this context Nāgārjuna was not deployed as a model of emulation for elite Chinese monks who sought to localize Indian models of saintly scholarship. Rather, here he served as an object of veneration for Chinese adepts with a taste for ostensibly Indian thaumaturgic and alchemical rituals that provided apotropaic, therapeutic, material, and spiritual benefits. Though recognizably accordant with the liturgical conventions of local Chinese religions, Nāgārjuna's ritual programs were expressly labeled Indian Buddhist and thus rendered the preserve of Chinese Buddhists. In this way Nāgārjuna was made to instantiate Chinese models of divinity and soteriology while showing how Buddhist gods and rites were the best means of securing the benefits that all Chinese supplicants valued most.

Chapter 5 illustrates a similar dynamic in the case of Aśvaghoṣa, who by the mid- to late-Tang came to be represented as an Indian god of silkworms and silk production. In this guise Aśvaghoṣa, like Nāgārjuna, was localized in Chinese ritual arenas to provide a variety of tangible boons—though often revolving around the process and products of sericulture. And also like Nāgārjuna, as local Indian deity, Aśvaghoṣa in his Chinese apotheosis illustrates the interdependent nature of religious genres like hagiography, Dharma genealogy, and ritual manual. Aśvaghoṣa's ritual prescriptions as presented in manuals attributed to him, which were promoted as practicable for ritual specialists and common sericulturists alike, closely accorded with the manner in which he was portrayed in hagiographies circulated by the Chinese Buddhist clergy—especially the early ninth-century *Tradition of the Baolin* [*Temple*] (*Baolin zhuan* 寶林傳). As such, Aśvaghoṣa was not bifurcated along social lines in medieval China, as scholars sometimes assume, with his patriarchal persona serving the interests of clerical elites and his divine manifestation working for the wellbeing of popular religionists. Instead, Chinese sources depicted the same Aśvaghoṣa playing both roles at once, and several others besides, all of which were advertised to Chinese religious adepts across social and lay-monastic boundaries. In addition, as Aśvaghoṣa was said to have invented sericulture in ancient India, he functioned to render this most ubiquitous Chinese enterprise into a fundamentally Buddhist occupation. In this way traditional Chinese deities and rituals for ensuring healthy silkworms and abundant silk crops could be supplanted by Buddhist rites and ritualists, thus securing for the Chinese Buddhist institution a lucrative revenue stream in the form of patronage from silk producers.

Lastly, with the preceding chapters having examined specific instances in which Aśvaghoṣa, Nāgārjuna, and Āryadeva served broader Chinese efforts to negotiate the gap between ancient India and latter-day China, chapter 6 offers a more synoptic perspective on the Indian patriarchs as both models for emulation and objects of veneration in medieval China. In this chapter I aim to articulate the unique sorts of power and authority that Chinese Buddhists invested in the Indian patriarchs, as opposed to other Indian holy beings and in relation to competing Chinese models of sainthood and divinity. On the one hand, as discussed in chapters 4 and 5, the Indian patriarchs served as objects of veneration in medieval China, much like other Indian figures and Chinese deities and saints. In this guise as local gods, Aśvaghoṣa and Nāgārjuna functioned to Indianize time-honored Chinese models of divinity, thus making these models the preserve of Chinese Buddhists. On the other hand, the patriarchs were most often represented as "Goldilocks saints" of sorts, who lived neither too close to nor too far from either the Buddha or latter-day Chinese adepts. This made the Indian patriarchs both authoritative representatives of original Indian Buddhism and proximal exemplars of Buddhist sainthood for the generations after nirvāṇa. Aśvaghoṣa, Nāgārjuna, and Āryadeva thus provided models for emulation in China, unlike the arhats or celestial bodhisattvas, and served as vehicles through which Chinese Buddhists could lay claim to the most venerable Chinese repertoires of saintly attainment. These dynamics illustrate how Chinese Buddhists developed models of Buddhist sanctity as means of bridging the Sino-Indian divide, showing how great Buddhist saints could be created in the centuries after nirvāṇa, whether in India or China; how ancient Indian holy beings had become immanent presences in China; and how the avowedly foreign religion of Buddhism actually represented—from its ancient Indian inception and through its greatest Indian saints—the most vaunted Chinese ideals of sanctity and salvation.

1
Buddhist Sainthood in Dharmic History

PRIOR TO THE FIFTH CENTURY, information available to the Chinese about post-*parinirvāṇa* Buddhist India was scant. There were numerous records describing the life of the Buddha, disciples, and royal patrons who helped propagate the religion around the time of its founder. Hundreds of scriptures of both *Āgama* and Mahāyāna varieties, translated from the Eastern Han to the Eastern Jin, recounted fantastic tales of figures and events that marked the earliest history of Indian Buddhism. *Jātaka* tales of the Buddha's previous lives stretched this history into the cosmic past, and *Abhidharma* treatises pushed it slightly forward with the activities of the Buddha's personal disciples. But what happened to Buddhism in India over the centuries after Śākyamuni's departure? What of the intervening half-millennium, or more, before the religion was finally transmitted to China? Who kept Buddhism alive during this crucial period, and what lessons could they offer Chinese Buddhists who likewise worked to propagate the Dharma in a world without a Buddha? These were questions that preoccupied Chinese Buddhist authors of the early fifth century. With issues of fidelity to Indian Buddhism having come to the fore especially from the time of Daoan 道安 (312–385), and with mounting disquiet over the authenticity of Chinese modes of Buddhist thought and practice, leaders of the Chinese sangha became increasingly focused on the spatiotemporal gap that separated them from the ancient Indian fount of Buddhist truth.

Early Chinese secular records and translations of Indic sources would only scratch the surface in ensuing efforts to delineate the contours of this gap. Prior to the travelogue of the intrepid pilgrim Faxian 法顯 (ca. 337–422), completed in 416 at the Eastern Jin capital of Jiankang 建康,[1] the state of Buddhism in contemporary India was only vaguely understood. The *Historical Records* (*Shiji* 史記) and *Book of the Han* (*Hanshu* 漢書) recounted the Western travels of the famous emissary Zhang Qian 張騫 (ca. 167–114 BCE)—providing details of Central and South Asia pertinent to commercial, political, and military expeditions—but the current religious climate of India did not go on official record until the *Book of the Later Han* (*Hou Hanshu*

1. On Faxian's travelogue, see especially Deeg 2005.

後漢書) of the mid-fifth century.[2] Of course, a number of well-known Western missionaries, such as An Shigao 安世高 (fl. 148 CE), Lokakṣema (Zhi Loujiachen 支婁迦讖; fl. 150 CE), and Fotucheng 佛圖澄 (d. 348), had demonstrated by their very presence the continued existence of Buddhism across the Western Regions, and they doubtless regaled their Chinese audiences with accounts of the religion in their home countries.[3] Otherwise, for Chinese Buddhists at the turn of the fifth century, the main sources of knowledge about post-*parinirvāṇa* Buddhist India included a handful of potentially disconcerting scriptural prophecies concerning the fate of the Dharma, and the more heartening if somewhat conflicted stories from the *Tradition of King Aśoka* (*Ayuwang zhuan* 阿育王傳; *Aśokāvadāna*).

Already from the Eastern Han, Chinese Buddhists had access to translated sūtras that recorded the Buddha's predictions about the gradual decline of the Dharma over the centuries after his death. These scriptures often provided specific timelines for this decline, foretelling Buddhism's demise some five hundred or one thousand years after nirvāṇa, and sometimes describing its devolution from "True Dharma" (*zhengfa* 正法) to "Semblance Dharma" (*xiangfa* 像法) periods. The exact causes of this devolution were not always specified, though a number of traditions claimed that the teaching was diminished through corruption in the sangha or persecution by evil kings.[4] Overall, however, such texts offered a rather sparse depiction of Indian Buddhism in the generations after nirvāṇa, usually glossing over kingdoms and centuries in a few brief episodes and providing little detail about the vicissitudes of the religion. Nevertheless, these sources did paint a general picture of darkness and decay that would deeply influence Chinese representations of this period of Indian Buddhist history. Also important in this regard was the *Aśokāvadāna*, first translated into Chinese at the beginning of the fourth century, which narrated the exploits of the (in)famous Mauryan king, Aśoka. As Aśoka was generally thought to have lived one hundred years after the Buddha (Lancaster 1991, 455), this was perhaps the only text of its time that elaborated the trials and triumphs of Indian Buddhism post-*parinirvāṇa*. The *Aśokāvadāna* mostly depicted Buddhists in this period as full of vim and vigor—though it did present its own brief decline narrative like the sūtras I mention—and it included the earliest account in China of an Indian Buddhist patriarchate that upheld the Dharma after Śākyamuni's departure.

Together with its description of Aśoka's efforts to patronize Buddhism, the *Aśokāvadāna*'s summary tales of the Dharma masters Mahākāśyapa, Ānanda, Madhyāntika, Śāṇavāsa, and Upagupta provided the first explicit

---

2. For the *Shiji*, see Watson 1969, 274–299; for the *Hanshu*, see Hulsewé and Loewe 1979; for the *Hou Hanshu*, see Hill 2003.

3. On An Shigao and Lokakṣema, see most recently Nattier 2008, 38–72, 73–89; on Fotucheng, see Wright (1948) 1990.

4. On early timelines of Dharma decline and its purported causes, see Hubbard 2001, chap. 2 and 3; Lamotte 1988, 192–202; and Nattier 1991.

narrative in China of what happened to Buddhism in India after the Buddha. It recounted the construction of famous monasteries, the courting of royal patrons, the conversion of kingdoms, and especially the exploits of those holy men who carried forth the teachings bequeathed by Śākyamuni.[5] However, the *Aśokāvadāna* only focused on the first century after nirvāṇa, and many of the patriarchs that it described had themselves practiced at the feet of the Buddha and thus vividly recalled a world illuminated by his presence. But how did this history progress? What of the later generations of Buddhist devotees who had never seen the Buddha and who worked to uphold the Dharma through the centuries of darkness that so many sūtras portended? These questions were crucial to fifth-century Chinese Buddhists, who counted themselves among those devotees facing the daunting challenge of propagating the teaching in a world without a Buddha. Earlier Western missionaries and translated Indic sources had yet to offer a complete picture of post-*parinirvāṇa* Buddhist India, or satisfactory models of Buddhist practice for devotees living in such circumstances. So when the great Kuchean master Kumārajīva arrived at the Later Qin capital of Chang'an in the winter of 401–402,[6] and Chinese adepts gathered in his company to forge a more authentic Buddhist canon to guide the Chinese sangha, one major avenue of inquiry was the plight of the Indian patriarchs who had spanned that crucial gap separating latter-day China from ancient India.

This preoccupation is apparent in a number of translations and writings produced by Kumārajīva and his Chinese associates, including especially Sengrui 僧叡 (ca. 352–436), Sengzhao 僧肇 (ca. 374–414), and Huiyuan 慧遠 (ca. 334–416).[7] Kumārajīva was charged by the Qin emperor Yao Xing 姚興 (r. 394–416) with producing new and authoritative translations of some of the most influential Buddhist scriptures of the time, such as the *Lotus*, *Vimalakīrti*, *Pure Land*, and *Perfection of Wisdom* sūtras, but his own predilection for the exegesis of latter-day saints is indicated by the selection of

5. *Ayuwang zhuan* 阿育王傳, T no. 2042, 50:111b–121b. Summarized in Lamotte 1988, 206–210; French trans. Przyluski 1923, 308–369. The sixth-century *Scripture of King Aśoka* (*Ayuwang jing* 阿育王經, T no. 2043, 50:149b–162c) contains a similar narrative; trans. Li 1993, 91–152. Several other early translations of the Aśoka legend are listed in the *Chu sanzang jiji*, most of which are now lost; see Zürcher (1959) 2007, 423n162.

6. Useful secondary sources on the life and works of Kumārajīva include Chou 2000; Lu 2004; Pelliot 2002; Robinson 1967, chap. 3; and Tang 1938, chap. 10.

7. On Sengrui, see Chou 2000, 19–35; Chou 2004, 287–295; and Robinson 1967, 115–117. The *Gaoseng zhuan* 高僧傳 contains separate biographies of Sengrui (T no. 2059, 50:364a–b) and Huirui 慧叡 (T no. 2059, 50:367a–b), treating them as distinct individuals of the north and south, respectively. Both of these accounts are translated by Wright 1957b, who (following Ōchō Enichi 横超慧日) shows that they actually refer to the same individual. On Sengzhao, see Liebenthal 1968 and Robinson 1967, 123–155, 210–232. For more recent discussions of his career, see Liu 1994, 37–39, and Sharf 2002, 31–32. On Huiyuan, see Hurvitz 1957; Robinson 1967, chap. 4; Tang 1938, chap. 11; and Zürcher (1959) 2007, 204–239. His *Chu sanzang jiji* (T no. 2145, 55:109b–110c) and *Gaoseng zhuan* (T no. 2059, 50:357c–361b) biographies are translated in Zürcher (1959) 2007, 240–253.

treatises that he introduced to his Chinese audience. These included Āryadeva's *Hundred Treatise* (*Śata śāstra*) and Nāgārjuna's *Middle Stanzas* (*Madhyamakakārikās*) and *Twelve Gates Treatise* (*Dvādaśamukha śāstra*), providing the foundation for what would later become known as the East Asian "Three Treatise" (Sanlun 三論) tradition.[8] Also from Nāgārjuna's ostensive oeuvre Kumārajīva translated the *Expanded Treatise on the Ten Stages* (*Daśabhūmikavibhāṣāśāstra*) and the *Great Perfection of Wisdom Treatise* (*Mahāprajñāpāramitāśāstra*), the latter of which would become the most influential Indian treatise in China.[9] Finally, with his translation of the *Scripture on Seated Dhyāna Samādhi,* Kumārajīva introduced the poetry of Aśvaghoṣa, whose verses graced this compendium of meditation instructions.[10] As consequential as these translations were, however, equally important to Chinese adepts of the time were the models of Buddhist practice provided by the Indian authors of these texts. The life stories of these masters filled a glaring lacuna in the history of latter-day Indian Buddhism, while fleshing out the early Chinese *imaginaire* of post-*parinirvāṇa* Buddhist sainthood. These tales thus offered valuable resources for latter-day Chinese adepts who sought to articulate their own place in Sino-Indian

---

8. The Sanskrit title of Āryadeva's *Śataśāstra* is reconstructed from the Chinese *Bai lun* 百論 (T no. 1569; trans. Qiang 1997, Tucci [1929] 1976), translated in 402 and revised in 404, the only version in which it is extant. According to Sengzhao's preface (*Bai lun* 百論, T no. 1569, 30:168a; *Chu sanzang ji ji* 出三藏記集, T no. 2145, 55:77c; trans. Robinson 1967, 211), Kumārajīva translated only the first ten chapters of an original that had twenty chapters of five verses each—thus the "hundred" of the title. This translation consists largely of commentary on Deva's verses by a certain bodhisattva Vasu (Posou 婆藪). The earliest extant version of Nāgārjuna's *Madhyamakakārikās* is imbedded within Kumārajīva's translation in 409 of the *Zhong lun* 中論 (*Madhyamakaśāstra*, T no. 1564; trans. Bocking 1995), which contains 449 of Nāgārjuna's *kārikās* and an extensive commentary by someone named Qingmu 青目 ("Blue Eye[s]"), which is extant only in Chinese. For the identity of this individual see Bocking 1995, 395–405; cf. Funayama 2000, 348, 352n6. Nāgārjuna's *Dvādaśamukhaśāstra* was rendered into Chinese in 409 as the *Shi'ermen lun* 十二門論 (T no. 1568; trans. Cheng 1982), also the only version that has come down to us.

9. The *Expanded Treatise on the Ten Stages* (*Daśabhūmikavibhāṣāśāstra*) was translated as *Shizhu piposha lun* 十住毘婆沙論, T no. 1521. Extant only in Chinese; partial trans. Inagaki 1998. This is an exposition of the first two of the bodhisattva's ten stages that were introduced in the *Daśabhūmika* chapter of the *Avataṃsakasūtra*, which circulated independently of the sūtra in translations made first by Dharmarakṣa (*Pusa shizhu xingdao pin* 菩薩十住行道品, T no. 283) and later by Kumārajīva (*Shizhu jing* 十住經, T no. 286). The *Mahāprajñāpāramitāśāstra* was translated as *Da zhidu lun* 大智度論, T no. 1509. This commentary was translated in conjunction with Kumārajīva's retranslation of the *Pañcaviṁśati*, which is interspersed throughout and constitutes some 30 percent of the 700 Taishō pages and 100 scrolls of the *Da zhidu lun*. Both translations were completed in February of 406. On the compilation and authorship of the *Da zhidu lun* see Chou 2000 and 2004, which argue convincingly that parts of the present text are recorded discussions between Kumārajīva and his Chinese associates over problems of interpretation. French trans. of the first thirty-four scrolls by Lamotte 1944–1980.

10. *Zuochan sanmei jing* 坐禪三昧經, T no. 614; trans. Yamabe and Sueki 2009. The contents of this text are outlined in Sengrui's "Preface to the *Dhyāna* Scriptures Translated within the Passes" (*Guanzhong chu chanjing xü* 關中出禪經序, in *Chu sanzang jiji*, T no. 2145, 55:65a–b).

Dharmic history, as well as the roles that they should strive to fulfill in their own challenging times so far removed from the epicenter of Buddhist enlightenment.

Within the writings of Kumārajīva's Chinese associates we find the earliest surviving depictions of Aśvaghoṣa, Nāgārjuna, and Āryadeva in any Buddhist canon.[11] In prefaces to translated Indian treatises, recorded dialogues interspersed throughout other commentarial works, and more explicitly hagiographic writings, Sengrui, Sengzhao, and Huiyuan in particular emphasized aspects of these Indian patriarchs' careers that were deemed pertinent to the ideals and aspirations of contemporary Chinese Buddhists. The theme that predominated in these sources was the dire state of Indian Buddhism in the centuries after nirvāṇa and the charge of Buddhist masters to uphold the teachings amid the encroaching darkness. Kumārajīva and his disciples most frequently situated Aśvaghoṣa, Nāgārjuna, and Āryadeva in specific centuries after the Buddha's death, at times when his teachings had fallen into decay. However, the degradations characteristic of this latter age served primarily as a backdrop against which the great accomplishments of the Indian patriarchs were emphasized. In such dark times Aśvaghoṣa, Nāgārjuna, and Āryadeva alone were able to clear the path of the True Dharma and reestablish Śākyamuni's teachings throughout Jambudvīpa. And much like India in the centuries after nirvāṇa, Kumārajīva's Chinese compatriots characterized their own time and place as teeming with false dogmas that threatened to obliterate the increasingly distant Buddhist truth. Nevertheless, they asserted that Aśvaghoṣa, Nāgārjuna, and Āryadeva had brought renewed hope of liberation—through both their translated treatises and models of Buddhist practice—thus mitigating any concerns that Chinese Buddhists might harbor about their own inability to adequately grasp the teachings of the Buddha.

How exactly did Aśvaghoṣa, Nāgārjuna, and Āryadeva revive an otherwise failing Buddhadharma? What specific practices did these Indian masters model for Chinese Buddhists living in similarly dark times, long after Śākyamuni's death? Perhaps not surprisingly, these patriarchs instantiated a repertoire of practices not unlike those most valued by the Chinese intellectual elite of the time, which included Sengrui, Sengzhao, and Huiyuan. These luminaries of the Chinese sangha were well-known for their intellectual prowess and mastery of classical Chinese literature and fields advanced by *xuanxue* 玄學 (study of the profound) adepts of earlier generations, as well as practices championed by contemporary literati gentlemen across religio-philosophical traditions, such as *qingtan* 清談 (pure conversation) public debate, authorship of philosophical treatises,

11. I am aware of only one reference to Nāgārjuna that may predate the sources discussed in this chapter. This reference, apparently drawn from Daoan's long-lost *Xiyu zhi* 西域志, occurs in Daoshi's 道世 (ca. 596–683) *Fayuan zhulin* 法苑珠林 (T no. 2122, 53:589a) of 668. This is a brief story about Nāgārjuna retrieving a jewel-encrusted stūpa from an undersea dragon palace. See Lamotte 1944–1980, 3:xxxviii–xxxix; and Shanhui 1979, 136.

meditation, and eremitism. These are also among the practices most frequently highlighted in the earliest Chinese accounts of Aśvaghoṣa, Nāgārjuna, and Āryadeva. Through these biographies the defining vocations of the medieval Chinese scholar-gentleman were projected back into post-*parinirvāṇa* India as the concrete means by which the greatest Buddhist masters of the time had saved a dying Dharma. So by advancing practices for which they were already most renowned—and by advocating a particularly Buddhist inflection for these longstanding endeavors of the Chinese literati—Buddhist adepts such as Sengrui, Sengzhao, and Huiyuan could likewise resurrect the True Dharma in latter-day China and thereby join their Indian predecessors as the greatest Buddhist saints across the Sino-Indian divide.

Chinese Chronologies of Indian Sainthood

As much as anything else, the earliest Chinese hagiographies of Aśvaghoṣa, Nāgārjuna, and Āryadeva were about Buddhist history. These accounts almost always endeavored to situate their protagonists within specific historical circumstances—signaled at the outset by a chronology begun with Śākyamuni's passing—and, as a result, they filled a longstanding gap in the medieval Chinese understanding of the vicissitudes of Indian Buddhism after nirvāṇa. Reflecting numerous predictions offered by the Buddha in earlier scriptures, and in other works transmitted by Kumārajīva, these patriarch biographies represented Indian Buddhist history as cyclical in nature, marked by a repeated rise and decline of the Dharma and the appearance of holy beings at significant junctures in this cycle. These holy beings would precipitate the resurrection of a failing Buddhadharma in their own trying times, much as Śākyamuni had done in reintroducing the lost teachings of past buddhas, and bequeath traces of their brilliance to future generations. Nominally depicting the progression of this Dharmic history in post-*parinirvāṇa* India, the Chinese biographies of Aśvaghoṣa, Nāgārjuna, and Āryadeva also heralded the trajectory of the Dharma in latter-day China and furnished models of Buddhist sainthood tailored specifically to their medieval Chinese audience. In this regard the patriarch accounts resonated with age-old Chinese traditions according to which the true Way would wax and wane and great saints would appear in the world to set it straight. But unlike these earlier Chinese traditions, the accounts of Aśvaghoṣa, Nāgārjuna, and Āryadeva offered specific means by which Chinese adepts themselves could overcome the darkness, resurrect the truth, and thereby stand among the greatest saints in history.

Kumārajīva's disciple Sengzhao provides a clear example of the tendency to historicize the patriarchs in post-*parinirvāṇa* India and emphasize their great triumphs in reviving a dying Buddhadharma through practices most esteemed by medieval Chinese scholar-monks. In his preface to Kumārajīva's translation of Āryadeva's *Hundred Treatise*, Sengzhao presented the only extant account of this patriarch that can be confidently dated to the early fifth century.[12] Here Sengzhao emphasized Āryadeva's temporal remove from the Buddha and the degradation of the Dharma during Āryadeva's generation. Despite this handicap, Āryadeva was uniquely equipped to stem the tide of false views and resurrect the true teaching in the land of the Buddha's birth. Sengzhao stresses that Āryadeva rescued the deluded masses during this dark time primarily by composing the *Hundred Treatise*, thus providing an early indication of how important the patriarchs' models of authorship were to their Chinese proponents:

> Eight hundred and some years after the Buddha's nirvāṇa there was a great master named [Ārya]deva who left home [to become a monk]. His profound mind was singularly enlightened and his genius was outstanding. His Way illumined his time and his spirit surpassed the mundane. Thus he was able to unlock the double bars from the Threefold Canon and level the abstruse road of the twelve [sections of the canon].[13] He strode freely through Kapilavastu and became a moat to the City of Dharma.
>
> At that time, non-Buddhists ran riot, heterodoxies arose in conflict, and false debates imperiled the truth so that the True Way was nearly lost in confusion. Then, looking up he lamented the decline of the saintly teaching, and looking down he grieved that the strayed multitude was given over to delusion. With the intention of rescuing far and wide those who were drowning, he composed this treatise in order to buttress the true and check the false, making the ultimate principles thoroughly clear. Thus due to his [efforts] the correct teaching was exalted and false ways declined. Who but one endowed with all sublime qualities could do such a thing?[14]

> 佛泥洹後八百餘年, 有出家大士, 厥名提婆. 玄心獨悟, 俊氣高朗. 道映當時, 神超世表. 故能闢三藏之重關, 坦十二之幽路. 擅步迦夷, 為法城塹.
>
> 于時外道紛然, 異端競起, 邪辯逼真, 殆亂正道. 乃仰慨聖教之陵遲, 俯悼群迷之縱惑. 將遠拯沈淪, 故作斯論, 所以防正閑邪, 大明於宗極者矣. 是以正化以之而隆, 邪道以之而替. 非夫領括眾妙孰能若斯?[15]

Like most of the Chang'an Indian patriarch accounts, Sengzhao began his presentation of Āryadeva's career with a timeline of Dharmic history, locating the patriarch some eight hundred years after nirvāṇa. Āryadeva

---

12. This preface was likely written shortly after the revision of the *Hundred Treatise* in 404. The independently circulating biography of Āryadeva preserved in the Taishō canon (*Tipo pusa zhuan* 提婆菩薩傳, T no. 2048) was probably produced at least a half-century later. See chapter 2 and appendix 2.

13. Jizang 吉藏 (549–623) explained in his *Hundred Treatise Commentary* (*Bailun shu* 百論疏, T no. 1827, 42:233c) that the "double bars" to understanding the scriptures were either 1) the falsities of non-Buddhists and 2) the grasping at essences by Lesser Vehicle adherents, or the tendency of Lesser Vehicle followers to 1) grasp the words but miss their meaning and 2) miss both words and meaning (Robinson 1967, 303n7).

14. Trans. Robinson 1967, 210–211, with minor modifications.

15. *Bai lun*, T no. 1569, 30:167c–168a; *Chu sanzang jiji*, T no. 2145, 55:77b–c.

was dated not according to regnal years, imperial reign titles, or the sexagenary cycle of Celestial Stems and Terrestrial Branches (*ganzhi* 干支), as was standard practice from Han times with local figures both religious and secular. Rather, Āryadeva was dated in terms of his remove from the time of Śākyamuni's death. This chronology followed an ancient Indian model of dating Buddhist masters based on the *parinirvāṇa* year, as found in a number of Pāli texts and later Chinese translations of Sanskrit literature.[16] For the Chinese, such timelines had clear soteriological implications in that they signaled an historical devolution of the True Dharma through epochs often termed the Semblance Dharma (*xiangfa*) and Final Dharma (*mofa* 末法), or Final Age (*moshi* 末世).[17] Here Sengzhao did not use these terms, but he was explicit about the soteriological perils of Āryadeva's generation: "non-Buddhists ran riot, heterodoxies arose in conflict, and false debates imperiled the truth so that the True Way was nearly lost in confusion." However, this temporal remove from the Buddha did not lessen Āryadeva's worth in the eyes of his biographer. Rather, Āryadeva's dire circumstances made his achievements all the more vaunted; he was "singularly enlightened" (*duwu* 獨悟) in the sense—quite prominent in these early patriarch accounts—that only he was capable of truly grasping the Buddhist truth in such degenerate times.[18]

Finally, what was Āryadeva's response to the soteriological mire in which he found himself? He wrote. He "rescued far and wide those who were drowning," not by miraculous bodily transformations or public displays of magical power, but by composing the *Hundred Treatise*. Of course, Sengzhao's account occurs in the preface to the *Hundred Treatise*, so one might expect this text to be his focus. Nevertheless, exegetical composition was clearly a defining function of the latter-day Indian patriarchs, much as it was for the Chinese scholar-monks by and for whom such accounts were propagated. Aśvaghoṣa, Nāgārjuna, and Āryadeva left behind writings that were upheld by Kumārajīva himself as models of authorship at a distance from the word of the Buddha. The writings of these patriarchs were to be both venerated and emulated throughout medieval China, a world where the power of the written word was always seen as paramount.

The next important example of this tendency to historicize the Indian patriarchs is provided by Sengrui, who was Kumārajīva's primary amanuensis from the time they both arrived in Chang'an at the beginning of

16. See Lamotte 1988, 203–205.

17. As shown by Nattier (1991, 110–111), an explicit tripartite scheme of *zhengfa*, *xiangfa*, and *mofa* was not developed until the sixth century. However, all of these terms are present within the works of Kumārajīva and his associates, and they played a significant role in how the Indian patriarchs were conceived at the time.

18. This is Jizang's interpretation; see Robinson 1967, 303n5. *Duwu* typically referred to those who were awakened on their own, without being taught—that is, buddhas or *pratyekabuddhas*. This may have been Sengzhao's meaning, which would further support the hypothesis that Kumārajīva and his associates did not see Āryadeva as Nāgārjuna's direct disciple. See the discussion later in this chapter.

402. Sengrui was intimately involved in the translation of Aśvaghoṣa's, Nāgārjuna's, and Āryadeva's works, and he left behind a number of writings in which he delineated the repertoires of these post-*parinirvāṇa* Buddhist saints. Sengrui's preface to the *Great Perfection of Wisdom Treatise* in particular emphasized the gradual decline of the teaching through True and Semblance Dharma periods and placed Aśvaghoṣa and Nāgārjuna at the ends of these periods.[19] Sengrui stressed that although these patriarchs worked in dark times of soteriological degradation, they made the teachings of the Buddha flourish once again:

> Aśvaghoṣa appeared during the remainder of the True Dharma [period] and Nāgārjuna was born at the end of Semblance Dharma [period]. In the remainder of the True [Dharma period] it was easy to propagate [the Dharma]. Thus [Aśvaghoṣa] directly exploited the heritage bequeathed [by the Buddha]; he needed only polish it a bit. But at the end of the Semblance [Dharma period false teachings] proliferated. Therefore, [Nāgārjuna] left his traces among ordinary people and taught the awakening of beings through gradual [methods].
>
> Further, he availed himself of the light of the dragon palace[20] to illumine wisdom in search of the profound, and he devoted himself to the study of the secret depth in order to exhaust the marvel of the subtle words. Then, modeled on the canon of wisdom,[21] he composed this exposition. It opened the great road in such a manner that the carriage of the Greater Vehicle could advance straight ahead along the tracks [of the Way]. It specified the true aspect in such a way that those confused by false views would not stray far before returning [to the origin] on their own . . .
>
> An Indian tradition says, "At the end of the Semblance and True [Dharma periods], if not for Aśvaghoṣa and Nāgārjuna the teaching of the Way would have fallen into desuetude."[22] Why is this? Because without these two to harmonize the subtle [Dharma], false methods prospered. Empty words arose together with the true teaching. The steep path contended tracks with the great road. Those who had just entered [on the True Path] were converted [to false teachings] and went astray; those who were progressing towards the Way were deceived and roamed aimlessly. Without these two master-workmen [Aśvaghoṣa

19. This preface was probably composed not long after the translation of the *Da zhidu lun* was completed in February, 406 (Shih 1981, 737).

20. See the subsequent discussion on Nāgārjuna's sojourn to the dragon palace.

21. *Zhidian* 智典 perhaps refers to the *Prajñāpāramitā* text upon which the *Da zhidu lun* was based, the *Pañcaviṁśati*; see Shih 1981, 744n12.

22. On this Indian tradition: Robinson (1967, 23), Shih (1981, 747), and Yamano (2009, 68) take "*Tianzhu zhuan* 天竺傳" to be the title of a specific text. Ochiai (2000, 632), Robinson (1967, 25), and Shih (1981, 747n35) all speculate that this information was related to Sengrui by Kumārajīva, which is as good a guess as any. Robinson (1967, 22) further asserts that this *Tianzhu zhuan* attests the independently circulating biography of Nāgārjuna (*Longshu pusa zhuan* 龍樹菩薩傳, T no. 2047), which is traditionally attributed to Kumārajīva. However, this suggestion exceeds the evidence. See appendix 2.

and Nāgārjuna], who could have set it right? Therefore all the kingdoms in India built temples in homage to them and worshipped them like buddhas.

Also, [Nāgārjuna] was eulogized in verse:

"The sun of wisdom had been eclipsed,
but this man caused it to shine again;
the world had long been asleep in darkness,
but this man awoke it."

This being so, one may indeed say that his merits are comparable to a tenth-stage [bodhisattva] and his Way is equal to the next buddha! Passing down [such examples] and eulogizing them, is this not also fitting?[23]

馬鳴起於正法之餘, 龍樹生於像法之末. 正餘易弘, 故直振其遺風, 瑩拂而已. 像末多端, 故乃寄跡凡夫, 示悟物以漸.

又假照龍宮, 以朗搜玄之慧; 託聞幽祕, 以窮微言之妙. 爾乃憲章智典, 作茲釋論. 其開夷路也, 則令大乘之駕, 方軌而直入. 其辨實相也, 則使妄見之惑, 不遠而自復 . . .

天竺傳云, "像正之末, 微馬鳴龍樹, 道學之門, 其淪胥溺喪矣." 其故何耶? 寔由二未契微, 邪法用盛. 虛言與實教並興. 嶮徑與夷路爭轍. 始進者化之而流離; 向道者惑之而播越. 非二匠其孰與正之? 是以天竺諸國, 為之立廟, 宗之若佛.

又稱而詠之曰:

"智慧日已頹,
斯人令再曜;
世昏寢已久,
斯人悟令覺."

若然者, 真可謂, 功格十地, 道牟補處者矣! 傳而稱之, 不亦宜乎?[24]

This preface again demonstrates the early Chinese preoccupation with placing the Indian patriarchs on a timeline that began with the death of the Buddha. In the centuries after nirvāṇa, as Sengzhao, Sengrui, and others frequently asserted, false teachings flourished, potential converts to the true Way were led astray, and people were thereby hindered in their ability to achieve awakening. In this instance Sengrui did not provide specific after-nirvāṇa dates for the patriarchs; rather, he placed them directly within their respective Dharma Periods—near the end of the True Dharma for Aśvaghoṣa and at the end of the Semblance Dharma for Nāgārjuna. How did Sengrui understand these periods, and what time frames did he have in mind for their duration? According to the passage I quoted, in the True Dharma period it was easy to propagate the teaching, so Aśvaghoṣa "needed only polish it a bit." During the Semblance Dharma numerous false dogmas proliferated, so in order to save sentient beings Nāgārjuna was forced to employ expedient methods. Later in the passage Sengrui declared in no uncertain

23. Trans. Shih 1981, 744, 747–748, with minor modifications. Cf. trans. Lü 1996, 234–237 and Robinson 1967, 23.

24. *Chu sanzang jiji*, T no. 2145, 55:74c–75a; *Da zhidu lun*, T no. 1509, 25:57a–b.

terms that the ends of both eras were characterized by false teachings that obscured the truth. And while this preface offered no indication of the duration of these periods, in his *Treatise on Resolving Doubts* (*Yuyi lun* 喻疑論) Sengrui clearly stipulated that the True and Semblance Dharma were made up of consecutive half-millennium blocks, explaining that in the former age many people achieved enlightenment, while in the latter period the Dharma "was but a likeness and not genuine."[25]

Indeed, this division of the Dharma into consecutive five-hundred-year True and Semblance periods was commonplace in fifth-century Chang'an, as seen in a number of Kumārajīva's translations. The *Diamond Sūtra*, for example, twice mentions a five-hundred-year period following the death of the Buddha,[26] and Kumārajīva's version of the *Lotus Sūtra* contains several references to half-millennium divisions of Buddhist history, some with a pronounced rhetoric of decline.[27] A number of *Lotus* passages describe a so-called latter evil age (*hou e shi* 後惡世), "when the Dharma was about to perish" (*fa yu mie shi* 法欲滅時), indicating a vision of soteriological decay similar to that which marked the Indian patriarch accounts.[28] In addition, Kumārajīva's translations of the *Great Perfection of Wisdom Treatise* and *Middle Treatise* provide comparable chronologies that were perhaps more likely sources for Sengrui's timeline. The former text explained that "when the Buddha was in the world sentient beings had sharp faculties and were easily awakened," but then "five hundred years after the Buddha's extinction, in the Semblance Dharma [period], sentient beings . . . descended into attachment to dharmas."[29] And according to the *Middle Treatise*, "after the extinction of the Buddha, in the latter five-hundred years of the Semblance Dharma, people's faculties became dull and they were deeply attached to the myriad dharmas."[30]

These sources clearly indicate that, for Kumārajīva and his associates, the Semblance Dharma period began five hundred years after the Buddha's extinction, lasted for another five hundred years, and was characterized by soteriological degradation. This is the context in which the Indian

---

25. *Chu sanzang jiji*, T no. 2145, 55:41c. See Ochiai 1996, 566; 2000, 623. This treatise was most likely composed after Sengrui fled to the Eastern Jin capital of Jiankang in 418 (Wright 1957b, 287).

26. *Jin'gang boreboluomi jing* 金剛般若波羅蜜經, T no. 235, 8:749a: "After the extinction of the Thus Come One, in the latter five hundred years" 如來滅後後五百歲; 750b: "In the coming age of the latter five-hundred years" 來世後五百歲. See the discussion by Nattier (1991, 33–37), where she translates *hou wubai sui* 後五百歲 as "five hundred after-years" and speculates that the text envisions only five hundred years of perduring Dharma after the Buddha's death, rather than one thousand years divided into two five-hundred-year periods.

27. See, e.g., *Miaofa lianhua jing* 妙法蓮花經, T no. 262, 9:61a; 61b, trans. Hurvitz 1976, 333.

28. See Nattier 1988, 340–347.

29. *Da zhidu lun*, T no. 1509, 25:681b: 佛在世時, 眾生利根易悟. 佛滅度五百年後, 像法中, 眾生愛著佛法, 墮著法中.

30. *Zhong lun*, T no. 1564, 30:1b–c: 佛滅度後, 後五百歲像法中, 人根轉鈍, 深著諸法; cf. trans. Bocking 1995, 104. These last two references are from Nattier 1991, 47.

patriarchs were invariably placed in early fifth-century Chinese writings, including Sengrui's preface to the *Great Perfection of Wisdom Treatise* as well as the preface that Kumārajīva's disciple Tanying 曇影 (ca. 348–418) wrote for the *Middle Treatise*:

> Arriving at the end of the age, during the Semblance Teaching [period], people's faculties were shallow and their understanding of the Way was dim. Accordingly, they discarded the fish but kept the trap,[31] perceived the finger but forgot the moon.[32] Seeing the teaching of emptiness they said that both sins and merits were destroyed; hearing talk of external marks they took these to be the ultimate truth. Thus they made existence and non-existence give rise to one another, arising and cessation mutually contend. All the extremes of nihilism and eternalism flourished in confusion.
>
> At that time there was a great master named Nāgārjuna. When he went to the ocean palace he attained the forbearance of birthlessness.[33] His mind focused on [refuting] biased schools, he brought about the prosperity of the teaching bequeathed [by the Buddha]. Therefore, he composed this treatise to bend [extreme views] to the middle.[34]

流至末葉, 象[35]教之中, 人根膚淺, 道識不明. 遂廢魚守筌, 存指忘月. 睹空教, 便謂罪福俱泯; 聞相說, 則謂之為真. 是使有無交興, 生滅迭爭, 斷常諸邊, 紛然競起.

時有大士, 厥號龍樹. 爰託海宮, 逮無生忍. 意在傍宗, 載隆遺教. 故作論以折中.[36]

Two crucial questions remain: Where did Kumārajīva's Chinese associates see themselves on this Dharmic timeline, and why were the exploits of the Indian patriarchs so important to them in this regard? If Aśvaghoṣa, Nāgārjuna, and Āryadeva worked to resurrect the Dharma amid the chaos of their own times in India—500, 800, or even 1000 years after nirvāṇa and at the ends of the True and Semblance Dharma periods—how were these

31. *Zhuangzi* 莊子 26 (*Zhuangzi jinzhu jinyi* 莊子今注今譯, 725): "The fish trap exists because of the fish; once you've gotten the fish, you can forget the trap. . . . Words exist because of meaning; once you've gotten the meaning, you can forget the words." 筌者所以在魚, 得魚而忘筌. . . . 言者所以在意, 得意而忘言. Trans. Watson 1968, 302.

32. From the *Da zhidu lun*, T no. 1509, 25:125b, 726a. The former passage (125b) is translated in Lamotte 1944–1980, 1:538, who cites a similar analogy in the *Laṅkāvatāra Sūtra*.

33. Also known as the "forbearance of non-arising dharmas" (*wusheng fa ren* 無生法忍), according to the *Da zhidu lun* (T no. 1509, 25:662b–c) this is the understanding that dharmas neither arise nor cease, without attachment to views of nonarising and noncessation. The attainment of this forbearance reportedly marked the adept's entrance onto the bodhisattva path. Cf. Ciyi 1988–1989, 6:5089a–c; Mochizuki 1954–1963, 5:4835b–4836b; and Nakamura 1981, 1330d–1331a, 1331a–b. For a brief but insightful discussion of "forbearance" or "tolerance" (*kṣānti*) in Buddhist thought, see Thurman 1976, 5.

34. Cf. trans. Lü 1996, 250–251.

35. Reading *xiang* 像 for *xiang* 象, as in the Song, Yuan, and Ming editions used in Taishō collating (*Chu sanzang jiji*, T no. 2145, 55:77n8).

36. *Chu sanzang jiji*, T no. 2145, 55:77a–b. This preface was probably written around 409, when the *Middle Treatise* was translated.

patriarchs understood to affect the fortunes of Buddhist adepts at even later times in China? The answer to this first question of course depends on when Kumārajīva and his disciples considered the Buddha to have died. Several scholars have remarked that the preoccupation of medieval Chinese Buddhists with determining their own place on this timeline of Dharma decline was one major impetus for their attempts to determine the Buddha's dates. Such attempts especially gained momentum from the sixth century, as seen with authors such as Wei Shou 魏收 (507–572), Fei Zhangfang 費長房 (d. after 598),[37] and Huisi 慧思 (515–568), but already by the early fifth century various dating schemes had developed. At that time it was generally held that the Buddha was born in the tenth year of King Zhuang 莊 of the Zhou dynasty (686 or 687 BCE), which, since Śākyamuni was thought to have lived for eighty years, put the *parinirvāṇa* date at 607 BCE.[38] Then if we add five centuries for each of the True and Semblance Dharma periods, the Semblance Dharma would have reached its conclusion around 392 CE, roughly a decade before Kumārajīva's team convened in Chang'an. Where did this leave them?

While some have speculated that in fact this Chang'an group had a different reckoning of the *parinirvāṇa* date that kept them well within Semblance Dharma territory,[39] the fact remains that at least Sengrui believed Nāgārjuna to have appeared at the end of the Semblance Dharma, and there is no indication that Kumārajīva's followers saw Nāgārjuna as a contemporary. In fact, Nāgārjuna's independently circulating biography, traditionally ascribed to Kumārajīva, concluded that "from [the time of Nāgārjuna's] departure from this world until today, one hundred years have passed."[40] But regardless of specific dating schemes, members of this Chang'an community clearly saw themselves as either in the midst of the Semblance Dharma or living in its immediate wake, and given the numerous depictions of the darkness of this period, they would seemingly have viewed their own situation as rather dire.

Another important consideration was Chang'an's geographical remove from the origin of Buddhism. While Aśvaghoṣa, Nāgārjuna, and Āryadeva were all situated across the Indian subcontinent, and sometimes in more specific locales marked by momentous events in early Buddhist history, Chinese adepts were quite conscious of their own distance from

37. I follow Chen 2002, 17–18n21 for the reading of this name as Zhangfang rather than Changfang, and the date of 598 rather than the conventionally accepted 597.

38. On medieval Chinese traditions concerning the dates of the Buddha, see Durt 1991; Franke 1991; Lancaster 1991; and Zürcher (1959) 2007, 271–274; 1982, 18–19.

39. According to an entry in *Guang hongming ji* 廣弘明集 (T no. 2103, 52:142a), by Daoxuan 道宣 (596–667), Kumārajīva amended the *parinirvāṇa* date to 637 BCE. See Lamotte 1944–1980, 3:li; and Robinson 1967, 22–23.

40. *Longshu pusa zhuan*, T no. 2147, 50:185b, 186b: 去此世已來至今, 始過百歲. Cf. trans. Corless 1995, 531; and Li 2002c, 27. See also de Jong 1971, 105–106; and Robinson 1967, 22. As I discuss in appendix 2, this biography as a whole probably dates to the sixth century, though we cannot discount the possibility that it preserves some elements from Kumārajīva's time.

this Dharmic Middle Kingdom (*zhongguo* 中國; *madhyadeśa*).[41] In addition to living in an intermediate period between buddhas, medieval Chinese Buddhists suffered from another of the so-called eight difficulties (*banan* 八難; *aṣṭāvakṣaṇāḥ*), or conditions least conducive to attaining enlightenment: they were situated on the "borderlands" (*biandi* 邊地; *pratyanta janapada*) where the True Dharma had not reached or had become diluted beyond recognition.[42] This sentiment was expressed, for example, in Sengrui's preface to the *Commentary on the Vimalakīrti-nirdeśa*, in which he attributed Chinese misunderstandings of Buddhist teachings to "the deviant mind of the borderland, where comprehending the Truth is difficult."[43] Daoan, Kumārajīva, and Faxian also labeled China a "peripheral kingdom,"[44] and the status of Chang'an as a Buddhist hinterland was a prominent theme in at least two more of Sengrui's writings. In his preface to the *Middle Treatise*, Sengrui exclaimed, "How fortunate that this land of China has suddenly had Numinous Vulture [Peak] (Gṛdhrakūṭa) transported here to be our chief mountain, and that deviant minds in this outlying area can receive the flowing light of its surplus of kindness."[45] And in his *Great Perfection of Wisdom Treatise* preface, Sengrui carried the theme one step further, situating China beyond even the frontiers of the Indian center: "How fortunate that here beyond the central and frontier [regions of India] we have suddenly obtained this treatise in its entirety."[46]

However, a striking feature of both of these statements is how happy Sengrui seems about the situation. "How fortunate!" he proclaimed, that Nāgārjuna's works had found their way so far beyond the bounds of Dharmic

---

41. On the various self-referential uses of this term in ancient and medieval China see Wilkinson 2000, 132. In early translations such as the *Sishi'erzhang jing* 四十二章經 (T no. 784, 17:723c), *zhongguo* also referred to India. For this and other references see Zürcher (1959) 2007, 266. See also Lamotte (1988, 8–9) for a brief discussion of *madhyadeśa* versus *pratyanata janapada* ("borderland") in Indic Buddhist literature.

42. See, e.g., *Chang ahan jing* 長阿含經 (*Dīrghāgama*), T no. 1, 1:55c; *Zhong ahan jing* 中阿含經 (*Mādhyamāgama*), T no. 26, 1:613b. The other six of the eight difficulties are 1) being born in the hells; 2) in the animal realm; 3) as a hungry ghost; 4) in the long-life heavens where distracting pleasures abound; 5) born deaf, dumb, or blind; and 6) as a worldly philosopher absorbed in logical views. Cf. Chou 2004, 323; and Mochizuki 1954–1963, 5:4221c–4222b.

43. *Chu sanzang jiji*, T no. 2145, 55:58c–59a: 邊情險詖, 難可以參契真言. Trans. Chou 2004, 324–325; cf. Robinson 1967, 297n22.

44. Daoan's "peripheral kingdom" statement is in the *Chu sanzang jiji*, T no. 2145, 55:45a (trans. Robinson 1967, 297n22). For Kumārajīva's assessment of Huiyuan's writings, in which he refers to him as a "man from a peripheral kingdom," see the *Gaoseng zhuan*, T no. 2059, 50:360a (trans. Zürcher [1959] 2007, 249; and Robinson 1967, 297n22). For Faxian's comments see the *Gaoseng Faxian zhuan* 高僧法顯傳, T no. 2085, 51:859a (trans. Li 2002a, 174); 860c (trans. Li 2002a, 182); and 864c (trans. Li 2002a, 203). Cf. Hu-von Hinüber 2011, 231–236.

45. *Chu sanzang jiji*, T no. 2145, 55:77a; *Zhong lun*, T no. 1564, 30:1a: 幸哉此區之赤縣, 忽得移靈鷲以作鎮; 險詖之邊情, 乃蒙流光之餘惠. Trans. Robinson 1967, 207, with minor changes. As Robinson (1967, 297n21) notes, citing Jizang as authority, "The *Middle Treatise* is metaphorically represented as a sacred mountain" being transmitted to China.

46. *Chu sanzang jiji*, T no. 2145, 55:75a; *Da zhidu lun*, T no. 1509, 25:57b: 幸哉此中鄙之外, 忽得全有此論. Trans. Shih 1981, 748, with minor modifications.

civilization. And in a similar vein, Sengrui remarked in his preface to the *Twelve Gates Treatise*, "How fortunate are the students of later times! The level road is already made plain, and the dark pass is already opened."[47] Indeed, far from being overly concerned about their own position at the periphery of the Buddhist heartland, or at the end of the soteriological chronology in which Aśvaghoṣa, Nāgārjuna, and Āryadeva were invariably placed, the Chinese monks of the Chang'an community appear rather content with their lot. In order to understand how this might be the case, it is useful to further examine the rhetoric of decline in the sources, as well as the implications of the Indian patriarchs' resurrection of the Dharma in their own dark times and places.

First of all, it is noteworthy that early scriptural accounts of Dharma decline, such as those in the *Diamond* and *Lotus* sūtras, almost always occur together with admonishments to receive and uphold the scripture itself.[48] Adepts who followed these sūtras amid the particularly evil times five centuries after nirvāṇa would accrue immeasurable merit, eventually achieve the same enlightenment as the Buddha, and ensure the perpetuation of the Dharma into the indefinite future. As Jamie Hubbard explains, "The *Vajracchedikā* speaks of the 'latter five-hundred years, when the true teaching is in the process of decay' only as an opportunity to contrast its own continued efficacy." And, "Much like the *Vajracchedikā* . . . the *Lotus* uses the theme of decline as an opportunity to assert that even in such a period, due to the power of the sutra itself, there will still be those who will gain innumerable merits and enter into nirvana *if* they recognize its truth" (Hubbard 2001, 49, 52). Hubbard thus emphasizes that the vision of soteriological degradation presented within such sūtras is best understood as a rhetorical posture—rather than an actual prediction of Dharma's death—assumed to promote the saving power of that text alone within the generations following the "latter five-hundred years."

The depictions of Dharma decline in the *Great Perfection of Wisdom Treatise* and *Middle Treatise* also readily lend themselves to such an interpretation. In the former text the weakness of beings in the Semblance Dharma period was highlighted in order to explain why Subūti pressed the Buddha for an explanation of how good and evil could exist while all dharmas were empty. Only with the Buddha's subsequent teaching of emptiness in the *Perfection of Wisdom* (*Prajñāpāramitā*) literature were the benighted masses of future generations saved from their attachment to dharmas. And in this way, of course, the *Prajñāpāramitā* class of Buddhist scriptures was promoted above all others. Similarly, in the *Middle Treatise* the dull faculties of adepts in the latter five hundred years were emphasized in order to explain why Nāgārjuna was moved to compose this text. With Nāgārjuna's teachings in hand, as Sengrui exclaimed, "deviant minds in [this] outlying area can

---

47. *Chu sanzang jiji*, T no. 2145, 55:77c; *Shi'ermen lun*, T no. 1568, 30:159b: 遇哉後之學者! 夷路既坦, 幽塗既開. Trans. Robinson 1967, 209.

48. See Hubbard 2001, 49–52; and Nattier 1991, 106.

receive the flowing light of its surplus of kindness." The Dharma was at death's door in Nāgārjuna's generation, and only by virtue of his profound treatises were beings of his time awakened to the Truth. And in the same way, it was Nāgārjuna alone who allowed the true light of the Buddhadharma to shine eastward, assuaging any concerns that fifth-century Chinese adepts might harbor about the evils of the Semblance Dharma period lingering on, into their own latter age and peripheral kingdom.

One finds this same strategy employed within almost every account of the Indian patriarchs' trials and triumphs. Sengzhao emphasized that in Ārydeva's generation non-Buddhists and false views were running amok, precisely so he could foreground Āryadeva's singular capacity for quelling specious dogmas and upholding the Dharma. Likewise, Tanying lamented that in Nāgārjuna's time "all the extremes of nihilism and eternalism flourished in confusion"[49] as a means of highlighting Nāgārjuna's unsurpassed command of the Buddha's teachings. And in addition to Sengrui's assertion in his preface to the *Great Perfection of Wisdom Treatise* that the Dharma would have died if not for Aśvaghoṣa and Nāgārjuna, there is a similar sentiment in his *Middle Treatise* preface:

> That the Way and the worldly are not unified and that the two extremes are not obliterated is what grieves the bodhisattva. Therefore the great master Nāgārjuna equalized them with the Middle Path, enabling students who had confused the goal to see the profound pointer[50] and utterly transform [their ways]. He encompassed them with [the principle of] identity with transformations,[51] and caused the clients of abstruse understanding to lose their plans and deliberations in the morning's clear rays.[52]

> 道俗之不夷，二際之不泯，菩薩之憂也. 是以龍樹大士，折之以中道，使惑趣之徒，望玄指而一變. 括之以即化，令玄悟之賓，喪諮詢於朝徹.[53]

In other accounts of the Indian patriarchs overcoming the tribulations of their times, the foils for their triumphs were only vaguely identified: non-Buddhists, heterodoxies, and confused minds, for the most part. But here Sengrui hinted more clearly at the traditions against which Nāgārjuna's work should be measured. These were the "clients of abstruse understanding" (*xuanwu zhi bin* 玄悟之賓), which, according to the famous Three Treatise exponent Jizang, referred both to Indian non-Buddhists and the *xuanxue* adepts of Sengrui's generation. With the expression "the morning's clear rays" (*zhaoche* 朝徹) Sengrui drew upon the *Zhuangzi* 莊子, which was one

---

49. *Chu sanzang jiji*, T no. 2145, 55:77a.

50. For the expression *xuanzhi* 玄指 (profound pointer) see Robinson (1967, 296n13), who, following Jizang, equates it with the *Middle Treatise*.

51. The *Chu sanzang jiji* has 恬之以即化 while the *Zhong lun* has 括之以即化, which has been followed here. See Robinson 1967, 296n14.

52. Trans. Robinson 1967, 206, with minor changes.

53. *Chu sanzang jiji*, T no. 2145, 55:76c; *Zhong lun*, T no. 1564, 30:1a.

primary focus of *xuanxue* discourse, wherein the Woman Crookback explained how Buliang Yi 卜梁倚 achieved a state of sublime illumination called *zhaoche*.[54] Sengrui thus implied not only that Nāgārjuna was singularly capable of converting the non-Buddhists of ancient India but also that he was the sole agent through whom contemporary Chinese *xuanxue* proponents could truly fathom the profound insights of their own tradition. As such, Nāgārjuna's discourse was lauded as holding sway across eras, continents, and religiophilosophical traditions, with his unparalleled treatises having revived the Dharma in post-*parinirvāṇa* India while also being uniquely suited to the exigencies of latter-day China.

And along similar lines, this whole discourse about the Indian patriarchs arising at end times to resurrect the lost Truth—advanced at every turn by Sengrui, Sengzhao, and others of their cohort—resonated both with the prophesies of translated Indic scriptures and with several Chinese traditions concerning the sage's appearance in history. Aśvaghoṣa, Nāgārjuna, and Āryadeva arose in India to revive a dying Buddhadharma in much the same way that Confucian sage-kings or Daoist messiahs arose in cyclical fashion when the Way was weak and the masses in peril. Through these Indian patriarch accounts Kumārajīva's associates deployed a catholic rhetoric, representing their Indian forebears as the paragons of both Indian Buddhist and native Chinese models of sainthood in time. In prototypical bodhisattva fashion, Aśvaghoṣa, Nāgārjuna, and Āryadeva arose to liberate all beings, regardless of time, place, or sectarian affiliation; they were invaluable resources for all who claimed to seek the truth. But not only did the Indian patriarchs shine Zhuangzi's clear rays across the Sino-Indian divide with their sublime treatises, they also provided models of sainthood by which Chinese adepts themselves could rise to the ranks of world saviors in dark times. In this regard the patriarchs were unlike the sage-kings of old or the Daoist divinities that descended to save the elect. The patriarchs were objects of both veneration and emulation, as the practices that they upheld mirrored the favored occupations of spiritually inclined Chinese literati.

Several well-known Chinese models of sainthood in history were available to scholar-monks of the early fifth century. Mencius famously elaborated a cosmic cycle wherein the principles of sageliness would wax and wane and true sage-kings would only arise every five hundred years, as seen with the successive appearances of Yao 堯 and Shun 舜, King Tang 湯 and King Wen 文.[55] By the early centuries CE, the notion was prevalent in Chinese sources that humanity could prosper only after cycles of decay, as seen for example in the writings of *xuanxue* proponent Xi Kang 嵇康 (223/24–262) (Middendorf 2010, 151, 170n121). Similar notions of a cyclical rise and decline of the Way were also common fare in Daoist sources

54. See Jizang's *Zhongguan lun shu* 中觀論疏, T no. 1824, 42:4a; cited by Robinson 1967, 296n15. For the *Zhuangzi* passage in question, see Watson 1968, 83, who translates *zhaoche* as "the brightness of dawn."

55. See Legge (1895) 1970, 232, 279–283, 501–502.

from early medieval times, with texts like the *Scripture of Great Peace* (*Taiping jing* 太平經) and the *Xiangr Commentary on the Laozi* (*Laozi Xiangr zhu* 老子想爾注) outlining a progressive degeneration of the Dao and human moral order, to be rectified only through the maintenance of certain ethical norms and self-cultivation practices. The *Central Scripture of the Most High Lord Lao* (*Taishang Laojun zhong jing* 太上老君中經) described cosmic cycles with temporal nodes marked by natural disasters and the appearances of sages (*xianren* 賢人), saints (*shengren* 聖人), and perfected ones (*zhenren* 真人). The *Scripture of Laozi's Transformations* (*Laozi bianhua jing* 老子變化經) explained the cosmic origins, powers and descents of Laozi into the world at various historical junctures in order to save humankind. Specific dates, or at least sexagenary designations, were provided for the arrival of the messiah Li Hong 李弘—the avatar of Lord Lao, or Laozi apotheosized—in Yang Xi's 楊羲 (b. 330) influential *Purple Texts Inscribed by the Spirits* (*Lingshu ziwen* 靈書紫文) as well as the *Scripture of Spirit Spells from the Abyss* (*Dongyuan shenzhou jing* 洞淵神咒經). Both of these texts predicted the advent of their savior in a *renchen* 壬辰 year, which then corresponded to either 392 or 452—the former year also marking for some the end of the Semblance Dharma period.[56]

With all these accounts of sainthood in history, however, their main protagonists were objects of veneration rather than models for emulation. Yao, Shun, or Li Hong represented the will of Heaven or the compassion of the Dao itself; they were divine, or at least semidivine, manifestations of cosmic forces that transcended the capacities and aspirations of even the greatest mortal men. These were godlike figures to be admired and worshipped, not the types of beings that local devotees could themselves strive to become.[57] And in fact, in Robert Campany's recent study of the early medieval quest for transcendence, he notes that adepts in this tradition were never depicted appearing in grand cycles of cosmic time—like Mencius' sage-kings or the Lord Lao of so many Daoist scriptures—precisely because *xian* identity was supposed to be attainable: "For Ge Hong [葛洪] in the early fourth century C.E., at least, transcendents were to be understood as sharply differentiated from such beings . . . One of Ge Hong's reasons for taking such care to make this point clear was his opposition to any view of transcendents that saw them as born, not made, and hence as so elevated in their cosmic station that transcendence became an impossible goal" (2009, 50n31). And in the same way, the Indian patriarchs were represented in their earliest biographies as down-to-earth, having been born as mortal men—naturally brilliant, but men nonetheless—who through specific models of

---

56. On these Daoist sources and related eschatological traditions, see Bokenkamp 1994; 1997, 29–148, 275–372; Hendrichke 2000, 143–159; Lo 2010, 321–322; Seidel 1969–1970; and Zürcher 1982, 2–6, 20.

57. One exception to this rule was the practice of visualizing and manifesting the spirits of the body, which sometimes included Laozi. In this way the practitioner could become Laozi himself. See Puett 2010.

practice had risen to the ranks of holy beings capable of saving the world in its direst moments of need. The patriarchs were made, not born as such, even as they reflected age-old Chinese traditions of divine descent into world history, and Chinese adepts could therefore emulate the practices perfected by their Indian forebears in order to stem the tide of Dharmic devolution.

The Indian Patriarchs' Early Repertoire

In their earliest Chinese hagiographies the post-*parinirvāṇa* Indian patriarchs were represented as having perfected a specific repertoire of practices that was deemed most effective for eliminating false teachings and saving sentient beings at times when the Dharma was in peril. It is no coincidence that these practices were standard fare as well among (aspiring) literati gentlemen across religiophilosophical traditions in medieval China, by and for whom these Indian patriarch accounts were disseminated. Kumārajīva's Chinese associates—especially Sengrui, Sengzhao, and Huiyuan—traveled in circles of the intellectual elite and frequented the courts of princes and kings. They were renowned for their accomplishments in public debate, scholarship, and authorship—demonstrating mastery of both Indian Buddhist and native Chinese literary traditions—and they esteemed such preoccupations of "high-minded gentlemen" as eremitic reclusion and meditative contemplation. It comes as no surprise, then, that these same practices were most often highlighted in the Chang'an accounts of Aśvaghoṣa, Nāgārjuna, and Āryadeva. This is not to suggest that these biographies must have originated with their Chinese proponents, nor even in China at all; Sengrui, Sengzhao, and Huiyuan merely stressed specific aspects of the patriarchs' careers that they deemed apropos at the time. And while it is never safe to ascribe motives to agents long past, the obvious effect of emphasizing these particular practices in the Indian patriarch accounts was to valorize the preferred occupations of elite Chinese scholar-monks as the foremost means of upholding the true Way through pernicious times.

Debate and Conversion

Of their time, Sengrui, Sengzhao, and Huiyuan were certainly scholar-monks par excellence, and as John Kieschnick remarks in his study of Chinese monastic biographies, the ideals and practices of such figures were closely tied to those of the secular literati.[58] One favorite pastime of the latter class, especially through the Wei-Jin period (220–420), was the practice known as *qingtan*—or *qingyan* 清言 in contemporary sources—public debate intended to display the eloquence, rhetorical skill, and thus cultural cachet of its practitioners. Literati gentlemen would convene at one another's estates and organize discursive sparring matches on favored *xuanxue* topics such as the *Laozi*, *Zhuangzi*, and *Book of Changes* (*Yijing* 易經) or Buddhist sūtras like the

58. Kieschnick 1997, 113. This is also the main theme of Cao 1994.

Prajñāpāramitās or the *Vimalakīrti-nirdeśa*.[59] As seen in the primary record of *qingtan* debate, the *New Account of Tales of the World* (*Shishuo xinyu* 世說新語), the participation of Buddhist monks at these gatherings was a common occurrence. Dozens of episodes from this text featured representatives of the sangha, such as Zhu Daoqian 竺道潛 (286–374), Zhu Fatai 竺法汰 (320–387), Yu Fakai 于法開 (ca. 310–370), and most frequently the multitalented Zhi Dun 支遁 (314–366).[60] And in fact, Kumārajīva's southern associate Huiyuan also appeared in this collection, discussing the substance of the *Yijing* with governor Yin Zhongkan 殷仲堪 (d. 399).[61]

Throughout this period, public debate played an important role in the intellectual lives of many educated Chinese, regardless of whether they had "left home" to become monastics (*chujia* 出家), and by the early fifth century a long tradition had already developed of oral disputation as an avenue for legitimizing philosophical positions and their proponents. From at least the fourth-century BCE there were documented debates between Confucians and Mohists over the propriety of their respective traditions, and through the Qin and Han dynasties (221 BCE–220 CE) debates at court had become prevalent forums for the development of sociopolitical policy (Kroll 1985, 119, 121–122). From the fourth century, evidence emerges of Buddhists debating local rulers over the proper relationship between state and sangha, and debates between Buddhists and Daoists were staged to nominally determine which religious institution deserved imperial patronage. The winners of such contests could gain state support for their monasteries and positions at court, significantly improve their social standing, and also at times claim the allegiance of the defeated.[62]

Although early records often depict scholar-monks engaged in debate, in medieval China this was not a specifically Buddhist occupation.[63] This is not to suggest parallels with the Tibetan Buddhist tradition, for example, in which debate has long played a central role in the education of monks and the development of doctrinal traditions.[64] Sengzhao, Sengrui, and Huiyuan were all renowned for their skill in oral disputation because they were great scholars, not necessarily because they were Buddhist monks.[65] Nevertheless, they employed this talent in service of their chosen vocation, striving to demonstrate the superiority of the Buddha's teachings over competing religiophilosophical traditions through overt doctrinal discourse and narratives of their Indian forebears' triumphs in this arena.

---

59. On this latter text in *qingtan* debates and in relation to *xuanxue* ideals, see Mather 1968.

60. See Tang 1991, 248–261.

61. See Mather 2002, 131.

62. See the introduction to Kohn 1995; and Zürcher (1959) 2007, 231, 293–294.

63. For discussion of Buddhist debate as illustrated in the *Gaoseng zhuan* series, see Kieschnick 1997, 123–127.

64. See especially Dreyfus 2003, chap. 10–12.

65. On the oratorical skills of Sengzhao, Sengrui, and Huiyuan, see, e.g., Robinson 1967, 104, 117, and 123.

One of the earliest examples of the Indian patriarchs engaged in oral debate occurs in Sengzhao's commentary on Kumārajīva's translation of the *Vimalakīrti-nirdeśa*—a scripture whose central narrative also famously revolves around argumentation.[66] It is significant that in this example, involving Aśvaghoṣa in particular, the patriarch was depicted losing his debate. This is because, although he was naturally intelligent, educated, and eloquent, he did not yet adhere to the Buddhist truth. This was in fact a tale of conversion, through public debate, of one of the greatest Buddhist masters in history. And as a narrative propagated by elite Chinese scholar-monks in a world of disputatious lay literati, the subtext for this tale was argument with the haughty, opinionated *xuanxue* adepts often encountered by members of the Chang'an group and represented by Aśvaghoṣa before he realized the superiority of the Buddhist truth:

> Kumārajīva said, "This is like when six hundred years after the Buddha's nirvāṇa there was a man who left home [to become a monk] at the age of sixty. Not long thereafter he could recite[67] the whole Threefold Canon exhaustively. He then composed an exegesis of the Threefold Canon.[68] After composing this treatise he thought, 'What other undertakings does the Buddhadharma entail? There are only the methods of *dhyāna*; I should practice these.'
>
> Thereupon he received the methods of *dhyāna* and made a vow to himself, 'If I do not attain the Way and do not become endowed with all the merits of settled *dhyāna*, then I will never lie down to rest.'
>
> His side never touched the ground, so he was called *bhikṣu* Side (Pārśva). After a short while he was able to become an arhat endowed with the three insights and six penetrations.[69] He was very eloquent and excellent at debating.

---

66. This commentary was compiled sometime between 406, when the translation was completed, and 410, when Sengzhao mentioned it in a letter to the recluse Liu Chengzhi 劉程之 (a.k.a. Liu Yimin 劉遺民, 354–410) on Mount Lu 廬山 in the south. See *Zhao lun* 肇論, T no. 1858, 45:155c–156a; trans. Robinson 1967, 137; and Liebenthal 1968, 92. The received edition of the *Vimalakīrti Commentary* (*Zhu weimojie jing* 注維摩詰經, T no. 1775) is comprised mostly of Sengzhao's and Kumārajīva's exegesis, as well as a number of statements by Huiyuan's disciple Daosheng 道生 (ca. 360–434), which were likely inserted at a later date. See Liebenthal 1968, 10n36, 83n356; and, more recently, Lo 2002.

67. Taking *song* 頌 as an error for the homonymous *song* 誦 (Pulleyblank 1991, 293).

68. According to the *Da zhidu lun* (T no. 1509, 25:748c), Pārśva composed an "*upadeśa* (exegesis) on the four Āgamas" (*si ahan youpotishe* 四阿含優婆提舍), which is probably what is referred to here. In later sources Pārśva is said to have compiled the *Vibhāśāśāstra* (*Piposha lun* 毘婆沙論), purportedly composed by five hundred arhats at a council convened by King Kaniṣka. This text was first translated by Buddhavarman (Futuobamo 浮陀跋摩; fl. 424–453) and Daotai 道泰 (fl. 437–439) in 437 (T no. 1546), and again by Xuanzang 玄奘 (602–664) from 656 to 659 (T no. 1545). On these translations see Ono 1933–1936, 1:32b–33b, 37d–38b. Their compilation seems to have first been attributed to Pārśva (in Chinese sources) in Xuanzang's *Da Tang xiyu ji* 大唐西域記 (T no. 2087, 51:886b–887a; trans. Beal 1884, 1:151–56; and Li 1996, 101–106). See also the entry on Pārśva in Mochizuki 1954–1963, 1:559b–560a.

69. The "three insights" (*sanming* 三明) overlap with the "six penetrations" (*liutong* 六通); they are powers gained at advanced stages of meditation. See Muller 1995– (s.v. "*liu shentong* 六神通").

There was a non-Buddhist master named Aśvaghoṣa who had sharp faculties, wisdom, and completely understood all of the scriptures. He was also greatly eloquent and could refute all arguments. He had heard the name of *bhikṣu* Side, so brought all of his disciples to where [the *bhikṣu*] was. He announced, 'I can refute all arguments. If I cannot refute your claims, I will cut off my head in admission of defeat.' As *bhikṣu* Side heard this assertion he remained silent without saying a word.

Aśvaghoṣa then became conceited, 'This man has but an empty name; in fact he knows absolutely nothing.' He and his disciples then abandoned [*bhikṣu* Side] and departed. Along the road, after some consideration [Aśvaghoṣa] said to his disciples, 'That man has exceedingly deep wisdom; I have been defeated!' His disciples thought this strange and asked, 'Why do you say so?' He answered, 'I spoke [even though] all words can be refuted, so I refuted myself. He did not speak so there was nothing to be refuted.'

He then returned to where *bhikṣu* Side was and said to him, 'I have been defeated, so I am a fool. I do not need the head of a fool; you should cut it off. If you do not sever my [head] then I will cut it off myself.' *Bhikṣu* Side said, 'Do not cut off your head, you should cut off your topknot; this [tie to the] world is no different than death.' [Aśvaghoṣa] then let his hair fall and became the disciple of *bhikṣu* Side.

[Aśvaghoṣa's] wisdom and eloquence were unmatched throughout the world. He broadly composed treatises on the scriptures and greatly propagated the Buddhadharma. At that time people said that he was the second Buddha."

什曰, "如佛泥洹後六百年, 有一人年六十出家. 未幾時頌三藏都盡. 次作三藏論議. 作論已思惟言, '佛法中復有何事? 唯有禪法, 我當行之'

於是受禪法, 自作要誓, '若不得道, 不具一切禪定功德, 終不寢息.' 脅不著地, 因名脅比丘. 少時得成阿羅漢, 具三明六通. 有大辯才, 善能論議.

有外道師, 名曰馬鳴. 利根智慧, 一切經書皆悉明練. 亦有大辯才, 能破一切論議. 聞脅比丘名, 將諸弟子, 往到其所. 唱言, '一切論議, 悉皆可破. 若我不能破汝言論, 當斬首謝屈.' 脅比丘聞是論, 默然不言.

馬鳴即生憍慢, '此人徒有空名, 實無所知.' 與其弟子, 捨之而去. 中路思惟已, 語弟子言, '此人有甚深智慧. 我墮負處.' 弟子怪而問曰, '云何爾?' 答曰, '我言一切語言可破, 即是自破. 彼不言則無所破.'

即還到其所, 語脅比丘言, '我墮負處, 則是愚癡. 愚癡之頭, 非我所須, 汝便斬之 若不斬我, 我當自斬.' 脅比丘言, '不斬汝頭, 當斬汝結髮. 比於世間, 與死無異.' 即下髮為脅比丘作弟子.

智慧辯才, 世無及者. 廣造經論, 大弘佛法. 時人謂之, 為第二佛."[70]

This combined biography of Pārśva and Aśvaghoṣa was inserted as commentary to the famed silence of Vimalakīrti, illustrated near the end of the sūtra's ninth chapter entitled "Entering the Gate of Non-dualism." In this chapter, a number of bodhisattvas stepped forward to answer Vimalakīrti's

70. *Zhu weimojie jing*, T no. 1775, 38:399b.

query about how a bodhisattva should go about entering the gate of non-dualism. Finally Vimalakīrti's main interlocutor Mañjuśrī replied, "To my way of thinking, all dharmas are without words, without explanations, without purport, without cognition, removed from all questions and answers. In this way one may enter the gate of non-dualism."[71] At this Vimalakīrti demonstrated his unsurpassed wisdom by actualizing Mañjuśrī's verbal, and thus artificially limiting, exposition—he remained silent without speaking a word. The story of debate between Pārśva and Aśvaghoṣa thus offered apropos commentary on Vimalakīrti's non-response to Mañjuśrī. The victor in the patriarchal debate, and thus the master responsible for converting him who would become the "second Buddha," was the participant who in fact refused to debate. In this way the Buddhist truth was shown to transcend the petty arguments upon which *xuanxue* and *qingtan* adepts staked their reputations, as once Aśvaghoṣa realized the profundity of the True Dharma he changed his arrogant ways and followed Vimalakīrti into the silent abyss.

Another prominent example of Aśvaghoṣa's conversion through debate occurred in his earliest independently circulating biography, preserved in Japan at Nanatsu-dera 七寺 (Nagoya) and elsewhere, which was probably first disseminated within this Chang'an group.[72] This biography began by introducing Aśvaghoṣa as a Brahman, born some three hundred years after the death of the Buddha in eastern India. Aśvaghoṣa was a precocious youth, and as per Indian custom at the time he wandered from province to province looking for worthy opponents in debate. Eventually he heard of an arhat, possessed of the six penetrations and three insights, by the name of Pūrṇa (Fulouna 富樓那), and sought him out to challenge him in debate. In response to this challenge Pūrṇa sat unmoved in complete silence, leaving Aśvaghoṣa to withdraw and ponder the results of this encounter. Realizing that the silence of his opponent could not be defeated and that he himself had "not yet escaped the fetters of words," Aśvaghoṣa returned to Pūrṇa to offer his head in admission of defeat. However, Pūrṇa stopped him from doing this and instead suggested that he become a follower of the Buddha. Aśvaghoṣa thus took the tonsure, received the monastic precepts, and soon became a great Buddhist master who "composed many treatises in millions of words that glorified the Buddhadharma."[73]

Apart from the obvious discrepancies between Aśvaghoṣa's position in Dharmic history (six or three hundred years after nirvāṇa) and his Buddhist preceptor (Pārśva or Pūrṇa)[74] the central themes and storylines of

---

71. *Weimojie suoshuo jing* 維摩詰所說經 (*Vimalakīrtinirdeśa*), T no. 475, 14:551c; trans. Watson 1997, 110.

72. See appendix 1 for a brief discussion and complete annotated translation of this biography. For convenience I call it the Nanatsu-dera biography to distinguish it from the *Tradition of Aśvaghoṣa Bodhisattva* (*Maming pusa zhuan* 馬鳴菩薩傳) appearing in the Taishō canon, which is a completely different text.

73. See the translation in appendix 1.

74. I discuss these discrepancies in appendix 1.

these two accounts are nearly identical. In both stories Aśvaghoṣa began as a truly exceptional talent but only in lesser, non-Buddhist sorts of learning, and his excessive arrogance was readily manifest as a result. His exceptional talents were both a curse and a blessing. He had clearly become an accomplished master, as was evident through his track record in debate and his crowds of disciples, but this made him haughty and overconfident. He sought an accomplished arhat to challenge in debate, announcing his superior talents and offering to decapitate himself if defeated. In response to this challenge the arhat remained completely silent, which led Aśvaghoṣa to recognize the fallibility of any discourse and offer his head in admission of defeat. Declining this bloody token, the arhat asked Aśvaghoṣa to cut off his hair rather than his head and follow the teachings of the Buddha. Aśvaghoṣa did as requested and soon became a great Buddhist master who saved countless beings primarily by composing doctrinal treatises.

Ironically, however, after realizing the ultimate futility of argumentation and converting to Buddhism, Aśvaghoṣa followed in the footsteps of his master Pārśva (Pūrṇa) by resuming his debating ways. The *Vimalakīrti Commentary* concluded by noting that his eloquence was unmatched, and the Nanatsu-dera biography emphasized that he would remain "undefeated in essential discourse." As such, Aśvaghoṣa's proclivity for debate per se was not the problem; rather, these accounts took issue with his initial desire to argue for argument's sake alone. Once the Buddhadharma and the salvation of beings were at stake, so the underlying rhetoric would have it, debate was a necessary expedient means for propagating the truth. In other words, as long as one was right (i.e., Buddhist), he could argue his points. Otherwise, he was wasting everyone's time with pointless webs of words and logics. Proponents of other traditions, such as *xuanxue* and *qingtan*, debated only for self-aggrandizement. Buddhist debate masters like Sengrui, Sengzhao, and Huiyuan were well within their right to dispute the positions of their contemporaries, precisely because only the former were on the side of truth. They sought not to condemn or even curb the practice of doctrinal disputation, but to co-opt it as appropriate only for propagating the Buddhadharma.

In another tale involving Nāgārjuna's confrontation with an unnamed non-Buddhist, the *Vimalakīrti Commentary* presents a similar example of debate as *upāya* (expedient means), which could be employed effectively only by Buddhist masters. Sengzhao and Kumārajīva adduced this story as commentary on the beginning of the sūtra's "Expedient Means" chapter, wherein Vimalakīrti was described as a rich layman who in past lives made offerings to countless buddhas so was endowed with extensive merit, understanding of the Buddhist truth, and was able to "disport himself with spiritual penetrations" (*youxi shentong* 遊戲神通).[75] In explanation of this last attribute Sengzhao related an anecdote told by Kumārajīva about Nāgārjuna engaged in debate:

75. *Weimojie suoshuo jing*, T no. 475, 14:539a; cf. trans. Watson 1997, 32.

Kumārajīva said, "Because of his spiritual penetrations [Vimalakīrti] could extend his efforts to convert [the people]. Also by the power of his spiritual penetrations he could prove his eloquence.

This is like Nāgārjuna debating with a non-Buddhist. The non-Buddhist asked, 'What are the gods doing now?' [Nāgārjuna] answered, 'The gods are now at war with the *asuras* [titans].' [The non-Buddhist] again asked, 'How can you prove this?'

The bodhisattva then manifested proof, as broken halberds, shattered swords, the bodies and heads of *asuras* came falling down from the sky. They also saw the gods and *asuras* in the sky lined up in battle array facing one another. After the non-Buddhist saw this proof he submitted before [Nāgārjuna's] eloquence. Spiritual penetrations serve as proof in debate, as in this case."[76]

什曰, "因神通廣其化功. 亦以神通力證其辯才.

如龍樹與外道論議. 外道問曰, '天今何作?' 答曰, '天今與阿修羅戰.' 復問, '此何以證?'

菩薩即為現證, 應時摧戈, 折刃, 阿脩身首, 從空中而墜落. 又見天與阿脩羅, 於虛空中列陣相對. 外道見證已, 乃伏其辯才. 神通證辯, 類如此也."[77]

Here Nāgārjuna was presented as a wielder of *shentong* 神通, by which he was able to convince his non-Buddhist opponent of the truth of his assertions in debate. Employed in Chinese Buddhist texts to translate Sanskrit terms such as *ṛddhi* or *abhijñā*, *shentong* was an expression that already carried a considerable semantic range by the early fifth century. It could mean various forms of omnipotence—transcendent powers of physical, spiritual, and mental varieties—supernormal attainments gained through meditative trance, or simply wisdom or skill that exceeded that of normal human beings.[78] Moreover, this term was ubiquitous in medieval Daoist literature, and was in fact derived from the *Zhuangzi* several centuries before Buddhism arrived in China (Sharf 2002, 175, 323n98). Thus *shentong* carried not only Buddhistic associations of *dhyāna* attainments or merits accrued through eons of paying obeisance to tathāgatas, but also fell under the purview of Daoist transcendents and Chinese sages from time immemorial. *Shentong* also transcended any boundaries that one might imagine between more mundane and scholarly pursuits, such as formal debate or textual composition, and supernatural abilities like flying through the air or conjuring magical beings. Sober scholarship and perspicacity in philosophical rhetoric did not preclude the application of magical power; the former in fact demanded the latter.

The multivalence of *shentong* was clearly demonstrated in the above tale of Nāgārjuna's debate as related to its context in the *Vimalakīrti* "Expedient Means" chapter. Immediately preceding the assertion in the sūtra that

---

76. Cf. trans. Lo 2002, 98.

77. *Zhu weimojie jing*, T no. 1775, 38:339a.

78. On the range of meaning of *shentong*, with reference to a variety of early Buddhist sources in which it appears, see Nakamura 1981, 794a–b. Cf. Luo 1987–1995, 4437b–c.

Vimalakīrti could "disport himself with spiritual penetrations," was the seemingly disparate account of his "unhindered eloquence." The apparent incongruity of this juxtaposition compelled Kumārajīva to offer further explanation for his disciples, and led Sengzhao to insert Kumārajīva's exposition (followed by his own) at this point in the commentary. Skill in debate was buttressed by "spiritual penetrations," as indicated by the closing statement of the above passage and as illustrated by the episode involving Nāgārjuna and the falling body parts. This anecdote demonstrated exactly what sort of spiritual penetrations were at issue: Nāgārjuna could both see the gods and *asuras* battling in heaven and make others see the same. As indicated by the title of the sūtra chapter in which this episode was inserted, Nāgārjuna employed this power as an expedient means to convert and thus liberate the nonbeliever, just as Vimalakīrti did with his "unhindered eloquence" and ability to "disport himself with spiritual penetrations." In this regard Nāgārjuna's debate scene shared an affinity with the above accounts of Aśvaghoṣa's conversion. All of these stories evinced an effort on the part of their proponents to co-opt religious debate as a form of Buddhist *upāya*. And because Nāgārjuna was able to fortify his position with the powers of *shentong*, presumably gained through mastery of the Buddha's teachings, he showed how the Buddhist path not only legitimized oral disputation but also ensured success in the debate arena.

The Power of Commentary

For fifth-century Chinese scholar-monks, by far the most important aspect of the Indian patriarchs' repertoire was the writing of exegetical commentary. Treatises written by latter-day Indian masters such as Aśvaghoṣa, Nāgārjuna, and Āryadeva were the only tangible traces of post-*parinirvāṇa* Indian Buddhism available to Chinese adepts. These texts expressly manifested the teachings and practices that kept the Dharma alight in the land of the Buddha's birth during the centuries after his death. Many of the patriarchs' writings modeled the kind of dialogic structure befitting such great debate masters—with opposing positions raised and refuted throughout their expositions—and in fact Āryadeva's *Hundred Treatise* would later be deemed a blow-by-blow transcript of his debates with non-Buddhists. Indeed, the doctrinal contents of these treatises were seen to be determined by the historical contexts in which the Indian patriarchs worked. Doctrine and hagiography were always mutually reinforcing. Most importantly in the present context, just as Aśvaghoṣa, Nāgārjuna, and Āryadeva were valorized as world saviors in dark times, their treatises were upheld as the principal vehicles for the propagation of the Dharma when it was seriously imperiled. The practice of doctrinal authorship itself, as much as the specific doctrines espoused by the patriarchs, was promoted as the best means of liberating sentient beings in pernicious circumstances (literacy rates notwithstanding, apparently). And again, it is not surprising that, through the accounts of their Indian forbears, Chinese scholar-monks advocated scholarship as the foremost Buddhist practice for a world without a Buddha. Just as the Indian patriarchs had saved their benighted contemporaries with writings like the *Middle Treatise*, latter-day Chinese adepts could best serve their own generation by exercising their already prodigious talents in manipulating the powers of the written word.

I have already discussed several examples of this tendency in the earliest Indian patriarch accounts to uphold doctrinal exegesis as the primary means of resurrecting the True Dharma in post-*parinirvāṇa* India. According to Sengzhao, when "false debates imperiled the truth so that the True Way was nearly lost in confusion," Āryadeva composed his *Hundred Treatise* to "rescue far and wide those who were drowning."[79] At the end of the Semblance Dharma period, as Sengrui exclaimed, Nāgārjuna's *Great Perfection of Wisdom Treatise* "opened the great road in such a manner that the carriage of the Greater Vehicle could advance straight ahead along the tracks [of the Way]."[80] And Tanying emphasized that when the "extremes of nihilism and eternalism flourished in confusion," Nāgārjuna wrote his *Middle Treatise* to "bend [these extreme views] to the middle."[81] Further, as recounted in both the *Vimalakīrti Commentary* and Aśvaghoṣa's Nanatsu-dera biography, after converting to Buddhism Aśvaghoṣa propagated the True Dharma primarily through written discourse. The latter text highlighted the soteriological perils of Aśvaghoṣa's generation, when peoples' capacity for enlightenment was diminished and their grasp of scriptural teachings incomplete. Therefore—in a manner prefiguring the famously laconic *Mahāyāna Awakening of Faith* (*Dasheng qixin lun* 大乘起信論)—"Aśvaghoṣa abbreviated superfluous words that strayed from the truth and omitted flowery expressions that [merely] implied meaning . . . his skillfully composed texts were direct in their expression." Through his extensive oeuvre, which was universally revered and "taken as a model of composition," Aśvaghoṣa "rescued the weak and dying from this dream world." For his exegetical efforts Aśvaghoṣa was praised by the bodhisattvas, venerated as a buddha, and renowned like Confucius's disciple Zixia 子夏 (ca. 507–420 BCE), whose wisdom reportedly equaled that of Confucius himself.[82]

However, for Kumārajīva's associates this fervent praise of Aśvaghoṣa's vast corpus must have rung somewhat hollow. This is because Chinese scholar-monks of the time had seen only a handful of Aśvaghoṣa's verses in the *Scripture on Seated Dhyāna Samādhi*. With Nāgārjuna's *Middle Treatise, Great Perfection of Wisdom Treatise, Twelve Gates Treatise,* and *Treatise on the Ten Stages* all introduced by Kumārajīva, as well as Āryadeva's *Hundred Treatise,* the fifth-century Chang'an group clearly had a sizeable sampling of these two patriarchs' writings. But from Aśvaghoṣa they had next to nothing. There was a notable discrepancy between the dearth of Aśvaghoṣa's writings at the time

79. *Bai lun,* T no. 1569, 30:167c; *Chu sanzang jiji,* T no. 2145, 55:77b.
80. *Chu sanzang jiji,* T no. 2145, 55:74c; *Da zhidu lun,* T no. 1509, 25:57a.
81. *Chu sanzang jiji,* T no. 2145, 55:77a–b.
82. See the translation in appendix 1.

and the account of their proliferation in his Nanatsu-dera biography. This discrepancy apparently prompted later observers to read into this biography the title of another treatise associated with Aśvaghoṣa, the *Treatise on the Great Adornment Scripture* (*Da zhuangyan jing lun* 大莊嚴經論, *Kalpanāmaṇḍitikā* or *Sūtrālaṃkāraśāstra*?), which is a collection of *avadānas* and *jātakas* ostensibly translated by Kumārajīva.[83]

However, this text is notably absent from Sengyou's 僧祐 (445–518) *Collected Notes on the Production of the Threefold Canon* (*Chu sanzang jiji* 出三藏記集), which faithfully catalogued all of the Buddhist translations known in the early sixth century, and there is otherwise no evidence that the Chang'an group had any knowledge of it at all. Fajing's 法經 (fl. 594) *Catalogue of All the Scriptures* (*Zhongjing mulu* 眾經目錄), compiled almost two centuries after Kumārajīva's team was active, was the earliest source to ascribe the *Treatise on the Great Adornment Scripture* to Aśvaghoṣa and Kumārajīva.[84] But it was Fei Zhangfang's *Record of the Three Jewels through the Ages* (*Lidai sanbao ji* 歷代三寶紀) that first provided some context for this attribution:

> The *Record of the Sarvāstivāda* (*Sapoduo ji* 薩婆多記) says, "Aśvaghoṣa Bodhisattva was born a Brahman in eastern India some three-hundred years after the death of the Buddha." He left home [to seek the Way] and defeated all non-Buddhists. He composed the *Da zhuangyan lun* in several hundreds of verses, broadly propagating the Buddha's teachings. There is a separate biography that records this. [His birth] is estimated to correspond to this time.[85]
>
> 薩婆多記云, "馬鳴菩薩, 佛滅後三百餘年, 生東天竺婆羅門種." 出家破諸外道. 造大莊嚴論數百偈, 盛弘佛教. 有別傳載. 計當此時.[86]

As his source of Aśvaghoṣa information Fei cited the *Record of the Sarvāstivāda*, which was compiled by Sengyou at the turn of the sixth century but has since been lost.[87] From Fei's quotation it is clear that this text drew upon Aśvaghoṣa's Nanatsu-dera biography, since the line about Aśvaghoṣa's date, caste, and place of birth is a near-verbatim copy. However, because Sengyou's *Collected Notes* has no record of any *Da zhuangyan* (*jing*) *lun*, it is safe to assume that his *Record of the Sarvāstivāda* did not mention such a text. Therefore, in his attribution of the *Da zhuangyan jing lun* to Aśvaghoṣa, Fei probably misinterpreted either the Nanatsu-dera biography itself—which is doubtless the text mentioned at the end of Fei's brief entry—or the reproduction of this biography in the *Record of the Sarvāstivāda*.

---

83. T no. 201. French trans. Huber 1908; cf. Ono 1933–1936, 7:269a–270c.

84. *Zhongjing mulu* 眾經目錄, T no. 2146, 55:141a; compiled ca. 594. See Tomomatsu 1931, 143, 163.

85. Cf. trans. Suzuki 1900, 2–3. The time that Fei refers to in his concluding sentence is the nineteenth year of Zhou King Nan 赧王 (r. 314–256 BCE), or 315 after nirvāṇa.

86. *Lidai sanbao ji* 歷代三寶紀, T no. 2034, 49:28a.

87. The preface for and lists of patriarchs chronicled in the *Sapoduo ji* are preserved in the *Chu sanzang jiji*, T no. 2145, 55:88c–90b. See chapter 2.

How could Fei have misread these texts? Just after Aśvaghoṣa's conversion the biography states, "He composed many treatises in millions of words that glorified the Buddhadharma" (作莊嚴佛法諸論數百萬言). The text here is indeed ambiguous. It could be referencing a specific text with the title *Zhuangyan fofa* 莊嚴佛法, which Aśvaghoṣa composed among many others, or *zhuangyan fofa* could be an adjectival phrase modifying his "many treatises" (*zhulun* 諸論), as I have indicated in my translation ("that glorified the Buddhadharma").[88] However, in light of the fact that the *Da zhuangyan jing lun* is not attested in any other source before the *Catalogue of All the Scriptures*, it is doubtful that this phrase referred to a specific text. Further, the Nanatsu-dera biography was also first ascribed to Kumārajīva in these late sixth-century catalogues.[89] So Fajing and Fei Zhangfang probably had this biography to hand, which they associated with Kumārajīva, and they had the *Da zhuangyan* (*jing*) *lun*, which most likely appeared after Sengyou's catalogue and was otherwise unattributed. They then drew the connection between this treatise, Aśvaghoṣa, and Kumārajīva, based on the phrase *zhuangyan fofa* used in Aśvaghoṣa's Nanatsu-dera biography to describe his oeuvre. But before Fajing and Fei Zhangfang, no one else had drawn this connection, probably because the *Da zhuangyan* (*jing*) *lun* did not yet exist. Despite the thousands of verses that Aśvaghoṣa supposedly composed, Chinese adepts of the early fifth century had only a sampling of his work on *dhyāna* practice, which no doubt forged a perception of Aśvaghoṣa as a meditation master of some renown.

Another important legacy of Aśvaghoṣa's writings, as indicated in the Nanatsu-dera biography, was the longstanding association that they prompted between him and Nāgārjuna. As previously discussed, in Sengrui's preface to the *Great Perfection of Wisdom Treatise*, these two patriarchs were closely tied to one another. Sengrui described how Aśvaghoṣa and Nāgārjuna appeared near the ends of the True and Semblance Dharma periods respectively, and how they were both worshipped like buddhas for their efforts at preserving the Dharma. However, without recourse to Aśvaghoṣa's Nanatsu-dera biography, the connection between these two patriarchs in Sengrui's preface appears to come from nowhere. Sengrui gave no reason why Aśvaghoṣa and Nāgārjuna, separated by half a millennium, would be seen to share such spiritual affinity, apart from the assertion that they both succeeded in reviving a dying Dharma. It would seem more fitting for Nāgārjuna and Āryadeva to have been joined instead. But Nāgārjuna also played an important role in the Nanatsu-dera biography of Aśvaghoṣa. After summarizing Aśvaghoṣa's conversion through debate and triumph at upholding the

88. In his initial article on this portion of the text, Ochiai (1993, 44) understands *Zhuangyan fofa* as a reference to the *Da zhuangyan jing lun* attributed to Aśvaghoṣa and Kumārajīva, as did Fei Zhangfang and presumably Fajing before him. In his later work Ochiai (2000, 640; Ochiai and Saitō 2000, 276, 293) reads *zhuangyan fofa* as an adjectival phrase, but offers no explanation for his change of heart.

89. *Zhongjing mulu*, T no. 2146, 55:146a; *Lidai sanbao ji*, T no. 2034, 49:79a.

Dharma, this biography turned to a brief account of Nāgārjuna's exploits. It explained how Nāgārjuna arose five centuries after Aśvaghoṣa and "made the Way of the Greater Vehicle [flourish] once more throughout Jambu[dvīpa], again proclaiming the teaching of non-attachment during the Final Dharma [period]." The biography then explained the connection between these two patriarchs: "Each time [Nāgārjuna] inked his quill and began composing treatises, he never failed to pay the utmost respect to Aśvaghoṣa. He composed verses for personally taking refuge and expressed his wish to rely on [Aśvaghoṣa's] profound illumination so as to become enlightened himself."[90]

This must have seemed an odd claim at the time, because none of Nāgārjuna's treatises mentioned Aśvaghoṣa at all, much less offered such fervid expressions of praise. I am aware of no other assertions in medieval Chinese sources of Nāgārjuna's reliance on Aśvaghoṣa's works.[91] However, there is a close affinity between the Sanskrit writings of these patriarchs that seems not to have been translated into Chinese with their treatises. According to E. H. Johnson, a number of Nāgārjuna's treatises often borrowed liberally from the writings of Aśvaghoṣa, in particular the latter's verses about the conversion of the Buddha's half-brother Nanda, titled *Saundarananda*.[92] Only fragments of this text were translated in three different Chinese compilations attributed to Kumārajīva—the *Scripture on Seated Dhyāna Samādhi*, *Essential Exposition of Dhyāna Methods* (*Chanfa yaojie* 禪法要解), and the *Scripture on the Bodhisattva's Methods of Censuring Sexual Desire* (*Pusa he seyu fa jing* 菩薩訶色欲法經)[93]—and although Sengrui outlined Aśvaghoṣa's contribution to this first compilation, none of these texts were known to have been derived from the *Saundarananda*; the latter two were not associated with Aśvaghoṣa at all. Indeed, nowhere aside from the Nanatsu-dera biography did Kumārajīva or his disciples elaborate any direct connection between the writings of Nāgārjuna and Aśvaghoṣa. Therefore, it appears that on this point the biography preserved a tradition not otherwise found in the literature translated into Chinese and attributed to these patriarchs. Rather, this particular connection between Nāgārjuna and Aśvaghoṣa must have been transmitted orally by Kumārajīva or in other documents that have not come down to us. These patriarchs were thus bonded initially through their shared faith in the power of written exegesis to save the world, and this bond would hold steadfast throughout Chinese Buddhist history.

The Practice of *Dhyāna*

While debate and authorship were clearly the two most prominent aspects of the Indian patriarchs' repertoire, as indicated by their earliest Chinese biographies, these sources also advocated *dhyāna* as an important practice

90. See the translation in appendix 1.

91. Cf. Ochiai 2000, 631.

92. Johnson (1936) 1984, xxix–xxx. *Saundarananda* trans. Johnson 1932.

93. See Yamabe 1999, 79, 83n67.

for aspiring Buddhist saints in the centuries after nirvāṇa. This practice was noted in early accounts of Nāgārjuna's career, but it was Aśvaghoṣa who garnered particular renown for his expertise in *dhyāna* cultivation. The earliest evidence for Aśvaghoṣa's mastery of meditation was provided in Sengrui's "Preface to the *Dhyāna* Scriptures Translated within the Passes" (*Guanzhong chu chanjing xü* 關中出禪經序). Sengrui composed this preface to accompany his revision of the *Dhyāna Essentials of All the Schools* (*Zhongjia chanyao* 眾家禪要), which was a meditation manual that Kumārajīva compiled shortly after his arrival in Chang'an.[94]

> Dharma-master Kumārajīva arrived in Chang'an from Guzang on the 20th day of the 12th month of the *xinchou* year (February 8, 402). Then on the 26th day of that month (February 14) I received [from him] the methods of *dhyāna*. . . .
>
> Before long I obtained a selection of *Dhyāna Essentials of All the Schools*, compiled into these three scrolls. The first forty-three verses were composed by Kumāralāta. The concluding twenty verses were composed by Aśvaghoṣa Bodhisattva. Therein the five gateways came from among the compiled *Dhyāna Essentials* of Vasumitra, Saṅgharakṣa, Upagupta, Saṅghasena, *bhikṣu* Side (Pārśva), Aśvaghoṣa and Kumāralāta.[95] The verses within the [section on the] six kinds of thought are those cultivated by Aśvaghoṣa Bodhisattva in order to explain these six thoughts.[96] The initial contemplations of the marks of desire, anger and delusion and then of their three gateways were all compiled by Saṅgharakṣa. The six elements of *ānāpāna-smṛti*[97] were spoken by all [of these] discourse masters. The middle and latter bodhisattva methods for practicing *dhyāna* were also based on the *Vasudharasūtra* and [used to] augment the *Twelve Causes and Conditions* in one scroll and the *Essential Exposition* in two scrolls, which were compiled and published at another time."[98]

---

94. Sengrui's revision was completed on January 29, 407; see *Chu sanzang jiji* (T no. 2145, 55:65b): "the fifth day of the intercalary month of the ninth year of the Hongshi [era]" 弘始九年閏月五日.

95. The "five gateways" all appear in the first scroll of the present *Zuochan sanmei jing* (T no. 614, 15:271c–277b). They are listed in Yamabe and Sueki 2009, xvi, and translated pp. 10–41. For these Sanskrit reconstructions I follow Yamabe and Sueki 2009, xvi. Bhikṣu Side (Pārśva) is here translated/transliterated as Le biqiu 勒比丘. Although Pārśva is more commonly known as Xie 脅 (lit. "side" or "rib"), Le can also mean "side" (Luo 1987–1995, 1076a); cf. Yamabe 1999, 79n62.

96. The "six kinds of thoughts" that must be eliminated constitute the fourth of the five gateways. See Yamabe and Sueki 2009, 18–27.

97. I.e., practices of breathing meditation. See Lü 1996, 207n8 and Yamabe and Sueki 2009, 27–30.

98. *Vasudharasūtra*: *Chishi jing* 持世經, T no. 482; trans. attributed to Kumārajīva. *Twelve Causes and Conditions* probably refers to the *Shier yinyuan guan jing* 十二因緣觀經, trans. attributed to Kumārajīva but no longer extant; see Ono 1933–1936, 5:180b. *Essential Exposition*: *Chanfa yaojie* 禪法要解, T no. 616; trans. attributed to Kumārajīva. Cf. trans. Lü 1996, 202–203; and Minowa 2003, 177–178. The preface is paraphrased by Yamabe 1999, 78–79.

究摩羅法師, 以辛丑之年十二月二十日, 自姑藏至常[read 長]安. 予即以其月二十六日, 從受禪法. . . .

尋蒙抄撰, 眾家禪要, 得此三卷. 初四十三偈, 是究摩羅羅陀法師所造. 後二十偈, 是馬鳴菩薩之所造也. 其中五門, 是婆須蜜, 僧伽羅叉, 漚波崛, 僧伽斯那, 勒比丘, 馬鳴, 羅陀禪要之中, 抄集之所出也. 六覺中偈, 是馬鳴菩薩修習之, 以釋六覺也. 初觀婬恚癡相及其三門, 皆僧伽羅叉之所撰也. 息門六事, 諸論師說也. 菩薩習禪法中後, 更依持世經, 益十二因緣一卷, 要解二卷, 別時撰出.[99]

As Minowa Kenryō 蓑輪顕量, Nobuyoshi Yamabe, and others have shown, it is clear from a comparison between the contents outlined here by Sengrui and those of the current *Scripture on Seated Dhyāna Samādhi* that this is the text described by Sengrui as containing verses composed by Aśvaghoṣa.[100] This text thus corresponds to the *Dhyāna Essentials of All the Schools* that Sengrui received from Kumārajīva (and perhaps helped to compile) almost immediately after they arrived in Chang'an at the beginning of 402. As a scholar-monk for some thirty-five years prior to his discipleship under Kumārajīva, Sengrui had developed strong convictions about the state of Buddhism in China, which aspects of Buddhist practice were most important, and the areas in which it was most deficient. In particular, he considered meditation to be a practice of great worth and thus lamented the fact that he and his Chinese colleagues lacked effective instructions for its advancement.[101]

Sengrui traveled to Chang'an from Mount Lu 廬山 in the south when he learned that Kumārajīva was being brought to the northern capital, and upon their arrival Sengrui immediately beseeched the Kuchean master to provide Indic texts elaborating procedures for *dhyāna* practice. Shortly thereafter the *Dhyāna Essentials of All the Schools* was produced, and Sengrui set himself to the task of applying their principles. In Sengrui's focus upon improving the fidelity of *dhyāna* practice in early fifth-century Chang'an, one can see cause for him to have fostered a sense of indebtedness to the Indian patriarchs noted in his preface. And, judging from his description of the text's contents and his attribution of its different sections to the seven Indian masters, Aśvaghoṣa was thought to have made the largest contribution. Moreover, although Sengrui does not say so explicitly, it appears that some of Aśvaghoṣa's verses also found their way into another of the extant *dhyāna* texts attributed to Kumārajīva, the *Essential Exposition of Dhyāna Methods* (*Chanfa yaojie*), which Sengrui noted was later compiled in part from the

99. *Chu sanzang jiji*, T no. 2145, 55:65a–b.

100. Minowa 2003; Yamabe 1999, 76–84. Yamabe and Sueki (2009) also indicate correspondences to Aśvaghoṣa's *Saundarananda* throughout their translation of the *Zuochan sanmei jing*.

101. These sentiments are expressed in Sengrui's biography in the *Gaoseng zhuan* (T no. 2059, 50:364a; trans. Wright 1957b, 274–275) and in his "*Dhyāna* Scriptures" preface (*Chu sanzang jiji*, T no. 2145, 55:65a).

"bodhisattva methods for practicing *dhyāna*" of the *Scripture on Seated Dhyāna Samādhi.*[102]

Therefore, in addition to the conceptions of Aśvaghoṣa discussed above, according to which he was a master of non-Buddhist learning converted to Buddhism through debate with his silent interlocutor Pārśva (Pūrṇa), as well as a great champion of the True Dharma at a time when the teaching had fallen into decay, Aśvaghoṣa was also seen as a purveyor of *dhyāna* essentials to a Chinese sangha that had long been deficient in this regard. With the brief account of Aśvaghoṣa in the *Vimalakīrti Commentary*, in which his master Pārśva became an "arhat endowed with the three insights and six penetrations" in particular through his focus on *dhyāna* practice, one can see whence Aśvaghoṣa would have gained his *dhyāna* mastery and authority to transmit it in verse. Indeed, although there was no indication of a formal transmission lineage of *dhyāna* practice across the seven Indian masters listed in Sengrui's preface, Pārśva did appear immediately before Aśvaghoṣa as one author of the "*dhyāna* essentials" comprising the *Scripture on Seated Dhyāna Samādhi.* As such, these patriarchs illustrated for their Chinese descendants the importance of meditation practice for Buddhist adepts living in a world without a Buddha.

Another prominent account of Aśvaghoṣa's *dhyāna* mastery was included in Huiyuan's "Comprehensive Preface to the *Dhyāna* Scriptures on the Cultivation of Expedient Means Translated at Mount Lu" (*Lushan chu xiuxing fangbian chanjing tongxu* 廬山出修行方便禪經統序).[103] In addition to one of the first explicit statements of Dharma lineage in Chinese Buddhist history, for which it has drawn the attention of modern scholars, this preface also provides the earliest extant evidence of transmission beyond Chang'an of the Aśvaghoṣa imagery promoted by Kumārajīva's disciples. Like Sengrui's "Preface to the *Dhyāna* Scriptures Translated within the Passes," Huiyuan presented Aśvaghoṣa as a great *dhyāna* master who dispensed invaluable meditation instructions when they were particularly lacking in China:

> I always grieved that since the great teaching had been disseminated eastward, techniques of *dhyāna* were very rare, the three trainings [of *śīla*, *samādhi*, and *prajñā*?] thus lacked their complete order, and the Way was in danger of dying out. Then Kumārajīva promulgated Aśvaghoṣa's exposition, such that this discipline [of *dhyāna* (*samādhi*)] appeared [in China]. Although his Way has not yet been fully disseminated, [it can eventually be established just as] a mountain

102. See the *Chengshi lun* 成實論 (*Satyasiddhiśāstra*), trans. Kumārajīva (T no. 1646, 32:372a), which attributes verses to Aśvaghoṣa that are found in the *Chanfa yaojie* (T no. 616, 15:294b) but not in the *Zuochan sanmei jing.*

103. Preserved in the *Chu sanzang jiji*, T no. 2145, 55:65b–66a. It also appears as the preface to Buddhabhadra's (359/60–429) translation of the *Damoduoluo chan jing* 達摩多羅禪經 (T no. 618, 15:300c–301b), which was probably completed in 410 (Zürcher [1959] 2007, 223). Portions of this preface have been translated into English by Liebenthal 1950, 249; and McRae 1986, 81–82 (on which see Barrett 1990, 91), and into modern colloquial Chinese by Lü 1996, 208–216.

starts with but a single basket [of earth].[104] It is a joyous occasion to encounter this timely arrival, as we can [finally] experience the wondrous purport of such a person. He relinquished his arguments for overcoming [opponents] and instead embraced the wordless teaching.[105] Thereupon he vowed to take on the *saṃnāha* (armor) [of the bodhisattva's resolve to liberate beings],[106] and made it his personal charge to achieve ultimate tranquility (i.e., nirvāṇa). Embracing the virtues and never forgetting them, he bequeathed his teachings to this land.

每慨大教東流, 禪數尤寡, 三業無統, 斯道殆廢. 頃鳩摩耆婆, 宣馬鳴所述, 乃有此業. 雖其道未融, 蓋是為山於一簣. 欣時來之有遇, 感寄[107]趣於若人. 捨夫制勝之論, 而順不言之辯. 遂誓被僧那, 以至寂為己任. 懷德未忘, 故遺訓在茲.[108]

Huiyuan's "Comprehensive Preface" exhibits many of the same concerns that Sengrui expressed about the dearth of adequate meditation instructions in early fifth-century China, as well as a sense of debt to Aśvaghoṣa for helping to remedy the situation. Of the seven *dhyāna* masters that Sengrui noted in his "*Dhyāna* Scriptures" preface, Huiyuan singled out Aśvaghoṣa in particular for extended praise, even though Aśvaghoṣa was not part of the lineage that Huiyuan (presumably following Buddhabhadra) outlined elsewhere in this text.[109] In this regard Huiyuan perpetuated the notion, emphasized by Kumārajīva's disciples, of temporal distance between Aśvaghoṣa and the Buddha Śākyamuni that was *not* bridged by a direct line of Dharma transmission. As I will explore in chapter 2 in connection with the *Tradition of the Causes and Conditions of the Dharma-Treasury Transmission* (*Fu fazang yinyuan zhuan* 付法藏因緣傳), the placement of Aśvaghoṣa, Nāgārjuna, and Āryadeva within lineage histories such as this would significantly alter their function for medieval Chinese Buddhists. These patriarchs

104. Adapted from the *Analects* 9.18: "Confucius said: 'It is like creating a mountain: If I stop with only one basket left to complete the job, it is my stopping. It is like leveling the ground: If I continue even though I have dumped only one basket, it is my advancement.'" 子曰: "譬如爲山, 未成一簣止, 吾止也! 譬如平地, 雖覆一簣進, 吾往也!" Cf. trans. Lau 1979, 98–99 (where the passage is 9.19). The point is that continual effort is required in one's endeavors, even if only in small steps, just as Aśvaghoṣa's teachings of *dhyāna* practice can be made to flourish in China with determined effort.

105. Perhaps echoing Sengzhao's *Vimalakīrti Commentary*, in which Pārśva's "thunderous silence" defeated Aśvaghoṣa in debate. Cf. McRae (1986, 82), who notes Huiyuan's emphasis elsewhere in this preface on the ineffability of the Buddhadharma.

106. *Sengna* 僧那 is short for *sengna sengnie* 僧那僧涅, which transliterates the Sanskrit *saṃnāha saṃnaddha. Saṃnāha* means "armor," *saṃnaddha* means "to don" or "to wear," and the compound indicates the bodhisattva's great vow to save all beings. See Mochizuki 1954–1963, 1:677a; and Nakamura 1981, 875d.

107. Reading *qi* 奇 for *ji* 寄, as in the *Damoduoluo chan jing*, T no. 618, 15:301a. I owe this reading to Chen Jinhua (personal communication).

108. *Chu sanzang jiji*, T no. 2145, 55:65c–66a. See also the slightly different rendering in the *Damoduoluo chan jing*, T no. 618, 15:301a–b.

109. For discussion of this brief lineage statement, see especially Adamek 2007, 34–36; and McRae 1986, 80–82.

became transmitters of the teaching that they had received directly from their own masters, through a lineage extending back to the Buddha himself, rather than reviving a Dharma that before them had fallen into decay. Nevertheless, in Huiyuan's "Comprehensive Preface," Aśvaghoṣa still fit within the same Dharmic history as in the earlier Chang'an accounts, as did Nāgārjuna in Huiyuan's preface to his abridged *Great Perfection of Wisdom Treatise.* Like the patriarch accounts in the writings of Kumārajīva's disciples, with Aśvaghoṣa emerging in dark times far from the Buddha and causing the True Dharma to flourish once again, Huiyuan's "Comprehensive Preface" also portrayed Aśvaghoṣa as a great master who helped save a Buddhist tradition—*dhyāna* practice in fifth-century China—when it was in danger of dying out. In this way, following Sengrui's "*Dhyāna* Scriptures" preface, Huiyuan conceived Aśvaghoṣa first and foremost as a master of Buddhist meditation. This facet of Aśvaghoṣa's repertoire was thus central to his early fifth-century representations, and as will be discussed in detail, it was one reason why he would later be associated with the celebrated *Mahāyāna Awakening of Faith.*

Men of the Cliffs, Caves, and Dragon Palaces

The eminent monk Huiyuan was one of the leaders of the Buddhist establishment in southern China during the early fifth century, and as such he had regular contact with Kumārajīva and his disciples in the north. From this group in Chang'an, Huiyuan learned much about the teachings and practices of Nāgārjuna and Aśvaghoṣa, and in his writings he elaborated the repertoires of these post-*parinirvāṇa* Indian masters. The most prominent of Huiyuan's writings on the Indian patriarchs is his preface to an abridged edition of the *Great Perfection of Wisdom Treatise,* which includes the fullest biography of Nāgārjuna that can be confidently dated to the early fifth century.[110] In this preface Huiyuan reiterated all of the themes examined above—revolving around Dharma revival in the centuries after nirvāṇa through a specific repertoire of literati practices—while also highlighting different aspects of Nāgārjuna's career that reflected Huiyuan's own vision of the exemplary Buddhist master:

> There was a high-minded gentleman[111] of the Greater Vehicle named Nāgārjuna. He was born in India and came from the Brahman caste. His sincerity

110. *Dazhi lun chao xu* 大智論抄序, preserved in the *Chu sanzang jiji,* T no. 2145, 55:75b–76b; trans. Robinson 1967, 200–205. Robinson (1967, 113), following Liebenthal (1950, 248), surmises that at least part of this preface was written after Huiyuan saw Sengzhao's *Prajñā Has No Knowing* (*Bore wuzhi lun* 般若無知論) in 408. Huiyuan's abridged version of the *Great Perfection of Wisdom Treatise,* from one hundred scrolls to twenty, as well as his preface to the full version of the same—written at the behest of Qin ruler Yao Xing around 406—are no longer extant; see Zürcher (1959) 2007, 212, 249, 410n97.

111. On "high-minded gentleman": as Robinson (1967, 287n12) notes, *gaoshi* 高士 was an archaic translation of bodhisattva. However, this term was also suggestive of Nāgārjuna's penchant for eremitism, which Huiyuan emphasized throughout.

accumulated through former ages fitted his mind to existence in this [world]. He lived during the ninth century [after nirvāṇa], at a moment when [the Dharma] was decadent and weak. He was grieved at the benightedness of the multitudes, and treading the steep path, he did not falter.

Thereupon, he secluded himself in a private mode of life[112] and roamed cloudlike through Kapilavastu. He grieved that his cultured brilliance had not yet been revealed, and that although his thoughts might leap they were not put to use.[113] Then he said with a deep sigh, "When the heavy night is darkening, the firefly's light cannot illuminate it.[114] Though the white sun has put its light to rest, one can still continue by the bright moon." Accordingly, he made his vows, took the tonsure, and adopted the dark garments [of a monk]. He dwelt in seclusion in the woods and swamps, lived as a hermit and practiced *dhyāna*. He stilled his mind and studied the subtle, his thoughts penetrating the supra-normal.

Consequently he had an awakening and said, "I have heard in previous discourses that the Great Square has no limits.[115] There may be someone who has gone beyond it." He suddenly turned his steps towards the snowy mountains, revealing his spiritual brilliance in order to pursue his resolve. He was about to pass through a place frequented by transcendents of old when he suddenly met a *śramaṇa* (renouncer) beneath a cliff. He questioned him about points on which he had doubts, and first came to know Greater Vehicle teachings (*vaipulya*).

When he proceeded to the dragon palace, there was no important canon or secret text that he did not master. When the roots of his impediments had been pulled up, his name crowned the stages of the [bodhisattva] path, and by his virtue he became endowed with the three forbearances.[116] Only then did he open up the nine fords in the mighty abyss and, befriending the scaly species, roam together with them.[117] His students were like [the trees in] a forest,

112. On "a private mode of life": The expression *hengmen* 衡門 (gate with a horizontal beam) derives from the *Shi jing* 詩經; it connotes reclusion and retirement from worldly affairs. See Luo 1987–1995, 1909b; and Robinson 1967, 287n15. On *Chize* 赤澤 (red swamp) as a gloss for Kapilavastu and synecdoche for India, see Robinson 1967, 287n16.

113. See Robinson (1967, 287n18) for the sentence 思忽躍而勿用 and its potential source in the *Yijing*. In light of the *Yijing* prototype, Robinson reads *huo* 或 for *huo* 惑, which is the variant for *hu* 忽 in the Song, Yuan and Ming editions used in Taishō collating (*Chu sanzang jiji*, T no. 2145, 55:75n19).

114. From the *Weimojie suoshuo jing* (*Vimalakīrtinirdeśa*), T no. 475, 14:541a: 無以日光, 等彼螢火 "Do not take the light of the sun to be the same as the firefly's glimmer" (Robinson 1967, 288n19).

115. Cf. *Daode jing* 道德經: "The Great Square has no corners" 大方无隅 (Henricks 1989, 102–103; Robinson 1967, 288n22).

116. The "three forbearances" (*sanren* 三忍) refer to a number of different attainments; see Ciyi 1988–1989, 1:571c–572b; Mochizuki 1954–1963, 2:1656c–1658b; and Nakamura 1981, 484c–d. Here Huiyuan appears to follow Tanying's preface to the *Middle Treatise*, according to which Nāgārjuna attained the forbearance of birthlessness (*wusheng ren* 無生忍) in the dragon palace.

117. Robinson (1967, 288n26) speculates that the "nine fords in the mighty abyss" (*jiujin yu zhongyuan* 九津於重淵) are the nine interstices between the ten stages of the bodhisattva path.

and the talented and accomplished inevitably gathered [around him]. Consequently, the non-Buddhists esteemed his manner, and famous gentlemen submitted to his dictates. From this time, the enterprise of the Greater Vehicle flourished again.[118]

有大乘高士, 厥號龍樹. 生于天竺, 出自梵種. 積誠曩代, 契心在茲. 接九百之運, 撫頹薄之會. 悲蒙俗之茫昧, 蹈險跡而弗吝.

於是卷陰衡門, 雲翔赤澤. 慨文明之未發, 思忽躍而勿用. 乃喟然嘆曰, "重夜方昏, 非熒燭之能照. 雖白日寢光, 猶可繼以朗月." 遂自誓落簪, 表容玄服. 隱居林澤, 守閑行禪. 靖慮研微, 思通過半.

因而悟曰, "聞之於前論, 大方無垠. 或有出乎其外者." 俄而迴步雪山, 啟神明以訊志. 將歷古仙之所遊, 忽遇沙門於巖下. 請質所疑, 始知有方等之學.

及至龍宮, 要藏祕典, 靡不管綜. 滯根既拔, 則名冠道位, 德備三忍. 然後開九津於重淵, 朋鱗族而俱遊. 學徒如林, 英彥必集. 由是外道高其風, 名士服其致. 大乘之業, 於茲復隆矣.[119]

In many respects, Huiyuan's preface mirrored the thematic emphases of Sengrui's and Sengzhao's accounts of Nāgārjuna. Nāgārjuna was placed in the ninth century after nirvāṇa, which followed both the Nanatsu-dera biography of Aśvaghoṣa—with Aśvaghoṣa born three hundred years after nirvāṇa and Nāgārjuna five centuries later—and Sengrui's preface to the *Great Perfection of Wisdom Treatise*, which placed Nāgārjuna near the end of the Semblance Dharma period, or the first millennium after nirvāṇa. Further, according to Huiyuan, during this time the Dharma was "decadent and weak" and Nāgārjuna "was grieved at the benightedness of the multitudes," just as in the accounts of the Semblance Dharma period provided by Kumārajīva's disciples. And as one might expect, the rise of Nāgārjuna during these dark times brought about a renewal of the teachings. How did Nāgārjuna rescue the Dharma when it was in peril? According to Huiyuan, he steeled himself through the practice of *dhyāna*, he made famous gentlemen submit to his dictates, presumably through public debate, and he composed the *Great Perfection of Wisdom Treatise*.[120] But most central to Huiyuan's account was Nāgārjuna's proclivity toward reclusion and his solitary peregrinations through the wild haunts of ancient sages.

In the early Chang'an accounts Aśvaghoṣa and Āryadeva were shown following a peripatetic lifestyle—with the former roaming the kingdoms of India and the latter "striding freely through Kapilavastu"—but in Huiyuan's Nāgārjuna biography this kind of eremitic wandering was given special emphasis. With his recognition that the Dharma was in decline and that the masses could not but wallow in their own ignorance, Nāgārjuna "secluded himself in a private mode of life" and "roamed cloudlike" throughout the

---

118. Trans. Robinson 1967, 201, with minor changes.

119. *Chu sanzang jiji*, T no. 2145, 55:75b–c.

120. The saving power of this treatise is emphasized elsewhere in Huiyuan's preface; see Robinson 1967, 202.

land. He then took the tonsure and donned the robes of a Buddhist monk, after which he "dwelt in seclusion in the woods and swamps" and lived as a hermit. This led to an awakening of sorts, which drove Nāgārjuna toward the "snowy mountains" (of the Himalayas?), to places "frequented by transcendents of old," and along the way into the company of a cliff-dwelling *śramaṇa* who further instructed him in the teachings of the Buddha. Finally Nāgārjuna proceeded to the dragon palace, where he received all of the most profound Buddhist scriptures and perfected his bodhisattva qualities.

In this way Nāgārjuna was closely aligned with age-old Chinese traditions of eremitism, represented by figures variously called "men of the cliffs and caves" (*yanxue zhi shi* 巖穴之士), "men in reclusion" (*yinshi* 隱士), "men of the mountains and forests" (*shanlin zhi shi* 山林之士), and so on, who appeared throughout the ancient classics and were celebrated in medieval hagiographic compilations like the *Traditions of High-Minded Gentlemen* (*Gaoshi zhuan* 高士傳) and *Traditions of Disengaged Persons* (*Yimin zhuan* 逸民傳).[121] Characters of this sort punctuated Nāgārjuna's peregrinations, but he himself would soon become foremost among them, drawing to his side the most talented and accomplished disciples. It may seem contradictory to measure the worth of a recluse by the size of his entourage. But the strength of character so often associated with worldly withdrawal in Chinese sources made such figures the paradoxical centers of attention. As Alan Berkowitz (2000, 2010) and Robert Campany (2009) have shown, eremitism was a social role and political posture utterly meaningless apart from cultural norms, and the social interactions of nominally reclusive adepts were commonplace in the accounts of their lives. Further, in premodern China, eremitism was often defined in particular as withdrawal from public service and refusal to accept court appointments; it was one form of protest against the corruption of officialdom (Berkowitz 2000, 2–4, 7; Vervoorn 1990, 8–14). In this regard it is noteworthy that Nāgārjuna's well-known triumph over secular authority—in particular an episode from his later biographies in which he converted a South Indian king—was entirely absent from Huiyuan's account.[122] Here Nāgārjuna's withdrawal was not from the state apparatus; rather, in prototypical Buddhist fashion he renounced the *sahā* (endurance) world of suffering and delusion. Nevertheless, with Huiyuan's narrative and terminology clearly drawing upon Chinese eremitic traditions, Nāgārjuna here struck the figure of a Chinese recluse roaming the sacred lands of the Buddha's own peregrinations.[123]

Whether or not Nāgārjuna's eremitic tendencies were invented by Huiyuan, the ideals that they illustrated were very much in line with Huiyuan's own religious ambitions, and with his conception of the exemplary Buddhist

121. On the traditions of these figures through the Han, see Vervoorn 1990. For their development during the Six Dynasties, see Berkowitz 2000.

122. See chapter 2 and appendix 2.

123. Morrison (2010, 211) makes a similar point about Huiyuan's depiction of Ānanda and his successors.

adept as "a stranger beyond the world [of men]" (*fangwai zhi bin* 方外之賓).[124] Huiyuan himself sought to cultivate a life of "noble retirement" (*jiadun* 嘉遁)[125] at the tender age of twenty, away from the political intrigue and social chaos of northern China in the mid-fourth century, and throughout his career he seems to have kept his distance from the hustle and bustle of the mundane world. Before settling on Mount Lu around 380, Huiyuan lived in a number of secluded mountain retreats described in Ge Hong's (283–343) *Master Who Embraces Simplicity* (*Baopuzi* 抱朴子) as especially suitable for quiet meditation and the concoction of alchemical elixirs. Huiyuan eventually moved to Mount Lu, where he would remain until his death in 416, in part because of this mountain's already hallowed tradition as a dwelling place of hidden sages, as well as its natural beauty and serenity far (enough) from the city centers of the south (Zürcher [1959] 2007, 207–208). Whether or not Huiyuan cultivated this image of withdrawal for the sociopolitical capital that it may have garnered him and his community—he did in 404 get caught up in local struggles for political power—he would have had the same interest in depicting Nāgārjuna as likewise concerned to seclude himself in the wilderness to perfect his qualities.[126] In more fully developed biographical traditions of Nāgārjuna that began perhaps from the late fifth century and that crystallized in the sixth, this episode in Nāgārjuna's career of restless wandering born of spiritual yearning would become standard fare in Chinese conceptions of this Indian patriarch—a crucial turning point between his foolish parading as a precocious youth and his profound transformation in the depths of the sea dragon palace.

In Huiyuan's account, Nāgārjuna's solitary travels finally led him to this oceanic dwelling place of the famed dragon kings of Buddhist lore, which was functionally analogous to such mythic Chinese locales as Penglai 蓬萊, Yingzhou 瀛洲, and Kunlun 崑崙—where the secrets of transcendence were kept—and every abyssal cavern of magical purport in which Daoist gods stored esoteric scriptures for the coming of worthy adepts. Early Buddhist sources such as the *Lotus Sūtra*, the *Great Perfection of Wisdom Treatise*, and the *Scripture Spoken by the Buddha on the Sea Dragon King* described wish-fulfilling jewels, Buddha relics, caches of scriptures, and other Dharmic treasures being hidden away in the palaces of dragons.[127] Similarly, Daoist scriptures, talismans, sacramental regalia, and the like were often ensconced deep within remote grottoes, as when, for example, Thearch Ku 帝嚳 stored

124. See Zürcher (1959) 2007, 211, 396n156.

125. This expression appears in Huiyuan's *Chu sanzang jiji* and *Gaoseng zhuan* biographies; see Zürcher (1959) 2007, 403n7.

126. On Huiyuan's dealings with the Eastern Jin official Huan Xuan 桓玄 (369–404), who in 404 usurped the throne in the southern capital Jiankang, see Hurvitz 1957 and Zürcher (1959) 2007, 211–217, 231–239.

127. For the *Lotus Sūtra*, see *Miaofa lianhua jing*, T no. 262, 9:35a–b. For the *Great Perfection of Wisdom Treatise*, see *Da zhidu lun*, T no. 1509, 25:181c. For the *Scripture Spoken by the Buddha on the Sea Dragon King*, see *Foshuo hailongwang jing* 佛說海龍王經, T no. 598, 15:144b–146a; trans. Dharmarakṣa (fl. 266–313) in 285.

the *Scripture of the Five Numinous Treasure Talismans* (*Lingbao wufu jing* 靈寶五符經) in a mountain cave for discovery by Yu the Great 大禹.[128] Also, in Chinese sources such caverns were sometimes designated as the abodes of dragon kings, where rituals, offerings, and prayers could be performed to elicit a variety of benefits. But more frequently these grottoes were equated with various levels of heaven, with esoteric structures of the human body, and described as quiescent sanctuaries within which methods of self-cultivation could be perfected.[129] Dragon palaces of Buddhist myth were likewise places where ultimate truth was found—in the form of scriptural caches or through the perfection of spiritual qualities—and Nāgārjuna was depicted early on as having attained both therein.[130]

The dragon palace scene in Huiyuan's Nāgārjuna biography evoked these various traditions of religious sanctity ensconced, while also alluding to Sengrui's preface to the *Great Perfection of Wisdom Treatise* and Tanying's *Middle Treatise* preface. Sengrui wrote that Nāgārjuna "availed himself of the light of the dragon palace to illumine wisdom in search of the profound," and Tanying explained that "when he went to the ocean palace [Nāgārjuna] attained the forbearance of birthlessness."[131] Huiyuan's biography elaborated on these accounts, specifying that within the dragon palace Nāgārjuna mastered all of the most important Buddhist scriptures and completed the stages of the bodhisattva path. In this way Nāgārjuna's eremitic wanderings reached their culmination, as he finally came to that secret place where the most profound teachings were hidden. And as a corollary to the equation between nominal secrecy and increased sociocultural cachet—as when scriptures and their teachings were esotericized through the motif of inaccessibility—masters who could discover and reveal these secrets were accorded utmost sanctity.[132] Such was the case with Nāgārjuna, who was valorized as the lone adept accepted into the dragon palace to access these foremost Buddhist teachings and disseminate them throughout the world.

Conclusion: Early Chinese Portraits of Indian Buddhism

Throughout the Indian patriarch accounts discussed in this chapter, one sees a concerted effort on the part of their authors to delineate the contours of post-*parinirvāṇa* Indian Buddhism. These biographies of Aśvaghoṣa,

---

128. See Campany 2009, 93.

129. See Hahn 2000, 695–698.

130. For further discussion of dragon palaces in Buddhist myth, including a number of other relevant primary sources, see Ciyi 1988–1989, 7:6385b–6386a; Mochizuki 1954–1963, 5:4984a–4985c (s.v. "Ryū 龍"), 10:1156b–1158a; and Zürcher 1982, 28–29n51. Buswell (1989, 50–52) discusses how later tales of Wŏnhyo disseminating the *Vajrasamādhisūtra* drew upon this aspect of Nāgārjuna's legend. This episode appears in Nāgārjuna's canonical biography, *Longshu pusa zhuan*, T no. 2047, 50:184c, 186a.

131. *Chu sanzang jiji*, T no. 2145, 55:74c; *Da zhidu lun*, T no. 1509, 25:57a. *Chu sanzang jiji*, T no. 2145, 55:77a.

132. See Campany 2009, 94–100.

Nāgārjuna, and Āryadeva focused first and foremost on the historical circumstances of their protagonists, providing specific chronologies and describing the soteriological conditions of the times. And as much as anything else, these accounts presented a bracing vision of Buddhism in India after the Buddha's death. Without the First Jewel to light the way, the Dharma and sangha were gradually weakened, until several centuries after nirvāṇa, false teachings flourished and benighted non-Buddhists covered the lands. Chinese scholar-monks of the early fifth century depicted their own time and place along similar lines, emphasizing their spatiotemporal distance from the Buddha and decrying the dim wits and deluded views that thereby surrounded them. But before them, Aśvaghoṣa, Nāgārjuna, and Āryadeva had shown how this kind of post-*parinirvāṇa* darkness could be overcome. These patriarchs toiled and triumphed in the land of the Buddha's birth, which made them authoritative representatives of Buddhist sainthood, but the models of practice that they provided were equally effective for upholding the Dharma in latter-day China. The Indian patriarchs instantiated a specific repertoire of practices—including especially doctrinal authorship, public debate, meditative contemplation, and eremitism—that was shown to be ideally suited to propagating Buddhism in a Buddhaless world, regardless of where that world might be.

On the one hand, then, the Indian identity of the patriarchs was muted. Foregrounded primarily was their temporal distance from the Buddha, which their latter-day Chinese proponents shared, so the plights of these Buddhist adepts over the centuries after nirvāṇa were largely accordant across the Sino-Indian divide. On the other hand, the Indian identity of Aśvaghoṣa, Nāgārjuna, and Āryadeva played crucial roles in the ways they were conceived at this stage in China. For one, their Indianness expressly entailed the vestiges of pure Buddhist origins, rendering them intrinsically emblematic of Dharmic truth. And at the same time, the Indian identity of these patriarchs made them vehicles through which the practices that they modeled could be redefined as quintessentially Buddhist. I emphasized above how Sengrui, Sengzhao, and Huiyuan were the foremost Buddhist scholars of their time, and as such they upheld the favored activities of spiritually inclined Chinese literati as the primary means of sustaining Buddhism. Having come of age amid the traditions of *xuanxue* and *qingtan*—and of the "men of the cliffs and caves"—Kumārajīva's associates were masters of the practices that these figures valued most. Sengrui, Sengzhao, and Huiyuan then showed how the great Buddhist patriarchs of post-*parinirvāṇa* India had likewise perfected a cognate repertoire and thereby saved the world. In this way the practices of debate, authorship, meditation, and eremitism were accorded a hallowed Indian Buddhist pedigree. Through the Indian patriarchs these time-honored vocations of the Chinese literati were redefined as fundamentally Buddhist, and the Chinese sangha was thus implicitly promoted as their rightful custodian and foremost bastion.

As such, in the early fifth century Aśvaghoṣa, Nāgārjuna, and Āryadeva were essentially represented as Indian literati gentlemen who had awakened to the truth, converted to Buddhism, and perfected their bodhisattva qualities such that they could revive the True Dharma when it had fallen into decay. This was the model of Buddhist sainthood advanced by Sengrui, Sengzhao, and Huiyuan, and it gives us a good baseline for assessing later developments in the Chinese imagery of these Indian patriarchs. First of all, as Michel Strickmann emphasizes, medieval Chinese sources that dwelled on the end times frequently offered as antidote to the encroaching evil a range of therapeutic and apotropaic techniques. These methods included spells, talismans, divination, exorcistic rites, and the like, which were the preserve of adepts across religious traditions, who sometimes competed with the Buddhist ecclesiastic elite. Scriptures of this sort were often apocryphal, advanced by millenarian or other potentially subversive groups, and produced from the margins of mainstream religious institutions (Strickmann 1990). The earliest representations of Aśvaghoṣa, Nāgārjuna, and Āryadeva similarly highlighted the decline of the Dharma, but the practices that they advanced as most effective for such times were anything but marginal. In later sources that elaborated the repertoires of these Indian patriarchs, however, thaumaturgic expertise was expressly foregrounded, making them speak to a different range of Chinese religious concerns. Secondly, while the earliest biographies of Aśvaghoṣa, Nāgārjuna, and Āryadeva repeatedly emphasized the decline of the Dharma during their generations—thus presenting a cyclical, wax-and-wane model of Indian Buddhist history—later accounts of these patriarchs would radically reconstruct this historical context. Instead of depicting the patriarchs arising in pernicious times to save a dying Dharma, subsequent accounts showed them standing in long lines of Indian masters who maintained the teaching in the same pristine condition as when Śākyamuni walked the earth. The earliest example of Aśvaghoṣa, Nāgārjuna, and Āryadeva being placed within such Dharma lineages was the *Tradition of the Causes and Conditions of the Dharma-Treasury Transmission.* It is to this text and its contexts that I now turn.

2
An Indian Lineage Severed

AROUND THE YEAR 500, Buddhist historiographer and Vinaya specialist Sengyou 僧祐 (445–518) compiled more than one hundred Indian patriarch biographies into a compendium titled *Record of the Masters and Disciples of the Sarvāstivādin Sect* (*Sapoduo bu shizi ji* 薩婆多部師資記; hereinafter *Record of the Sarvāstivāda*).[1] This compendium was lost sometime during the Tang (Funayama 2000, 345), but its preface and lists of patriarchs remain. As indicated by the terms *shizi* 師資 (masters and disciples) and *xiangcheng* 相承 (mutually presenting/receiving) in the text's titles, these patriarch lists constituted transmission lineages in the Sarvāstivādin Vinaya tradition. In his preface to this lineage history, Sengyou stressed the crucial role played by its constituents in preserving Buddhism after nirvāṇa and providing models of practice for latter-day Chinese Buddhists:

> The age of the Great Saint's splendor is in the distant past. It is only because of the Vinaya that the Dharma and sangha have not fallen away. When the canon of the Vinaya was first compiled, everyone learned it in the same manner. Then in the middle ages differences arose and the five sects split from one another. After that [monks] learned and practiced according to the traditions of their own masters. Only the Sarvāstivādin sect is prevalent in the land of Qi (China), because it originated in India and spread to Kāśmīra, and the light of its former saints and latter sages shines so brightly. The virtue of some was to rise through the [bodhisattva] stages; the Way of others was to attain the four fruits.[2] Some manifested signs to show their beneficence; others concealed their traces to appear as ordinary people. All of them upheld the standards of the Vinaya and propagated the Dharma. An old record recounts [the careers of] fifty-three people. After them, more wise men arose in succession, together continuing the glories of the past and setting models for us today. Following

1. This title is given in the *Chu sanzang jiji* 出三藏記集, T no. 2145, 55:82c. It is also titled *Sapoduo bu ji* 薩婆多部記 (*Chu sanzang jiji*, T no. 2145, 55:89a) and *Sapoduo bu xiangcheng zhuan* 薩婆多部相承傳 (*Chu sanzang jiji*, T no. 2145, 55:87b). For its date see Funayama 2000, 326–327.

2. This distinction between the bodhisattva stages and four fruits marked the Sarvāstivādin patriarchs as either Mahāyāna or Hīnayāna in orientation. Most of the masters listed after this preface were labeled arhats or bodhisattvas, which, according to Wang (1994, 193n19), also indicated their Mahāyāna or Hīnayāna affiliation.

> these, the five assemblies in the last period established their doctrines.[3] The graceful bearing and glories left by them can be readily traced. As one shaded by a tree protects its roots, and one drinking from a spring respects its source, how can we bear in mind these profound teachings without recording the lives of the men [who propagated them]?[4]
>
> 大聖遷輝, 歲紀綿邈. 法僧不墜, 其唯律乎. 初集律藏, 一軌共學. 中代異執, 五部各分. 既分五部, 則隨師得傳習. 唯薩婆多部, 偏行齊土, 蓋源起天竺, 流化罽賓, 前聖後賢, 重明疊耀. 或德昇住地; 或道證四果. 或顯相標瑞; 或晦跡同凡. 皆秉持律儀, 闡揚法化. 舊記所載, 五十三人. 自茲已後, 叡哲繼出, 並嗣徽於在昔, 垂軌於當今. 季世五眾, 依斯立教. 遺風餘烈, 炳然可尋. 夫蔭樹者護其本, 飲泉者敬其源, 寧可服膺玄訓, 而不記列其人哉?[5]

Immediately following this preface Sengyou presented two overlapping lineages, one the "old record" of fifty-three saints and another of fifty-four recounted by the Indian missionary Buddhabhadra (359/60–429). Many of the Sarvāstivādin masters appeared in both lists, with their sequence sometimes rearranged, after which Sengyou appended biographies of six Western missionaries, who had transmitted the teaching to China, and twenty Chinese Vinaya masters who upheld it there. On this last point it is worth noting that the *Record of the Sarvāstivāda* is often overlooked in favor of Guanding's 灌頂 (561–632) seventh-century Tiantai 天台 lineage as the first attempt in Chinese history to connect genealogies of Indian and Chinese Buddhist masters (see chapter 3). But most important for our present purposes is the related vision of post-*parinirvāṇa* Indian Buddhism and paradigm of Buddhist sainthood that this text advanced. Like the earlier accounts of Kumārajīva's associates, Sengyou emphasized the distance of the Buddha's splendor, but rather than beginning an inexorable descent into darkness, in this account Śākyamuni's departure initiated the rise of an Indian patriarchate that preserved his teachings undimmed. This represented a significant revaluation of Indian Buddhist history and of what it meant to be a Buddhist saint in the centuries after nirvāṇa. Sengyou adduced the Indian Buddhist "middle ages" (*zhongdai* 中代), when the sangha had split along sectarian lines, but this development did not signal any deterioration in the Dharma. Instead, because of the Vinaya regulations that the Buddha had stipulated, and the succession of patriarchs that carried them forth, the Dharma persevered undiminished through post-*parinirvāṇa* India and into latter-day China. From this standpoint, the most important task of Buddhist adepts living in a world without a Buddha was to uphold traditional Vinaya regulations and hand them down to future generations. Given that Sengyou

3. The five assemblies were fully ordained monks and nuns, novice monks and nuns, and ordained practitioners between the ages of eighteen and twenty who accepted the six precepts against killing, stealing, sex, lying, alcohol, and eating at improper times. See Muller 1995– (s.v. "*wu zhong* 五眾"). Different five-fold divisions of the sangha are discussed by Benn 2009, 18–21.

4. Trans. Wang 1994, 192–193, with modifications.

5. *Chu sanzang jiji*, T no. 2145, 55:89a.

was a Vinaya master in particular, this characterization of the Indian patriarchs comes as no surprise.

But Sengyou's *Record of the Sarvāstivāda* was not the first Chinese source to depict Indian Buddhist history as marked by perennial prosperity, maintained by a long line of patriarchs who transmitted the teaching after nirvāṇa. Similar models of Dharmic history and Buddhist sainthood were advanced some decades prior in the *Tradition of the Causes and Conditions of the Dharma-Treasury Transmission* (*Fu fazang yinyuan zhuan* 付法藏因緣傳; hereinafter *Dharma-Treasury Transmission*). Like the *Record of the Sarvāstivāda*, this earlier text recounted the formation of a single line of Indian patriarchs, illustrating the careers of some two dozen masters who handed down the teaching from one to the next and thereby preserved the Dharma for centuries after nirvāṇa. And also like Sengyou's compendium, the compiler (or compilers) of the *Dharma-Treasury Transmission* probably aimed to codify the haphazard fragments of Indian Buddhist history and hagiography that had come to proliferate in China, as well as provide for contemporary Chinese Buddhists an authoritative model of Dharma propagation for a world without a Buddha. However, where the *Dharma-Treasury Transmission* diverged most fundamentally from Sengyou's work was in emphasizing that the Indian lineage had been severed long before it ever got to China. According to the *Dharma-Treasury Transmission*, the twenty-third and final patriarch, *bhikṣu* (monk) Siṃha (Shizi 師子), was murdered by an anti-Buddhist king in Kashmir before he could transmit the Dharma and continue the succession of Buddhist saints.

The question, then, is why would a Chinese history of the Indian patriarchate depict that patriarchate being cut off before it ever reached China? At the time that the *Dharma-Treasury Transmission* was created, what purposes would have been served by a *severed* Indian lineage in particular? And how were the Indian patriarchs themselves understood before being appropriated by Chan and Tiantai ideologues in particular as links along chains of Dharma transmission connecting Chinese sectarian traditions with the Buddha himself? Answers to these questions are suggested, first of all, by the contents and contexts of the *Dharma-Treasury Transmission* itself. Similar to the *Record of the Sarvāstivāda*, this text was compiled at a time when the rhetoric of Dharma decline was widespread. Sengyou sometimes advertised his compilations as forestalling the disappearance of Buddhism in China,[6] and in fact it was a common strategy of the time to foreground impending soteriological doom in order to advance specific texts or teachings as the only effective defense. The *Dharma-Treasury Transmission* evinces a similar tactic, but instead of presenting genealogical transmission as the antidote to Dharma's demise, I argue that this text deployed what we might call a *Lotus Sūtra* soteriology. Just as the Buddha's absence was explained in this scripture as a form of *upāya* (expedient means) devised to encourage self-reliance, the *Dharma-Treasury Transmission* emphasized the severance of the Indian

6. See Durt 2006, 53n3.

patriarchate in order to exhort latter-day Chinese Buddhists to redouble their efforts at upholding the Dharma. Further, as the *Dharma-Treasury Transmission* was first compiled under imperial patronage right after one of the most violent state suppressions of Buddhism in Chinese history, it aimed to promote a mutually beneficent relationship between Chinese monastic and imperial institutions. From this standpoint, the Indian masters of this text—who were often depicted converting and advising kings—served to exemplify the myriad benefits that the sangha could provide for the Chinese state.

These discursive agendas are evidenced both in the current canonical recension of the *Dharma-Treasury Transmission* and in its oldest extant rendition, which is in fact a visual representation of the Indian lineage preserved at a once high-profile monastery complex that has since fallen into disuse and been largely forgotten. This is the complex known as Lingquan monastery 靈泉寺, which was also a state-sponsored project that fell victim to imperial persecution and was rebuilt ostensibly to ensure the continued prosperity of Buddhism in China. A number of Buddhist monuments were cut into the limestone hillsides surrounding this monastery, including most prominently a cave-temple that may have been used for rites of *Buddhanāma* (Buddha-name) recitation, confession, and repentance. Titled "Cave of Great Perduring Saints" (Dazhusheng ku 大住聖窟) and dated by inscription to 589, this cave contains the first known iconographic depiction of the Indian Buddhist patriarchate in China as well as the earliest extant citation of any kind—textual or visual—from the *Dharma-Treasury Transmission*.[7] Based on the context of the iconographic, epigraphic, and devotional programs in which these rock-cut Indian patriarchs were placed, as well as possible ritual prescriptions in the *Dharma-Treasury Transmission* itself, it appears that the Cave of Great Perduring Saints functioned not only to instantiate the central didactic message of this source text but also to manifest its protagonists as immanent presences in latter-day China.

Like the earlier writings of Kumārajīva's associates, the *Dharma-Treasury Transmission*, the Cave of Great Perduring Saints, and the *Record of the Sarvāstivāda* all exemplify broader processes through which medieval Chinese Buddhists adduced their greatest Indian forebears in service of local agendas. One central preoccupation in Chinese Buddhist sources over the fifth and sixth centuries was to elaborate the Chinese *imaginaire* of post-*parinirvāṇa* (final nirvāṇa) Indian Buddhist sainthood. In the decades following Kumārajīva's introduction of Aśvaghoṣa, Nāgārjuna, and Āryadeva, the vicissitudes of Indian Buddhism over the centuries after nirvāṇa began to receive much fuller treatment. The division of the sangha into various sects, for example, which Sengyou mentioned, was described in fifth-century translations like the *Scripture on the Questions of Śariputra* and the *Great*

7. There may be earlier representations of parts of the *Dharma-Treasury Transmission* at the Yungang 雲崗 caves in Datong 大同, but these only depict a few brief episodes of the text (if they were indeed drawn from this text at all). See Ch'en 1964, 167; Mizuno 1968; and Nagahiro 1994.

Collection Scripture.[8] Sengyou himself detailed the history of these Indian sectarian developments in several other compilations such as the *Newly Collected Records of the Vinaya Divided into Eighteen Sects.*[9] Further, translations of Indic *avadāna* literature, like the *Scripture on the Storehouse of Sundry Treasures*, recounted tales of figures and events important to the history of Buddhism through India's "middle ages."[10] Sengyou's *Genealogy of the Śākya*, best known for providing the earliest extant anthology of materials concerning the life of the Buddha, also included several stories about Śākyamuni's disciples and the development of Buddhism after nirvāṇa.[11] And Fei Zhangfang's sixth-century *Record of the Three Jewels through the Ages* presented a linear chronology of significant Buddhist personages and events during and after the Buddha's lifetime, all corresponded to Chinese regnal years.[12]

Several Chinese sources produced during this period also focused on elaborating the achievements of the Indian patriarchs in particular. In addition to the *Record of the Sarvāstivāda*, which provided a lineage of masters in this specific Vinaya tradition, fifth-century translations of the *Mahāsāṃghika vinaya* and *Samantapāsādikā* likewise included genealogies of Indian masters who were important to their propagation.[13] The earliest extant lineage of a *dhyāna* tradition was advanced in the *Meditation Scripture of Dharmatrāta*, which listed nine Indian proponents who were said to have transmitted its teachings.[14] The first five of these patriarchs corresponded to the original "masters of the Dharma" (*dharmācārya*), who immediately succeeded Śākyamuni in several early translations such as the *Saṃyuktāgama* and *Aśokāvadāna.*[15] The latter source, which initially appeared in Chinese

8. *Shelifu wen jing* 舍利弗問經 (*Śāriputraparipṛcchāsūtra* or *Scripture on the Questions of Śariputra*; T no. 1465, 24:900b–c); trans. toward the end of the Eastern Jin (317–420). This text provides a complete history of the division of the sangha into eighteen sects; see Wang 1994, 170. *Daji jing xukong mu fen* 大集經虛空目分 (*Great Collection Scripture*), T no. 397.10, 13:159a–b; trans. Dharmakṣema (385–433) between 414 and 426. This contains an oft-cited prediction by the Buddha that the sangha would split into five or six sects; see Wang 1994, 171.

9. *Xinji lü fenwei shibabu jilu* 新集律分爲十八部記録; not extant but summarized in the *Chu sanzang jiji*, T no. 2145, 55:20a. See Wang 1994, 173–174.

10. *Za baozang jing* 雜寶藏經 (*Scripture on the Storehouse of Sundry Treasures*), T no. 203; trans. Tanyao 曇曜 (ca. 410–485) and Kiṅkara (Jijiaye 吉迦夜; fl. 460–472) in 472 (*Chu sanzang jiji*, T no. 2145, 55:13b). English trans. Willemen 1994.

11. *Shijia pu* 釋迦譜, T no. 2040. On this text, see Cao 1999, 149–153; and Durt 2006.

12. *Lidai sanbao ji* 歷代三寶紀, T no. 2034; see especially Juan 1990.

13. *Mohe sengqi lü* 摩訶僧祇律 (*Mahāsāṃghika vinaya*), T no. 1425, 22:492c–493a; *Shanjian lü piposha* 善見律毘婆沙 (*Samantapāsādikā*), T no. 1462, 24:684b–685a. The latter is a Vinaya commentary closely related to the extant Pāli Vinaya. See Funayama 2000, 333; McRae 1986, 298n197; and Morrison 2010, 24n38.

14. *Damoduoluo chan jing* 達摩多羅禪經, T no. 618, 15:301c; trans. Buddhabhadra (359/60–429) ca. 410. Prefaces by Huiyuan and Buddhabhadra's disciple Huiguan 慧觀 (d. ca. 440), which include similar lists, are also preserved in the *Chu sanzang jiji*, T no. 2145, 55:65b–66a, 66b–67a. See McRae 1986, 79–82.

15. *Za ahan jing* 雜阿含經 (*Saṃyuktāgama*), T no. 99, 2:177b; trans. Guṇabhadra (392–468) between 435 and 443 (Lamotte 1988, 206). *Ayuwang zhuan* 阿育王傳 (*Aśokāvadāna*), T no. 2042; trans. An Faqin 安法欽 (fl. 281–306) ca. 306 (French trans. Przyluski 1923).

at the beginning of the fourth century, was retranslated in the early sixth century to include a more elaborate description of the first post-*parinirvāṇa* patriarchs.[16] And in addition to these early lineage statements, individual Indian masters of later generations were singled out and given their own separate biographies. Harivarman, introduced into China with Kumārajīva's translation of the *Satyasiddhiśāstra*, was memorialized in a biography by the southern Sanlun adept Xuanchang 玄暢 (416–484).[17] The famous Yogācāra master Vasubandhu was accorded substantial biographical treatment by the Indian missionary Paramārtha.[18] And it appears that sometime during the sixth century, biographies of Aśvaghoṣa, Nāgārjuna, and Āryadeva were excerpted from earlier compilations and disseminated as separate documents attributed to Kumārajīva (see appendices 1–2).

Indeed, over the fifth and sixth centuries, this particular triad of post-*parinirvāṇa* patriarchs gained considerable notoriety in China and was elicited to serve a number of interests beyond those initially advanced by Kumārajīva and his associates. In the sources examined in this chapter—especially the *Dharma-Treasury Transmission* and Cave of Great Perduring Saints—Aśvaghoṣa, Nāgārjuna, and Āryadeva were merged with their predecessors and successors in the Indian patriarchate as exemplars of Dharma transmission and state-sangha relations. Unlike the accounts of Kumārajīva's associates, in which Aśvaghoṣa, Nāgārjuna, and Āryadeva were singled out as the sole revivalists of a dying Dharma in specific centuries after nirvāṇa, here they handed down the teaching that before them had been preserved by their own masters. In the earlier writings of Sengrui, Sengzhao, and Huiyuan, these post-*parinirvāṇa* patriarchs were considered valuable resources because of their perceived proximity to latter-day China in Dharmic history and their resultant affinity with the plight of Chinese Buddhists in striving to revive a tradition in decline. But in the *Dharma-Treasury Transmission*, Aśvaghoṣa, Nāgārjuna, and Āryadeva stood within an Indian lineage that was conceived as soteriologically efficacious largely because it was long gone, much like Śākyamuni in the *Lotus Sūtra*. Then in the Cave of Great Perduring Saints the Indian patriarchs were brought back to life—also like the Buddha in the *Lotus*—manifested as immanent presences who could provide for medieval Chinese Buddhists a more direct means of perpetuating the Dharma in a world without a Buddha.

---

16. *Ayuwang jing* 阿育王經 (*Aśokarājasūtra*), T no. 2043; trans. Sanghapāla (460–524) in 512 (English trans. Li 1993).

17. For Kumārajīva's translation, see *Chengshi lun* 成實論 (*Satyasiddhiśāstra*), T no. 1646. Harivarman appears to have been largely ignored by Kumārajīva's associates, who wrote brief biographies for all the other Indian masters whose treatises they helped translate. A no-longer-extant preface to the *Chengshi lun* was attributed to Sengrui, but this attribution is doubtful; see Robinson 1967, 26. Xuanchang's biography is preserved in the *Chu sanzang jiji*, T no. 2145, 55:78b–79b; see Wang 1994, 194n22.

18. Cf. Funayama 2008, esp. 174–177.

Contents and Contexts of the *Dharma-Treasury Transmission*

Initially compiled in the latter half of the fifth century, the *Dharma-Treasury Transmission* was the most influential medieval Chinese chronicle of post-*parinirvāṇa* Indian Buddhism. Although it drew upon earlier sources that included partial accounts of patriarchal lineage, especially the *Aśokāvadāna*, the *Dharma-Treasury Transmission* was the first Chinese text occupied from beginning to end with recounting the transmission of the Dharma along a single line of Indian masters over the centuries after nirvāṇa. This text was considered an authentic translation of an Indian chronicle produced by a respected Western missionary and a well-placed Chinese collaborator—and some even labeled it a sūtra—so it was seen as an authoritative record of Indian Buddhist history and sainthood. When later sectarian historiographers began compiling Dharma genealogies for their own traditions, which would claim ancient Indian origins for local Chinese teachings through long master-disciple lineages, they drew heavily on the *Dharma-Treasury Transmission* and its tales about the Indian succession. The problem for these Chinese authors constructing Sino-Indian Dharma lineages, however, was that the *Dharma-Treasury Transmission* was explicit about the severance of the lineage. This text was well-known and trusted, so it could not be simply ignored, but something had to be done about its vexing tale of the last patriarch's murder. Early Chan ideologues responded by asserting that Siṃha had actually transmitted the Dharma before his death,[19] and in so doing they created an altogether new kind of lineage history.

While the sectarian patriarchal histories of the Sui-Tang period (581–907) functioned largely to legitimize local teachings by linking them genealogically with Śākyamuni himself, the *Dharma-Treasury Transmission* was clearly not intended to demonstrate the origins of Chinese traditions. Because their line had been severed, the Indian patriarchs did not transmit the Dharma to China directly. So what purposes *was* this text intended to serve, and what did the Indian patriarchate mean for Chinese Buddhists before it was a Dharma conduit spanning the Sino-Indian divide? First of all, in part because the translation of the *Dharma-Treasury Transmission* was credited to the "sangha regulator" (*sengzheng* 僧正) Tanyao, who was a prominent figure in the restoration of Buddhism after the Northern Wei 北魏 (386–534) persecutions of the mid-fifth century,[20] the text has long been seen as a product of the fever-pitch drive to revitalize the religion in the wake of imperial suppression. This line of thought first appeared in the

19. See, most recently, Adamek 2007, 104–106; and Morrison 2010, 69–70.

20. See *Chu sanzang jiji*, T no. 2145, 55:13b; French trans. Maspero 1911, 133–134. This entry also asserts that the Central Asian monk Kiṅkara helped Tanyao with the translation, and that it was completed in 472. Later catalogues discuss two or three editions of the *Dharma-Treasury Transmission*: one translated by Baoyun 寶雲 (367–449), another by Tanyao alone in 462, and a third by Tanyao and Kiṅkara together. See especially Maspero 1911, and more recently Matsuyama 2009a, 200–206. On Tanyao and the Northern Wei persecution, see Ch'en 1964, 147–158; Mather 1979; Tang 1938, 493–500; and Tsukamoto (1942) 1957.

Record of the Three Jewels through the Ages, compiled in 598, which described the Northern Wei abolition and reparation of Buddhism before explaining that Tanyao translated this lineage history and other texts in order to preserve the Dharma in perpetuity.[21] Later sources asserted that the *Dharma-Treasury Transmission* actually appeared before the persecution, was lost in the chaos of the 440s, and then reconstructed from memory by Tanyao and associates after Buddhism had been restored.[22] From this perspective, the purpose of the *Dharma-Treasury Transmission* was to protect Buddhism from future persecution by demonstrating to secular rulers the wondrous merits of the Indian patriarchate and the whole of the Buddhist sangha by extension, which righteous monarchs had long employed for the benefit of their kingdoms.

Modern scholars have often elaborated this age-old association between the *Dharma-Treasury Transmission* and imperial persecution, taking the text's political context as a primary means of explaining its *raison d'être* and especially its jarring account of the last patriarch's death. Linda Penkower, for one, asserts that the murder of Siṃha by an anti-Buddhist king and termination of the Dharma-treasury lineage due to state suppression were but a "veiled allusion" to the evils wreaked upon the Buddhist institution by Wei Emperor Taiwu 太武帝 (r. 424–451).[23] Penkower and Whalen Lai both speculate that the text's emphasis on lineal succession served to rebut charges by the Confucian official Cui Hao 崔浩 (381–450), who instigated the purge of the Buddhist clergy, that the continuity of Indian Buddhism could not be verified (Penkower 2000, 250; Lai 1990, 201n40). Matsuyama Sadayoshi 松山貞好 likewise stresses the legitimizing function of the Indian lineage for Chinese Buddhism in the eyes of the Wei court, arguing that the tale of Siṃha's murder was intended to admonish those in power not to repeat the mistakes of their anti-Buddhist predecessors (2009a, 208, 212; 2009b, 806). Along similar lines, Henri Maspero maintains that the *Dharma-Treasury Transmission* was revised in the sixth century to include mention of the infamous Hephthalite king, Mihirakula, who brutally persecuted Buddhists in India until his defeat around 530.[24] And following Maspero in favoring a sixth-century compilation date, Wendi Adamek views the text as a product of "'final age' pessimism" stemming from sociopolitical instability after the fall of the Northern Wei in 534 (2007, 101).

---

21. *Lidai sanbao ji*, T no. 2034, 49:85a–b; trans. Maspero 1911, 136–137.

22. This story first appeared in the *Baolin zhuan* 寶林傳 of ca. 801 and was repeated in later Chan sources. These sources aimed to discredit the *Dharma-Treasury Transmission*—as being a Chinese compilation rather than a translation from an Indian original—because it claimed that the lineage had ended. See Adamek 2007, 101–102; and Morrison 2010, 176–177.

23. Penkower 2000, 250. A similar case is made by Barrett 1990, 91–92.

24. *Fu fazang yinyuan zhuan* 付法藏因緣傳, T no. 2058, 50:321c; Chinese trans. Li 1997a, 409. The text here claims that the last patriarch was killed by a king named Miluojue 彌羅掘, which may be a transliteration of Mihirakula. See Maspero 1911, 142, 146. For a brief introduction to Mihirakula and his Hephthalite Huns, see Nattier 1991, 111–113.

Indeed, whether finally compiled in the fifth or sixth century, the *Dharma-Treasury Transmission* is often understood as reflecting contemporary Buddhist concerns about the advent of this so-called "final age" (*moshi* 末世). A number of sources produced during this period predicted the coming of Buddhism's last days, several centuries after nirvāṇa, when evil teachings would overrun the Dharma and the world would fall into darkness. For example, the *Mahāmāyāsūtra*, which in some respects echoed the themes of the *Dharma-Treasury Transmission*, described a line of outstanding Buddhist saints that marked the first seven of fifteen centuries over which the Dharma would gradually deteriorate and eventually disappear.[25] Such foreboding scriptures contributed to the development of a local rhetoric of decline, whereby Chinese Buddhists lamented the foregone arrival of this final age—termed in some sources the "final Dharma" (*mofa* 末法) period—in order to advance specific ideologies or programs of praxis. In chapter 1, I discussed how early fifth-century Buddhist writings underscored Dharma decay as a means of promoting the works of Aśvaghoṣa, Nāgārjuna, and Āryadeva in particular. But more broadly, one strategy prevalent within Chinese eschatologies of the time was to foreground the signs of Buddhism's demise as a rallying cry for Chinese Buddhists to bear down in their practice. The complete annihilation of the Dharma could always be prevented, these texts maintained, if latter-day Buddhists kept faith in the Three Jewels and strove diligently to uphold the teachings.[26]

In a similar fashion, the *Dharma-Treasury Transmission* emphasized Dharma devolution and asserted the end of the patriarchate as a means of encouraging Chinese Buddhists to rededicate themselves to the charge of propagating the teaching. As Elizabeth Morrison illustrates, the *Dharma-Treasury Transmission* was shot through with references to declining Dharma and lamentations over the progressive degeneration of people's capacities.[27] But the most prominent sign of this text's concern with failing Dharma is its vivid tale of Siṃha's beheading, which was followed by a flat assertion that the teaching would be wiped out and Buddhist saints would disappear altogether.[28] However, as Morrison also emphasizes, what is most striking about this episode is the heartening discourse that followed it. After this stark pronouncement of Buddhism's end, the text digressed at length about the wondrous power of the Dharma to endure despite the fate of its human proponents, and it assured its audience that if Buddhist devotees exerted

25. *Mohemoye jing* 摩訶摩耶經 (*Mahāmāyāsūtra*), T no. 383; trans. Tanjing 曇景 (fl. 479–502) during the Xiao Qi 蕭齊 dynasty (479–502). On this scripture see Durt 1994, 51–53; 2007; 2008; and Nattier 1991, 50–51, 168–170. See also the discussion to come. Adamek (2007, 102) likewise notes the "conceptual similarity" between this text and the *Dharma-Treasury Transmission*.

26. Nattier (1991, 184, 198) also discusses the Chinese proclivity for emphasizing the staying power of the Dharma rather than its inevitable demise.

27. See Morrison 1996, 10–12. I would like to thank Dr. Morrison for sending me this manuscript.

28. *Fu fazang yinyuan zhuan*, T no. 2058, 50:321c; Chinese trans. Li 1997a, 411.

themselves diligently, the Dharma would in fact live on.[29] In this regard the *Dharma-Treasury Transmission* fit in quite well with many other ostensibly eschatological writings of the fifth and sixth centuries. These texts dwelled on the death of the Dharma as a warning to Buddhist devotees, who were otherwise exhorted to grit their teeth and gird their raiment before battling the encroaching darkness. In the *Dharma-Treasury Transmission,* the untimely end of the Indian lineage functioned to exhort latter-day Chinese Buddhists to carry on the torch even if—and especially because—their Indian forebears had *not* transmitted it directly to them.

Modern scholarship has often focused on the ways in which the *Dharma-Treasury Transmission* was incorporated into Chan and Tiantai lineage histories of the seventh and eighth centuries,[30] but here one sees that it was more akin to the Buddhist eschatological literature of its own time. The text did valorize a single line of Buddhist saints and so seemingly prefigured the exclusivism of later sectarian genealogies, but then it terminated the line and admonished its audience to venerate the patriarchs and emulate their models of Dharma propagation. It set no limits on who could properly uphold the Dharma in the absence of the patriarchate, and as a result, its agenda would appear to diverge from the exclusivist use to which it was put in later sectarian traditions. Proponents of these traditions appropriated the *Dharma-Treasury Transmission* in an effort to demarcate True Dharma transmission—culminating, of course, in none other than their own masters—from other groups that they decried as misrepresenting and corrupting the Buddha's teachings. In contrast, judging by its concluding exhortations, the *Dharma-Treasury Transmission* was far more catholic in its expectations of how the Indian patriarchate might be employed. Here the patriarchs were presented as models for all, objects of both emulation and veneration for the whole of the Chinese sangha. In fact, the more devotees who revered the patriarchs and followed their examples, the better the chance that Buddhism would persevere in perpetuity. This ecumenical agenda is evidenced in the *Dharma-Treasury Transmission* itself,[31] and is also confirmed by its representation in the Cave of Great Perduring Saints. Within this cave the Indian patriarchs could provide a potentially limitless fount of True Dharma, having been placed in a space for devotional

29. *Fu fazang yinyuan zhuan,* T no. 2058, 50:321c–322b; Chinese trans. Li 1997a, 411–421. Cf. Adamek 2007, 106.

30. See especially the series of articles by Tanaka (1962; 1981a; 1981b; 1983, 61–106), which focus on Tang Dunhuang manuscripts of the *Dharma-Treasury Transmission* and how it was employed in sectarian genealogies of the time. More recent discussions along similar lines include those of Adamek 2007, 101–110; Cole 2009, 55–56; Matsuyama 2009a, 208–211; Morrison 2010, 30–38, 68–73; and Penkower 2000.

31. In this interpretation of the *Dharma-Treasury Transmission,* I part with Adamek (2007, 98–110), who argues that the text's focus on lineal patriarchy evinces an exclusivist agenda against the backdrop of widespread bodhisattva precepts practices and Pure Land devotionalism, which threatened to cut the Chinese sangha out of the loop of Buddhist salvation.

practices such as *Buddhanāma* recitation, merit making, and confession and repentance—practices that were intended to provide the greatest possible access to enlightenment. Illuminating the path to enlightenment for all, especially in the absence of the great saints who succeeded Śākyamuni, was one main agenda that the *Dharma-Treasury Transmission* itself claimed.[32]

The other principal aims of this text—promoting Dharma propagation through master-disciple transmission, advantageous state-sangha relations, and a *Lotus Sūtra* soteriology of absence—necessitated the wholesale reconception of the Indian patriarchs introduced by Kumārajīva and his associates. Aśvaghoṣa, Nāgārjuna, and Āryadeva had been the primary representatives of post-*parinirvāṇa* Buddhist sainthood for nearly a century in China, so they were accorded a certain pride of place in the *Dharma-Treasury Transmission*. Aside from the first five *dharmācārya*, for whom there was extensive source material from the *Aśokāvadāna* and elsewhere to fill out the *Dharma-Treasury Transmission*, Aśvaghoṣa, Nāgārjuna, and Āryadeva received the most detailed treatment of all the patriarchs in the lineage. But in the earlier accounts of Sengzhao, Sengrui, and Huiyuan, this triad of patriarchs had no dealings whatsoever with secular authority, their master-disciple relationships were largely undeveloped, and their influence derived from their perceived proximity to latter-day China rather than the salvific hollow engendered by their absence. On these counts and others, the *Dharma-Treasury Transmission* considerably expanded the hagiographies of Aśvaghoṣa, Nāgārjuna, and Āryadeva, making their accounts in this text useful indices to the overarching concerns of its compiler (or compilers).

In some respects, the images of these patriarchs first presented by Sengzhao, Sengrui, and Huiyuan were reinscribed in the *Dharma-Treasury Transmission*, but otherwise the hagiographies of Aśvaghoṣa, Nāgārjuna, and Āryadeva in this latter text are unprecedented. The *Dharma-Treasury Transmission* accounts of Nāgārjuna and Āryadeva are very similar to the independently circulating hagiographies of these masters later attributed to Kumārajīva, so scholars have long assumed that Tanyao (or some later anonymous editor) simply followed these.[33] However, there is little evidence for this assumption, and it is more likely that these separate hagiographies were excerpted from the *Dharma-Treasury Transmission* sometime during the sixth century. This is largely because the representations of Nāgārjuna and Āryadeva (as well as Aśvaghoṣa) in the *Dharma-Treasury Transmission* are far more accordant with the overarching themes of this text than with the agendas evinced in the writings of Kumārajīva's associates.

First of all, in the accounts produced by Sengzhao, Sengrui, and Huiyuan, the Indian patriarchs were all dated several centuries after nirvāṇa,

32. One indication of this agenda is the fact that the text described itself as a "good friend" (*shan zhishi* 善知識; *kalyāṇamitra*) because it guided people to liberation after the patriarchs' demise. See Matsuyama 2009b, 806–807.

33. This conjecture has been repeated for a hundred years, from Maspero (1911, 142) to Matsuyama (2009a, 207).

when Śākyamuni's teachings had long been left to ruin. The emergence of these masters in particular brought about a renewal of the Dharma. They steeled their faculties through eremitic wanderings and *dhyāna* practice, defeated countless non-Buddhists in debate, and produced profound doctrinal treatises that allowed the Buddhist truth to flourish once more. In the *Dharma-Treasury Transmission*, Aśvaghoṣa, Nāgārjuna, and Āryadeva instantiated much the same repertoire of practices, but they did not thereby resurrect a failing Dharma. Instead, they perpetuated the teaching that had been upheld by their own masters, through all the generations separating them from the time of the Buddha. In some of its episodes the *Dharma-Treasury Transmission* dwelled on declining Dharma—particularly where it followed the *Aśokāvadāna* and in its concluding account of Siṃha's murder—but its biographies of Aśvaghoṣa, Nāgārjuna, and Āryadeva were wholly innocent of this concern. This is especially telling because the demise of the Dharma was such an important theme in the earlier accounts by Kumārajīva's associates. In this regard the *Dharma-Treasury Transmission* did not follow these earlier patriarchal narratives, which emphasized a cyclical, wax-and-wane model of Indian Buddhist history and sainthood. Instead, it depicted a lineal progression of Buddhist history, illustrating how the Dharma persevered over the centuries after nirvāṇa because the greatest masters of each generation received, upheld, and transmitted it in succession.

Secondly, the *Dharma-Treasury Transmission* diverged sharply from the earlier accounts of Aśvaghoṣa, Nāgārjuna, and Āryadeva by emphasizing their roles as counselors and even subjugators of Indian kings. While Kumārajīva's associates never discussed any connection between these patriarchs and the secular authority of their time, in the *Dharma-Treasury Transmission* this dynamic was central to the accounts of all three. As I have previously noted, one significant thrust of the *Dharma-Treasury Transmission* as a whole was to demonstrate the command of patriarchs over kings, or at least illustrate the mutually beneficial relationship that could inhere between monastic and imperial institutions. In this regard, the *Dharma-Treasury Transmission* shared a strong affinity with its main source text, the *Aśokāvadāna*, which likewise appears to have been aimed at securing the allegiance of the "Wheel of State" (*ājñācakra*) to the "Wheel of Dharma" (*dharmacakra*).[34] This reading of the *Dharma-Treasury Transmission* is clearly evidenced in its accounts of Aśvaghoṣa, Nāgārjuna, and Āryadeva, all of whom were depicted either converting anti-Buddhist kings or propitiating rampaging monarchs with Dharmic treasures. Here these patriarchs illustrated how both the Chinese and Indian states and sanghas were equally dependent upon those who worked to perpetuate the True Dharma.

With this refashioning of Aśvaghoṣa, Nāgārjuna, and Āryadeva to promote master-disciple transmission and state-sangha symbiosis, the repertoires of these patriarchs were greatly elaborated and their earlier biographical traditions were adopted and merged with other elements of unknown

34. See Strong 1983, especially chap. 3.

origin. In addition to exemplifying public debate, exegetical authorship, meditation and eremitism, here they also instantiated paradigms of Dharma transmission and Buddhist-imperial relations and modeled a wide range of practices such as self-immolation, spell-casting, musical composition, and the concoction of alchemical elixirs. But overall, in the *Dharma-Treasury Transmission* and especially the Cave of Great Perduring Saints, Aśvaghoṣa, Nāgārjuna, and Āryadeva were represented less as singular exemplars of these practices than as interchangeable members of the broader, corporate whole of the Indian Buddhist patriarchate. From this perspective the distinctions between periods of Dharmic history and related models of Buddhist sainthood were largely erased. These distinctions were crucial to both earlier and later Chinese Buddhist conceptions of their Indian forebears. But here Aśvaghoṣa, Nāgārjuna, and Āryadeva played much the same role as not only Śākyamuni's immediate disciples but also the rest of the patriarchs down to Siṃha. All of these masters shared the charge of preserving the Dharma over the centuries after nirvāṇa, through master-disciple transmission and by securing state patronage. Then, with the severance of their line and their eventual disappearance, the patriarchs transmitted one last message: that propagating the Dharma was now the charge of latter-day Chinese Buddhists, who could thereby take their place among the greatest saints in Buddhist history.

Aśvaghoṣa in the *Dharma-Treasury Transmission*: Patriarchs and the Imperium

In contrast to the earlier Indian patriarch accounts written by Kumārajīva's associates, the *Dharma-Treasury Transmission* does not appear geared toward audiences steeped in recondite *xuanxue* 玄學 or Buddhist doctrinal discourses. It was not composed with the doctrinal complexity, allusive vocabulary, or prosodic sophistication that characterized the writings of literati gentlemen or elite scholar-monks like Sengrui, Sengzhao, or Huiyuan. Rather than working to incorporate erudite allusions to Chinese classics or Buddhist sūtras, the author (or authors) of the *Dharma-Treasury Transmission* focused on presenting vivid and engaging stories—written in straightforward prose—which showed how the teachings that liberated beings and bolstered regimes were transmitted in succession by the greatest saints ever known. For medieval Chinese rulers in particular, this text would have served to demonstrate how the most powerful kings of old had converted to Buddhism, lavishly supported the sangha, and thereby ensured the prosperity of their kingdoms for generations. This agenda is especially evident in the *Dharma-Treasury Transmission* account of Aśvaghoṣa, which reinscribed the earlier tales of his Buddhist conversion and added a detailed narrative of his dealings with kings of the Western Regions.

Given its focus on lineal transmission and master-disciple relations, it is no surprise that the *Dharma-Treasury Transmission* drew upon the stories in Sengzhao's *Vimalakīrti Commentary* and Aśvaghoṣa's Nanatsu-dera biography about his defeat in debate at the hands of Pārśva and Pūrṇa. However, the *Dharma-Treasury Transmission* added to the list of Aśvaghoṣa's preceptors, claiming that it was a certain Puṇyayaśas (Funashe 富那奢) who vanquished his arguments and converted him to Buddhism.[35] While Pūrṇa was entirely absent from the *Dharma-Treasury Transmission*, Pārśva appeared as the ninth patriarch in the lineage. This account of his career followed both the *Great Perfection of Wisdom Treatise* and *Vimalakīrti Commentary*,[36] as in all three sources he became an arhat endowed with the "six spiritual penetrations" and earned the name *bhikṣu* Side for fulfilling his vow to never lay down on his side to rest. The *Dharma-Treasury Transmission* also introduced an interesting twist to the earlier accounts of Pārśva becoming a monk at the age of sixty, as it described him being born with white hair and beard after sixty years in the womb.[37]

Between Pārśva and Aśvaghoṣa the *Dharma-Treasury Transmission* inserted the tenth patriarch Puṇyayaśas, whom Aśvaghoṣa tracked down to challenge in debate. However, unlike the earlier Chang'an accounts, the ensuing row did not revolve around the profound silence of the Buddhist interlocutor. Aśvaghoṣa and Puṇyayaśas actually debated the two truths—conventional and absolute—and the ontological status of the self. Representing the Buddhist doctrines of emptiness and no-self, Puṇyayaśas emerged victorious. Although Aśvaghoṣa acknowledged his defeat, offered to sever his tongue (rather than head) as penalty, and left home to become a monk, he remained ashamed and embittered and did not fully assent to the superiority of the Buddhadharma. For Aśvaghoṣa's final conversion, a demonstration of magical ability was required, as the blinding light of Puṇyayaśas' "spiritual power" (*shenli* 神力) overwhelmed Aśvaghoṣa's non-Buddhist "techniques" (*jishu* 技術) to illuminate a dark room full of scriptures. Then the encounter between master and disciple drew to a close, with Puṇyayaśas sensing his approaching nirvāṇa and formally transmitting the Dharma to Aśvaghoṣa:

> All the sages and saints have forever defended [the teaching]. They entrusted it to one another until it came down to me. Now I uphold this superlative [True

35. For this Sanskrit reconstruction I follow Yampolsky 1967, 8. This may be an anachronistic reading, as it is informed by the Funayeshe 富那夜(or 耶)奢 of the *Lidai fabao ji* 曆代法寶記 (T no. 2075, 51:180a) and *Baolin zhuan* (Yanagida 1983, 39), which in turn were followed by all the Song Chan and Tiantai lineage histories. However, it seems unlikely that Funashe here renders Pūrṇa, as Lévi (1908, 94–95) asserts. If the author (or the authors) of the *Dharma-Treasury Transmission* intended to describe the same master of Aśvaghoṣa as in his earlier biography, I see no reason why they would have used a different transliteration than Fulouna 富樓那.

36. *Da zhidu lun* 大智度論 (*Mahāprajñāpāramitāśāstra*), T no. 1509, 25:748c; *Zhu weimojie jing* 注維摩詰經, T no. 1775, 38:399b.

37. *Fu fazang yinyuan zhuan*, T no. 2058, 50:314c; Chinese trans. Li 1997a, 291. Cf. *Zhu weimojie jing* (T no. 1775, 38:356c), which also recounted the tradition according to which the Buddha's son Rāhula remained in his mother's womb for six years, until Gautama attained Buddhahood. Another parallel is the legend of Laozi being born with white hair after an eighty-one-year gestation period; see Kohn 1998.

> Dharma] eye and transmit it to you. You must henceforth do your utmost to preserve it, and allow future generations to universally obtain its boundless benefit.
>
> 諸賢聖人, 常加守護. 共相委囑, 乃至於我. 我以勝眼, 持用付汝. 汝當於後, 至心受持, 令未來世, 普得饒益.[38]

After this standard pre-nirvāṇa exhortation from master to disciple, which appeared in similar form at each juncture along the lineage, Aśvaghoṣa received transmission of the teaching and traveled to Pāṭaliputra (Huashi cheng 華氏城) to propagate it further. To this end he became a famous musician who composed Buddhist ballads that propounded the teachings of suffering, emptiness, and no-self. Aśvaghoṣa then donned white robes (which may signal his identity as a layman)—prefiguring his later Chinese and Japanese iconographic forms—before playing in the orchestra himself. Thus he enticed five hundred local princes to join the sangha through his beautifully enlightening music. Fearful that at this rate his land would soon be devoid of householders, the king of Pāṭaliputra commanded that Aśvaghoṣa's music never again be played within city precincts.[39]

The final episode of Aśvaghoṣa's biography introduced Caṇḍa-Kaniṣka (Zhantanjinizha 栴檀罽昵吒) as the king of Yuezhi 月支 (Indo-Scythia), who besieged Pāṭaliputra and demanded 900,000 gold pieces as ransom. In order to propitiate him, the king of Pāṭaliputra offered up Aśvaghoṣa, the begging bowl of the Buddha, and a chicken so compassionate that it refused to drink water with insects in it—each of which was said to be worth 300,000 gold pieces. With these grand prizes in tow, the merit of each capable of defeating all enemies, Caṇḍa-Kaniṣka happily withdrew his armies and returned to his kingdom.[40]

At this point the *Dharma-Treasury Transmission* provided an extended treatment of Caṇḍa-Kaniṣka, recounting numerous episodes in which he promoted the Buddhadharma over other non-Buddhist teachings. Aśvaghoṣa reappeared once in the middle of these Kaniṣka chronicles—to assure the king that if he followed Buddhism his great sins and hellish retributions would be expurgated—and again at the end—where the narrator explained that because Kaniṣka listened to Aśvaghoṣa's teachings he was reborn as a great thousand-headed fish. However, because of Kaniṣka's past evil deeds, this fish incarnation was dogged by a wheel of swords that continuously cut off its heads, only to have them grow back and be severed again—an ignominious fate to be sure, but one that was eventually allayed by the sounding

38. *Fu fazang yinyuan zhuan*, T no. 2058, 50:315a; cf. Chinese trans. Li 1997a, 299. This whole debate and conversion episode has been translated into English by Suzuki 1900, 28–31.

39. *Fu fazang yinyuan zhuan*, T no. 2058, 50:315a–b; Chinese trans. Li 1997a, 301–303; and trans. Suzuki 1900, 35–36. For further analysis of this episode see Inui 1990.

40. *Fu fazang yinyuan zhuan*, T no. 2058, 50:315b; Chinese trans. Li 1997a, 303–305; and trans. Suzuki 1900, 11–12.

of a monastery bell.[41] The *Dharma-Treasury Transmission* then returned to the patriarchal succession, describing Aśvaghoṣa's death and transmission of the Dharma to a certain *bhikṣu* Biluo 比羅 (Vīra?).[42]

This biography of Aśvaghoṣa in the *Dharma-Treasury Transmission* both drew upon and diverged considerably from the earlier accounts of his exploits. The beginning of the *Dharma-Treasury Transmission* narrative mostly matched the *Vimalakīrti Commentary* and Aśvaghoṣa's Nanatsu-dera biography: Aśvaghoṣa was a brilliant but arrogant non-Buddhist who prided himself on his prowess in public debate; he sought out a renowned Buddhist master to challenge in debate and lost, then was converted to Buddhism. However, the discrepancies in language and narrative structure between Aśvaghoṣa's earlier biographies and the *Dharma-Treasury Transmission* suggest a different agenda and intended audience for this latter text. First of all, as with the *Dharma-Treasury Transmission* accounts of Nāgārjuna and Āryadeva, it described the career of Aśvaghoṣa in the most straightforward language, with a consistent four-character prosodic structure that could be readily followed without extensive knowledge of Buddhist or non-Buddhist philosophy or literature. This is in contrast to the Nanatsu-dera biography of Aśvaghoṣa, which like Sengrui's prefaces was highly allusive and full of abstruse vocabulary.

Also, the *Dharma-Treasury Transmission* account of Aśvaghoṣa, like that of Āryadeva compared with his separate biography, was replete with what one might call medieval Chinese "pop" Buddhist philosophy. There were no elaborate discourses on recondite doctrinal issues, but rather brief, simplistic, and rote outlines of Buddhist ideas that by the late fifth or sixth century had become commonplace. So rather than having the Buddhist opponent Pārśva or Pūrṇa sit in thunderous silence while Aśvaghoṣa barked challenges—a response that would require detailed commentary, as it did with Vimalakīrti—the *Dharma-Treasury Transmission* simply asserted that Aśvaghoṣa believed in a substantial self and that Puṇyayaśas knew about "emptiness," "no-self," and the "two truths." Therefore, after only the briefest, stock explanation of these concepts, Aśvaghoṣa recognized his own failings and Puṇyayaśas easily won the debate. But Puṇyayaśas winning this battle of ideas did not mean that Aśvaghoṣa would thereby immediately assent, as it did in the Chang'an accounts. Instead, his conversion to Buddhism required a display of surpassing spiritual power, which in this case went hand-in-hand with skill in philosophy and debate but also meant eye-popping magic—paired with but superior to the techniques that Aśvaghoṣa had

41. *Fu fazang yinyuan zhuan*, T no. 2058, 50:315b–317a; Chinese trans. Li 1997a, 305–333.

42. The standard reading of Biluo as Kapimala (Jiapimoluo 迦毘摩羅), followed by Yampolsky (1967, 8) and others, is clearly anachronistic; Jiapimoluo is not attested until the ninth-century *Baolin zhuan* (Yanagida 1983, 43). Nevertheless, it is unclear whom the *Dharma-Treasury Transmission* author (or authors) intended with the transliteration Biluo. Earlier sources mention no disciple of Aśvaghoṣa or master of Nāgārjuna. The suggestion of Vīra is from Maspero (1911, 141), who notes the similarity with Weiluo 韋羅 in Sengyou's Sarvāstivādin lineage lists (and, we might now add, the Nanatsu-dera biography of Aśvaghoṣa).

learned before his Buddhist conversion. The fact that Aśvaghoṣa acquiesced only after witnessing the victory of true spiritual power over his ostensibly ersatz (if sometimes effective) magic, rather than through logical argument or thunderous silence, signals an intended audience for the *Dharma-Treasury Transmission* that would have been less concerned with elaborate doctrinal exegesis and more interested in the supernormal powers of Buddhist adepts. In this regard one might also note that the earlier preoccupation with Aśvaghoṣa's extensive literary output was entirely absent from this account.

That the *Dharma-Treasury Transmission* was not aimed at a literati audience is indicated by its simple language and de-emphasis of philosophical discourse, but its intended readership of secular and monastic political leaders is evident in its new focus on Aśvaghoṣa's dealings with East Indian and Central Asian kings. His connection to the king of Pāṭaliputra was in this account more nebulous than it would become in his later canonical biography (see appendix 1), but the *Dharma-Treasury Transmission* elaborated in some detail Aśvaghoṣa's relations with the Indo-Scythian king, Caṇḍa-Kaniṣka. In this the *Dharma-Treasury Transmission* appears to have followed the *Scripture on the Storehouse of Sundry Treasures*, which was also attributed to Kiṅkara and Tanyao. This text included a story of Kaniṣka and his three wise ministers, one of whom was Aśvaghoṣa. At the outset of this tale Aśvaghoṣa counseled the king, explaining that if he followed Buddhism his kingdom would prosper and he would forever be free from evil destinies. However, the king followed the advice of another minister and was thereby able to conquer much of India. During these campaigns Kaniṣka killed millions of people, and as a result his evil karma weighed heavily upon him. Fearful of his forthcoming retribution, Kaniṣka soon changed his ways and began to support the Buddhist sangha, constructing monasteries and making offerings to the clergy. Nevertheless, his ministers doubted that these good acts could counter the grave sins that he had accumulated during his military conquests, so the king gave an example to allay their skepticism. He boiled water in a cauldron for seven days and then dropped a ring into the scalding water, asking his ministers if any of them could retrieve it. Finally one minister did by pouring ice water into the cauldron. Just so, exclaimed the king, was the cooling effect of his virtuous acts upon his burning cauldron of past evil—present good will outweighs past evil and can forever free one from unhappy destinies.[43]

This same story appeared in slightly different form in the lengthy account of Kaniṣka that bisected Aśvaghoṣa's biography in the *Dharma-Treasury Transmission*.[44] The difference was that in the latter text, Kaniṣka's optimism about the efficacy of his good deeds was tempered by the appearance of an unnamed arhat, who conjured images of all the hells for the king to witness. This shocked the king into true repentance for his countless murders, just

---

43. *Za baozang jing*, T no. 203, 4:484b–c; trans. Willemen 1994, 183–185. Cf. Suzuki 1900, 10.

44. *Fu fazang yinyuan zhuan*, T no. 2058, 50:316b–c; Chinese trans. Li 1997a, 321–325.

in time for Aśvaghoṣa to reappear on the scene and assure Kaniṣka that if he followed Aśvaghoṣa's teachings, his evil karma would be eliminated and he would be freed from his hellish retributions. Kaniṣka did, and as a result his heavy sins were wiped away. Therefore, together with the other interactions between king and patriarch outlined previously, in which Kaniṣka was propitiated by the gift of Aśvaghoṣa and other Dharmic treasures, the text insisted that rulers of the secular world must seek the counsel of Buddhist preceptors in order to ensure the prosperity of their reigns and the well-being of their future incarnations after committing the necessary evils of kingship.[45]

In addition to its emphasis on state-sangha relations and paradigms of Buddhist kingship, another indication of the *Dharma-Treasury Transmission*'s imperial aspirations is its central focus on the figure of the patriarch. In other contexts, scholars have stressed that the medieval Buddhist preoccupation with lineal patriarchy derived in part from the same Confucian-based kinship models that formed the ethico-political foundation for the Chinese imperium. With dynastic and monastic institutions engaging the same relational hierarchies and familial terminology—*jia* 家 (house/school), *zu* 祖 (ancestor/patriarch), *dizi* 弟子 (brother-son/disciple), for example—the sangha mirrored both family and state in its attempt to secure the allegiance of local social establishments.[46] The *Dharma-Treasury Transmission* was similarly aimed at cementing an alliance between state and sangha, and this may have been the impetus behind its focus on patriarchal lineage as a means of aligning Buddhism with the sociopolitical norms of the state. From the standpoint of the Chinese imperium, patriarchs represented a known commodity—a familiar, stable, and respected fount of authority—and by depicting such figures as cornerstones of the Buddhist institution as well, the *Dharma-Treasury Transmission* molded the religion in a manner most palatable to secular rulers.

One indication that the Chinese state was receptive to this message is the fact that, around the turn of the sixth century, a number of pro-Buddhist emperors and officials embraced these Indian patriarchs as paragons of mainstream Buddhist authority. For example, in his preface to a commentary on the *Prajñāpāramitāsūtra*, Liang Emperor Wu 梁武帝 (464–549; r. 502–549) lauded Nāgārjuna's efforts at liberating beings through his discourse on perfect wisdom.[47] Northern Wei Prime Minister (*zaixiang* 宰相) Cuiguang 崔光 (449–522) exclaimed in his preface to the *Treatise on the Ten Stages Scripture* that its author Vasubandhu followed the lofty examples of Aśvaghoṣa and Nāgārjuna.[48] And the famous Prince Xiao Ziliang 蕭子良 (460–494) of

45. See also Zürcher 1968 for discussion of these and related Kaniṣka (Yuezhi) accounts in Chinese sources.

46. See especially Jorgensen 1987 and more recently Yu 2005, chap. 5. Cf. Morrison 2010, 3, and the sources cited therein.

47. *Zhujie dapin xu* 注解大品序; in the *Chu sanzang jiji*, T no. 2145, 55:54b.

48. *Shidi jing lun* 十地經論 (*Daśabhūmikasūtraśāstra*), T no. 1522, 26:123a.

the Southern Qi 南齊 dynasty (479–502) singled out Aśvaghoṣa, Nāgārjuna, Āryadeva, and Harivarman as having saved the world when it was falling into darkness.[49] These prominent Chinese statesmen reinscribed images derived from earlier monastic writings, in which the Indian patriarchs were advanced as exemplifying the primary occupations of the Chinese ecclesiastic elite. And indeed, these patriarchs represented exactly the brand of Buddhism that the empire sought to support—one that promoted normative ideals and practices, as opposed to other more marginal and potentially subversive elements of the religion. The Indian masters from the *Dharma-Treasury Transmission* and elsewhere illustrated how, from its inception, the Buddhist sangha was firmly grounded in the same patriarchal principles as Chinese society, and thus they helped shape Buddhism into a legitimate, respectable institution and a most felicitous party to Chinese imperial rule.

Nāgārjuna in the *Dharma-Treasury Transmission*: A Daoist Death for a Buddha?

The main agendas that informed Aśvaghoṣa's biography in the *Dharma-Treasury Transmission* are also readily discernible in this text's representation of Nāgārjuna. For the first time in Chinese sources, the *Dharma-Treasury Transmission* depicted Nāgārjuna as immediately preceded and followed by venerable Buddhist masters in the Indian patriarchal lineage. And also for the first time, it showed him converting and counseling a South Indian king.[50] The *Dharma-Treasury Transmission* thus advanced its vision of Dharma propagation through master-disciple relations and state-sangha symbiosis while it negated the emphases on post-*parinirvāṇa* chronology and failing Dharma that marked Nāgārjuna's earlier Chinese accounts. Further, in line with the drive to represent Buddhism as accordant with time-honored Chinese traditions, the *Dharma-Treasury Transmission* foregrounded aspects of Nāgārjuna's career that ostensibly demonstrated congruency between ancient Buddhist and native Chinese models of religious sanctity. Several episodes in this biography are worth extended analysis—and some will be revisited in the following chapters—but mirroring the themes of Nāgārjuna's earlier Chinese accounts, the episode recounting the scene of Nāgārjuna's death in particular illustrates how the *Dharma-Treasury Transmission* presented Nāgārjuna as a valuable resource for Chinese adepts across religious traditions.

49. *Chu sanzang jiji*, T no. 2145, 55:85b.

50. As Yamano (2009, 85) points out, Nāgārjuna's *Suhṛllekha* (*Friendly Epistle*, addressed to a king) was translated into Chinese in the first half of the fifth century (T nos. 1672, 1673), so his royal connections may have been known in China by then. Nevertheless, the *Dharma-Treasury Transmission* was the first (extant) source to explicate those connections in hagiographic narrative.

While much of Aśvaghoṣa's biography in the *Dharma-Treasury Transmission* revolved around his conversion by a great Buddhist master, as did the earlier Chang'an accounts, Nāgārjuna's relations with his master, Vīra, received relatively little attention. Like Puṇyayaśas before Aśvaghoṣa, Vīra was given a most summary treatment, including the standard exaltations of his wisdom, merit, and skill in defeating the arguments of non-Buddhists. After briefly recounting the transmission of the Dharma from Vīra to Nāgārjuna, the text launches into a lengthy account of this latter patriarch, which is very similar to the canonical *Tradition of Nāgārjuna Bodhisattva* (*Longshu pusa zhuan*) in both structure and content, at times matching word for word. According to the *Dharma-Treasury Transmission*, Nāgārjuna was an aristocratic Brahman from southern India. He was born under a tree and obtained true wisdom from a dragon, so he was called "Dragon Tree." At a young age he was surpassingly brilliant, and had mastered the four Vedas and all the arts of astronomy, geography, divination, and so on.[51]

Having perfected the branches of learning available to him as a highborn Brahman, Nāgārjuna and three like-minded friends hatched a scheme to transgress their social mores and engage in the pursuit of sensual pleasure. The best way to do so, they figured, was to sneak into the palace harem and have their way with the king's women. Nāgārjuna concocted an elixir of invisibility, which, when smeared on their eyelids would allow him and his friends to enter the palace undetected. Before long, many of the palace maidens became pregnant and reported this to the king. The king then ordered that sand be spread across the floors of the palace so that the intruders' footsteps could be seen. Sure enough, when Nāgārjuna and friends returned they were spotted, and the palace guards converged with swords flailing. Only Nāgārjuna escaped the onslaught, having stood rigid and silent right next to the observing king.[52]

At this point the *Dharma-Treasury Transmission* appears to have drawn on Huiyuan's preface to the abridged *Great Perfection of Wisdom Treatise*, in which Nāgārjuna wandered the wilds and met a Buddhist hermit who upgraded his scripture collection. In the *Dharma-Treasury Transmission*, after Nāgārjuna escaped the palace he vowed to find a *śramaṇa* from whom he could receive ordination rites to renounce household life. He entered the mountains and found a Buddhist stūpa, where he formally left home to follow the Buddhadharma. Within ninety days Nāgārjuna mastered all of the scriptures that he could find in Jambudvīpa, and as in Huiyuan's account he then proceeded to the Himalayas where he came across a monk who revealed to him the teachings of the Mahāyāna (*vaipulya* in Huiyuan's version). However, while in Huiyuan's narrative Nāgārjuna then traveled to the dragon palace to perfect his qualities, in the *Dharma-Treasury Transmission* his mastery of the Buddhist teachings and countless victories in debate made him arrogant, and he came to think of himself as omniscient. Then,

51. *Fu fazang yinyuan zhuan*, T no. 2058, 50:317b; Chinese trans. Li 1997a, 335–337.
52. *Fu fazang yinyuan zhuan*, T no. 2058, 50:317b–c; Chinese trans. Li 1997a, 337–343.

in an episode unique to the *Dharma-Treasury Transmission*, Nāgārjuna "wished to enter through Gautama's Gate"[53]—indicating the highest conceit of considering himself equal to the Buddha—and was confronted by the god of this gate who chided him for his insolence. After this rebuke, Nāgārjuna's incomplete knowledge was again confirmed by one of his own disciples, who opined that, since Nāgārjuna was a follower of the Buddha, he clearly had more to learn. Following this cue, Nāgārjuna set out to remedy the deficiencies of Buddhism and establish his own teachings, complete with new precepts and monastic garb.[54]

A great dragon bodhisattva observed Nāgārjuna in this endeavor and pitied him in his presumptuousness. He took Nāgārjuna to his undersea palace, where he showed him a vast cache of unspecified scriptures that expounded the doctrines of ultimate nondifferentiation (*fangdeng* 方等; *vaipulya*). Within ninety days Nāgārjuna thoroughly mastered all of the scriptures in the dragon palace, after which he "deeply penetrated birthlessness and became endowed with the two endurances"[55]—a construction that appears to combine Tanying's and Huiyuan's earlier accounts of Nāgārjuna's dragon palace attainments. Finally, discerning that Nāgārjuna had at last found the right scriptures to engender his enlightenment, the dragon bodhisattva sent him back to southern India to propagate the Dharma.[56]

At that time, according to the *Dharma-Treasury Transmission*, the king of South India was an avid patron of non-Buddhist teachings, so Nāgārjuna took it upon himself to convert him to Buddhism. In order to get the king's attention, Nāgārjuna marched around in front of him for seven years carrying a red flag—a tale reminiscent of Buddhamitra's (Fotuomiduo 佛陀蜜多) encounter elsewhere in the *Dharma-Treasury Transmission* with another non-Buddhist king.[57] When the king finally asked who this flag-toting character was, Nāgārjuna replied that he was an omniscient one, and this time he was apparently right. The king wanted proof of this, so he asked about the present activities of the gods—just like the non-Buddhist debating with Nāgārjuna in Sengzhao's *Vimalakīrti Commentary*. And also like Kumārajīva's commentary (through Sengzhao) on Vimalakīrti's "spiritual penetration," Nāgārjuna answered that the gods were battling the *asuras* in heaven, and this was proven by weapons and body parts falling from the sky. With Nāgārjuna's omniscience thus demonstrated, the South Indian king, as well as thousands of Brahmans observing from atop the king's palace,

53. *Fu fazang yinyuan zhuan*, T no. 2058, 50:317c: 欲往從瞿曇門入. Cf. *Chang ahan jing* 長阿含經 (*Dīrghāgama*), T no. 1, 1:12c, which explained how places that the Buddha frequented were often named after him, including a city gate. Cf. Yamano 2009, 80–81.

54. *Fu fazang yinyuan zhuan*, T no. 2058, 50:317c–318a; Chinese trans. Li 1997a, 345–347.

55. *Fu fazang yinyuan zhuan*, T no. 2058, 50:318a: 深入無生, 二忍具足.

56. Chinese trans. Li 1997a, 347–349.

57. *Fu fazang yinyuan zhuan*, T no. 2058, 50:314a; Chinese trans. Li 1997a, 283. See Walleser (1923) 1979, 33.

submitted themselves to Nāgārjuna's superior wisdom and became followers of Buddhism.[58]

After a brief account of Nāgārjuna's ensuing victories in debate over hordes of non-Buddhists, the text turned to an equally summary description of his oeuvre. This included an "exegesis" (*upadeśa*, *youpotishe* 優波提舍), probably referring to the *Great Perfection of Wisdom Treatise*, the *Middle Treatise*, and what appear to be titles of three other texts: *Adorning the Path of the Buddha* (*Zhuangyan fodao* 莊嚴佛道), *Expedient Means of Great Compassion* (*Daci fangbian* 大慈方便), and the *Treatise on Fearlessness* (*Wuwei lun* 無畏論), from which the *Middle Treatise* was said to have been drawn.[59] However, as K. V. Ramanan suggests, these may be classes of texts rather than individual titles, and the purpose of this brief outline was not bibliographic but rather to emphasize Nāgārjuna's unsurpassed ability to propagate the Dharma through his profound treatises.[60]

With Nāgārjuna having thus been depicted as a master of all sorts of non-Buddhist learning—the traditional sciences, alchemy, and even the pursuit of pleasure—as well as the most sublime teachings of the Buddha, the *Dharma-Treasury Transmission* then turned to his facility with spells (*zhou* 咒). This talent was demonstrated in a contest between Nāgārjuna and an arrogant Brahman, which was advertised as a doctrinal debate but quickly turned into a battle of magical powers. The first volley was offered by the Brahman, who created a large pond with a thousand-pedaled lotus upon which he sat. He taunted Nāgārjuna, saying, "You are sitting on the ground like an animal, while I am on a lotus flower, wise and pure. How dare you match words with me in debate?"[61] In response, Nāgārjuna conjured a six-tusked white elephant that trampled through the Brahman's pond, uprooting the lotus and throwing the Brahman to the ground. Injured and humiliated, the Brahman submitted before the superior power of Nāgārjuna and became his follower.[62]

Finally, the *Dharma-Treasury Transmission* recounted the death of Nāgārjuna and transmission of the Dharma to his disciple Āryadeva. It so happened that there was a Dharma-master of the Lesser Vehicle (*Hīnayāna*,

---

58. *Fu fazang yinyuan zhuan*, T no. 2058, 50:318a–b; Chinese trans. Li 1997a, 349–353.

59. The title *Zhuangyan fodao* suggests a relation to Nāgārjuna's *Shizhu piposha lun*, as it similarly appears focused on the bodhisattva path. However, no such equation is attested elsewhere. *Daci fangbian* is reminiscent of the *Fangbian xin lun* 方便心論 (T no. 1632), which appears in the *Chu sanzang jiji* (T no. 2145, 55:13b) as a translation by Kiṅkara and Tanyao in 472. However, this text does not seem to have been attributed to Nāgārjuna until *Shi'ermen lun zongzhi yi ji* 十二門論宗致義記 by Fazang 法藏 (643–712) (T no. 1826, 42:214b). I know of no possible equivalent in Chinese sources for the *Wuwei lun*, but Ramanan (1966, 34) notes a similarly titled text in the Tibetan Buddhist canon that is also attributed to Nāgārjuna. See Yamano (2009, 88) for Tiantai exponent Zhanran's 湛然 (711–782) brief explanation of these titles.

60. Ramanan 1966, 34. *Fu fazang yinyuan zhuan*, T no. 2058, 50:318b; Chinese trans. Li 1997a, 353–355.

61. *Fu fazang yinyuan zhuan*, T no. 2058, 50:318c: 汝處於地，類同畜生，我居花上，智慧清淨. 寧敢與吾，抗言議論?

62. *Fu fazang yinyuan zhuan*, T no. 2058, 50:318b–c; Chinese trans. Li 1997a, 355–357.

xiaosheng 小乘) who was jealous of Nāgārjuna. Nāgārjuna asked him whether he would be glad if Nāgārjuna remained in the world. The Dharma-master answered that, frankly, he would not, so Nāgārjuna withdrew to a quiet chamber and did not emerge for days. His disciples thought this strange so went to his room to find out the matter. After getting no response to their knocks and calls, Nāgārjuna's disciples broke down the door, looked inside and saw that their master had departed, like a cicada shedding its husk (*chantui er qu* 蟬蛻而去). Temples for Nāgārjuna were built in all the states of India and he was worshipped like a buddha. But before this, the text explained, Nāgārjuna transmitted the Dharma treasury to his to greatest disciple Āryadeva, or Kāṇadeva (Jianatipo 迦那提婆) as he was called here.[63]

The compilers of this Nāgārjuna biography in the *Dharma-Treasury Transmission* appear to have taken to heart the assertion in earlier sources that he was treated like a buddha, for this account was clearly traced along the lines of Śākyamuni's biographical template (Corless 1995, 525–526). In the *Dharma-Treasury Transmission* Nāgārjuna was depicted as a precocious youth of aristocratic stock who experienced the utmost sensual pleasures through his escapades in the palace harem, as did the young prince Gautama. Through this experience Nāgārjuna first came to realize that desire is the root of all suffering, and he left home to seek the truth. He wandered the forests and mountains and eventually found a monk who helped him along the path, but whose teachings did not lead to true enlightenment—much like Gautama's encounters with the meditation masters Ārāḍa Kālāma and Udraka Rāmaputra. Then, just as Śākyamuni first turned the Dharma-wheel in the deer park outside Vārāṇasī, Nāgārjuna turned the Dharma-wheel a second time—as Huiyuan announced—after the *vaipulya* scriptures were bequeathed to him in the undersea palace of a great dragon bodhisattva. Finally, while there were various suspects for what had caused the Buddha's final nirvāṇa, including a promise to Māra and a simple slab of bad pork, one tradition maintained that Śākyamuni departed the world because his attendant Ānanda failed to request his continued presence.[64] Similarly, in the *Dharma-Treasury Transmission* Nāgārjuna's death was of his own choosing, and was precipitated by a Hīnayāna master who did not ask Nāgārjuna to remain in the world.

At this point, however, scholars have imagined the intrusion of Daoist ideas into this otherwise prototypically Buddhist hagiography.[65] While the trajectory of Nāgārjuna's career followed that of the Buddha, Nāgārjuna was shown exiting the world in the manner of a Daoist transcendent—he "molted like a cicada and departed" (*chantui er qu* 蟬蛻而去). Although it is unclear exactly how this phrase was intended—was this some kind of "postmortem immortality," to use Anna Seidel's (1987) apt expression?—scholars have generally understood the trope of the sloughed cicada husk to indicate

63. *Fu fazang yinyuan zhuan*, T no. 2058, 50:318c; Chinese trans. Li 1997a, 357–361.
64. E.g., *Sifen lü* 四分律 (*Dharmaguptaka Vinaya*), T no. 1428, 22:967c.
65. See Corless 1995, 526.

the Daoist process of "corpse deliverance," or *shijie* 尸解. The meaning of this term, however, has also prompted a good deal of debate. "Should we interpret it as deliverance of a person *from* the mortal coil of his corpse," asks Ursula-Angelika Cedzich, "as deliverance *of* a person's body from death and putrefaction, or as deliverance *by means of* a corpse?" (2001, 2). In considering all of these possibilities—freedom of a perduring spirit from its corporeal prison, preservation of the physical form and thus life of the individual, or feigned death via a substitute body—Cedzich examines a number of ancient and medieval sources to illustrate the multivocality of *shijie* as part of the broader Daoist quest for transcendence.[66] Further, Cedzich informs us that the "cicada metaphor is one of the earliest and most frequent images associated with 'corpse deliverance,'" and Bernard Faure and Robert Sharf both assert that the molted cicada husk remains a "Daoist metaphor" even when used to describe mummified Buddhist saints.[67]

But is this the context within which *chantui* should be read in the present case—against the backdrop of *shijie* and Daoist transcendence? Did Nāgārjuna undergo a form of "corpse deliverance," however interpreted, and would *chantui* have necessarily been read in the fifth or sixth century as a Daoist metaphor? It seems clear that these questions must be answered in the negative. First of all, if this were indeed intended as an instance of *shijie*, then Nāgārjuna would have been placed on a fairly low rung of the Chinese spiritual hierarchy. At least from the time of the famous scholar-official and practitioner of transcendence arts, Ge Hong, *shijie* was ranked lowest among three means of "divine transcendence" (*shenxian* 神仙), after "celestial transcendence" (*tianxian* 天仙) and "earthbound transcendence" (*dixian* 地仙).[68] Understood in this context, *chantui* as *shijie* would indeed appear too base a means of departure for a character as exalted as Nāgārjuna. Secondly, considering that most other patriarchs in the *Dharma-Treasury Transmission* were said to have attained nirvāṇa (*niepan* 涅槃; *miedu* 滅度) after conferring the Dharma, it seems most likely that here the image of the cicada husk was used to signal this prototypically Buddhist ending. The same was the case with Nāgārjuna's disciple Āryadeva, whose nirvāṇa (*mie* 滅) was also described with the phrase *chantui er qu*.[69] Further, in Buddhist canonical literature throughout the medieval period, the expression *chantui* was not entirely uncommon, and was used to indicate the "death" of Buddhist adepts in all three *Traditions of Eminent Monks* collections.[70]

But the argument here is not that *chantui* in Daoist texts necessarily meant "corpse deliverance" while in Buddhist texts it must have equaled

66. Of course, as Campany (2009, 35–36) argues, not all ideas and practices associated with immortality or transcendence were necessarily "Daoist."

67. Cedzich 2001, 12; Faure 1991, 158; Sharf 1992, 7–8.

68. See Campany 2002, 59, 75–80.

69. *Fu fazang yinyuan zhuan*, T no. 2058, 50:319c.

70. *Gaoseng zhuan* 高僧傳, T no. 2059, 50:410a, 387c, 397b; *Xu gaoseng zhuan* 續高僧傳, T no. 2060, 50:562a, 660c; and *Song gaoseng zhuan* 宋高僧傳, T no. 2061, 50:845c, 886a. See also Campany 2009, 59; and Cole 2009, 150–151.

nirvāṇa. I doubt that in either context its semantic value was ever so fixed. Rather, the point is that the expression *chantui* and the image of the molting cicada were parts of a common stock of Chinese cultural imagery upon which followers of any religious tradition could draw. Indeed, from time immemorial the various cultural associations of the cicada—deriving from the distinctive sounds of its stridulation, its seasonal appearance, and its life cycle and suggestive molting process—have been mainstays in Chinese literature of all genres and generations, and the visual image of the cicada has graced Chinese artworks of many varieties since ancient times.[71] That the metaphor of the cicada husk was thus applied to adepts of both Daoist and Buddhist traditions would seem of little surprise. The cicada sloughing off a husk that looked very much like its living body was a powerful image of death-that-was-not-death, and was thus an especially apposite marker of "departure" for religious practitioners who were thought to have transcended mortality, as both Buddhists and Daoists claimed. In this way the *Dharma-Treasury Transmission* advanced another key theme of the earlier Nāgārjuna accounts, especially those in Sengrui's *Middle Treatise* preface and Huiyuan's preface to his abridged *Great Perfection of Wisdom Treatise.* All of these sources adorned Nāgārjuna with imagery common to different Chinese religious traditions—even as he followed the standard life path of the Buddha—which served to advertise him as worthy of adulation by Chinese adepts from all walks of religious life.

Āryadeva in the *Dharma-Treasury Transmission*: An Eye for Eyes

The account of Āryadeva in the *Dharma-Treasury Transmission,* which is similar to his separate biography later attributed to Kumārajīva (see appendix 2), is entirely different than the brief biographical excerpt provided in Sengzhao's preface to the *Hundred Treatise.* As with Aśvaghoṣa and Nāgārjuna in the *Dharma-Treasury Transmission,* Āryadeva was completely removed from the earlier context of Dharma decline and was instead depicted propagating the teaching through patriarchal transmission and by securing state patronage. This biography in the *Dharma-Treasury Transmission* also provided the foundation for three principal attributes that would come to define Āryadeva in medieval China: being the greatest disciple of Nāgārjuna, a formidable Buddhist debater and converter of non-Buddhists, and an exemplar of Buddhist self-immolation. Here I examine this last aspect of Āryadeva's repertoire, which later centered the hagiographies of Aśvaghoṣa and Nāgārjuna as well and thereby added another compelling dimension to the Chinese *imaginaire* of post-*parinirvāṇa* Buddhist sainthood.[72] The tale

71. See Hopkins and Hobson 1912 and Liu 1950.

72. See chapter 5 for analysis of Aśvaghoṣa's *Baolin zhuan* hagiography, in which he transformed his body into silkworms and then relinquished his life so that the poor and destitute could have silk clothing. Nāgārjuna was first depicted in the seventh-century *Xiyu ji* cutting off his own head and giving it to a prince who requested it; see chapter 3.

of Āryadeva's self-immolation in the *Dharma-Treasury Transmission* revolved around his encounter with the Brahmanical god Maheśvara.[73] Through Āryadeva's example, this text advanced an understanding of immolated bodies as structurally analogous to religious icons. Both flesh and stone were infused with a numinous essence—sometimes called *shen* 神 (spirit or divinity)—and both were ultimately insubstantial so rightfully effaced in service of the greater good.

This episode in the *Dharma-Treasury Transmission* opened with Āryadeva visiting a temple in southern India and admonishing the worshippers there about how they should understand its golden statue of Maheśvara. This particular image had a reputation for efficacy—which elicited Āryadeva's interest in it—and upon Āryadeva's arrival Maheśvara rolled his eyes and glared angrily at him.[74] However, Āryadeva insisted that the god and golden image were fundamentally dissimilar: "This god is truly divine, but what I see now is greatly inferior. Divinities should subdue the masses with their essential numen, but here gold and *sphaṭika* (crystal) are used as adornments to confuse the people."[75] Āryadeva then climbed up the statue and bored out its eye, to the great dismay of the throngs of onlookers. He explained to the people, "This god's wisdom is boundless, so he used these superficial means to test me. I deeply understood his intention, so I climbed this mound of gold and bored out its *sphaṭika* jewel to make you all understand that essential numen is pure and not dependent upon form and substance."[76]

The only modern scholar to comment on this scene, Yamakami Sōgen, applauds Āryadeva's role "as the destroyer of idol-worship which was the root of the numerous superstitions in India at his time."[77] Leaving aside the critique of modern discourse on "idolatry," which Robert Sharf has recently encapsulated (2001, 9–12), is it possible that Sōgen has a point here? Was Āryadeva railing against the worship of images? On the one hand, it would certainly seem that he was. He admonished that people should understand and respect the "essential numen" (*jingling* 精靈) of Maheśvara himself, and not be fooled by the mere adornments of gold and crystal, the "form and substance" (*xingzhi* 形質) of the wrought image. He then climbed

73. *Fu fazang yinyuan zhuan*, T no. 2058, 50:318c–319b; Chinese trans. Li 1997a, 361–369.

74. *Fu fazang yinyuan zhuan*, T no. 2058, 50:319a: 天動其眼, 怒目視之 The canonical biography (*Tipo pusa zhuan* 提婆菩薩傳, T no. 2048, 50:186c) has 天像搖動其眼, 怒目視之, "the *image* of the god rolled its eyes and glared angrily at him."

75. *Fu fazang yinyuan zhuan*, T no. 2058, 50:319a: 天實神矣, 然今相觀, 甚大卑劣. 夫為神者, 當以精靈偃伏群類, 而假黃金, 頗梨為飾, 熒惑民物.

76. *Fu fazang yinyuan zhuan*, T no. 2058, 50:319a: 神明遠大, 近事試我. 我深達彼心所念, 故登金山聚, 出頗梨珠, 咸令一切, 皆悉了知, 精靈純粹, 不假形質. Here the use of *shan* 山 rather than *xiang* 像 is suggestive, perhaps serving to further distance the external form of the statue from the pure numen of the god: a mere "mound of gold" rather than an actual "likeness" or "image" of the god.

77. Sōgen 1912, 188. In his synopsis of Āryadeva's canonical biography for the *Kokuyaku issaikyō*, Hasuzawa Shōjūn 蓮澤成淳 (1936, 465) says only that he was also called Kāṇadeva because he gave one of his eyes to a god.

atop the statue and actually dug out its eye—a dramatic act of apparent desecration that would certainly seem to preclude any respect for the sanctity of a "living image."[78] On the other hand, there was no indication that people's prayers to this Maheśvara statue were *not* answered as claimed, and Āryadeva never said that they should not worship Maheśvara through his golden image.[79] It was only a question of how they should understand the god's pure essence infusing the superficial form and substance of the icon. Indeed, as indicated by the statue's angry glare at the outset of this episode and the next scene in which Maheśvara appeared before Āryadeva, which Sōgen otherwise ignores, the actual god and its sculpted image were seen to share a close if ambiguous connection.

The miracle part of this tale involved the statue of Maheśvara only indirectly, and served in part to verify Āryadeva's earlier insight into the relationship between the god and its image. After Āryadeva left the temple, Maheśvara paid him a visit in a "bodily form" (*roushen* 肉身) that, because of Āryadeva's earlier demonstration for the worshippers, was likewise missing one eye. While Āryadeva explained to the people that he carved out the statue's eye in order to demonstrate that the true god was not dependent upon its image, when the god later appeared he was missing one eye precisely because his statue in the temple was equally deformed. But this did not necessarily invalidate Āryadeva's earlier lecture about essential numen versus form and substance, for this "bodily form" in which Maheśvara appeared to Āryadeva was, like the statue, something "wrought" (*zuo* 作),[80] and thus also not to be seen as capturing the true essence of the god. In other words, both statue of metal and body of flesh were equally "image," and Maheśvara praised Āryadeva for his ability to distinguish between the ghost and the shell: "Well done, great master! You deeply grasped my mind and displayed your offerings with wisdom; now you truly have reverent faith in me. The people of the world are foolish and ignorant, only grasping my form."[81]

---

78. It would not have been lost on a medieval Chinese reader that Āryadeva attacked the eye of the statue in particular because that was seen as the locus of an image's power. From at least the early sixth century there are indications that Chinese monks practiced the ancient rite of image consecration, or "establishment" (Skt. *pratiṣṭhā*), in which the eyes of images were ritually "opened" (*kaiguang* 開光) and the images thereby brought to life (Kieschnick 2003, 60). On the importance of painted or inlaid eyes in the creation (and destruction) of Buddhist images, see also Faure 1991, 169–171; Gombrich 1966, 1978; Kieschnick 2003, 66; Strickmann 1996, chap. 3; Swearer 2004, 94–107; and Tambiah 1984, 255–257.

79. A similar juxtaposition between the illusory nature of wrought images and the great benefits of making and worshiping them is seen in a number of early Chinese Buddhist sources; see Kieschnick 2003, 69–80.

80. *Fu fazang yinyuan zhuan*, T no. 2058, 50:319a: 大自在天作一肉形 (Maheśvara created a bodily form); cf. *Tipo pusa zhuan*, T no. 2048, 50:187a: 大自在天貫一肉形 (Maheśvara was clad in a bodily form). Only the Kōshō-ji 興聖寺 edition of the latter text gives *wan* 完 (complete, perfect) rather than *rou* 肉 (bodily).

81. *Fu fazang yinyuan zhuan*, T no. 2058, 50:319a: "善哉大士! 深得吾心, 以智見供; 汝今真是, 敬信我者. 世人愚癡, 唯得吾形."

This equation between the external forms of gold and flesh was further solidified with the god's subsequent request that Āryadeva give the "utmost gift" (*shangshi* 上施) of his own flesh: his left eye to replace that which he took from the golden statue. Āryadeva of course obliged, gladly digging out his eyeball only to have it grow back due to Maheśvara's divine power. Āryadeva then popped out this new eyeball and another replaced it. This went on for some ten thousand rounds—evoking a macabre image of god and patriarch wading through heaps of bloody eyeballs—before Maheśvara finally praised Āryadeva for his unparalleled generosity. Therefore, just as the crystal eye of the golden statue could be removed without affecting the god's pure numen, even though the god was indeed present therein, the bodily form of Āryadeva's own eyes was recognized as insubstantial and unworthy of attachment. This interpretation of Āryadeva's self-immolation was confirmed toward the end of the account in both the *Dharma-Treasury Transmission* and Āryadeva's separate biography, in which he admonished against attachment to the illusion of perduring self.[82] Further, there is reason to believe that the compiler (or compilers) of this episode drew upon the same source that much of the *Dharma-Treasury Transmission* followed, the *Aśokāvadāna*, which included the tale of Aśoka's son Kuṇāla and his beautiful eyes as source of attachment, and a vehicle for similar discourses on insubstantiality.

In this connection, Hasuzawa Shōjūn 蓮澤成淳 draws our attention to Jizang's *Hundred Treatise Commentary*, which recounted this story of Āryadeva's self-immolation in explanation of how he got the name Kāṇadeva (literally meaning "one-eyed god"). Jizang then recited another tradition according to which Āryadeva plucked out his eye for the benefit of an admiring woman, who was smitten with his beautiful eyes. He did this to teach her about the impurity of the physical form so she could relinquish her attachment to it and thereby attain the Way.[83] This tradition about Āryadeva (or Kāṇadeva) to which Jizang referred has apparently not come down to us, but in outline bears a certain resemblance to the account of Aśoka's son Kuṇāla in the *Aśokāvadāna*. Born with the most beautiful eyes that anyone had ever seen, Kuṇāla soon became the object of a queen's amorous affection. When Kuṇāla spurned her advances, however, she grew embittered and sought to take revenge on the prince. While Kuṇāla was abroad she ordered that his beautiful eyes be gouged out, which contrary to her intentions actually enabled his enlightenment. With his eyes in hand and blood streaming from his empty sockets, he came to realize the truth of impermanence and the folly of attachment to physical form.[84] It is uncertain whether this was the source of Jizang's account or the eye-for-eyes episode

82. *Fu fazang yinyuan zhuan*, T no. 2058, 50:319c; *Tipo pusa zhuan*, T no. 2048, 50:187c.

83. Hasuzawa 1936, 465; *Bailun shu* 百論疏, T no. 1827, 42:233b–c.

84. *Ayuwang zhuan*, T no. 2042, 50:108a–110b; trans. (French from Chinese) Przyluski 1923, 281–295; trans. (English from Sanskrit) Strong 1983, 268–285; and *Ayuwang jing*, T no. 2043, 50:144a–147b; trans. (English from Chinese) Li 1993, 63–79.

from the *Dharma-Treasury Transmission*, but all three stories clearly shared the same concern with illustrating the insubstantiality of physical form, which in turn bears upon the interpretation of Āryadeva (or Kāṇadeva) engaging in self-immolation vis-à-vis Maheśvara's golden statue.

The pairing of Āryadeva's destruction of the statue with his like method of self-immolation indicates that Maheśvara's golden statue and bodily form, as well as Āryadeva's physical body, were all structurally equivalent and equally insubstantial. Āryadeva dug out both eyes of crystal and flesh in order to demonstrate that "essential numen is pure and not dependent upon form and substance." This interpretation accords with the emphasis on perfect generosity in Āryadeva's act of self-immolation, as indicated by Maheśvara's repeated praise of Āryadeva's "utmost gift." The same emphasis is apparent in numerous *jātaka* and *avadāna* tales, in which bodhisattvas gave freely of their own flesh in order to alleviate the suffering of others.[85] As in these accounts, Āryadeva's eyeball immolation proved that he could truly see: flesh and blood are ultimately insubstantial but furnish the perfect vehicle for genuine renunciation—a dynamic that also recalls Aśoka's discourse on good conduct as the physical body's one true "essence" (*sāra*).[86] But here this understanding of self-immolation was advanced through a unique and ingenious association between Āryadeva's bodily form and the golden statue of Maheśvara. Both were "alive"—equally animated by *shen*—but both were evanescent, so unworthy of attachment. Āryadeva thus expressed his devotion to Maheśvara by gouging out both the statue's eyes and his own, exemplifying the proper understanding of bodies human and divine, flesh and stone, and of the bodhisattva's practice of self-immolation.

Like Aśvaghoṣa and Nāgārjuna, the *Dharma-Treasury Transmission* depicted Āryadeva—in accessible language with minimal philosophical flourish—as a foremost exemplar of the practices that transformed mere human beings into eminent Buddhist saints. Aside from Kumārajīva's translation of the *Hundred Treatise* and Sengzhao's brief biographical statement in his preface to this translation, Āryadeva was by and large born to the Chinese audience with the *Dharma-Treasury Transmission*. He was already known through these earlier sources as a brilliant philosopher and converter of non-Buddhists, but in this text he became a model of Buddhist self-immolation, another converter of kings (see appendix 2), and for the first time the chief disciple of Nāgārjuna in this lineage of patriarchs that perpetuated the Dharma after nirvāṇa. In service of the central agendas animating the *Dharma-Treasury Transmission*, the images of Aśvaghoṣa and Nāgārjuna were also markedly expanded from their early

85. In his commentary on the *Lotus Sūtra*, which included famous tales of self-immolating bodhisattvas (see Benn 2007, chap. 2), Jizang adduced Āryadeva's act of eye gouging as an example of the bodhisattva's "substantial gift" (*zhongshi* 重施). See the *Fahua yi shu* 法華義疏, T no. 1721, 34:474b. On the theme of the bodhisattva's bodily sacrifice in Indic Buddhist literature, see Ohnuma 2007. On self-immolation in China see Benn 2007.

86. See Strong 1983, 148–160.

fifth-century accounts. Aśvaghoṣa remained an arrogant Brahman humbled and converted to Buddhism through debate, but also became a musician in Pāṭaliputra and a confidant of Caṇḍa-Kaniṣka. Nāgārjuna's dragon palace adventure became a central climatic episode in the *Dharma-Treasury Transmission*, which otherwise greatly elaborated his repertoire in a variety of fields and presented him as a Buddha-like figure who transcended the bounds of specific religious traditions. In these ways Aśvaghoṣa, Nāgārjuna, and Āryadeva were individuated in the *Dharma-Treasury Transmission*, made to stand head and shoulders above the other masters in the lineage who received relatively little attention. But for the most part this saintly triad was subsumed within the broader corporate body of the Indian Buddhist patriarchate. The function of this unit as a whole is indicated by the contents and contexts of the *Dharma-Treasury Transmission* itself but is also exemplified by the manner in which it was situated in the Cave of Great Perduring Saints (Dazhusheng). The Indian patriarchs in this cave were perhaps conceived to provide a potentially limitless fount of Dharma propagation, tailor-made for Chinese Buddhists living in a world without a Buddha.

The *Dharma-Treasury Transmission* in the Cave of Great Perduring Saints

The visual representation of the Indian Buddhist patriarchate in the Cave of Great Perduring Saints takes the form of a floor-to-ceiling stele-like carving on the interior of the cave's entrance wall, which includes images of twenty-four Indian masters fixed in poses of perpetual Dharma transmission. Standing more than two meters tall and roughly a meter wide, the stele is segmented into twelve horizontal registers of alternating text and image. Carved in relief along each of its six pictorial registers are two pairs of patriarchs facing one another in conversation. Between each conversing pair and also linking the two pairs on each row is either a jewel-in-the-lotus or a mushroom-like column, which apparently symbolized the Dharma commuting between each master along the line (Kucera 2006, 65–66). The patriarchs themselves are clearly depicted as monkish figures, with shaved heads and simple robes, sitting cross-legged on plain square mats. Beneath each register of carved figures is another register filled with blocks of inscribed text. These blocks are aligned with the individual patriarchs such that each is identified by name and number in the transmission lineage. In most cases a few details about the patriarchs' lives are also given. A vertical inscription at the top right of the stele identifies them as "Saintly masters who transmitted the Dharma after the World-Honored One departed the world" (*Shizun qushi chuanfa shengshi* 世尊去世傳法聖師) (see figure 1).[87] The specific order of patriarchs indicated by their inscribed labels, and the content of the inscriptions themselves clearly show that the stele was based

87. Photograph from Chen and Ding 1989, 181.

Figure 1. The Dazhusheng Indian Patriarch Stele. *Zhongguo Meishu Quanji*, vol. 13 (Beijing: Wenwu Chubanshe, 1989), pl. 214.

on the *Dharma-Treasury Transmission*.[88] Dating to 589, the Cave of Great Perduring Saints thus provides invaluable evidence for how this lineage history and its main protagonists were conceived in China before the burgeoning of Sino-Indian Dharma genealogies, and at a time when the traumatic end of the Indian patriarchate was something to be carefully heeded rather than flatly denied.

The Dazhusheng Indian patriarch stele instantiated at least one central message from the *Dharma-Treasury Transmission*—that the severed Indian

88. The *Dharma-Treasury Transmission* includes twenty-three patriarchs in direct succession, relegating Madhyāntika to a collateral line after Ānanda and before the third patriarch Śaṇavāsa. However, in Guanding's famous introduction to the *Mohe zhiguan* 摩訶止觀, which was the first attempt to connect the Indian patriarchs from the *Dharma-Treasury Transmission* to local Chinese masters, Madhyāntika was inserted into the main lineage as the third patriarch for a new total of twenty-four. See Penkower 2000, 249. The Dazhusheng cave likewise includes twenty-four patriarchs rather than twenty-three, with Madhyāntika as the third in succession—perhaps for reasons of visual symmetry as much as anything else. Since according to Penkower (2000, 271) Guanding's lineage statement appeared no earlier than 607, the Dazhusheng cave was probably the forerunner in this regard. For more on the shifting numbers of patriarchs in these and related sources, see Tanaka 1983, 66–73.

lineage offered admonition and encouragement for Chinese Buddhists living in a time of declining Dharma. This text both warned of impending danger and exhorted Buddhists of latter-day China, whose own efforts at Dharma propagation were made paramount by the absence of their Indian predecessors. This discursive function of the *Dharma-Treasury Transmission* was actualized in the context of the Dazhusheng cave, where Buddhist adepts could engage the Indian patriarch stele as part of a broader ritual program of *Buddhanāma* recitation, veneration, confession, and repentance. In addition, this proposed interaction between practitioner and patriarch stele indicates a heretofore unrecognized ritual application of the *Dharma-Treasury Transmission*. This text provided more than just a didactic message; it also prescribed rites of devotion to the Indian patriarchs themselves, as means of ensuring enlightenment in dark times. Through iconic representation and liturgical performance in the Cave of Great Perduring Saints, the long-departed patriarchs of the *Dharma-Treasury Transmission* could be brought back to life, made manifest within the precincts of the cave and invoked to confer blessings upon their latter-day Chinese descendents.

The Indian patriarchs at Dazhusheng did not convey the Dharma to China in a lineal master-disciple fashion, as later claimed by Chan and Tiantai ideologues. Rather, as a single unit, the patriarchate instantiated the process and power of Dharma-treasury transmission, and together its constituents could be entreated to bestow the seal of Buddhist sainthood. In this respect the Indian patriarchs paralleled the numerous buddhas and bodhisattvas sculpted throughout the Cave of Great Perduring Saints. All were immanent presences, superhuman beings capable of manifesting the Dharma through all time and space, and as a result they were objects of veneration within the cave. At the same time, however, the Indian patriarchs maintained their humanity, their proximity, and familiarity to medieval Chinese Buddhists through their shared experience of having toiled to preserve the Dharma in the centuries after the Buddha's departure. Through their success in this endeavor the patriarchs had ascended into the airy realms of Buddhist transcendence, but long ago in ancient India they struggled with the same problem that now vexed latter-day Chinese Buddhists. In this regard the Indian patriarchs of Dazhusheng were models of emulation as well, providing for the practitioner an image of ideal Buddhist sainthood to be carried forth as she or he ventured out into a world of declining Dharma.

The Cave of Great Perduring Saints is part of the Lingquan monastery complex, which sits at the eastern foot of Mount Bao 寶山 (Treasure Mountain) in the precincts of the medieval capital of Ye 鄴 (near modern Anyang 安陽 city, Henan 河南 province).[89] The monastery was established un-

89. Originally called Baoshansi 寶山寺, the monastery's name was changed in 591 by Sui Wendi 隋文帝 (541–604; r. 581–604) in honor of the monk Lingyu 靈裕 (518–605), who that same year had been invited to the capital to confer the bodhisattva precepts upon the emperor and empress. See Henan Sheng Gudai Jianzhu Baohu Yanjiusuo 1992, 63.

der imperial patronage by the eminent "Stages Treatise" (Dilun 地論) master Daoping 道憑 (488–559) in the fourth year of the Eastern Wei 東魏 (534–550) Wuding 武定 era (546). It was badly damaged during the Northern Zhou 北周 (557–581) religious persecutions of 574–578, after which Daoping's chief disciple Lingyu 靈裕 (518–605) oversaw its restoration. As part of this project, Lingyu commissioned the Cave of Great Perduring Saints, which instantiated a number of devotional, iconographic, and epigraphic innovations. It represented several novel features carried over from the formative Northern Qi 北齊 (550–577) period, including its abundance of inscribed scriptural excerpts, its architectural design, and its main Buddha triad of Vairocana, Amitābha, and Maitreya. Also, engraved on its wall is the earliest extant example of a class of ritual manuals centering on *Buddhanāma* recitation, and it appears to be one of the first cave-temples ever constructed for the performance of the liturgical program evinced by this manual.

Aside from having designed this cave and its ritual program, Lingyu was best known for his proficiency in a number of Buddhist scholarly traditions, especially those surrounding the *Avataṃsakasūtra, Nirvāṇasūtra,* and Vinaya corpuses. He was said to have composed no less than thirty commentaries on these and other texts, including the *Sukhāvatīvyūha, Śrīmālādevī, Mahāsaṃnipāta,* and a number of Maitreya sūtras. In other writings such as the *Record of the Destruction of the Dharma* (*Miefa ji* 滅法記) and the *Records of Retribution for Destroying Temples* (*Sipo baoying ji* 寺破報應記), Lingyu exhibited a clear preoccupation with "final age" eschatology.[90] This concern is evident as well in the sūtra inscriptions, relief carvings, and Buddha images that he selected to adorn the walls of the Dazhusheng cave. Lingyu personally experienced the Northern Zhou persecution, during which tens of thousands of temples were razed, hundreds of thousands of monks and nuns were laicized, and countless Buddhist scriptures and images were destroyed. Having been closely aligned with the Northern Qi ruling family—in particular the governor Lou Rui 婁叡 (532–570), first cousin to emperor Wenxuan 文宣 (r. 550–559) and chief benefactor of Baoshan (Lingquan) monastery—Lingyu saw lavish imperial patronage quickly turn to bitter suppression, and he was forced from the capital monasteries to practice his religion in hiding. This traumatic episode is seen to have profoundly affected Lingyu's outlook on the fate of the Dharma in China, as well as the ritual programs that he devised as most appropriate for Buddhists living in the "final age."[91]

90. This emphasis on *mofa* thought underlying Lingyu's Lingquansi projects appears as early as his *Xu gaoseng zhuan* biography (T no. 2060, 50:497b). The *Miefa ji* and *Sipo baoying ji* are also mentioned therein (T no. 2060, 50:497c), but like most of Lingyu's writings they are no longer extant.

91. The most comprehensive study of Lingyu is Makita 1964. Lingyu's epitaph at Lingquansi is transcribed in Ōuchi 1997, 329–332. See also Mochizuki 1954–1963, 5:5032c–5033b; Ciyi 1988–1989, 7:6939b–c; and Lee 1999, 4–5.

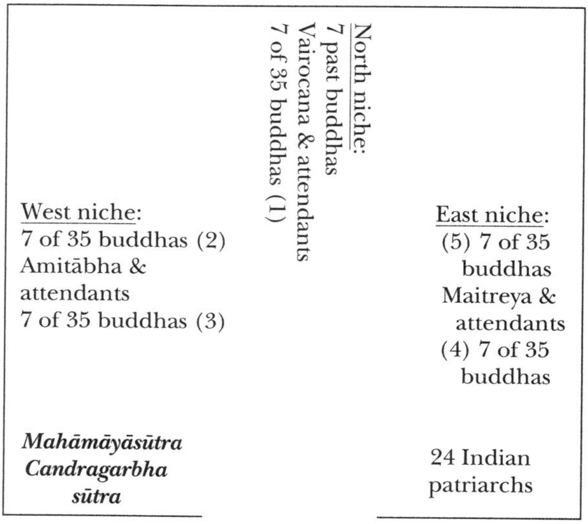

Figure 2. Layout of the Dazhusheng Cave.

By far the most famous project undertaken by Lingyu at Lingquan monastery is the Cave of Great Perduring Saints, which bears all the marks of Lingyu's personal history: his specialization in *Avataṃsaka* and *Nirvāṇa* corpuses, his interest in Amitābha and Maitreya devotionalism, his development of confession and repentance rites, and his concern with "final Dharma" eschatology. The cave was dug out of the limestone on the southern slope of Mount Bao about a half kilometer from the central monastery. It is roughly 3.4 meters deep and wide, 2.6 meters in height, and has statues of Vairocana, Amitābha, and Maitreya occupying the majority of its three interior walls.[92] One enters the cave facing north. Straight ahead is a large niche that takes up most of the north wall and houses a seated image of Vairocana flanked by a disciple and a bodhisattva. The west wall is covered by a niche in which a seated Amitābha with two attendant bodhisattvas reside. Another large niche for Maitreya and his attendant bodhisattva and disciple fill the east wall. The seven buddhas of the past and the thirty-five eternal buddhas are depicted in six columns of seven small nooks that flank each of the three large Buddha niches. The Indian patriarch stele is carved on the east side of the south wall entranceway, while the west side is filled with two inscribed scriptures: the *Mahāmāyāsūtra* and *Candragarbhasūtra*. Finally, the ceiling is adorned with a lotus flower surrounded by *apsarases* (celestial maidens), and the center of the cave appears to have always been empty (see figure 2).[93]

92. This triadic grouping is unusual for medieval Chinese cave-temples on the whole; it was first used in the Northern Qi caves around Ye, and may be at Xiaonanhai 小南海, Xiangtangshan 響堂山, and another cave at Lingquansi. See Howard 1996, 16, 19–20; and Kim 2011.

93. A more detailed description of the Dazhusheng cave is provided in Henan Sheng Gudai Jianzhu Baohu Yanjiusuo 1992, 15–18, 62–64, 146–151, and 283–299. See also Chen and Ding 1989, 170–182, for high-quality color photographs of the cave, which are partially reproduced in Lee 1999, 43–52. Figure 2 follows Lee 1999, 27.

The exterior of the cave is blanketed with inscriptions and carvings, which similarly reflect Lingyu's varied interests and also offer important clues as to the intended purposes of the cave. Excerpts from a number of famous scriptures are engraved there, including the *Śrīmālādevī*, *Lotus*, *Nirvāṇa*, and *Candragarbha* sūtras,[94] as well as a number of *Buddhanāma* rosters, a repentance liturgy, and a dedicatory inscription. At first sight, however, the cave is most striking for the unique pair of guardian figures carved in intaglio along the walls flanking its entranceway. Standing nearly two meters tall and brandishing swords and spears, "divine kings" (*shenwang* 神王), Kapila (Jiapiluo 迦毘羅) and Nārāyaṇa (Naluoyan 那羅延), are imposing figures of martial prowess and they appear to have functioned as sentries for the cave. They are among the most conspicuous indicators of the cave's broader iconographic and devotional programs focused on protecting the Dharma through the perilous "final age."

This emphasis is also apparent in the biography of Lingyu compiled by Daoxuan 道宣 (596–667), who titles the cave "Jingang xingli zhuchi Naluoyan ku" 金剛性力住持那羅延窟.[95] As Lee Yu-min 李玉珉 points out, this title clearly drew upon the "Building Stūpa-Temples" (Jianli tasi 建立塔寺) chapter of the *Candragarbhasūtra*—an early Buddhist eschatology from which two separate excerpts were carved on the walls of the cave. In this particular chapter, the Buddha described a number of stūpa-temples that were constructed by buddhas of the past and forever protected by great bodhisattvas, which present and future Buddhists should emulate as sacred spaces to preserve the Dharma. One of these stūpas was called the "Cave of Nārāyaṇa" (Nalouyan ku 那羅延窟),[96] named after the same "divine king" who stands guard at the entranceway of the Dazhusheng cave, and who was described elsewhere in the *Candragarbha* as a great Dharma protector residing in China.[97] Together with the lengthy excerpts from this sūtra inscribed on the cave walls, this title in Lingyu's biography indicates that his cave was ideologically indebted to the *Candragarbhasūtra*, and was constructed in emulation of the Cave of Nārāyaṇa described therein. "Jingang xingli zhuchi" means that the cave manifested the power of the adamantine (Vajra) nature of all the buddhas and bodhisattvas to forever protect the Dharma. In light of this clear scriptural connection, the *zhu* of the title Dazhusheng—which is carved above the cave's entranceway—likewise signals the central theme of enduring Dharma, given the ceaseless protective power of its immanent custodians.[98]

---

94. For more on these scriptural excerpts see Lee 1999, 12–13, 28–29.

95. *Xu gaoseng zhuan*, T no. 2060, 50:497b.

96. *Daji jing Yuezang fen* 大集經月藏分 (*Candragarbhasūtra*), T no. 397.15, 13:373c–374a.

97. *Daji jing Yuezang fen*, T no. 397.15, 13:394a. This same sūtra (368b–c) also describes Kapila, the other divine king carved outside the cave, as having been dispatched by the Buddha to China to protect the Dharma there. It is also noteworthy that Yang Jian 楊堅 (541–604), who would become Sui Emperor Wen and patron of the Dazhusheng cave, was called Nārāyaṇa as a youth. See Chen 2002, 79.

98. For analysis and *Candragarbha* references I follow Lee 1999, 8–9, 16.

These custodians are therefore the *sheng* (saints) of the cave's inscribed title, and like the buddhas and bodhisattvas watching over the Cave of Nārāyaṇa in the *Candragarbhasūtra*, they were seen to protect and preserve the Dharma by remaining eternally present in the precincts of the cave. Who exactly were these saints? Fortunately, the cave gives a precise roster, with extensive lists of Buddha names inscribed on its exterior walls as well as a dedicatory inscription detailing the contents of its interior:

> Cave of Great Perduring Saints
> Reverently constructed in the ninth year of the Kaihuang era of the Great Sui, a *jiyou* year (589), the cave [excavation] cost 1600 cash, while the 24 [patriarch] images and world-honored ones cost 900 cash.[99]
>
> > [The main images in the cave are:] Vairocana, world-honored one, one niche;
> > Amitābha, world-honored one, one niche;
> > Maitreya, world-honored one, one niche;
> > the thirty-five Buddhas, world-honored ones, thirty-five niches;
> > the seven Buddhas, world-honored ones, seven niches;
> > the saints who transmitted the Dharma, great Dharma masters, twenty-four men.
>
> The Verses in Praise of the Three Jewels say:
>
> > (for the Buddha Jewel) The concentration and wisdom of the Thus Come One are limitless;
> > His spiritual penetrations are broad and expansive, his wonder difficult to conceive.
> > The bright light of his excellent marks surpasses the net of the world,
> > thus he causes the triple world to universally take refuge.
> > (for the Dharma Jewel) The Dharma-jewel is pure as empty space.
> > Perfect tranquility is profound and inexhaustible;
> > not born and not extinguished, not departing and not coming;[100]
> > nirvāṇa, the departure from defilements, is difficult to conceive.
> > (for the sangha Jewel) The sea of merit of the saints and myriad arhats
> > extirpates all the outflows (i.e., karmic residue) [caused by] strife;
> > [their] discipline and concentration are pure and flawless.[101]

---

99. I am not sure what *yonggong* 用功 means here. I follow McNair 2007, 59, in reading 功 as "cash." Angela Howard (1996, 20) and Ding Mingyi (1998, 64, 66n2) both understand 功 to mean "workers," but this seems unreasonable for a cave so small. Wendi Adamek (2007, 103) thinks that 1624 is the number of images in the cave (not separating 24 from 1600, as I have) and that 900 is the number of days taken to complete the project. I thank Dr. Kim Sunkyung for sharing her thoughts on the matter.

100. The inscription at this point is unclear so the translation "not departing and not coming" is tentative.

101. See also the translations of this inscription in Adamek 2007, 103, and Ding 1998, 64–65, both of which I follow in part.

大住聖窟[102]
大隋開皇九年己酉歲敬
造窟用功一千六百廿四
像世尊用功九百
盧舍那世尊一龕
阿彌陀世尊一龕
彌勒世尊一龕
三十五佛世尊三十五龕
七佛世尊七龕
傳法聖大法師廿四人
歎三寶偈言

如來定慧无邊際
神通廣大妙難思
相好光明超世綱
故令三界普歸依
法寶清淨如虛空
善寂[103]甚深无窮盡
无生无滅无往无[?][104]來
寂滅離垢難思議
聖眾應[105] 真功德海
斷滅一切諸諍流
戒定[106] 清淨无瑕[107]

102. For this transcription I follow Ding 1998, 65–66; Henan Sheng Gudai Jianzhu Baohu Yanjiusuo 1992, 16, 62, and rubbing of the inscription, 293; Lee 1999, 34; and my own photographs of the inscription.

103. The character *ji* 寂 ("tranquility"), appearing here and later, appears as an unusual variant in the inscription; see Ding 1998, 66, and Lee 1999, 34. This variant looks much like *jia* 家 ("home" or "family") and has been transcribed as such in Henan Sheng Gudai Jianzhu Baohu Yanjiusuo 1992, 16. This misreading presumably accounts for the translation "good home" in Adamek 2007, 103.

104. There is a gap here in the inscription. It is difficult to tell whether more characters were originally carved and have since worn away, or if this spot was left blank to begin with. Ding 1998, 66; Lee 1999, 34; and Henan Sheng Gudai Jianzhu Baohu Yanjiusuo 1992, 16 all transcribe the sentence as if there were no gap.

105. This character has become highly eroded. Lee (1999, 34) supplies *ying* 應, which is supported by my photographs of the inscription and the context of the sentence—*yingzhen* 應真 being one Chinese translation of arhat. Adamek (2007, 103) suggests "images" (presumably *xiang* 像).

106. Lee (1999, 34) transcribes these characters as *miezhi* 滅之 rather than *jie ding* 戒定. Although the inscription here is slightly eroded, the first character lacks the water radical as well as the vertical enclosure stroke (*pie* 丿) on the left side of the *ge* 戈 radical, while the second character is clearly a variant of *ding* (宀/之). Ding concurs (1998, 66).

107. These "Verses in Praise of the Three Jewels" were apparently intended to consist of three quatrains of seven-character lines, one each for the Buddha, Dharma, and sangha. However, whether due to erosion or mistaken carving, the third lines of the second and final quatrains contain the wrong numbers of characters. Also, the final quatrain should include one more line of seven characters. Space was left and template squares were carved on the cave wall after the third line of this quatrain, but these squares are now blank. Lee

In addition to the "Great Perduring Saints" named here—including Vairocana, Amitābha, and Maitreya, the groups of thirty-five and seven buddhas, and the twenty-four Indian patriarchs, all of whom inhabit the cave—inscriptions along the exterior wall include rosters of twenty-five, fifty-three, and thirty-five buddhas, as well as the buddhas of the ten directions.[108] The function of these Buddha names is signaled by a ritual manual inscribed next to them, which is titled "The Abridged Text of the Repentance for Venerating [the Buddhas and Their Names] in Seven [Stages]" (Lüe li qi[jie foming] chanhui deng wen 略禮七[階佛名]懺悔等文). This inscription represents a class of liturgy used in programs of meditative visualization, *Buddhanāma* recitation, confession, and repentance, which proliferated in northern China during the sixth century, particularly within the Dilun and Sanjie 三階 ("Three Levels") traditions.[109] The Dazhusheng liturgy directs the practitioner to first call upon and pay homage to eight rosters of buddhas, including those inscribed in entirety on the wall; she or he should then confess and repent of various transgressions in the presence of these buddhas before dedicating any merits accrued to all sentient beings.[110] At the conclusion of this rite the buddhas were expected to appear in full bodily form before the practitioner and directly confer upon him the seal of enlightenment.

By ritually engaging these sets of buddhas, then, latter-day Chinese practitioners could ideally attain perfect enlightenment and be thus equipped to preserve Buddhism through the perilous "final Dharma" period. This cave bears the imprint of Lingyu's rhetorical disquiet over the fate of the Dharma but otherwise displays most prominently his conviction that the right ritual program—if performed with utmost devotion—could harness the power of the buddhas to ensure the Dharma's continued efflorescence. The Cave of Great Perduring Saints was designed, like the Cave of Nārāyaṇa in the *Candragarbhasūtra*, to protect and preserve the Dharma through difficult times. As evidenced by the *Buddhanāma* repentance text inscribed on the cave's wall, Lingyu constructed this space to facilitate what he considered

---

(1999, 34) supplies the character *hui* 穢 after *xia* 瑕 at the end of this third line, as well as a fourth line that reads *bazhong gongde futian seng* 八種功德福田僧 (merit-field sangha of the eight kinds of merit). However, none of this appears in the extant inscription.

108. Rubbings of these Buddha rosters are reproduced in Henan Sheng Gudai Jianzhu Baohu Yanjiusuo 1992, 297–298; transcriptions in Lee 1999, 36, 38–39. Scriptural sources are discussed in Lee 1999, 10; and Williams 2005, 44–46.

109. On the Sanjie school, its founder Xinxing 信行 (541–594), and his ritual programs of confession and repentance, see especially Hubbard 2001. Connections between the Dilun and Sanjie traditions, and between Lingyu and Xinxing as co-disciples of Daoping, were first drawn by Tokiwa 1943–1944, 1:181–198.

110. See Williams (2005, 40–70) for a reconstruction, translation, and insightful discussion of this repentance text. I follow Williams's suggested translation of its title, rather than the more commonly accepted "Abridged Text of the Repentance for Venerating [the Buddha Names] of the Seven [Registers]." This is because, as Williams argues, few texts of this ilk actually contain seven registers of Buddha names, while they do often prescribe a seven-step ritual program. The Dazhusheng repentance text is transcribed in Lee 1999, 39; and a rubbing of it is reproduced in Henan Sheng Gudai Jianzhu Baohu Yanjiusuo 1992, 296.

the most appropriate ritual program for Buddhists living in such times.[111] This cave provided the necessary tangible support for these rituals, through which the "Great Perduring Saints" could be invoked, manifested, and entreated to restore the True Dharma and confer it upon the practitioner.

How did the Indian patriarch stele and *Dharma-Treasury Transmission* fit into all of this? If a ritual program of *Buddhanāma* repentance was central to the interaction between the cave's practicants and its sculpted buddhas, one might surmise that the visual images of the Indian patriarchs were engaged in a similar process. Just as the ritual practitioner could invoke the sets of three, seven, and thirty-five buddhas within the cave and perform rites of obeisance and repentance before them, she or he may have similarly entreated the twenty-four Indian patriarchs from the *Dharma-Treasury Transmission*—who were expressly equated with these buddhas as "Great Perduring Saints" in the cave's dedicatory inscription. This is not to suggest that the Indian patriarchs transmitted the Dharma directly to their Chinese descendents in the same way that they once did among themselves in ancient India. But it does seem plausible that this stele served as a site where the patriarchs could be invoked, manifested within the cave, and entreated to bestow Dharmic blessings upon their devotees. Admittedly, such a ritual program involving the Indian patriarchate is unattested elsewhere, although in other contexts similar sets of Indian masters were depicted visually and apparently used in devotional practice.[112] And on the whole, the Cave of Great Perduring Saints was indeed a site of innovation—the patriarch stele itself and several other cave features were firsts for their time—and the iconographic and epigraphic contexts in which the stele was placed suggest that here it constituted a unique addition to an otherwise well-known ritual program.

Understood in relation to the buddha images sculpted throughout the cave, and in the context of the cave's broader program of *Buddhanāma* ritual repentance, the Indian patriarch stele may have served to facilitate rites of liturgical invocation. The Cave of Great Perduring Saints perhaps indicates an otherwise unrecognized ritual application of the *Dharma-Treasury Transmission* itself. As previously discussed, after the death of the last Indian patriarch, this text concluded with ebullient praise of the supreme

111. Lingyu's emphasis on the need for repentance rituals in dark times is also evident in his "Verses for General Repentance of the Ten Evils" (Zongchan shi'e jiewen 総懺十惡偈文). Here Lingyu laments that in such dire circumstances people cannot possibly become awakened through their own efforts; instead, the buddhas' infinite wisdom is needed to illuminate the truth. Especially when false views obscure the True Teaching, the buddhas are forsaken and the precepts broken, the greatest sin, says Lingyu, is not to repent. As such, one must confess all transgressions before the buddhas and pray that they might in their boundless compassion eliminate one's defilements and assist in the complete realization of the True Dharma-realm. See *Fayuan zhulin* 法苑珠林, T no. 2122, 53:918c–919a; partial trans. Williams 2005, 62. Cf. Lee 1999, 24.

112. See especially Kucera 2006, which discusses the Kanjingsi 看經寺 and Leigutai Central 擂鼓台中 caves at Longmen 龍門, which date to the eighth century and include sculpted images of the Indian patriarchs that may have been used in rituals of circumambulation. See also Foulk and Sharf 1993–1994 and Joo 2007.

Dharma and enjoined the faithful to redouble their efforts at propagating it throughout the world. Amid these concluding exhortations were passages that may have been taken literally as calls to invoke the Indian patriarchs themselves, perform rites of obeisance in their honor, and thereby receive blessings directly from them. For example, the text enjoined:

> If there is a person who can give rise to reverent faith, draw near to these saints and sages, listen to and uphold this wondrous Dharma, because of the meritorious causes and conditions of hearing this Dharma she or he will remove the stains of desire and obtain supreme bliss. This is why these men [the patriarchs] are called good and virtuous friends (*kalyāṇamitra*). One should exhaust oneself in striving to be ever near them and in making offerings [to them], and one will certainly be made to leave behind the suffering of the three evil [destinies].
>
> 若有人能起信敬心, 親近賢聖, 聽受妙法, 由聽斯法功德因緣, 出欲淤泥, 受最勝樂. 是故此人, 名善知識. 宜應勤心, 習近供養, 必能令人離三惡苦.[113]

After this devotional prescription, the *Dharma-Treasury Transmission* concluded with a story of a Brahman who traveled around Pāṭaliputra hawking human skulls. The local lay Buddhists consented to buy only those skulls with open ear holes, reckoning that such skulls were those of wise men who, when alive, had personally heard and fully grasped the wondrous Dharma. The laymen then enshrined the skulls in stūpas and made offerings to them, thereby attaining rebirth in the heavens. The compiler (or compilers) of the *Dharma-Treasury Transmission* then provided the moral of the story:

> Those *upāsakas* were reborn in heaven just because they erected stūpas for the skulls of those who listened to the Dharma. How much more [the merits of] those who wholeheartedly listen to and uphold this Dharma [themselves], and make offerings in reverence to those who preserved the [teachings of the] scriptures? This kind of blessed reward is hard to exhaust; in the future they will certainly achieve the unsurpassed Way.
>
> 此優婆塞, 以聽法人髑髏起塔, 尚生天上. 況能至心聽受斯法, 供養恭敬持經人者? 此之福報, 甚難窮盡; 未來必當, 成無上道.[114]

The Dazhusheng Indian patriarch stele may have been sculpted to facilitate just this kind of performance. With the patriarchs depicted iconically transmitting the Dharma along the registers of the stele, the practitioner could draw near to them, make offerings to them, and thereby attain good rebirths and eventually "the unsurpassed Way." It is unclear exactly what kind of rites would have been performed in the presence of the Indian patriarchs, or whether these masters were engaged in the same way as the various buddhas carved throughout the cave. However, the patriarchs'

113. *Fu fazang yinyuan zhuan*, T no. 2058, 50:322a; cf. Chinese trans. Li 1997a, 413.
114. *Fu fazang yinyuan zhuan*, T no. 2058, 50:322b; cf. Chinese trans. Li 1997a, 419–421.

function here was apparently analogous to that of the buddhas invoked in Lingyu's repentance liturgy. These hosts of buddhas were inscribed on the exterior wall of the cave and sculpted throughout cave's interior, where they could receive offerings of obeisance and oversee rites of repentance before finally conferring the Dharma upon the successful practitioner. Likewise, the Indian patriarchs were sculpted in the entrance-wall stele in full bodily form—striking Dharma-transmission poses in perpetuity—while the *Dharma-Treasury Transmission* said that by being in their presence and making offerings to them one could be sure to attain enlightenment. Again, although the specifics of such procedures cannot be elaborated with certainty, the fact that this stele was placed inside a cave designed primarily for *Buddhanāma* repentance rites suggests that the Indian patriarchs may have functioned as part of this program—particularly since they were represented in iconographic fashion, like the buddhas throughout the cave.

However, each of the patriarchs, as well as the hagiographic collection from which they were derived, was also represented in the form of inscribed text. In this regard the *Dharma-Treasury Transmission* and its lineage of Indian masters corresponded most closely with the other texts engraved inside the cave: the *Candragarbha* and *Mahāmāyā* sūtras, which occupy the same south-side wall across the cave's entranceway. While these scriptures may have been recited orally within the cave as part of its presumed ritual program, we have no reason to assume that they themselves were objects of devotion. Rather, the soteriological message that they propounded was most likely their raison d'être. Both of these passages highlighted the prevailing darkness of the "final age" precisely in order to set in clear relief the enduring power of the True Dharma, harnessed through the earnest effort of devout practitioners. The selection from the *Mahāmāyāsūtra* in this cave provided an extended meditation on suffering and impermanence before encouraging its readers to follow the Buddhist teachings and seek nirvāṇa.[115] The excerpt from the *Candragarbhasūtra* predicted that the Dharma would gradually diminish over the centuries after nirvāṇa but concluded by promising that great merits could still be earned and sainthood attained.[116] Such was the same with the *Dharma-Treasury Transmission*, which was initially explicit about the downfall of Buddhism but then reversed course in emphasizing the Dharma's ultimate staying power. The Indian patriarch stele, as inscribed text, thus instantiated within the cave this central message from the *Dharma-Treasury Transmission*.

This stele provided a perfect match on the east side of the entranceway for the *Candragarbha* and *Mahāmāyā* sūtras on the west side. Together these

115. Here the cave wall matches *Mohemoye jing*, T no. 383, 12:1005b–1006a. The inscription is mostly reproduced in the rubbing in Henan Sheng Gudai Jianzhu Baohu Yanjiusuo 1992, 294; transcribed in Lee 1999, 41–42.

116. The excerpt inscribed in the cave is a verbatim copy of *Daji jing Yuezang fen*, T no. 397.15, 13:363a–b. A rubbing is reproduced in Henan Sheng Gudai Jianzhu Baohu Yanjiusuo 1992, 294; transcribed in Lee 1999, 40–41. This particular prophesy of Dharma decline is discussed in Nattier 1991, 54–55. For more on the *Candragarbhasūtra* see Nattier 1991, esp. 170–188.

texts framed the most prominent feature of the south wall as the practitioner completed his ritual rounds and turned back toward the cave's exit. This feature was of course the world out there—the hills, vegetation and sunlight streaming over the profane lands through which the adept sought to perpetuate the Dharma. In their full versions, these texts offered bracing commentary on the state of this world during the centuries after the Buddha's death, and on the pressing tasks of the faithful within such a world. As excerpts framing this view of the outside world facing the cave's practitioner, they offered a similar if somewhat more exigent perspective. The *Dharma-Treasury Transmission*, together with the *Candragarbha* and *Mahāmāyā* sūtras across the entranceway, warned the practitioner of looming darkness in the world of "final Dharma," but they also ardently encouraged him to bear down in his practice and maintain unwavering faith in the eternal salvific capacity of the True Dharma and its timeless champions. These texts demonstrated that even after Śākyamuni's departure, the Dharma could be made to endure for generations through an otherwise defiled world, as long as righteous practitioners strove to uphold the teachings that they had been bequeathed.

These two interpretations of the *Dharma-Treasury Transmission* in the Cave of Great Perduring Saints—as ritual performance and discursive exhortation—would not have been mutually exclusive for the practitioners within this cave. As a set of visual images juxtaposed with the buddhas sculpted throughout the cave, the Indian patriarch stele perhaps functioned in liturgical performance, ensuring salvation in latter-day China through a program of ritual obeisance. As an inscribed text corresponding with the eschatological scriptures across the entrance wall, the stele functioned as didactic performance—its redemptive message enacted as it braced the practitioner to reenter the outside world. In this latter respect the protagonists of the *Dharma-Treasury Transmission* within the Dazhusheng stele modeled the ideal means of Dharma propagation for a world without a Buddha. Upon exiting the sacred space of the cave, the practitioner would strive to follow these examples set forth by his Indian forebears, transmitting the Dharma bequeathed for the benefit of all living beings. The message of this text was thus redemptive *because of* the fact that the Indian lineage had been severed with Siṃha. Just as the Buddha's nirvāṇa was depicted in the *Lotus Sūtra* as a mere expediency (*upāya*) devised to encourage self-reliance, the disappearance of the Indian lineage was seen to provide the necessary means for Chinese Buddhists to stave off complacency in their practice, and generate great merit thereby. And also like the Buddha in the *Lotus Sūtra*, the Indian patriarchs in fact never really left. Counted among the "Great Perduring Saints" throughout the cave, they remained in eternal Dharma-transmitting stasis, thus ensuring that the Dharma would always endure through the "latter evil age" in China.

Conclusion: Competing Chinese Portraits of Indian Buddhism

Together with the accounts of Aśvaghoṣa, Nāgārjuna, and Āryadeva produced by Kumārajīva's associates, the *Dharma-Treasury Transmission* provided the foundation for the medieval Chinese *imaginaire* of post-*parinirvāṇa*

Indian Buddhism. The repertoires of the Indian patriarchs were well filled out by these fifth- and sixth-century sources, which were largely reinscribed by later Chinese authors who sought to adduce paradigms of Indian Buddhist history and sainthood in service of local agendas. Indeed, in Chinese Buddhist writings of the medieval period, models of Buddhist sainthood were often developed in lockstep with perceived trajectories of Dharmic history. Specific kinds of Buddhist saints were fashioned in specific soterio-historical circumstances, which in turn were integrally shaped by the appearance of these saints. In early fifth-century sources, Indian Buddhism waxed and waned with the rise and demise of the foremost Buddhists holy beings, who were identified as such by their triumphs at reviving a Dharma in decline. Then with the *Dharma-Treasury Transmission* and other sources like Sengyou's *Record of the Sarvāstivāda*, Indian Buddhism prospered uninterrupted because of the linked succession of Buddhist patriarchs, who were defined by their positions in lineages that propagated the Dharma in perpetuity. Chinese Buddhists of the time were fundamentally concerned with the problem of how to uphold the Dharma at a remove from the fount of Buddhist enlightenment. One strategy for addressing this problem was to delineate the history of Indian Buddhism and the means by which Indian masters had succeeded in upholding the Dharma after nirvāṇa. The two models of sainthood in time are outgrowths of these medieval Chinese efforts to devise programs of practice most appropriate for Buddhists living in a world without a Buddha.

Such is the case with the Cave of Great Perduring Saints, which was similarly constructed, as a means of engendering enlightenment and resurrecting the True Dharma for Buddhists in latter-day China. Here, however, although Lingyu conceived this cave as a site for protecting the Dharma through the latter, evil age, the buddhas and patriarchs that adorned its walls were essentially timeless. Within this ritual space, the history of the Dharma in India or China was rendered mostly moot. Kumārajīva's associates had conceived Aśvaghoṣa, Nāgārjuna, and Āryadeva as proximal figures in a Dharmic-historical sense, given that these patriarchs also lived several centuries after nirvāṇa when the Dharma was in decline. Then the *Dharma-Treasury Transmission* emphasized the distance between its Chinese audience and the Indian patriarchs, who had long ago departed the world. The Cave of Great Perduring Saints partially reflected (and advanced) this perspective from the *Dharma-Treasury Transmission*, but then also represented its protagonists as transcending the vicissitudes of Dharmic history. Here these long-departed masters could be invoked and manifested in the immanent present, from whence they would ensure the prosperity of the Dharma into the indefinite future.

In some respects, the Dazhusheng cave represents a transitional moment in Chinese Buddhist conceptions of the Indian patriarchs. Pulled from the pages of the *Dharma-Treasury Transmission* and set in stone—through both iconographic and epigraphic forms—the patriarchs were anomalous and liminal figures. Paralleling in perceived power and iconic representation the numerous buddhas carved throughout the cave, the patriarchs were ancient yet timeless, transcendent and immanent, evoked in solemn rite to imbue the present with a sacred power of old. They were "Great *Perduring* Saints." Also depicted iconographically as eminently *human* beings, gentle and fragile, and described in inscription as having transmitted the Dharma "after the World-Honored One departed the world," the patriarchs were mortal men who had toiled through a Buddhaless age. Simultaneously venerable and sympathetic, exalted and familiar, the Indian patriarchs represented both the grim plight of latter-day Chinese Buddhists and their greatest hopes of spiritual achievement within such circumstances. By virtue of having struggled to uphold the Dharma without the Buddha to light their way, the Indian patriarchs remained proximal figures to the medieval Chinese. The patriarchs offered encouragement that the task could be fulfilled and great attainments could be won as long as Chinese Buddhists kept the faith and followed the examples they had been given. These were the messages signaled by the Indian patriarch stele in the Cave of Great Perduring Saints, through which the *Dharma-Treasury Transmission* could be ritually performed and its Indian patriarchs made manifest to resurrect the Dharma that was otherwise fading into oblivion.

In other sources that perhaps began to appear from the sixth century, the Indian Buddhist patriarchs were similarly represented as local, immanent presences that could be invoked in ritual contexts to provide a variety of benefits. In chapters 4 and 5 I examine such sources that bear on the figures of Aśvaghoṣa and Nāgārjuna in particular. But for the most part, through the ensuing Sui-Tang period, these Indian patriarchs were firmly situated within the two paradigms of Indian Buddhist history and sainthood outlined previously. Aśvaghoṣa, Nāgārjuna, and Āryadeva were again singled out above and against their compatriots in the Indian patriarchal lineage, even as their expanded repertoires from the *Dharma-Treasury Transmission* were reinscribed and developed further. The individuation of these three patriarchs was also achieved by their independently circulating biographies, which perhaps appeared in the decades following the *Dharma-Treasury Transmission*. And although Sui-Tang Buddhism would later become well-known for its patriarchal lineage histories, in which individual Indian masters were less important than the genealogies they constituted, this particular triad of post-*parinirvāṇa* patriarchs was also often adduced to advance the agendas of contemporary exegetical authors. In the next chapter, I will show how these authors amalgamated patriarchal paradigms—of Dharma resurrection amid soteriological decline and preservation of the teaching through direct lineal succession—in the process of re-conceiving Aśvaghoṣa, Nāgārjuna, and Āryadeva as singular exemplars of Buddhist sainthood who helped instantiate in China the highest truth of ancient Indian Buddhism.

3

Salvation in Writing and the Annex of Indian Buddhism

THE SEVERED INDIAN LINEAGE of the *Dharma-Treasury Transmission* was first extended to latter-day Chinese masters within the Cave of Great Perduring Saints, which was excavated near the Northern Qi capital of Ye in 589. Together with the myriad buddhas represented at this site, the twenty-four Indian patriarchs carved inside the cave were rendered as immanent holy beings who could be entreated to confer blessings upon their Chinese descendents. This cave was part of a series of projects—textual, architectural, and ritual—orchestrated by the monastic and secular elite of the incipient Sui 隨 dynasty (581–618) to localize the means of Buddhist enlightenment within the newly unified kingdom of China.[1] Having finally annexed the territory of the southern Chen 陳 dynasty (557–589) in 589, Sui emperor Wen 文 (541–604; r. 581–604) sought to legitimize his "restoration" of imperial rule in part by conjoining state and sangha, pouring resources into sociopolitical and religious infrastructure and strengthening efforts to simultaneously expand and regulate the Buddhist institution. To this end the Sui court engaged the services of all the most important monks of the kingdom, including Jingying Huiyuan 淨影慧遠 (523–592), Tanqian 曇遷 (542–607), Yancong 彥琮 (557–610), Zhiyi 智顗 (538–597), Jizang 吉藏 (549–623), and many others. These monks aided in the establishment of imperial Buddhist monasteries, the compilation of scriptural canons, the distribution and enshrinement of Buddha relics, the performance of Buddhist rituals, and other projects designed to represent the new Sui emperor as a Buddhist "wheel-turning king" (*cakravartin*) in the image of Aśoka.[2] In this way, not only were the Sui court and sangha jointly empowered in their dominion, but also the entire Chinese kingdom was ostensibly transformed from a Buddhist hinterland into a new epicenter of Buddhist enlightenment.

With the reunification of the empire and centralization of power under the Sui and ensuing Tang regimes, China was no longer to be seen as a soteriological wasteland, hopelessly removed in time and space from

1. On Sui patronage of this cave, see Henan Sheng Gudai Jianzhu Baohu Yanjiusuo 1992, 62–63.

2. See Chen 2002; Wright 1957a; and Xiong 2006, 151–157.

the Indian cradle of Buddhist civilization. Like the Sui founder, his successor Sui Yangdi 煬帝 (569–618; r. 604–617) and emperors of the Tang and Zhou 周 interregnum (690–705) worked to legitimize their reigns by incorporating the vast resources of the Buddhist institution and centering their kingdoms in Buddhist cosmographic terms.[3] Leaders of the Chinese sangha often worked in concert with these imperial courts in organizing further reliquary enshrinements, relocating illustrious Indian bodhisattvas to famous Chinese mountains, identifying Chinese rulers as buddhas incarnate, and constructing Dharma transmission lineages to demonstrate that the "total truth of the Indian Buddhist tradition had recently come to China, where it was perfectly lodged in the bodies of contemporaneous Chinese men."[4] Through these efforts on the part of Sui-Tang imperial courts and monastic elites, the kingdom of China would come to be seen as the equal to India in harboring the media and means of Buddhist enlightenment. And as Sino-Indian transmission lineages functioned to relocate the truth of Indian Buddhism within Chinese masters—especially of the nascent Chan tradition—the Indian patriarchs who constituted these lineages were made to play prominent roles in the redefinition of China as a center of Buddhist civilization.

As discussed in chapter 2, the severance of the Indian patriarchal lineage was one key to the soteriological message provided by the *Dharma-Treasury Transmission*. Like the *Lotus Sūtra* before it, this text emphasized the absence of these great Indian saints in order to exhort latter-day Buddhists to redouble their efforts at propagating the Dharma. The Buddha and his patriarchal successors were all long gone, the world was dark and the Dharma imperiled, so now it was up to Chinese Buddhists to uphold the light for their benighted contemporaries. Then in the Dazhusheng cave this message was both perpetuated and nullified. On the one hand, the Indian patriarch stele ended with Siṃha, the inscription beneath his image recounted his murder,[5] and the lineage appeared adjacent to prophesies of Dharma decline. But on the other hand, the cave's dedicatory inscription clearly identified the Indian patriarchs as "great *perduring* saints," and they may have functioned as part of a ritual program in which a host of Buddhist holy beings could be brought before local supplicants to receive offerings of obeisance. In this way absence gave way to immanence, and the Indian lineage of the *Dharma-Treasury Transmission* was extended beyond Siṃha to sanctify the Buddhist masters of latter-day China. This proposed

3. See, e.g., Chen 2002, chap. 3; Forte 1976; Weinstein 1987; and Xiong 2006, 157–171.

4. Cole 2009, 1. On these other examples, see the discussion in Sen 2003, chap. 2. Similar campaigns had been organized by previous dynastic regimes—especially the Southern Liang and Northern Wei—but never on such a broad scale. See, most recently, Ku 2010 and Pearce 2012.

5. "The twenty-fourth [patriarch] Siṃha bhikṣu; in the kingdom of Kaśmīra he performed great Buddhist deeds and was cut down by a king" 第廿四師子比丘; 于罽賓國, 大作佛事, 為王所絕. Transcribed in Henan Sheng Gudai Jianzhu Baohu Yanjiusuo 1992, 18; and Lee 1999, 42.

ritual engagement was not the same sort of direct master-disciple encounter so valued in the later Chan tradition, and the Indian lineage of the *Dharma-Treasury Transmission* was not extended through missionary patriarchs who personally brought the Dharma to China, as with the Bodhidharma of so many Chan genealogies. But both models of lineal Dharma transmission and ritual invocation functioned to bridge the chasm between Indian and Chinese Buddhism—as posited in the *Dharma-Treasury Transmission* and elsewhere—and to establish new sources of enlightenment in local Chinese masters and paradigms of Buddhist practice.

Many of the same ecclesiastic elites who participated in the aforementioned state-sangha building projects also developed another means by which the Indian patriarchs would help instantiate Śākyamuni's truth in China. This method did not involve face-to-face encounters between Indian masters and Chinese disciples, or rites of obeisance before sculpted images, but rather the transmission of Indian doctrinal treatises and models of exegetical authorship. The most prominent exemplars of this transmission method were Aśvaghoṣa, Nāgārjuna, and Āryadeva, who were first depicted as authors of doctrinal commentaries in a world of declining Dharma in order to resurrect the true teaching. Then, in the Sui-Tang period, these patriarchs were similarly represented as brilliant exegetes whose profound writings transmitted the highest truth of Indian Buddhism to China. For example, the eminent Tiantai master Guanding 灌頂 (561–632) famously claimed Nāgārjuna's *Great Perfection of Wisdom Treatise* as the primary medium through which Śākyamuni's teachings were instantiated in the figure of Zhiyi. And the great Three Treatise exponent Jizang likened Aśvaghoṣa, Nāgārjuna, and Āryadeva to the Buddha himself for their efforts at propagating the teaching through doctrinal exegesis. Just as Śākyamuni appeared when the Dharma was lost and preached sūtras to reintroduce it to the world, these patriarchs arose when the Dharma was imperiled and composed *śāstras* to perpetuate it for their own and future generations.[6]

As these and many other examples illustrate, despite the fact that master-disciple transmission lineages were coming to proliferate in Sui-Tang China, at this time Aśvaghoṣa, Nāgārjuna, and Āryadeva were most often represented not as placeholders in Sino-Indian Dharma genealogies but as singular exemplars of Buddhist sainthood through doctrinal scholarship. Lineage histories like the *Record of the Dharma-Jewel through the Ages*, the *Platform Sūtra of the Sixth Patriarch*, or the *Tradition of the Baolin* [*Temple*][7] downplayed the patriarchs' individual accomplishments by negating their roles as epoch-altering figures and deploying them largely as Dharma conduits to bridge the gap between Śākyamuni and Chinese Buddhist traditions.

---

6. See, e.g., Jizang's *Dasheng xuan lun* 大乘玄論, T no. 1853, 45:69c; and *Zhongguan lun shu* 中觀論疏, T no. 1824, 42:13c, 18c.

7. *Lidai fabao ji* 歷代法寶記, T no. 2075 (trans. Adamek 2007); *Tan jing* 壇經, T no. 2007 (trans. Yampolsky 1967); *Baolin zhuan* 寶林傳 (see chapter 5).

However, in contrast to the homogenizing tendency of these patriarchal historiographies, even when Aśvaghoṣa, Nāgārjuna, and Āryadeva were placed in serial lineages they were made to stand out above the faceless patriarchal crowd. The writings of these patriarchs would therefore be valorized as arising from the most significant junctures of post-*parinirvāṇa* Buddhist history. For instance, Jizang's *Commentary on the Scripture of Benevolent Kings* (*Renwang bore jing shu* 仁王般若經疏) explains that over the first five hundred years after nirvāṇa, twenty-five unnamed Indian patriarchs transmitted the Dharma, while the seventh and eighth post-*parinirvāṇa* centuries were marked by Aśvaghoṣa and Nāgārjuna alone.[8] Similarly, Jizang's disciple Qi fashi 磧法師 (fl. 590–618) excerpted the line of Aśvaghoṣa, Vīra, Nāgārjuna, and Āryadeva from the *Dharma-Treasury Transmission* before connecting it to China through the person of Kumārajīva, who purportedly received the teaching directly from Āryadeva.[9] And the Buddhist convert and polemicist Falin 法琳 (572–640) provided a brief history of Indian Buddhism by tracing a line from the Lesser Vehicle teachings of Kātyāyana and Harivarman to the "Mahāyāna pillars" Aśvaghoṣa, Nāgārjuna, and Āryadeva.[10]

But aside from the focus on genealogical historiography, these accounts also exemplify the widespread tendency throughout Sui-Tang China of singling out members of this patriarchal triad from the host of Indian masters that abounded in Buddhist sources. Aśvaghoṣa, Nāgārjuna, and Āryadeva had already received special attention from the time of Kumārajīva, but their popularity increased greatly over the following centuries with the appearance of nearly two dozen treatises to their names,[11] as well as a pair of influential prophesies in the *Mahāmāyā* and *Laṅkāvatāra* sūtras. According to the former, Aśvaghoṣa and Nāgārjuna would appear in succession at six-hundred and seven-hundred years after nirvāṇa, destroy false dogmas, and re-light the lamp of the True Dharma.[12] And in the latter, Nāgārjuna was destined to champion the Greater Vehicle after Śākyamuni's departure, eventually attaining the first bodhisattva stage of joy (*huanxi di* 歡喜地; *pramuditā bhūmi*) and rebirth in the Land of Bliss (Anle guo 安樂國; Sukhāvatī).[13] With the addition of such sources that prominently advertised

---

8. *Renwang bore jing shu* 仁王般若經疏, T no. 1707, 33:357c. This periodization follows the *Mahāmāyāsūtra*.

9. *Sanlun youyi yi* 三論遊意義, T no. 1855, 45:116c–117a. Cf. Morrison 2010, 30–31.

10. *Bianzheng lun* 辯正論, T no. 2110, 52:493a: 大教之棟幹.

11. See the list of Chinese texts attributed to Aśvaghoṣa, Nāgārjuna, and Āryadeva provided at the beginning of the bibliography.

12. *Mohemoye jing* 摩訶摩耶經 (*Mahāmāyāsūtra*), T no. 383, 12:1013c.

13. *Ru lengqie jing* 入楞伽經, T no. 671, 16:569a. Completed by Bodhiruci in 513, this was the third of four Chinese translations of the *Laṅkāvatāra*. The first translation is no longer extant; the second omits this prophesy; and the fourth, translated by Śikṣānanda in 700, contains a similar passage (*Dasheng ru lengqie jing* 大乘入楞伽經, T no. 672, 16:627c). In the Sanskrit version, this prophecy refers to a certain Nāgāhvaya, or "the one called Dragon," which was translated as Longshu 龍樹 and always taken in China to mean Nāgārjuna. See Abé 1999, 506n83; Suzuki 1932, 239–240; and Walleser (1923) 1979, 21.

these patriarchs as the foremost Mahāyāna champions after nirvāṇa—indeed, as foretold by the Buddha himself—it comes as no surprise that so many Buddhist authors of the Sui-Tang period would uphold Aśvaghoṣa, Nāgārjuna, and Nāgārjuna's chief disciple, Āryadeva, as paragons of Indian Buddhist authority. And just as these patriarchs were represented in the early fifth century as literati-gentlemen first and foremost—mirroring the preferred occupations of their Chinese hagiographers—Sui-Tang Buddhist exegetes likewise lauded these Indian masters for propagating the Dharma through doctrinal exegesis in particular.

In the present chapter, I examine these images of Aśvaghoṣa, Nāgārjuna, and Āryadeva as promoted by some of the most influential Chinese scholar-monks from the sixth century to the eighth—the period during which these Indian patriarchs became truly ubiquitous in Chinese Buddhist discourses across traditions. I focus on several important developments in Sui-Tang Buddhist appropriations of these figures—including Guanding's genealogy of the Tiantai tradition, the attribution of the *Awakening of Faith* (*Dasheng qixin lun* 大乘起信論) to Aśvaghoṣa, and the patriarchal tales recounted by the famous pilgrim Xuanzang 玄奘 (602–664)—all of which illustrate how Buddhist authors worked to valorize local Chinese traditions vis-à-vis the Indian heartland. While earlier representations of Aśvaghoṣa, Nāgārjuna, and Āryadeva evince a central concern with articulating ideals of Buddhist sainthood for a world without a Buddha, Sui-Tang writings about these figures were part of a broader effort to localize the Indian sources of Buddhist truth to create, potentially, a world with many buddhas. In this context the Indian patriarchs not only provided models of Buddhist practice suited to dark times full of dim wits; they also conveyed the apex of Indian truth eastward to help redefine China as a center of Buddhist civilization. Together with the relics, icons, scriptures, buddhas, bodhisattvas, and all the other instruments of Indian sanctity that were now firmly rooted in Chinese soil, Aśvaghoṣa, Nāgārjuna, and Āryadeva were seen to contribute the foremost Indian doctrinal treatises and models of exegesis. With these great works of the Indian patriarchs readily available in China, India was no longer the sole locus of profound Buddhist exegesis. Now Chinese scholar-monks also had the means to elucidate the True Dharma and thereby join the ranks of the greatest Buddhist saints across the Sino-Indian divide.

Exegesis Saves

> Question: Now, from the [time of the] True Teaching to the Semblance Dharma [period], the men who upheld and transmitted [the Dharma] in succession were many. Now whom shall we select as the men [most capable of] destroying heresy and clarifying the truth? Answer: Generally speaking, there are no more than four men. The first is the Tamer, the World-Honored One, who is the master of the teaching. The other three are saints who aided the Buddha in spreading [the Dharma]. These three are named Aśvaghoṣa Bodhisattva, Nāgārjuna, and Āryadeva.

問: 爰及正化, 迄平[14] 像法, 傳持紹繼, 其人不少. 今定取何人, 破邪顯正. 答: 大格為論, 不出四人. 一是調御世尊, 是能化主. 其餘三聖, 助佛宣揚. 三者所謂馬鳴開士, 與龍樹提婆也.[15]

This brief dialogue, excerpted from Jizang's *Treatise on the Profundity of the Mahāyāna* (*Dasheng xuan lun* 大乘玄論), appears amidst a lengthy discussion of what it meant to "destroy heresy and clarify the truth," both during and after the time of the Buddha.[16] According to Jizang, second only to Śākyamuni in fulfilling this charge were Aśvaghoṣa, Nāgārjuna, and Āryadeva, who Jizang further portrayed as upholding the teaching and saving the world in particular through doctrinal exegesis. This claim reflects a common interest among Sui-Tang Buddhist exegetes in promoting these Indian masters and their writings as the greatest manifestations of post-*parinirvāṇa* Buddhist sainthood. By elevating this triad above and against the host of Indian patriarchs who transmitted the teaching through the True and Semblance Dharma periods, Jizang expressly contravened lineage histories like the *Dharma-Treasury Transmission*, which largely compressed all of the patriarchs into a single mold. As previously noted, Chinese scholar-monks of this time most often represented Aśvaghoṣa, Nāgārjuna, and Āryadeva not as placeholders in genealogies of Dharma transmission but as singularly talented exegetical authors who liberated their benighted contemporaries by writing doctrinal commentaries. These commentaries and models of exegesis were especially important to Buddhist authors who affirmed, with the *Dharma-Treasury Transmission*, that the Indian patriarchal lineage had been severed before ever reaching China. Given this fact, and also given the common understanding that the patriarchs after Aśvaghoṣa, Nāgārjuna, and Āryadeva had grown progressively weaker, Sui-Tang Buddhist authors maintained that the writings of this triad were the sole vehicles through which the perfect truth of Indian Buddhism had been conveyed to China.

Although Aśvaghoṣa, Nāgārjuna, and Āryadeva had been acclaimed since the time of Kumārajīva, it was Jizang in particular who did the most to popularize this patriarchal triad during the Sui-Tang period. Best known to posterity as a champion of Three Treatise teachings, Jizang was also an expert in all the major exegetical traditions of his day—especially those surrounding the *Vimalakīrti*, *Avataṃsaka*, *Lotus*, and *Nirvāṇa* sūtras—and was one of the most famous and powerful scholar-monks in all the kingdom. Through the Sui and early-Tang dynasties, Jizang enjoyed the patronage of high officials, princes, and emperors, having been invited to reside at several capital monasteries, and was eventually appointed one of the official Ten Monks of Great Virtue (*shi dade* 十大德) to oversee the Chinese

14. Reading *ping* 平 as an error for *hu* 乎, as suggested by the Taishō editors (*Dasheng xuan lun* 大乘玄論, T no. 1853, 45:69n1).

15. *Dasheng xuan lun*, T no. 1853, 45:69a.

16. For discussion of *Treatise on the Profundity of the Mahāyāna*, see Koseki 1977.

sangha.[17] Against this backdrop it is not difficult to see Jizang's works as dovetailing with the ambitions of the Sui and Tang imperial courts to define Buddhist orthodoxy across the Sino-Indian divide. In this regard, Jizang had much in common with the other scholar-monks discussed in this chapter, who were likewise closely aligned with the secular authority of their times and regularly adduced the Indian patriarchs as paragons of mainstream, elite monasticism and thus stable forms of authority in the eyes of the Chinese state. And just as the Sui and Tang regimes sought to consolidate sociopolitical power in part by centering their kingdoms in Buddhist cosmographic terms, Jizang and his contemporaries likewise worked to localize the paradigms of Indian Buddhist authority provided by Aśvaghoṣa, Nāgārjuna, and Āryadeva.

Modern scholars have often characterized the period of the sixth century through the eighth as one in which Chinese Buddhists and their state patrons sought to consolidate the dizzying array of Buddhist scriptural and doctrinal traditions that had haphazardly filtered into China since the second century. In traditions ranging from ordination platforms and ritual programs to theorized stages of meditative attainment and models of Buddhist sainthood, Chinese Buddhists of this period worked to make sense of disparate Indic traditions that circulated during their time and reshape them to suit contemporary exigencies. Perhaps the best known of these Chinese Buddhist efforts at systematization was the process of *panjiao* 判教, or "classifying the teachings." *Panjiao* essentially involved ordering and explicating the different doctrines found in important Buddhist scriptures according to the time at which the Buddha supposedly preached them, his methods of instruction, or the scriptures' thematic content. Later Indian scholastic traditions were similarly classified according to their doctrinal emphases, such as Sarvāstivādin notions of causality versus the teaching of provisional existence in the *Satyasiddhiśāstra*, and the emptiness of the Madhyamaka.[18] This practice of *panjiao* was begun by Chinese scholar-monks in the early fifth century, and it became a central preoccupation of famous sixth- to eighth-century exegetes such as Jingying Huiyuan, Zhiyi, Jizang, Kuiji 窺基 (632–682) and Fazang 法藏 (643–712)—all of whom also played significant roles in the development of Indian patriarchal imagery during their times.[19]

The historical component of the *panjiao* classification method typically involved only the forty-five years during which Śākyamuni preached the Dharma. The soteriological import of a given scripture was seen to be directly affected by the time at which the Buddha preached it—especially

17. On Jizang's career, see especially Chen 1999, chap. 1 and 4; and Liu 1994, chap. 3.

18. See, for example, the discussion by Liu (1994, 116–117, 210–211) on the "four creeds" and "four teachings" delineated by Dilun and Tiantai masters, respectively.

19. Useful discussions of the *panjiao* schemes developed within this period include Gregory 1991, 93–170; Liu 1994, 110–135 (focusing on Jizang), 196–217 (focusing on Zhiyi); and Mun 2006.

whether, for example, this occurred just after his enlightenment or just before his nirvāṇa. And although similar efforts at classifying the teachings of later Indian masters lacked this historical dimension, the *panjiao* process of consolidating disparate views of Dharmic history during the Buddha's lifetime was carried over to like efforts at collating the chronologies of post-*parinirvāṇa* Indian Buddhism. From the sixth century, Chinese Buddhist authors worked to systematize the numerous historical statements found in earlier sources concerning the True and Semblance (and sometimes Final) Dharma periods, or the various chronologies emphasizing specific centuries after nirvāṇa that were marked by epoch-altering events or personages. As Jamie Hubbard explains, the underlying motive for these efforts to systematize the history of the Dharma was "the simple need for harmonizing (or at least making sense of) the various schemes that presented themselves in translated texts, exactly the same need that fueled the great systematization of . . . *panjiao*" (Hubbard 2001, 68–69). And in the same way, the attempts of this period to organize earlier accounts of the Indian patriarchs' historical contexts are best understood as part of this widespread movement toward simultaneously consolidating and elaborating Buddhist traditions of all varieties.

One important result of these attempts to harmonize earlier Indian patriarch accounts was the merging of Dharma decline narratives—which first framed the tales of Aśvaghoṣa, Nāgārjuna, and Āryadeva—with models of direct master-disciple transmission, which later presented a radically different vision of Dharmic history and thus paradigm of Buddhist sainthood. A prominent example of this fusion is found in the *Commentary on the Prajñā Scripture of Benevolent Kings Who Defend the Country* (*Renwang huguo bore jing shu* 仁王護國般若經疏), which was attributed to Zhiyi but likely compiled by an anonymous Tiantai exegete between the mid-seventh century and the mid-eighth:[20]

> Within one hundred years of the Buddha's departure, five men maintained [the Dharma]. The first was Kāśyapa, the second Ānanda, and the third Madhyāntika. These three men saw the Buddha in the world, and maintained [the Dharma] from one to the next. [Thus] through sixty years the practice of the Dharma was not extinguished. Next were Śāṇakavāsa and Upagupta. These two men did not see the Buddha, but still maintained [the Dharma] from one to the next. [Thus] over [the next] forty years the Dharma of proper decorum was extinguished. Therefore, it is said that by this time there was no Buddha, Dharma, or sangha.

20. On the dating and authorship of this commentary, see Satō (1961) 2005, 665–674. My thanks to Dan Stevenson for this reference. This section of the text may have been drawn from Jizang's *Renwang jing* 仁王經 commentary, which combined narratives of Dharma decline and lineal transmission in nearly identical fashion. See *Renwang bore jing shu*, T no. 1707, 33:357c.

As for what is termed "the eight hundred years," during the True Dharma period, twenty masters maintained the Buddhadharma. All were saintly men and the dharma was not extinguished. At six hundred years [after nirvāṇa, there was] Aśvaghoṣa Bodhisattva, and at seven hundred years Nāgārjuna. Both were bodhisattvas, so the Dharma was still not extinguished. By eight hundred years [after nirvāṇa] evil teachings came to flourish. Therefore, at this time [the Dharma] was bequeathed to kings. Deva Bodhisattva sounding the king's drum to propagate the Dharma was [an instance of] this. Eight thousand years [after nirvāṇa] is the time of the Final Dharma, when the Semblance Dharma has been exhausted. Sentient beings believe in falsehoods, so the Dharma is extinguished.

佛去百年內, 五人住持. 一迦葉, 二阿難, 三末田地. 三人見佛在世, 相次住持. 經六十年, 法行不滅. 次商那和修, 優波鞠多. 此二人不見佛, 相次住持. 經四十年, 威儀法滅. 故於此時, 言無佛法僧也.

言"八百年"者, 正法年內, 二十師住持佛法. 並是聖人, 法不滅. 第六百年馬鳴菩薩, 第七百年龍樹。皆是菩薩, 法亦不滅. 八百年中, 邪宗極盛. 故於此時, 付囑國王. 提婆菩薩, 聲王鼓申法是也. 八千年者, 像法盡末法時. 眾生信邪, 故法滅.[21]

Here commenting on the "Entrustment Chapter" (*zhulei pin* 囑累品) of the *Scripture of Benevolent Kings*, an influential Chinese Buddhist apocryphon, this text explained the Buddha's admonition to King Prasenajit about the destruction of the Three Jewels and the need to transmit the profound wisdom of this scripture to future kings and Buddhist disciples. The Buddha predicted successive stages of Dharma decline at eighty, eight hundred, and eight thousand years after nirvāṇa,[22] which accounts for the periodization described here. However, while the source text detailed the decay of the Dharma and emphasized the need for future generations to uphold and transmit the teaching in order to prevent its collapse, the superimposition of lineal master-disciple transmission upon this chronicle of declining Dharma was the work of its commentator. He included the earliest disciples of the Buddha who kept the Dharma in its most pristine state for sixty years after nirvāṇa, but then with Śāṇakavāsa and Upagupta a certain decline was evident. This is because these two had not actually met the Buddha in person, and thus could not maintain "proper decorum" (i.e., fidelity to Vinaya regulations) in the same way that his direct disciples could. The commentator then explained the Buddha's eight-hundred-year prophesy by emphasizing that because of the saintly character of the twenty patriarchs who transmitted the teaching through the True Dharma period—presumably spanning five centuries—it suffered no further decline. Then at six hundred and seven hundred years after nirvāṇa, respectively, Aśvaghoṣa and Nāgārjuna appeared, and they were able to maintain the Dharma untarnished because, simply stated, they were bodhisattvas. But at eight

21. *Renwang huguo bore jing shu* 仁王護國般若經疏, T no. 1705, 33:285b.
22. See Orzech 1998, 287.

hundred years after the Buddha's departure, the winds of Dharma had again changed, and now it was time for great kings, august defenders of nations, to take the reins in perpetuating the Buddhist truth. This period was exemplified by Āryadeva, whose king-conversion episode from the *Dharma-Treasury Transmission* now served to illustrate Dharma decline amidst lineal patriarchy.

In this way the *Commentary on the Scripture of Benevolent Kings* amalgamated the paradigms of Indian Buddhist history and sainthood presented in the writings of Kumārajva's associates and in the *Dharma-Treasury Transmission*. The earliest accounts of Aśvaghoṣa, Nāgārjuna, and Āryadeva frequently emphasized these patriarchs' triumphs in dark times, several centuries after nirvāṇa, when the Dharma was nearly lost to a world populated by fools. Then in the *Dharma-Treasury Transmission*, which described a lineage of Indian patriarchs spanning some two dozen generations after nirvāṇa, Aśvaghoṣa, Nāgārjuna, and Āryadeva were shown living in a world uplifted by True Dharma transmitters. These two visions of Dharmic history were both advanced in (ostensibly) Indic scriptures and were equally compelling for Chinese Buddhists trying to determine how best to propagate the Dharma in their own time and place. Thus these schemes had to be reconciled with one another in terms of how Indian patriarchal models were conceived—models that became increasingly important to the localization of Buddhist enlightenment. One way to resolve this discrepancy, as in this commentary and elsewhere, was to assert that the decline of the Dharma continued inexorably even though the greatest Indian masters had transmitted the teaching in succession since the time of Śākyamuni.[23] As such, the decline prophesy from the *Scripture of Benevolent Kings*, the lineal succession of the *Dharma-Treasury Transmission*, and the chronologies of the earliest Indian patriarch accounts were all properly reconciled, while Aśvaghoṣa, Nāgārjuna, and Āryadeva alone were advanced as upholding the teaching after the True Dharma period.

While this melding of Dharmic histories served to resolve discrepancies between earlier authoritative sources, it also laid the groundwork for countering the implication in the *Dharma-Treasury Transmission* that the highest truth of Indian Buddhism had never finally reached China. Although evil teachings had come to flourish and the Dharma would still devolve through the Semblance and Final periods, Aśvaghoṣa, Nāgārjuna, and Āryadeva propagated the teaching before its most precipitous decline. This was an important point for the numerous Chinese scholar-monks who in particular promoted the writings of these Indian patriarchs. Aśvaghoṣa, Nāgārjuna, and Āryadeva could not be allowed to just blend in with the crowd of Indian masters, as they did in the *Dharma-Treasury Transmission*,

23. This model had partial precedent in the writings of Lushan Huiyuan (Adamek 2007, 35), the *Mahāmāyā Sūtra*, and the *Dharma-Treasury Transmission*, which also included scattered references to Dharma decline (if not in its accounts of Aṣvaghośa, Nāgārjuna, or Āryadeva).

and the profundity of their treatises could not be asserted only in doctrinal terms. Rather, these works had to be seen as arising from the most significant junctures of Indian Buddhist history, when only the doctrinal discourse of the greatest Buddhist saints could save the world from destruction. Thus it made sense for Buddhist exegetes to reassert the sort of Dharmic history that Kumārajīva's associates first employed in their Indian patriarch accounts, according to which the Dharma was nearly extinguished before Aśvaghoṣa, Nāgārjuna, and Āryadeva arose to set things right.

Indeed, many scholar-monks of the Sui-Tang period reinscribed this narrative of Dharma decline in order to valorize the writings of their post-*parinirvāṇa* Indian predecessors. Jizang, for one, often claimed that Nāgārjuna and Āryadeva composed their treatises in order to check the heretical teachings that had arisen over the generations after nirvāṇa.[24] And in the same way, the *Awakening of Faith* commentaries attributed to Huiyuan and composed by Fazang both asserted that Aśvaghoṣa wrote his *magnum opus* in order to save sentient beings mired in evil times.[25] As the former commentary explained:

> During the time of the True Dharma, the Great Saint's departure was recent, so people had the capacity for genuine faith and there was no heterodoxy. Seven hundred years later, the Great Saint's departure was distant and all of the saintly disciples had followed[26] the Buddha into extinction, so people had [only] the capacity for shallow faith. Because of this decline of the times, non-Buddhist heterodoxies flourished throughout the world. . . . For this reason Aśvaghoṣa Bodhisattva then appeared, taking pity on sentient beings dragged into inhuman streams [of rebirth]. Fearing that the Buddha's ultimate purpose would sink into oblivion, based on the *Laṅkāvatāra Sūtra* [Aśvaghoṣa] produced the *Treatise on the Awakening of Faith.*
>
> 正法之時, 大聖去近, 人根厚信, 故無異端. 七百歲後, 大聖去遠, 聖弟子眾, 遂佛滅度, 人根薄信. 以世衰故, 外道異端, 競興於世. . . . 是故復出, 馬鳴菩薩, 愍傷眾生, 拕非人流. 慼[厂@煩]佛出極意潛沒, 依楞伽經, 造出起信論.[27]

Thus, Aśvaghoṣa, Nāgārjuna, and Āryadeva were not to be seen as garden-variety patriarchs who handed down the Dharma undimmed over the generations after nirvāṇa, as in the *Dharma-Treasury Transmission* and elsewhere. This triad did not live in the halcyon days of the Buddha's light kept bright by the lineage of True Dharma transmitters. Rather, even though

24. E.g., *Zhongguan lun shu*, T no. 1824, 42:13a–b; and *Bailun shu*, T no. 1827, 42:233a–c (trans. Robinson 1967, 23–24).

25. The ascription of the *Dasheng qixin lun yishu* 大乘起信論義疏 to Huiyuan is considered spurious; see Lai 1975, 193. Even so, it could not have been composed later than the seventh century. For Fazang's comments see *Dasheng qixin lun yiji* 大乘起信論義記, T no. 1846, 44:246a; trans. Vorenkamp 2004, 57.

26. Here reading *sui* 遂 as *zhu* 逐.

27. *Dasheng qixin lun yishu*, T no. 1843, 44:175c–176a.

the model of master-disciple succession was beginning to make inroads in Chinese attempts to propagate Buddhism locally, and this model had become integrated within commentarial traditions elaborating the careers of the Indian patriarchs, Dharma degradation nevertheless remained the primary order of the day. Aśvaghoṣa, Nāgārjuna, and Āryadeva were thus elevated above the rest of the Indian patriarchs in part because they championed the True Dharma within singularly trying times. And as the accounts of Jizang, Huiyuan (?), and Fazang also emphasized, these great masters were seen to have resurrected the Buddhist truth in post-*parinirvāṇa* India with the very same exegetical treatises that subsequently served as focal points for contemporary Chinese Buddhist doctrinal discourse—the *Great Perfection of Wisdom Treatise*, the *Middle Treatise*, the *Hundred Treatise*, and the *Awakening of Faith*.

In fact, Chinese scholar-monks of the time considered it the primary duty of the greatest patriarchs-*cum*-bodhisattvas who lived after the Buddha to compose doctrinal treatises in order to rescue deluded beings and transmit the truth to future generations. Huiyuan, for one, defined *lun* 論 in precisely these terms, as opposed to lesser sorts of writings such as "interpretive essays" (*yizhang* 義章) that the common rabble composed.[28] In dark times after Śākyamuni's departure, sentient beings ultimately depended on these *lun* in order to obtain liberation. Just as beings at the time of the Buddha were most suited to liberation through the scriptures that he preached, the karmic conditions of beings in the latter age dictated that they would require the sort of doctrinal commentary that the Indian patriarchs offered in their writings. Consequently, one should revere doctrinal treatises of the latter age just the same as scriptures preached by the Buddha himself.[29] The greatest Indian patriarchs did what was most appropriate for their times, composing exegetical commentaries suited to the weakened proclivities of contemporary beings and thereby upholding the Buddhist truth for future generations through the vehicle of the written word. And given access to the treatises that Aśvaghoṣa, Nāgārjuna, and Āryadeva had authored to save the benighted beings of their own times, Buddhist adepts of later generations could likewise benefit from the truth transmitted. These points are made clear in Jizang's *Commentary on the Twelve Gates Treatise* (*Shi'ermenlun shu* 十二門論疏):

> Sentient beings have confused the teaching, and their erroneous interpretations have obscured the true scriptures. Now wishing to requite on high the benevolence of the Buddha, his great purpose is briefly explained. The present text [of Nāgārjuna's *Twelve Gates Treatise*] is concise and easy to understand;

28. *Dasheng qixinlun yishu*, T no. 1843, 44:175c.

29. This line of reasoning is stressed, for example, in Jizang's *Sanlun xuanyi* 三論玄義, T no. 1852, 45:10a; *Shi'ermenlun shu* 十二門論疏, T no. 1825, 42:179a; and *Weimo jing yi shu* 維摩經義疏, T no. 1781, 38:911b.

it can be *forever transmitted to distant generations*.[30] Thus the *Māyā Scripture* says, "Nāgārjuna Bodhisattva lit the lamp of the True Dharma, and destroyed the banners of false views."[31] Dharma-master Kumārajīva said, "Nāgārjuna Bodhisattva made the great Dharma of the Thus Come One arise for the third time in Jambudvīpa."[32] A biography of Nāgārjuna says:

"The sun of wisdom had been eclipsed
but this man caused it to shine again;
the world had long been asleep in darkness,
but this man awoke it."[33]

眾生迷教，邪義覆於正經．今欲上報佛恩，略明大意．今文約而易顯，久傳於遐代．故摩耶經云，"龍樹菩薩，燃正法炬，滅邪見幢．" 什法師云，"龍樹菩薩，令如來大法，三啟閻浮．" 龍樹傳云:

"智慧日已頹，
斯人令再耀；
世昏寢已久，
斯人悟令覺."[34]

In light of sources indicating that the Indian patriarchate was ultimately unable to prevent the decline of the teaching, such assurances that Aśvaghoṣa's, Nāgārjuna's, and Āryadeva's doctrinal treatises succeeded in transmitting the Dharma would lead Chinese Buddhists to uphold these patriarchs' writings in lieu of direct master-disciple succession as the best means of propagating Buddhism locally. On the one hand, as previously noted, the Indian patriarchate of the *Dharma-Treasury Transmission* had already been severed long before it reached Chinese masters, so a direct master-disciple link between India and China would require refuting this well-known and authoritative Indic translation (and "sūtra," according to some). On the other hand, the eventual severance of the lineage in the *Dharma-Treasury Transmission* turned out to be of little consequence, since after Aśvaghoṣa, Nāgārjuna, and Āryadeva the Dharma was thought to have declined precipitously through the succeeding generations of Indian patriarchs. Therefore, aside from the scriptures preached by the Buddha himself, the treatises of this patriarchal triad were lauded as representing

30. Empahsis added.

31. *Mohemoye jing*, T no. 383, 12:1013c.

32. Qi fashi attributed a similar statement to Sengrui. See the *Sanlun youyi yi*, T no. 1855, 45:119a, according to which the Buddha was first to propagate the True Dharma, Aśvaghoṣa was second, and Nāgārjuna third.

33. This statement is preserved in Sengrui's preface to the *Da zhidu lun* (大智度論 [*Mahāprajñāpāramitāśāstra*], T no. 1509, 25:57b; *Chu sanzang jiji* 出三藏記集, T no. 2145, 55:75a); see chapter 1 of the present volume. As suggested by Chen Jinhua (personal communication), it would make sense for 悟令覺 in the last line to read 令悟覺, in parallel with 令再耀, which appears above it. However, only the former reading is attested in all other sources that quote these verses.

34. *Shi'ermenlun shu*, T no. 1825, 42:180a.

the highest expression of Buddhist truth available to latter-day Chinese adepts. And, as Jizang asserted, the karmic conditions of beings during the latter age were no longer suited to enlightenment through scriptural revelation; rather, these beings were karmically connected to the Indian patriarchs and the sort of doctrinal discourse that their treatises provided. Such texts, then, would be the most appropriate means for Chinese Buddhists to propagate the Dharma in their own time and place. These treatises had, in fact, freed the Buddhist truth from the trajectory of decline that the Indian patriarchate could no longer prevent, and they represented a moment in Buddhist history when the Dharma had not yet deteriorated beyond recognition—precisely because Aśvaghoṣa, Nāgārjuna, and Āryadeva championed the truth in otherwise pernicious times. So now their texts could serve as a new starting point for Chinese Buddhists to begin their own transmission lineages, and the written word would form the primary link between the apex of the Indian patriarchate and Chinese masters working to localize the means of Buddhist enlightenment.

Guanding's Introduction to the *Great Calming and Contemplation*

This juxtaposition between the images of Aśvaghoṣa, Nāgārjuna, and Āryadeva as propagating the teaching through exegetical authorship, as shining beacons in an otherwise dark portrait of declining Dharma, and as links in a failed Dharma lineage, was doubtless one important factor underlying the first known Chinese claim to lineal descent from the Indian patriarchs of the *Dharma-Treasury Transmission*. This claim was advanced by the eminent Tiantai master Guanding, who in his introduction to the *Great Calming and Contemplation* (*Mohe zhiguan* 摩訶止觀) connected his Tiantai predecessors Zhiyi, Huisi 慧思 (515–568) and Huiwen 慧文 (fl. 550s) to the *Dharma-Treasury Transmission* lineage—and the Buddha Śākyamuni thereby—not through direct master-disciple transmission but through Nāgārjuna's *Great Perfection of Wisdom Treatise*. Guanding affirmed the account of the *Dharma-Treasury Transmission* according to which the last patriarch of the Indian lineage, *bhikṣu* Siṃha, was killed before transmitting the teaching any further. Thus Guanding made no attempt to link Siṃha's generation with this newly formed line of Chinese patriarchs, as would the Chan historiographers of the eighth and ninth centuries. But because his Tiantai masters had based their teachings on the *Great Perfection of Wisdom Treatise*, so Guanding claimed, the "high ancestral master" (*gaozushi* 高祖師)[35] of the Tiantai tradition was none other than Nāgārjuna, whose written exegesis thus formed a crucial link between the Indian origins of Buddhism and the greatest Buddhist saints of China.

---

35. *Mohe zhiguan* 摩訶止觀, T no. 1911, 46:1b; trans. Donner and Stevenson 1993, 107; and Penkower 2000, 259.

Much like his contemporary Jizang, Guanding was a well-known and highly regarded scholar-monk whose efforts at defining Buddhist orthodoxy intertwined with projects orchestrated by the Sui regime to strengthen its claims to power.[36] In the years following the death of the illustrious Zhiyi, who himself enjoyed lavish imperial patronage, Guanding took to compiling and editing a series of literary encomia for his deceased master. These included the official biography of Zhiyi,[37] Zhiyi's lectures constituting the *Great Calming and Contemplation*, and a collection of documents relating to the Tiantai community based around Guoqing monastery 國清寺.[38] As several scholars have shown, these works were aimed in part at securing continued state support for the Tiantai institution after Zhiyi's death. One way to do this was to assert that Zhiyi and thus the Tiantai tradition that he left behind were the principal Chinese representatives of original Indian Buddhism, which the imperial court likewise sought to uphold and incorporate. Guanding made this assertion in his newly compiled documents by associating Zhiyi with several different founts of Indian Buddhist authority, including the Indian missionary Buddhabhadra, the Buddha's preaching of the *Lotus Sūtra* on Vulture Peak, and especially the Indian patriarchal lineage of the *Dharma-Treasury Transmission*.[39] In this way, just as Sui emperors Wen and Yang worked to transform their kingdom into a new epicenter of Buddhist enlightenment, Guanding's writings served to negotiate "the transference of Real Buddhism from India to China" and thereby improve the standing of his Tiantai tradition in the eyes of the imperial court (Cole 2009, 39).

Among these projects initiated by Guanding to imbue his tradition with the aura of Indian authority, the introduction to the *Great Calming and Contemplation* has drawn particular attention as a "watershed" in the development of Chinese Buddhist "sectarian consciousness" (Penkower 2000, 246), as it inaugurated a series of similar efforts to valorize local Chinese traditions by connecting them with the Indian patriarchate. While Guanding's brief Tiantai genealogy was not necessarily "the first known attempt of any kind to define a Chinese teacher (or text) in terms of a succession theory" (ibid., 268; Morrison 2010, 32), as we saw with Sengyou's *Record of the Sarvāstivāda* (*Sapoduo bu ji* 薩婆多部記), it was nonetheless an important precursor to the Chan and Tiantai master-disciple lineages that began to proliferate during the Tang. Linda Penkower provides a thorough account of Guanding's early Tiantai lineage, offering a convincing argument for when and why it was produced—in terms of changes in temple inheritance

36. On Guanding's relations with the Sui court, which to some extent were overblown by later biographers, see Chen 1999, 46–53.

37. *Sui Tiantai Zhizhe dashi biezhuan* 隋天台智者大師別傳, T no. 2050; compiled ca. 601–605. See also Cole 2009, 43–49; and Shinohara 1992.

38. *Guoqing bailu* 國清百錄, T no. 1934; compiled ca. 601–607. See Cole 2009, 39–42; and Shinohara 1992.

39. On Buddhabhadra, see Morrison 2010, 33–35. On the Buddha's preaching on Vulture Peak, see Cole 2009, 45–46; and Penkower 2000, 261–262.

structures and contemporary drives to consolidate religio-political power in the wake of Zhiyi's death and during the transition from the Sui dynasty to the Tang.[40] And although Penkower also details the processes by which Guanding's introduction coalesced into the structure that has come down to us, her analysis leaves room for further consideration of the role that Nāgārjuna's *Great Perfection of Wisdom Treatise* played in this construct. In particular, two fundamental questions remain: Why, for one, did Guanding see Indian doctrinal treatises in general as the most effective means of connecting Western and Eastern patriarchal lineages, and why did he choose Nāgārjuna's *Great Perfection of Wisdom Treatise* in particular? By considering the niche that Chinese Buddhists were carving for Indian doctrinal treatises—particularly as juxtaposed with Dharma transmission through master-disciple lineages—as well as Nāgārjuna's importance to Chinese scholar-monks of all persuasions since the early fifth century, one can see in sharper focus the reasons for Guanding's choice of this particular Indian master and treatise.

In order to understand Guanding's reliance on an Indian treatise to connect the *Dharma-Treasury Transmission* lineage with his Chinese masters, we might first recall how contemporary sources decried the inability of the Indian patriarchate to forestall the decline of the Dharma. Given this fact, it makes sense that Guanding would not have considered the latter patriarchs of the *Dharma-Treasury Transmission* to be the most propitious starting point for his own Dharma lineage. And although he did recount the death of Siṃha from the end of the *Dharma-Treasury Transmission*, Guanding did not appear overly concerned with the fact that the Indian lineage was terminated at that point. Instead, he lauded the efforts of all members of the patriarchate and proclaimed the benefits of hearing their teachings.[41] In this regard as well, Guanding followed the *Dharma-Treasury Transmission*, upholding the saving power of the Dharma regardless of the ultimate fate of its transmission lineage. However, by singling out the work of Nāgārjuna as the foundation for his own tradition, Guanding made a similar move as his contemporaries in conceiving the Indian lineage as an arc rather than a flat line—with Nāgārjuna's *Great Perfection of Wisdom Treatise* representing the apex of all the patriarchs' accomplishments. And since such treatises were upheld in contemporary accounts as the most effective means of eliminating confusion during the Indian patriarchs' own times, as well as perpetuating the truth for future generations, Guanding would no doubt have seen these texts as a most appropriate link between Indian and Chinese

40. Penkower (2000, 271) argues that the extant lineage statement "may have appeared as early as 607 but was probably completed not long before Guanding's death in 632." Cf. Cole 2009, 49n40.

41. *Mohe zhiguan*, T no. 1911, 46:1b; trans. Donner and Stevenson 1993, 103. Morrison (2010, 37; following Barrett 1990, 93) similarly argues that Guanding was "indifferent to the seeming demise of the dharma because he believe[d] it to have been continued elsewhere"—with Nāgārjuna's writings.

patriarchs, especially since the *Dharma-Treasury Transmission* clearly stated that the Indian lineage was severed with Siṃha.

This general consideration of Nāgārjuna's placement at the apogee of the Indian patriarchate provides a good starting point for explaining Guanding's focus on the *Great Perfection of Wisdom Treatise* in particular. But for more specific reasons underlying Guanding's selection of this text, scholars often turn to the aforementioned thesis of sectarian competition. This thesis basically runs as follows: Guanding's main competition for imperial patronage at the time was Jizang and his Sanlun tradition; Jizang and Guanding saw themselves as representing mutually exclusive Buddhist traditions, each with a claim to absolute truth and each with its own Indian basis of authority—primarily the Three Treatises for Jizang and the *Lotus Sūtra* for Guanding; so Guanding appropriated Jizang's Indian textual foundation—-i.e., the writings of Nāgārjuna—as a sectarian *coup de maître* aimed at unseating Sanlun at court and establishing Tiantai in its place. Penkower provides a compelling example of this line of thought, building on the work of several Japanese scholars who maintain that "the natural affinity between Tiantai and the Madhyamaka-oriented ideas of the Sanlun and Silun 四論 traditions . . . may have combined with political realities to influence Guanding to designate Nāgārjuna, the founder of the Madhyamaka school in India, to the position of 'high ancestor' of Tiantai" (Penkower 2000, 282). Alan Cole also argues that Guanding's use of Nāgārjuna "as the crucial Indian pivot appears all the more aggressive, and derivative, as Nāgārjuna had already been claimed by Guanding's rival [Jizang] in this game of truth-by-ancestors" (Cole 2009, 61). And along similar lines, according to Elizabeth Morrison, "Just as Sanlun advocates reacted to the prominence of other schools, like the Chengshi [成實; Satyasiddhi] . . . the growing prestige of the Sanlun in the late sixth century prompted a response from the nascent Tiantai community" to produce this lineage connecting Zhiyi to the Buddha through Nāgārjuna (Morrison 2010, 32).

However, while it certainly makes sense to view this well-documented competition between Guanding and Jizang as a proximal cause for Guanding's appropriation of the *Great Perfection of Wisdom Treatise*—especially since Guanding appears to have "borrowed" from Jizang's writings on several other occasions (as Jizang had done with Zhiyi)[42]—this particular line of influence has perhaps been overdetermined. For centuries before Guanding and Jizang, the figure of Nāgārjuna, his corpus of writings and especially the *Great Perfection of Wisdom Treatise* had been employed by Chinese exegetes of all traditions to authorize Buddhist ideals and practices across a broad spectrum. Nāgārjuna had never been the exclusive property of any one Chinese Buddhist tradition, and he was never viewed, even by Jizang or other Sanlun advocates, as the founder of a specific sect such as the Madhyamaka. His *Great Perfection of Wisdom Treatise* in particular contained detailed exegesis of doctrines and practices that far exceeded the bounds of

42. See, e.g., Penkower 2000, 289–291.

exclusively Madhyamaka or Sanlun concerns—concerns that were, moreover, determined largely in a medieval Japanese context and later read into the writings of fifth- to seventh-century Chinese exegetes. From the time of Kumārajīva, Chinese authors always represented Nāgārjuna as a master of all Buddhist (and non-Buddhist) teachings, as both his hagiographies and voluminous writings clearly attested, and by the Sui-Tang period he had become a synecdoche for all things Mahāyāna. As such, Jizang's claim to the authority of this Three Treatise master was but one of many such claims throughout Chinese Buddhist history, and Guanding had equal right and ample precedent to assert the importance of Nāgārjuna's exegesis to his own Tiantai tradition.

In addition, while Guanding's use of the *Great Perfection of Wisdom Treatise* accords with this general trend throughout medieval China of eliciting Nāgārjuna to support all kinds of Buddhist teachings, there are also more specific congruencies between the early hagiographic depictions of Nāgārjuna and the ways in which Guanding attempted to portray his master Zhiyi. In particular, Penkower and Wendi Adamek emphasize how Guanding worked to cement Zhiyi's legacy both by portraying him as the recipient of Buddhist tradition through the Indian lineage and by highlighting his innate brilliance and personal discovery of the Buddhist truth. This latter basis for Zhiyi's authority was indicated by tales of his miraculous birth, his portentous physiognomy (having double pupils), and his self-awakening achieved through a meditative repentance practice based on the *Lotus Sūtra*.[43] Similarly, the earlier tale of Zhiyi and Huisi personally attending Śākyamuni's *Lotus* sermon on Vulture Peak underscored their direct access to the Buddhist truth, without need for further instruction from Indian masters or commentarial treatises. As such, according to Penkower, Guanding claimed for Zhiyi what had been claimed for the Buddha Śākyamuni, "namely, that his authority is sufficient unto itself and does not rely on what he has learned from a teacher" (Penkower 2000, 262). Nevertheless, Guanding's rehearsal of the *Dharma-Treasury Transmission* and claim to Nāgārjuna as Tiantai's "high ancestral master" also ensured that Zhiyi was joined with the Buddha in quasi-genealogical fashion. This juxtaposition, as Adamek puts it, provided "an elegant solution to the problem of validating both the continuity of transmitted teachings and the discontinuity of individual insight" (Adamek 2007, 112). But it also served to create a clear resonance between Zhiyi and the earlier hagiographic imagery of Nāgārjuna. Just as Zhiyi was chosen to carry on the Dharma-Treasury transmission by virtue of his own innate brilliance, as Guanding implied, Nāgārjuna was likewise depicted as both a self-made saint and a recipient of Buddhist tradition through patriarchal transmission.

---

43. *Mohe zhiguan*, T no. 1911, 46:1b; trans. Donner and Stevenson 1993, 104–105. Double pupils were a mark of sanctity from ancient times in China, especially for sage-kings; see Cole 2009, 44n31.

At several points so far I have noted the tension in medieval China between representing Aśvaghoṣa, Nāgārjuna, and Āryadeva as singular exemplars of Buddhist sainthood and as placeholders in lineages of master-disciple succession. Kumārajīva's associates first depicted these patriarchs as lone beacons of light in the darkness, while the *Dharma-Treasury Transmission* showed them standing in a long line of similarly brilliant saints. But in the case of Nāgārjuna, this latter hagiography also instantiated the former model of Buddhist sanctity, albeit without the emphasis on decline and revival that marked Nāgārjuna's earliest accounts. As outlined in the previous chapter, the *Dharma-Treasury Transmission* was the first Chinese source to claim that Nāgārjuna directly succeeded another master, as he ostensibly received Dharma transmission from Vīra. But at the same time, according to this account, Nāgārjuna was awakened to the Buddhist truth through his own efforts at mastering a cache of scriptures revealed to him in the undersea palace of a great dragon bodhisattva. This tale of Nāgārjuna's dragon-palace sojourn, akin to the earlier prefaces by Sengrui, Tanying, and Huiyuan, would therefore seem at odds with the emphasis on master-disciple Dharma transmission. But this discrepancy arises only if we understand that model as signaling the necessity of Buddhist preceptors for the realization of Buddhist truth. However, since Nāgārjuna achieved enlightenment through his own study of the *vaipulya* scriptures, his receipt of the Dharma-treasury transmission was portrayed as the effect rather than the cause of his sanctity. Nāgārjuna's placement in the lineage did not indicate his reliance on Vīra, who did not confer any truths that Nāgārjuna did not already know; rather, Vīra simply sanctioned the awakening that Nāgārjuna had achieved on his own. From this standpoint the lineal succession was one of discovery rather than transmission, with Dharma masters simply finding and announcing the next great talent rather than teaching their disciples the means to true enlightenment. As such, Nāgārjuna's dragon-palace enlightenment and his meeting with Vīra were complementary aspects of his career, with his induction into the Dharma-treasury lineage serving both to validate his self-realization and invest within him the totality of Indian Buddhist tradition.

Such was the case with Guanding's portrayal of Zhiyi in the introduction to the *Great Calming and Contemplation*, which recounted both sources of Nāgārjuna's authority before repeating them in the figure of Zhiyi.[44] Guanding's text thus followed Nāgārjuna's modes of hagiographic representation at the same time that it emphasized how Zhiyi instantiated Nāgārjuna's model of doctrinal exegesis. Here Zhiyi's placement at the

44. *Mohe zhiguan*, T no. 1911, 46:1a: 法付龍樹 . . . 龍成法身 "The Dharma was transmitted to Nāgārjuna . . . a dragon completed his Dharma-body." Cf. trans. Donner and Stevenson 1993, 102. Also, while Donner and Stevenson here have Kapimala as Nāgārjuna's master (following Yampolsky 1967), this is probably not the proper rendering of Guanding's Piluo 毘羅. As noted in the previous chapter, Yampolsky's (1967, 8) Kapimala is based on the Jiapimoluo 迦毘摩羅 of the ninth-century *Baolin zhuan*, not the Biluo 比羅 of the *Dharma-Treasury Transmission* itself.

Chinese end of the Dharma-treasury lineage functioned to sanction his innate brilliance and his sermons constituting the *Great Calming and Contemplation*, rather than indicating his reliance on the line of Indian masters. Similarly, Guanding adduced Nāgārjuna and his *Great Perfection of Wisdom Treatise* as analogues to Zhiyi and his *Great Calming and Contemplation*, with the former sanctioning the latter as equals rather than serving as requisite instructional guides. As such, Guanding's use of these Indian media in fact signaled a move away from Indian sources of authority and toward the creation of local Chinese founts of Buddhist enlightenment—as in the person, practices, and teachings of Zhiyi. The *Great Calming and Contemplation*, otherwise advertised as an "integrated systemization of the totality of received tradition" (Penkower 2000, 278), was here presented as the Chinese equivalent to Nāgārjuna's *Great Perfection of Wisdom Treatise*, which was widely viewed as the paragon among Indian doctrinal treatises of the same sort of comprehensive, universalist teaching that Zhiyi (via Guanding) claimed to deliver. In this way, Zhiyi's natural brilliance and self-realization were perfectly encapsulated within his exegetical *magnum opus*,[45] which was validated by the *Dharma-Treasury Transmission* lineage and Nāgārjuna especially as a foremost source of Dharmic truth on a par with anything produced in India. And now with the *Great Calming and Contemplation* to hand, Chinese scholar-monks and secular rulers could look no further than their own borders for the greatest manifestation of Buddhist enlightenment.

The *Awakening of Faith* in Aśvaghoṣa's Repertoire

In much the same way that Nāgārjuna's *Great Perfection of Wisdom Treatise* was seen to transmit the epitome of Indian Buddhist tradition to latter-day China—instantiating both the culmination of the Indian patriarchate and the unique content of Nāgārjuna's dragon-palace enlightenment—Aśvaghoṣa's most famous doctrinal treatise was likewise conceived to localize the highest truth of Indian Buddhism. I previously noted the proliferation of texts attributed to Aśvaghoṣa, Nāgārjuna, and Āryadeva after the time of Kumārajīva, which both resulted from and contributed to the widespread popularity of these Indian patriarchs in China. Without doubt the most important of these texts was Aśvaghoṣa's *Treatise on the Mahāyāna Awakening of Faith*, which was a ubiquitous source of Indian authority in Chinese doctrinal discourses throughout the Sui-Tang period. Purportedly translated by Paramārtha (499–569) in the early 550s and again by Śikṣānanda (652–710) around the beginning of the eighth century, this text has long been identified as a Chinese apocryphon.[46] As such, modern scholars have

45. A similar point is made by Cole 2009, 50.

46. Liebenthal (1959) provides the fullest discussion in English on the provenance of the *Awakening of Faith*. He largely follows Demiéville's (1929) masterful work in French on the same issue, as well as Japanese scholars such as Mochizuki (1922, 1938) and Tokiwa (1943–1944) who pioneered the modern debate over the text's authenticity. The most thorough ex-

most often viewed it as an important index to the doctrinal concerns of medieval Chinese Buddhists, especially of the Dilun and Yogācāra traditions. Less attention has been paid, however, to the role that this ostensibly Indian doctrinal treatise played in Sui-Tang Chinese efforts to localize Indian paradigms of Buddhist sainthood. Alan Cole, for one, maintains that the central agenda of the *Awakening of Faith* was to encapsulate the entirety of Indian Buddhist truth and tradition and make it accessible to Chinese adepts without further need for Indian scriptural or patriarchal authority. Given that the text was nonetheless attributed to a famous Indian patriarch, Cole (2005, 12) reads it as one of several medieval Chinese examples of "relying on India to end reliance on India"—as with Guanding's use of Nāgārjuna to show that the totality of Indian Buddhism was perfectly enshrined within the works of Zhiyi. But while Cole (ibid., 4) offers a promising analysis of this text's agenda in terms of its doctrinal focus on the embryo of Buddhahood inherent within all sentient beings—and thus always already present in China—Aśvaghoṣa's role in this agenda deserves further consideration. In particular, if this treatise was intended to relocate the crux of Indian Buddhism to China, as Cole argues, what would Aśvaghoṣa have been seen to contribute to this transmission? Why would this particular patriarch have been selected as the most appropriate Indian author for the *Awakening of Faith*, and what was the relationship between the paradigms of Buddhist sainthood that Aśvaghoṣa exemplified and the contents and contexts of this purportedly Indian doctrinal treatise?

Modern scholarly consensus is that only three extant texts were actually composed by Aśvaghoṣa: the *Acts of the Buddha* (*Buddhacarita*), *Nanda the Fair* (*Saundarananda*) and the fragmentary *Play on Śāriputra* (*Śāriputraprakaraṇa*).[47] All three are classical Sanskrit poems that elaborate early Buddhist teachings; they evince little concern with even prototypical Mahāyāna ideals, much less the sort of intricate synthesis of advanced Mahāyāna constructs that characterizes the *Awakening of Faith*.[48] Therefore, scholars typically banish the notion that Aśvaghoṣa authored such a text, arguing that this preeminent Indian poet and Hīnayāna devotee could not possibly have written a philosophical tract having to do with "storehouse consciousness" (*ālayavijñāna*; *alaiye shi* 阿賴耶識) or the "embryo/womb of

---

amination of this debate is found in Kashiwagi (1981, 61–182), and handy English synopses are provided by Grosnick (1989, 65–66) and Lai (1990, 186–189). See also, more recently, Aramaki 2000, 78–84 (cited in Chen 2002, 37n72, 130n56); Girard 2004; and Seok 2010.

47. See Hakeda 1967, 5–6; and Johnson (1936) 1984, xviii.

48. Yamabe (2003, 227), for one, questions this standard assessment, arguing that "the methods of meditation practice described in the latter portion of the *Saundarananda* are closely related to those in the *Śrāvakabhūmi* section of the *Yogācārabhūmi*." In light of this similarity, Yamabe (2003, 243) asserts, "it seems very likely that Aśvaghoṣa was close to the meditative tradition that later formed the Yogācāra school." Nevertheless, Yamabe does not go so far as to suggest that Aśvaghoṣa might have actually composed the *Awakening of Faith*—Yogācāra characteristics of this treatise notwithstanding. Cf. Kashiwagi (1981, 106), who also notes similarities between the *Saundarananda* and *Awakening of Faith* in terms of their Yogācāra proclivities.

Buddhahood" (*tathāgatagarbha*; *rulai zang* 如来藏)—advanced Mahāyāna doctrines that were developed long after Aśvaghoṣa's death.[49] Medieval Chinese Buddhists, however, expressed no doubt about Aśvaghoṣa's authorship of the *Awakening of Faith*.[50] And in fact, given the hagiographic imagery of this patriarch that had developed up until the beginning of the seventh century, it would have made perfect sense to Chinese Buddhists of the time for Aśvaghoṣa to have composed this treatise.

Not long after the *Awakening of Faith* appeared in the late sixth century, it was hailed as a seminal exposition of the most important Mahāyāna principles, and many prominent Buddhist exegetes of the Sui-Tang period drew upon this text as an authority in explicating a variety of Mahāyāna ideals. Much like Nāgārjuna's and Āryadeva's treatises before it, the *Awakening of Faith* came to be seen as one of the most fundamental expressions of Mahāyāna truth produced after the time of the Buddha. And given this fact, it is instructive to recall the previously quoted statement by Jizang, according to which Aśvaghoṣa, Nāgārjuna, and Āryadeva alone aided Śākyamuni in propagating the Dharma after nirvāṇa. Similarly, Guanding joined Aśvaghoṣa with Nāgārjuna as the keystones of Mahāyāna Buddhism as a whole, and Jingying Huiyuan frequently invoked this pair of patriarchs to illustrate various points of Mahāyāna doctrine.[51] But these are just a few examples of the ubiquitous tendency in medieval Chinese sources to treat Aśvaghoṣa as a foundational figure for Mahāyāna exegesis across the board, and as joined particularly with Nāgārjuna (and Āryadeva) to form a dynamic duo (or triad) of post-*parinirvāṇa* Mahāyāna patriarchs. And while these examples all likely appeared after the *Awakening of Faith* had been attributed to Aśvaghoṣa—and thus could be seen primarily as testimony to the influence of this text alone—they nevertheless carried forth an age-old tradition of joining Aśvaghoṣa with the Three Treatise exegetes as the greatest champions of Mahāyāna Buddhism over the centuries after nirvāṇa.

While the attribution of the *Awakening of Faith* to Aśvaghoṣa greatly increased the popularity of this patriarch and effectively solidified his image as an unparalleled doctrinal author, Aśvaghoṣa was selected from among the host of available Indian patriarchs as author for this text precisely because he had already been celebrated since the time of Kumārajīva as one of the greatest Mahāyāna exegetes in Buddhist history. In early fifth-century

---

49. See, e.g., Demiéville 1929, 63–65; Hakeda 1967, 6; and Kashiwagi 1981, 101.

50. Fajing 法經 (n.d.) listed the *Awakening of Faith* as "suspect" (*yihuo* 疑惑) in his *Zhongjing mulu* 眾經目錄 (T no. 2146, 55:142a) of ca. 594; however, Fajing only doubted whether Paramārtha translated it, not that Aśvaghoṣa authored it. See Demiéville 1929, 4; Girard 2004, xxxiii; and Liebenthal 1959, 158. Also, later Japanese authors quoted a certain Huijun 慧均 (7th century) as saying that the *Awakening of Faith* was composed by a northern Chinese Dilun exegete. See Demiéville 1929, 66–67; Grosnick 1989, 65; and Liebenthal 1959, 156–157. However, this quote is not attested anywhere in medieval Chinese sources, nor is its skepticism concerning the text's Indian authorship.

51. For Guanding, see *Guoqing bailu*, T no. 1934, 46:817b. For Jingying Huiyuan, see, e.g., *Dasheng yizhang* 大乘義章, T no. 1851, 44:718b.

sources, Aśvaghoṣa was said to have unified the Greater and Lesser Vehicles rather than promoting the former above and against the latter. But over the following centuries in China, it came to be taken for granted that Mahāyāna masters harmonized all of Śākyamuni's teachings—which included both Vehicles—while only Hīnayāna advocates were exclusivist in their outlook on the Dharma. And since Aśvaghoṣa was depicted from the outset as ecumenical in his approach to the Buddha's teachings, he would by the sixth century be seen as the quintessential Mahāyāna bodhisattva who understood Śākyamuni's need to tailor his teachings to the proclivities of individual sentient beings.[52]

It was a common refrain within both the *Awakening of Faith* itself and its early commentaries that this text was composed to suit the weakened capacities of people living during the latter age of Buddhist history, when the True Dharma was nearly overrun by non-Buddhist dogmas. Of course, this was fairly standard rhetoric in a variety of Chinese sources produced around the beginning of the seventh century, when many Chinese Buddhists claimed to be living at the end of the Semblance Dharma period or amidst the Final Dharma. But because Aśvaghoṣa was so often depicted as a great savior and reviver of the Dharma within similarly pernicious times, it would have seemed perfectly sensible to sixth- and seventh-century Chinese Buddhists that the *Awakening of Faith* was the very text with which this patriarch had once demonstrated his skill in means. And again, because he was so closely connected with Nāgārjuna since the time of Kumārajīva, Aśvaghoṣa would have appeared to the anonymous Chinese author (or authors) of the *Awakening of Faith* as a most propitious choice for the author of a treatise composed to share the niche long occupied by texts like the *Middle Treatise* and *Great Perfection of Wisdom Treatise*—Indian doctrinal treatises written by the greatest Mahāyāna masters since Śākyamuni. And finally, with Aśvaghoṣa having been depicted from the outset as first and foremost a master of meditation practice, the *Awakening of Faith* would have further seemed an ideal match for this particular patriarch's expertise, given that this treatise was likewise conceived in part as a meditation manual intended to guide practitioners toward realization of the "One Mind" (*yixin* 一心). In these ways Aśvaghoṣa was the most logical choice for medieval Chinese

52. Kashiwagi (1981, 103–105) in particular assumes a firm delineation between Hīnayāna and Mahāyāna traditions in his attempt to locate early Chinese indications of Aśvaghoṣa's scholastic affiliation. Kashiwagi focuses especially on the two Indian lineages in Sengyou's *Record of the Sarvāstivāda*. In the first lineage the name Aśvaghoṣa appeared twice, while in the second it was listed only once; in both cases he was labeled a bodhisattva. Kashiwagi suspects that the second Aśvaghoṣa was omitted from the second list because its Chinese redactor (or redactors) took this Aśvaghoṣa to be a Mahāyāna master and thus inappropriate to this otherwise Hīnayāna list. However, as Wang (1994, 177–178, 193n19) rightly notes, in early Chinese sources a given master's vinaya or *nikāya* affiliation did not necessarily have any bearing on his perceived doctrinal persuasion (Hīnayāna or Mahāyāna). Further, medieval Chinese Buddhists never considered Aśvaghoṣa to be anything other than Mahāyāna, even if he was said to follow the Sarvāstivādin Vinaya—as were Nāgārjuna, Āryadeva, Vasubandhu, Kumārajīva, and many other famous Mahāyāna masters.

Buddhists as the author of the newly composed *Awakening of Faith*. With this seminal treatise thus ascribed to Aśvaghoṣa, not only did it serve to localize the means to enlightenment within latter-day China—through a program of meditative practice designed to awaken the embryo of Buddhahood inherent within every individual mind—but it also sanctioned Chinese Buddhist efforts to liberate beings through the practice of doctrinal authorship. With the *Awakening of Faith* to hand, Chinese scholar-monks now had access to the foremost means by which Buddhism had been saved in India and transmitted to China, as well as a model of exegetical writing that would enable them to propagate the True Dharma without further need for recourse to Indian authority.

The Aśvaghoṣa-Nāgārjuna Connection

The few scholars who have devoted some attention to Aśvaghoṣa's authorship of the *Awakening of Faith* have also noted in passing how his association with Nāgārjuna influenced Chinese conceptions of his prowess as a Mahāyāna exegete.[53] However, these brief comments do little justice to the fundamental impact of this connection on Aśvaghoṣa's early Chinese imagery. I have already cited several examples of the close relationship between these two patriarchs in Chinese sources from the time of Kumārajīva, and even a cursory search through the Chinese Buddhist canon reveals numerous instances of Aśvaghoṣa and Nāgārjuna being paired as the foremost champions of Mahāyāna Buddhism. From his introduction in China, Aśvaghoṣa was depicted as the predecessor and even acknowledged master of Nāgārjuna, who was otherwise the greatest Indian Mahāyāna champion known to the Chinese. Then, over the Sui-Tang period, this patriarchal association became common knowledge, as Aśvaghoṣa and Nāgārjuna were increasingly depicted upholding the Buddhist truth against all encroachment, or cited as authority in Chinese Buddhist discourse on all things Mahāyāna. With Aśvaghoṣa having been thus represented, the application of his name to the newly composed *Awakening of Faith* would surely have legitimized this text and its central agendas in the eyes of contemporary Chinese Buddhists. And in this regard we can point to one important factor underlying the *Awakening of Faith*'s ascription to Aśvaghoṣa—the simple need for the authority of a respected Indian master. But Aśvaghoṣa offered a certain brand of Indian authority, and one that was especially appealing to the medieval Chinese author (or authors) and audiences of the *Awakening of Faith*. This was the authority of the predecessor and teacher of Nāgārjuna, who was otherwise the archetype of Mahāyāna sainthood who reportedly followed Aśvaghoṣa's example of upholding the Dharma in dark times through the vehicle of the written word.

Together with the quasi-genealogical statements previously cited, according to which Aśvaghoṣa preceded Nāgārjuna in reviving the True

53. See, e.g., Demiéville 1929, 64; and Kashiwagi 1981, 111–112.

Dharma in specific centuries after nirvāṇa, a clear hierarchical relationship was established between these two patriarchs in the biography of Aśvaghoṣa preserved at Nanatsu-dera. In particular, this biography asserted, "Each time [Nāgārjuna] inked his quill and began composing treatises, he never failed to pay the utmost respect to Aśvaghoṣa. He composed verses for personally taking refuge and expressed his wish to rely on [Aśvaghoṣa's] profound illumination so as to become enlightened himself" (see appendix 1). I noted in chapter 1 that this is an otherwise unknown tradition in Chinese sources—of Nāgārjuna expressing such fervent praise for Aśvaghoṣa—but that it may be a remnant of the close stylistic relationship between Nāgārjuna's treatises and Aśvaghoṣa's *Saundarananda*. Nevertheless, this assertion of Nāgārjuna's dependence on Aśvaghoṣa's "profound illumination," in an almost master-disciple fashion, indeed reflects the otherwise well-known historical precedence of Aśvaghoṣa over Nāgārjuna in propagating the Mahāyāna in a world without a Buddha. Because medieval Chinese sources rarely suggested that Nāgārjuna personally met Aśvaghoṣa, Nāgārjuna's acknowledgment here of the debt owed Aśvaghoṣa would seemingly refer in particular to the writings that Aśvaghoṣa had bequeathed—in a manner not unlike Guanding's association between Zhiyi and Nāgārjuna's *Great Perfection of Wisdom Treatise*. But despite this and similar indications elsewhere of Aśvaghoṣa's impressive literary output, early Chinese Buddhists had only a small sampling of his work. In part because Nāgārjuna himself extolled Aśvaghoṣa's writings with such reverence, Chinese adepts would no doubt have longed to see more of the profound Mahāyāna exegesis that Aśvaghoṣa was said to have produced.

At the beginning of the fifth century, a number of Nāgārjuna's doctrinal treatises were translated into Chinese—including, most notably, the *Great Perfection of Wisdom Treatise*, the *Middle Treatise*, and the *Twelve Gates Treatise*, which accounted for two of the famous Three Treatises. Over the following centuries many more works attributed to Nāgārjuna would appear in China, thus providing tangible evidence for the numerous hagiographic assertions that Nāgārjuna resurrected the Dharma through doctrinal authorship. However, the similar hagiographic statements about Aśvaghoṣa must have rung somewhat hollow for fifth-century Chinese readers, who had only brief excerpts of his writings in the *Scripture on Seated Dhyāna Samādhi* (*Zuochan sanmei jing* 坐禪三昧經), and then somewhat later the *Buddhacarita* and *Sūtrālaṃkāra*—neither of which would have satisfied Chinese appetites for Indian Mahāyāna exegesis.[54] In this way, a demand was created for Aśvaghoṣa's foundational Mahāyāna treatises, which had been advertised

54. The *Buddhacarita* is a poetic biography of the Buddha, and the *Sūtrālaṃkāra* is a collection of *jātakas* and *avadānas*. Neither evinces any concern with Mahāyāna doctrine. The *Buddhacarita* appeared in Chinese translation during the first half of the fifth century; two versions were made, the *Fo suo xing zan* 佛所行讚 (T no. 192) and the *Fo benxing jing* 佛本行經 (T no. 193). On these translations, see Beal 1883 and Kanakura 1959, 303. The Chinese translation of the *Sūtrālaṃkāra* (*Da zhuangyan jing lun* 大莊嚴經論, T no. 201) was probably executed after ca. 515, when Sengyou completed his *Chu sanzang jiji*. See chapter 1.

as demonstrating a brilliance paralleled only by Nāgārjuna's own writings, and which could thus fit into the niche that works such as the *Middle Treatise* had already long occupied.

The *Awakening of Faith* was probably intended to share this Chinese niche for Indian Mahāyāna exegesis rather than to co-opt it outright. By the middle of the sixth century, Nāgārjuna and his treatises were already too well established as integral to the development of Mahāyāna Buddhism to be unseated or denigrated in any way. In fact, as previously demonstrated in the case of Guanding's introduction to the *Great Calming and Contemplation*, even when quasi-sectarian battles were taking place and it may have been in one party's interest to denounce his opponent's fount of authority, Guanding would not seek to undermine Jizang by attacking Nāgārjuna. Instead, Guanding likewise claimed Nāgārjuna's writings as the foundation for his Tiantai tradition. Further, nowhere in Chinese sources do we see any attempts to situate Aśvaghoṣa above and against Nāgārjuna or depict these two in any way as at odds with one another, even after the *Awakening of Faith* had gained a foothold in Chinese Buddhist discourse. Just as Nāgārjuna was not only a Mādhyamika, but rather encapsulated the entirety of Mahāyāna Buddhism, Aśvaghoṣa was likewise seen as transcending any doctrinal differentiations that had arisen among Mahāyāna proponents—particularly since the *Awakening of Faith* was composed as a synthesis of many prevailing modes of Buddhist thought and practice. For these reasons we should not view Nāgārjuna's expressions of reverent praise for Aśvaghoṣa as a sectarian polemic intended to devalue Nāgārjuna's own writings.[55] Rather, these statements were part and parcel of the broader trend throughout medieval China of linking these two patriarchs in succession as the greatest champions of Mahāyāna Buddhism over the centuries after nirvāṇa.

Aśvaghoṣa's *Dhyāna* Expertise

While both Aśvaghoṣa and Nāgārjuna were depicted predominantly as the greatest post-*parinirvāṇa* champions of Mahāyāna Buddhism across sectarian bounds, at the same time these patriarchs did have their own specific doctrinal identities. Particularly as author of the *Great Perfection of Wisdom Treatise*—a voluminous commentary on a wide array of Buddhist teachings—Nāgārjuna was certainly seen as possessing expertise in many areas aside from his Mādhyamika specialization. Nevertheless, since he had also

55. Grosnick (1989, 85–86), for one, notes the possibility that one of Paramārtha's disciples attributed the *Awakening of Faith* to Aśvaghoṣa in order to "win sympathy" for Paramārtha's new Yogācāra translations, which had been suppressed by monks at Jiankang who favored *Prajñāpāramitā* and Mādhyamika ideals. However, if this were the case, the application of Aśvaghoṣa's name would not have served to promote Yogācāra teachings above and against the Madhyamaka—since Aśvaghoṣa had long been depicted as Nāgārjuna's ally—though it may have helped place the former tradition on a more equal footing with the latter. In any event, as previously noted, Chinese Buddhists did not see Nāgārjuna as solely Mādhyamika and Aśvaghoṣa as Yogācāra, in contradistinction to one another; rather, these patriarchs were both depicted as representing the entirety of the Mahāyāna.

authored doctrinal tracts such as the *Middle Treatise* and the *Twelve Gates Treatise,* Chinese commentators viewed Nāgārjuna in particular as a proponent of quintessentially Mādhyamika doctrines such as the "middle way" and the "two truths." With this celebrated body of Mādhyamika literature in Chinese translation, Nāgārjuna's own doctrinal proclivities were fairly well-defined for Chinese Buddhists, even if he was otherwise considered an expert on all things Mahāyāna. Because of this, Nāgārjuna would perhaps have been seen as an unlikely author of the *Awakening of Faith,* which integrated ideals such as the *ālayavijñāna* that were understood to contravene Nāgārjuna's orthodox Mādhyamika doctrinal position. Aśvaghoṣa, in contrast, was depicted from the very beginning as specializing in areas that would have made him an appropriate choice as Indian author for this newly composed Chinese treatise.

It is well known that the fourth and fifth divisions of the *Awakening of Faith* were devoted to explicating methods of practice by which one could realize the doctrinal insights outlined earlier in the text. While these doctrinal insights have received the lion's share of attention in the subsequent commentarial tradition—and rightfully so, considering their abstruse nature—the text's practical emphasis was perhaps equally important to Aśvaghoṣa's selection as its author. In chapter 1, I discussed how fifth-century sources commended Aśvaghoṣa in particular for his expertise in *dhyāna* cultivation, and how the only examples of Aśvaghoṣa's writings available to Chinese Buddhists at the time were instructions for meditation practice. Sengrui's "Preface to the *Dhyāna* Scriptures Translated within the Passes" outlined the contents of a meditation manual that has come down to us in the form of the *Scripture on Seated Dhyāna Samādhi.* Sengrui wrote that this compilation of "*dhyāna* essentials" was comprised in large part of verses that Aśvaghoṣa wrote in order to explain meditation practices known as the "five gateways" and the "six kinds of thought," as well as other forms of breathing meditation. Then in his "Comprehensive Preface to the *Dhyāna* Scriptures on the Cultivation of Expedient Means Translated at Moun Lu," Huiyuan similarly praised Aśvaghoṣa for having bequeathed his instructions for *dhyāna* cultivation to future generations. While I have not found any specific correlations between the *Scripture on Seated Dhyāna Samādhi* and the meditation practices described in the *Awakening of Faith,* it seems clear that Aśvaghoṣa's early depiction as a meditation master was one important factor in his subsequent claim to fame as author of this sixth-century Mahāyāna doctrinal synopsis and meditation primer.

How to Write for Dimwitted Readers

A third major factor underlying the attribution of the *Awakening of Faith* to Aśvaghoṣa was this patriarch's early and oft-repeated depiction as savior of the benighted masses during the latter age of Buddhist history. I have already cited several examples in which Aśvaghoṣa was described generally as working to benefit beings whose distance from the fountainhead of enlightenment had lessened their spiritual capacities; and I have also noted instances in which Aśvaghoṣa was stated more specifically to have liberated his benighted contemporaries by authoring doctrinal treatises. One such instance is worth repeating here, since it prefigured most directly the manner in which the *Awakening of Faith* was said to conform to the weakened proclivities of its intended audience. The Nanatsu-dara biography of Aśvaghoṣa explained:

> At that time, although the end of the True Dharma [period] was approaching, people's minds could still attain [the Way]. Their ability to realize it themselves was insufficient, and awakening through texts and words was still incomplete. Therefore, Aśvaghoṣa abbreviated superfluous words that strayed from the truth and omitted flowery expressions that [merely] implied meaning. He pronounced the supple teaching through clear principles and related their essentials and fundamentals with the utmost beauty. How could this not be the case? His skillfully composed texts were direct in their expression, and he was without match in his excellence. At that time [his writings] were praised and revered throughout the world, taken as models of composition (See appendix 1).

Compare this with the justification for composing the *Awakening of Faith* offered at the outset of the text:

> Though this teaching is presented in the sūtras, the capacity and the deeds of men today are no longer the same, nor are the conditions of their acceptance and comprehension. That is to say, in the days when the Tathāgata was in the world, people were of high aptitude and the Preacher excelled in his form, mind, and deeds, so that once he had preached with his perfect voice, different types of people all equally understood; hence, there was no need for this kind of discourse. But after the passing away of the Tathāgata, there were some who were able by their own power to listen extensively to others and to reach understanding; there were some who by their own power could listen to very little and yet understand much; there were some who, without any mental power of their own, depended upon the extensive discourse of others to obtain understanding; and naturally there were some who looked upon the wordiness of extensive discourses as troublesome, and who sought after what was comprehensive, terse, and yet contained much meaning, and then were able to understand it. Thus, this discourse is designed to embrace, in a general way, the limitless meaning of the vast and profound teaching of the Tathāgata. This discourse, therefore, should be presented (Hakeda 1967, 26–27).

修多羅中, 雖有此法, 以眾生根行不等, 受解緣別. 所謂如來在世, 眾生利根, 能說之人, 色心業勝, 圓音一演, 異類等解, 則不須論. 若如來滅後, 或有眾生, 能以自力, 廣聞而取解者; 或有眾生, 亦以自力, 少聞而多解者; 或有眾生, 無自心力, 因於廣論, 而得解者; 自有眾生, 復以廣論, 文多為煩, 心樂總持, 少文而攝多義, 能取解者. 如是此論, 為欲總攝如來廣大深法無邊義. 故應說此論.[56]

56. *Dasheng qixin lun* 大乘起信論, T no. 1666, 32:575c.

Aśvaghoṣa himself was notably absent from this statement of Dharmic history and justification for authoring the *Awakening of Faith*, and in fact his name appeared nowhere in the body of the extant text.[57] Nevertheless, the obvious congruencies between this passage and the Nanatsu-dera biography of Aśvaghoṣa, as regards the proclivities of beings who are distant from the Buddha and the expediencies that treatise masters must thereby employ, would seem to suggest that the *Awakening of Faith*'s author (or authors) bore Aśvaghoṣa's early hagiographic imagery firmly in mind. Both of these quoted texts described the weakened capacities of people who lived over the centuries after nirvāṇa—which was a common sentiment in Chinese sources during the fifth and sixth centuries—but the explanation of how treatise authors should thus tailor their writings was somewhat more specific to Aśvaghoṣa's Nanatsu-dera biography and the *Awakening of Faith*. According to the former source, Aśvaghoṣa "abbreviated superfluous words" and "omitted flowery expressions," so "his skillfully composed texts were direct in their expression." Likewise, the supposed Indian author of the *Awakening of Faith* wrote in a way that was "comprehensive, terse, and yet contained much meaning," in particular for readers "who looked upon the wordiness of extensive discourses as troublesome." Similarly, the commentary on the *Awakening of Faith* attributed to Jingying Huiyuan explained that Aśvaghoṣa used "abbreviated wording" (*wen lüeshao* 文略少) to compensate for the shortcomings of earlier treatises, which were too verbose and allusive for contemporary beings to follow.[58] And in what would later become the definitive commentary on Aśvaghoṣa's *magnum opus*, Fazang wrote:

> Lamenting the snares of decadence and grieving over this sinkhole [of *saṃsāra*, Aśvaghoṣa] wished to explain the wondrous meaning of the profound scriptures to again illuminate dark roads, reprimand those holding perverted views, and thereby cause them to return to the True Path. He enabled those intent on returning to the source to get back to the origin without deviation. At that time he composed a broad range of treatises for the far-reaching benefit of the multitudes. But, because the words were numerous and the meanings abstruse, they were not discernable by those of shallow intellect. So, out of compassion for the deluded of this last age, he also composed this treatise. We can say that the meaning [of the *Awakening of Faith*] is rich though the text is concise, and it unites both understanding and practice. Because of this work, even those with less than average capacities can attain awakening.[59]

57. Aśvaghoṣa was mentioned in the preface to the text, which was attributed to Paramārtha's disciple Zhikai 智愷 (or Huikai 慧愷, 518–568). However, this preface is considered spurious; see Demiéville 1929, 8, 11–15; and Girard 2004, xviii, lxvii.

58. *Dasheng qixin lun yishu*, T no. 1843, 44:175c–176a.

59. Translation adapted from Vorenkamp 2004, 26.

> 慨此頹綱, 悼斯淪溺. 將欲啟深經之妙旨, 再曜昏衢; 斥邪見之顛眸, 令歸正趣. 使還源者, 可即返本非遙. 造廣論於當時, 遐益群品. 既文多義邈, 非淺識所闚. 悲末葉之迷倫, 又造斯論. 可謂義豐文約, 解行俱兼. 中下之流, 因茲悟入者矣.[60]

Here Fazang appears to have combined Aśvaghoṣa's early hagiographic depictions with the soterio-historical justification offered within *Awakening of Faith* itself, explaining (in language that also echoed Sengrui's *Great Perfection of Wisdom Treatise* preface) how Aśvaghoṣa adopted a simplified approach for his exegetical masterpiece so that beings of shallow intellect during the latter age could comprehend it easily—an ironic claim considering how the laconic quality of the *Awakening of Faith* has often caused such difficulty in interpretation. In any event, given the manner in which the *Awakening of Faith* as well as its early commentaries rationalized its style in terms of its moment in Dharmic history—as tailored to suit the weakened capacities of beings after the death of the Buddha—it is clear that Aśvaghoṣa's early hagiographic imagery would have made him an ideal match for this treatise. Aśvaghoṣa had been depicted from the outset as likewise having saved his dimwitted contemporaries by authoring doctrinal treatises, and the Nanatsu-dera biography in particular described how he did this by excising flowery expressions and elucidating the Buddhadharma in a straightforward manner—precisely the style that the *Awakening of Faith*'s author sought to emulate. Therefore, together with Aśvaghoṣa's age-old connection with the archetypal Mahāyāna master Nāgārjuna, and his early depiction as a meditation master first and foremost, the soterio-historical association between Aśvaghoṣa and the *Awakening of Faith* made this patriarch a most viable candidate to serve as a front for the Chinese author of this ostensibly Indian Mahāyāna treatise.

The attribution of the *Awakening of Faith* to Aśvaghoṣa verified the numerous hagiographic assertions that this celebrated Indian patriarch had saved the world by authoring doctrinal treatises. And with this text to his name, the reasons why Aśvaghoṣa had always been intimately associated with Nāgārjuna—and in fact why Nāgārjuna so fervently praised Aśvaghoṣa's writings—were thereby brought to light. Aśvaghoṣa's advertised brilliance in both doctrinal analysis and practical training were made manifest for a Chinese audience. Around the end of the sixth century, when we first have indisputable evidence that Chinese Buddhists attributed the *Awakening of Faith* to Aśvaghoṣa,[61] the popularity of this Indian patriarch soared, and

---

60. *Dasheng qixin lun yiji*, T no. 1846, 44:241a. In his commentary on the *Twelve Gates Treatise* (*Shi'ermen lun zongzhi yi ji* 十二門論宗致義記, T no. 1826, 42:212b–c), Fazang described Nāgārjuna in very similar terms. My thanks to Chen Jinhua for this reference.

61. Candidates for earliest reference to Aśvaghoṣa's authorship of this text include the preface attributed to Zhikai, or Huikai (*Dasheng qixin lun*, T no. 1666, 32:575a–b); the commentary attributed to Tanyan (*Qixin lun yishu* 起信論義疏, Z 1:71:3:265a; see Liebenthal 1958); and the commentary attributed to Jingying Huiyuan (*Dasheng qixin lun yishu* 大乘起信論義疏, T no. 1843). However, the authenticity of all these texts has been questioned. The earliest

Chinese exegetes had more concrete means to elicit his name as authority in discourse on Mahāyāna ideals. While the *Awakening of Faith* was ascribed to Aśvaghoṣa precisely because of the ways in which he had been depicted from the earliest times in China, with this seminal treatise to his name Aśvaghoṣa would forever be remembered primarily as an unparalleled Buddhist philosopher and doctrinal author. And according to Jingying Huiyuan, Jizang, Fazang, and their contemporaries, the greatest post-*parinirvāṇa* patriarchs were, in fact, defined in large part by their function as treatise masters who liberated beings with their writings amidst difficult soteriological circumstances. With the *Awakening of Faith* now available for Chinese adepts to personally read, practice, and adduce in their own doctrinal commentaries, Aśvaghoṣa was thus seen to have fulfilled this function for both ancient Indian and contemporary Chinese Buddhists.

As indicated, one purpose of the *Awakening of Faith* was to relocate the highest truth of Indian Buddhism within latter-day China and thus eliminate the need for further reliance on Indian founts of Buddhist authority. Focusing on the embryo of Buddhahood always already present at the core of every sentient being, and offering the practical means by which Chinese adepts could personally realize their potential Buddhahood, this ostensibly Indian treatise ideally obviated any further mediation between India and China. And as part of this agenda, the Chinese author (or authors) of the *Awakening of Faith* ascribed this treatise to Aśvaghoṣa in order to instantiate in China another Indian model of Buddhist awakening. This was the model of post-*parinirvāṇa* sainthood through doctrinal scholarship, according to which great bodhisattvas were made by mastering the conventions of exegetical authorship and saving beings through the vehicle of the written word. With Aśvaghoṣa having shown how the vast Indian scriptural and commentarial tradition could be condensed into one convenient textual package, which best suited the proclivities of human beings living far from the Buddha, Chinese scholar-monks were now given the means to elucidate the truth without further need for recourse to Indian authority. The *Awakening of Faith* conveyed the doctrine of innate Buddhahood and the meditative means to awakening—thus cutting the rest of Indian tradition out of the loop of Buddhist salvation—and in the same way Aśvaghoṣa modeled the exegetical means of this conveyance, thus sanctioning the efforts of Chinese scholar-monks who likewise sought to liberate beings through writing. And with more than one hundred and seventy commentaries written on the *Awakening of Faith* in China, Korea, and Japan over the following centuries (Hakeda 1967, 5), it appears that scholar-monks across East Asia took up Aśvaghoṣa's charge of illuminating this path to sainthood through Buddhist doctrinal scholarship.

---

undisputed source to connect Aśvaghoṣa with the *Awakening of Faith* is Huiyuan's *Dasheng yizhang* (T no. 1851, 44:473a–b), which was completed around 590 (Demiéville 1929, 62; Grosnick 1989, 66, 86).

Indian Patriarchs in Xuanzang's True Buddhism

Perhaps the most celebrated attempt in Chinese Buddhist history to effect the transmission of Real Buddhism from India to China was made by the eminent pilgrim and translator Xuanzang. Similarly focused on the saving power of Buddhist texts and doctrinal authorship, Xuanzang famously journeyed for some sixteen years (ca. 629–645) through the Western Regions in order to locate the most authentic textual representations of Indian Buddhism and bring them back to China. Xuanzang's pilgrimage was ostensibly motivated by his perception of confusion and disjointedness in the Chinese Buddhist doctrinal traditions of his day, which he thought would be righted by one final transmission—and proper translation—of the foremost Indian sources of Buddhist truth.[62] With the enormous cache of Indian scriptures, treatises, and other sacred items hauled back to China by Xuanzang and his retinue, Chinese Buddhists would finally have access to the greatest manifestations of Śākyamuni's True Dharma, and the continued import of Indian sources of Buddhist authority would no longer be necessary.

Upon his return to the capital Chang'an, Xuanzang was reportedly received with great fanfare and was subsequently housed by Tang emperor Taizong 太宗 (r. 626–649) in the imperial Hongfu monastery 弘福寺, established in honor of Taizong's mother, where Xuanzang could begin translation of the 657 Sanskrit texts that he had retrieved (Weinstein 1987, 24). The rest of his life was spent translating these texts and composing his own doctrinal commentaries—also under the patronage of Taizong's successor emperor, Gaozong 高宗 (r. 650–683)—in order to remedy the perceived deficiencies of the extant Buddhist canon and ensure that Chinese Buddhists could thenceforth consult the most authentic expressions of Indian enlightenment.[63] In addition, at Taizong's request, Xuanzang compiled his famous *Great Tang Record of the Western Regions* (*Da Tang xiyu ji* 大唐西域記), which outlined the geographies, climates, industries, sociopolitical and economic structures, cultural mores, and religious proclivities of more than one hundred different kingdoms that Xuanzang traversed across South and Central Asia. And at the same time that Xuanzang's travelogue served to satisfy imperial appetites for diplomatic intelligence, it also provided for both state and sangha the fullest portrait ever seen of Indian Buddhist history, sacred geography, institutional structure, and traditions of *doxa* and praxis prevalent over the centuries after Śākyamuni's departure.

While Xuanzang's massive body of translation work was the primary means by which he sought to relocate the truth of Indian Buddhism within the imperial-monastic institutions of Tang China, through his *Record of the Western Regions* Xuanzang also worked to redefine the Chinese paradigms

62. *Da Tang Da Ci'ensi Sanzang fashi zhuan* 大唐大慈恩寺三藏法師傳, T no. 2053, 50:221a (trans. Li 1995, 6–7), 261a (trans. Li 1995, 227–228); cf. Barrett 1990, 94–95. *Da Tang xiyu ji* 大唐西域記, T no. 2087, 51:868b, 869c; trans. Beal 1884, 1:5, 15 and Li 1996, 12, 19–20.

63. See the list of works associated with Xuanzang in Lusthaus 2002, 554–573.

of Indian Buddhist sainthood that had developed up until his time, vis-à-vis the Indian patriarchal tales that he recounted from various sites along his journey. For the present analysis, it makes no difference whether these tales were actually told to Xuanzang in the manner that he recorded or whether he embellished or invented them outright. Of interest here is the fact that Xuanzang chose to present stories about the Indian patriarchs in the manner that he did, which in the context of his travelogue lent them the same authority that Xuanzang claimed for all his other works. Just as Xuanzang's translations were advertised as approximating the original Sanskrit better than any preceding Chinese works, and his exegetical writings were born of years of study under the greatest Indian masters of Nālanda, Xuanzang's new-and-improved Indian patriarch accounts were ostensibly gleaned from the very sites where Śākyamuni once travailed and where the patriarchs had left their own veritable traces. And with the most authentic narratives of the Indian patriarchs thus transmitted to China, Chinese adepts would finally be equipped with the foremost models of Buddhist sainthood for the generations after nirvāṇa.

Throughout his *Record of the Western Regions,* Xuanzang recounted numerous tales of Śākyamuni's disciples and other great Buddhist masters who championed the Dharma in post-*parinirvāṇa* India, such as Asaṅga, Dharmapāla, Dignāga, Pārśva, and Vasubandhu. Given Xuanzang's predilection for Yogācāra and "consciousness only" teachings, one might expect Asaṅga and Vasubandhu to have received special attention in Xuanzang's *Record*; and indeed, therein Xuanzang did have a good deal to say about these famous Indian masters. But also among the most prominent Indian patriarchs depicted in this text were Nāgārjuna and Āryadeva, two of the "four suns that illuminated the world."[64] In the case of the former, who was doubtless the most celebrated Indian patriarch in China and whose hagiographies had received considerable attention since the time of Kumārajīva, Xuanzang offered no less than a wholesale reinvention—even going so far as to change Nāgārjuna's Chinese name.[65] In some respects reinscribing the themes of the *Dharma-Treasury Transmission* and the hagiography ascribed to Kumārajīva but through completely different narrative arcs, Xuanzang's tales of Nāgārjuna emphasized the symbiotic relationship between kings and Buddhist masters. And equally significant but perhaps more surprising is the attention that Xuanzang lavished upon Āryadeva, who was confirmed in this account as the foremost disciple of Nāgārjuna and master of public debate who displayed for imperial patrons the superiority of Śākyamuni's teachings.

64. *Da Tang xiyu ji,* T no. 2087, 51:942a: 四日照世; trans. Beal 1884, 2:302–303 and Li 1996, 370. The other two "suns" were Aśvaghoṣa and Kumāralāta, similar to the Nanatsudera biography of Aśvaghoṣa (see appendix 1).

65. *Da Tang xiyu ji,* T no. 2087, 51:912c: 唐言龍猛，舊譯曰龍樹非也 ("Dragon-valor," in the language of the Tang; the archaic translation of "Dragon-tree" is incorrect). Cf. trans. Li 1996, 231.

Given Xuanzang's heritage in high officialdom and his close personal relationship with Tang emperors Taizong and Gaozong,[66] it comes as no surprise that his *Record of the Western Regions* would emphasize how these Indian patriarchs were likewise closely allied with the prerogatives of the state. Xuanzang's account of Nāgārjuna, for example, centered on this patriarch's relations with a certain king of the Sātavāhana dynasty.[67] Known in particular for his skill in alchemy, Nāgārjuna concocted an elixir of longevity that enabled both himself and his patron king to live for several hundreds of years.[68] In appreciation of Nāgārjuna's efforts, the king constructed for him an enormous mountain monastery, replete with storied pavilions, channeled waterfalls, golden life-sized images of the Buddha, and countless jeweled adornments.[69] But part way through construction, the king's treasury was exhausted and work had to be halted for lack of funds. Nāgārjuna again put his alchemical talents to good use, composing an elixir that could transform rock into gold and thus create sufficient funds to complete monastery construction.[70] And just as these episodes depicted Nāgārjuna providing for his royal patron the most coveted of alchemical boons—immortality and aurification—Nāgārjuna's death was likewise portrayed as a great gift to the imperial family. There was a prince who feared that he would never become king because of his father's extreme longevity. The prince asked Nāgārjuna to end his own life, and thus the life of the king, so that the prince could finally take the throne. Manifesting the bodhisattva's perfect generosity, Nāgārjuna gladly severed his own head for the benefit of the prince, thereby allowing the imperial succession to follow its natural course.[71]

Much more could be said about Xuanzang's tales of Nāgārjuna—and in the following chapter, I discuss their relation to Nāgārjuna's image as an alchemist—but for now, it is sufficient to note that the primary aim of this account was to establish its protagonist, as well as the religious institution that he represented, as a valuable commodity to be cherished and

66. See Li 1996, 1; and Weinstein 1987, 24–31.

67. Xuanzang gives this king's name as "Suoduopohe ('Leading to Righteousness' in the language of the Tang)" 娑多婆訶(唐言引正) (*Da Tang xiyu ji*, T no. 2087, 51:929a). The identity of this king has received a great deal of attention in modern scholarship, particularly in the effort to date Nāgārjuna. For a recent discussion and citation of relevant sources, see Walser 2005, 61–68.

68. *Da Tang xiyu ji*, T no. 2087, 51:929b; trans. Beal 1884, 2:212; and Li 1996, 309–310. On the theme of Nāgārjuna's longevity in relation to Indian models of Buddhist sanctity, see Ray 1997.

69. The name and location of this monastery have long been points of scholarly contention, to the extent that they bear on Nāgārjuna's historical and geographic contexts. See, most recently, Walser 2005, 66, 294n32.

70. *Da Tang xiyu ji*, T no. 2087, 51:929c–930a; trans. Beal 1884, 2:214–217; and Li 1996, 311–313.

71. *Da Tang xiyu ji*, T no. 2087, 51:929b–c; trans. Beal 1884, 2:212–214; and Li 1996, 310–311. Cf. Benn (2007, 93, 282n70), who mentions this episode in relation to similar tales of self-immolation.

supported by the state. While Nāgārjuna's royal connections had been elaborated in Chinese sources since the *Dharma-Treasury Transmission*, Xuanzang's narrative reinvention of this celebrated Indian patriarch was truly audacious, given how well known and influential Nāgārjuna's earlier hagiographic traditions had become. In Xuanzang's account, Nāgārjuna was not a solitary wanderer who found his way to the dragon palace. No mention was made of his vast *oeuvre* of doctrinal treatises, and he was not part of a Dharma-transmission lineage, nor was he shown resurrecting the Dharma in specific centuries after nirvāṇa. Instead, according to Xuanzang, Nāgārjuna was almost exclusively an exemplar of Buddhist sainthood at the imperial court, which of course reflected Xuanzang's own station in the Tang monastic-imperial complex. Another factor underlying this hagiographic reinvention of Nāgārjuna may have been Xuanzang's general disapprobation of the works produced by Kumārajīva. Just as Xuanzang believed Kumārajīva's earlier translations to have been inaccurate to the point of distortion, he perhaps suspected that Kumārajīva's tales of Nāgārjuna similarly misrepresented their original Indian sources. So now with this new account derived from the very kingdom where Nāgārjuna himself lived—and where Śākyamuni formerly traveled and an Aśokan stūpa remained (Kośala)[72]—Xuanzang's Chinese audiences would at last know the "real" story of how this celebrated Indian patriarch propagated the Truth for the generations after nirvāṇa.

Like Nāgārjuna in the *Record of the Western Regions*, the aforementioned post-*parinirvāṇa* Indian patriarchs who also appeared in Xuanzang's travelogue largely served to illustrate ideal state-sangha relations, and Āryadeva in particular was depicted winning imperial allegiance through his prowess in public debate. Xuanzang thus solidified Āryadeva's earlier image as a great debate master and converter of non-Buddhists—as advanced especially in the *Dharma-Treasury Transmission*—and also confirmed that Āryadeva's debating talents were honed under the tutelage of Nāgārjuna. The earliest Chinese accounts of Āryadeva never actually claimed that Nāgārjuna was his master; the *Dharma-Treasury Transmission* was the first source to assert a direct master-disciple relationship between these two patriarchs. Later writings that similarly focused on transmission lineage largely repeated the *Dharma-Treasury Transmission* in this regard (e.g., Guanding's introduction to the *Great Calming and Contemplation*). Other texts that instead foregrounded soteriological degradation elided this notion of direct transmission while maintaining earlier chronological progressions (e.g., situating Nāgārjuna at seven hundred years after nirvāṇa and Āryadeva a century later). A third approach was to amalgamate these positions by highlighting the close personal relationship between Nāgārjuna and Āryadeva while asserting simultaneously that the differences between them were determined by their respective stages in Dharmic history.

72. *Da Tang xiyu ji*, T no. 2087, 51:929a; trans. Beal 1884, 2:209–210; and Li 1996, 307–308.

This last approach was exemplified most prominently in the writings of Jizang, who emphasized Āryadeva's temporal distance from the Buddha and emergence amidst difficult soteriological circumstances. Along the lines of the aforementioned commentaries on the *Scripture of Benevolent King*—according to which Āryadeva's circumstances at eight hundred years after nirvāṇa had worsened considerably from the time of Nāgārjuna—Jizang elsewhere asserted that Āryadeva's particular brand of doctrinal exegesis was especially suited to a world teeming with benighted heretics. Thus when Jizang addressed the issue of Nāgārjuna's and Āryadeva's ostensive target audiences—with the former refuting the mistaken views of Lesser Vehicle adherents and the latter dealing especially with non-Buddhists—he argued that Āryadeva was forced to gear his philosophical disputation toward non-Buddhists precisely because so many of them had come to flourish during his time.[73]

In thus explaining Āryadeva's particular debate focus in terms of his soterio-historical context, Jizang echoed at least two common concerns of his time regarding the status of the post-*parinirvāṇa* Indian patriarchs. On the one hand, he re-emphasized the contention that Nāgārjuna's and Āryadeva's doctrinal writings were products of pernicious circumstances—and the most significant junctures of post-*parinirvāṇa* Buddhist history. On the other hand, Jizang further exemplified the tension in Chinese accounts of these patriarchs concerning their relationship with one another. Did these two work in concert to quash false views and revitalize the truth, as master and disciple, or did they in fact arise at different stages of Dharmic history and thus tailor their teachings to disparate audiences? Clearly Jizang himself was somewhat torn over this question. Throughout his *Hundred Treatise Commentary*, for example, Jizang maintained that Āryadeva's main purpose was to defeat the misguided arguments put forth by the myriad non-Buddhists who ran amok during his day, while Nāgārjuna instead focused on undoing the attachments to various viewpoints that contemporary Hīnayāna masters had come to harbor. Jizang accounted for this difference by asserting that the central problem of Nāgārjuna's time was that people held to the Lesser Vehicle while shunning the Greater, while in Āryadeva's time—as much as two centuries later—the most pressing concern was to manage the non-Buddhists who had since taken over the world.[74] However, in direct contrast to this stipulated historical gap between Nāgārjuna and Āryadeva, elsewhere in this same commentary Jizang reasserted their master-disciple relationship, even as he acknowledged that the sources available to him were conflicted on this question.[75] It is therefore clear that during Jizang's time Āryadeva's purported discipleship under Nāgārjuna was a disputed issue, and in fact it was more commonly accepted that there was a

73. *Dasheng xuan lun*, T no. 1853, 45:72b.
74. *Bailun shu*, T no. 1827, 42:233b.
75. Ibid., 233a; trans. Robinson 1967, 23.

historical disjuncture between the two that explained why they tailored their respective teachings to different audiences.

In Xuanzang's *Record of the Western Regions*, however, this earlier confusion about Nāgārjuna's and Āryadeva's master-disciple relationship was finally dispelled, while the oft-repeated narrative of Dharma decline was further deployed to contextualize the works of these patriarchs. In two separate episodes, Xuanzang described direct encounters between Nāgārjuna and Āryadeva, with the former patriarch instructing the latter in matters of Buddhist doctrine and debate. One of these episodes detailed the first meeting between Nāgārjuna and Āryadeva, in which Āryadeva arrived at Nāgārjuna's abode and was presented with a bowl of water. Āryadeva silently dropped a needle into the bowl, symbolizing his ability to pierce to the heart of Nāgārjuna's all-encompassing wisdom. With that, Nāgārjuna accepted Āryadeva as his disciple and began training him in the teachings of the Buddha.[76] In another episode, Xuanzang described a longstanding debate between the Buddhists and non-Buddhists of Pāṭaliputra, which Āryadeva, with the help of Nāgārjuna, would eventually come to settle.

In former times the Buddhists of this kingdom were strong, wise, and able to silence their non-Buddhist opponents in debate. But since then the sangha had become weak, incapable of maintaining the True Dharma, so the non-Buddhists grew powerful and arose to a position of supremacy. The king of Pāṭaliputra oversaw a public debate at which the non-Buddhists emerged victorious and demanded that the bell in the Buddhist monastery no longer be struck. At that time Āryadeva told his master Nāgārjuna that he could defeat the non-Buddhists' erroneous views. Nāgārjuna tested Āryadeva's skill in debate by assuming the non-Buddhists' positions. Āryadeva eventually won, so he ventured off to Pāṭaliputra to challenge the non-Buddhists. There Āryadeva sounded the monastery bell in order to attract the attention of the king and the non-Buddhist masters. The king then assembled everyone for a debate, stipulating that the defeated debater would pay with his life. In short order Āryadeva vanquished all of the non-Buddhists, so the king declared the superiority of Buddhism and had a great monument constructed in Āryadeva's honor.[77]

In this way Xuanzang confirmed both Āryadeva's discipleship under Nāgārjuna and expertise in debate, while illustrating how this great Indian patriarch had won imperial support for Buddhism at a time when the sangha had otherwise grown weak. Xuanzang also described Āryadeva's doctrinal debates in at least four other episodes throughout the *Record*.[78] One of these

76. *Da Tang xiyu ji*, T no. 2087, 51:929a–b; trans. Beal 1884, 2:210–212; and Li 1996, 308–309.

77. *Da Tang xiyu ji*, T no. 2087, 51:912c–913a; trans. Beal 1884, 2:97–99; and Li 1996, 231–233.

78. *Da Tang xiyu ji*, T no. 2087, 51:891b (trans. Beal 1884, 1:189; and Li 1996, 127–128); 929a–b (trans. Beal 1884, 2:210–212; and Li 1996, 308–309); 931b (trans. Beal 1884, 2:227–228; and Li 1996, 319). On the relationship between Maitreya and the arhats described in this last episode, see Shih 2002, 150–151; cf. De Visser 1923, 20.

served to advertise Āryadeva's *Expanded Hundred Treatise* (*Guang bailun* 廣百論)—which Xuanzang translated upon his return to China—as the veritable record of this patriarch's debate prowess.[79] Xuanzang thus echoed earlier efforts by Jizang to connect Āryadeva's tangible writings with his doctrinal debates, which were illustrated in earlier hagiographies. I described in chapter 1 how Sengzhao supplied a brief context for Āryadeva's authorship of the *Hundred Treatise,* explaining that, eight hundred years after nirvāṇa, "non-Buddhists ran riot, heterodoxies arose in conflict, and false debates imperiled the truth so that the True Way was nearly lost in confusion." Therefore, "with the intention of rescuing far and wide those who were drowning," Āryadeva composed his *Hundred Treatise,* which was arranged as a sort of Socratic dialogue between "insider" (*nei* 內) and "outsider" (*wai* 外).[80] As such, rather than elaborating its theses through dry philosophical monologue, the *Hundred Treatise* offered a compelling cast of characters that cried out for an equally vivid setting and background story for how its patriarchal protagonist emerged victorious. Sengzhao's preface met this demand to some extent, but the *Dharma-Treasury Transmission* and Āryadeva's independently circulating hagiography later did a much better job.

The accounts of Āryadeva's debates in these two later hagiographies are nearly identical to one another in structure and content. One substantial difference between them is that the *Dharma-Treasure Transmission* depicted Āryadeva's debates as an examination before a south Indian king, while according to the separate biography, Āryadeva had already won the king's allegiance by demonstrating his supernormal powers. In both accounts, after having defeated all the arguments of his non-Buddhist opponents, Āryadeva retired to a quiet forest to compose his doctrinal treatises—either the *Hundred Treatise Scripture* (*Bai lun jing* 百論經), according to the *Dharma-Treasury Transmission,*[81] or two separate texts, according to the separate biography: the *Hundred Treatise* and the *Four Hundred Treatise* (see appendix 2). Neither of these accounts claimed that Āryadeva's writings were direct records of his earlier debates; it was Jizang who first asserted that Āryadeva "excerpted and compiled the discussions from that occasion to make the *Hundred Treatise.*"[82] Thus, like his contemporaries in the case of Aśvaghoṣa's *Awakening of Faith,* Jizang made manifest the link between

79. *Da Tang xiyu ji,* T no. 2087, 51:897b; trans. Beal 1884, 1:231; and Li 1996, 156–157. Xuanzang's translation is titled *Guang bailun ben* 廣百論本 (T no. 1570), completed in 647 or 650. Xuanzang also translated a commentary on this text by Dharmapāla, titled *Dasheng guang bailun shi lun* 大乘廣百論釋論 (T no. 1571).

80. Robinson (1967, 33–34) provides a handy content summary of this text; Tucci (1929) 1976 translates it in full.

81. *Fu fazang yinyuan zhuan* 付法藏因緣傳, T no. 2058, 50:319b. According to Jizang (*Zhongguan lun shu,* T no. 1824, 42:168c), the *Dharma-Treasury Transmission* said that Āryadeva composed the *Four Hundred Treatise* (*Sibai lun* 四百論). Since this is what the separate biography of Āryadeva now says, Jizang's assertion may further indicate that the latter text (*Tipo pusa zhuan* 提婆菩薩傳, T no. 2048) was in fact excerpted from the *Dharma-Treasury Transmission.*

82. *Sanlun xuanyi,* T no. 1852, 45:13b: 撰集當時之言, 以為百論.

Āryadeva's hagiographies and his doctrinal exegesis, illustrating how Āryadeva's philosophical *magnum opus* was integrally intertwined with the central elements of his life story. And by associating Āryadeva's *Expanded Hundred Treatise* with the very site at which this patriarch once silenced non-Buddhists in debate, Xuanzang similarly integrated doctrine and hagiography, showing how both Āryadeva's writings and the stories about their composition instantiated the means by which this patriarch had helped save Buddhism in India and convey it to China.

Like the texts of Guanding, Huiyuan, Jizang, and other elite monastic authors of the Sui and early-Tang dynasties, Xuanzang's works were part of a longstanding and widespread effort to localize the highest truth of Indian Buddhism within the imperial-monastic institution of China, thus generating a new, proximal locus of Buddhist enlightenment. Ostensibly concerned that inaccurate translations and doctrinal obfuscations had further distanced latter-day Chinese Buddhists from their Indian heritage, Xuanzang ventured west to study under the greatest living Indian masters and return to his kingdom with the most authentic manifestations of Śākyamuni's teachings. At the same time, Xuanzang's pilgrimage also presaged later Chan efforts to bridge the Sino-Indian divide through the bodies and minds of the greatest Buddhist saints who ever lived. Xuanzang claimed for himself the status of foremost transmission medium by virtue of having brought the Dharma to China—like the Indian missionaries of later Chan lineage histories—while Chan ideologues assumed the mantle of True Dharma bearers by asserting a genealogical link to Śākyamuni through the Indian patriarchs. But also like the authors of these Chan lineage histories, Xuanzang deployed the Indian patriarchs to instantiate within his own person and tradition the authority of hallowed Indian origins. Throughout his *Record of the Western Regions*, Xuanzang recounted tales of Indian figures who were already well known in China—especially Nāgārjuna and Āryadeva—but he reshaped these figures to suit his own interest in securing state patronage. Within the context of his travelogue, these Indian patriarch accounts were accorded a unique brand of authority. By situating his stories of Nāgārjuna and Āryadeva at the sacred Indian sites where these patriarchs themselves once dwelled, and where Xuanzang had personally visited, Xuanzang rendered his texts and the ideals they exemplified unassailable. And on the strength of these Indian patriarch accounts, Xuanzang's own efforts to integrate sangha and state would be valorized as the foremost means to Buddhist sainthood for the generations after nirvāṇa.

Conclusion: Locating India in China

Much like the tales of the Indian patriarchs advanced by Kumārajīva's associates, the works of Chinese scholar-monks of the Sui and early Tang often focused on the difficult soteriological circumstances in which Aśvaghoṣa, Nāgārjuna, and Āryadeva travailed. One difference between the fifth-century accounts and those discussed in this chapter is that the latter were written in contradistinction to the model of master-disciple Dharma transmission. Chinese scholar-monks of Kumārajīva's time had not yet seen any full-blown accounts of Buddhist lineal patriarchy, much less those that included Aśvaghoṣa, Nāgārjuna, and Āryadeva in particular. But by the time of Jizang, his contemporaries. and his successors, these patriarchs had long been accorded prominent positions in Indian transmission lineages—most notably in the *Dharma-Treasury Transmission*—which extended from the Buddha himself and thus maintained the Dharma in its original, pristine condition. Therefore, by reasserting earlier conceptions of Indian Buddhist history in their accounts of Aśvaghoṣa, Nāgārjuna, and Āryadeva and by re-emphasizing Dharma degradation as against lineal propagation, sixth- to eighth-century Chinese exegetes elevated these patriarchs above their predecessors and successors in the Indian patriarchate. In depicting twenty-three (or twenty-four) Indian masters all playing essentially the same role, and all living within equally propitious circumstances, lineage histories like the *Dharma-Treasury Transmission* had a homogenizing effect. But for subsequent Chinese Buddhist exegetes who sought to promote the works of Aśvaghoṣa, Nāgārjuna, and Āryadeva in particular, these patriarchs had to be seen as standing head and shoulders above their compatriots in the transmission lineage. Thus the Chinese authors discussed in this chapter responded to the *Dharma-Treasury Transmission* by re-emphasizing how Aśvaghoṣa, Nāgārjuna, and Āryadeva had in fact worked within singularly trying times, liberating their benighted contemporaries and transmitting the Dharma to future generations by composing the most profound doctrinal treatises in Indian Buddhist history.

Another major difference between the Indian patriarch accounts of the early fifth century and those of the Sui-Tang period has to do with shifting Chinese perspectives on the relationship between Indian and Chinese Buddhism. In previous chapters, I described how Chinese representations of Aśvaghoṣa, Nāgārjuna, and Āryadeva often developed in concert with discourses about the historical trajectory of Buddhism in post-*parinirvāṇa* India. Whether as a rhetorical stance assumed to promote specific teachings or as a heartfelt "form of paranoia" about the fate of Buddhism (Barrett 1990, 95), Chinese authors of the fifth and sixth centuries often foregrounded the decline of the Dharma in India after the Buddha, as well as in their own soteriological hinterland far removed from the Indian Middle Kingdom. Similarly, models of Buddhist sainthood that developed through the figures of Aśvaghoṣa, Nāgārjuna, and Āryadeva often functioned as responses to—or rhetorical deployments of—this claim to grievous embattlement. The Indian patriarchs were shown to have devised their teachings in particular to forestall the demise of the Dharma, thus serving as vehicles through which specific paradigms of practice could be promoted for Chinese Buddhists similarly perched on the precipice of end times. Through all of this, Chinese images of Indian Buddhism more broadly—its historical trajectories and saintly champions—were marshaled primarily as criteria for delineating norms of Buddhist practice in the ostensive soteriological wasteland of latter-day China. Chinese Buddhist authors of the fifth and sixth centuries prioritized fidelity to the traditions of India, the heartland of perfect Buddhist enlightenment, without which the authenticity, salvific efficacy, and sociopolitical cachet of Chinese Buddhism were all but lost.

Over the ensuing Sui-Tang period, one can observe a similar effort to negotiate the relationship between Buddhism in China and in the land of its birth. The images of Aśvaghoṣa, Nāgārjuna, and Āryadeva produced during this period likewise functioned in part as responses to the rhetoric of decline and the concomitant Chinese "borderland complex," although these issues would become less prominent over time. And, in fact, as opposed to the earlier emphasis on providing models of Buddhist practice suited to these spatiotemporal handicaps, in the Sui-Tang period the Indian patriarchs were represented as having conveyed to China the full truth of Indian Buddhism. As such, Chinese Buddhists no longer needed to concern themselves with Dharma's devolution or China's distance from the Indian motherland. Rather, with Aśvaghoṣa, Nāgārjuna, and Āryadeva having transmitted the means and media of Indian enlightenment across the Sino-Indian divide, the True Dharma could now flourish in latter-day China. And by the same token, from this standpoint India was no longer just a distant cradle of bygone sanctity, or a model against which local Chinese teachings were measured. Rather, India itself had become localized in China, which was increasingly represented as a new center of Buddhist civilization. Relics of the Buddha, Indian icons, ritual practices, buddhas, arhats, and bodhisattvas, sūtras and *śāstras* had all become widespread and readily available in Sui-Tang China. Together with all these instruments of Indian sanctity instantiated in the Chinese imperium, Aśvaghoṣa, Nāgārjuna, and Āryadeva contributed the foremost Indian doctrinal writings and models of post-*parinirvāṇa* Buddhist sainthood. And at the same time, as we will see in the following chapters, Aśvaghoṣa and Nāgārjuna themselves were localized in latter-day China, and made imminent in Chinese ritual arenas to personally provide to religious adepts across traditions a wide array of tangible boons—from mountains of riches to magical powers and protection from baleful influences.

4

Nāgārjuna Divine and the Alchemy of Hagiography

By the ninth century, Aśvaghoṣa and Nāgārjuna had undergone a dramatic metamorphosis in China that would influence their East Asian personae into modern times. From their introduction into China at the beginning of the fifth century, these patriarchs were depicted primarily as eminent exemplars of Buddhist sainthood for the generations after the Buddha's nirvāṇa. In Kumārajīva's time Aśvaghoṣa, Nāgārjuna, and Āryadeva were shown reviving a dying Dharma in post-*parinirvāṇa* India, which made them proximal models for latter-day Chinese Buddhists who viewed their own situation as similarly dire. In the *Dharma-Treasury Transmission*, these Indian patriarchs served as placeholders in a master-disciple succession that upheld Śākyamuni's teaching after his departure, but their absence and distance from China were emphasized with the severance of their lineage. Then, in the sources discussed in the previous chapter, Aśvaghoṣa, Nāgārjuna, and Āryadeva were employed in a series of projects aimed at localizing Indian paradigms of exegetical authorship and state-sangha symbiosis within the newly reunified Empire of China. At the same time, in Chinese sources that both overlapped with and diverged from the elite monastic writings I have examined, Aśvaghoṣa and Nāgārjuna began to appear as local deities who brought to China the same supernormal powers that were illustrated in their earlier hagiographies and doctrinal treatises. Aśvaghoṣa became, among other things, a god of silkworms, or a species of patron saint for the sericulture industry, promising unprecedented silk yields and bounty of silkworm stock and even offering to assuage the guilt that some sericulturists felt over murdering millions of little silkworms. Nāgārjuna's deification progressed along more general lines, not having been linked to any particular industry, but he likewise appeared personally in Chinese ritual arenas to equip local devotees with a broad range of Indian spells, talismans, and alchemical elixirs. In this way, much like the illustrious Indian bodhisattvas Avalokiteśvara, Samantabhadra, Mañjuśrī, and Kṣitigarbha, who were said to reside on sacred Chinese mountains, Aśvaghoṣa and Nāgārjuna were literally moved to China, instantiating within this new Buddhist Middle Kingdom a repertoire of Indian ritual practices that would benefit Chinese religious adepts across traditions.

As with the writings of Kumārajīva's associates and those of Guanding, Jizang, and Xuanzang, as well as in the *Dharma-Treasury Transmission* and the decorations of the Cave of Great Perduring Saints, the sources examined in this chapter deeply implicate the Indian patriarchs in broader Chinese efforts to define the relationship between Indian and Chinese Buddhism. The early hagiographies of Aśvaghoṣa, Nāgārjuna, and Āryadeva served in part to delineate the contours of post-*parinirvāṇa* Indian Buddhism, illustrating the fate of the Dharma in the land of Śākyamuni's birth over the centuries after his death. By making examples of their Indian forebears who had triumphed in such circumstances, Chinese Buddhists advanced paradigms of practice that they deemed appropriate to their own Buddhaless land. In these accounts India was largely a distant paragon of religious authority, a land sanctified by the traces of the Buddha and his foremost descendents and thus a model of enlightened civilization against which China often paled in comparison. But then with the centralization of imperial power and reunification of Chinese territory under the Sui and Tang regimes, Chinese Buddhists' strategies for dealing with their distance from India underwent a gradual shift in orientation. Buddhist authors became less interested in decrying their horrific Final Dharma circumstances and lamenting their ineluctable remove from the Indian fount of Buddhist enlightenment. Instead, they increasingly worked to localize the sources of Indian Buddhist authority and redefine China as the heartland of Buddhist civilization. In this context, elite Chinese scholar-monks with royal connections deployed Aśvaghoṣa, Nāgārjuna, and Āryadeva to valorize local paradigms of Buddhist sainthood through doctrinal scholarship and imperial appointment, as discussed in the previous chapter. The present and following chapters examine how contemporary Buddhist writings of different genres and authorships similarly represented the Indian patriarchs as immanent sources of Buddhist truth, but through starkly divergent magical repertoires that situated these patriarchs within broader fields of Chinese religious practice.

Early Chinese hagiographies of Aśvaghoṣa and Nāgārjuna accorded these masters a wide range of talents and interests. Nāgārjuna was depicted as a textual scholar and exegetical author, a master of debate and converter of kings. He revived the Dharma when it was dying and perpetuated it through master-disciple transmission. He also was a solitary wanderer admitted to the famed undersea dragon palace, and he was a master of "spiritual penetrations" who learned the art of invisibility through alchemy, observed the workings of heavenly beings, and conjured magical creatures through the use of Buddhist spells. Aśvaghoṣa was similarly well-versed in Buddhist doctrinal scholarship, authorship, and debate, and he renewed and transmitted the True Dharma and served as advisor to kings. He also was a world-renowned *dhyāna*-master, lyricist, and musician and the possessor of "magical techniques." Further, both of these patriarchs were depicted as prodigies in various non-Buddhist arts before converting to Buddhism and becoming beings of high spiritual attainment—usually bodhisattvas and sometimes even buddhas—which enabled them to wield supernormal powers that would surpass those of any given god. The preceding chapters examined how Chinese monastic elites foregrounded aspects of these patriarchs' repertoires that accorded with the occupational priorities of traditional Chinese literati-gentlemen—especially doctrinal authorship, public debate, eremitism, meditation practice, and the fostering of normative social relations between master and disciple, ruler and subject. In what follows, we will see how the therapeutic, apotropaic, and other divine salvific powers of Aśvaghoṣa and Nāgārjuna were instead emphasized in various Buddhist sources that advanced ritual rather than scholarly Buddhist endeavors and advertised their protagonists as local deities to be venerated rather than models of sainthood to be emulated.

These representations of the Indian patriarchs were clearly devised to cut across the boundaries of elite and popular, mainstream and marginal, and Buddhist and non-Buddhist, and to some extent it would appear that they actually did so. Aśvaghoṣa's and Nāgārjuna's spiritual powers and divine manifestations were expressly advertised as accessible to anyone who could follow the ritual procedures that they prescribed, whether high-minded monk, lay supplicant, or practical technician of any denomination. These images of the patriarchs also appeared in the writings of eminent Chinese scholar-monks, in sources from the fringes of the Chinese sangha, and in non-Buddhist texts of various kinds. And indeed, the methods advanced by Aśvaghoṣa and Nāgārjuna were closely aligned with the ritual technologies developed across religious traditions in China, although the Indianizing etiology of these methods also lent them a distinctly Buddhist flavor. While the Indian patriarchs provided spells, talismans, seals, elixirs, and procedural stipulations that would have been equally at home in a variety of Chinese ritual settings—and recognized as such by medieval Chinese adepts—these methods were rendered ostensibly Buddhist by their assignment of ancient Indian origins. Through the figures of Aśvaghoṣa and Nāgārjuna, Chinese Buddhist authors laid claim to the most venerable, efficacious technologies for obtaining a wide range of apotropaic, exorcistic, therapeutic, material, and salvific benefits. In this way the Indian patriarchs were insinuated into the religious practice of Chinese supplicants across social and sectarian divisions.

In addition, these images of Aśvaghoṣa and Nāgārjuna blurred the distinctions that scholars often assume between religious genres like doctrinal treatise, ritual manual, and hagiography. Just as the *Awakening of Faith* (*Dasheng qixin lun* 大乘起信論) was ascribed to Aśvaghoṣa because of his reputation for post-*parinirvāṇa* exegesis, his affiliation with Nāgārjuna, and his *dhyāna* expertise, and as Āryadeva's *Hundred Treatise* was seen as a verbatim transcript of the debates described in his hagiographies, the nature of the Indian patriarchs' magical prowess was directly related to their early hagiographic representations and doctrinal writings. In the case of Aśvaghoṣa, his association with horses by virtue of his peculiar appellation—usually translated literally as "Horse Neigh" rather than transliterated like other

Indian names—was a key component of his *Baolin zhuan* hagiography depicting him as a compassionate silkworm saving horse-people, which was likewise implicated in his role as a Chinese sericulture god (see chapter 5). Nāgārjuna's divine talents were more wide-ranging, as were their hagiographic and exegetical sources. On the basis of his purported expositions in the *Great Perfection of Wisdom Treatise* and *Expanded Treatise on the Ten Stages*, the *Laṅkāvatāra* prophecy of his bodhisattva attainments and Pure Land rebirth, and the widespread tales of his facility with spells and elixirs, Nāgārjuna came to be seen as a local deity who provided Chinese adepts with the best Indian methods of repelling evils, attracting boons, and attaining rebirth in the Western paradise of Amitābha. As seen in the Chinese writings about these Indian patriarchs, doctrinal exegesis, ritual manual, and religious biography were often mutually constitutive genres. The career trajectories, doctrinal dispositions, and thaumaturgic prescriptions of Aśvaghoṣa and Nāgārjuna all went hand in hand, and from the ancient hagiographies of these long-departed masters were fashioned immanent deities to ensure the wellbeing of local Chinese devotees.

Nāgārjuna in the Land of Bliss

One salient means by which Nāgārjuna was seen to personally liberate medieval Chinese adepts was through his involvement in Pure Land devotional practice. Nāgārjuna was adduced as authority in the writings of all the most influential Chinese Pure Land masters, including Tanluan 曇鸞 (ca. 476–572), Daochuo 道綽 (562–645), Jiacai 迦才 (fl. ca. 620—650), and Shandao 善導 (613–681), and he was eventually placed at the head of a Japanese Pure Land patriarchate developed by advocates of Jōdo Shinshū 浄土真宗 in the thirteenth century.[1] The oft-cited *loci classici* for Nāgārjuna's Pure Land interests are passages from his *Great Perfection of Wisdom Treatise* and *Expanded Treatise on the Ten Stages*, which were taken together as proof texts for the practice of reciting paeans to buddhas in order to gain access to their Pure Lands.[2] While the former text explained the nature of buddha-fields (*focha* 佛刹, *buddhakṣetra*) and their presiding buddhas, including Amitābha and Sukhāvatī,[3] the latter text was especially popular with Pure Land adepts

1. See Dobbins 1989, 2–3. A caveat is in order with regard to the sources attributed to these famous Pure Land masters. Many of these sources were preserved only in Japan, so their medieval Chinese provenance remains open to question. While there is no strong reason to doubt any particular text cited in this chapter, one must remain cautious in staking any firm conclusions on their authority. Nevertheless, in terms of how these texts depicted Nāgārjuna, they indeed appear consonant with broader trends apparent in other sources confidently placed in Sui-Tang China.

2. Unlike modern scholars, medieval Chinese Buddhists never questioned Nāgārjuna's authorship of *Expanded Treatise on the Ten Stages*; the earliest extant source to ascribe it to Nāgārjuna and Kumārajīva was the *Chu sanzang jiji* 出三藏記集, T no. 2145, 55:8b, 11a.

3. See, e.g., *Dazhidu lun* 大智度論 (*Mahāprajñāpāramitāśāstra*), T no. 1509, 25:134b (trans. Lamotte 1944–1980, 1:601), and 309a (trans. Lamotte 1944–1980, 5:2308); otherwise, Amitābha was mentioned repeatedly throughout this treatise, as were many other buddhas.

who took its "Easy Practice Chapter" (Yixing pin 易行品) as quasi-scriptural justification for their favored devotional programs. In this chapter Nāgārjuna prescribed a program for worshipping a host of buddhas and bodhisattvas (also including Amitābha), visualizing them, and reciting their names and verses in their honor, which he described as expedient means of attaining the stage of non-regression (*aweiyuezhi* 阿惟越致, *avinivartanīya*) and eventually perfect enlightenment.[4] In this way Nāgārjuna was linked to Pure Land devotionalism through his exegetical treatises, which scholars often highlight as important to the development of East Asian Pure Land doctrine.[5] However, in medieval China these texts were influential not only in doctrinal terms, and Nāgārjuna's contributions to Pure Land practice extended far beyond his commentarial writings. In fact, these sources and their offshoots led to Nāgārjuna himself becoming an object of Pure Land devotion—with some even claiming that he presided over his own buddha-field[6]—and they furnished evidence to support the *Laṅkāvatāra* prophecy that Nāgārjuna had become a resident of Sukhāvatī. Indeed, perhaps by the seventh century this prophecy was treated as history, and Nāgārjuna was called upon to descend from his Pure Land perch to personally retrieve the faithful and usher them into this most coveted post-mortem paradise.

The *Great Perfection of Wisdom Treatise* and *Expanded Treatise on the Ten Stages* demonstrated to their medieval Chinese audiences not only that Nāgārjuna knew all about the Pure Land, but also that he knew how best to get there. Daochuo, for one, cited the former treatise to confirm that by reciting the *Amitābha Sūtra* one could be sure to meet the Buddha at death.[7] Tanluan adduced the latter source in emphasizing the importance of personal devotion to Amitābha and vows to obtain Pure Land rebirth.[8] And Jiacai equated Nāgārjuna's Pure Land paeans with the buddhas unfurling their enormous tongues and emitting light from their eyebrows as powerful means of guiding beings to salvation.[9] In fact, these verses in praise of

---

4. *Shizhu piposha lun* 十住毘婆沙論 (*Daśabhūmikavibhāṣāśāstra*), T no. 1521, 26:40c–45a; trans. Inagaki 1998, 137–164.

5. For example, Dobbins 1989, 4; Gómez 1996, 119–120; Pas 1995, 53–55; and Tanaka 1990, 10–12.

6. *Foshuo dasheng wuliangshou zhuangyan jing* 佛說大乘無量壽莊嚴經 (*Sukhāvatīvyūhasūtra*), T no. 363, 12:326a; trans. Dharmabhadra (d. 1001) in 991.

7. *Anle ji* 安樂集, T no. 1958, 47:18b. Cf. *Dazhidu lun*, T no. 1509, 25:127a (trans. Lamotte 1944–1980, 1:556). For more on Daochuo and the *Anle ji*, see especially Chappell 1976.

8. E.g., *Wuliangshou jing youpotishe yuansheng jie zhu*, T no. 1819, 40:826a–b; trans. Corless 1973, 89–90. This text has gone by a variety of names (see Ono 1:377c–d, 6:60a–b); it is attested in the sixth-century *Zhongjing mulu* (T no. 2146, 55:148a) as *Wuliangshou lunjie zhujie* 無量壽論偈注解. The *Taishō* text was based on a Tokugawa-era (1603–1868) print that included annotations referencing earlier source manuscripts (T no. 1819, 40:826n5). Several other editions of this text have been preserved in Japan, including a recently discovered Kongō-ji 金剛寺 manuscript dating to 1138; see Miyake 2008.

9. *Jingtu lun* 淨土論, T no. 1963, 47:102b. The *Taishō* edition of this text was based on a seventeenth-century Japanese print, collated with a xylographic copy from Jinling 金陵 (i.e., Nanjing, Jiangsu); see T no. 1963, 47:83n1. A number of other recensions of this text are extant; see Sowa 2006. On the Jinling Buddhist Press, see Wu 2006.

various buddhas from Nāgārjuna's *Expanded Treatise on the Ten Stages* would by Tang times be developed into a concise liturgy of twelve stanzas titled "Nāgārjuna's Text of Obeisance to Amitābha Buddha" (Longshu zanli Emituofo wen 龍樹讚禮阿彌陀佛文).[10] Like the earlier treatise on which they were based, these stanzas functioned to actuate through ritual performance their semantic, doctrinal contents, thus setting their readers on the path to salvation while also describing the nature of that path and its end. For example, according to the *Expanded Treatise on the Ten Stages*:

> If a person, at life's end, attains birth in this [Pure-] land
> He or she will at once be endowed with immeasurable merit
> Thus I take refuge
>
> If a person can be mindful of this Buddha's immeasurable power and virtue
> He or she will at once enter the stage of non-regression
> Thus I am always mindful
>
> Though the people of this land [i.e., Jambudvīpa] may suffer upon death
> They will not fall into the evil hells (because of the Buddha's teachings)
> Thus I prostrate in homage[11]
>
> 若人命終時　得生彼國者
> 即具無量德　是故我歸命
> 人能念是佛　無量力威德
> 即時入必定　是故我常念
> 彼國人命終　設應受諸苦
> 不墮惡地獄　是故歸命禮[12]

These verses thus described Pure Land residents as endowed with immeasurable merit and free from rebirth in hell, while emphasizing the need for Buddha-mindfulness in order to join their ranks. In this way the text served as a doctrinal primer for Pure Land practice, and it was taken as such by medieval Chinese adepts.[13] But at the same time, these verses were performative, intended for recitation, and as such their performance

10. First appearing in Jiacai's *Jingtu lun* (T no. 1963, 47:96b–97a), this text was also titled *Shi'er li* 十二禮. It was printed as an independent text in the *Dainippon zokuzōkyō* 大日本續藏經 (Z 1:2:2:195) and preserved in manuscript form at Dunhuang: see manuscript no. 8503 (果 088) from Dunhuang held in the National Library, Beijing; and *Dunhuang baozang* 敦煌寶藏, ed. Huang Yongwu, 1981–1986, 110:470. Cf. Ciyi 1988–1989, 1:347a–b; and Mochizuki 1954–1963, 3:2345a.

11. Translation adapted from Inagaki 1998, 150.

12. *Shizhu piposha lun*, T no. 1521, 26:43a.

13. See, e.g., Tanluan's *Wuliangshou jing youpotishe yuansheng jie zhu* (T no. 1819, 40:830c; trans. Corless 1973, 153) and Huiyuan's *Guan wuliangshou jing yishu* 觀無量壽經義疏 (T no. 1749, 37:182b–c; trans. Tanaka 1990, 174–175). On the provenance of this latter text, see Tanaka 1990, chap. 3.

set in motion the devotional program that they prescribed. This is indicated in part by the use of the first person to conclude each refrain—"Thus I take refuge"; "Thus I am always mindful"; "Thus I prostrate in homage"—which invited the reader to take Nāgārjuna's place as incanter. In addition, the semantic content of these verses, which detailed the virtues of the buddhas and their Pure Lands, served to aid in the practice of "calling to mind" (*nian* 念, *smṛti*) that was supposed to accompany oral recitation, as Jiacai explained.[14] Nāgārjuna's verses actualized in the mind of the practitioner the buddhas and buddha-fields that they illustrated, which further facilitated the attainment of the salvific boons promised. A similar dynamic is evident in "Nāgārjuna's Text of Obeisance to Amitābha Buddha," which was more clearly intended for liturgical use:

I bow to him who is honored by celestials and humans
The transcendent Amitābha, supreme among two-legged creatures
Dwelling in his wondrous Land of Ease and Bliss
Surrounded by a countless assembly of buddhas' children
I pray for all sentient beings
To be reborn in the Land of Ease and Bliss

His golden body pure like a mountain king
His *śamatha* (calm-abiding) practice like an elephant's stride
His two eyes pure like blue lotus flowers
Thus I pay homage to the Buddha Amitābha
I pray for all sentient beings
To be reborn in the Land of Ease and Bliss

His face perfectly round and pure like the full moon
His majestic light resembles a thousand suns and moons
His voice like both a heavenly drum and *kokila* bird [cuckoo]
Thus I pay homage to the Buddha Amitābha
I pray for all sentient beings
To be reborn in the Land of Ease and Bliss[15]

稽首天人所恭敬　阿彌陀仙兩足尊
在彼微妙安樂國　無量佛子眾圍遶
願共諸眾生　往生安樂國
金色身淨如山王　奢摩他行如象步
兩目淨若青蓮華　故我頂禮彌陀佛
願共諸眾生　往生安樂國
面善圓淨如滿月　威光猶如千日月
聲如天鼓俱翅羅　故我頂禮彌陀佛
願共諸眾生　往生安樂國[16]

14. *Jingtu lun*, T no. 1963, 47:95a.
15. Translation adapted from Robinson 1954, 64.
16. *Jingtu lun*, T no. 1963, 47:96c; *Shi'er li*, Z 1:2:2:195a.

The remaining verses of Nāgārjuna's liturgy follow this same pattern, describing Amitābha, his Pure Land, and its residents, while placing repetitive, formulaic prayers and statements of devotion in the mouths of its readers. First cited by Jiacai as a translation by the Gandhāran missionary Jñānagupta (523–600),[17] this liturgy found a prominent place in the Pure Land devotional program devised by Shandao, whereby the practitioner would perform rites of confession and repentance and recite paeans to Amitābha from various sources at each of six periods of the day and night. "Nāgārjuna's Text of Obeisance to Amitābha Buddha" was to be recited at midnight.[18] And while Nāgārjuna's verses would function as Shandao prescribed in the ritual programs of medieval Chinese devotees, in the Pure Land liturgy developed by Tanluan, Nāgārjuna himself became an object of devotion:

Homage to Amitābha, Buddha of the West, I wholeheartedly take refuge
The original teacher Nāgārjuna *mahāsattva* (great being)
Born at the beginning of Semblance [Dharma period]
He restored the severed link [to the Buddha]
Shutting the doors of perversion and opening the path of righteousness
Acting as the eyes [for all beings] in Jambudvīpa
At the Buddha's word[19] he achieved the stage of joy
Relying upon Amitābha to be born in [the Land of] Ease and Bliss
I pray for all sentient beings
To be reborn in the Land of Ease and Bliss
Homage to Amitābha, Buddha of the West, I whole-heartedly take refuge
Just as when the dragon moves the clouds must follow[20]
And Jambudvīpa spawns one hundred kinds of blossoming flowers
Homage to the venerable and compassionate Nāgārjuna
I wholeheartedly bow down and take refuge
I pray for all sentient beings
To be reborn in the Land of Ease and Bliss[21]

南無至心歸命禮西方阿彌陀佛
本師龍樹摩訶薩　　誕形像始理頹綱
關閉邪扇開正轍　　是閻浮提一切眼
伏承尊悟歡喜地　　歸阿彌陀生安樂
願共諸眾生往生安樂國

17. *Jingtu lun*, T no. 1963, 47:96b. On Jñānagupta, see Muller 1995– (s.v. "Shenajueduo 闍那崛多").

18. *Wangsheng lizan jie* 往生禮讚偈, T no. 1980, 47:442a–c; see Pas 1995, 110–112. Cf. *Ji zhujing lichan yi* 集諸經禮懺儀, by Zhisheng 智昇 (fl. 700–786), T no. 1982, 47:469c–470a, which largely reproduced Shandao's program.

19. Reading *yu* 語 for *wu* 悟.

20. Cf. *Yijing*, first hexagram (*qian*) 乾: 雲從龍, 風從虎, 聖人作而萬物覩 ("As the clouds follow the dragon and the wind follows the tiger, all living things observe the activities of the sage"). My thanks to Chen Jinhua for this reference.

21. Cf. trans. Corless 1990, 130–131.

南無至心歸命禮西方阿彌陀佛
譬如龍動雲必隨　閻浮提放百卉舒
南無慈悲龍樹尊　至心歸命頭面禮
願共諸眾生往生安樂國[22]

Here Tanluan singled out Nāgārjuna for extended praise and humble devotion, expressly reinscribing in liturgical format the earlier hagiographic narratives of Nāgārjuna reviving the teaching during the Semblance Dharma period, as well as the *Laṅkāvatāra* prophecy of his achievements on the bodhisattva path and rebirth in Sukhāvatī. In fact, aside from the standard Pure Land duo of Avalokiteśvara and Mahāsthāmaprāpta, Nāgārjuna was the only bodhisattva invoked by name in Tanluan's liturgy—as the "original teacher" (*benshi* 本師) who took refuge in Amitābha. In addition, according to a biography of Tanluan recounted by Jiacai, Tanluan often worshipped Nāgārjuna in particular, and for that he was rewarded with a personal visit and prophecy from this great Pure Land denizen:

> [Tanluan] encouraged the people, both monastic and lay, to resolutely seek rebirth [in the Pure Land], where they could see the myriad buddhas. He always prayed to Nāgārjuna Bodhisattva that he would attain awakening at death. Just as he had wished, when his retribution in this world was about to end [i.e., when he was approaching death], in the middle of the sky there appeared an image of a saintly monk, who suddenly entered [Tanluan's] chamber and said, "I am Nāgārjuna," and then spoke these words:
>
> "A leaf that has already fallen cannot be put back on the branch.
> Grain that has not yet been bundled cannot be sought in the storehouse.
> Like 'a white steed that flits past a crack,'[23] it cannot stay for a moment.
> What is already gone cannot be reached.
> The future cannot be pursued.
> What is here now in the present?
> The white steed is hard to turn back."
>
> Profoundly grasping the meaning of these words, the Dharma-master thereupon announced his [imminent] death. So, in the middle of the night he dispatched a messenger to tell all his lay disciples in the village and his monastic disciples in the monastery, and at once some three hundred people gathered like rain clouds. The Dharma-master bathed and put on new, clean clothes, held a censer in his hand, and sat facing west. He instructed his disciples to follow the practices [for attaining rebirth] in the Western [Pure Land].

22. *Zan Emituofo jie* 讚阿彌陀佛偈, T no. 1978, 47:424a. Part of this text is attested in Daochuo's *Anle ji* (T no. 1958, 47:19b); for a brief discussion in English of its extant recensions, see Corless 1989, 263.

23. *Zhuangzi* 莊子 22 (*Zhuangzi jinzhu jinyi* 莊子今注今譯, 570); trans. Watson 1968, 240. Cf. Luo 1987–1995, 4813a.

At daybreak the great assembly chanted in chorus the name of Amitābha Buddha as [Tanluan's] life came to an end. . . . He certainly attained birth in the Western [Pure Land].

勸道俗等, 決定往生, 得見諸佛. 恒請龍樹菩薩, 臨終開悟. 誠如所願, 此方報盡, 半霄之內, 現聖僧像, 忽來入室, 云: "我是龍樹." 便為說曰:

"已落之葉, 不可更附枝也;
未束之粟, 不可倉中求也.
'白駒過隙,' 不可暫時留也.
已去叵可及,[24]
未來未可追.
現在今何在,
白駒難可迴!"

法師妙達言旨, 如是告終. 即半夜內, 發遣使者, 遍告諸村白衣弟子, 及寺內出家弟子, 可三百餘人, 一時雨雲集. 法師沐浴, 著新淨衣, 手執香爐, 正面西坐. 教誡門徒, 索西方業.
日初出時, 大眾齊聲, 念彌陀佛. 便即壽終. . . . . 定得生西方也.[25]

Here the manner of Tanluan's obeisance to Nāgārjuna was only vaguely outlined. He entreated Nāgārjuna for enlightenment and Pure Land rebirth, but it is unclear if he recited Nāgārjuna's verses or his own Pure Land liturgy, performed rites of confession and repentance, or engaged votive images of Nāgārjuna. Only Nāgārjuna's appearance at midnight would suggest a resonance with the devotional program later outlined by Shandao. Further, the details of Nāgārjuna's identity were apparently assumed, and his precise role in Tanluan's death and rebirth was left undefined. Did Nāgārjuna ensure Tanluan's Pure Land rebirth or directly effect his salvation in some way? Did he serve as intermediary between Tanluan and Amitābha? Did he respond in particular to the rituals of obeisance presumably performed by Tanluan? In any event, clearly it was because Tanluan "always prayed to Nāgārjuna" that this particular Pure Land resident appeared personally to communicate his enigmatic prophecy. In another, later version of Tanluan's encounter with Nāgārjuna, the reasons for the latter's visit were similarly vague, and Nāgārjuna again did little more than predict Tanluan's death (albeit with poetic flourish). But this time Nāgārjuna's appearance followed immediately on the heels of Tanluan's decision to forsake Chinese "transcendence scriptures" (*xianjing* 仙經) and take up Pure Land practice instead. This tale thus signaled another salient theme of Tanluan's career as well as Nāgārjuna's Chinese manifestation: competition between religious traditions.

---

24. The reading of *keji* 可及 is from the Jinling edition of the text; the Japanese edition has *fan* 反 instead (*Jingtu lun*, T no. 1963, 47:97n4). The former is preferable in maintaining the pentasyllabic structure of Nāgārjuna's verses.

25. *Jingtu lun*, T no. 1963, 47:97c–98a.

Dharma-master Tanluan of the Qi dynasty lived near Wutai [modern Shanxi]. He deeply understood the myriad teachings. Having obtained ten scrolls of Chinese transcendence scriptures, he wished to visit Tao Hongjing 陶弘景 [456–536] and study the arts of transcendence. Later he met a Trepiṭaka bodhisattva and asked him, "Does the Buddhadharma include methods for attaining longevity and transcending death that surpass the transcendence scriptures of this land?" The Trepiṭaka scoffed and said to Tanluan, "Where in this place are there methods for attaining longevity and transcending death? Even if you live a long life, when your years are exhausted you must die." He then gave to Tanluan the *Sūtra on the Contemplation of the Buddha of Immeasurable Life* and said, "If one follows and practices this great method of transcendence, he will forever obtain liberation and release from birth and death." Tanluan then burned his transcendence scriptures.

Suddenly in the middle of the night he saw an Indian monk enter his chamber. [This monk] said to Tanluan, "I am Nāgārjuna Bodhisattva," and he spoke these verses:

"Leaves that have already fallen cannot be returned to their branches.
Future grain cannot be sought in the storehouse.
Like 'a white steed that flits past a crack,' it cannot stay for a moment.

齊朝曇鸞法師, 家近五臺. 洞明諸教. 因得此土仙經十卷, 欲訪陶隱居, 學仙術. 後逢三藏菩薩, 問曰, "佛法中有長生不死法, 勝此土仙經否?" 三藏唾地驚曰, "此方何處有長生不死法? 縱得延壽, 年盡須墮." 即將無量壽觀經, 授與鸞曰, "此大仙方, 依而行之, 長得解脫, 永離生死." 鸞便須火, 遂焚仙經.

忽於半夜, 見一梵僧入房. 語鸞曰, "我是龍樹菩薩." 便說偈,

"已落葉, 不可更附枝.
未來粟, 不可倉中求.
'白駒過隙,' 不可暫駐. [26]

As in Jiacai's earlier rendition, Tanluan understood the meaning of Nāgārjuna's words, gathered his disciples, and told them to worship the Pure Land, and then died while they chanted Amitābha's name. But the obvious differences here are Tanluan's interest in longevity and immortality and his encounter with a "Trepiṭaka bodhisattva" who chided him for this misguided interest before selling him on the Pure Land way of escaping death. This portion of the tale was drawn from Daoxuan's *Continued Biographies of Eminent Monks*, which similarly emphasized Tanluan's early Daoist proclivities as well as his dramatic act of burning all his Daoist texts before devoting himself to Amitābha.[27] But only in Tanluan's later Pure Land biography was

26. *Wangsheng xifang jingtu ruiying zhuan* 往生西方淨土瑞應傳, T no. 2070, 51:104a–b; compilation attributed to Shaotang 少唐 (d. 805) and Wenshen 文諗 (n.d.). For more on this text see Ono 1:358c–d and Mochizuki 1954–1963, 1:338a.

27. *Xu gaoseng zhuan* 續高僧傳, T no. 2060, 50:470a–c; briefly summarized by Corless 1987, 36–37. The quest for longevity and transcendence was in itself no more Daoist than

his conversion to Buddhism followed by the appearance of Nāgārjuna. One might initially suspect that the mysterious "Trepiṭaka bodhisattva" who gave Tanluan the *Sūtra on the Contemplation of the Buddha of Immeasurable Life* was in fact Nāgārjuna—especially since Jizang once related this text directly to Nāgārjuna's dragon-palace adventure.[28] However, Daoxuan identified this Trepiṭaka as Bodhiruci (fl. 508–535), translator of Vasubandhu's *Commentary on the Sūtra of Immeasurable Life* (*Wuliangshou jing youpotishe* 無量壽經優波提舍 [*Sukhāvativyūhopadeśa*]), and otherwise made no mention of Nāgārjuna at all.[29] It was Tanluan's later Pure Land hagiographers who associated his sectarian about-face with the figure of Nāgārjuna, thus situating this Indian patriarch at the juncture between Chinese and Buddhist models of sanctity and salvation. The same was the case with another tale of Nāgārjuna's Pure Land prowess, in which he appeared personally before a certain *dhyāna*-master Daoquan (n.d.) to convey the life-sustaining power of Amitābha:

> Shi Daoquan was a man of unknown origin. As a youth he was praised for his excellence in doctrinal study. He took the *Perfection of Wisdom Treatise* as his mind's essence and Nāgārjuna as his teacher and patriarch. He made a vow, saying:
>
> "The great master Nāgārjuna
> received the Buddha's assurance
> that he would achieve the stage of joy
> and rebirth in the Land of Ease and Bliss.
> To assist Amitābha in teaching
> and protecting the beings of the ten directions,
> I pray [that the Buddha will] bestow pity and compassion,
> [enabling me] to attain rebirth in that land!"
>
> He further constructed a three-foot image [of Nāgārjuna] and made offerings of incense and flowers, focusing his mind in prayer.
>
> He had a dream of a *śramaṇa* who said, "Your Pure Land practices are certainly beyond question; after three years you will be reborn in the Land of Ease and Bliss."

---

rice—*pace* Sivin (1978, 319), and as Campany (2009, 35–36) also emphasizes—but the association with a vaunted scriptural tradition and with Tao Hongjing in particular (on whom see Strickmann 1979) surely signaled more strictly Daoist connotations. On Daoism as defined by the creation of a scriptural canon, see Ōfuchi 1979 and Schipper 1995.

28. See Jizang's *Guan wuliangshou jing yishu* 觀無量壽經義疏, T no. 1752, 37:237b. Corless (1987, 43n6) doubts that the "*Guanjing* 觀經" in Daoxuan's account referred to the *Contemplation Sūtra* in particular (*Guan wuliangshou jing* 觀無量壽經, T no. 365), suggesting rather that it indicated several Pure Land texts. However, the tale in the *Wangsheng xifang jingtu ruiying zhuan* more specifically stated *Guan wuliangshou jing*—like the title that Jizang gave. See Yamabe 1999 for more on the genre of *guanjing* in general.

29. *Xu gaoseng zhuan*, T no. 2060, 50:470b. *Commentary on the Sūtra of Immeasurable Life, Wuliangshou jing youpotishe* 無量壽經優波提舍 (*Sukhāvativyūhopadeśa*), T no. 1524; trans. 529. This text led medieval Chinese Buddhists to associate Vasubandhu with Pure Land devotionalism.

Daoquan said, "I have a teacher and friend. How can I relinquish my life before him?"

The *śramaṇa* said, "I must report this to Amitābha Buddha; I will return to tell you the result."

After [Daoquan] awoke he prayed further, "May I relinquish my life after my teacher and friend."

After three days had passed, he again dreamed of the *śramaṇa*, who came to tell Daoquan, "I reported what you said to Amitābha Buddha. The Buddha said that your teacher will die after twelve years, you will die after seventeen years, and your mother will die in twenty years. But through the wondrousness of your vow, your life will be extended for another three years, in addition to [your mother's] twenty years. So you will be born in this [Pure] Land after twenty-three years. The teaching of the Buddha is like this."

[Daoquan] again asked, "Will my mother, father, and teacher and friend be born in the Pure Land?"

[The *śramaṇa*] answered, "If they make this vow with the same [determined] mind, they will certainly be born there without doubt."

Daoquan happily inquired again, "Who are you, sir?"

[The *śramaṇa*] answered, "I am Nāgārjuna, the thirteenth [patriarch] in the Dharma-treasury transmission. You constructed an image of me, so I urgently came to report this to you."

Twenty-three years later, on the fifteenth day of the first month, [Daoquan] died.

釋道詮, 不知何處人. 少有義學嘉譽. 以智度論為心要, 以龍樹為師宗. 發願云:

"大士龍樹,
蒙佛誠言,
證歡喜地,
往安樂國.
補彌陀化,
十方攝生,
願垂哀愍,
得生彼國!"

更造三尺形像, 香花供養, 專心祈願.
夢感一沙門云, "汝淨土業, 必定無疑, 卻後三年, 方往生安樂國."
詮云, "我有師友. 豈先捨壽. 此事如何?"
沙門曰, "須白阿彌陀佛; 還來告其實."
夢覺彌祈請, "我及師友, 捨壽先後."
經三日後, 又復夢沙門, 來告詮曰, "以汝言白阿彌陀佛, 佛言汝師卻後十二年卒, 汝卻後十七年方卒, 汝母二十年方卒. 但汝願微妙, 須延三年壽, 加二十年. 卻後二十三年, 方生此國. 佛教如斯."
復問, "我父母師友, 生淨土否?"
答, "同心發願, 必生無疑."
詮歡喜復問, "君何人?"
答, "我是龍樹, 付法藏中第十三. 汝造我像, 頻來告之."
其後二十三年, 正月十五日而卒.

Upon Daoquan's death, as Nāgārjuna had prophesied, music emanated from the heavens, purple clouds gathered, and other auspicious omens verified that the Land of Bliss had indeed gained another blessed resident. Purportedly drawn from a certain *Traditions of the Pure Land* (*Jingtu zhuan* 淨土傳), this tale was titled "The Sympathetic Resonance of *Dhyāna*-Master Shi Daoquan Constructing an Image of Nāgārjuna and Being Reborn in the Pure Land."[30] Compared with the aforementioned hagiographies of Tanluan, this tale more clearly circumscribed Nāgārjuna's role in Pure Land practice and salvation. Nāgārjuna was invoked by name in the Pure Land vow; he was represented in iconic form, given offerings of incense and flowers, and solicited directly; he appeared personally to communicate with the devotee; and he served as emissary for Amitābha and the other exalted bodhisattvas of Sukhāvatī. At the same time, the author of this tale expressly maintained Nāgārjuna's earlier Chinese roles—as member of the master-disciple lineage and as singularly brilliant doctrinal exegete—and clearly foregrounded his Indian identity by restating his position in the Dharma-treasury transmission. But what is new and especially intriguing in this account is the manner in which it situated Nāgārjuna within broader Chinese paradigms of bureaucratic divinity and processes of augmenting one's pre-allotted life span (*ming* 命). Incorporating widespread Chinese notions of destiny, filial piety, and heavenly hierarchy, this tale deployed Nāgārjuna to further integrate Pure Land soteriology into Chinese society and position the Chinese sangha as the institution best equipped to protect people's lives and loved ones.

As recently explained by Christine Mollier, from ancient times in China the notion was prevalent that every person was born with a predetermined but flexible allotment of years.[31] In heaven there was a "life-account" (*suan* 算) for each individual that gradually diminished but was also affected by sins and good deeds. The question of what constituted a merit or demerit was variously answered across traditions, but essentially one could expect that if she or he did something wrong or right, it would affect

30. "Shi Daoquan chanshi zao Longshu pusa xiang sheng jingtu ganying" 釋道詮禪師造龍樹菩薩像生淨土感應; preserved in *Sanbao ganying yaolüe lu* 三寶感應要略錄, by Feizhuo 非濁 (d. 1063), T no. 2084, 51:856a-b (on which see Chen 1979 and Ono 1933–1936, 4:114d–116a). The origin of this tale is uncertain; I have not found it recounted elsewhere. *Jingtu wangsheng zhuan* 淨土往生傳 (T no. 2071), by Jiezhu 戒珠 (985–1077), which is referenced in Song writings as *Jingtu zhuan*, includes no such account of Daoquan. There is also a *Jingtu zhuanji* 淨土傳記, mentioned in Sui-Tang sources, that is no longer extant; see, e.g., *Jingtu shiyi lun* 淨土十疑論, T no. 1961, 47:77b. The matter is further complicated by the obscurity of this figure Daoquan. Could this be the same Daoquan mentioned by Zongmi 宗密 (780–841) as residing at Zanghai monastery 藏海寺 in Beidu 北都 (Taiyuan) (*Da fangguang yuanjue xiuduoluo liaoyi jing lüeshu* 大方廣圓覺修多羅了義經略疏, T no. 1795, 39:528b); or the Daoquan of Qizhou 齊州 (in present-day Shandong), who according to Daoxuan was a contemporary of the monk Huihai 慧海 (548–609) and was known for his images of Amitābha (*Xu gaoseng zhuan*, T no. 2060, 50:515c); or the Daoquan who reportedly authored Abhidharma commentaries and was affiliated with Fugan monastery 福感寺 in present-day Sichuan (Chen 1999, 143n8)?

31. Mollier 2008, 100–106; cf. Campany 2005.

proximity to death. In both Buddhist and Daoist sources, this life-account was sometimes conceived as a granary or treasury in heaven, which when depleted would signal the end of one's days but which could also be replenished through various forms of ritual obeisance. A divine bureaucracy was often tasked with the management of these accounts, with the so-called Directors of Destiny (Siming 司命) overseeing everyone's deeds, making reports, and adjusting their registers accordingly. The means employed to curry favor with these Directors and their ilk varied widely, from the thaumaturgic and ritual to the more strictly ethical, and these means would affect more than just lifespan; health, wealth, career, offspring, and other markers of worldly prosperity were also implicated in this otherworldly economy. Many sources were produced in medieval China that ascribed to the Buddha various methods of attaining longevity, despite Buddhist admonitions from the likes of Bodhiruci that death was ultimately unavoidable. And although Pure Land rituals usually focused more on post-mortem salvation than on lengthening one's current lifespan, in this case these two aims were clearly complementary.

Here Daoquan's desire for longevity was justified by the ethic of filial piety, as he prayed for a longer life only to avoid deserting his venerable teacher and parents. Thus Daoquan performed two good deeds in order to ensure that his lifespan would be increased: he displayed true devotion to his forebears and he enacted the proper Pure Land rites. In some respects Daoquan's plight resonated with tales of Śākyamuni's disciple Maudgalyāyana, that most filial of Indian masters, who was instructed to make offerings to the sangha in order to save his mother from post-mortem torture.[32] Daoquan's elders were still alive and in no imminent danger, but his tale similarly advanced Buddhist rituals as the most effective means of ensuring his family's wellbeing. Toward this end—and as guarantor of Daoquan's increased longevity—Nāgārjuna played a quasi-bureaucratic role akin to that of the Directors of Destiny. He mediated between earth and the upper levels of heaven and conveyed reports from on high about amendments to Daoquan's lifespan.[33] Of course, as per the standard logic of karmic causality, Nāgārjuna ascribed operative agency for Daoquan's longevity not to himself or Amitābha but to the meritorious quality of Daoquan's Pure Land vows. Nevertheless, the author of this story also maintained that Daoquan's life was extended—and his eventual liberation secured—only because he performed rites of obeisance to the denizens of Sukhāvatī. As such, this tale advanced age-old Chinese ideals of prosperity, morality, divinity, and salvation, while at the same time revaluating them within a particularly Pure Land soteriological framework. Through the figure of Nāgārjuna in particular, Daoquan's biography demonstrated how Buddhist deities and rituals were the most effective means of procuring what Chinese supplicants

32. See Teiser 1988.

33. For an insightful discussion of the bureaucratic model of Chinese divinity, see Hymes 2002.

from all religious traditions valued most: longevity, family wellbeing, and ultimate salvation in paradise.

Nāgārjunian Spell-Craft

Another popular device that Nāgārjuna supplied to facilitate Pure Land rebirth was also closely related to his earlier hagiographies and treatises, as well as his Pure Land liturgies and function in Chinese ritual practice. This was Nāgārjuna's "spirit-spell for uprooting all karmic hindrances and attaining birth in the Pure Land," which he reportedly received in a vision from Amitābha Buddha.[34] According to two (Six Dynasties?) texts in which this spell was preserved, the Pure Land aspirant should bathe and clean her teeth, light incense before an image of the Buddha, kneel with palms pressed together, and recite this spell thirty-seven times at each of the six periods of day and night. If performed regularly with sincere devotion, this rite would completely erase all of the adept's sins, protect her from disturbances by evil spirits, and guarantee rebirth in the Land of Bliss. While Nāgārjuna here again played the role of mediator between Amitābha and his earthbound devotees, as in Daoquan's filial drama, it was Nāgārjuna in particular who transmitted this spell for Pure Land salvation. But Nāgārjuna's association with Buddhist spell-craft extended far beyond his specialization in Pure Land soteriology, and his efficacious incantations were advertised by and for a broad range of medieval Chinese adepts toward a wide variety of material, apotropaic, and therapeutic ends. In this regard Nāgārjuna once again joined forces with his long-time partner Aśvaghoṣa, who likewise provided a host of occult technologies aimed at repelling evils and attracting boons. In tandem these Indian patriarchs-*cum*-deities appeared personally in Chinese ritual arenas to benefit supplicants in this life and the next, employing ritual procedures that were prevalent across religious traditions but also demonstrating how Buddhist masters were most adept at unlocking their powers.

In his early Chinese hagiographies and commentarial writings, Nāgārjuna demonstrated both his authoritative understanding of Buddhist spells—*chi* 持, *jue* 決, or *zhou*; *dhāraṇī*, mantra, or *vidyā*—as well as his unmatched ability to devise and deploy them. Perhaps the best-known early hagiographic tale of Nāgārjuna's spell-craft appeared in the *Dharma-Treasury*

34. This spell and its instructions for use were appended to the *Taishō* edition of the *Smaller Sukhāvatī-vyūha* (*Foshuo Emituo jing* 佛說阿彌陀經, T no. 366, 12:348b), following a Dunhuang manuscript of this text. Here it is called the "spell spoken by Amitābha Buddha for rebirth in the Pure Land" (Wuliangshoufo shuo wangsheng jingtu zhou 無量壽佛說往生淨土呪). Another version of this spell was given as the *Ba yiqie yezhang genben desheng jingtu shenzhou* 拔一切業障根本得生淨土神咒 (T no. 368), which says that it was excerpted from the *Smaller Sukhāvatī-vyūha*. These texts claimed that either Guṇabhadra (392–468) or Narendrayaśas (ca.490–589) transmitted the spell to China, where it was promulgated by a certain Dharmamaster Xiu 銹法師 of Tianping monastery 天平寺 in the Northern Qi capital of Ye. See Mochizuki 1954–1963, 1:71a–c (s.v. "Amida ju 阿彌陀咒").

Transmission and his independently circulating biography, in which he defeated an arrogant Brahman by casting a spell to conjure a six-tusked white elephant.[35] In Jizang's extended remix of this tale, the Brahman followed Nāgārjuna's elephant apparition by producing a ten-headed *rākṣasa* (ogre). Nāgārjuna then manifested the heavenly king Vaiśravaṇa to scare away the *rākṣasa*, and the Brahman followed with a poisonous dragon that rained down boulders. Nāgārjuna concluded the battle by transforming the boulders into heavenly flowers.[36] Thus Nāgārjuna showed some of the more spectacular effects of his potent spells while also illustrating how the superiority of Buddhism was sometimes best proven thaumaturgically. Such sectarian considerations were similarly foregrounded in later Chinese sources that prescribed ritual worship of Nāgārjuna and advertised his vast repertoire of spells and talismanic seals, including those for controlling elephants and invoking Vaiśravaṇa.[37] These sources advanced powerful models of magical practice that were common to both Chinese Buddhist and Daoist traditions, but then ascribed them to Nāgārjuna (together with other famous Indian saints) in order to render them the preserve of Buddhist adepts alone.

Like most other areas of Buddhist soteriology, cosmology, and theology, Nāgārjuna's vast knowledge of Buddhist spell-craft was demonstrated first and foremost in his *Great Perfection of Wisdom Treatise*. As Paul Copp (2008) and Richard McBride (2005) have recently emphasized, this was one of the most important sources for Chinese scholastic understandings of *dhāraṇī* as theorized and utilized in the Indian Buddhist tradition.[38] Chinese Buddhist exegetes relied heavily on this treatise in formulating their own discourses on *dhāraṇī*, as with Huiyuan's elaboration on the four-fold *dhāraṇī* classification of the *Bodhisattvabhūmi* (*Pusa dichi jing* 菩薩地持經).[39] Throughout the *Great Perfection of Wisdom Treatise*, Nāgārjuna (via Kumārajīva, Sengrui, and others) provided his authoritative pronouncements on the nature and function of *dhāraṇī*, and at several points he defined them as one attainment or spiritual capacity of the bodhisattva, like concentration or forbearance. The bodhisattva's power of *dhāraṇī*, as the text explained, was his ability to "grasp" (*chi*) and keep hold of all good dharmas as well as "block out" (*zhe* 遮) any evil dispositions.[40] Copp argues that the basic meaning of "grasp" underlay the various permutations of the term *dhāraṇī*—as a kind of mnemonic device, a form of spiritual capacity, or a magical incantation—which were all, according to Nāgārjuna, the province of buddhas and

35. See chapter 2; Chaudhuri 2008, 22; Corless 1995, 529–530; and Li 2002c, 25.

36. *Dasheng xuan lun* 大乘玄論, T no. 1853, 45:77a–b.

37. *Longshu wuming lun* 龍樹五明論, T no. 1420, 21:963a, 966b.

38. For the present discussion it matters only that Chinese readers thought this text was Indian; we do not know how much of it actually was.

39. See *Dasheng yizhang* 大乘義章, T no. 1851, 44:685a–c; discussed by McBride 2005, 96–102.

40. See, e.g., *Dazhidu lun*, T no. 1509, 25:95c–97c; Copp 2008, 500–506; and Lamotte 1944–1980, 1:317–328. For an in-depth study of *dhāraṇī* in medieval China, see Copp 2014.

bodhisattvas. In his earliest Chinese hagiographies, Nāgārjuna was himself labeled a bodhisattva, so by his own definition he would have been equally endowed with such *dhāraṇī*. And who better to prescribe specific spells than the bodhisattva who authored one of their most influential doctrinal expositions? Indeed, together with Nāgārjuna's early hagiographies, the *Great Perfection of Wisdom Treatise* helped shape the Chinese image of this Indian patriarch as a master of Buddhist spell-craft, and other sources of less scholarly persuasion built on this image in advancing Nāgārjuna as a local deity who could be entreated directly to bestow the thaumaturgic fruits of his labor.

Another aspect of Nāgārjuna's early Chinese repertoire that closely related to his facility with spells was his penchant for Pure Land paeans. As already discussed, the *Expanded Treatise on the Ten Stages* and "Nāgārjuna's Text of Obeisance to Amitābha Buddha" provided devotional verses that functioned both as Pure Land doctrinal primers and as liturgical performances devised to effect Pure Land rebirth. The exact mechanism of these potent utterances was variously conceived, whether as following the natural laws of karma, engaging the power of Amtābha's vows,[41] or, as per Tanluan's formulation, instantiating identical ontological realities. That is, according to Tanluan, while some words were just arbitrary labels for things, with no effective relationship between signifier and signified, other words were exactly the same as the things they represented. These kinds of words when uttered would directly affect reality according to their nature. That was why the practice of *Buddhanāma* recitation actually brought the Buddha Amitābha before the practitioner: the name Amitābha and Amitābha himself were no different from one another. Tanluan also argued that *dhāraṇī* and spells (*jinzhou* 禁咒) functioned the same way, instantiating the ontological modes or entities that they ostensibly signified.[42] Similarly, Nāgārjuna's paeans to Amitābha operated in a manner analogous to his "spirit-spell for uprooting all karmic hindrances and attaining birth in the Pure Land." Both were intended for oral recitation and both worked to manifest Amitābha within the ritual arena and ensure the supplicant's Pure Land rebirth. And while on linguistic grounds it may be improper to posit an equation between these *zan* 讚 (paeans) and *zhou*—especially since the former were translated into straightforward Chinese while the latter was transcribed into nonsensical strings of exotic characters—following Tanluan's reasoning these utterances were structurally analogous as well. In any event, Nāgārjuna's liturgies and spells were clearly seen to work in concert with one another, especially in a Pure Land ritual setting. But for those not so inclined toward Amitābha worship or Pure Land rebirth, Nāgārjuna's efficacious incantations could do much else besides.

41. See, e.g., Shandao's *Wangsheng lizan jie*, T no. 1980, 47:438c.

42. *Wuliangshou jing youpotishe yuansheng jie zhu*, T no. 1819, 40:835c; see also Corless 1987, 40.

Without doubt the most comprehensive medieval Chinese source for spells and talismanic seals devised by this Indian patriarch-*cum*-local deity was *Nāgārjuna's Treatise on the Five Sciences*. Set during the reign of King Aśoka, at a time of widespread famine, pestilence, and destitution, this text provided a vast array of thaumaturgic methods for warding off evils, attaining powers and riches, and healing afflictions. These methods were advanced as requisite expediencies in the dark centuries after Śākyamuni's departure, when the technologies of all magical-medico traditions were needed to save beings in peril. In fact, near the beginning of this text, an unnamed Buddhist monk and former non-Buddhist was introduced as a transmitter of various techniques for securing health and wealth, which he expressly labeled both Buddhist and "other."[43] These techniques were then incorporated by the greatest king of Buddhist lore and promulgated by two of the most famous post-*parnirvāṇa* Indian patriarchs: Aśvaghoṣa and Nāgārjuna. This text thus reinscribed earlier narratives of these masters saving the world in dark times, but instead of emphasizing how they dispelled confusion with their doctrinal treatises, here they employed spells and talismans to eliminate demons, curses, sickness, and poverty. As such, unlike the earlier accounts by Kumārajīva's associates, this text accords with the Six Dynasties eschatologies studied by Michel Strickmann, in which therapeutic and apotropaic remedies were provided to save the world in end times.[44] This emphasis suggests an authorship and intended audience for *Nāgārjuna's Treatise on the Five Sciences* that extended beyond the ranks of the Buddhist ecclesiastic elite, especially as Aśvaghoṣa and Nāgārjuna were advertised as directly accessible to any "ordinary person" (*fanren* 凡人) who wished to engage their services.[45]

Nāgārjuna's Treatise on the Five Sciences identifies itself as the sole remaining fragment of an enormous text some ten thousand scrolls long, which was composed by Aśvaghoṣa and Nāgārjuna during (or after?) the time of Aśoka.[46] These remnants now constitute a mere two scrolls (spanning thirteen *Taishō* pages), which carry no translator attribution and which were preserved only in a single Japanese manuscript.[47] Strickmann speculates that the text was composed in northern China during the sixth century, though he is uncharacteristically coy about his reasoning (2002, 170). He would appear to follow the suggestion of Osabe Kazuo 長部和雄 that *Nāgārjuna's Treatise on the Five Sciences* was excerpted from a certain *Treatise*

43. *Longshu wuming lun*, T no. 1420, 21:956c: 我昔尋外法中, 有利益人民之法. 今日出家入佛法中, 亦有利益眾生之法 ("The non-Buddhist teaching that I once followed includes methods for benefiting the people. Now I have left home and entered into the Buddhadharma, which also has methods for benefiting sentient beings").

44. See Strickmann 1990; 2002, 50–62.

45. *Longshu wuming lun*, T no. 1420, 21:957b, 967b; cf. Davis 2001, 135–136.

46. The attribution to Aśvaghoṣa and Nāgārjuna occurs toward the end of the main body of the text (*Longshu wuming lun*, T no. 1420, 21:967b).

47. The *Taishō* text is based on a Heian 平安 period (794–1185) manuscript from the Ishiyama-dera 石山寺 canon, Kyoto (*Longshu wuming lun*, T no. 1420, 21:956n1).

on the Five Sciences (*Wuming lun* 五明論), which was listed in the Sui-Tang Buddhist catalogues as a translation completed in 558 by Jñānabhadra (n.d.) and Jinayaśa (n.d.) at the Bhagavat monastery (Poqie si 婆伽寺) in Chang'an.[48] Osabe admits that this connection is pure conjecture, since the *Treatise on the Five Sciences* is long lost and so cannot be compared with the extant manuscript. But the same Buddhist catalogues defined the fourth and fifth sciences of the former text as "spell-craft" (*zhoushu* 咒術) and "talismanic seals" (*fuyin* 符印), which would indeed seem a likely source for *Nāgārjuna's Treatise on the Five Sciences*. If this is so, then when and why were these particular collections of techniques excerpted from a more comprehensive manual and ascribed to Nāgārjuna?

Although we cannot determine precisely when Nāgārjuna was connected with the *Wuming lun*, there are a few clues that point to the mid-Tang dynasty. First of all, there is a passing reference by the Buddhist layman Li Tongxuan 李通玄 (ca. 635–730) to Nāgārjuna's talismanic seals,[49] which may attest *Nāgārjuna's Treatise on the Five Sciences* since no other sources of the time included seals ascribed to Nāgārjuna. Secondly, this text's depiction of Nāgārjuna and Aśvaghoṣa joining forces as purveyors of magical rites suggests a connection to the eighth- or ninth-century *Scripture on the Power and Virtue of Prince Kumbhīra* (*Jinpiluo tongzi weide jing* 金毘羅童子威德經; hereinafter *Scripture on Kumbhīra*). This text similarly portrayed Nāgārjuna and Aśvaghoṣa together prescribing ritual techniques for the attainment of material and salvific boons, which, according to Osabe, may have inspired some unknown editor to ascribe related portions of the *Treatise on the Five Sciences* to this patriarchal duo (Osabe 1982, 243). Finally, in his *Kaiyuan Record of Śākyamuni's Teachings*, Zhisheng 智昇 (fl. 700–786) noted that the *Wuming lun* of earlier catalogues had since been lost, and he explained how another text, called *Brahmanical Astronomy* (*Poluomen tianwen* 婆羅門天文), was excised from the Chinese *Tripiṭaka* because it was insufficiently Buddhist.[50] While Zhisheng did not say whether the *Treatise on the Five Sciences* had been similarly censored, it is possible that some viewed it as equally endangered. As Osabe notes, medieval Chinese sources differentiated between Buddhist and non-Buddhist forms of the "five sciences," and this text was usually associated with the latter.[51] So it is not difficult to imagine, in light of what

48. Osabe 1982, 236. See the *Lidai sanbao ji* 歷代三寶紀 of 598 (T no. 2034, 49:100b); the *Da Tang neidian lu* 大唐内典錄 of 664 (T no. 2149, 55:271c); and the *Kaiyuan shijiao lu* 開元釋教錄 of 730 (T no. 2154, 55:544c). Edward Davis (2001, 134) cites Ōmura Seigai 大村西崖 (1918, 5:17) as the authority in associating Nāgārjuna's text with the sixth-century *Treatise on the Five Sciences*. Ōmura, however, only lists the latter text and says nothing about Nāgārjuna.

49. *Xin huayan jing lun* 新華嚴經論, T no. 1739, 36:895b.

50. *Kaiyuan shijiao lu*, T no. 2154, 55:544c: 今以非三藏教，故不存之 This *Poluomen tianwen* was listed in earlier catalogues (*Lidai sanbao ji*, T no. 2034, 49:100b and *Da Tang neidian lu*, T no. 2149, 55:271c), but the *Kaiyuan shijiao lu* was the first to claim its demise.

51. Osabe 1982, 236. The Buddhist and non-Buddhist five sciences were variously defined. One standard delineation, which Osabe follows, had grammar, logic, philosophy,

happened to the *Brahmanical Astronomy*, that some anonymous editor excerpted his favorite sections from the "non-Buddhist" *Treatise on the Five Sciences* and ascribed them to Nāgārjuna in order to ensure their preservation. To the extent that any of this is feasible, it stands to reason that this happened around the time that the *Treatise on the Five Sciences* and the *Brahmanical Astronomy* went missing from the canon.[52]

In addition, by the middle of the Tang, Nāgārjuna had become associated with broader canons of Buddhist spell-craft and was incorporated into the lineage of the burgeoning Esoteric Buddhist tradition. According to the *Great Tang Biographies of Eminent Monks Who Sought the Dharma in the Western Regions*, completed in 691 by Yijing 義淨 (635–713), Nāgārjuna was said to have preserved the essence of the enormous *Vidyādharapiṭaka* (*Chi mingzhou zang* 持明咒藏; literally "Canon of the Spell-Wielders"), which was a legendary source of Buddhist incantation recipes. This he apparently handed down to a disciple named Nanda (Nantuo 難陀), who therefrom compiled some twelve thousand verses of *dhāraṇī* texts for use by later adepts.[53] While Yijing described a succession of Indian and Chinese masters who studied the *Vidyādharapiṭaka*—Nāgārjuna, Nanda, Dignāga (ca. 480–540), Daolin 道琳 (fl. 7th century), and himself—he did not specify whether they formed a discrete transmission lineage for this body of spell literature. But in the following century, Nāgārjuna was expressly drawn into the newly formed lineage of the "mantras and dharma-seals of the Vajra crown, king of the secret teachings of yoga" (*Jin'gang ding yuqie mimi jiao wang zhenyan fayin* 金剛頂瑜伽祕密教王真言法印)—indicating the tradition variously known as Vajrayāna, Tantra, or Esoteric Buddhism—which reportedly passed from the Buddha Vairocana to Vajrapāṇi, Nāgārjuna, Nāgabodhi, and the most renowned Indian Esoteric masters in China: Vajrabodhi (671–741) and Amoghavajra (705–774).[54] And, in fact, according to a biography of Vajrabodhi written by his lay follower Lü Xiang 呂向 (d. after 744), Vajrabodhi

---

medicine, and mathematics as "orthodox" (*nei* 內), and substituted spell-arts and talismanic seals for logic and philosophy in the "heterodox" (*wai* 外) system. Cf. Muller 1995– (s.v. "*wuming* 五明") and the lexicographic sources cited therein.

52. This would also accord with Osabe's (1982, 246) tentative conclusion that the present text, though based in part on Six Dynasties materials, was finally compiled in the mid- or late Tang dynasty. While the eighth-century *Kaiyuan shijiao lu* listed the *Wuming lun* as lost, at least part of the latter text remained in circulation at Dunhuang for some time thereafter. It was quoted in the Dunhuang manuscript *Zhujing yao lüewen* 諸經要略文 (T no. 2821, 85:1205b; S. 779), which Giles (1957, 202–203) dates to the early ninth century.

53. *Da Tang xiyu qiufa gaoseng zhuan* 大唐西域求法高僧傳, T no. 2066, 51:6c–7a; trans. Lahiri 1986, 65–67. Also, from this canon Nāgārjuna was said to have excerpted the *Chimingzang yuqie dajiao Zunna pusa daming chengjiu yigui jing* 持明藏瑜伽大教尊那菩薩大明成就儀軌經, T no. 1169. See Ono 1933–1936, 4:302a–c. For a useful discussion of the *Vidyādharapiṭaka* in medieval China, see Copp 2014, chap. 4.

54. *Bukong xingzhuang* 不空行狀, T no. 2056, 50:292b, written in 774 by Amoghavajra's lay disciple Zhao Qian 趙遷 (d. after 775). A similar lineage was presented in an epitaph for Amoghavajra written in 781 by another of his lay disciples, Yan Ying 嚴郢 (d. 782). See Chen 2010, 103–107.

received instruction from Nāgārjuna's disciple Nāgabodhi in the *Vajraśekhara Sūtra* (*Jin'gang ding jing* 金剛頂經), the *dhāraṇī* methods of Vairocana, and the *Treatise on the Five Sciences*.[55]

From all of this it seems fairly clear why Nāgārjuna would have been identified as the author of this text. By the eighth century Nāgārjuna was one of the most famous Indian masters in China. He had long been associated with Buddhist spell-craft through his *Great Perfection of Wisdom Treatise* and *Dharma-Treasury Transmission* hagiography, he was instrumental in preserving the mother of all Indic spell collections, and he had assumed a prominent position in the lineage of high Esoteric Buddhism. So if we are inclined toward the hypotheses that *Nāgārjuna's Treatise on the Five Sciences* was excerpted from the earlier *Wuming lun*, and that the latter was removed from the canon for being too "non-Buddhist," then it makes sense to assume that this text's sections on spells and talismans were ascribed to Nāgārjuna in order to properly Buddhicize and legitimize them. But at the same time, Nāgārjuna played a substantive role in authorizing and empowering the thaumaturgic methods prescribed throughout the body of this text; his name was not just tacked onto its title. Amidst these prescriptions we also find specific rituals devised to invoke and manifest Nāgārjuna himself, perhaps offering more concrete details of the procedures through which adepts like Tanluan and Daoquan reportedly succeeded in localizing this ancient Indian patriarch within the Chinese ritual arena.

As Osabe points out, *Nāgārjuna's Treatise on the Five Sciences* appears to have taken its spells, talismans, and ritual prescriptions from several earlier sources that are no longer extant.[56] These sources include at least two ascribed to Nāgārjuna in particular: *Nāgārjuna Bodhisattva's Scripture of Secret Charts and Incantations* (*Longshu pusa mijue tu jing* 龍樹菩薩祕決圖經) and *Nāgārjuna Bodhisattva's Treatise on the Five Luminous Seals* (*Longshu pusa wu mingyin lun* 龍樹菩薩五明印論).[57] The first scroll of *Nāgārjuna's Treatise on the Five Sciences* apparently drew in part from the former source in supplying talismans and Sanskrit-style *dhāraṇī* to command astral deities of twelve directions, which corresponded to the twelve "hours" of the traditional Chinese day. In order to deploy these spells and talismans, practitioners were directed to first purify themselves, perform obeisance with utmost sincerity, avoid pungent foods, and take care to never speak reviling words. Then they should build an oratory in which to install an altar for Nāgārjuna's image (Longshu *zuo* 龍樹座). The practitioners would place offerings of mixed fruit, milk congee, and incense upon this altar, which was affixed with a sign on its southwestern side (perhaps to identify Nāgārjuna or to empower

55. Preserved in the *Zhenyuan xinding shijiao mulu* 貞元新定釋教目錄, T no. 2157, 55:875b; cf. Chen 2010, 103n67.

56. Osabe 1982, 236. Ritual texts in manuscript format are often bricolages of this sort; see Copp 2011.

57. *Longshu wuming lun*, T no. 1420, 21:958b; and *Longshu wuming lun*, T no. 1420, 21:963a. On the talismanic function of these "charts," which "express the inherent, hidden, and real aspect of the things of the world," see Raz 2012, 143–146.

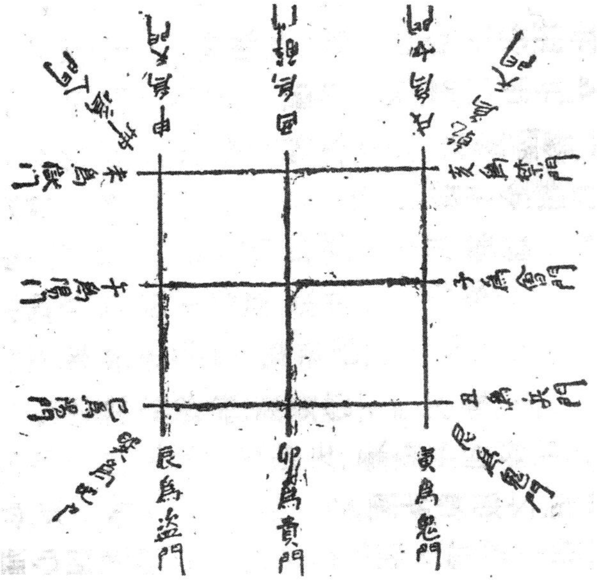

Figure 3. Nāgārjuna's Oratory. *Longshu wuming lun*, T no. 1420, 21:958b.

the altar). From this apparent center of the ritual arena, the adepts would then mark the directions of the twelve astral deities radiating out along six segmentary lines of a square grid, plus gates for heaven, earth, ghosts, and humans at each end of the two diagonal axes (see figure 3).[58] They would then point "Nāgārjuna's Divine Talismans of the Twelve Hours" (Longshu shi'ershi shenfu 龍樹十二時神符) toward each direction depending on the desired result. Thereby one could attain longevity, "divine transcendence" (*shenxian* 神仙), command over gods and ghosts, curative powers, worldly wealth, and many other fantastic benefits.[59] As Strickmann (2002, 171) and Edward Davis (2001, 134–135) both emphasize, this process incorporated long-standing Chinese astronomical and ritual conventions, which would have lent this ostensibly Indian text a most familiar flavor to its medieval Chinese audience.

The second scroll of *Nāgārjuna's Treatise on the Five Sciences* opened with "Nāgārjuna Bodhisattva's twenty methods" (Longshu pusa chu ershi fa 龍樹菩薩出二十法), including an apotropaic rite through which Nāgārjuna would appear in person and, with a snap of his fingers, cause one's enemies to bind and flog themselves before donning snake heads and bleating like sheep.[60] After describing several more similar procedures, the text then turned to *Nāgārjuna Bodhisattva's Treatise on the Five Luminous Seals*. As its title would suggest, this source provided instructions for creating and

58. Ibid., 958b.
59. Ibid., 958b–c.
60. Ibid., 962a.

deploying five talismanic seals, which were drawn in *Nāgārjuna's Treatise on the Five Sciences.*[61] They were to be were engraved on wooden stamp-blocks and worn on one's person, or dipped in vermilion and impressed upon various parts of the body to heal or imbue with special powers. For example, if pressed on the face, the "Seal of the Sky-Flying Bodhisattva" (Pusa chengkong yin 菩薩乘空印) would cure all sickness; if used with an accompanying spell, Nāgārjuna would personally grant all wishes; if worn at the chest, the user would be welcomed into imperial palaces; Nāgārjuna and other "beneficent deities" (*shanshen* 善神) would confer enlightenment; and, finally, if worn on the head, one could fly up into the sky.[62]

Here and elsewhere Nāgārjuna promised his personal intervention for the wellbeing of devoted practitioners—often indicated by the first-person singular "I" (*wo* 我)—but further on the text provided more specific procedures for invoking this powerful master, who was variously termed a "bodhisattva," "beneficent deity," "saint" (*shengren* 聖人), or "divine king" (*shenwang* 神王).[63] At one point the devotee was instructed to make offerings to both Nāgārjuna and a particular wooden seal within a purified oratory for a period of forty-nine days. Thus imbued with the recompense of Nāgārjuna's personal empowerment, this seal could then be used to obtain a variety of useful results. Sealing the forehead, the devotee would become invisible; sealing the feet, he would be able to walk on water; sealing the mouth, he could convert anyone with a single Dharma-talk; and sealing the eyes, he could witness both the past and future travails of all sentient beings.[64] But the grand finale of ritual worship of this bodhisattva-*cum*-deity was not presented until Aśvaghoṣa joined him on the scene. If the "ordinary person" wished to practice the methods of these twin bodhisattvas, the text advised, he must first seek out a beautifully adorned space in which to construct a purified oratory. The practitioner should paint this hall green and its floor white, hang jeweled canopies and multicolored banners all around, and place incense burners at each of the four corners. Then he should set up votive statues of the bodhisattvas Aśvaghoṣa and Nāgārjuna and their divine attendants. Five-colored sashes were to be draped on these statues and additional incense burners placed before them. The supplicant was instructed to align tables in front of the images, cover the tables with offerings, and with utmost reverence offer obeisance to these bodhisattvas. Here the strictest standards of purity had to be maintained. The practitioner must avoid contact with women, children, and animals, and persons of reckless demeanor must be kept clear of the ritual implements. In fact, for a period of one hundred days, the practitioner ought not to leave the oratory at all, and was to subsist on the stock of ritual offerings only after the bodhisattvas and other recipient deities had had their fill. If the supplicant burned

61. Ibid., 963a–964c.

62. Ibid., 964b. On these *shanshen*, see Campany 2012b, 162.

63. These last two labels are given at, e.g., *Longshu wuming lun*, T no. 1420, 21:965b.

64. Ibid., 965a; cf. Strickmann 2002, 175.

incense and incanted spells without cease, presenting offerings with the deepest sincerity, Aśvaghoṣa and Nāgārjuna would respond by dispatching deities to the ritual arena who would do whatever the supplicant commanded.[65]

But this was not yet the limit to Aśvaghoṣa's and Nāgārjuna's munificence. If one wished to heal the afflicted, he should submit a formal petition to these bodhisattvas, conveyed in the rising smoke of burning incense, and recite their spells before the sick or injured party. The text then instructed the practitioner to seal the site of the patient's affliction with the "Vajra Heart Seal" (Jin'gang xinyin 金剛心印), which was drawn and described earlier in the text, and perform obeisance for seven days. He must gird his raiment stoutly, never lie upon the ground, never relax his determination, and never cry or wail but instead shut his eyes in deep prayer. If any of these strictures were not firmly upheld, all involved parties would increase in misfortune. But should the practitioner observe these admonitions to the letter, never eating meat, drinking alcohol, behaving licentiously, or uttering slanderous words, and he reverently intoned Nāgārjuna's spells while constantly holding this bodhisattva in mind, Nāgārjuna would personally appear in the ritual arena and grant whatever the practitioner desired. And of course, Nāgārjuna would ensure that the sickness of the patient was spontaneously cured. Finally, should the supplicant wish to further invoke the bodhisattvas Aśvaghoṣa and Nāgārjuna for whatever reason, he need only procure a variety of implements required to create the "Divine Talisman of the Heavenly Emperor" (Tiandi shenfu 天帝神符), draw it in vermilion on white paper, and place it upon their effigies.[66]

Thus *Nāgārjuna's Treatise on the Five Sciences* promoted Aśvaghoṣa and Nāgārjuna as local deities who would personally provide their apotropaic services to the supplicant who invoked them through the proper ritual channels. In depicting these bodhisattvas in this way, the text offered specific procedures for performing many of the same techniques that Nāgārjuna was shown to have mastered in his earlier hagiographies. For example, the text offered a seal that could be used to make one's body invisible so as to enter the dwelling of a king unseen,[67] just as Nāgārjuna did in the *Dharma-Treasury Transmission* when he sought to defile the ladies of the palace harem. Another seal-spell combination could foil the designs of any non-Buddhist with whom the practitioner debated,[68] much as Nāgārjuna's early hagiographies showed him defeating an arrogant Brahman in debate. Other techniques were offered for observing the activities of beings within the different paths of rebirth[69]—an ability that Nāgārjuna often demonstrated by showing the

65. *Longshu wuming lun*, T no. 1420, 21:967b–c. Cf. Davis 2001, 135; and Strickmann 2002, 177.

66. *Longshu wuming lun*, T no. 1420, 21:967c–968a; cf. Strickmann 2002, 177.

67. *Longshu wuming lun*, T no. 1420, 21:963b; cf. Strickmann 2002, 172.

68. *Longshu wuming lun*, T no. 1420, 21:964c; cf. Strickmann 2002, 175.

69. *Longshu wuming lun*, T no. 1420, 21:965a.

gods and *asuras* battling in the sky. And in more general terms, the fact that *Nāgārjuna's Treatise on the Five Sciences* described its own contents as partially non-Buddhist would seem to recall Nāgārjuna's broad talents as a Brahman youth prior to "leaving home," when he had mastered all the arts of divination, astronomy, prophecy, and alchemy. Indeed, this career trajectory was clearly recalled in the figure of the monk and former non-Buddhist who offered King Aśoka his pan-sectarian methods of saving beings in dark times.

Nāgārjuna's Treatise on the Five Sciences illustrated how its namesake bodhisattva put these multiple talents to good use for contemporary Chinese adepts, be they card-carrying Buddhists or not. Given that it referred to its would-be practitioners as "ordinary people" and nowhere asserted the necessity of clerical officiants, the text appears pitched toward local-level ritualists or lay supplicants across denominations. Indeed, as Davis (2001, chap. 6) illustrates, by Song times local spirit-mediums would employ Nāgārjuna's spells and seals to exercise demons and heal afflictions. *Nāgārjuna's Treatise on the Five Sciences* thus continued the trend of making Aśvaghoṣa and Nāgārjuna accessible to a broader range of Chinese supplicants in addition to the elite Buddhist scholar-monks by and for whom the earliest patriarchal writings were promulgated. Further, this text presented a wide variety of thaumaturgic techniques that would have been recognized as consonant with—if not identical to—contemporary Daoist ritual practices, but it also included Indian ritual conventions and Sanskrit-style spells devised to create an Indian veneer. Indeed, every modern commentator on this text has been struck by the degree to which it integrated elements commonly found in both Daoist and Tantric ritual manuals.[70] But by depicting Nāgārjuna as the author of these various ritual technologies, the text insinuated that only Buddhist adepts could both master all non-Buddhist methods as well as incorporate the most efficacious Buddhist thaumaturgy from ancient India. In this context Nāgārjuna was no longer just an author of ancient texts—a distant paragon of Indian authority and Buddhist sainthood. Now, in response to detailed procedures of ritual obeisance, Nāgārjuna would personally deliver the magic of ancient India to China, providing for local devotees the most powerful methods of defeating enemies, curing diseases, and securing any benefit that one could possibly desire.

The Alchemist and Minister

As previously noted, the *Dharma-Treasury Transmission* and Nāgārjuna's independently circulating biography both began with a story about Nāgārjuna's youth, in his pre-Buddhist days, when he and three friends hatched a scheme to sneak into the local palace harem and have their way with the king's concubines. They figured that the best way to accomplish this task was to procure an elixir of invisibility, so they visited their local "sorcerer" (*shujia* 術家)

70. Davis 2001, 134–136; Osabe 1982, 234, 241, 244; Strickmann 2002, 170–171, 178; and Xiao 1994, 399–406.

to request an appropriate recipe. Seizing on this chance to secure highbred clientele on a long-term basis, the sorcerer supplied the Brahmans with only a small sample of his invisibility elixir. He instructed them to mix it with water and smear it on their eyelids to make their bodies invisible, expecting that when they used up their allotted batch they would have to come back for more. But as soon as Nāgārjuna got hold of the sample he was able to discern each of its ingredients in their exact quantities, just by smelling its aroma. Awed and humbled by Nāgārjuna's innate brilliance in alchemical composition, the sorcerer gave up his recipe to the Brahmans, who then proceeded with their plan to become invisible rapists. As outlined in chapter 2, Nāgārjuna's friends were eventually caught and killed, which led Nāgārjuna to realize the equation between desire and suffering and go on to become the greatest Buddhist saint since Śākyamuni.[71] And in fact, this portion of Nāgārjuna's hagiography has been compared to that of the Buddha, who likewise experienced the pleasures of the palace harem before realizing the inevitability of old age, sickness, and death. But another important aspect of this tale was Nāgārjuna's proven expertise in the field of alchemy, which led later Chinese authors to advertise his efficacious elixirs as another valuable means by which he could personally ensure health, longevity, and a panoply of spectacular boons.

Already at the beginning of the sixth century there appeared a text called *Nāgārjuna Bodhisattva's Methods of Blending Aromas* (*Longshu pusa hexiang fang* 龍樹菩薩和香方), which is now lost but would seem by its title to have drawn on this tale of Nāgārjuna's olfactory acumen from the *Dharma-Treasury Transmission*.[72] And indeed, several sources produced over the following centuries evince a widespread Chinese interest in Nāgārjuna's apothecarial talents, as first demonstrated in this account. For example, the seventh-century *History of the Sui Dynasty* (*Sui shu* 隋書) catalogued another no-longer-extant text that apparently offered a wide variety of Nāgārjuna's "medicinal prescriptions" (*Longshu pusa yaofang* 龍樹菩薩藥方); the Tang poet Yuan Zhen 元稹 (779–831) adduced "Nāgārjuna's methods" in connection with the esoteric elixirs and medical practices of a certain *bhikṣu* Yi 比丘溢; and poems composed by the famous Bai Juyi 白居易 (772–846) and Qi Ji 齊己 (863–937) both lauded Nāgārjuna's facility with eye medicines in particular.[73] On this last count we might note that *Nāgārjuna's Treatise on the Five Sciences* likewise included a recipe for curing blindness with orpiment smeared on a talismanic seal (Strickmann 2002, 176). But by the late Tang dynasty, this

71. This summary is based on the *Dharma-Treasury Transmission*. For English translations of this episode in the *Longshu pusa zhuan* 龍樹菩薩傳 (T no. 2047, 50:184a–b, 185b–c), which varies only slightly, see Chaudhuri 2008, 18–20; Corless 1995, 527–528; and Li 2002c, 21–22.

72. See *Lidai sanbao ji*, T no. 2034, 49:86b–c, which claims that the text was translated by Ratnamati (d. ca. 513) in Luoyang in 508. It was also listed in the *Sui shu* 隋書; see Jan 1970, 145.

73. On the *Sui shu* entry see Jan 1970, 145. The poems are found in *Quan Tang shi* 全唐詩, 12:4489, 13:5031 (noted in Deshpande 2000, 372), 24:9540.

patriarch was associated with ophthalmology most prominently in *Nāgārjuna Bodhisattva's Eye Treatise* (*Longshu pusa yan lun* 龍樹菩薩眼論), which provided etiologies, indications, and surgical and pharmaceutical treatments for a host of eye ailments.[74] This last source perhaps indicates a burgeoning Chinese tendency to delineate Nāgārjuna's medicinal skill set from his thaumaturgy and alchemy, but at the same time his depiction as an eye doctor clearly overlapped with his talents at producing curative spells, talismans, and elixirs. Indeed, for the most part, Nāgārjuna's wide-ranging techniques and powers were deployed in concert and advertised as all-encompassing. Just as Nāgārjuna's spells and talismans could accomplish almost anything, his alchemical elixirs, which often worked together with his incantations, were said to provide all manner of therapeutic, apotropaic, material, and salvific boons.

Perhaps the fullest account of Nāgārjuna's alchemical expertise was provided in the aforementioned *Scripture on Kumbhīra*.[75] Like *Nāgārjuna's Treatise on the Five Sciences*, this text depicted Nāgārjuna together with Aśvaghoṣa prescribing thaumaturgic recipes for accomplishing a wide variety of practical and extravagant tasks, from making ice in summer to resurrecting the dead and transforming people into rabbits. Here this patriarchal duo appeared alongside the exalted bodhisattvas Avalokiteśvara and Bhaiṣajyarāja, the Buddha's personal physician Jīvaka, and Śākyamuni himself, all of whom likewise exercised their apotropaic and therapeutic powers in order to save beings mired in pernicious circumstances. Further, as Xiao Dengfu 蕭登福 emphasizes, the *Scripture on Kumbhīra* incorporated various ritual procedures, behavioral strictures, alchemical recipes, and other instructions that accorded with the contents of both medieval Buddhist and Daoist ritual manuals (Xiao 1994, 320–322, 326–327). But in contrast to Xiao's analysis, the author of the *Scripture on Kumbhīra* was concerned not to parse out its Buddhist and Daoist elements, but rather to incorporate a broad spectrum of prevalent ritual practices and assert that they all originated with Śākyamuni (in the guise of Prince Kumbhīra) and the eminent bodhisattvas of his retinue. These practices were largely alchemical in nature and they were prescribed to treat a variety of ailments, especially with Śākyamuni/Kumbhīra beginning the text with therapeutic exhortations and with Jīvaka and the Medicine King Bodhisattva playing prominent roles throughout. The *Scripture on Kumbhīra* also continued the drive to localize the Indian patriarchs in latter-day China, as Nāgārjuna offered to personally instruct local devotees in the preparation of his alchemical recipes. As such, this scripture

74. See Deshpande 2000 and Yamano 2011.

75. *Foshuo Jinpiluo tongzi weide jing* 佛說金毘羅童子威德經, T no. 1289; trans. attributed to Amoghavajra. The *Taishō* text is based on a print dating to the Kyōhō 享保 reign period (1716–1736) from the Buzan University 豐山大學 library, now housed at Taishō University, Tokyo. The *Taishō* editors collated this with a manuscript from the Kōzan-ji 高山寺 canon (Kyoto), which dates to 1203 (T no. 1289, 21:367n2). The Buzan University print includes a colophon indicating that the text upon which it was based was copied in 1172 (T no. 1289, 21:374a).

further demonstrates that by the mid-Tang dynasty Aśvaghoṣa and Nāgārjuna had become immanent agents in the fortunes of local Chinese adepts, as Buddhist authors sought to interject these patriarchs into Chinese ritual practices of the most eclectic variety.

Although we cannot be certain whether the *Scripture on Kumbhīra* was translated by Amoghavajra as claimed, its Tang provenance was attested by the Shingon monk Jōgyō 常曉 (d. 865), who traveled through China in 838–839 and returned to Japan with a catalogue of Chinese Buddhist texts. Included in this catalogue was the *Essential Methods of the Power and Virtue of Prince Kumbhīra*,[76] which is not quite the same as the "scripture spoken by the Buddha" that we have today. But that Jōgyō had a similar text to hand is indicated by the brief content summary he provided in connection with a sculpted image of Kumbhīra that he also catalogued. He wrote that this image was one of Śākyamuni's bodily transformations, and then he quoted a scripture as saying that when the Buddha preached before a grand assembly, he changed into this form of Prince Kumbhīra in order to subdue a pack of wild heretics.[77] This is the same storyline preceding the current *Scripture on Kumbhīra*'s ritual mélange, which therefore probably also dates to the early ninth century. Additionally, the Tiantai adept Zhanran 湛然 (711–782) mentioned a "golden elixir" (*jindan* 金丹) recipe prescribed by Nāgārjuna, which appears similar to that which Nāgārjuna presented before Kumbhīra's assembly in the *Scripture on Kumbhīra*.[78]

The *Scripture on Kumbhīra* opened with this scene of the Buddha preaching to a vast assembly of bodhisattvas, disciples, gods, *asuras*, and other Indian mythological creatures. After assuming the form of the thousand-armed and thousand-headed Prince Kumbhīra, the Buddha instructed his assembly that if they wished to alleviate the suffering of the world, become great healing kings, cure the sickness of the masses, and defeat heretics and demons, they should construct a pure oratory according to certain specifications and temporal and behavioral strictures. Kumbhīra then presented a collection of spells to enlighten all in attendance, and some of the great bodhisattvas from his assembly stepped forth to add their own ritual prescriptions to the mix.[79] First was the Medicine King Bodhisattva, who described the spells and elixirs that he had perfected over the eons, as well as the spectrum of benefits that his ritual methods could provide.[80] With the Medicine King's prescription thus filled—and after his heroic promise (following the *Lotus Sūtra*) to burn his own body if his methods failed—the text

76. *Jōgyō kasho shōrai mokuroku* 常曉和尚請來目錄, T no. 2163, 55:1069c: 金毘羅童子威德要法. This text was repeated in *Sho ajari shingon mikkyō burui sōroku* 諸阿闍梨真言密教部類總錄, by Annen 安然 (841–ca. 889), T no. 2176, 55:1128a.

77. *Jōgyō kasho shōrai mokuroku*, T no. 2163, 55:1070b.

78. *Zhiguan fuxing chuanhong jue* 止觀輔行傳弘決, T no. 1912, 46:445c. According to Penkower (1993, 82) this text was completed by 765.

79. *Foshuo Jinpiluo tongzi weide jing*, T no. 1289, 21:368c–369b.

80. Ibid., 369b–370a.

turned to its next protagonist bodhisattva. This was Nāgārjuna, who began his presentation by telling the Buddha about his own past life under the tutelage of the primordial Buddha Dīpaṃkara. At that time there was a king who wanted to kill Nāgārjuna, so Nāgārjuna "manifested great divine transformations" (*huaxian dashenbian* 化現大神變) to make the king revere and promote the Buddhist teachings. Now that Nāgārjuna was able to hear the Dharma from the present Buddha, he wished to continue doing all that he could to aid in its dissemination.[81]

With Śākyamuni's exuberant approval, Nāgārjuna offered his own prescriptions for various alchemical elixirs, which together with the proper spells could produce an abundance of miraculous effects for sentient beings ensnared in this evil world of defilements. According to Nāgārjuna, one must first procure twelve yellow myrobalan fruits, a measure of honey, and a certain type of partially boiled water, and blend them in a precise manner while reciting spells in order to produce an elixir. If taken at the right time of night, this elixir would cause the practitioner to produce gold by coughing it out of his mouth. If the practitioner bathed in the elixir he would become invisible—recalling the previously related tale from the *Dharma-Treasury Transmission*—and by adding a dash of cow milk and bathing once more, he could become visible again. Then the practitioner was instructed to blend in various other ingredients, bring the elixir before an image of Śākyamuni, recite a spell six thousand times, fast for seven days, and then ingest a large spoonful of it. That night Nāgārjuna would personally appear in a vision to clearly explain all of his ritual methods. Further, by employing Nāgārjuna's elixirs in certain ways—smeared on parts of the body or ingested in specific amounts at specified times, sometimes while reciting spells—the practitioner could obtain extreme longevity, worldly riches, and vast wisdom; cure all sorts of illnesses; raise the dead, from three-day-old to seven-day-old and hundred-day-old corpses; make ice in summer; conjure a dragon or white elephant; reverse the flow of a river; control the weather; travel one thousand *li* in a day; and transform himself into a snake, a lion king, a white rabbit, or another animal. Finally, Nāgārjuna concluded by promising that if his methods proved ineffective, he would gladly relinquish his status as bodhisattva and take the place of all sentient beings in their worldly suffering.[82]

After a similar presentation by the bodhisattva Avalokiteśvara, the text turned to its next protagonist: Aśvaghoṣa. Like the preceding bodhisattvas, Aśvaghoṣa began by telling the Buddha that he was also possessed of numerous wonderful methods for liberating the masses bound to this evil world of suffering. The Buddha praised Aśvaghoṣa and entreated him to share his sublime techniques. Aśvaghoṣa then explained that if sentient beings wished to depart from the realms of birth and death, they should first procure a

81. Ibid., 370a–b.
82. Ibid., 370b–371a.

variety of exotic ingredients in specific quantities and boil them in water within a temple or stūpa while reciting several spells. The mixture was then to be placed in an unused vessel and buried underground for fourteen days before being unearthed and placed before an image of the Buddha. For three days the practitioner should pay obeisance to the Buddha, maintaining the strictest standards of purity, and after three thousand more spell recitations he or she should consume only a half portion of the elixir. Within the next seven days his or her body would ascend into the sky and he or she would be able to fly around at will, eventually transforming into a bird and taking off into the heavens. Aśvaghoṣa then went on to catalogue the various other uses of his elixirs, given certain adjustments in ingredients, quantity and timing of ingestion, and accompanying spell recitations. By following his instructions, one could attain great wisdom and knowledge of previous lives, eliminate retribution for past sins, cure various illnesses, become adorned with the thirty-two marks of perfection, reach three thousand years of age, master the spell-arts or all the Mahāyāna scriptures, and attain clairvoyance, invisibility, and all forms of worldly wealth.[83] The *Scripture on Kumbhīra* concluded with a presentation by Jīvaka,[84] who offered a roster of prescriptions much the same as those of the bodhisattvas Bhaiṣajyarāja, Nāgārjuna, Avalokiteśvara, and Aśvaghoṣa before him.

In depicting Nāgārjuna alongside these illustrious Buddhist holy beings, as an interlocutor with the Buddha himself, and with a cosmic lifespan extending back to the Buddha Dīpaṃkara, the *Scripture on Kumbhīra* radically reconceived the career trajectory of this Indian patriarch. Rather than being a converted Brahman who resurrected (or transmitted) the Dharma in post-*parinirvāṇa* India, here Nāgārjuna was counted among the most advanced bodhisattvas who transcended time and space and could thus be called upon to personally appear before local devotees. But at the same time that the *Scripture on Kumbhīra* redefined Nāgārjuna's capacities along this cosmic continuum, it also expressly reinscribed his earlier hagiographic representation as an Indian Buddhist convert who lived in the centuries after nirvāṇa. Nāgārjuna's facility with elixirs in the *Scripture on Kumbhīra* clearly resonated with his account in the *Dharma-Treasury Transmission* as well as with the tales of his alchemical talents in Xuanzang's *Records of the Western Regions.* As discussed in the previous chapter, this latter text included two episodes illustrating Nāgārjuna's skill in concocting alchemical elixirs. In one episode he was able to extend his lifespan as well as that of his patron king with an elixir of longevity, while in the other episode he created gold by smearing a certain concoction upon rocks so that the king would have sufficient funds to construct a Buddhist monastery. Longevity and aurification were also among the powers gained from Nāgārjuna's alchemy

83. Ibid., 372a–c.

84. The transcription here is Qipo 祁婆 (or Zuopo 祚婆, in another recension), which I take to be a variant of the more common rendering of Jīvaka, Qipo 耆婆. On this figure see, most recently, Salguero 2009.

in the *Scripture on Kumbhīra*.[85] But what distinguished this text from earlier accounts of Nāgārjuna's elixirs was that here, in response to specific programs of ritual obeisance, Nāgārjuna would personally transmit his alchemical recipes to Chinese practitioners in need.

Conclusion: Nāgārjuna's Chinese Indianness

As I have noted, *Nāgārjuna's Treatise on the Five Sciences* variously labeled its namesake protagonist a "bodhisattva," "saint," "beneficent deity," and "divine king." The *Scripture on Kumbhīra* placed Nāgārjuna at the feet of both the past Buddha Dīpaṃkara and the present Buddha Śākyamuni, as well as in the oratories of contemporary Chinese adepts. The Pure Land biography of Daoquan invoked Nāgārjuna's *Great Perfection of Wisdom Treatise* and his position as thirteenth Indian patriarch of the *Dharma-Treasury Transmission* while also claiming that he responded in person to Daoquan's ritual entreaties. These and other sources discussed in this chapter illustrate how many different roles Nāgārjuna was made to play in medieval China. Nāgārjuna simultaneously instantiated several different models of sainthood and divinity as he developed gradually from a distant paragon of Indian authority to an immanent agent in the fortunes of contemporary Chinese adepts. But throughout this development, Nāgārjuna's earliest Chinese images were continually reinscribed. By the ninth century Nāgārjuna's role as Dharma transmitter had become thoroughly routinized in Chan and Tiantai lineage histories, and the application of his name to a host of newly translated or composed doctrinal treatises continued to provide unquestioned authority. I have emphasized how Nāgārjuna's talents as described in his early hagiographies were carried over into ritually oriented texts that advertised Nāgārjuna as a powerful local deity. Nāgārjuna's initial repertoire of doctrinal authorship, public debate, eremitism, and meditation, as well as his roles in resurrecting a dying Dharma, transmitting the teaching undimmed, converting and counseling imperial rulers, and other notable acts, were all upheld in Chinese sources that also worked to transform Nāgārjuna into an object of ritual obeisance.

In this way Nāgārjuna's Chinese manifestations are perhaps best understood in terms of Prasenjit Duara's (1988) model of "superscription," according to which both cohering and conflicting images were superimposed upon a set of core attributes of a single figure in order to suit the needs of different people at different times. Indeed, the question of multiple

85. Nāgārjuna's association with alchemy is well known in Indo-Tibetan Buddhist traditions as well; see, e.g., White 1996, 60–77. The analysis I have provided should not be taken to deny possible lines of influence from these Western traditions on Chinese representations of Nāgārjuna's facility with elixirs. Rather, I aim to show how the sources available to a Chinese audience would have informed their understanding of this patriarch. I am not positing any absolute origins of these images; the point is that with few exceptions medieval Chinese practitioners would have had access only to those sources written in or translated into Chinese.

Nāgārjunas, which has long preoccupied modern scholars,[86] was never an issue for medieval Chinese Buddhists. In Chinese sources the same Nāgārjuna was clearly capable of authoring doctrinal treatises, prescribing talismanic seals, and animating votive icons constructed by the likes of Daoquan. But unlike with the figure of Guan Yu 關羽 (d. 219) in Duara's study, it is difficult to determine precisely which social groups were responsible for which of Nāgārjuna's Chinese images. While Nāgārjuna's earliest accounts were clearly produced by and for the Chinese literati elite, and the contents of the *Dharma-Treasury Transmission* suggest monastic authors writing for a target audience of imperial patrons, texts like *Nāgārjuna's Treatise on the Five Sciences* and the *Scripture on Kumbhīra* appear aimed at anyone and everyone. I have suggested that *Nāgārjuna's Treatise on the Five Sciences* was authored by and for local-level ritualists and perhaps lay supplicants, but it could just as easily have been employed by members of the ecclesiastic elite, who were equally interested in health, wealth, longevity, and protection from baleful forces. Indeed, as seen in the writings of eminent Pure Land masters like Tanluan and Jiacai, it is clear that Nāgārjuna's divine incarnation was advertised by some of the most accomplished Chinese scholar-monks of the kingdom.

But while it is difficult to pin down the social groups responsible for many of the ritual texts concerning Nāgārjuna, the sectarian agendas of these sources are more readily discernible. Previous studies of *Nāgārjuna's Treatise on the Five Sciences* and the *Scripture on Kumbhīra* have all emphasized the degree to which these sources mimicked the ritual conventions of medieval Daoist texts while also including linguistic and procedural elements commonly found in Tantric ritual manuals. However, as I have argued, by asserting that all of their prescriptions originated with Nāgārjuna or other Indian bodhisattvas and at the time of Śākyamuni or Aśoka in ancient India, these sources implied either that the most efficacious Daoist thaumaturgic methods were actually ancient Indian or that only Buddhist adepts were capable of mastering both Daoist and Buddhist ritual technologies. In this way, like Tanluan's Pure Land biography in which Nāgārjuna appeared only after Tanluan had forsaken his Daoist scriptures, here Nāgārjuna was situated at the juncture between Chinese and Indian models of sainthood and soteriology. And also like the earlier account of Nāgārjuna in the *Dharma-Treasury Transmission*, which depicted him as a Buddha-like figure who died in the manner of a Chinese transcendent, these ritual sources represented Nāgārjuna as a valuable resource for Chinese adepts of all religious traditions.

Nevertheless, Nāgārjuna's Indian identity was expressly maintained in the representations examined in this chapter; this was one core attribute upon which Nāgārjuna's various images were superscribed. Throughout the previous chapters, I have emphasized how Aśvaghoṣa, Nāgārjuna, and Āryadeva were utilized in Chinese Buddhist efforts to negotiate the gap be-

86. See Jan 1970; White 1996, 66–70; and Walser 2005, 69–70.

tween ancient India and latter-day China. In broad outline, the earliest Chinese representations of the Indian patriarchs evince a concerted effort to delineate models of Buddhist sainthood for a world removed from the Indian fount of Buddhist enlightenment. But not long thereafter—and especially with the Sui-Tang reunification of China—Chinese Buddhists and their imperial patrons worked to localize Indian Buddhist sources of authority, including those provided by the post-*parinirvāṇa* Indian patriarchs. In the present chapter, I have argued that Nāgārjuna's Chinese apotheosis illustrates a similar drive to localize Indian paradigms of Buddhist sanctity, although with Nāgārjuna as an object of ritual devotion rather than a model of saintly practice. But in this context, even as an immanent deity who personally appeared in the Chinese ritual arena, Nāgārjuna's Indian identity remained as important as ever to his Chinese proponents. One of Tanluan's biographies explicitly labeled Nāgārjuna an "Indian monk"; the account of Daoquan expressly foregrounded Nāgārjuna's Indianness; and both *Nāgārjuna's Treatise on the Five Sciences* and the *Scripture on Kumbhīra* situated their ritual prescriptions in ancient India. This Indian identity imbued Nāgārjuna with the hallowed origins of Buddhist sanctity and made him a vehicle through which Chinese Buddhists could lay claim to the plethora of ritual technologies circulating in China. Having illustrated how these dynamics inhered in the figure of Nāgārjuna, in the following chapter I examine similar processes at work with the silkworm god Aśvaghoṣa, through whom Chinese Buddhists could demonstrate the Indian origins of silk production and thus insinuate themselves into the religious dimensions of the Chinese sericulture industry.

5

An Indian Silkworm God in China

Nāgārjuna's treatise on the *Five Sciences* (*Longshu wuming lun* 龍樹五明論) and the *Scripture on Kumbhīra* (*Foshuo jinpiluo tongzi weide jing* 佛說金毘羅童子威德經) both worked to localize Aśvaghoṣa in the Chinese ritual arena as an Indian bodhisattva who personally conveyed a wide array of occult technologies. This shift in Aśvaghoṣa's Chinese imagery appears more abrupt than in the case of Nāgārjuna, whose early hagiographic and doctrinal sources clearly not only illustrated his talents in alchemy and spell-craft but also emphasized his expertise in all branches of Buddhist and non-Buddhist learning. The earliest Chinese sources detailing Aśvaghoṣa's career were fairly tame by comparison, as they focused mostly on his facility in meditation, debate, and doctrinal authorship. Nevertheless, in most respects the Chinese apotheoses of Aśvaghoṣa and Nāgārjuna ran parallel courses. As with Nāgārjuna, sources that promoted Aśvaghoṣa's divine manifestation and thaumaturgic prowess appear devised to cut across social, sectarian, and lay-monastic boundaries. Aśvaghoṣa was represented as accessible to anyone who followed his ritual prescriptions, and this representation was advanced in a wide variety of sources—Buddhist and otherwise. Further, as in the case of Nāgārjuna, Aśvaghoṣa's depictions as a local deity illustrate the interdependent nature of religious genres like hagiography, lineage history, and ritual manual. Texts that promoted Aśvaghoṣa's ritual techniques were closely related to those that elaborated his career accomplishments and position in the Indian Buddhist patriarchate. And, also like Nāgārjuna, in his guise as a local godlike figure, Aśvaghoṣa simultaneously instantiated various models of sainthood and divinity. By the late Tang 唐 dynasty (618–907), Aśvaghoṣa was at once an ancient Indian exemplar of salvation through scholarship, master-disciple transmission, and state-sangha symbiosis. He was also an object of ritual obeisance through whom the greatest otherworldly and this-worldly benefits could be obtained.

As opposed to Nāgārjuna's ritual techniques, however, which were advertised as limitless in scope, Aśvaghoṣa's thaumaturgic and apotropaic powers eventually came to center around one specific material commodity: silk. In medieval China this ancient Indian *dhyāna*-master, transmitter of the Dharma-treasury, and author of the seminal *Awakening of Faith* (*Dasheng qixin lun* 大乘起信論), was also represented as an immanent deity who specialized in rituals for promoting silk production. The factors contributing to this expansion of Aśvaghoṣa's Chinese repertoire are less readily apparent than with Nāgārjuna. Aśvaghoṣa's early hagiographies and doctrinal treatises entailed no obvious connections with silk or silkworms, even if his association with horses proved sufficient for Chinese devotees to assert his utility to the sericulture industry. Nevertheless, as in the case of Nāgārjuna, the depictions of Aśvaghoṣa as a local god reflect broader processes, through which models of religious sanctity were expressly defined as ancient Indian and represented as having been transplanted into Tang China. Aśvaghoṣa's widespread popularity in medieval China and status as synecdoche for all things Mahāyāna led to him being counted among the foremost sources of Indian Buddhist authority. Consequently, elite Chinese scholar-monks conceived the *Awakening of Faith* to instantiate Aśvaghoṣa's model of post-*parinirvāṇa* doctrinal exegesis. And in a similar fashion, Chinese sources of more wide-ranging authorship and intended readership served to localize Aśvaghoṣa himself as a divine benefactor of the Chinese silk trade.

The question of how to understand this Chinese transformation of Aśvaghoṣa has long preoccupied modern scholars, even if only a few have engaged the topic to date. The universal scholarly response to Aśvaghoṣa's seemingly disparate Chinese representations has been to bifurcate them along social lines, positing one Aśvaghoṣa as revered forebear of the monastic institution, ancient Indian author, and counselor of kings; and another Aśvaghoṣa as silkworm god invented by Chinese sericulturists. However, the evidence indicates that for both monastic and lay devotees, the same Aśvaghoṣa was capable of performing both roles at once, and many others besides. Silk producers themselves reportedly worshipped the Indian patriarch Aśvaghoṣa as a local god of sericulture, and the architects of sectarian Buddhist genealogies also promoted Aśvaghoṣa as an invaluable boon to the Chinese silk industry. While Chinese scholar-monks may have been more invested in Aśvaghoṣa's doctrinal exegesis, and silk producers more interested in his sericulture rituals, it appears nonetheless that both groups were complicit in conceiving him as a local deity capable of ensuring healthy silkworms and abundant silk crops.

Promoted by representatives of the Buddhist institution in order to secure the patronage of silk producers, entreated by sericulturists to assist in their trade, Aśvaghoṣa was a unique addition to the prodigious pantheon of Chinese sericulture deities. Aśvaghoṣa was the only silkworm god in China who reportedly hailed from ancient India, and as such he was the only one who could supply the most advanced Indian Esoteric procedures for warding off baleful influences and securing material prosperity. As I will detail, Aśvaghoṣa reportedly prescribed prototypical Esoteric ritual programs, replete with Indian spells, icons, and *mudras* (hand gestures). But Aśvaghoṣa's brand of Esoteric technology was designed specifically for the advancement of silk production. In this way Aśvaghoṣa's ritual prescriptions functioned to ensure bountiful silk as well as to supplant, or at least supplement, traditional Chinese procedures for entreating age-old silkworm deities. And while it may appear to the modern observer that Aśvaghoṣa was thoroughly "Sinified" through this process—made to take on evermore Chinese characteristics in order to address specifically Chinese concerns—for Aśvaghoṣa's Chinese proponents it was precisely his ancient Indian identity that allowed him to advance these Esoteric Buddhist technologies.

By the same token, Aśvaghoṣa's unique combination of foreignness and familiarity in medieval China made him an ideal medium through which Chinese Buddhists could stake their claim on the religious dimensions of the sericulture industry. On the one hand, Aśvaghoṣa's Chinese hagiographies accounting for his unusual appellation—literally meaning "Horse Neigh" and translated into Chinese as such—tied him into age-old currents of Chinese mythic, cosmological, and astrological thought. On the other hand, these same hagiographies deliberately foregrounded Aśvaghoṣa's foreignness, and his status as an ancient Indian master of unparalleled spiritual attainment. Especially in later Chinese hagiographies that connected Aśvaghoṣa with sericulture, his foreignness was crucial to his perceived role as patron saint of silk production. For Buddhists in particular sericulture was problematic because it involved killing countless silkworms. One solution to this problem was to radically reconfigure sericulture on Indian Buddhist moral, mythic, and soteriological grounds by claiming that it was in fact invented by Aśvaghoṣa in ancient India. In this way Chinese Buddhists could redefine sericulture as a normative Indian Buddhist activity, making it fully consonant with traditional Mahāyāna ideals of the bodhisattva path, merit production, and expedient means. As such, the crucial moral problem of silkworm murder could be ameliorated and sericulture could be reconceived as the true heritage of Chinese Buddhists alone. Aśvaghoṣa was a key figure in these efforts to reconcile Buddhism and sericulture, and in the following I examine the underlying factors and important repercussions of his transformation from an ancient Indian patriarch into a local god of silk.

Chinese Sericulture Religion, Silkworms, and Horses

By the time Buddhism was transmitted to China, silk had long been the lifeblood of the kingdom. Over the course of at least two millennia prior, silk production, use, and trade had spread to every corner of the Chinese imperium, and sericulture had grown into a truly ubiquitous commodity industry. During the medieval period, as Buddhism developed into one of the most influential and widespread religions in China, the role of sericulture as Chinese socioeconomic and material-cultural cornerstone was further solidified. In addition to being one of the most important commercial enterprises in all of China, sericulture also entailed prominent religious dimensions. Like most agrarians and tradespeople in premodern China, silk producers depended heavily on the unseen world and its inhabitants for the success of their work. Ritual interactions with various gods and goddesses accompanied every major stage of the sericulture process, from the hatching of silkworm eggs in early spring, through the molting stages of the silkworm caterpillars, to the reeling of silk from their cocoons. If crops were good and silk abundant in a given season, offerings of thanks were made to the appropriate gods or goddesses; if a season had gone awry for whatever reason, propitiatory sacrifices to various deities were the necessary next steps. Sericulture was simply unthinkable without the constant participation of otherworldly agents, both at the level of the imperial court and in rural households throughout the kingdom. And as a result, there was always a strong demand for rituals and deities with efficacy in this arena. Chinese Buddhists sought to meet this demand by advancing one of their most prominent Indian forebears as a powerful god of silkworms. This was Aśvaghoṣa, who helped promote Buddhism as integral to the well-being of the Chinese silk industry—as providing the proper moral and soteriological framework within which to understand silkworm rearing (and killing), and as the ritual tradition most efficacious in ensuring abundant silk harvests.

Throughout recorded Chinese history, the demand for sericulture deities and rituals spread to all corners of the kingdom—through the four major silk-producing regions of Sichuan, Shandong, the Jiangnan region, and Guangdong delta—and across all social strata, from rural peasant households and large elite manors to urban workshops, state-run factories and even the imperial family.[1] The latter institutions often focused on producing fine silk brocades for official use, utilizing raw materials obtained from households across the land in the form of taxes. From Zhou times (ca. 1045–256 BCE) through the Ming dynasty (1368–1644), Chinese central governments taxed their citizenry in various agricultural and textile goods, usually including sizeable quantities of silk cloth and yarn. From the fifth century through the early Tang, an "equal field" (*juntian* 均田) land allocation system was instituted to provide every eligible household with a standard-sized plot for farming. Some of these plots were called "mulberry fields" (*sangtian* 桑田) and designated for planting mulberry trees, which supplied food for the vast numbers of silkworms being raised across the land (Twitchett 1970, 1–4). In addition to such government policies mandating widespread silk and mulberry production, silk was also a standard medium of exchange through much of Chinese history—legal tender that often circulated as much as strictly monetary currency. Overall, silk was required in huge quantities by the state, to clothe court officials according to rank, to pay members of vast bureaucracies and standing armies, and as diplomatic offering and medium of exchange when negotiating or trading with neighboring kingdoms. Silk was in enormous demand across all other social strata as well, whether for clothing, as medium for writing and painting, trade, or to pay taxes. As a result, sericulture was nearly everywhere in premodern China.

For many people, particularly rural peasant farmers or urban workshop employees, the ability to make a living often hinged on the success of a given season's silkworm crop. And since silk was a major form of currency and

1. This outline largely follows Bray 1997 and Needham 1988.

taxation, the state depended on its abundant production for financial solvency. But the process of sericulture was a capricious one, dependent upon numerous factors, such as weather and silkworm health, that were beyond people's control. These factors were seen to fall under the purview of the sericulture pantheon, those gods and goddesses who, for various reasons, had some stake in silkworm raising and silk production. Given the importance of sericulture for so many people, it was crucial that these deities be constantly involved, through offerings and prayers made in ritual settings. Rites to entreat these deities for blessings were performed at the imperial court and in peasant households across the land, though to varying degrees of formality and expense.

The earliest written evidence of sericulture in China includes invocations of a certain "silkworm deity" (*canshen* 蠶神), as seen in oracle bone records dating to the Shang 商 period (ca. 1600–1100 BCE) (Needham 1988, 250–252). Over the centuries this *canshen* would be associated with various semimythic figures, patron saints of sorts, who were seen to have played important roles in the development of sericulture. During the Han dynasty (206 BCE—220 CE) this "silkworm deity" was identified with a legendary "first sericulturist" (*xiancan* 先蠶), also known as either Lady Yuanyu 菀窳 or Princess Yu 寓, and imperial sacrifices were made in her honor before the first ceremonial feeding of the imperial silkworms (Needham 1988, 253; Sterckx 2002, 62). Such ceremonies followed stipulations found in the *Record of Rites* (*Liji* 禮記) and *Rites of Zhou* (*Zhouli* 周禮), according to which the empress and emperor's consorts should inaugurate the sericulture season with rituals to ensure plentiful harvests (Needham 1988, 247, 252–253). These ceremonies were performed from the Han to the Song (960–1279) dynasties, paralleling the emperors' annual agriculture rites. From the third century CE, there is clear evidence that imperial altars for the "first sericulturist" were established and "silkworm palaces" (*cangong* 蠶宮) were built for raising imperial silkworms. Six "silkworm mothers" (*canmu* 蠶母) or "silkworm maidens" (*canniang* 蠶娘) were selected to feed and clean the silkworms, under the supervision of the emperor's chief consort, as the imperial household modeled the sericulture process that it mandated throughout the kingdom (Needham 1988, 254, 264). From Han times through the late-imperial period, successive Chinese dynasties both practiced sericulture and conducted state rituals intended to ensure the prosperity of silk production across the land.

Since ancient times rank-and-file silk producers have also performed rituals to elicit blessings from a variety of silkworm deities. By the Han at the latest, sericulturists made sacrifices to the "first sericulturist" and other silkworm deities. From the fifth century on, there is clear evidence that local temples dedicated to silkworm deities were built to provide sites where sericulturists could make prayers and sacrifices (Broadwin 1999, 26; Needham 1988, 248, 265). People would offer fish, pork, fowl, or wine to the appropriate deities when silkworm eggs were ready for hatching, or place faux cocoons made of rice or newly hatched silkworms on altars in front of deity images (Needham 1988, 268–269). Offering sacrifices, burning incense, kowtowing, and praying were the most common ways to show respect to the silkworm deities and ask them to bless one's silkworms (Broadwin 1999, 112). Since sericulture was a seasonal endeavor, timed according to the life cycle of the silkworms, silk producers often performed such rites on a fixed schedule. People in medieval times prayed for healthy silkworms on the fifteenth day of the first lunar month, when the sericulture season was approaching; they asked for skill in weaving on the seventh day of the seventh month, after the silk had been processed from the cocoons; and they performed rites of thanks to silkworm deities during the tenth month (Como 2009, 138).

A variety of gods and goddesses were the recipients of this obeisance offered by silk producers. In addition to the previously mentioned Lady Yuanyu and Princess Yu, the deity Tiansi 天駟, named after an astral constellation; the legendary first emperor, Huangdi 黃帝; and his principal wife, Lady Xiling 西陵 were all at some point worshipped as the "first sericulturist" or as more generic "silkworm deities" (Kuhn 1984). But one of the most popular silkworm deities throughout premodern China was a figure known as the horse-head maiden (matou niang 馬頭娘). First evidenced in Han-era stone-wall carvings discovered in the area of modern Sichuan (Niu 2004), this horse-head maiden has long been situated at the forefront of the sericulture pantheon. Her story is told in an oft-repeated myth called the "Record of the Silkworm Horse from High Antiquity" (Taigu canma ji 太古蠶馬記), which may have originated in Sichuan and is preserved in the fourth-century *Record of the Search for the Supernormal* (*Soushen ji* 搜神記).[2] This story tells of a young girl who promised to marry a horse if it could bring back her long-lost father. The horse did as asked, but when it returned for its reward the girl reneged on her promise. Eventually the father learned of the arrangement and slew the horse, skinning it and hanging its hide in the courtyard to dry. Later, when the father went off on another journey, his daughter went out to play with the hide. She kicked it and mocked it, saying what a fool the horse was to think that it could actually marry a human. As she spoke, the horse's hide rose up, wrapped itself around the young girl and took her into the limbs of a nearby tree. After several days of searching, the local villagers finally found her and the horse hide together in the tree, where they had transformed into a giant silkworm spinning a cocoon. "Therefore, people named this tree *sang* 桑 (mulberry), since *sang* is [a homophone of] *sang* 喪 (lost). Because of this everyone rushed to plant from it, and this is [the mulberry tree that sericulturists] cultivate today. It is said that [today's] mulberry silkworms are descended from that ancient silkworm."[3]

2. See Needham 1988, 264; and Sterckx 2002, 304n89.

3. *Soushen ji*, 104: 因名其樹曰"桑." 桑者喪也. 由斯百姓競種之, 今世所養是也. 言桑蠶者, 是古蠶之餘類也. Cf. trans. Birrell 1993, 200; Como 2009, 186–187; and DeWoskin and Crump 1996, 166. For a useful analysis of the mythic tropes of this tale from structuralist perspective, see Miller 1995.

One of numerous sericulture etiologies current in premodern China, this tale is important for our present purposes because it inscribed in mythic format the age-old Chinese association between horses and silkworms. The compiler of the *Record of the Search for the Supernormal* attempted to explain this association through a number of astro-, cosmo-, and ontological links between the silkworm and horse, offering rather opaquely that "*chen* is the horse star" constellation and that when the moon is in "great fire" silkworms must be culled and graded.[4] As it turns out, "great fire" was one of twelve sections of the celestial equator, which included the *chen* (otherwise known as "heart" [*xin* 心]) constellation as well as the "chamber" (*fang* 房) and "tail" (*wei* 尾) constellations of the so-called Azure Dragon (*canglong* 蒼龍) in the eastern sky. This "chamber" constellation was also known as the "heavenly team of four horses" (*tiansi* 天駟), which was frequently depicted hovering above the pantheon of sericulture deities in block-print illustrations dating to the late-imperial period (Kuhn 1984, 228–231; Needham 1988, 260–263). This constellation consisted of the stars β (*beta*), δ (*delta*), π (*pi*), and ν (*nu*) of Scorpius, and "according to legend, could also have been the spirit of the First Sericulturalist" (Needham 1988, 260–261). Because the *chen* (heart) and chamber (or four-horse) constellations were adjacent to one another within "great fire," *chen* was also called the "horse star" constellation or "heavenly team of four horses." The moon was in "great fire" when these constellations were at their zenith in the night sky, which occurred during the second month of the agrarian calendar or the spring equinox. This was when the sericulture season usually began, with the culling and grading of newly hatched silkworm larvae. Through this complex web of astronomical and seasonal associations "the interpretation may have sprung up that the '[heavenly] team of four horses' represented the animal spirit of the silkworm (*canjing* 蠶精)," and Chinese commentators since ancient times would assert that horses and silkworms shared the same modality of *qi* 氣.[5]

Further, the thirteenth-century literatus Dai Zhi 戴埴 (fl. ca. 1241) included in his collection of extraordinary tales titled *Fresh Rat* (*Shupu* 鼠璞) a brief chapter called "The Common Origin of the Silkworm and Horse" (*Can ma tong ben* 蠶馬同本), in which he summarized the "Record of the Silkworm-Horse" in order to explain the inception of the horse-head maiden. Dai noted that the people of Shu 蜀 (Sichuan) would often pray to this goddess for the well-being of their silkworms, and that she was represented with a statue of a woman wearing a horsehide.[6] Indeed, the horse-head maiden

4. *Soushen ji*, 104: 案天官, "辰為馬星." 蠶書曰, "月當大火, 則浴其種"; trans. DeWoskin and Crump 1996, 166.

5. Needham 1988, 261. Huang (1991, 393n7) provides a detailed explanation of these astrological observations, which I mostly follow here. Cf. Como 2009, 142, and van Gulik 1935, 41. Further, the ancient Confucian philosopher Xunzi 荀子 (340–245 BCE) wrote that the silkworm's head resembles that of a horse, and it was commonly believed that silkworms nodded their heads in the same way as horses. See Broadwin 1999, 25; Knoblock 1988, 3:200; and Needham 1988, 265.

6. *Songdai biji xiaoshuo* 宋代筆記小說, 23:80: 蜀中寺觀, 多塑女人披馬皮, 謂馬頭娘, 以祈蠶.

was often considered the divine manifestation of the young girl in the silkworm-horse myth, who was cocooned within a horsehide to become the progenitor of silkworms, and she is worshipped to the present day in silk-producing regions across China.[7] As noted, this horse-head maiden was seen as relevant to the sericulture industry in large part because of ancient Chinese cosmological connections between horses and silkworms. And in the same way, it was Aśvaghoṣa's close association with horses, stemming from a number of hagiographic traditions as well as his peculiar name—literally "Horse Neigh"—that made him a most suitable figure through whom Chinese Buddhists could assert the utility of their religion to the sericulture industry.[8]

Aśvaghoṣa as God of Silk

Appearing near the end of a small prayer booklet discovered in the library cave at Dunhuang is a brief formulary bearing the title "Silkworm Feast Prayer Text" (*Canyan yuanwen* 蠶筵願文).[9] Like many such prayer texts found at Dunhuang, this formulary or "model text" (*fanben* 範本) was apparently intended as a guide for liturgical recitation at a communal fete sponsored for a specific purpose—in this case the advancement of a patron's sericulture business.[10] This document is of interest here because it includes Aśvaghoṣa among an eclectic host of deities whose services were sought for the benefit of silk producers:

> Submit your heart to the Ox King *śramaṇa*[11] and prostrate yourself before Aśvaghoṣa Bodhisattva, and all that you hope for in sericulture and agriculture will measure up to your wishes. The silk cocoons will fulfill your desires, you will reap double the amount of silk fabrics and pongees for many years,

7. On the relationship between the silkworm-horse myth and the horse-head maiden, see Bodde 1975, 271; Broadwin 1999, 22–25; Iyanaga 2002, 518; Kuhn 1984, 232–233; Shimizu 1937, 84–85; and Xiao 1994, 201–205.

8. This point is also made by Iyanaga 2002, 523; Strickmann 2002, 302n31 (actually Ursula-Angelica Cedzich, who wrote the footnotes for this chapter); and Xiao 1994, 201. Further, by late-imperial times Aśvaghoṣa was sometimes conflated with the horse-head maiden. See Broadwin 1999, 25; Pan 1993, 110; and van Gulik 1935, 46.

9. *Yinyuan lun* 因緣論 (*Treatise on Causes and Conditions*) is the title on the cover of this booklet (S 5639), which is followed by Giles (1957, 184). Dunhuang Yanjiu Yuan (2000, 175) calls it a *Shimen yingyong wenfan* 釋門應用文範 (*Buddhist Usage Formulary*), and suspects that the title *Yinyuan lun* was given by Jiang Xiaowan 蔣孝琬 (d. 1922), who was an assistant to Aurel Stein (1862–1943). The *Dunhuang baozang* 敦煌寶藏 calls it a *Shimen yingyong wen* (*Buddhist Usage Text*) or *Qingdiao wen* 慶弔文 (*Congratulations or Condolences Text*). I follow Huang and Wu (1995, 208) in reading *yan* 筵 rather than *yan* 延 in the title of the silkworm prayer text. The original manuscript has the latter character.

10. For a useful discussion in English on the genre of *yuanwen*, see Teiser 2004.

11. On the Ox King (a.k.a. Ox God, *niushen* 牛神) as divine protector of draft animals in China, see Werner 1932, 331–332; and Yin and Yin 2002, 224–229. This could also be a reference to the Buddha's disciple Gavāṃpati, whose name was sometimes glossed as Niu wang 牛王; see Mochizuki 1954–1963, 1:618b–c; and Ciyi 1988–1989, 7:6063a–b.

and your silk [production] will completely surpass that of previous years. . . . [The sound of] silkworms eating will be like the wind and rain, and the cocoons will pile up like marchmounts and mountains. In one harvest [you will obtain] ten-thousand-fold floss silks, and your silk [will produce] a thousand boxes of fine, patterned silks.[12]

傾心於牛王沙門，啟（稽）首向馬鳴菩薩，所希蠶農稱意. 絲繭遂心，繆紬倍穫於常年，絹白（帛）全勝往歲. . . . 蠶食如風如雨，成繭乃如岳如山；一收萬倍之絲綿，絹白（帛）千箱之羅綺.[13]

Probably dating to the tenth century, this brief liturgy is one of the earliest explicit examples of Aśvaghoṣa being elicited in rituals directed toward the betterment of the sericulture industry.[14] Over the following centuries there were sporadic claims that Aśvaghoṣa had some stake in the fate of silkworms and the production of silk. The Buddhist layman Wang Rixiu 王日休 (d. 1173), for example, likewise invoked Aśvaghoṣa as he provided a sobering contrast to this formulary's exuberance with a stern admonition for the reapers of silkworms:

Exhortation to Sericulturists:

Those who raise silkworms should think to themselves: silkworms make silk so that people will have clothing—this is surely an abiding worldly truth—but it also involves killing living beings. Common people base [their sericulture practice] on Aśvaghoṣa Bodhisattva. But having examined the scriptures, [I found that] they in fact lack this tradition. They only say that the Buddha admonished his disciples to not take clothes of silk or use leather for footwear because living beings are killed in their production. How can people who raise silkworms for a living not be ashamed? They should often repent, invoke the Buddha Amitābha and make a great vow, saying, "I vow that after I see the Buddha and achieve the Way I will completely liberate all of the silkworms that I have killed since becoming a sericulturist."

勸養蠶者:

養蠶者當自念云: 蠶為絲以為人衣—此固世間常理—然亦是殺害物命. 世人以為馬鳴菩薩. 考於藏經，本無此說. 唯說佛訓弟子，不得衣綿絹，及用皮為鞋履，為殺物命而得.

12. Cf. Japanese trans. Iyanaga 2002, 525.

13. *Dunhuang baozang*, 44:96; available online at the International Dunhuang Project website, http://idp.bl.uk (accessed June 6, 2012). Transcription, punctuation, and character amendments following Huang and Wu 1995, 208.

14. The approximate date of the tenth century is given by Giles 1957, 184; and Huang and Wu 1995, 221–222. The latter base their dating on semantic and stylistic similarities between this and other more confidently dated formularies, as well as specific terminology in the present text.

人既以養蠶為業，豈可不知慚愧？當常懺悔，念阿彌陀佛，發大願云，"願我見佛，得道之後，盡度養蠶以來所殺一切蠶命."[15]

Further, in Dai Zhi's *Fresh Rat* chapter on silkworms and horses, he noted how "commoners say that Aśvaghoṣa Bodhisattva is a silkworm god,"[16] and the widely circulating morality book (*shanshu* 善書) *Tract of the Most Exalted on Action and Retribution* (*Taishang ganying pian* 太上感應篇) likewise elicited Aśvaghoṣa in its admonition against wasting silk cloth.[17] Of course, neither these brief statements nor Wang's exhortation provide more than the barest indication of what common people of the time believed about Aśvaghoṣa's link to the fortunes of sericulture. And throughout the following analysis of earlier documents that appear to have provided the foundation for Aśvaghoṣa's identification as a silkworm deity, I will indeed have little more to say about what sericulturists themselves actually did or thought. Nevertheless, together with the Dunhuang formulary, in which silk producers were directed to personally entreat Aśvaghoṣa to fatten their silkworms, these statements lend credence to the impression given by prescriptive ritual manuals, that Aśvaghoṣa had indeed become an immanent agent in the fortunes of medieval Chinese sericulturists, offering silken blessings in exchange for personal obeisance.

These glimpses of lay Buddhist worship of the silkworm god Aśvaghoṣa have contributed to modern scholarly assumptions that there were two distinct Aśvaghoṣas in premodern China, one venerated as a deity by sericulturists themselves and another honored as patriarch by the Buddhist clergy. Perhaps the earliest example of this bifurcation is Mochizuki Shinkō's 望月信亨 (1869–1948) pioneering *Encyclopedia of Buddhism* (*Bukkyō daijiten*). Mochizuki's conviction that we should posit a clean break between Buddhist patriarch and silkworm god is clearly illustrated in the structure of his encyclopedia entries: one entry for Aśvaghoṣa, the Indian historical personage, contemporary of King Kaniṣka (ca. 128–151 CE) and author of the *Buddhacarita*, and a separate entry for Aśvaghoṣa *Bodhisattva*, also known as "Horse Luminescence Bodhisattva" (Maming pusa 馬明菩薩), who was worshipped as a "folk" (*zoku* 俗) deity of sericulture (Mochizuki 1954–1963, 5:4862a–4893a and 4863a–c). This arrangement was copied in the *Encyclopedia of the Buddha's Light* (*Foguang da cidian*), which was largely based on Mochizuki's work, and its assumption of disjuncture between Buddhist historical personage and mythic invention of popular religion has informed

15. *Longshu zengguang jingtu wen* 龍舒增廣淨土文, T 1970, 47:271c. This text was completed in either 1161–62 or 1173; see Hirosato 1951, 70–71. Longshu is present-day Shucheng 舒城 city, in Anhui province.

16. *Songdai biji xiaoshuo* 23:80: 俗謂蠶神為馬明菩薩. The names Maming 馬鳴 and Maming 馬明 seem to have been used interchangeably, as is discussed later in this chapter.

17. *Taishang ganying pian* 太上感應篇, DZ 1167, fasc. 836, 5a–6b. This text is attributed to Li Changling 李昌齡 (937–1008). See Schipper and Verellen 2005, 2:740–742.

almost all subsequent Chinese and Japanese scholarship concerning Aśvaghoṣa's apotheosis.[18]

However, while it may seem perfectly reasonable to assert that an ancient Indian personage and a medieval Chinese deity are not the same thing, there is no indication that Chinese devotees themselves saw Aśvaghoṣa the Buddhist patriarch and Aśvaghoṣa the silkworm god as two distinct characters.[19] Mochizuki's strategy of distinguishing the two by labeling only the latter a bodhisattva is completely at odds with the sources he cites, which frequently described the ancient Indian Aśvaghoṣa as a great bodhisattva as well. Neither is there any correlation between the names "Horse Neigh" (Maming 馬鳴) and "Horse Luminescence" (Maming 馬明) and the patriarch and silkworm god, as Mochizuki implies,[20] since *ming* 明 was confused with the homophonous *ming* 鳴 in a variety of sources. For example, in *Nāgārjuna's Treatise on the Five Sciences* the names Maming 馬鳴 and Maming 馬明 were both used to refer to the same bodhisattva, and the *Comprehensive History of the Buddhas and Patriarchs* inadvertently substituted *ming* 明 for *ming* 鳴 in the name of the transcendent Ma Mingsheng 馬鳴生.[21] Examples of this sort—including such character substitutions in different editions of the same text—are readily multiplied. Perhaps individual authors had their own ideas about the difference between Maming 馬鳴 and Maming 馬明, but nowhere in the extant literature was this discussed, and there certainly seems to be no consistency in the application of these names across texts—both *ming* 明 and *ming* 鳴 were used for Aśvaghoṣa's name in sources discussing sericulture ritual and in those concerning the Indian patriarchate.[22]

18. Ciyi 1988–1989, 5:4350a–c; 4350c–4351b. See Iyanaga 2002, 523; Mikkyō Daijiten Saikan Iinkai 1979, 3:2153b; Sawa 1975, 670; Shimizu 1937, 74, 81; and Xiao 1994, 201.

19. There are discussions in medieval Chinese texts of multiple individuals named Aśvaghoṣa, but none of these has anything to do with silkworm gods. See the *Chu sanzang jiji* 出三藏記集, T no. 2145, 55:88c–89c; *Qixin lun shu bixue ji* 起信論疏筆削記, T no. 1848, 44:314b–c; and *Shi moheyan lun* 釋摩訶衍論, T no. 1668, 32:594b–c. This final source is probably a Korean text (Buswell 1989, 98); Suzuki (1900, 7–9n1) provides an English translation of its discussion of multiple Aśvaghoṣas. Cf. Hou 1999, 247–248.

20. Mochizuki 1954–1963, 5:4863c: 恐らく馬明馬鳴音相通ずるに依り、好事者之を彼の馬鳴論師に附託し僞作せしものならん ("Perhaps due to the similarity in pronunciation between 馬明 and 馬鳴, some dilettante falsely associated this [silkworm god] with the treatise-master Aśvaghoṣa").

21. Or Maming sheng, as Campany (2002, 595) has it? See the *Longshu wuming lun* 龍樹五明論, T no. 1420, 21:967b; and *Fozu tongji* 佛祖統紀, T no. 2035, 49:459b.

22. There may also have been some convergence between Aśvaghoṣa and the Vidyārāja (Brilliant King [of Wisdom], Mingwang 明王) Hayagrīva, whose name was often translated as Matou 馬頭 (horse-head). Introduced into China during the seventh century, this figure played a prominent role in a number of Tang Buddhist ritual texts, in which he was often called Matou mingwang. In late-imperial sources we find deities called Maming wang, Maming da 大 wang or Maming wang pusa 菩薩, including both 明 and 鳴, who may represent some amalgamation of Aśvaghoṣa and Hayagrīva. See Howard 1999; Iyanaga 2002, 497–503; Pan 1993, 110; van Gulik 1935, 46–75; and Yin and Yin 2002, 220–223, 240–245.

Indeed, clear-cut distinctions between Aśvaghoṣa the Buddhist patriarch and Aśvaghoṣa the silkworm god are found only in modern scholarship, and are nowhere supported in premodern Chinese texts. In fact, as I will illustrate, Chinese sources exhibit a clear continuity between these two facets of Aśvaghoṣa's character—they were represented as two overlapping stages of his bodhisattva career. Aśvaghoṣa was worshipped in China as a sericulture deity—if we accept the accounts of Wang Rixiu, Dai Zhi, and the Dunhuang formulary—in part because he was seen to have demonstrated a particular affinity for sericulture through past-life triumphs as an ancient Indian master along the bodhisattva path. These triumphs were illustrated in hagiographies advanced by some of the same Chinese scholar-monks who developed the Indian Buddhist patriarchate. Viewed in the round, Chinese sources thus demonstrate a clear progression in the association between Aśvaghoṣa and sericulture—due primarily to his horse connections—from hagiographies touting his sericulture prowess to ritual manuals intended to ensure the same silken benefits for local supplicants that he once provided in ancient India. In this way, as in the case of Nāgārjuna, Aśvaghoṣa's silkworm persona was superscribed upon his earlier hagiographic images, as Chinese adepts gradually expanded his saintly repertoire to include occult technologies that would speak to a broad range of local religious concerns.

Perhaps the most prominent Chinese Buddhist source to directly connect Aśvaghoṣa with silk production was the ninth-century *Tradition of the Baolin [Temple]* (*Baolin zhuan*; hereinafter *Baolin Tradition*). This text is now best known as the lineage history of the so-called Hongzhou 洪州 school of Chan Buddhism, which standardized the list of twenty-eight Indian and six Chinese patriarchs, culminating in the shadowy figure of Huineng 慧能 (638–713). Purportedly compiled around 801 by the monk Zhiju 智炬 (or Huiju 慧炬, n.d.) of the Baolin temple 寶林寺 at Mount Caoxi 曹溪山 (Guangdong), this new Chan history "virtually swept away the laboriously compiled [lineage] works of the eighth century" (Yampolsky 1967, 52) and subsequently served as the basis for the most important Chan genealogies of the Song, such as Daoyuan's 道原 (fl. ca. 1004) *Jingde [Era] Record of the Transmission of the Lamp* (*Jingde chuandeng lu* 景德傳燈錄) and Qisong's 契嵩 (1007–1072) *Record of the True Lineage of Dharma Transmission* (*Chuanfa zhengzong ji* 傳法正宗記).[23]

The *Baolin Tradition* thus stood in a long line of Chinese Buddhist genealogies in which hagiographies of the greatest Indian (and later Chinese) masters were strung together to establish discrete lineages of Dharma transmission extending back to the Buddha himself. It is important to emphasize that in this context Aśvaghoṣa remained just as much a "patriarch" as in

23. On the structure, content and textual history of the *Baolin zhuan*, see, e.g., Foulk 1999, 222–233; and Yampolsky 1967, 47–57. For recent assessments of its authorship, see Jia 2006, 84–86; and Jorgensen 2005, 640–649. Scrolls one to six and eight (of ten), which were rediscovered in the early 1930s, are reproduced in Yanagida 1983; they have been translated into Japanese by Tanaka 2003.

any other Buddhist lineage history: he was explicitly labeled *zu* 祖 (ancestor) and he stood amid a procession of singularly talented Buddhist saints who worked to transmit the Dharma to its latter-day champions. This is noteworthy because the *Baolin Tradition* provided the earliest extant indication of Aśvaghoṣa's association with sericulture, and thus militates strongly against the perception instilled by Mochizuki and others that Aśvaghoṣa's silkworm connections were somehow confined to the religion of sericulturists and distinct from his role as patriarch of the Chinese sangha. Instead, according to Zhiju (?) and later Daoyuan, Qisong, and others,[24] Aśvaghoṣa the ancient Indian patriarch once transformed his body into a silkworm and spun silk so that the destitute masses might have sufficient clothing—a formulation that clearly prefigured ritual manuals in which Aśvaghoṣa was invoked as a local god of silkworms.

The account of Aśvaghoṣa in the *Baolin Tradition* extended over its fifteenth and sixteenth chapters: "The Chapter on the Eleventh Patriarch Puṇyayaśas: Examining Aśvaghoṣa" (Di shiyi zu Funayeshe zhang: cha Maming 第十一祖富那夜奢章: 察馬鳴) and "The Chapter on the Twelfth [Patriarch] Aśvaghoṣa: Manifesting a Sun Disk" (Di shi'er Maming pusa zhang: xian rilun 第十二馬鳴菩薩章: 現日輪). The first of these chapters described Aśvaghoṣa's reception of the Dharma from his Buddhist master Puṇyayaśas, and consisted largely of a tale of Aśvaghoṣa's former life. Set in Vārāṇasī (Boluonai 波羅奈), the central Indian site of Śākyamuni's first sermon, this chapter introduced Aśvaghoṣa as a brilliant elder who followed Buddhism and was thus able to overcome false views of essentialism. Puṇyayaśas had just arrived in Vārāṇasī from Pāṭaliputra in the east, and as he encountered Aśvaghoṣa he related a tale according to which Aśvaghoṣa had once transformed himself into a silkworm to produce clothing for the poor "horse-people" of Vaiśāli (Pi[she]li 毗[舍]離):

> Among your former lives you were once born in Brahma heaven, but because of your attachments you were reborn in the kingdom of Vaiśāli. The people there had no clothing, and the hair growing on their bodies resembled that of horses. Although they had mouths they could not understand speech. You gave rise to compassion and so transformed yourself into a small insect and multiplied yourself a million-fold. Atop the trees there you ate leaves, and in less than ten days [you produced] cocoons. There were three classes of people in that kingdom. The highest issued forth bright light from their bodies and they could speak. Whatever clothing they thought of could be provided spontaneously. The middle class of people had no bright light issuing forth from their bodies, and they had to seek clothing themselves. The bodies of the lowest [class] had the form of horses and they were called "horse-people." They gathered the cocoons from

24. See the *Jingde chuandeng lu*, T no. 2076, 51:209b; and *Chuanfa zhengzong ji*, T no. 2078, 51:725c–726a. The *Taishang ganying pian* (DZ 1167, fasc. 836, 5a) also reemphasized Aśvaghoṣa's position in the Indian patriarchate while at the same time associating him with sericulture through a retelling of his *Baolin zhuan* hagiography.

atop the trees and used them to produce clothing. They called these cocoons "godling clothes."[25] In this land [of contemporary Vārāṇasī, such cocoons] are [spun by] silkworm larvae. Because the horse-people of the whole kingdom [were able to] produce clothing and you enabled them to obtain this benefit, you were reborn in the Middle Kingdom (Madhyadeśa). When you previously left the kingdom [of Vaiśāli] the horse-people were overcome with emotion, so they all cried out [in grief]. Your heart was moved so you spoke these verses:

"I was once born in Brahma Heaven,
but because of my petty attachments
I descended to the kingdom of Vaiśāli
to share your gloom and suffering with you.
I saw that you had no clothing,
so in my heart arose the good (karmic) reward of protection
and I manifested my transformations in cocoons
so that all might attain liberation."

After you recited these verses you were born in Vārāṇasī. You were destined to turn the Dharma wheel, becoming the twelfth [patriarch] in succession. Because of this emotional response [by the horse-people], you were called "Horse Neigh" [Aśvaghoṣa].[26]

汝先世中，曾生梵天，而為愛故，生毗離國中. 人無衣服，身生其毛，猶似其馬. 雖有其口，不解言說. 汝興慈故，而化小蟲，分身萬億，於彼樹上，而食其葉. 不經旬日，而有窠圍. 彼國人眾，而有三等. 最上之者，身有光明，而能言說. 所念衣服，而能自資. 中等人者，身無光明，自求衣服. 最下之者，身形如馬，號為馬人. 於此樹上，拾其窠圍，將充衣服. 此窠圍者，彼號天子衣. 即此土，蠶子是也. 因此一國馬人，而充衣服，為獲此利，而生中國. 昔離彼國，馬人感故，而共鳴喚. 汝心感故，而說偈曰:

"我昔生梵天，
為有小愛故
而墮毗離國
與汝同憂苦.
我見汝無衣，
心生善報護
示化於窠圍
當得諸濟度."

說誦此偈已，便生波羅奈. 汝合轉法輪，次第當十二. 因此所感，故號於馬鳴.[27]

Zhiju then described the transmission of the Dharma from Puṇyayaśas to Aśvaghoṣa, complete with a "transmission verse," a genre for which the *Baolin Tradition* and later Chan lineage histories have become so well-known.

---

25. Probably because the cocoons were the transformed body of Aśvaghoṣa, who, having descended from Brahma heaven, was considered a "godling" (*tianzi* 天子, *devaputra*).

26. Cf. Japanese trans. Tanaka 2003, 127–128.

27. Chinese text reproduced from Yanagida 1983, 40d–41b.

Aśvaghoṣa reverently received the Dharma and Puṇyayaśas passed into nirvāṇa. This was said to have happened in the fourteenth year of King An 安 of the Ji Zhou 姬周 dynasty, or 388 BCE.[28]

The Buddhist Ethic of Silkworm Murder

Numerous aspects of this brief past-life story are worthy of comment, not least of which is its spirited, eclectic blend of traditional Chinese and Buddhist mythic tropes and conventions of genre. The *Baolin Tradition* here followed a long line of Chinese hagiographies of Aśvaghoṣa and explanations of his strange name, but broke entirely new ground in this narrative direction; no extant hagiography prior to this text represented Aśvaghoṣa in a similar manner. At the same time, this tale both continued and recast an age-old Chinese tradition of mythic sericulture etiology, asserting that silk production in fact began in ancient India out of the compassion of this great bodhisattva. In this regard, also noteworthy is the obvious resonance between this image of cocoon-harvesting horses and the "Record of the Silkworm Horse from High Antiquity." Both tales accounted for the origins of silk production through strikingly peculiar equine associations and dramatic metamorphoses that recalled the uncanny life cycle of the silkworm moth itself. Further, the *Baolin Tradition* insinuated Aśvaghoṣa into this ancient Chinese matrix of silkworm-horse connections in a manner reminiscent of ancient Indian *jātakas*, or past-life tales of the Buddha Śākyamuni. By selflessly donating his own body and relinquishing his life in order to ease the suffering of sentient beings—in this case the naked horse-people of Vaiśāli who harvested silk from his presumably ravaged silkworm bodies—Aśvaghoṣa manifested the unparalleled generosity of a Buddha-to-be.[29] In this way the *Baolin Tradition* likened Aśvaghoṣa to Śākyamuni as principal exemplar of the bodhisattva path, while at the same time radically reconceiving the plight of silkworms on traditional Buddhist mythic, moral, and soteriological grounds. This last point in particular represented a major shift in Chinese Buddhist attitudes toward sericulture, justifying on Buddhist

---

28. Ibid., 41c–d. The text claimed that this was a *wuxu* 戊戌 year, but the fourteenth year of Zhou King An was a *guiyi* 癸巳 year. The nearest *wuxu* year was the nineteenth year of King An, or 383 BCE.

29. On the general theme of self-sacrifice in Buddhist literature, see especially Benn 2007 and Ohnuma 2007. By the time of the *Baolin Tradition*, numerous similar *jātaka* tales had been rendered into Chinese—tales in which Śākyamuni once lived as an animal who gave up his body to help others. According to Xuanzang's *Da Tang xiyu ji* 大唐西域記, Śākyamuni was once a rabbit who offered to jump into a fire so his cooked body could feed an old man (T no. 2087, 51:907b; trans. Beal 1884, 2:59–60; and Li 1996, 205–206), and he formerly lived as a deer king who offered to take the place of a pregnant doe in line for sacrifice (T no. 2087, 51:906a–b; trans. Beal 1884, 2:50–51; and Li 1996, 199–200). Another *jātaka* translated in the third century *Liudu jijing* 六度集經, describes how Śākyamuni once voluntarily transformed himself into a fish so that other fish could eat his body and avoid starvation (T no. 152, 3:1c-2a; trans. Chavannes 1910–1934, 1:11–12). Such examples that predate this Aśvaghoṣa hagiography abound in the Chinese Buddhist canon.

terms what had largely been depicted as a grossly immoral, soteriologically defeating means of making a living.

I have already mentioned the "exhortation to sericulturists" written by Buddhist layman Wang Rixiu, who sternly admonished silk producers to repent of their murderous ways, as well as the *Tract of the Most Exalted on Action and Retribution*, which emphasized the great debt owed to the thousands of silkworms who lost their lives for but a single article of silken clothing.[30] Both of these sources were compiled sometime after the *Baolin Tradition*, which indicates the continued conflict over the propriety of sericulture in religious circles, despite this apparent attempt to justify it. But several Buddhist texts that expressed similar sentiments were written before this Aśvaghoṣa hagiography. The best-known example is that of the great Vinaya master Daoxuan, who argued forcefully against the use of silk for monastic robes, largely because of the countless silkworms that were killed in the sericulture process.[31] Sui-Tang commentaries on the *Scripture of Benevolent Kings* (*Renwang jing* 仁王經) included sericulture in a list of twenty-eight offenses against the Buddhadharma—a list that also included such transgressions as drinking alcohol, neglecting one's parents, teachers, or elders, and intentionally giving rotten food to mendicants.[32] Further, the fifth-century *Scripture on Upāsaka Precepts* (*Youposai jie jing* 優婆塞戒經) warned that sericulture is a sin for Buddhist laypersons, and the *Great Universal Dhāraṇī Scripture* (*Da fangdeng tuoluoni jing* 大方等陀羅尼經) admonished against even associating with silk producers.[33] Finally, the *Dharmaguptaka Vinaya* (*Sifen lü* 四分律), translated into Chinese in the early fifth century, included a story about monks who went begging for silk floss so that they could make new silk beds. They arrived at the home of a sericulturist, who told them to wait while he boiled the silkworm cocoons to collect their silk. The monks stood by and watched while the cocoons sank into the scalding water and the silkworm pupae let out tiny yelps of agony in their death throes. Buddhist laypersons who observed this scene reviled the monks as shameless murderers, and the Buddha rebuked them for failing to uphold the Dharma.[34] While this story as a whole may have been more about proper monastic deportment than the propriety of sericulture, its emphasis on the horrible suffering of silkworms in the process accurately reflected the general Buddhist disapprobation—at least on a rhetorical level—of the silk industry's wanton disregard for the fates of its most valuable resources.

But in the hagiography of Aśvaghoṣa in the *Baolin Tradition*, silkworms were a different class of being altogether, and the sericulture process thus

30. *Taishang ganying pian*, DZ 1167, fasc. 836, 5a: 大抵片衣蠶千命, 按如佛說, 身服絲帛, 尚當還債.

31. See Kieschnick 2003, 98–99; and Suwa 1988, 99–182.

32. *Renwang huguo bore jing shu* 仁王護國般若經疏, T no. 1705, 33:282c; and *Renwang bore jing shu* 仁王般若經疏, T no. 1707, 33:349b.

33. *Youposai jie jing* 優婆塞戒經 (*Upāsakaśīlasūtra*), T no. 1488, 24:1050b (trans. Shih 1994, 83); and *Da fangdeng tuoluoni jing* 大方等陀羅尼經 (*Pratyutpannabuddhasaṃmukhāvasthitasamādhi-sūtra*), T no. 1339, 21:657c.

34. *Sifen lü* 四分律 (*Dharmaguptaka Vinaya*), T no. 1428, 22:613c–614a.

entailed completely different moral connotations. As in other, perhaps more mercantile understandings of sericulture, Aśvaghoṣa's silkworms lived only to die for silk, but here they were no mere commodities. Rather than being hapless victims of the slaughter, these silkworms were self-aware agents of compassion, leaping into the fire with eyes wide open. They were the bodies of bodhisattvas transformed, the manifestation of unparalleled generosity unleashed upon the evils of worldly suffering. Silkworms voluntarily and gladly give up their bodies, their lives, in a glorious act of self-sacrifice that was essential to ease the terrible pains of destitution. Silkworms represented the path of the Buddha, and the seeds of their virtuous deaths would beget the greatest holy beings of Buddhism. In this way, the process of sericulture and especially the killing of silkworms was depicted as a noble sacrifice, enabling the fulfillment of bodhisattva vows and promoting the greater Buddhist goods of perfected compassion, generosity, and the ultimate end of suffering. Silk production was therefore just as ethically and soteriologically as it was economically uplifting, so long as it was understood in the way intimated by Aśvaghoṣa's *Baolin Tradition* hagiography.

Another strategy that this account simultaneously employed to justify silk production was its Indianizing etiology of the sericulture process. Set in the distant Indian past, the *Baolin Tradition* described a time when this technology was unknown to human kind, and showed how a great Buddhist saint of Vaiśāli introduced silkworms, cocoons, and the production of silken clothing for the first time in human history. To see in clear relief the repercussions of this exoticizing strategy, it is instructive to compare this account with a brief text from the Daoist canon, which likewise laid claim to the origins of sericulture but instead insisted that the responsible party was a certain Daoist Perfected (*zhenren* 真人):

> At one time the Heavenly Worthy of Numinous Treasure was on Horse-Trail Mountain in the Land of Pure Luminosity with an assembly of hundreds of millions of Transcendents and Perfected. They followed him to the Palace of Red Luminosity [where they convened] a great assembly. As he was expounding the Law, one Perfected from among the assembly, named Lunar Purity, arose from his seat, approached solemnly, and addressed the Heavenly Worthy saying, "Today I see that the suffering and happiness of the people of the world are unequal, and some cannot obtain clothing. How shall we save them?"
>
> The Heavenly Worthy felt sympathy at this request, and dispatched the Perfected of the Mysterious Name to transform his body into a silkworm moth. It produced its silk and enabled the people to harvest abundantly. He taught them weaving and tailoring to make clothing. Moreover, he supplied a divine talisman to expurgate evil demons. The Perfected further addressed the Heavenly Worthy saying, "What will I gain in return for [teaching] sericulture to these worldlings?"
>
> The Heavenly Worthy replied, "Several years after you have transformed this body you will return to your original body and fly around at will, coming and going through space."

Thereupon the Perfected of the Mysterious Name addressed the various worldlings, "This silkworm moth is my body transformed. I looked with pity upon the masses suffering in cold and hunger, so I came to save them. You should devoutly honor [this silkworm body] and not irreverently discard me. If you give rise to irreverence you will return to suffering. If you increase [your] reverence you will obtain great wealth and honor. The more [silkworms] you rear the more you will get. [Even with] little rearing you will reap a bountiful harvest." The faithful and reverent who were pure of heart all rejoiced.

After this scripture was spoken, the Perfected, Immortals and rest of the assembly bowed their heads before the Heavenly Worthy and respectfully withdrew.

爾時, 靈寶天尊, 在淨明國土, 馬跡山中, 與諸仙眾, 及諸真人, 百千萬眾. 隨從到赤明宮中大會. 說法是時, 眾中有一真人, 名曰月淨, 從座而起, 端簡前進, 上白天尊曰, "今見世間人民, 苦樂不均, 衣無所得. 將何救濟?"

天尊憫其所請, 乃遣玄名真人, 化身為蠶蛾. 口吐其絲, 與人收甚. 教其經絡機織, 裁製為衣. 復以神符鎮貼, 以斷邪魔. 真人重告天尊曰, "世人所養蠶蛾, 為復有何報對?"

天尊答曰, "此身變化之後, 經餘年歲, 復歸本身, 飛行自在, 來往虛空."

於是玄名真人, 告諸世人, "其蠶蛾是我之身變化, 憫見眾生, 饑寒困苦, 故來救濟. 汝可精心虔敬, 不得輕慢, 將我拋棄. 若生輕慢, 當復困苦. 若加敬重, 得獲大富貴, 多養多得, 少養廣收." 精心信敬, 咸皆歡喜.

說是經畢, 真仙等眾, 稽首天尊, 奉辭而退.[35]

This Daoist canonical text, which includes a diagram of the previously mentioned talisman to protect silkworms, is titled *Wondrous Scripture Spoken by the Most High* [*Lord Lao*] *for the Multiplication of the Silkworm King* and is associated with the (Song dynasty?) Orthodox Unity (Zhengyi 正一) tradition.[36] It is structured more like a Mahāyāna sūtra than a *jātaka* tale, with the Heavenly Worthy of Numinous Treasure (in place of the Buddha) surrounded by a vast assembly of the most spiritually advanced adepts, one of whom he dispatched to another world to provide blessings for the beings there. Nevertheless, this text clearly bears a strong resemblance to the past-life tale of Aśvaghoṣa in the *Baolin Tradition*. Both stories depicted great saints who looked down upon the suffering masses, felt compassion for their plight, and transformed themselves into silkworms so that the impoverished could produce silken clothing to cover their nakedness. Both stories therefore offered justification for silk production by identifying the death of silkworms with the compassionate vows of sacred beings. In the Daoist version, however, rather than an Indian bodhisattva in a prior incarnation introducing sericulture to the world, the Perfected of the Mysterious Name was given the honor of first offering this great blessing to humanity.

35. *Taishang shuo liyi canwang miaojing* 太上說利益蠶王妙經, DZ 365, fasc. 180.

36. Both Ren Jiyu (1995, 274) and John Lagerwey (in Schipper and Verellen 2005, 2:960) provide brief content summaries of this text; I follow Lagerwey for the English translation of its title.

In this way the *Wondrous Scripture for the Multiplication of the Silkworm King* supplanted the similar Buddhist etiological myth in the *Baolin Tradition,* both of which were perhaps composed in order to bolster their respective traditions by crediting them with the founding of one of China's most important commercial industries.

As opposed to this Daoist origin myth and moral justification for sericulture, which remained firmly rooted in Chinese soil, Aśvaghoṣa's hagiography in the *Baolin Tradition* radically resituated the silk industry in ancient Indian history. According to the *Baolin Tradition,* sericulture was not originally a Chinese enterprise at all, and was thus not subject to traditional Chinese cultural mores or ethical standards. It could not be judged as immoral or murderous according to common Chinese conceptions of life and death or right and wrong. Rather, sericulture was most fundamentally an Indian Buddhist enterprise, given to the world by a great Buddhist master on the hallowed ground where Śākyamuni once lived, so its ethical framework could only be delimited by the expedient means and meritorious intentions of the most holy Buddhist beings. As such, this tale skillfully foregrounded the foreignness of Buddhism in general and Aśvaghoṣa in particular in order to completely reinvent sericulture historically, ethically, and soteriologically. The *Baolin Tradition* reshaped sericulture as a most virtuous enterprise but only within this Indian ethical framework, thus making it the exclusive heritage of the Buddhist institution and its representative branches in medieval China.

While the *Baolin Tradition* is typically understood as the foundational lineage history of Hongzhou Chan, serving primarily to establish the orthodoxy of this school over its competitors, here one sees that it entailed other agendas as well. One of these may have been to claim the sericulture industry as a fundamentally Buddhist enterprise. This text offered the requisite moral justification, divine agency, and ideological foundation for the development of advanced Buddhist ritual technologies that could ensure healthy silkworms and abundant silk crops. Indeed, new sericulture rituals were devised on the basis of Aśvaghoṣa's hagiography in this seminal Chan lineage history. The affiliation between Aśvaghoṣa and sericulture clearly derived from ancient Chinese currents of astro-agricultural thought, as well as age-old tales about the horse-head maiden as silkworm transformed, which extended beyond the Chinese Buddhist institution and its preoccupation with Indian patriarchy. But at the same time, the fact that Aśvaghoṣa's role as compassionate silkworm was so prominently displayed in this foundational Chan lineage history clearly indicates that his sericulture associations had penetrated deep into discourse of the Chinese Buddhist clergy. Aśvaghoṣa's silkworm connections were not confined to local sericulture cults—even if there is evidence that silk producers themselves worshipped him for the betterment of their trade—and his status as a revered Indian patriarch was directly connected to his past life as cocoon-spinning larvae. And in a similar fashion, the specific blessings that Aśvaghoṣa offered the ancient Indian horse-people in his *Baolin Tradition* hagiography were promised to Chinese sericulturists by Buddhist authors through ritual manuals touting Aśvaghoṣa's immanent presence.

The Ritual Manuals of Aśvaghoṣa Bodhisattva

Within modern editions of the Chinese Buddhist canon are two texts that enthusiastically celebrated Aśvaghoṣa's role as a powerful deity who offered *mudrās*, mantras, icons, and ritual procedures that could be wielded in order to ward off baleful influences, greatly increase one's silkworm harvest, and obtain vast riches including a wide variety of fine silks. Presented as Chinese translations by Vajrabodhi and Amoghavajra, respectively, these texts are titled *Ritual Instructions for the Recitation of the Incomparably Efficacious Method of the Divine Power of Aśvaghoṣa Bodhisattva* (*Maming pusa dashenli wubiyanfa niansong guiyi* 馬鳴菩薩大神力無比驗法念誦軌儀; hereafter *Ritual Instructions*)[37] and *The Perfect Siddhī Recitation of Aśvaghoṣa Bodhisattva* (*Maming pusa chengjiu xidi niansong* 馬鳴菩薩成就悉地念誦; hereafter *Siddhī Recitation*).[38] These texts share many defining characteristics of medieval Chinese Buddhist and Daoist ritual manuals, and they appear to have continued an effort observable within both traditions of proclaiming their importance to the well-being of the sericulture industry. These texts extended the development of advanced Buddhist ritual technologies into the arena of silk production, offering new-and-improved Esoteric rites to supersede traditional procedures for entreating silkworm deities.

The *Ritual Instructions* in particular drew upon Aśvaghoṣa's earlier hagiographic tales in the *Baolin Tradition*, illustrating how Aśvaghoṣa could provide for contemporary adepts the same benefits that he once offered the destitute masses of ancient India. This actualization of a bodhisattva's hagiographic talents is also seen in a number of ritual texts centering on Avalokiteśvara, for example, demonstrating how the salvific boons that this bodhisattva promised in earlier tales could be manifested in the present through certain devotional practices.[39] The *Siddhī Recitation* continued the

---

37. *Maming pusa dashenli wubiyanfa niansong guiyi* 馬鳴菩薩大神力無比驗法念誦儀軌, T no. 1166; translated in appendix 3. The *Taishō* text is based upon a Japanese print dating to the Kyōhō 享保 reign period (1716–1736) and preserved in the library of Buzan University 豐山大學 (T no. 1166, 20:674n7).

38. *Maming pusa chengjiu xidi niansong* 馬鳴菩薩成就悉地念誦, Z 1:3:5; also translated in appendix 3. As indicated in its colophon, the *Zokuzōkyō* text is based on a Japanese print dating to 1804 that was copied from an earlier manuscript in the Kōzanji 高山寺 canon (Kyoto). The author of the colophon, a monk named Jijun 慈順 (1735–1816), wrote that the Kōzanji text bore Japanese reign titles which pushed its date back as far as 1099. A note appended to the title of the text says that it was brought to Japan by the famous Nāra court minister Kibi no Makibi 吉備真備 (695–775), who traveled through China from 717 to 734. *Siddhī*, transliterated here as *xidi*, means "attainment," "consummation," or "perfection." It is essentially synonymous with and is frequently paired with *chengjiu*, as in the title of this text, and indicates the attainment of some good through ritual practice. See Mochizuki 1954–1963, 2:1951c–1952c; and Ciyi 1988–1989, 5:4562a–c.

39. See Reis-Habito 1994 and Strickmann 1996, 136, 146.

theme of silken riches offered by Aśvaghoṣa, while at the same time expanding his repertoire to include a broad range of apotropaic procedures. Together with the sources attesting Aśvaghoṣa's role as patron saint of the silk industry, these ritual manuals support the foregoing interpretation of Aśvaghoṣa's *Baolin Tradition* hagiography as serving to justify the sericulture process. Aśvaghoṣa was indeed seen to wholeheartedly endorse silk production as a morally and soteriological upright enterprise, and Buddhist ritual specialists presented him as the otherworldly agent most capable of providing divine support to those who counted their blessings in silken currency.

Aśvaghoṣa's *Ritual Instructions*

Although attributed to Vajrabodhi in the first half of the eighth century, scholars have long been in agreement that the *Ritual Instructions* was not the work of this great Indian ritual specialist.[40] Instead, given its thematic affinity with Aśvaghoṣa's hagiography in the ninth-century *Baolin Tradition*, the *Ritual Instructions* may have been compiled after this Chan genealogy and ascribed to Vajrabodhi for purposes of legitimacy.[41] Further, assuming that the *Baolin Tradition* presented its Buddhist sericulture etiology in part because it was compiled in one of the most important sericulture centers in China, it is logical to surmise that the *Ritual Instructions* likewise originated in a silk-producing region like southeastern Jiangnan. In any event, this latter text clearly emerged in a time and place at which Chinese ritual manuals of the sort that modern scholars commonly describe as Tantric or Esoteric—texts that share a close affinity with the *Ritual Instructions*—had long been an important part of the Buddhist canonical repertoire. This impression is supported by the highly cursory and patchwork nature of the *Ritual Instructions* as a whole, which suggests that the text arose in a context where ritual practitioners were already quite familiar with the sorts of technologies described therein—only a few brief cues were necessary to fit Aśvaghoṣa's specific prescriptions within well-established structures of ritual practice.

Like most Mahāyāna sūtras and their sub-class of *dhāraṇī* texts, the *Ritual Instructions* opened by populating one of the stock Buddhist stages—in this case under the Bodhi tree in Bodhgayā—with the standard Buddhist players: the Buddha Śākyamuni and a vast assembly of the most spiritually advanced beings. Next the story's protagonist bodhisattva, whose name adorned the title of the text, approached the Buddha to offer the great spells that he had acquired through countless eons of bodhisattva practice. Śākyamuni responded with excited praise of the bodhisattva's efforts and

40. See Endo 2001, 201; Iyanaga 2002, 523–524; Mikkyō Daijiten Saikan Iinkai 1979, 3:2154a; and Mochizuki 1954–1963, 5:4863c. Mochizuki was apparently the first to doubt the text's authenticity, on the grounds that its "clumsy wording" (*bunji setsuretsu* 文辭拙劣) does not match the style of other works confidently ascribed to Vajrabodhi.

41. Cf. Iyanaga 2002, 528.

the unsurpassed power of his spells, and entreated the bodhisattva to share with the world his efficacious incantations. The bodhisattva then bowed in honor and joyously intoned his wondrous *dhāraṇī*, often to the accompaniment of brilliant lights, raining flowers, and auspicious earthquakes. Such was the standard opening of a medieval Chinese *dhāraṇī* text, which the *Ritual Instructions* reproduced faithfully if somewhat hurriedly.

The *Ritual Instructions* here differed from other *dhāraṇī* texts, however, in Aśvaghoṣa's declaration that during the Semblance and Final Dharma periods his spell could assure that "the masses of the low and destitute and the myriad sentient beings who are naked will be clothed." As Michel Strickmann notes, it was common for such *dhāraṇī* texts to situate themselves during the time when Śākyamuni walked the earth, while looking forward to an apocalyptic future in which demons run wild and the Dharma is imperiled (2002, 104). The *Ritual Instructions* adhered to this standard *dhāraṇī* text format, while simultaneously reinscribing Aśvaghoṣa's age-old hagiographic association with Semblance and Final Dharma eschatology. But the text's interest in clothing the impoverished masses within such circumstances clearly recalled Aśvaghoṣa's past-life as compassionate silkworms described in the *Baolin Tradition*, in which he sacrificed himself to produce clothing for the naked horse-people of Vaiśāli. The *Ritual Instructions* later went on to describe the various fine silks procured through the recitation of Aśvaghoṣa's *dhāraṇī*, in combination with other ritual procedures. One can presume that these silken goods were intended to fulfill the bodhisattva's promise to clothe the poor during the Semblance and Final Dharma periods—periods that for medieval Chinese Buddhists often corresponded to their own place in Dharmic history.

After Aśvaghoṣa spoke his powerful spell, the narrative of the *Ritual Instructions* jumped to another venue. Until the presentation of the spell, the text was set in ancient India—during the time of the Buddha—and the speaker would appear to have been Ānanda or a member of Śākyamuni's grand assembly, even if the standard opening of "Thus have I heard" was not there to signal the auditor's voice. After the spell, the text leapt forward to its reader's present time, and the narrator became an anonymous contemporary with specialized knowledge of Aśvaghoṣa's rites. First, this narrator explained, one must follow a master who could transmit the spell just presented and a *mudrā* I will soon describe. This indicates that the text was not intended for professional ritual officiants; rather, here it appears to be a guide for the uninitiated layperson. But then after instructing this layperson to seek out a ritual master, it provided all the information that this master would need to perform Aśvaghoṣa's rituals. In this respect the text presented itself as a manual for ritualists. As such, the *Ritual Instructions* was apparently devised to encourage lay supplicants, with the help of their local ritual specialists, to personally entreat Aśvaghoṣa for the hoards of luxurious silks and other riches that this bodhisattva had to offer.

In order to obtain these blessings, the text further prescribed the proper iconography for Aśvaghoṣa and directed the practitioner to paint his visage.

Aśvaghoṣa was said to have white skin, he sat upon a white lotus flower on a white horse, and, as in the *Dharma-Treasury Transmission*, he was clad completely in white (see chapter 2).[42] He wore a floral crown, he sat with one leg pendant and his palms were pressed together. With the proper iconography thus described, the text then instructed the practitioner to set up an altar and begin ritual obeisance from the third day of the third month. It specified that one must set up the image facing west and make all sorts of offerings to it for a period of twenty-eight days. Finally, up until the one-hundredth day the practitioner must cleanse and purify himself or herself—a standard requisite for Chinese rituals of all varieties.[43]

At that point the text again switched gears, and Aśvaghoṣa appeared personally to take over narration. He first described the benefits that could be accrued by properly performing the rites just outlined, and then went on to add a few more ritual procedures and admonitions to the mix. The narrative remained in the present time of the reader, thus quite literally bringing Aśvaghoṣa home to his text's audience. If the practitioner recited his mantra and worshiped his image, Aśvaghoṣa promised, "I will always shine great rays of light upon [his or her] household," and "she or he will obtain all kinds of rich brocades, patterned silks, money, firm silks, and fine woven silks. Treasures of gold will pile up like a mountain for all the world to enjoy!" This was in keeping with Aśvaghoṣa's "original vow" (*benyuan* 本願), so he said, made when he first set forth upon the bodhisattva path eons ago, to ensure that "all would be adorned with riches" (see appendix 3).

Aśvaghoṣa then provided the standard admonition to maintain unwavering faith in his original vow, cautioning the reader that any doubts would lessen the efficacy of the methods prescribed. Practicing Aśvaghoṣa's rites with the proper resolve, however, the supplicant was assured of the bodhisattva's personal protection, and of course all the riches that she or he could desire. But that was not all. So as to include all "three mysteries" (*sanmi* 三密, *trīṇi guhyāni*) of the standard Esoteric ritual process—the mysteries of mind, speech, and body engaged through contemplation of an icon, recitation of *dhāraṇī*, and formation of *mudrās*, respectively[44]—Aśvaghoṣa also described his own *mudrā* to be placed before the practitioner's heart as she or he faced the painted image and incanted Aśvaghesa's mantra I have

42. In the *Xu gaoseng zhuan* 續高僧傳 biography of Tanyan 曇延 (516–588) (T no. 2060, 50:488a–b), Aśvaghoṣa was also described as wearing white clothes and riding a white horse. This was repeated in the *Fayuan zhulin* 法苑珠林 (T no. 2122, 53:467c). Medieval Chinese sources provide scant evidence for Aśvaghoṣa's iconography; for further discussion of related Japanese sources, see Endo 2001 and Iyanaga 2002, 528–532.

43. I have found no evidence to indicate whether Aśvaghoṣa's rituals were intended for men, women, or both. However, as sericulture has often been considered women's work throughout East Asia, there is a distinct possibility that women were involved in these rites. As Como (2009, 184) notes, "Throughout the premodern period women at virtually every level of Chinese society participated in sericulture rites." On the topic of sericulture and gender, see especially Bray 1997, 183–272; and Como 2009, 109–192.

44. See, e.g., Gimello 2004, 231.

quoted here. With this, Aśvaghoṣa's ritual repertoire was complete, and the practitioner was empowered to accrue all of the material, salvific, and apotropaic benefits that this bodhisattva promised. Finally, lest the emphasis on silk and sericulture be forgotten, the text concluded with the alternate title, "Instructions for the Rites for Perfect Silkworm Cultivation."

On the whole, the *Ritual Instructions* presented a montage of elements commonly associated with Esoteric Buddhist practice—*mudrās*, mantras, and image iconography—pieced together to form a semicoherent practical formula for invoking the bodhisattva Aśvaghoṣa and attaining the wondrous boons that he offered, some of which were related to sericulture. I suggested that Aśvaghoṣa's ritual efficacy here derived from earlier hagiographic tales preserved in the *Baolin Tradition*, following a trend in medieval China of instantiating through ritual practice the salvific benefits that popular bodhisattvas were said to have provided in ancient India. As the text of the *Ritual Instructions* currently stands, however, its connection to Aśvaghoṣa's past-life tale as compassionate silkworm remains somewhat tenuous, and its utility for medieval Chinese sericulturists is admittedly less than obvious. The text did declare that Aśvaghoṣa could clothe the naked masses during dark times, it prominently advertised all of the fine silks accrued through Aśvaghoṣa's rites, and it carried the alternate title "Instructions for the Rites for Perfect Silkworm Cultivation." But the text also strayed considerably from such sericulture-related aims, promising most frequently that the faithful would be adorned with great riches of a more general sort. At the same time, there is evidence that the *Ritual Instructions* once carried more of the emphasis on sericulture that its current version only partially suggests. The fourteenth-century Japanese iconographic compendium *Pure Treasures Recorded from Oral Tradition*, for example, quoted extensively from the *Ritual Instructions* and included passages not found in its extant editions. These passages further asserted the text's efficacy in improving the practitioner's silkworm crop, and they included another vow made by Aśvaghoṣa: "I vow that for those impoverished and unclothed persons in this evil age I will make silken thread to adorn their bodies and [in this way] adorn the Buddha's work."[45]

Here there is a somewhat clearer connection to Aśvaghoṣa's past-life tale in the *Baolin Tradition* as he renewed his ancient vow to clothe the impoverished with silk—this time in the first person for his medieval Chinese audience—and demonstrated a familiar economy of compassion according to which the plight of unclothed humans eclipsed that of boiling silkworms. Further, with this vow and Aśvaghoṣa's assurance (via the *Byakuhōkushō*) that the supplicant's "silkworm cultivation will be as he or she wishes,"[46] one can see more clearly how the *Ritual Instructions* would have worked for

45. *Byakuhōkushō* 白寶口抄, T no. 3119, 92 (*Zuzō* supplement vol. 7): 256b: 我有誓願, 惡世為貧窮裸形眾生, 作絲線莊嚴其身, 及莊嚴佛事; English translation adapated from Birnbaum 1983, 114. Context indicates that this was Aśvaghoṣa's vow, not the practitioner's, as Birnbaum asserts.

46. *Byakuhōkushō*, T no. 3119, 92 (*Zuzō* supplement vol. 7): 256b: 蠶養如意.

sericulturists to enhance their trade. The *Ritual Instructions* thus continued a drive apparent in other Buddhist and Daoist canonical sources to assert the importance of their respective ritual traditions to the prosperity of the Chinese sericulture industry. I have discussed how the *Wondrous Scripture for the Multiplication of the Silkworm King* was perhaps composed as a Daoist sericulture etiology in competition with the *Baolin Tradition*; there are likewise a handful of medieval Daoist Heavenly Master (Tianshi 天師) ritual manuals that prescribed rites for improving one's silkworm crop (Verellen 2004, 310–311); and the *Scripture on the Propagation of Sericulture Spoken by the Heavenly Worthy of Numinous Treasure* (*Lingbao tianzun shuo yangcan yingzhong jing* 靈寶天尊說養蠶營種經) instructed sericulturists to protect their silkworms by enlisting Daoist priests to perform exorcistic rites.[47] Similarly, the *Scripture Spoken by the Buddha on Prolonging Life* [*by Worshiping*] *the Seven Stars of the Northern Dipper* (*Foshuo beidou qixing yanming jing* 佛說北斗七星延命經) promised that by revering the text itself one could ensure the fecundity of his or her silkworms; the *Ritual Instructions of the Earth Goddess Pṛthivī* (*Jianlao ditian yigui* 堅牢地天儀軌) prescribed a certain *homa* (immolation) rite by which the practitioner could successfully cultivate silkworms by the ton; and the *Brahma Heaven Horoscope of the Nine Luminaries* (*Fantian huoluo jiuyao* 梵天火羅九曜) offered astrological calculations to assist ministers and kings whose lands were faltering in silk production.[48] Apparently preserving ritual and textual traditions that date to the Tang,[49] these sources perhaps worked in tandem with Aśvaghoṣa's ritual manuals and in competition with their Daoist counterparts for a share in the medieval Chinese market of supernormal technology designed for the promotion of sericulture.

Aśvaghoṣa's *Siddhī Recitation*

I have previously noted how the *Siddhī Recitation* prescribed rituals for invoking Aśvaghoṣa and enlisting his aid in raising silkworms while also expanding in various directions the services that this bodhisattva could provide. The *Siddhī Recitation* thus further asserted the utility of Buddhist rites to the prosperity of the sericulture industry and simultaneously interjected Aśvaghoṣa into broader fields of ritual practice—much like *Nāgārjuna's Treatise on the Five Sciences* and the *Scripture on Kumbhīra* before it. In addition to providing a variety of silken riches and helping to avert the decline of silk production throughout the kingdom, here Aśvaghoṣa

47. *Lingbao tianzun shuo yangcan yingzhong jing* 靈寶天尊說養蠶營種經, DZ 360, fasc. 179; see Schipper and Verellen 2005, 2:959.

48. *Foshuo beidou qixing yanming jing* 佛說北斗七星延命經, T no. 1307, 21:426b (trans. Orzech and Sanford 2000, 391); *Jianlao ditian yigui* 堅牢地天儀軌, T no. 1286, 21:355a; and *Fantian huoluo jiuyao* 梵天火羅九曜, T no. 1311, 21:461b; compiled by Yixing 一行 (683–727).

49. On the *Fantian huoluo jiuyao*, see Ono 1933–1936, 10:223c–d; and Ciyi 1988–1989,5:4628a–b. On the *Foshuo beidou qixing yanming jing*, see most recently Mollier 2008, chap. 4; on the *Jianlao ditian yigui*, see Ono 1933–1936, 3:166a–b.

could eliminate "the retribution of utmost destitution [accumulated] through rebirth after rebirth"; he could alleviate "the grave injury caused by curses of loathing, evil demons and . . . spirits of the dead"; and he could ensure that the supplicant would be reborn in the Land of Bliss. Also, similar to Aśvaghoṣa's *Ritual Instructions,* the *Siddhī Recitation* further emphasized the efficacy of this bodhisattva's prescribed rites for lay supplicants in particular: "a good man or good woman who is either a householder or a renunciant, who receives and upholds but one word of this sublime mantra," would benefit from the various apotropaic services that Aśvaghoṣa offered (see appendix 3).

The provenance of the *Siddhī Recitation* is unknown. It presents itself as a translation by Amoghavajra that was brought to Japan by Kibi no Makibi in the eighth century, and I have found no definitive evidence to either confirm or refute these claims. Given its structural and thematic affinities with the *Ritual Instructions* and other Tang ritual texts that advanced Aśvaghoṣa's divine powers, we cannot reject offhand its claims to Tang provenance, although with the dearth of available evidence we can do little more than speculate. Even more than the *Ritual Instructions,* the *Siddhī Recitation* is best described as a pastiche. It lurches forward from general prescriptions for practice to benefits accrued and then to opaque descriptions of its protagonist bodhisattva, the appropriate ritual platform, and a specific mantra and *mudrā,* all without any apparent concern for segues. There are also at least two places where the text appears to end—both where it promises comprehensive wish fulfillment (*ruyi* 如意)—only to be followed by more formulaic prescriptions for practice and resultant benefits. It thus gives the appearance of a text pieced together with passages taken from a variety of sources. This appearance is strengthened by the fact that aside from its title, the text contains no mention of the name Aśvaghoṣa. It includes a brief and apparently corrupt iconographic description of "the bodhisattva" that diverges considerably from Aśvaghoṣa's iconography in the *Ritual Instructions,* and apart from a few benefits related to sericulture there is nothing that specifically connects the text to Aśvaghoṣa. The *Siddhī Recitation*'s murky textual history and fragmented structure thus warrant caution in staking any firm conclusions upon its medieval Chinese provenance. Here I remain content to take it as a secondary and tentative example of Aśvaghoṣa's role as a Chinese silkworm god.

Like the *Ritual Instructions* but in even more abbreviated fashion, the *Siddhī Recitation* opens in the ancient past with the bodhisattva addressing Śākyamuni and offering his profound *dhāraṇī* to liberate sentient beings in the coming Final Dharma period. The Buddha praises him, the *dhāraṇī* is spoken, and auspicious omens ensue. The bodhisattva then assumes first-person narration, assuring the reader that if she or he recites just one word of this mantra and hears the bodhisattva's name only once, she or he will have his or her evil karma completely erased and will dwell in happiness through present and future incarnations. But lest the reader conclude that salvation is just that easy, the text goes on to repeatedly qualify these exuberant promises and add a number of other ritual prescriptions to the fold.

One must also maintain resolute faith in the bodhisattva's methods, never allow them to be transmitted to those who do not believe in the bodhisattva's vow, and pay careful attention to the sequence of procedures described in the text. One must make offerings to the Three Jewels, the ancestors of nine generations, and to all beggars. One must receive the transmission of the *dhāraṇī* from a master, treat this master like a Buddha, and donate all of one's belongings to him. After the bodhisattva's *dhāraṇī* is provided, the text then instructs the supplicant to paint an image of him. His body is red; he has six arms; he sits upon a lotus flower and white horse; and has six attendants surrounding him.[50] Although the text is unclear on this point, it would seem that the painted image should be set atop a ritual altar, which is given specific dimensions and described as smeared with ox dung and surrounded by incense burners. "If kings, great ministers and the various rulers, at times when the living things upon their lands are completely withered, the harvest of the five grains is meager, the silkworms do not produce rich brocades, and money and silks are lacking, put this method into practice for three months out of the year . . . making offerings of all sorts of food and drink . . . all the people of their kingdoms will be completely fulfilled with the joy of heavenly beings." Finally, the bodhisattva prescribes a specific *mudrā* to seal five parts of the body (usually forehead, left and right shoulders, heart and throat) and thereby protect the practitioner from all sorts of evil influences (see appendix 3).

While I would submit that the *Siddhī Recitation* drew upon the *Ritual Instructions* and Aśvaghoṣa's hagiographic tradition in highlighting this bodhisattva's association with silken riches, it also attributed to him to a wide variety of apotropaic functions, from eliminating bad karma to warding off malignant spirits and shielding the practitioner from evil curses. It also followed the *Ritual Instructions* in emphasizing the good that this bodhisattva could attract in place of the baleful forces that he repelled: mountains of treasure, merit, abundant harvests, government office, longevity, rebirth in the Pure Land, and whatever else the practitioner desired. Were this the only ostensibly medieval Chinese text to claim such broad powers for Aśvaghoṣa, one might be more inclined to disregard its assertion of Tang provenance and treat it as a Japanese apocryphon—since it only survives in Japan and Aśvaghoṣa seems to have been a relatively popular deity there as well.[51] However, as I have previously shown, both *Nāgārjuna's Treatise on*

50. Pan 1993, 1:110 includes a color photograph of a statue of the "Great King Aśvaghoṣa" (Maming dawang 馬鳴大王) atop an altar in a modern Horse King temple (Mawang miao 馬王廟), Shaanxi 陝西 province, that partially fits this description. It is red, has six arms and sits on a horse. This is the only Chinese image of Aśvaghoṣa I have found that matches the *Siddhī Recitation* iconography; I have seen at least four such Japanese drawings that combine this iconography with that of the *Ritual Instructions.*

51. This possibility is also suggested by Shimizu 1937, 86. For discussion of Aśvaghoṣa as silkworm god in Japan, see Birnbaum 1983, 112–114; Endo 2001; Hardacre 2002, 202–206; Iyanaga 2002, 528–532; Mochizuki 1954–1963, 5:4863; and Shimizu 1937. Important primary sources on Aśvaghoṣa's ritual and visual imagery in medieval Japan include the

the Five Sciences and the *Scripture on Kumbhīra* also advertised Aśvaghoṣa's ability to provide a similar range of material, salvific, and protective benefits. In the same way as these texts, the *Ritual Instructions* and *Siddhī Recitation* perhaps worked to localize Aśvaghoṣa as an Indian deity in the Chinese ritual arena, supplying for this great bodhisattva a wide range of advanced Esoteric ritual technologies. But by emphasizing the silk-related benefits to be accrued through Aśvaghoṣa's rites, the *Ritual Instructions* and *Siddhī Recitation* furthered the effort evidenced in the *Baolin Tradition* and other medieval Chinese sources to secure for Buddhism a niche in the ubiquitous sericulture industry. These texts thus worked to supplant traditional Chinese sericulture rites with competing Buddhist ritual technologies, while further promoting Aśvaghoṣa as an efficacious god of silkworms.

Conclusion: Indianizing Sericulture along Aśvaghoṣa's Bodhisattva Path

Against the backdrop of the age-old Chinese sericulture etiologies studied by Dieter Kuhn, according to which silk was invented by the ancient sages as a fundamental building block of Chinese civilization, it is striking to see Chinese authors working to redefine sericulture as an ancient Indian innovation. Nonetheless, this revisionist history indicates how conflicted some Chinese Buddhists were over living in a land of silk. On the one hand, Buddhist authors expressed great consternation over the fact that sericulture demanded the deaths of so many living creatures, and that silk symbolized the worldly pleasures that strengthened people's deluded desires. On these counts silk was understood to contravene traditional monastic ideals, if not universal moral standards. On the other hand, Chinese Buddhists were practical-minded products of a sociocultural environment in which sericulture was widely extolled and silk was ubiquitous. Buddhist involvement in the silk industry was simply unavoidable, at least to some degree, and it also presented a host of socioeconomic and soteriological opportunities of which the monastic community often availed itself.[52] Chinese sources depicting Aśvaghoṣa as a sericulture deity likewise exhibit a mixture of ethical

---

thirteenth-century *Asabashō* 阿娑縛抄 (T no. 3190, 94 [*Zuzō* supplement vol. 9]: 296c–298a), the twelfth-century *Bessonzakki* 別尊雜記 (T no. 3007, 88 [*Zuzō* supplement vol. 3]: 310c, 328a–b, 329), and the fourteenth-century *Byakuhōkushō* 白寶口抄 (T no. 3119, 92 [*Zuzō* supplement vol. 7]: 255a–257b).

52. Scholars have only begun to examine Buddhist involvement in the Chinese silk trade. Chinese Buddhist attitudes toward sericulture, ritual and commercial uses of silk, and debates about materials for monastic attire have been summarized in a handful of studies. We know in broad outline that the Chinese monastic community produced, traded, stocked, and received as offerings large quantities of silk; Buddhist clergy and laity alike were active players in this omnipresent industry, despite the conflicts that this involvement sometimes generated. For some introductory explorations of these issues, see Kieschnick 1997, 32; 2003, 98–99; Liu 1996; Sen 2003, 182–186; Suwa 1988, 92–128; and Walsh 2010, 63–64.

handwringing and a sort of religious entrepreneurship. While some of these sources focused on the crucial moral problem of silkworm murder, some also worked to transform this killing into a Buddhist virtue—a vehicle for the unparalleled compassion and generosity of the great bodhisattva. With this ethical dilemma properly framed in Buddhist doctrinal terms, the path was cleared for Aśvaghoṣa to personally proffer his magical services to silk producers, vowing to clothe the destitute masses and prescribing spells, icons, and ritual procedures to ensure plentiful silk crops. In this way Buddhists touted their own powerful silkworm god and program of efficacious sericulture rites, which could compete with existing sericulture deities and rituals to secure for the Buddhist monastic community a new revenue stream in the form of patronage from silk producers.

Mercantile agendas of this nature were not necessarily inimical to the moral and soteriological concerns of medieval Chinese Buddhists. According to the time-honored Mahāyāna logics of merit production and expedient means, expanding the institutional presence of the monastic community through increased material wealth was the most effective way to make Buddhism accessible to all, thus liberating the greatest number of beings. Individual donors who facilitated this process reaped great rewards in terms of merit, or wholesome karma, generated for themselves and their families. Good monastic business and orthodox Mahāyāna soteriology went hand in hand, and the case of Aśvaghoṣa as silkworm god demonstrates how these ideals may have been applied to Buddhist involvement in the silk trade. Nevertheless, while ethics and economics were inextricably intertwined, and the financial clout of the sangha was necessitated in the name of spiritual salvation, the sericulture industry was still problematic for Buddhist devotees because it involved so much silkworm killing. Buddhists could not respond to this dilemma by denouncing the industry outright; silk production, trade, and use were just too widespread. Instead, as seen especially in the *Baolin Tradition* hagiography of Aśvaghoṣa, one Buddhist solution was to completely uproot sericulture from its traditional Chinese foundation and radically resituate it within a new historical, ethical, and soteriological framework that was explicitly labeled Indian and Buddhist. Having in fact originated in ancient India, at the hands of a great Buddhist master, sericulture would be fully consonant with traditional Mahāyāna ideals of the bodhisattva path, and would thus be the true heritage of Chinese Buddhists alone.

In this way, Aśvaghoṣa's foreignness was crucial to his ability to integrate Buddhism into the silk industry—or, rather, to redefine sericulture as an Indian Buddhist enterprise. Aśvaghoṣa's status as an accomplished bodhisattva of ancient Indian origin allowed him to effectively legitimize sericulture in the face of widespread moral outrage over unchecked silkworm murder. As a result, from the perspective of Chinese Buddhists themselves, Aśvaghoṣa was anything but "Sinified," and in fact he demonstrated how silk production was originally an Indian endeavor. Through the figure of Aśvaghoṣa, whose equine affiliations also closely resonated with ancient Chinese astro-agricultural thought, sericulture could be justified morally as an ancient Indian *upāya* devised by a great bodhisattva out of compassion for suffering beings. And by the same token, only because of his Indian identity could Aśvaghoṣa effectively prescribe Esoteric Buddhist technologies that would ideally obviate traditional Chinese rituals for augmenting silk production.

Who exactly was responsible for Aśvaghoṣa's silkworm metamorphosis? Unfortunately, it is impossible to identify any specific individuals or discrete social groups with ultimate agency in this transformation. One can, however, be relatively certain on two points. Firstly, Aśvaghoṣa's sericulture associations most likely began in China. There are no extant Indic sources that present similar images, and the ancient Chinese association between horses and silkworms was clearly influential in this development. Secondly, contrary to prior scholarly accounts that emphasize a clear demarcation between Aśvaghoṣa the Indian patriarch and Aśvaghoṣa the silkworm god, with the former being the preserve of Buddhist elites and the latter a product of local silkworm cults, evidence indicates that both scholar-monks and sericulturists shared agency in Aśvaghoṣa's Chinese transformation. Aśvaghoṣa's associations with sericulture were promoted (or at least acknowledged) by Buddhist authors and lay literati, and sericulturists themselves reportedly entreated him for the betterment of their trade. As such, Aśvaghoṣa's hagiographic and ritual imagery simultaneously trickled down and bubbled up, with the concerns of the clergy and laity, educated literati and silk producers alike infusing his silkworm persona. Representatives of the Buddhist institution upheld this figure as an effective means of securing patronage from sericulturists, who adopted him for the benefits that he might provide their silk production.

Sources that promoted Aśvaghoṣa's sericulture associations and divine incarnation also illustrated a merging of various different models of sainthood and divinity. The *Baolin Tradition*, much like earlier hagiographies of Aśvaghoṣa, represented him as an eminent exemplar of traditional monastic practices like authoring doctrinal treatises, preaching the Dharma, engaging in public debate, and propagating the teaching through master-disciple transmission. At the same time, the *Baolin Tradition* also illustrated a broader, multi-incarnation trajectory of Aśvaghoṣa's bodhisattva career, narrating his transition from a godling in Brahma heaven to a great savior in Vaiśāli to the twelfth post-*parinirvāṇa* patriarch in Vārānasī. Similarly, the *Scripture on Kumbhīra* depicted Aśvaghoṣa in the company of cosmic bodhisattvas like Avalokiteśvara and Bhaiṣajyarāja, as well as Śākyamuni himself, and Aśvaghoṣa's *Ritual Instructions* and *Siddhī Recitation* showed how their protagonist could leap directly from ancient India into the present time of his latter-day Chinese devotees. In all of these sources Aśvaghoṣa announced his bodhisattva vows to save all sentient beings, echoing earlier hagiographic sources that exalted his profound spiritual attainments and his status as a Buddha-to-be. Through all of this Aśvaghoṣa came to be represented not just as a distant paragon of Indian Buddhist sainthood but also as a cosmic bodhisattva who transcended time and space to personally appear before Chinese adepts and ensure their well-being.

Within the writings of Kumārajīva's associates and in the *Dharma-Treasury Transmission*, Aśvaghoṣa and Nāgārjuna were mostly depicted on the ground—removed by a continent and a few centuries, to be sure—but on a broader, cosmic scale well within the same spatiotemporal continuum as latter-day Chinese Buddhists. These patriarchs liberated sentient beings through their profound doctrinal writings and personal instruction, as all good Buddhist masters did. But they were also depicted wielding the mysteries of cosmic bodhisattvas—spirit-spells, magical elixirs, and profound bodily transformations—which they would employ to further aid sentient beings. In this way the Chinese ritual texts attributed to Aśvaghoṣa and Nāgārjuna were not so far removed from earlier Chinese conceptions of who and what these figures were. From the outset they straddled the human and divine—down-to-earth but far more powerful than most—and by the time of the sources examined here, Aśvaghoṣa and Nāgārjuna were at once ancient Indian patriarchs, cosmic bodhisattvas, and local gods.

But this was certainly not the end to the development of Aśvaghoṣa and Nāgārjuna as both patriarchs and deities in East Asian Buddhism. Throughout the Song dynasty, and in medieval Japan, the positions of these bodhisattvas as founding fathers of sectarian traditions—through the increasingly prevalent genre of Buddhist lineage history—became both thoroughly routinized and intensely controversial. Claims to their patriarchal authority were commonplace in all East Asian Buddhist traditions, whose members at times competed vociferously for the spiritual capital that the Indian patriarchs were seen to provide. And at the same time, their roles as local gods in both China and Japan continued to expand throughout the medieval and modern periods. Aśvaghoṣa became a mainstay in medieval Japanese ritual texts and iconographic compendia, as previously noted. He was worshipped as a sericulture deity throughout late-imperial China, and he continues to perform this function to some extent in modern East Asia. Nāgārjuna played a prominent role in Song dynasty exorcistic rites, also appeared in iconographic form at Dunhuang and in medieval Japanese ritual manuals, and he was placed alongside Laozi in paintings used in exorcistic rites in modern China.[53] But these are topics for another occasion. For now we return to medieval China, as we examine how Buddhist authors conceived these patriarchs as unique sorts of Indian holy beings, distinct from the early arhat-disciples of the Buddha and the so-called celestial bodhisattvas. The patriarchs were unusual among Indian figures in serving as both objects of veneration and models of emulation in China, thus providing an effective means by which Buddhist adepts could lay claim to the most venerable Chinese models of sainthood, divinity, and salvation.

53. Strickmann 2002, 320n68.

6

Buddhist Saints to Bridge the Sino-Indian Divide

Aśvaghoṣa, Nāgārjuna, and Āryadeva were many things to many people through their first five hundred years in China. From the writings of Kumārajīva's associates to the *Dharma-Treasury Transmission* (*Fu fazang yinyuan zhuan* 付法藏因緣傳) and Cave of Great Perduring Saints (Dazhusheng ku 大住聖窟), the accounts of Jizang 吉藏 (549–623), Guanding 灌頂 (561–632), and Xuanzang 玄奘 (602–664), the *Baolin Tradition* (*Baolin zhuan* 寶林傳) and *Scripture on Kumbhīra* (*Foshuo jinpiluo tongzi weide jing* 佛說金毘羅童子威德經), the Indian patriarchs played prominent roles in a wide variety of Buddhist discourses in medieval China. These patriarchs were deemed the founding fathers of Mahāyāna Buddhism as a whole; they authored some of the most seminal Indian Buddhist treatises available in Chinese translation; they single-handedly rescued the Dharma from the brink of oblivion; and they personally appeared at the behest of Chinese adepts to provide a host of tangible, immediate benefits. Aśvaghoṣa, Nāgārjuna, and Āryadeva provided models for Chinese adepts of how to become great Buddhist saints—how to champion the Truth through public debate and exegetical authorship; how to manage relations with secular authority; how to perpetuate the Dharma through direct master-disciple transmission; and most frequently how to uphold the teachings, through pernicious times, in a world without a Buddha. In addition to instantiating repertoires of Buddhist sainthood, modeling the means by which Chinese Buddhists could become great bodhisattvas in the centuries after nirvāṇa, the Indian patriarchs also served as objects of veneration through which Chinese adepts could secure health and longevity, family well-being, all forms of material prosperity, and ultimate salvation upon death.

Aśvaghoṣa, Nāgārjuna, and Āryadeva were ubiquitous in Chinese Buddhist writings throughout the medieval period. They appeared in a wide array of genres that reflected a broad range of authorships and intended readerships, including prefaces composed by elite scholar-monks and imperial patrons; Indian and Chinese doctrinal treatises and scriptural commentaries; hagiographies, master-disciple genealogies, and historiographies; and catalogues of ritual recipes that promised wondrous boons. The Indian patriarchs also made their mark on an assortment of non-Buddhist and extracanonical sources in China, from official dynastic histories and nominally secular poetry to memorial and reliquary inscriptions and even Daoist canonical texts.[1] These patriarchs played prominent roles in the development of Chinese religion in the realms of elite doctrinal and historiographic discourse, but they were also made accessible to Chinese adepts across social and sectarian divisions through ritual manuals and visual arts.[2] Through these tangible manifestations the patriarchs were ritually worshipped by local supplicants and summoned to specially constructed oratories, and some even said that they took up residence at world-famous Mount Wutai 五臺山 with Mañjuśrī and his associates.[3]

Ritually oriented sources that delineated the Indian patriarchs' roles as local deities largely functioned on different social and soteriological levels than the exegetical writings of a Sengrui or Jizang. To some extent these different Buddhist genres represented disparate idioms of Chinese Buddhism, and in the previous chapters I have attempted to explicate these differences. But there also was considerable overlap between the images of the Indian patriarchs advanced in these various sources. Texts that represented Aśvaghoṣa and Nāgārjuna as objects of ritual obeisance also often foregrounded their positions in the Indian patriarchate or talents at doctrinal authorship. Writings that advertised these Indian patriarchs as powerful, immanent presences also demonstrated familiarity with their earliest hagiographic images as presented by Kumārajīva's associates or in the *Dharma-Treasury Transmission*. Thus, the various genres discussed throughout this book are worth examining in tandem, because they provide complementary angles from which to approach the broader question of what the Indian patriarchs meant to medieval Chinese Buddhists.

There are several reasons why Aśvaghoṣa, Nāgārjuna, and Āryadeva were counted among the most important Indian historical figures across

1. On dynastic histories: see, e.g., *Chen shu* 陳書, 2:401; and *Sui shu* 隋書 (noted in chapter 4). On poetry: *Quan Tang shi* 14:5389 and 21:8469, in addition to the passages cited in Chapter 4. On inscriptions: Mather 1963, 346; and Suzhou Shi Wenguan Hui and Suzhou Bowuguan 1979, 21. On Daoist texts: see, e.g., *Huandan zhongxian lun* 還丹眾仙論, by Yang Zai 楊在 in 1052 (DZ 233, fasc. 113, 2b; see Ren 1995, 167–168, and Schipper and Verellen 2005, 2:856); *Lingjian zi yindao ziwu ji* 靈劍子引導子午記, Northern Song dynasty (960–1127) (DZ 571, fasc. 320, 11a; see Ren 1995, 413, and Schipper and Verellen 2005, 2:788); and the sources discussed in chapter 5.

2. In addition to the visual imagery of the Indian patriarchs discussed in chapters 2 and 5, especially noteworthy are the patriarchal processions carved along the interior walls of Kanjing si and Leigutai Central on the east side of the Yi 伊 River at Longmen 龍門 (Henan). Both of these caves date to the reign of Empress Wu Zetian 武則天 (690–705) and both include images of Aśvaghoṣa, Nāgārjuna, and Āryadeva. See Gong 2002, 341–50; Kucera 2006; and McNair 2007, 135. Also, Nāgārjuna appears in iconic form in an illustrated edition of the *Scripture on the Ten Kings* discovered at Dunhuang (Teiser 1994, 181), and he may be carved inside cave nine at Yungang 雲崗 (Shanxi) (Mizuno 1968; cf. Nagahiro 1994).

3. See Birnbaum 1983, 14–16. In Yanyi's 延一 (fl. ca. 1060) *Guang qingliang zhuan* 廣清涼傳 (T no. 2099, 51:1113c), Aśvaghoṣa and Nāgārjuna were said to inhabit a monastery on Mount Wutai together with all the most famous bodhisattvas in China, including Mañjuśrī, Avalokiteśvara, Bhaiṣajya-rāja, Samantabhadra, Mahāsthamaprāpta, and Kṣitigarbha.

these idioms of Chinese Buddhism. The breadth of the patriarchs' imagery was both a cause and effect of their increasing popularity in China from the fifth to tenth centuries. The patriarchs were introduced into China by perhaps the most famous Western missionary and translator in Chinese history, who promoted them and their writings as integral to the development of the Mahāyāna and the survival of Buddhism as a whole. This initial characterization led to their prominence in Chinese Buddhist discourses of a wide variety, especially during the Sui-Tang period, and their popularity soon spread beyond the clerical coteries of doctrinal specialists who followed Kumārajīva's lead in touting the patriarchs' accomplishments. From the beginning, the hagiographic imagery of Aśvaghoṣa, Nāgārjuna, and Āryadeva was elaborated together with their doctrinal discourse, and their early hagiographies depicted them as brilliant thinkers, invincible debaters, and prolific authors. But they were also shown to be masters of realms beyond the ken of intellectual and literary production: they were advanced *dhyāna* adepts who had achieved all the attendant "spiritual penetrations" (*shentong* 神通); they ventured to magical realms in search of the Buddhist truth; and they matched powers with kings and gods. Aśvaghoṣa, Nāgārjuna, and Āryadeva were invariably labeled bodhisattvas; some said that they had reached the highest stages of the bodhisattva path, and others even claimed that they were or would soon become full-fledged buddhas. With such a roster of accomplishments and accolades accorded them in only their first century in China, it is little surprise that these patriarchs would soon find a ready audience beyond the scholastic clergy that first introduced them into China. Much like Chinese religious figures such as Confucius 孔子 (551–479 BCE), Laozi 老子 (trad. 6th century BCE), or Huineng 慧能 (638–713), whose widespread devotional cults branched off from earlier literary traditions, Aśvaghoṣa and Nāgārjuna were accepted into broader fields of Chinese religiosity and ritual technology in part because they had already achieved such wide-ranging prominence in the discourses of clerical elites.

In addition, as I have emphasized in the preceding chapters, a more specific dynamic made these Indian patriarchs especially relevant to the concerns of medieval Chinese Buddhists. Aśvaghoṣa, Nāgārjuna, and Āryadeva had been promoted by the great Kumārajīva, and their personages encapsulated the entirety of the Mahāyāna more so than any other Indian figures. They were unparalleled exemplars of both doctrinal authorship and Buddhist supernormal power. But one of the most important and enduring images of these patriarchs in medieval China was as great Buddhist revivalists in times of soteriological decline. I have labeled Aśvaghoṣa, Nāgārjuna, and Āryadeva "historical figures" not as a concession to the modern scholarly consensus that they actually lived in India over the first few centuries of the Common Era. Rather, by "historical," I refer to the medieval Chinese consensus that these patriarchs lived as human beings in India during specific centuries after the Buddha's *parinirvāṇa*. For Chinese Buddhist authors, one of the most important aspects of the Indian patriarchs' careers was their broader historical contexts, which both filled out the medieval Chinese *imaginaire* of post-*parinirvāṇa* Indian Buddhism and foregrounded the patriarchs' great spiritual accomplishments. As ancient Indians who championed the True Dharma long after the Buddha's death, Aśvaghoṣa, Nāgārjuna, and Āryadeva were at once exotic and familiar to their Chinese proponents, and this juxtaposition had much to do with the patriarchs' early and sustained prominence in China.

While a central preoccupation of Chinese writings on Aśvaghoṣa, Nāgārjuna, and Āryadeva was to delineate their roles in ancient Indian Buddhist history, not all Chinese authors understood that history to have run the same course. On the one hand, Chinese commentators repeatedly emphasized the ways in which these Indian patriarchs resurrected the Dharma when it was in danger of dying out. The patriarchs converted kings, subdued non-Buddhists, and most importantly authored profound doctrinal treatises in order to forestall the collapse of the Dharma and return it to its former glory. On the other hand, other sources emphasized the patriarchs' roles as Dharma transmitters within lineages of Buddhist masters who together preserved the original integrity of the teaching. Aśvaghoṣa, Nāgārjuna, and Āryadeva handed down to their disciples the teaching that they had received from their masters, who likewise passed along the same True Dharma that Śākyamuni originally introduced into the world. Therefore, these variant depictions of the Indian patriarchs' careers also illustrate competing Chinese conceptions of Buddhist history in ancient India—one of precipitous Dharma decline after the Buddha's death and subsequent revival by the patriarchs, and another according to which the Dharma endured undimmed through the generations after nirvāṇa. These representations of Aśvaghoṣa, Nāgārjuna, and Āryadeva further indicate how Chinese Buddhists variously conceived Buddhist saints as forged within specific trajectories of post-*parinirvāṇa* Dharmic history, and thus how latter-day Chinese adepts themselves could ascend the ranks of Buddhist holy beings by perfecting practical repertoires ideally suited to the generations after nirvāṇa.

In the present chapter I recount how these and related concerns were fundamental to how medieval Chinese Buddhists conceived Aśvaghoṣa, Nāgārjuna, and Āryadeva as unique sorts of Indian holy beings. Having lived in ancient India neither too far from nor too close to the time of the Buddha, and having perfected repertoires of practices that were most valued across Chinese religious traditions, Aśvaghoṣa, Nāgārjuna, and Āryadeva fit within a distinctive Chinese niche for Indian Buddhist saints. These Indian patriarchs were unlike the arhat-disciples of the Buddha or the so-called celestial bodhisattvas, who had perfected their qualities in circumstances that were completely foreign to those of latter-day China. Only Aśvaghoṣa, Nāgārjuna, and Āryadeva had triumphed in a world much like that of their Chinese proponents—with hordes of heretics overrunning the True Dharma after Śākyamuni's departure—and consequently, they were especially apposite exemplars for medieval Chinese Buddhists who likewise sought to uphold the teaching during the latter, evil age. In the text to come, I examine how Chinese authors represented these Indian patriarchs in relation to other classes of Indian Buddhist saints, and in terms of native Chinese models of sainthood and divinity. Precisely because Aśvaghoṣa, Nāgārjuna, and Āryadeva served as exemplars in medieval China, unlike the arhats and celestial bodhisattvas, Chinese Buddhists could use them to demonstrate the ancient Indian heritage of time-honored Chinese religious ideals. Chinese authors advanced the Indian patriarchs as post-*parinirvāṇa* world-saviors who employed traditional Chinese practices, and also as Indian deities who functioned like local Chinese gods. These dynamics further illustrate how models of Buddhist sanctity and salvation were developed in medieval China, and how Buddhist proponents thereby negotiated their identities as representatives of an avowedly foreign religion in China and as Dharma-bearers in a world without a Buddha.

Indian Patriarchs, Buddhist Scholar-Monks, and Chinese Models of Sainthood

Medieval Chinese accounts of Aśvaghoṣa, Nāgārjuna, and Āryadeva were products of an environment in which different religious groups competed with one another for patronage from the gentry and ruling classes. Chinese Buddhist monks in particular worked to advance their vocation by associating themselves with repertoires of practices and values most favored by the Chinese elite, who developed paradigms of religious sanctity on the basis of these practices and values. Sengrui 僧叡 (ca. 352–436), Sengzhao 僧肇 (ca. 374–414), and Huiyuan 慧遠 (ca. 334–416), for example, who first introduced Aśvaghoṣa, Nāgārjuna, and Āryadeva to a Chinese readership, themselves came of age amid figures variously known as "high-minded gentlemen" (*gaoshi* 高士), "men of the cliffs and caves" (*yanxue zhi shi* 巖穴之士), "disengaged scholars" (*yishi* 逸士), and the like. These figures upheld Chinese gentry values of self-perfection through learning and contemplation, textual scholarship, public debate, and a certain degree of remove from worldly affairs. Kumārajīva's associates promoted their religion amid, above, and against such figures, in part by showing how Aśvaghoṣa, Nāgārjuna, and Āryadeva had propagated these same ideals and thereby saved the world. Then, in later sources such as the *Dharma-Treasury Transmission*, and in the writings of Sui-Tang exegetes like Guanding, Jizang, and Xuanzang, the Indian patriarchs similarly served to illustrate how Buddhist masters endorsed the core values of the Chinese elite. In these contexts and others, Aśvaghoṣa, Nāgārjuna, and Āryadeva were represented in a manner most akin to the Chinese Buddhist scholar-monk, demonstrating how traditional Chinese ideals were best upheld by those who pledged allegiance to Indian models of sainthood.

In medieval China there were several distinct yet overlapping ideals of what it meant to be an accomplished Buddhist monk. Scholars have often noted, for example, how the *Gaoseng zhuan* 高僧傳 series—begun by Huijiao 慧皎 (497–554) and continued by Daoxuan 道宣 (596–667) and Zanning

贊寧 (919–1001)—defined classes of "eminent monks" in terms of discrete categories of practice such as scriptural translation, doctrinal exegesis, meditation, spell-casting, and so on.[4] Some monks were eminent because of their prolific literary output and their accomplishments at elucidating the Dharma in writing; other monks were eminent because they effectively propagated the teaching by demonstrating unsurpassed magical power. John Kieschnick, for one, argues that the biographies in these *Gaoseng zhuan* collections exemplify three main practical repertoires—centering on asceticism, thaumaturgy, and scholarship—which constitute divergent Chinese ideals of Buddhist monasticism.[5] And in a similar fashion, different accounts of Aśvaghoṣa, Nāgārjuna, and Āryadeva emphasized different aspects of their careers, which both reflected and contributed to shaping different dimensions of the Chinese monastic ideal. But one common denominator of these Indian patriarch accounts, and of the various Chinese images of the Buddhist monk, was their claimed basis in ancient Indian models of sainthood. Chinese Buddhists were acutely aware of the foreign origins of their religion, which often led them to highlight its compatibility with traditional Chinese values. But at the same time, Chinese Buddhists embraced their ancient Indian heritage, which afforded a certain exotic mystique and cultural cachet that was unique among Chinese religious practitioners. This Indianness was a fundamental, defining feature of the Chinese Buddhist monk's cultural repertoire. And as a result, Chinese authors often emphasized the Indian identity of Aśvaghoṣa, Nāgārjuna, and Āryadeva, who exemplified ideals and practices that were ostensibly rooted in the Buddhist heartland and were thus the rightful heritage of Chinese Buddhists alone.

Kumārajīva's associates first recounted the careers of Aśvaghoṣa, Nāgārjuna, and Āryadeva in the linguistic and religious idioms of ancient Chinese classics like the *Daode jing*, *Zhuangzi*, *Analects*, and *Book of Changes*. Employing tropes, aphorisms, and turns of phrase from these and other foundational sources for the religious ideals of the Chinese literati, Sengrui, Sengzhao, and Huiyuan conceived their ancient Indian forebears in a manner most accordant with the "high-minded gentleman." Like these and related Chinese religious figures, the patriarchs were depicted most prominently as masters of debate in the style of *qingtan* 清談 (pure conversation), scholarship in the style of *xuanxue* 玄學 (the study of the profound), eremitic wandering, and contemplative practice. However, only after becoming Buddhist monks were the Indian patriarchs shown to have perfected their natural abilities in these endeavors. All three were originally non-Buddhist prodigies before recognizing the superiority of the Buddha's teachings, "leaving home" to join the sangha, and applying their prodigious scholarly and rhetorical talents toward the propagation of Buddhism. Thus, on the one hand, these images of the Indian patriarchs paralleled the conver-

4. See, e.g., Kieschnick 1997, 8–15; Shinohara 1994, 484–485; and Wright (1954) 1990, 82–84.

5. Kieschnick 1997.

gence in medieval China between the literati gentleman and Buddhist scholar-monk, illustrating how the Buddhist monastic vocation was likewise rooted in traditional Chinese modes of textual learning and measured renunciation toward the aim of self-perfection. On the other hand, having developed their qualities to the fullest only as agents of the Buddhadharma, the Indian patriarchs demonstrated the supremacy of Buddhism over competing avenues of spiritual and scholarly endeavor. But while Aśvaghoṣa, Nāgārjuna, and Āryadeva thus exemplified traditional Chinese religious practices, the patriarchs themselves were clearly not Chinese; in fact, Kumārajīva's associates often expressly foregrounded the Indian identity of their Buddhist forebears. And in so doing, not only did Sengrui and others show that Buddhism was founded in traditional Chinese values but these authors also implicitly transformed the practical repertoires of Chinese "high-minded gentlemen" into quintessentially Buddhist endeavors. These practices were thus rendered the preserve of Chinese scholar-monks alone, whose merging of Chinese and Indian saintly ideals was exemplified, and valorized, by the Indian Buddhist patriarchs.

Later Chinese accounts of Aśvaghoṣa, Nāgārjuna, and Āryadeva similarly showed how these masters had perfected a practical repertoire that closely mirrored that of elite Chinese scholar-monks. As seen especially in the *Dharma-Treasury Transmission* and the numerous Chinese sources that drew from it, the Indian patriarchs were not only great philosophical authors, debate masters, meditation specialists, and eremites; they also served as advisors to kings and propagated their religion through master-disciple transmission. But while these latter endeavors were certainly characteristic of Chinese Buddhist scholar-monks, religious practitioners of all sorts in medieval China similarly aimed to promote their traditions by courting imperial patrons and establishing lineages of genealogical succession. Models of the erudite religious seeking imperial audience had ancient precedent in China—most famously in the case of Confucius himself—and Chinese emperors and kings regularly employed elite religious adepts of many denominations. And in the same way, master-disciple lineages were certainly not the province of Chinese scholar-monks alone. Confucians, Daoists, and other religious devotees similarly grounded their traditions in ancient Chinese genealogical models. In these respects, the Indian patriarchs were much like the educated elites of many religious traditions in China. But what made Aśvaghoṣa, Nāgārjuna, and Āryadeva most akin to their counterparts in the Chinese sangha was, again, the manner in which both groups defined ancient Indian models of religious sanctity as comprising traditional Chinese values and practices. Like their Chinese Buddhist proponents, Aśvaghoṣa, Nāgārjuna, and Āryadeva demonstrated how the Buddhist sangha was firmly grounded in the same patriarchal principles as the rest of Chinese society—even though monks ideally renounced family life—and that the greatest kings of ancient India had ensured the ascendency of their reigns only by following Buddhist advisors and supporting the sangha in its mission to save the world.

At the same time, however, the Indian patriarchs of the *Dharma-Treasury Transmission* were more than imperial advisors, placeholders in master-disciple transmission lineages, and masters of traditional Chinese literati practices. Also like medieval Chinese monks, Aśvaghoṣa, Nāgārjuna, and Āryadeva were shown performing a wide variety of wondrous feats beyond the ken of literary or intellectual production. Aśvaghoṣa was a wielder of "magical arts" (*jishu* 技術), who liberated beings with his profound musical talents and produced relics for his disciples to worship. Nāgārjuna was a master of alchemy who perfected the art of invisibility, observed and revealed the activities of heavenly beings, cast spells to conjure magical creatures, and eventually transcended death. Āryadeva subdued the gods, ripped out his own eyes to no apparent detriment, gave Dharma-talks with his bowels spread out before him, and relinquished his body "like a cicada sheds its husk" (*chantui* 蟬蛻) (see chapter 2).

In these ways the Indian patriarchs instantiated a repertoire of practices more akin to the monastic thaumaturges of the *Gaoseng zhuan* and other miracle-tale collections, although scholarship and magic were certainly not mutually exclusive talents for the accomplished Chinese monk. Campany remarks that every such tale of wonder-working monks "implicitly positions these holy persons against an indigenous type—the wonder-working transcendent (*xian* 仙), or seeker of transcendence—and the two repertoires of attributed feats match up almost completely."[6] Indeed, the Indian patriarchs of the *Dharma-Treasury Transmission* clearly illustrated that the most spectacular magical powers were well within reach for those who followed the Buddha's teachings. Consequently, not only were Buddhist adepts the true masters of practices associated with Chinese high-minded gentlemen, but the former also rivaled the famous Chinese *xian* in perfecting supernormal powers and ultimately transcending death. And the fact that Buddhist masters perfected this range of repertoires made them far superior to both *gaoshi* and *xian*; having greatly surpassed the transcendent in scholarly prowess and the high-minded gentleman in thaumaturgy, only Buddhist monks demonstrated the full range of powers required of the foremost Chinese saint.

Like Chinese transcendents and wonder-working Buddhist monks, Aśvaghoṣa, Nāgārjuna, and Āryadeva were largely represented as human beings who had perfected their qualities through specific repertoires of practices that could, and should, be cultivated by Chinese religious adepts. In the writings of Kumārajīva's associates, Jizang, Guanding, Xuanzang, and others, and in the *Dharma-Treasury Transmission* and Cave of Great Perduring Saints, the Indian patriarchs were deployed, on the one hand, as models for emulation. The repertoires of Aśvaghoṣa, Nāgārjuna, and Āryadeva were most akin to those of Chinese literati gentlemen and transcendents—and Chinese Buddhist monks especially—precisely because, like these

6. Campany 2012b, 39.

figures, the Indian patriarchs were intended to exemplify the best means by which Chinese devotees could themselves attain liberation. But on the other hand, in many of these sources the Indian patriarchs were also conceived in accordance with age-old Chinese models of sainthood in cyclical time, which to some extent situated the patriarchs beyond the ken of human attainment and made them objects of veneration. Like the ancient Chinese sage-kings who, according to Mencius, arose every five hundred years to reinstitute enlightened civilization, or the Daoist divinities who periodically descended into the world to save the elect, the Indian patriarchs similarly appeared at significant junctures of Dharmic history, when the teaching was on the verge of collapse, in order to relight the lamp and liberate beings from delusion and death. In this way the patriarchs functioned much like buddhas as well, emerging in dark worlds to reintroduce the True Dharma, and the former also exhibited a similar blend of imitability and inimitability. Like the Buddha Śākyamuni, Aśvaghoṣa, Nāgārjuna, and Āryadeva were sometimes represented as eminently human beings who awakened to the truth, liberated others, and thereby achieved sainthood—in which case their imitability was emphasized—while at other times they functioned more like cosmic bodhisattvas or Chinese deities who responded to rites of obeisance with a wide variety of wondrous boons.

But by and large, for Kumārajīva's associates, the author of the *Dharma-Treasury Transmission*, and Sui-Tang Buddhist exegetes, the Indian patriarchs were great Buddhist monks who provided models of emulation for latter-day Chinese devotees. These models worked in competition with those of other Chinese religious adepts, against whom Buddhists were measured for their ability to perfect both scholarly and magical talents. And while there was thus considerable overlap between these different religious repertoires, what separated Aśvaghoṣa, Nāgārjuna, and Āryadeva from other Chinese religious figures was the fact that the former were compatriots of the Buddha and so modeled ancient Indian religious ideals—however familiar those ideals might have appeared to a Chinese audience. This Indianness was an integral component of the patriarchs' Chinese repertoire, much as it was for Chinese Buddhist monks. The Indian identity of Aśvaghoṣa, Nāgārjuna, and Āryadeva functioned as part of broader Chinese Buddhist discourses of origins, according to which ancient India represented the pure, untrammeled source of truths that only Chinese monks could instantiate. None but Chinese Buddhists could rightly claim ownership of the values and practices associated with the Indian patriarchs—and the hallowed origins of Buddhism thereby—which included much of what the Chinese ruling classes valued most. In these ways the Indian patriarchs reflected and contributed to shaping Chinese images of the exemplary Buddhist monk. And by following the examples of Aśvaghoṣa, Nāgārjuna, and Āryadeva, the most talented men in China could ensure that their natural abilities would be fully perfected and their efforts lavishly patronized in service of the Buddhist truth.

Indian Patriarchs as Homegrown Bodhisattvas

Chinese Buddhist monks ideally instantiated repertoires of values, practices, and attainments that closely overlapped with those of other Chinese religious types, such as the high-minded gentleman and transcendent. Chinese accounts of Aśvaghoṣa, Nāgārjuna, and Āryadeva illustrated the ancient Indian heritage of these religious repertoires, which would thus become the preserve of Chinese Buddhists alone. As a result, Chinese images of the Indian patriarchs were often most similar to those of Chinese Buddhist monks: eminently human figures who achieved sainthood by converting to Buddhism and cultivating practices like doctrinal authorship, public debate, and meditation, while upholding ideals of eremitism, master-disciple transmission, and state-sangha relations. However, Chinese Buddhist authors rarely referred to their great Indian forebears as mere "monks"; instead, Aśvaghoṣa, Nāgārjuna, and Āryadeva were almost always labeled "bodhisattvas." This prompts the question of how these Indian patriarch accounts reflected and affected broader Chinese conceptions of the bodhisattva. What exactly did this status signify, according to these accounts? To what extent was it something that Chinese Buddhists could themselves attain, and how did it relate to broader Chinese notions of Buddhist sainthood and divinity? Given that the Indian patriarchs spent their careers engaged in the very same practices that were associated with Chinese Buddhist monks, one might surmise that the patriarch accounts thus provided blueprints for the attainment of the status of bodhisattva in China. I argue that this was often the case. But how then did these kinds of local, "homegrown bodhisattvas" relate to famous "cosmic bodhisattvas" like Avalokiteśvara, Mañjuśrī, or Kṣitigarbha, the objects of longstanding devotional cults? And in other contexts where Aśvaghoṣa and Nāgārjuna clearly functioned much the same as these cosmic bodhisattvas—as otherworldly objects of ritual obeisance—how did the former then map onto local Chinese models of divinity?

Few medieval Chinese authors expressly theorized the patriarchs' status as bodhisattvas. The most salient example is provided by Jizang, who addressed this question with characteristic exegetical rigor in his commentaries to the treatises of Nāgārjuna and Āryadeva. In the case of the latter, Jizang unpacked the technical implications of Sengzhao's earlier statement that Āryadeva was a "great master who left home" (*chujia dashi* 出家大士). Jizang explained that while Hīnayāna and Mahāyāna followers both "left home," the appellation "great master" indicated that Āryadeva was in fact a Mahāyāna bodhisattva and one of the so-called four reliances (*siyi* 四依; *catvāri pratisaraṇāni*)—types of saints who guided beings in the Buddha's absence.[7] Jizang also attempted to classify Nāgārjuna along the lines of these "four reliances," incorporating earlier sources according to which

7. *Bailun shu* 百論疏, T no. 1827, 42:233b. The "four reliances" were variously defined; see Ciyi 1988–1989, 2:1702b–1703c, and Mochizuki 1954–1963, 2:1719b–1720c.

Nāgārjuna had attained specific bodhisattva "stages" (*di* 地; *bhūmi*). Jizang first quoted Sengrui and Huiyuan as claiming that Nāgārjuna was a tenth-stage bodhisattva, then the *Laṅkāvatāra* prophecy—according to which he was a first-stage bodhisattva—before citing the opinion of a certain Yao Dao'an 姚道安 (d. before 581) that Nāgārjuna guided other beings to the first stage but was himself of the tenth stage.[8] If Nāgārjuna was in fact a tenth-stage bodhisattva, then, he would be classified as the fourth, most exalted "reliance"; if he was actually a first-stage bodhisattva, then he would correspond to the second reliance.[9] But more in accordance with broader Chinese conceptions of the Indian patriarchs, and thus more important for our present discussion, Jizang concluded these analyses by emphasizing that Āryadeva and Nāgārjuna were at once bodhisattvas and monks. Śākyamuni did not distinguish between *śrāvaka* and bodhisattva sanghas, Jizang averred, so although the Indian patriarchs appeared in their external forms just like any other Buddhist monk, at heart they were great bodhisattvas who championed Dharma in the Buddha's stead.[10]

Medieval Chinese exegetes often followed suit in attempting to systematize different classes of Buddhist saints into schemes of four reliances, "four fruits" (*siguo* 四果; *catvāri phalāni*), ten or fifty-two bodhisattva stages, six or ten "perfections" (*boluomi* 波羅蜜; *pāramitā*), and so on. But Aśvaghoṣa, Nāgārjuna, and Āryadeva were rarely fit into these kinds of doctrinal schemes, which is why Jizang's exposition is mostly unindicative of how Chinese Buddhists conceived these Indian patriarchs. As I have previously shown, Aśvaghoṣa, Nāgārjuna, and Āryadeva were usually depicted as Indian historical figures, living in specific centuries after nirvāṇa, who saved

8. On Yao Dao'an, see *Xu gaoseng zhuan* 續高僧傳, T no. 2060, 50:628a–630b. The quote that Jizang attributes to him is otherwise unattested.

9. *Zhongguan lun shu* 中觀論疏, T no. 1824, 42:1c. In this same passage Jizang explained: "As for the Lesser Vehicle, the person who has not yet seen the Way and is still afflicted with defilements belongs to the first reliance; the *srota-āpanna* (stream-winner) and *sakṛd-āgāmin* (once-returner) belong to the second reliance; the *anāgāmin* (nonreturner) belongs to the third reliance; and the arhat belongs to the fourth reliance. Seen from the perspective of the Greater Vehicle, the ten dedications [of merit] belong to the first reliance; first-stage to seventh-stage [bodhisattvas] belong to the second reliance; eighth- and ninth-stage [bodhisattvas] belong to the third reliance; and tenth-stage [bodhisattvas] belong to the fourth reliance" 如小乘, 見道前具煩惱人是一依; 須陀洹, 斯陀含是二依; 阿那含是三依; 羅漢第四依. 約大乘望, 十迴向是一依; 初地至七地是二依; 八九地是三依; 十地第四依.

10. As Jizang put it in the *Bailun shu* passage, "Within Śākyamuni's Dharma there is no separate sangha of renunciant bodhisattvas. All join the assembly of voice-hearers (*śrāvakas*). Therefore, Mañjuśrī and Maitreya, while residing at Jetavana, followed the voice-hearers from highest to lowest in order" 釋迦法中, 無別出家菩薩僧. 皆入聲聞眾攝. 故文殊彌勒, 住在祇洹, 依聲聞高下次第也. Here Jizang followed the *Da zhidu lun* 大智度論 (T no. 1509, 25:311c): "Most often buddhas form sanghas of voice-hearers without separate bodhisattva sanghas. Thus Maitreya bodhisattva, Mañjuśrī bodhisattva, and others, because Śākyamuni Buddha had no separate bodhisattva sangha, entered the voice-hearer sangha and sat in order [of precedence]" 諸佛多以聲聞為僧, 無別菩薩僧. 如彌勒菩薩, 文殊師利菩薩等, 以釋迦文佛, 無別菩薩僧故, 入聲聞僧中次第坐. Cf. trans. Lamotte 1944–1980, 5:2335. Such was the same with Nāgārjuna and Āryadeva, in Jizang's estimation.

the Dharma from imminent death by authoring doctrinal treatises, defeating non-Buddhists, converting kings, and so on. This is how Jizang's analysis otherwise accorded with widespread Chinese accounts of the patriarchs' status as bodhisattvas. The patriarchs were, on the one hand, mortal men who had left home to join the sangha and don the mantle of Buddhist monks. And on the other hand, they became exalted bodhisattvas by reviving the teaching and liberating beings in dark times absent the Buddha. In this way the Indian patriarchs functioned as exemplars for latter-day Chinese Buddhists. Aśvaghoṣa, Nāgārjuna, and Āryadeva instantiated repertoires of practices that Chinese monks themselves could emulate, and the former had triumphed in Dharmic historical circumstances that were very similar to those of latter-day China—as Chinese Buddhist sources often claimed—several centuries after the Buddha, when non-Buddhist dogmas had come to flourish and the True Dharma was at death's door. Therefore, just as the patriarchs had become great post-*parinirvāṇa* bodhisattvas by authoring doctrinal treatises to save the world, latter-day Chinese Buddhists could similarly liberate their benighted generations through time-honored literati practices and thereby join the ranks of the greatest bodhisattvas in Sino-Indian Buddhist history.

From the perspective of medieval Chinese Buddhists, how exactly were these Indian patriarchs to be understood as "homegrown" bodhisattvas? The patriarchs were obviously not Chinese, their ancient Indian identity was often emphasized in Chinese sources, and their spatiotemporal distance from latter-day China was part of what made them foremost Buddhist authorities. But at the same time, it was the Indian patriarchs' *proximity* within Dharmic history that made them especially valued resources for medieval Chinese Buddhists. In many of their early hagiographies the patriarchs were located at sacred Indian sites like Kapilavastu, the land of the Buddha's birth; Vārāṇasī, the location of his first sermon; Vaiśāli, the site of the Second Council; and the great Himalayas overlooking the cradle of the Śākya clan. Having travailed within these hallowed stations of original Indian Buddhism, Aśvaghoṣa, Nāgārjuna, and Āryadeva were authorized to propound the fundamental essence of the religion. Further, the patriarchs' temporal remove from their medieval Chinese proponents and relative proximity to the time of Śākyamuni meant that they could represent the original tradition before it had been corrupted beyond recognition. Nevertheless, while the patriarchs' status as ancients and Indians was crucial to their perceived authority—their distance and difference from a medieval Chinese audience—the fact that they simultaneously shared a strong affinity with the historical circumstances, favored occupations, and ambitions of latter-day Chinese Buddhists is what made Aśvaghoṣa, Nāgārjuna, and Āryadeva especially pertinent exemplars. In this way, the Indian patriarchs differed most fundamentally from famous cosmic bodhisattvas like Avalokiteśvara (Guanyin 觀音), Bhaiṣajyarāja (Yaowang 藥王), Kṣitigarbha (Dizang 地藏), Samantabhadra (Puxian 普賢), or Mañjuśrī (Wenshu 文殊). These latter figures functioned mostly as objects of veneration rather than models of emulation,[11] being far removed from the soteriological circumstances and personal aspirations of latter-day Chinese Buddhists. Only Aśvaghoṣa, Nāgārjuna, and Āryadeva had toiled as human beings in the generations after nirvāṇa, and as such they were the only Indian figures to whom Chinese Buddhists could look for guidance in their own efforts to propagate Buddhism in a world without a Buddha.

Scholars often apply the labels "cosmic" or "celestial" to the aforementioned and other bodhisattvas who are described in Mahāyāna scriptures as residing in distant world-systems and travelling miraculously across the vast expanses of Buddhist time and space in order to save sentient beings.[12] Kṣitigarbha, for example, was sometimes shown commuting between his southern Lapis Lazuli Realm and the various hells; Avalokiteśvara often appeared in both in Amitābha's Pure Land and wherever his supplicants summoned him; and Bhaiṣajyarāja once dwelled in another Buddha-field where he burned his body to illuminate countless world-systems across the universe.[13] But these and other famous bodhisattvas were not just "out there" in the distant cosmos; they were also objects of widespread devotional cults in which their "real presence" was elicited here and now.[14] These bodhisattvas often appeared personally in the present world to aid supplicants and assume rebirth among them—a fact that is obscured by the use of the label "celestial." Further, as Paul Harrison argues, the phrase "celestial bodhisattva" has no equivalent in any Buddhist canonical language, and there was never any clear "qualitative distinction between two discrete categories of bodhisattva, the mundane and the celestial, between which a clear line can be drawn" (2000, 177). Indeed, one would be hard-pressed to find a bodhisattva warranting the designation "mundane." All bodhisattvas were exalted as great wonder-workers and world-saviors. Nevertheless, while the classification "cosmic bodhisattva" is problematic in these ways, and thus requires some qualification, for our present discussion it retains a certain heuristic value. On the whole, Chinese sources represented Aśvaghoṣa, Nāgārjuna, and Āryadeva quite differently than the aforementioned cosmic bodhisattvas. Unlike these latter figures, the Indian patriarchs were conceived as great men and "historical" figures first and foremost, who initially appeared in a world much like latter-day China and who earned their bodhisattva stripes by accomplishing what any ambitious Chinese monk could hope for—to uphold the Dharma in difficult times through eminently human conventions like master-disciple transmission, public debate, and written doctrinal exegesis.

11. One exception to this rule is the case of the Medicine King Bodhisattva, whose self-immolation in the *Lotus Sūtra* was emulated by medieval Chinese Buddhists in their efforts to become local bodhisattvas. See Benn 2007, 62.

12. See, e.g., Snellgrove 1987, 135–136.

13. On Kṣitigarbha, see Ng 2007, 258. On Avalokiteśvara, see, e.g., Hurvitz 1976, chap. 25; and Yü 2001, 102–106. On Bhaiṣajyarāja, see Benn 2007, 58–61.

14. See Campany 1993.

Famous cosmic bodhisattvas like Avalokiteśvara, Kṣitigarbha, or Mañjuśrī were introduced in China through some of the earliest translated Indic sūtras. Presented from the outset in sermons reportedly preached by the Buddha, these and other bodhisattvas were reverently praised and endorsed by this foremost Buddhist authority figure. But at the same time they were rendered somewhat alien to Chinese Buddhist aspirations for personal achievement. The bodhisattvas of these sūtras were often depicted amid throngs of the most advanced holy beings in audience with the Buddha, and they were party to inhuman displays of supernormal power—bending and connecting matrices of time and space, illuminating world-systems and beings in the paths of rebirth, past, present, and future—as numerous as the sands of the Ganges. When brief hagiographic statements about these bodhisattvas occurred, they most frequently emphasized the vast expanses of time through which their protagonists had cultivated the bodhisattva path. Then, as elaborate hagiographic accounts of these bodhisattvas later emerged, they also focused on the countless eons across which the bodhisattvas had achieved various perfections or stages along the path, under the tutelage of innumerable past buddhas. By the time these bodhisattvas emerged within Śākyamuni's world-system, they had already attained such spiritual heights that they no longer qualified as mere human beings. They appeared in the human realm and assumed human rebirth for the benefit of sentient beings, to be sure, but this was the work of beings far more powerful than those born as humans by virtue of their karmic causes and conditions. Of course, there are few firm boundaries between the paths of rebirth or the stages of cultivation along the Buddhist path, and sentient beings constantly traverse back and forth along these continuums of existence. Nevertheless, there can be little doubt that Chinese Buddhists saw these great bodhisattvas as having long transcended karma-induced existence in the human realm. This fact of having been depicted within early sūtras as cultivating the path across vast spatiotemporal expanses, amid hosts of contemporary buddhas and bodhisattvas, is what justifies the labels "celestial" or "cosmic" to describe figures such as these.

By contrast, the earliest Chinese sources in which Aśvaghoṣa, Nāgārjuna, and Āryadeva appeared were translation prefaces authored by Chinese monks, locally produced commentaries, and ostensibly translated hagiographies. Introduced through these genres of *xu* 序 (preface), *zhu* 注 (commentary), and *zhuan* 傳 (biography or tradition), which carried the authoritative stamp of Kumārajīva but not the same ancient, hallowed aura of the Buddha's own sūtras (*jing* 經), the patriarchs would have appeared from the outset as more local, familiar, and human figures than the cosmic bodhisattvas. Over the course of their careers the Indian patriarchs accomplished great deeds—converting kings and non-Buddhists to the True Dharma, authoring seminal doctrinal treaties, and transmitting the teaching to posterity—and they thereby earned the appellation "bodhisattva." Nevertheless, at the initial stages of their development in Chinese hagiographic traditions, Aśvaghoṣa, Nāgārjuna, and Āryadeva had only just begun their bodhisattva training under the aegis of Śākyamuni's waning Buddhadharma. Not until later sources would they develop a repertoire of past-life tribulations through which they had perfected their bodhisattva qualities. As a result, for roughly their first two centuries in China, these Indian patriarchs were seen primarily as human beings who became bodhisattvas within Śākyamuni's world-system—much like Chinese Buddhists themselves could hope to do—and they therefore differed from cosmic bodhisattvas who had already perfected their qualities across a vast spatio-temporal continuum that far exceeded the personal aspirations of latter-day Chinese Buddhists.

Further, the developmental trajectories of the Indian patriarchs and the cosmic bodhisattvas were markedly different across Chinese Buddhist sources. Scholars have noted how the cosmic bodhisattvas first appeared in China as tangential figures in early sūtra translations, were later individualized through elaborate past-life stories and made the central protagonists of sūtras named after them, and were eventually localized in Chinese miracle tales and iconic representations through which they appeared personally at the behest of local supplicants. The preeminent example of this trajectory is Avalokiteśvara (Guanyin), who first appeared as what Lewis Lancaster has termed an "audience bodhisattva" in second-century Chinese translations like the *Dharma-Mirror Scripture* (*Fajing jing* 法鏡經).[15] He was then given a specific personality that spanned a broad cosmic continuum in translated scriptures from the third century, such as Dharmarakṣa's (fl. 266–313) Chinese rendition of the *Lotus Sūtra* (*Zheng fahua jing* 正法華經), which detailed his salvific function in a chapter titled "Avalokiteśvara's Universal Gateway" (Guangshiyin pumen pin 光世音普門品). In fairly short order this text's prescriptions for worshipping Guanyin were followed by local Chinese adepts, whose personal encounters with the bodhisattva were recounted in collections of miracle tales by the fourth century (Yü 2001, 158). There is also a very similar developmental trajectory in the case of Kṣitigarbha (Dizang), who first appeared in fourth-century sūtra translations as a miscellaneous "audience bodhisattva;" was individualized with an ornate past-life history in sixth-century scriptures; and was shown personally aiding local Chinese adepts within miracles tales recorded by the eighth century (Ng 2007, 29, 169). With these and other celestial bodhisattvas in China there is a common evolutionary pattern: they emerge from the obscure mists of the vast Buddhist cosmos to find their own individual personalities and extensive *saṃsāric* histories as semimythic, superhuman beings, before being brought down to earth as immanent manifestations who personally aid local supplicants in need. As Chün-fang Yü emphasizes in the case of Guanyin, "the Chinese managed to transform Avalokiteśvara, the ahistorical bodhisattva who transcended temporal and spatial limitations as depicted in the Mahāyāna scriptures, into Guanyin, who . . . led lives in clearly definable times and locations on the soil of China" (2001, 294–295). One

15. See Lancaster 1981, 155; and Yü 2001, 33.

can observe a similar geographic localization in the cases of Aśvaghoṣa and Nāgārjuna, having been transformed from ancient Indian exemplars into local deity-like figures, as discussed in chapters 4 and 5. But these patriarchs first became bodhisattvas in an already localized spatiotemporal context, relative to the celestial bodhisattvas, and only later were they represented as having existed across the vast expanses of the Buddhist cosmos.

The transition that the cosmic bodhisattvas underwent in medieval China—from transcendent figures in ancient Indian scriptures to immanent presences in locally produced miracle tales—is quite the opposite of the developmental trajectory seen with the Indian patriarchs-*cum*-bodhisattvas. The latter first appeared in early fifth-century sources that avowedly originated long after nirvāṇa, wherein the patriarchs were depicted as eminently human figures who traversed the bodhisattva path in the present world alone. From these earliest stages the patriarchs received detailed biographical treatment, which served to familiarize them for a Chinese audience as models of post-*parinirvāṇa* Buddhist sainthood. It was not until the turn of the sixth century that the patriarchs were seen in ostensibly translated scriptures that claimed to recount the word of the Buddha—first in the *Mahāmāyā Sūtra*, and then in Bodhiruci's rendition of the *Laṅkāvatāra Sūtra*. However, in both of these texts the patriarchs were still situated in the centuries after nirvāṇa—here in the form of Śākyamuni's predictions about the future fate of the Dharma—and they were not yet given the expansive *saṃsāric* histories befitting celestial bodhisattvas. Around the turn of the ninth century Aśvaghoṣa and Nāgārjuna were finally accorded past-life tales—in the *Baolin Tradition* and the *Scripture on Kumbhīra*—and placed along a spatiotemporal continuum exceeding that of Śākyamuni's reign as Buddha in this world-system. At the same time, their imagery was expanded to include the sorts of immanent presence and magical efficacy that celestial bodhisattvas like Avalokiteśvara, Kṣitigarbha, and Mañjuśrī had long possessed in China. Therefore, on a narrower spatiotemporal scale, the Indian patriarchs were localized in Tang ritual texts—moving from India to China and a few centuries forward in time—but they were simultaneously distanced from a Chinese audience by being expanded across the vast reaches of Buddhist time and space. In this way the patriarchs were transformed from relatively local exemplars of Buddhist practice, who lived as human beings in historical circumstances familiar to the Chinese, into great cosmic bodhisattvas who had perfected their qualities over eons past and could thus appear at will in the human realm to aid local adepts.

Indian Patriarchs, Cosmic Bodhisattvas, and Chinese Gods

While the Indian patriarchs most often appeared in Chinese writings as homegrown bodhisattvas who provided models of Buddhist attainment for latter-day Chinese adepts, in some sources Aśvaghoṣa and Nāgārjuna were also represented in a manner akin to the celestial bodhisattvas. I have discussed how the ninth-century *Scripture on Kumbhīra* depicted Aśvaghoṣa and Nāgārjuna, at the feet of the Buddha Śākyamuni, prescribing a wide variety of alchemical recipes to match those provided by the bodhisattvas Avalokiteśvara and Bhaiṣajyarāja. This text further explained how Nāgārjuna once paid homage to the primordial Buddha Dīpaṃkara and also appeared personally before latter-day supplicants to instruct them in the use of his methods. At around the same time, the *Baolin Tradition* likewise described Aśvaghoṣa's past life along the bodhisattva path, when he descended from Brahma heaven to transform his body into silkworms and clothe the naked horse-people of Vaiśāli. And along similar lines, the eleventh-century *Summary Record of the Sympathetic Resonance of the Three Jewels* (*Sanbao ganying yaolüe lu* 三寶感應要略錄) included a tale about two brothers who vowed before the past Buddha Kāśyapa to forever be reborn as master and disciple and propagate the True Dharma. These former brothers eventually became Aśvaghoṣa and Nāgārjuna, who because of this ancient bodhisattva vow would always appear in *saṃsāra* together to liberate sentient beings.[16] While these later tales depicted their protagonists in novel fashion—at least as far as extant sources can tell—they nonetheless fleshed out earlier assertions about the Indian patriarchs' great spiritual accomplishments. As noted, Sengrui and Huiyuan described Nāgārjuna as a tenth-stage bodhisattva; Sengzhao's *Vimalakīrti Commentary* (*Zhu weimojie jing* 注維摩詰經) called Aśvaghoṣa the "second buddha"; the Nanatsu-dera biography (*Maming pusa zhuan* 馬鳴菩薩傳) said that both Aśvaghoṣa and Nāgārjuna were worshipped like buddhas; and in the *Dharma-Treasury Transmission* Nāgārjuna followed Śākyamuni's biographical template. It comes as no surprise, then, that medieval Chinese authors would uphold these Indian patriarchs as rivaling the most famous celestial bodhisattvas. Indeed, in his *Treatise on Discerning the Truth* (*Bianzheng lun* 辯正論), Falin 法琳 (572–640) joined Aśvaghoṣa and Nāgārjuna with Avalokiteśvara, Mañjuśrī, Maitreya, and Kṣitigarbha as the foremost Buddhist holy beings across the Sino-Indian divide.[17]

In this way the Indian patriarchs were accorded spiritual attainments, supernormal powers, and *saṃsāric* histories to match any of the celestial bodhisattvas. And also like these latter figures, Aśvaghoṣa and Nāgārjuna became objects of ritual obeisance in medieval China. In addition to the *Scripture on Kumbhīra* and *Nāgārjuna's Treatise on the Five Sciences* (*Longshu wuming lun* 龍樹五明論), which prescribed rites for invoking these patriarch-*cum*-bodhisattvas to obtain a wide variety of boons, Nāgārjuna was associated more specifically with Pure Land devotionalism and Aśvaghoṣa with the religious dimensions of sericulture. Nāgārjuna reportedly authored Pure Land liturgies, transmitted spells for Pure Land rebirth, and appeared personally in response to Pure Land prayers, so he was sometimes grouped together with Avalokiteśvara and Mahāsthāmaprāpta as helping local supplicants

---

16. *Sanbao ganying yaolüe lu* 三寶感應要略錄, T no. 2084, 51:856a.

17. *Bianzheng lun* 辯正論, T no. 2110, 52:524c. Kṣitigarbha and Nāgārjuna were here associated with China especially.

attain rebirth in Sukhāvatī.[18] In this context Nāgārjuna was represented as simultaneously transcendent and immanent, both light-years away in resplendent Buddha-fields and immediately on-call for Chinese Pure Land practitioners. Such was the case with Aśvaghoṣa Bodhisattva, who was sometimes associated with rituals devised to ensure healthy silkworms and abundant silk crops. Aśvaghoṣa's *Ritual Instructions* (*Maming pusa dashenli wubiyanfa niansong guiyi* 馬鳴菩薩大神力無比驗法念誦軌儀), for example, showed him prescribing a spell, icon, *mudrā*, and associated "rites for perfect silkworm cultivation," first at the behest of Śākyamuni Buddha and then in the presence of his own would-be devotees. In this way Aśvaghoṣa likewise joined the cosmic bodhisattvas in merging sacred pasts with immanent presents, bridging the gap between ancient India and latter-day China, and providing Chinese adepts with another avowedly Buddhist—and especially efficacious—object of ritual devotion.

In this latter guise as celestial bodhisattvas, Aśvaghoṣa and Nāgārjuna no longer functioned as models of emulation for latter-day Chinese Buddhists. For the most part, Chinese sources that emphasized the patriarchs' roles in post-*parinirvāṇa* Dharmic history were part of broader Chinese discourses about how to be Buddhist in a world without a Buddha. In these contexts the Indian patriarchs served as exemplars of Buddhist practice and attainment, showing how great Buddhist saints were made when times were darkest, whether in India or China. But Chinese sources that expanded the patriarchs' career arcs beyond the horizon of post-*parinirvāṇa* India—into distant world-systems, the time of Śākyamuni himself, or the oratories of local Chinese adepts—were less concerned with advancing this discourse of latter-day Buddhist embattlement. Instead, these sources aimed to promote their protagonists, and the Buddhist tradition that they represented, as the most powerful means of attaining what everyone in China valued most: health, wealth, protection from evil, and escape from death. In these same sources, the Indian patriarchs' practical repertoires came to include superhuman powers of the most spectacular variety. Some of the patriarchs' skill-sets were shared across their human and divine incarnations, such as Nāgārjuna's spell-craft and alchemy, but otherwise their past-life triumphs and association with all manner of cosmic beings brought supernatural abilities beyond the ken of human aspiration. In this regard, Chinese depictions of the Indian patriarchs accorded with earlier accounts of the Buddha Śākyamuni as otherworldly savior and as earth-bound exemplar. As Jan Nattier remarks, "the understanding of the Buddha as supermundane most often occurs in contexts in which Buddhists are not being encouraged to emulate him." Although "a supermundane concept of the Buddha can be very helpful in a context in which what is expected is worship of the Buddha . . . it can be distinctly unhelpful in a context in which people are being urged to become bodhisattvas, and thus to strive for Buddhahood,

18. See, e.g., *Emituo jing yishu* 阿彌陀經義述, by Huijing 慧淨 (578–645), T no. 1756, 37:310a.

themselves" (Nattier 2003, 177n13). Likewise, the Indian patriarchs were intended primarily as models of emulation in contexts in which they were represented as exemplary human beings, and as objects of veneration when they were shown to possess expansive *saṃsāric* histories and provide all the salvific benefits expected of cosmic bodhisattvas and local Chinese gods.

Further, when Aśvaghoṣa and Nāgārjuna were depicted along the lines of the great cosmic bodhisattvas—as objects of ritual devotion who provided all manner of salvific boons—these patriarchs also instantiated several different models of Chinese divinity. In fact, both patriarchs were expressly labeled "gods" (*shen* 神) in sources that emphasized their immanent presence and supernormal powers, reflecting the broad functional equivalence in medieval China between devotional bodhisattvas and deities. In general terms, Aśvaghoṣa and Nāgārjuna were represented in iconic form, given offerings and beseeched for various boons, and in this way they functioned much like local Chinese gods, Buddhist or otherwise. But these patriarchs also assumed more specific roles that were rare for cosmic bodhisattvas in China, like serving as functionaries in otherworldly bureaucracies and as patrons of specific industries or trades.[19] In chapter 4 I suggested that Nāgārjuna acted like the so-called Directors of Destiny who populated (some versions of) the Chinese celestial bureaucracy, conveying messages between *dhyāna*-master Daoquan and the Buddha Amitābha concerning adjustments to the former's allotted lifespan. But here Nāgārjuna also functioned according to a *personal* model of Chinese divinity, as outlined by Robert Hymes (2002, 4–5), in that his powers were inherent rather than delegated (as with heavenly bureaucrats) and his relationship with Daoquan was otherwise dyadic and based on principles of reciprocity. The case of Aśvaghoṣa-as-silkworm god, discussed in chapter 5, provides the only example I have seen of an avowedly Buddhist figure being cast as the founder of a traditional Chinese trade and thus its foremost patron saint. Most industrial enterprises in premodern China had their associated founding sages and pantheons of protective deities, but these figures were typically drawn from the ranks of ancient Chinese culture-bearers and apotheosized local cultural heroes.[20] Aśvaghoṣa was unique among Buddhist figures in standing alongside these deities of Chinese industry and thus instantiating age-old Chinese models of trade-based divinity.

Nevertheless, in these contexts, Aśvaghoṣa and Nāgārjuna were never actually represented as Chinese gods. Instead, they were almost always described as *Indian* bodhisattvas whose powers superseded those of Chinese gods. In this way the patriarchs served to Indianize religious realms that were typically the preserve of local Chinese deities, thus demonstrating Buddhist sovereignty over those realms. Much as Aśvaghoṣa, Nāgārjuna, and

19. Shahar and Weller (1996, 9), for example, note that Buddhist deities in China were usually nonbureaucratic. One exception to this was Dizang, who was sometimes associated with the bureaucracy of the underworld; see Ng 2007, 102–103.

20. See Li 1999.

Āryadeva first showed how traditional Chinese literati practices were actually rooted in ancient Indian models of sainthood—and were thus the rightful heritage of Chinese Buddhists alone—the patriarchs-*cum*-cosmic bodhisattvas illustrated how all manner of thaumaturgic, apotropaic, and divine salvific powers were in fact of Indian provenance and were thus the province of Buddhist holy beings above all others. In texts like *Nāgārjuna's Treatise on the Five Sciences* and the *Scripture on Kumbhīra*, both Aśvaghoṣa and Nāgārjuna were deity-like figures who brought to China the most efficacious magical rites of ancient India—rites that closely paralleled those of Chinese religious adepts. In Pure Land sources, Nāgārjuna demonstrated how family well-being, longevity, and ultimate salvation were most effectively secured through Indian religious practices. And in his guise as silkworm deity, Aśvaghoṣa established that sericulture was actually invented in ancient India and was thus most effectively served by Indian Buddhist deities. In all of these contexts, even though the Indian patriarchs and Chinese gods shared certain structural and functional similarities, the former were unique in serving to Indianize and thus Buddhicize time-honored Chinese models of divinity and salvation.

Patriarchs, Arhats, and Buddhist Authorship

As expressly non-Chinese holy beings, Aśvaghoṣa, Nāgārjuna, and Āryadeva were in some respects most akin to another group of Indian Buddhist figures that was greatly revered in medieval China: the original disciples of the Buddha, who had ideally attained the final fruit of *arhattva*. Like the Indian patriarchs, these arhats were largely depicted as eminently human beings who had become great saints through traditional Buddhist practices, and under the aegis of Śākyamuni's Buddhadharma. The arhats were then placed in lineages of master-disciple Dharma transmission, also like the Indian patriarchs, and in this context all of these figures functioned alike in demonstrating how Buddhism had been (and could be) preserved over the generations after nirvāṇa. Indeed, as Karil Kucera notes, Chinese genealogical writings—and the visual arts that followed them—often conflated these two classes of Buddhist holy beings (2006, 63). In sources like the *Dharma-Treasury Transmission*, the *Baolin Tradition*, Kanjingsi 看經寺 and Leigutai Central 擂鼓台中 at Longmen, or the Cave of Great Perduring Saints, Aśvaghoṣa, Nāgārjuna, and Āryadeva played much the same roles as arhats like Ānanda or Mahākāśyapa. However, as I discuss in chapter 2, this later patriarchal triad was given a certain pride of place in the *Dharma-Treasury Transmission*, and of the twenty-four Indian masters depicted at Dazhusheng, only Aśvaghoṣa, Nāgārjuna, and Āryadeva were labeled "bodhisattvas" in the inscriptions beneath them. "Arhat" was one term never applied to Aśvaghoṣa, Nāgārjuna, and Āryadeva in Chinese sources, which, on the whole, represented these three figures in a manner quite different than the earliest disciples of Śākyamuni. As with the Indian patriarchs versus the celestial bodhisattvas, one major factor distinguishing Aśvaghoṣa, Nāgārjuna, and Āryadeva from figures like Ānanda, Mahākāśyapa, Śāriputra or Maudgalyāyana was the locus of these groups in Dharmic history. Only the arhats had appeared in a world alight with the Buddha's splendor, learning the True Dharma direct from his golden mouth, and as such only the post-*parinirvāṇa* Indian patriarchs could show Chinese Buddhists how to properly uphold Buddhism in a world without a Buddha.

Ryan Bongseok Joo (2007) explains how, despite the fact that Chinese Buddhists have always claimed allegiance to Mahāyāna doctrinal positions, they nonetheless frequently venerated so-called Hīnayāna figures like the arhat-disciples of the Buddha. Indeed, the arhats were important players in Chinese Buddhist ritual worship—and in medieval Chinese conceptions of ancient Indian Buddhism—both before and after Kumārajīva introduced Aśvaghoṣa, Nāgārjuna, and Āryadeva on the Chinese scene. There are numerous examples of this phenomenon. For instance, the great assembly of five hundred arhats was known from early translated sources to have first codified Śākyamuni's teachings shortly after nirvāṇa.[21] Also, Kāśyapa and Piṇḍola were often depicted as eternally present in the world, personally aiding the faithful while awaiting the advent of Maitreya.[22] And from the mid-seventh century, when Xuanzang translated the *Record of the Perpetuity of the Dharma, Narrated by the Great Arhat Nandimitra* (*Da aluohan Nantimiduoluo suoshuo fazhu ji* 大阿羅漢難提蜜多羅所說法住記), the famous group of sixteen arhats was depicted in painting and sculpture and worshipped across China as great Dharma protectors.[23] Shih Jen Lang (2002, 117, 135) and John Strong (1979, 77, 88) emphasize that the arhats were conceived in medieval China as ideal Buddhist monks—having learned traditional teachings and practices from the founder himself—and they were revered as such throughout Chinese Buddhist history. So Joo is certainly right to highlight the arhats' wide-ranging roles as Chinese objects of veneration, especially since their Hīnayāna associations might otherwise be seen to have occasioned their general Chinese disapprobation.

Nevertheless, while the Mahāyāna-Hīnayāna divide seemingly held little purchase in Chinese Buddhist devotional settings, and Chinese arhat cults in particular show how such doctrinal delineations were often irrelevant,[24] the status of arhatship was still not something that Chinese Buddhists themselves hoped to achieve. Chinese monastics upheld the arhats as embodiments of the bhikṣu ideal and worshipped them in various ways toward various ends, but Buddhist monks in China did not strive to become arhats. What Chinese monks did often strive to become were homegrown bodhisattvas. The distinction between these two goals was not confined to the rarefied realms of Buddhist doctrine, nor did it necessarily correspond

21. See de Visser 1923, 21.

22. See Adamek 2007, 185–186; de Visser 1923, 77; and Strong 1979.

23. *Da aluohan Nantimiduoluo suoshuo fazhu ji* 大阿羅漢難提蜜多羅所說法住記 (*Nandimitrāvadāna*), T no. 2030. On this text, see especially Shih 2002.

24. See Joo 2007, 112.

to perceived differences between Hīnayāna and Mahāyāna teachings. This distinction also had to do with broader Chinese conceptions of Buddhist sainthood in Dharmic history. In these terms it was only during Śākyamuni's generation that arhats were made; bodhisattvas were those Buddhist holy beings who arose after his departure. And this was often what separated arhats like Kāśyapa or Piṇḍola from the patriarchs-*cum*-bodhisattvas Aśvaghoṣa, Nāgārjuna, and Āryadeva. Only the latter could provide models of Buddhist practice suitable for latter-day China, given that they arose long after the Buddha and became great bodhisattvas by reviving his teachings. By following these examples, latter-day Chinese Buddhists could likewise save the Dharma in Śākyamuni's absence and thus become the greatest bodhisattvas of their own time and place.

Another important function of the Indian patriarchs' Dharmic historical context, which further distanced them from both the arhats and cosmic bodhisattvas, was the primary means by which they went about liberating their benighted contemporaries and transmitting the Dharma to future generations: they authored doctrinal treatises, or *śāstras*. In addition to their temporal placement neither too far from nor too close to either the Buddha or latter-day Chinese Buddhists, Aśvaghoṣa, Nāgārjuna, and Āryadeva were distinguished from other sorts of Indian holy figures by the writings that they bequeathed to posterity. While the original arhat-disciples were responsible for compiling the entirety of the early Tripiṭaka, and the celestial bodhisattvas had a number of *dhāraṇī* texts and other Mahāyāna scriptures to their name, the Indian patriarchs alone left behind doctrinal treatises of a mold that Chinese Buddhists themselves could strive to emulate. The Tripiṭaka represented primarily the sermons of the Buddha as codified by his original disciples, who themselves were seldom viewed as authors of independent works, and the scriptures attributed to celestial bodhisattvas were likewise seen as products of Buddhist holy beings of a different order than latter-day Chinese adepts. Further, Chinese Buddhists usually considered Indian sūtras and *śāstras* as more authoritative than locally produced Buddhist writings—at least until the late-Tang dynasty when Chinese understandings of *buddhavacana* (word of the Buddha) were radically expanded to include the sermons of Chinese Buddhist masters.[25] Prior to this, apocryphal Buddhist scriptures were produced *en masse* in China, but these were cloaked in the standard garb of "Thus have I heard" and other accoutrements of earlier translated sūtras, such that they might appear to be genuine Indian products. Consequently, Chinese adepts of the early medieval period were by and large limited to Buddhist authorship of the commen-

25. A prominent example of this shift is the *Platform Sūtra of the Sixth Patriarch* (*Tan jing* 壇經), written around the turn of the ninth century, which claims the status of *buddhavacana* (as a sūtra) without any pretense to Indian provenance and which locates its teachings in the person of Śākyamuni only through a transmission lineage of enlightened masters culminating with Huineng.

tarial variety, and in this regard Aśvaghoṣa, Nāgārjuna, and Āryadeva served to show them how it was done.

In chapter 3 I emphasized that, according to Chinese Buddhist exegetes, these Indian patriarchs wrote *śāstras* in particular because human beings of the latter, evil age were most receptive to this kind of Dharmic packaging. And just as the historical conditions within which these patriarchs travailed were seen to share a strong affinity with the circumstances of their Chinese proponents, the specific brand of logical discourse through which Aśvaghoṣa, Nāgārjuna, and Āryadeva had liberated beings within their own times—as exemplified by the *Awakening of Faith* (*Dasheng qixin lun* 大乘起信論), *Great Perfection of Wisdom Treatise* (*Da zhidu lun* 大智度論), *Middle Treatise* (*Zhong lun* 中論), and *Hundred Treatise* (*Bai lun* 百論)—was likewise seen as especially appropriate to the weakened proclivities of human beings in latter-day China. These treatises were greatly valued as authoritative guides to the original inspiration of the Buddha, repackaged for beings living in a Buddha-less world, but equally important to Chinese Buddhists were the broader paradigms of Buddhist authorship that the Indian patriarchs offered. These paradigms of doctrinal exegesis as ideally suited to post-*parinirvāṇa* stages of Dharmic history is what the *śāstras* of the Indian patriarchs provided that Śākyamuni's original sūtras could not.

However, the patriarchs' treatises were not understood as working in competition with the translated scriptural literature; the former were not seen as transmitting a new Truth or superior Truth or even a more cogent articulation of the original Truth. The doctrinal exegesis of the Indian patriarchs in no way superseded the scriptures of the Buddha, which Chinese Buddhists usually valued over and above any other sorts of Buddhist writings. Rather, according to medieval Chinese commentators, the fundamental difference between the treatises of Aśvaghoṣa, Nāgārjuna, and Āryadeva and Śākyamuni's scriptures lay in the variant historical circumstances within which these two genres of Dharmic discourse were expounded. The patriarchs' treatises and the models of exegesis that they provided were to be upheld not above and against the sūtras, and not because they represented any sort of superior path to the True Dharma. Instead, *śāstras* were valued as expedient means of understanding the same Truth that the Buddha originally taught—expedient means necessitated by the weakened proclivities of beings living long after the Buddha's death. This, then, was the patriarchs' *upāya*—teaching the original Dharma through the sorts of logical discourse that people of the latter age could understand. And it was in large part by virtue of their unique combination of *prajñā* and *upāya*—through an unparalleled grasp of the True Dharma and of how to communicate it to the unenlightened—that Aśvaghoṣa, Nāgārjuna, and Āryadeva were seen to have risen above their human contemporaries and into the ranks of the most exalted homegrown bodhisattvas.

Just as the Indian patriarchs were largely seen to have become great bodhisattvas by authoring doctrinal treatises that were paragons of post-*parinirvāṇa upāya*, latter-day Chinese Buddhists could likewise ascend the

Buddhist hierarchy of spiritual attainment by producing written doctrinal exegesis. Again, Chinese Buddhists always valued Indian scriptures first and foremost as expressions of the wisdom of buddhas and cosmic bodhisattvas, and these were never wholly supplanted by post-*parinirvāṇa* patriarchal exegesis. But at least through the first half of the Tang dynasty, Chinese Buddhists did not see themselves as producing this sort of scriptural literature. Their task was to comment upon the *buddhavacana* of centuries past. Aśvaghoṣa, Nāgārjuna, and Āryadeva offered models for Chinese Buddhists of how to engage the Truth, how to make it accessible to latter-day adepts, through doctrinal authorship. By resurrecting the True Dharma and transmitting it to future generations through written exegesis in particular, these Indian patriarchs transformed themselves into great bodhisattvas. And by authoring Buddhist doctrinal analysis in the mold of the *Awakening of Faith*, *Great Perfection of Wisdom Treatise*, *Middle Treatise*, and *Hundred Treatise*, Chinese Buddhists could likewise become great bodhisattvas who perpetuated the True Dharma through expedient devices most appropriate to dire historical circumstances.

Conclusion: Emulating the Indian Other

In his seminal article on "The Rise and Function of the Holy Man in Late Antiquity," Peter Brown discusses how the desert fathers of the early Christian church were "deliberately not human." Depicted largely as otherworldly ascetics, whose "histrionic feats of self-mortification" were "long drawn out, solemn ritual[s] of dissociation—of becoming the total stranger," Late-Roman Christian saints were thereby able to function as objective mediators. Unbound to the mundane trappings of village life—to family relations, economic interests, local hierarchies, or even dietary norms—the eastern Mediterranean holy man was the one true compass in society, providing resolution to concerns that embroiled village insiders (Brown 1971, 91–92). In a subsequent essay, Brown takes a different but related approach to early Christian saints as exemplars, who otherwise modeled "the enduring images of order, of beauty, of respite" characteristic of the "Christ-carrying man" (1983, 13–14). On the one hand, then, Brown's early Christian saints were essentially inimitable, which allowed them to serve as the "other" ombudsmen for local societies. On the other hand, these holy men were the quintessential exemplars of Christian ideals that local patrons could ostensibly emulate. Along similar lines, Robert Cohn emphasizes how this "tension between imitability and inimitability, between likeness to us and otherness than us, lies at the core of the saint's identity" (1987, 1). And indeed, in medieval China the Indian patriarchs were "saints" in this very fashion: variously imitable and inimitable, serving in some contexts as objects of veneration, in others as models of emulation, and sometimes as both at once. But as religious exemplars in medieval China, these patriarchs also exhibited a unique brand of otherness that set them apart from the desert ascetics in Brown's formulation. The Indian patriarchs were not only "strangers" to their Chinese patrons in the "self-created" sense that Brown emphasizes—through intense religious practices that dissociated them from the mundane world. Aśvaghoṣa, Nāgārjuna, and Āryadeva were also ancient Indians, which doubly distanced them from latter-day Chinese Buddhists while also providing their *sine qua non* as Buddhist exemplars in China.

Indian holy beings were legion in Chinese Buddhist sources, as were models of spiritual attainment in Chinese religious traditions. And for the most part, the former were confined to the oratories of Chinese devotees as objects of ritual obeisance, while the latter exemplified practical repertoires that Chinese adepts could strive to emulate. Among the Indian figures that proliferated in medieval Chinese writings and visual arts, only the post-*parinirvāṇa* patriarchs functioned principally as exemplars of Buddhist teachings and practices that were tailor-made for the Dharmic historical circumstances of latter-day China. The arhats lived too close to the Buddha to demonstrate the path to sainthood after nirvāṇa, and the cosmic bodhisattvas were too "deliberately inhuman" to provide models of human practice. By contrast, Aśvaghoṣa, Nāgārjuna, and Āryadeva were the "Goldilocks saints" of medieval China: they provided the ideal middle ground between these other classes of Buddhist holy beings. Only the Indian patriarchs had lived in times and instantiated repertoires that perfectly matched the needs of latter-day Chinese Buddhists, and as a result, these patriarchs were the foremost Indian Buddhist exemplars in medieval China.

But by the same token, Aśvaghoṣa, Nāgārjuna, and Āryadeva were twice removed from their Chinese devotees in being both exalted bodhisattvas and ancient Indians. Chinese adepts could work to close the former gap by emulating the patriarchs' saintly repertoires, but the latter gap was unbridgeable. Chinese Buddhists could never become Indian. However, precisely because the patriarchs were nonetheless advanced as preeminent Buddhist exemplars in China, their ancient Indian identity—that aspect of their repertoires that would ostensibly have rendered them inscrutably alien—was expressly aligned with time-honored Chinese religious values and practices. Only by virtue of this Indian identity could Aśvaghoṣa, Nāgārjuna, and Āryadeva demonstrate how the most venerable religious ideals across Chinese traditions—which Chinese Buddhists likewise sought to incorporate—were deeply rooted in the land where Buddhism began. This assignment of ancient Indian heritage to Chinese models of sanctity and salvation thus allowed Buddhist advocates to annex these models in service of Śākyamuni's Truth. And along similar lines, when Aśvaghoṣa and Nāgārjuna were represented more as cosmic bodhisattvas than as human exemplars, their Indian identity functioned largely to Buddhicize age-old Chinese methods of securing health, wealth, and ultimate salvation. Having long served as guides for Chinese monastics along the path to Buddhist sainthood, and illustrating for potential Chinese patrons the ancient Indian heritage of traditional Chinese values, the Indian patriarchs eventually became objects of veneration across social and sectarian divisions as well. In these roles they further demonstrated the superiority of Buddhism for attaining the greatest of worldly and otherworldly boons.

While in this latter guise the Indian patriarchs functioned much like the arhats and cosmic bodhisattvas—providing specifically Buddhist and especially powerful objects of ritual devotion—Aśvaghoṣa, Nāgārjuna, and Āryadeva also filled a unique niche for Indian holy beings in medieval China. As deity-like figures who furnished the most efficacious magic of ancient India, the arhat-disciples, Indian patriarchs, and cosmic bodhisattvas all served to bridge the gap between the Indian roots of Buddhism its latter-day Chinese proponents. These Indian holy beings did so quite literally, appearing personally in Chinese oratories and wielding the ritual implements, procedures, and powers of Indian lore. But only the patriarchs served to merge Indian pasts with Chinese presents by providing models of Buddhist sainthood. Unlike the arhats and cosmic bodhisattvas, Aśvaghoṣa, Nāgārjuna, and Āryadeva showed Chinese adepts how to be Buddhist in a world without a Buddha, how to become great bodhisattvas in the generations after nirvāṇa, and how to manifest Indian models of sanctity on Chinese soil. The various Chinese images of the Indian patriarchs I have discussed—as homegrown bodhisattvas and Goldilocks saints, celestial bodhisattvas and local gods—were all equally implicated in Chinese Buddhist attempts to negotiate the chasm separating latter-day China from ancient India. These Indian patriarch accounts thus illustrate how Chinese Buddhist authors developed models of Buddhist sainthood and divinity in relation to local paradigms of religious sanctity, and as means of advancing an avowedly foreign religion in their own Middle Kingdom to the east.

Conclusion

WHAT DID IT MEAN to be Buddhist in medieval China? Certainly this identity had multiple dimensions, but one thing that it meant was to be partly non-Chinese. Buddhist adepts in medieval China laid claim to the religious heritage of ancient India, and in so doing they assumed a uniquely hybrid identity that demanded negotiations of boundaries both sociocultural and spatiotemporal. As well as incorporating scholarly repertoires of Chinese literati gentlemen, liturgical repertoires akin to those of local ritualists, and magical repertoires associated with Chinese transcendents (among others), members of the Buddhist sangha were the only medieval Chinese religionists to instantiate repertoires of Indianness. In some contexts this Indian association afforded for Chinese Buddhists a certain exotic mystique and authoritative otherness, but in other contexts it prompted accusations of inscrutability, inconsonance, and irrelevance for securing the spiritual and material wellbeing of China. The ancient sage-kings and hosts of Chinese holy beings from time immemorial had long since blazed the paths to sanctity and salvation for their descendents in the Divine Provinces; why uphold alien teachings above these native Chinese paths? Chinese Buddhist authors worked to mitigate these tensions in various ways, which were quite successful over the long term, developing paradigms of Buddhist thought, practice, sainthood, and divinity that they advertised as best meeting the needs and expectations of Chinese devotees. And in order to effect this transformation, rendering the teachings of alien worlds into universal truths that would also suit the specific exigencies of latter-day China, Buddhist authors expressly realigned the categories of "native" and "foreign," "Indian Buddhist" and "traditional Chinese," and thereby bridged the gap between themselves and the ancient Indian origins of their religion. Chinese Buddhists naturalized their vocation by aligning its Indian roots with the most vaunted religious ideals of medieval China, while at the same time they exploited (and encouraged) the empowering effects of their Indian identity as a marker of esoteric holiness and wondrous otherness.

Chinese Buddhists manifested a unique blend of Indianness and Chineseness, difference and sameness, and they conceived their ancient Indian forebears in analogous fashion—as amalgams of foreignness and familiarity.

Aśvaghoṣa, Nāgārjuna, and Āryadeva represented at once the hallowed founts of ancient Indian sanctity and the time-honored conventions of religious praxis associated with Chinese adepts across traditions. In addition, while the patriarchs' ancient Indian identity made them authorities on the true teachings of Śākyamuni, their placement in the generations after his nirvāṇa made them uniquely qualified exemplars for latter-day Chinese Buddhists, who likewise sought to uphold the tradition in its founder's absence. For Buddhist adepts in medieval China, the Sino-Indian divide represented both sociopolitical and soteriological challenges. On the one hand, this divide demanded that they reconcile their claimed Indian heritage with widespread sentiments of nativist cultural chauvinism. And on the other hand, the fact that they lived so far from the cradle of Buddhist salvation led them to question (at least rhetorically) the fidelity and thus efficacy of their own Buddhist practices. In order to address this latter concern, Chinese Buddhists worked to demonstrate that the means and media of Indian enlightenment were in fact readily available in China, and they did so in part by developing the hagiographic imagery of Aśvaghoṣa, Nāgārjuna, and Āryadeva.

In illustrating how these dynamics operated through Chinese hagiographies of the Indian patriarchs, this book has advanced a somewhat unusual approach to the study of premodern Buddhism. Rather than looking through Chinese (or other Asian) Buddhist sources in order to examine the history of Indian Buddhism, as scholars have typically done, this study has employed Indian figures in order to better understand the worlds of Chinese Buddhists. That is, I have focused on the question of how Chinese Buddhists themselves understood ancient India and its great Buddhist saints, thereby offering a novel perspective on Indian Buddhism as a contrivance fashioned to advance the causes of Buddhism in China. In foregrounding this perspective, however, I have had to set aside several other questions that readers might consider pertinent to a study of Indian Buddhist patriarchs. In particular, how do the Chinese conceptions these figures relate to their representations elsewhere in Asia? How do the dynamics illustrated in this book compare with other Asian Buddhist contexts? How did Buddhist authors in Tibet, Japan, or Korea, for example, conceive the hagiographic images of their great Indian forebears in ways that addressed local religious concerns? While these and related issues are certainly worth examining in depth, and they would no doubt yield a range of novel perspectives on premodern Asian Buddhism, they are nonetheless beyond the scope of the present study.

For an excellent example of the kind of approach that privileges such pan-Asian perspectives, one might look to Michael Radich's recent book on the Ajātaśatru narrative in Buddhist history. Radich traces the evolution of this narrative from ancient India through medieval China and into modern Japan, providing a thoroughgoing account of its transformation from an Indian regicidal tragedy into a Japanese familial psychodrama. He draws upon sources written in Pāli, Sanskrit, Chinese, and Japanese and produced over a time-span of more than two thousand years in order to address questions concerning the roles of narrative storytelling in Buddhist traditions and how locally circulating tales were part of a long and continuous process of Buddhist domestication across Asia (Radich 2011). Along similar lines, one might conduct a study of Aśvaghoṣa, Nāgārjuna, and Āryadeva that illustrates the transformation of their hagiographic imagery throughout Asian Buddhist history and cultures. These three Indian masters—and Nāgārjuna in particular—were well-represented in Buddhist writings from India, Tibet, China, Korea, and Japan, and as such these figures would readily lend themselves to such an investigation. I noted in the introduction that for more than a century Western scholars have focused their efforts on examining the extant hagiographies of these patriarchs, which were produced all across Asia over some fifteen hundred years. However, instead of using Chinese materials to study how Chinese Buddhists understood the Indian patriarchs and Japanese materials to study the Japanese context—as Radich does with Ajātaśatru—previous studies of Aśvaghoṣa, Nāgārjuna, and Āryadeva have utilized these East Asian sources in order study South Asia in particular. In this respect Radich's work represents a significant advancement, as his comparative approach accounts for the distinctive tonalities of the various cultures in which Ajātaśatru was developed, rather than looking through these East Asian contexts in order to elucidate their ostensive Indian origins.

Nevertheless, as I have indicated, the scope and methodology of the present book are significantly different than those of Radich's study. This is because the questions that he asks of his materials are quite different than those upon which I have based my investigation of the Indian patriarchs. Aśvaghoṣa, Nāgārjuna, and Āryadeva were ubiquitous in medieval Chinese Buddhist canons; extant Chinese sources concerning these figures are far more abundant than those produced in any other premodern Buddhist culture. Buddhist authors in medieval China were clearly quite interested in this triad of Indian patriarchs, and my study has aimed to account for this interest in the context of medieval Chinese religion. I have thus approached the materials of my study with an eye toward addressing questions like, how did medieval Chinese Buddhists themselves understand these ancient Indian patriarchs? Why did Chinese Buddhists focus their efforts on developing the hagiographic imagery of Aśvaghoṣa, Nāgārjuna, and Āryadeva? How did this imagery relate to local Chinese models of religious practice, sainthood, and divinity? What do the Chinese images of these Indian figures tell us about broader Chinese conceptions of ancient India? How did Chinese Buddhists imagine Indian Buddhism as a whole, and how did this relate to their understanding of Buddhist identity in China? Throughout this study, I have focused on answering such questions concerning Chinese Buddhists' conceptions of their ancient Indian heritage, and this research agenda has required that I examine the Chinese hagiographies of Aśvaghoṣa, Nāgārjuna, and Āryadeva, not in relation to their pan-Asian roots and branches but rather within the contexts of medieval Chinese culture and society.

This book has focused on such issues in large part because they had not yet been raised, much less substantively addressed, in previous studies of the Indian patriarchs or of Chinese Buddhism. There are numerous modern Buddhological studies of Aśvaghoṣa, Nāgārjuna, and Āryadeva, but the vast majority of these have endeavored to locate their subjects within Indian Buddhist history, doctrine, or society. Much has been learned in the process, for example, about Aśvaghoṣa's court poetry and Nāgārjuna's and Āryadeva's Madhyamaka system against the backdrop of contemporary Indian religious, literary, and philosophical developments. But the problem with these studies is that they have typically attempted to historicize the Indian patriarchs on the basis of medieval Chinese sources. Such projects are methodologically suspect because there is no way of knowing whether these Chinese sources are reflective of earlier Indian traditions, or whether they were wholly invented by medieval Chinese authors. The earliest extant Indic tales of Aśvaghoṣa, Nāgārjuna, and Āryadeva were composed several centuries later than the writings of Kumārajīva's associates, the *Dharma-Treasury Transmission*, and the patriarchs' independently circulating Chinese hagiographies. For the purposes of the present study, this distinction between original (Indian) reality and subsequent (Chinese) invention is wholly irrelevant—and theoretically problematic, as discussed in the introduction. But for scholars interested in fixing the historicity of the Indian patriarchs, this determination should matter a great deal.

In this book I examine the same Chinese sources that scholars have long used to reconstruct facts about the Indian patriarchs' careers. However, I approach these sources with the goal of addressing the aforementioned questions concerning Chinese Buddhist conceptions of ancient India. Consequently, I have shown how medieval Chinese authors adduced the Indian patriarchs as both exemplars of Buddhist sainthood for a world without a Buddha and immanent objects of veneration for the newfound Buddhist heartland of imperial China. I have illustrated how Aśvaghoṣa, Nāgārjuna, and Āryadeva played prominent roles in Chinese Buddhist efforts to negotiate the gap between ancient India and latter-day China. On the one hand, these Indian patriarchs functioned to localize ostensibly Indian models of Buddhist sanctity and salvation. By following the examples provided by these Indian masters, Chinese adepts could themselves become great Buddhist saints in the centuries after the Buddha's nirvāṇa. And on the other hand, Aśvaghoṣa, Nāgārjuna, and Āryadeva served to demonstrate that Indian Buddhist and traditional Chinese ideals of spiritual attainment were actually one and the same. In this way Buddhist adepts across the Sino-Indian divide would be the standard-bearers of normative Chinese values, and it was their claimed *Indian* heritage that would make Chinese Buddhists the foremost representatives of time-honored Chinese ideals and practices. Aśvaghoṣa, Nāgārjuna, and Āryadeva thus served as cornerstones in broader Chinese efforts to define Indian and Chinese identities, and to conceive ancient India as a site for authorizing Buddhist institutions in the competitive religious environment of medieval China.

I have not approached my main body of source materials—Chinese hagiographies of Indian saints—as data for comparing Indian and Chinese Buddhism or for documenting broad-scale religious transformations across sociocultural and geographic boundaries. And while I have argued against treating these sources as windows into Indian historical reality, neither can they be viewed as representing a purely Chinese imagination of ancient Indian Buddhism. In much the same way that I have examined how Chinese Buddhists themselves conceived the relationships between India and China, I have likewise approached these Chinese hagiographies with an eye toward understanding how they might have been viewed by their own authors and intended audiences. In this light, as represented by the Chinese authors who propagated them, these hagiographies were indeed grounded in Indian empirical reality while at the same time they served to validate local Chinese needs and expectations. There is no reason why medieval Chinese authors would not have seen veritable Indian history as coinciding perfectly well with the particular brands of Buddhist practice that they sought to promote. What was construed as empirical fact was the basis for didactic injunction, which, from the medieval Chinese standpoint, did not necessarily entail poetic invention or purposive imagining. These accounts would have been completely meaningless for their intended Chinese audiences, their normative prescriptions rendered null and void, if they were not seen to represent the veritable lives and times of the Indian patriarchs, at least to some extent. And at the same time, tales of Aśvaghoṣa, Nāgārjuna, and Āryadeva were indeed propagated by interested parties to serve a variety of purposes, which I have attempted to explicate in the preceding chapters. Thus, in this book I have treated the Indian patriarch hagiographies not as vehicles for conveying facts or fictions about ancient India but as medieval Chinese *exempla* that served to advance broader discourses about Buddhist sanctity across the Sino-Indian divide.

In addition, I have emphasized that as *exempla* these hagiographies instantiated Chinese collective representations of ancient India, and in this respect the accounts of Aśvaghoṣa, Nāgārjuna, and Āryadeva differed from Chinese tales of local holy beings. Hagiographies of transcendents and eminent Chinese monks, for example, were rooted in ancient Chinese biographical conventions; they followed fixed sets of structural characteristics, they were based upon common Chinese source materials, and they functioned as both models of and for traditional Chinese religious ideals. By contrast, the hagiographies of Aśvaghoṣa, Nāgārjuna, and Āryadeva were thought to have been transmitted from ancient India, so they were not expected share the same structural and thematic characteristics of Chinese biographical genres. The accounts of these Indian patriarchs ostensibly transmitted to China the foremost Indian models of Buddhist sainthood, and as such they functioned to integrate avowedly foreign religious ideals into local Chinese dialectics of mutually generative lives and narratives. And finally, I have argued that these hagiographies not only conveyed the life stories of Indian Buddhist patriarchs but also served to authorize doctrinal traditions and empower local deities. The Chinese hagiographies of Aśvaghoṣa, Nāgārjuna, and Āryadeva elaborated the contexts in which these masters had reportedly composed their exegetical magnum opuses, thereby illustrating the merging and mutually reinforcing nature of doctrinal and hagiographic exposition. By showing how the patriarchs' treatises had been composed in the most significant junctures of Dharmic history, these hagiographies served to promote the patriarchs' writings above all others. And in portraying the talents that these patriarchs had perfected long before in ancient India, which were closely aligned with the unique skill sets that they displayed as local gods, these accounts also show how hagiography often furnished the building blocks of deities in medieval China.

Now, having examined the Chinese hagiographies of Aśvaghoṣa, Nāgārjuna, and Āryadeva in the context of medieval China, might we briefly take a sideways glance at how these figures were conceived elsewhere in premodern Asia, or in later Chinese Buddhist history, in order to locate instructive comparisons? Unfortunately, given the current state of scholarship on these figures, such comparisons are impracticable. Short of conducting a thorough study of the numerous Buddhist sources across Asia that elaborated the careers of these Indian patriarchs, situating each source within its proximal religious and sociocultural contexts, it is difficult to know how Aśvaghoṣa, Nāgārjuna, and Āryadeva were conceived in India, Tibet, Japan, or anywhere else. For example, David Gordon White provides one of the few studies I have seen that foregrounds Indian sources in its discussion of Nāgārjuna's Indian identities—as a Vidyādhara, Siddha, Hindu master, and Jain alchemist, among other roles (1996, 74–75, 114–119). But while this study might have provided useful counterpoints to Nāgārjuna's assorted Chinese manifestations, White instead focuses his study on the modern scholarly question of how many "historical" Nāgārjunas can be excised from this body of Indian lore. He thereby ignores the viewpoints of his medieval Indian informants, who clearly had no such interest in parsing out Nāgārjunas. Otherwise, earlier studies that firmly situate the Indian patriarchs within their local contexts of conception are few and far in between. Phyllis Granoff (1988), for one, examines medieval Jain hagiographies that linked Nāgārjuna with important Jain pilgrimage centers. These hagiographies functioned for their authors and audiences to legitimize Jain sites as well as depictions of Nāgārjuna, and this process can be seen to parallel, for example, how Xuanzang associated the patriarchs with various sacred sites across India. In addition, Ryūichi Abé's monumental study of Kūkai 空海 (779–835), whose hagiographic reconstitution of Nāgārjuna served to authenticate the burgeoning Japanese Esoteric tradition, offers clear evidence that premodern Buddhist authors beyond medieval China similarly employed their Indian forebears as means of defining and deploying ancient Indian norms (Abé 1999, 228–232).

While these and other studies offer a few brief glimpses into the broader processes through which Aśvaghoṣa, Nāgārjuna, and Āryadeva were conceived across Asia, the investigation of these figures in later Chinese Buddhism has yet to begin. One notable example to the contrary is Francesca Tarocco's study of early twentieth-century Chinese receptions of Aśvaghoṣa's *Awakening of Faith* (Tarocco 2008). Otherwise, there is an abundance of Chinese materials from the Ming, Qing, Republican, and Communist eras that further elaborate the images of these Indian patriarchs but have yet to receive any scholarly attention. Here is not the place to enumerate this sizable body of literature, much less embark on any kind of in-depth examination, but a few modern and contemporary sources that I have spotted along the way offer intriguing avenues of investigation. One of these is a set of colophons appended to Republican-era prints of the independently circulating hagiographies of Aśvaghoṣa, Nāgārjuna, Āryadeva, and Vasubandhu. These colophons state exactly how much it cost to have each hagiography reprinted as well as who donated the money to do so, when, and why. One sponsor was the government official Wang Jitang 王揖唐 (1877–1948), who vowed that the merit accrued through his donation would go toward helping his relatives attain Pure Land rebirth.[1] Other contemporary Chinese sources concerning the Indian patriarchs include sets of popular books published by Fagu shan 法鼓山 and Foguang shan 佛光山 in Taiwan, which combine many of the medieval sources discussed here into concise accounts of the lives and works of Aśvaghoṣa, Nāgārjuna, and Āryadeva. Replete with elaborate graphic illustrations and forming long series of notably modernist biographies of premodern Buddhist saints, these books were compiled, in the estimation of Foguang founder Xingyun 星雲 (b. 1927), "to provide models for people to follow in their pursuit of the human spirit."[2] If nothing else, such sources clearly indicate the enduring importance of Aśvaghoṣa, Nāgārjuna, and Āryadeva in post-imperial China, and they invite a wide range of questions concerning modern Chinese conceptions of ancient Indian Buddhism.

Much could be learned from a detailed study of these Indian patriarchs as conceived throughout premodern Asia, and in late-imperial or modern China, but the present study has focused on examining their nature and function in medieval China—when and where their most widespread hagiographic images are first evidenced. Within this context the most salient issues surrounding Aśvaghoṣa, Nāgārjuna, and Āryadeva included the nature of Buddhist sainthood across the Sino-Indian divide, the delineation of Buddhist identity in times and places far removed from the origins of Buddhism, and how ancient India was conceived to suit the expectations and aspirations of latter-day Chinese Buddhists. In this last regard especially this book has advanced a relatively new and important research agenda in the field of Buddhist studies. Toni Huber, for example, in his recent account of Tibetan reinventions of Indian sacred geography, emphasizes how India itself constituted "an important type of cultural resource that

1. *Jin'gang bore jing po quzhao buhuai jiaming lun deng sizhong* 金剛波若經破取著不壞假名論等四種, unpaginated.

2. Lin 2000, 3. Other such books in these series include Hou 1999 and Mo 1999.

individuals and institutions in Tibetan societies have often drawn upon as agents in their own internal negotiations of power, authority, and legitimacy" (Huber 2008, 4). The present book has similarly aimed to illustrate, on the evidence of Chinese hagiographic representations of Aśvaghoṣa, Nāgārjuna, and Āryadeva, how medieval Chinese authors variously redefined ancient India in accordance with local exigencies. But this dynamic had multiple dimensions—far beyond the paradigms of Sino-Indian Buddhist sainthood illustrated by the Indian patriarchs—which have so far been investigated only in piecemeal fashion.[3] Buddhist authors in medieval China worked to reconcile their Indian and Chinese roots through a wide variety of projects that would be both grounded in ancient India and congruent with time-honored Chinese religious ideals. Such projects included developing ideals of monastic comportment, ritual programs, systems of meditation, and exegetical models, among others. Similarly, Buddhist authors across Asia have often invoked, or manufactured, ancient Indian origins as means of authorizing developments of all kinds in Buddhist thought, practice, and material culture. It is hoped that future studies will continue to shed light on these processes by which Asian Buddhists have long endeavored to determine the contours of their ancient Indian heritage.

3. Kieschnick and Shahar 2013 represents a solid step forward in this direction. I thank Professor Shahar for sharing an earlier version of this manuscript with me.

Appendix 1

The Nanatsu-Dera Tradition of Aśvaghoṣa Bodhisattva

IN MEDIEVAL CHINA there were several distinct yet overlapping biographical traditions of the Indian patriarch Aśvaghoṣa. These traditions are represented most prominently in the *Dharma-Treasury Transmission* (*Fu fazang zhuan* 付法藏傳), the *Baolin Tradition* (*Baolin zhuan* 寶林傳), the separate biography of Aśvaghoṣa preserved in the Taishō canon, and a little-known Chinese text extant only in Japanese monastery collections. In chapter 2 I examine the *Dharma-Treasury Transmission* and in chapter 5 the *Baolin Tradition*, which both foreground Aśvaghoṣa's position in the Indian Buddhist patriarchate. In this appendix, I introduce and translate the earliest independently circulating biography of Aśvaghoṣa, which details his conversion to Buddhism through public debate and his efforts to revive a failing Dharma by authoring doctrinal treatises. This version of Aśvaghoṣa's biography, titled *Maming pusa zhuan* 馬鳴菩薩傳 (Tradition of Aśvaghoṣa Bodhisattva), is preserved not in any printed canon but in a family of manuscripts copied in Japan (and is hereafter referred to as the Nanatsu-dera 七寺 edition, after the best-known monastery collection in which it appears). It is clearly attested in Sui-Tang sources and may have originated with Kumārajīva's disciples. By contrast, the biography of Aśvaghoṣa reproduced in the Taishō canon—also titled *Maming pusa zhuan*—is not evidenced before the tenth century and may have originated with the first printing of the Chinese Buddhist canon (Ochiai 2000, 5:635). This latter account also details Aśvaghoṣa's conversion through debate but otherwise emphasizes his royal connections and his skill as an orator. Following Ochiai Toshinori 落合俊典, who first brought the Nanatsu-dera edition to scholarly attention, I argue that this earlier biography is closely aligned with the writings of Kumārajīva's associates and thus likely stands among the earliest extant representations of the Indian Buddhist patriarchs.

In appendix 2, I discuss the provenance of the separate biographies of Nāgārjuna and Āryadeva—the *Longshu pusa zhuan* 龍樹菩薩傳 and *Tipo pusa zhuan* 提婆菩薩傳—which are both traditionally ascribed to Kumārajīva. In Buddhist catalogues from the late sixth century, these texts were grouped together with the *Maming pusa zhuan*, also attributed to Kumārajīva, and the *Tradition of Dharma-Master Vasubandhu* (*Poshupandou fashi zhuan* 婆藪槃

豆法師傳), translated by Paramārtha (499–569), to form a tetralogy of Indian patriarch biographies.[1] Through all the editions of the Chinese Buddhist canon, these were the only Indian patriarch biographies to be reproduced independent from larger compilations like the *Dharma-Treasury Transmission*—a fact that attests the unique importance of these Indian figures in China. But this biographical grouping was initially a product of Sui-era bibliographic exigencies; it was not Kumārajīva's arrangement. The patriarchal triad of Aśvaghoṣa, Nāgārjuna, and Āryadeva was apparently first drawn together by Kumārajīva and his disciples, but of the extant patriarch biographies only the Nanatsu-dera edition is likely to have circulated among this group. The *Longshu pusa zhuan* and *Tipo pusa zhuan* were perhaps excerpted from the late-fifth- or sixth-century *Dharma-Treasury Transmission*, while the *Maming pusa zhuan* preserved in the Taishō canon is a completely different text than its earlier namesake and has little in common with the extant writings of Kumārajīva's associates.

This latter Aśvaghoṣa biography is now readily accessible to English readers through translations done by myself (2002), Li Rongxi (2002b), and most recently Saroj Kumar Chaudhuri (2008). These translations are all based on the Taishō edition of the text, which probably derives from that included within the first printed edition of the Chinese *Tripiṭaka*—the Kaibao 開寶 canon of 972–983. That earlier version of Aśvaghoṣa's biography was reprinted in numerous editions of the Buddhist canon with relatively few stylistic or typographic variants.[2] According to this account, Aśvaghoṣa was a brilliant non-Buddhist from central India who challenged the Buddhists to prove their worth by defeating him in debate. None answered this call but the elder Pārśva, who sounded the local monastery bell to summon Aśvaghoṣa. In a week's time the two met before a grand assembly of Buddhist and non-Buddhist masters, court ministers, and the king himself. Pārśva offered the first volley, stipulating that "the world should be made peaceable, with a long-lived king, plentiful harvests, and joy throughout the land, with none of the myriad calamities."[3] Unable to refute this seemingly banal claim, Aśvaghoṣa lost the debate and was converted to Buddhism. In due course he became a great leader of the sangha and counselor to the king of central India (Pāṭaliputra, in the *Dharma-Treasury Transmission*). However, soon the kingdom was besieged by an Indo-Scythian (Yuezhi 月支) army, whose king—identified in the *Dharma-Treasury Transmission* as Caṇḍa-Kaniṣka—demanded Aśvaghoṣa and the Buddha's begging bowl as reparation. After returning to his kingdom with these great treasures in tow, the Yuezhi king sought to test Aśvaghoṣa's powers. To this end the king starved seven horses for six days, and then asked Aśvaghoṣa to preach the

1. See, e.g., *Zhongjing mulu* 眾經目錄, T no. 2146, 55:146a.

2. See Cai 1983, 234; and Young 2002. NB: I have not checked every edition of the text in every canon.

3. *Maming pusa zhuan* 馬鳴菩薩傳, T no. 2046, 50:183c: 當令天下泰平, 大王長壽, 國土豐樂, 無諸災患.

Dharma before them. Upon hearing Aśvaghoṣa's sermon, the horses were so overcome with emotion that they refused to eat even their favorite grass. The horses wept at the profundity of Aśvaghoṣa's words, which, according to this account, was how he got his name, which means "Horse Neigh."

In broad outline, this version of Aśvaghoṣa's biography bears some resemblance to both the Nanatsu-dera *Maming pusa zhuan* and the *Dharma-Treasury Transmission.* All three accounts detail Aśvaghoṣa's conversion to Buddhism through public debate, while the Taishō biography and the *Dharma-Treasury Transmission* both focus on Aśvaghoṣa's relations with Indian kings. But clearly these texts were all written by different hands; they share none of the same vocabulary and are stylistically dissimilar. Moreover, they present divergent narratives and emphasize different aspects of the episodes they do share.[4] The Nanatsu-dera edition begins by introducing Aśvaghoṣa as an East Indian Brahman born roughly three-hundred years after the Buddha's nirvāṇa. Aśvaghoṣa was renowned for his skills as an author and expositor, and traveled the country looking for wise men to vanquish in debate. He heard of an accomplished arhat by the name of Pūrṇa, whom he tracked down and challenged: "*Śramaṇa*, speak! If you dare offer any insights I will surely defeat you." But Pūrṇa just sat there in silence, leading Aśvaghoṣa to realize the fallibility of all discourse, admit his own failure, and submit to becoming Pūrṇa's disciple. At that time, according to this account, the True Dharma was in decline and people's intellectual and spiritual capacities had diminished. So Aśvaghoṣa composed clear, concise doctrinal treatises that enabled people to grasp the truth. For this he was renowned like the greatest disciples of Śākyamuni and Confucius and was worshipped like a buddha. At this point the text offers a brief account of Nāgārjuna, who appeared five centuries after Aśvaghoṣa and once again rejuvenated a declining Dharma by authoring doctrinal treatises. The text concludes by joining Aśvaghoṣa and Nāgārjuna with Dharma-masters Vīra and Kumāralāta as the greatest Buddhist saints from the four quarters of India: east, south, west and north, respectively.

Extant physical examples of this text held at Nanatsu-dera in Nagoya and Kōshō-ji 興聖寺 in Kyoto probably date to the twelfth and thirteenth centuries, respectively.[5] But how far back in Chinese history can it be confidently placed? As it turns out, this text is demonstrably archaic, certainly much older than the Taishō *Maming pusa zhuan* and probably predating the

---

4. On the textual history of the printed *Maming pusa zhuan*, see Ochiai 2000, 634–636; and Young 2002. For a comparison between the contents of the printed and manuscript versions, see Ochiai 2000, 640–641.

5. These manuscripts are examined in several articles by Ochiai, which are listed in the bibliography. For their dates, see, e.g., Ochiai 2000, 622; and Ochiai and Saitō 2000, 288. This version of the *Maming pusa zhuan* has also been preserved in the canons of Ishiyama-dera 石山寺, Myōren-ji 妙蓮寺 (Matsuo-sha 松尾社), and Saihō-ji 西方寺; see Kokusai Bukkyōgaku Daigakuin Daigaku Gakujutsu Furontia Jikkō Iinkai 2007, 325; and Ochiai 2000, 621. I have also consulted the Saihō-ji manuscript in preparing this appendix.

Dharma-Treasury Transmission as well. As Ochiai has shown, the evidence for its circulation during the Sui-Tang period is definitive. Fei Zhangfang's *Record of the Three Jewels through the Ages* (598), discussed in Chapter 1, briefly outlines Aśvaghoṣa's career in language that closely matches the extant manuscripts. The Buddhist encyclopedia *Grove of Pearls in a Dharma Garden,* completed by Daoshi (ca. 596–683) in 668, quotes extensively from a *Maming pusa zhuan* that was much the same as the first half of the Nanatsu-dera edition.[6] And the latter half of this text may also have existed during the Tang, as Huilin's 慧琳 (737–820) *Pronunciation and Meaning of* [*Terms in*] *the All the Scriptures* defines two terms that do not appear in Daoshi's work but are found in the Japanese manuscripts.[7] Several other sources verify that this version of Aśvaghoṣa's biography remained current in China through the tenth century, when the printed edition first appeared on the scene.[8] Ochiai has rightly hailed these manuscripts as conclusive proof that the canons of Nanatsu-dera and other Japanese monasteries are not just copies of the Chinese *Tripiṭaka* printed from Song times, but rather derive from Nara-period (710–794) manuscripts that preserve recensions of texts as they circulated in Tang times and earlier.[9] But for our present purposes this text is important as a testament to how the Indian patriarchs were conceived in China during the Sui-Tang period, at the latest, and probably from the time Kumārajīva first introduced them to his Chinese associates.

How far back before the sixth- and seventh-century works of Fei Zhangfang and Daoshi can we trace the Nanatsu-dera biography? It is first attested explicitly in the *Catalogue of All the Scriptures* of around 594, as previously noted, but what evidence do we have that it actually circulated in Kumārajīva's time, as the text itself claims? As argued by Ochiai and discussed later in this appendix, there is good reason to believe that a biography quite similar to the Nanatsu-dera text did exist in some form during the early fifth century in Chang'an. However, since no member of this early Chang'an group mentioned an independently circulating biography of Aśvaghoṣa, whether by the hand of Kumārajīva or not, and the title *Maming pusa zhuan* does not appear in the *Chu sanzang jiji* of ca. 515, we should remain cautious in assigning the text as a whole to this time and place. While it is difficult to defend every item of the Nanatsu-dera edition, and it may not have been an independently circulating document until the late sixth century,

6. *Fayuan zhulin* 法苑珠林, T no. 2122, 53:681b–c; see also Ochiai 2000, 623–624.

7. *Yiqie jing yinyi* 一切經音義, T no. 2128, 54:804a. See also Ochiai 1994, 16, 20; and Ochiai 2000, 624–625. It is possible that the latter portion of the text was added after Daoshi saw it and before Huilin's dictionary, compiled between 783 and 807. In the *Kaiyuan shijiao lu* 開元釋教錄 of 730 a note is appended to the *Maming pusa zhuan* entry that reads, "some lost sections have been gathered and placed in this separate edition" (T no. 2154, 55:623c: 拾遺編入單本).

8. See Ochiai 2000, 625–629. *Zongjing lu* 宗鏡錄, by Yanshou 延壽 (904–975) in 961 (T no. 2016, 48:658a), should be added to Ochiai's list of sources that quote the Nanatsu-dera *Maming pusa zhuan.*

9. See Ochiai 1991 and 2000.

it is plausible that some version of this text did exist in early-fifth-century Chang'an and thus represents this community's conceptions of Aśvaghoṣa and Nāgārjuna.

In a series of articles from 1992 to 2000, Ochiai presents a thorough comparative analysis of the *Maming pusa zhuan* preserved at Nanatsu-dera and Kōshō-ji, as well as a number of other texts containing similar narratives. Collating the variants in these copies of a presumed *ur*-text and determining the optimal reading based on internal and external evidence, Ochiai reconstructs the "original" *Tradition of Aśvaghoṣa Bodhisattva* and sets about comparing it to documents confidently ascribed to this fifth-century Chang'an group, especially those attributed to Sengrui 僧叡 (ca. 352–436). In his 1996 article "Sengrui and the *Tradition of Aśvaghoṣa Bodhisattva*," Ochiai discusses a number of similarities in language and structure that he found between this reconstructed *Maming pusa zhuan* and the prefaces composed by Sengrui.[10] He notes at least ten specific instances in which the wording of the reconstructed biography closely matches that of Sengrui's writings—most frequently his preface to the *Great Perfection of Wisdom Treatise*—and also highlights several thematic similarities between the biography and Sengrui's works. After examining the evidence and discussing possible interpretations, Ochiai concludes that the Nanatsu-dera edition was probably first transmitted orally by Kumārajīva and then transcribed and edited by Sengrui (1996, 567).

I will not rehash the linguistic component of Ochiai's comparative analysis; suffice it to say that he has certainly demonstrated a strong affinity between the language of the Nanatsu-dera edition and that of Sengrui's writings. However, his argument is not conclusive. In particular, as Ochiai himself confesses, it is possible that the biography was produced by a later hand and intentionally modeled on Sengrui's writing style (1996, 565). Further, there are two significant discrepancies between the Nanatsu-dera biography and another prominent account of Aśvaghoṣa that is confidently dated to Kumārajīva's time. This is the *Commentary on the Vimalakīrtinirdeśa* (*Zhu weimojie jing* 注維摩詰經, discussed in chapter 1), by Sengzhao 僧肇 (384–414) and Kumārajīva, which also describes how Aśvaghoṣa was vanquished in debate and converted to Buddhism. According to this account, the arhat who converted Aśvaghoṣa was Pārśva rather than Pūrṇa, as in the Nanatsu-dera edition; and, in the *Vimalakīrti Commentary*, Aśvaghoṣa arose in the seventh century after nirvāṇa rather than the fourth century.[11] These discrepancies would seemingly militate against the hypothesis that Kumārajīva's associates wrote the Nanatsu-dera edition, given that they certainly had a

10. Ochiai's essay is mostly reproduced in Ochiai 2000, 630–633.

11. The expression in the Nanatsu-dera edition is *sanbai yu nian* 三百餘年. According to Fei Zhangfang, this meant exactly 315 AN, which for Fei equaled 296 BCE since he took the *parinirvāṇa* date to be 611 BCE (or 297 years prior to the *dingwei* 丁未 year of Zhou dynasty King Nan's reign [r. 314–256], which is 314 BCE); see *Lidai sanbao ji* 歷代三寶紀, T no. 2034, 49:28a.

hand in the *Vimalakīrti Commentary*. Nevertheless, we can imagine at least one possible scenario to account for this contradiction. If we take the Nanatsu-dera edition to have been composed slightly later than the *Vimalakīrti Commentary*, which was compiled sometime between 406 and 410, and follow Ochiai's assertion that Sengrui was the architect of that later text, is it possible that he was simply correcting what he saw as errors in the account of Sengzhao and Kumārajīva? This would seem in line with Sengrui's character, as he is documented on more than one occasion to have disagreed with and amended Kumārajīva's interpretation in translation matters.[12]

If, as outlined in chapter 1, Chinese Buddhists of the early fifth century held the *parinirvāṇa* date to be sometime in the seventh century BCE, then six hundred years after nirvāṇa for Aśvaghoṣa plus five centuries for Nāgārjuna would put the latter in the fifth century CE, perhaps even some decades after this Chang'an group. Therefore Sengrui may have seen fit to adjust the figures, assigning Aśvaghoṣa to the early fourth century after nirvāṇa and thus moving Nāgārjuna back some two centuries before Kumārajīva's time in China. Aside from specific numbers, the presentation of Dharmic history in the Nanatsu-dera edition is quite in line with Sengrui's preface to the *Great Perfection of Wisdom Treatise*. In the Nanatsu-dera edition, Aśvaghoṣa lived when "the end of the True Dharma [period] was approaching," and people could still be enlightened if the proper methods were utilized. Likewise, when Nāgārjuna appeared a half-millennium later, times were much worse, and through his efforts the Buddhadharma flourished once again. Here, the Nanatsu-dera text does not use the phrase "Semblance Dharma," even if its description of Nāgārjuna's era matches the accounts of the Semblance Dharma period in Sengrui's writings; rather, it employs the phrase "Final Dharma" (*mofa* 末法), which was a rare if not altogether nonexistent expression of Dharma decline in early-fifth-century Chang'an.[13]

The discrepancy between Pārśva and Pūrṇa is somewhat more complex, and perhaps relates to how these patriarchs were conceived by Kumārajīva's associates. As described in the *Vimalakīrti Commentary* and *Great Perfection of Wisdom Treatise*,[14] Pārśva was a *śramaṇa* who left the household life at a very late age but was still able to accomplish great deeds as a Buddhist devotee. He became an expert in the Threefold Canon and composed an "*upadeśa* on the four Āgamas" before turning his attention to the perfection of *dhyāna* practice. As part of this effort, he vowed never to lay on his side to rest until attaining liberation, which is how he got the name Pārśva (Xie 脅 or Le 勒, meaning "side" or "rib"). Eventually he achieved the fruit of arhatship and became endowed with the "three insights and six penetrations," as the

12. See Chou 2000, 29–31.

13. See Nattier 1991, 91, 101n106.

14. See *Da zhidu lun* 大智度論 (*Mahāprajñāpāramitāśāstra*), T no. 1509, 25:748c.

Vimalakīrti Commentary has it, or the "six spiritual penetrations" (*liu shentong* 六神通) according to the *Great Perfection of Wisdom Treatise.*

The Pūrṇa of the Nanatsu-dera edition is most probably Pūrṇa Maitrāyaṇīputra (Fulounamiduoluonizi 富樓那彌多羅尼子), one of the ten principal disciples of the Buddha known as foremost among Dharma preachers. However, given the apparent historical incongruity in associating Aśvaghoṣa with one of the Buddha's original disciples, Ochiai tries to identify the Chinese transliteration "Fulouna" (富樓那) with an Indian figure who could have been Aśvaghoṣa's contemporary (Ochiai 1993, 32–33n1). Ochiai cites a number of later sources in which Aśvaghoṣa was associated with other Buddhist masters and suggests that the Fulouna of the Nanatsu-dera edition may have stood for the relatively unknown Pūrṇāśa, who apparently lived closer to Aśvaghoṣa's time (ca. 1st century CE). However, the Pūrṇa with whom the fifth-century Chang'an community would have been most familiar is certainly the famed Dharma preacher and disciple of the Buddha, Pūrṇa Maitrāyaṇīputra. This character figures prominently in a number of important Kumārajīva translations, including the *Perfection of Wisdom in 25,000 Lines* (*Pañcaviṁśati prajñāpāramitā*), the *Great Perfection of Wisdom Treatise,* and *Inquiry of Pūrṇa* (*Pūrṇa paripṛcchā*).[15] In the *Lotus Sūtra,* he is specifically associated with the attainment of "six penetrations and three insights."[16] Moreover, this Pūrṇa appears in the *Lotus* as a disciple-*cum*-arhat who assumes the guise of voice-hearer only as an expedient device to awaken beings to the Greater Vehicle, and he is the greatest of Dharma preachers because he had in fact propagated the True Dharma under millions of past buddhas and would continue to do so for eons to come.[17] In keeping with the avowed aim of the *Lotus Sūtra* to reconceptualize Buddhist history—particularly in its assertions of Śākyamuni's atemporality—Pūrṇa is explicitly removed from the timeframe of normal human existence and identified as a cosmic bodhisattva working to benefit beings across the vast expanses of Buddhist time and space. Therefore, it is certainly possible that Kumārajīva's associates saw Pūrṇa's attainments as enabling him to extend his lifespan well into Aśvaghoṣa's generation.

Why would Sengrui have felt compelled to substitute Pūrṇa for Pārśva? Aside from the obvious consideration that there could be no better master for one's patriarch than the foremost of True-Dharma preachers, in the *Inquiry of Pūrṇa* and *Great Perfection of Wisdom Treatise,* Pūrṇa is depicted as a purveyor of doctrines commonly associated with the Greater Vehicle. One must be cautious not to overstate the valorization of Greater Vehicle Buddhism over and against the Lesser Vehicle by Kumārajīva and associates. Nevertheless, there are indications that, for this group, a given patriarch's

15. Translated by Kumārajīva in 405, the *Fulouna hui* 富樓那會 was included as text number seventeen (scrolls 77–79) in the *Da baoji jing* 大寶積經 by Bodhiruci (ca. 572–727) in the early eighth century. See Ono 1933–1936, 9:237c–38b.

16. *Miaofa lianhua jing* 妙法蓮華經, T no. 262, 9:28a; trans. Hurvitz 1976, 159.

17. *Miaofa lianhua jing,* T no. 262, 9:27c; trans. Hurvitz 1976, 158.

association with the Mahāyāna rendered him worthy of praise, while exclusively Hīnayāna connections could be somewhat deleterious to one's reputation. We see this in the separation of four patriarchs mentioned in the Nanatsu-dera edition into two distinct camps: "The two Dharma-masters Kumāralāta and Vīra performed the meritorious act of [contributing to] the Threefold Canon, but they did not believe in the Greater Vehicle. Aśvaghoṣa and Nāgārjuna combined the Greater and Lesser [Vehicles] into one." Aśvaghoṣa and Nāgārjuna were not slavishly attached to the Greater Vehicle as the absolute truth; rather, they followed the prototypical Mahāyāna dialectic according to which reification of any dichotomy (here Greater versus Lesser Vehicles) was explicitly proscribed. In contrast, Kumāralāta, who is mentioned in Sengrui's "Preface to the *Dhyāna* Scriptures Translated within the Passes," and Dharma-master Vīra, who is otherwise largely unknown, were implicitly denigrated for not following the Greater Vehicle, a trait that was seemingly tied to their focus on the Threefold Canon.[18] Likewise, Pārśva was thought to have composed an "*upadeśa* on the four Āgamas"—a section of the canon particularly associated with Lesser Vehicle teachings—and his attainment of arhatship was not described as mere expedient means as with Pūrṇa. Thus we can see how Kumārajīva's associates may have considered Pūrṇa a more appropriate master for Aśvaghoṣa, even at three hundred years after the death of the Buddha, and substituted him for Pārśva sometime after the appearance of the *Vimalakīrti Commentary*. Such a switch would have been less likely in subsequent centuries, when there were concerted efforts to form discrete lineages of generational descent from the numerous arhats encountered throughout the early scriptural literature.

Nevertheless, even if the above scenario cannot be proven conclusively, it is clear that Aśvaghoṣa's placement in the fourth century after nirvāṇa and his association with Pūrṇa fit quite well with the beliefs of this Chang'an community. And, regardless of whether Sengrui actually altered the tradition preserved some years prior in Sengzhao's *Vimalakīrti Commentary*, it was not unusual for different notions of Aśvaghoṣa's dates and master to coexist at the same time and place in China. As I have demonstrated throughout this book, there were numerous traditions regarding these facts of Aśvaghoṣa's career, and it is certainly plausible that more than one of them had developed in India or Central Asia prior to the early fifth century and come to Chang'an with Kumārajīva or another of the Western missionaries who visited the Later Qin capital at the time. For even with these discrepancies, given the overwhelming thematic and stylistic similarities between the Nanatsu-dera edition and the writings of the Chang'an group,

18. The transliteration used for Kumāralāta in the biography—Jiumoluoluotuo 鳩摩羅羅陀—is only attested in Sengrui's "*Dhyāna* Scriptures" preface, a fact which lends further support to the attribution of the Nanatsu-dera edition to Sengrui, or at least its placement in early-fifth-century Chang'an.

particularly Sengrui, it remains most probable that the biography was produced at this time and place.

The remainder of this appendix provides a complete annotated translation of the Nanatsu-dera edition of the *Tradition of Aśvaghoṣa Bodhisattva*. I follow the reconstruction and transcription of the text provided by Ochiai and Saitō Takanobu 齊藤隆信, which I append to the end of the translation.[19] I closely consulted the Japanese translations of this text first done piecemeal by Ochiai (1992a, 1993, 1994) and later *in toto* by Ochiai and Saitō (2000, 275–277). Otherwise, the following is the only translation of the manuscript *Maming pusa zhuan* available in any language.

Tradition of Aśvaghoṣa Bodhisattva, one scroll
Translated by Kumārajīva

Aśvaghoṣa Bodhisattva was born a Brahman some three-hundred years after the death of the Buddha in the kingdom of Sāketa,[20] eastern India. As a youth he was greatly renowned, praised for his skill in letters. As per Indian custom, the masters of discourse and gentlemen of letters all proclaimed those aspects [of debate] in which they excelled in order to display their virtue. Following this custom, Aśvaghoṣa capped his walking staff with a sharp blade and thereunder inscribed this proclamation: "If there is any wise gentleman throughout the land who can gain my submission through any logical argument or vanquish me with any word, I will sever my own head with this blade."

He always carried this walking staff as he traveled throughout the various kingdoms. No gentleman of letters or debate dared contend with him in any discourse or oppose him in any word. At that time on Mount Indra[21] was an arhat possessed of the six penetrations and three insights. His

---

19. Ochiai and Saitō 2000, 268–271, with minor modifications.

20. Sangqiduo 桑岐多 is the transliteration used here for Sāketa in the Nanatsu-dera and Saihō-ji editions, the *Fayuan zhulin* (T no. 2122, 53:681b), and the *Fozu tongji* 佛祖統紀 (T no. 2035, 49:173b). There are variants in other editions of the text; see Ochiai 1992a, 7. This particular transliteration is indeed a strange bird, appearing nowhere but this biography and standing in for other more common renderings of the same place name. See, e.g., Akanuma 1967, 558–560; and Ochiai and Saitō 2000, 278–279n4. In light of later associations between Aśvaghoṣa and sericulture, it is tempting to see this rendering—literally "kingdom of many mulberry branches"—as no mere accidental selection of phonemes but rather the earliest literary connection between Aśvaghoṣa and silkworms. Sāketa was in northeastern India, in the ancient district of Kosala near the modern border with Nepal.

21. Mount Indra, or Indrakūṭa (Yuntuo shan 韻陀山), is so named because of its legendary designation as the abode of the god Indra and is located near the ancient city of Rājagṛha, in northeastern India (Ochiai 1992a, 11; Ochiai and Saitō 2000, 279n6). This transliteration does not appear in any lexicographic source of which I am aware, and the only primary sources in which I have found it are the *Fayuan zhulin* (T no. 2122, 53:681c) and *Zongjing lu* (T no. 2016, 48:658a), in both instances where they reproduce portions of the present biography.

name was Pūrṇa (Fulouna 富樓那).[22] There were no non-Buddhist terms or logical arguments that he had not thoroughly mastered.[23] Aśvaghoṣa went there to look for him and saw him sitting upright under the trees. [Pūrṇa's] aura of resolve lent him a lofty and distant appearance, as if unfathomable. He wore a retiring expression that made him seem like he could be brought to submission. Accordingly, [Aśvaghoṣa] said to him, "*Śramaṇa*, speak! If you dare offer any insights I will surely defeat you. If I am not victorious then I will cut my throat in admission of defeat."

The *śramaṇa* remained silent, and he had neither the appearance of the vanquished nor the countenance of the victorious. [Aśvaghoṣa] repeated this several times but [Pūrṇa] remained completely unmoved. Aśvaghoṣa withdrew and thought to himself, "I have been vanquished! He is the victor! He said nothing so he cannot be defeated. I said something even though I know that words can be defeated. Indeed, I have not yet escaped the fetters of words—how truly shameful!"

He approached to admit his defeat and intended to sever his own head with his blade. The *śramaṇa* stopped him. "As you would sever your own head in submission before me, you should follow my intention and shave your *cūḍā* (topknot) to become my disciple. If you approach you will be able to listen to the Way and purify your mind, and when you withdraw you can be undefeated in essential discourse."

For this reason [Aśvaghoṣa] submitted, took the tonsure and removed his hair ornaments, and received the full precepts. When settled he [composed] texts to proclaim the Buddhadharma; when traveling he explicated and converted others to the Way. He composed many treatises in millions of words that glorified the Buddhadharma,[24] and performed great deeds throughout India.

At that time, although the end of the True Dharma [period] was approaching, people's minds could still attain [the Way]. Their ability to realize it themselves was insufficient and awakening through texts and words was still incomplete.[25] Therefore, Aśvaghoṣa abbreviated superfluous words

---

22. This is most likely an abbreviation for Pūrṇa Maitrāyaṇīputra, as discussed earlier in this appendix. Cf. Mochizuki 1954–1963, 5:4508c.

23. I part with Ochiai in my interpretation of the sentence: 外道名理無不綰達. Ochiai (1993, 43) translates it as "there was no reason why the non-Buddhist's (Aśvaghoṣa's) name would not have reached the ear [of Pūrṇa]" (外道 [馬鳴] の名が知られわたっていないという道理はないであろう). However, because Pūrṇa is being introduced in the immediately preceding sentences, I believe that he is the topic here, not Aśvaghoṣa. Thus *waidao* 外道 refers not to Aśvaghoṣa in particular but to non-Buddhists in general. I have altered the punctuation of this sentence accordingly (moving the comma from after *ming* 名, as Ochiai has it, to after *li* 理).

24. See chapter 1 on the interpretation of this sentence (作莊嚴佛法諸論數百萬言) as a reference to the *Da zhuangyan jing lun* 大莊嚴經論 (*Kalpanāmaṇḍitikā* or *Sūtrālaṃkāraśāstra*), T no. 201.

25. The expression here "to realize" (*muji* 目擊) is perhaps drawn from the "Tian Zifang 田子方," chapter 21 of the *Zhuangzi* 莊子 (*Zhuangzi jinzhu jinyi* 莊子今注今譯, p. 533): "Confucius said, 'With that kind of man one glance tells you that the Way is there before you. What

that strayed from the truth and omitted flowery expressions that [merely] implied meaning. He pronounced the supple teaching through clear principles and related their essentials and fundamentals with the utmost beauty. How could this not be the case? His skillfully composed texts were direct in their expression, and he was without match in his excellence. At that time [his writings] were praised and revered throughout the world, taken as models of composition. Although when he returned to Xihe 西河 [Zixia 子夏] was confused with Confucius[26] and Śāriputra was taken for the Saintly Master,[27] [the renown of these disciples] did not surpass [that of Aśvaghoṣa].

Five-hundred years thereafter, Nāgārjuna Bodhisattva appeared in the world. His vast talents were unsurpassed, his clear discernment like that of a god. He invigorated *prajñā* amidst the bonds of great destruction[28] and grounded [the teaching of] birthlessness at the beginning of [the world's]

---

room does that leave for any possibility of speech?" (仲尼曰, "若夫人者, 目擊而道存矣, 亦不可以容聲矣?") Trans. Watson 1968, 223; cf. Luo 1987–1995, 4546a. My thanks to Chen Jinhua for this point. Here ends the presentation of variants in different editions of the text, *kundoku* 訓読 reading, and Japanese translation of the revised version in Ochiai 1993. Cf. the alternate punctuation, *kundoku*, and abbreviated translation in Ochiai and Saitō 2000, which I mostly follow.

26. As noted by Ochiai and Saitō (2000, 281n21), 復西河之亂孔父 refers to a well-known disciple of Confucius by the name of Zixia 子夏 (a.k.a. Bu Shang 卜商; ca. 507–420 BCE), who resided in the area of Xihe, modern Shaanxi province. Ochiai and Saitō assert that Zixia being confused with Confucius is an unknown tradition. However, as early as the *Li ji* 禮記 we find the tale of Zengzi 曽子 accusing Zixia of making the people of Xihe confuse him (Zixia) with Confucius. See Legge (1885) 1967, 1:135. This is also alluded to in the *Sanguo zhi* 三國志 (*juan* 巻 31) 4:867 ("At Xihe Zixia confused the teachings of the Sage" 子夏在西河疑聖人之論), and is repeated in later Buddhist texts such as *Beishan lu* 北山錄 by Shenqing 神清 (d. ca. 814) (T no. 2113, 52:622b).

27. Śāriputra was one of the ten principal disciples of the Buddha, known as being foremost among the wise. The Saintly Master here refers to the Buddha. 身子之疑聖師 could be interpreted to mean either that Śāriputra doubted the Buddha's teachings or that he himself was taken for (i.e., suspected to be) the Buddha. In the former case, the source for this allusion could be Kumārajīva's translation of the *Lotus Sūtra* (*Miaofa lianhua jing*, T no. 262, 9:6b), in which Śāriputra laments, "Of the multitude of voice-hearers / The Buddha has said that I am the first. / Now, with respect to my own knowledge, I / Cannot resolve my doubts / As to whether this is the ultimate Dharma" (trans. Hurvitz 1976, 27). The latter possibility could stem from conflicting traditions that take either Śāriputra or the Buddha himself as author of the Abhidharma. See Lamotte 1944–1980, 1:112–113; and Lamotte 1988, 190. I accept this latter possibility because it makes more sense as continued praise of Aśvaghoṣa's reputation. Ochiai and Saitō (2000, 281–282n22) speculate that the "Saintly Master" refers to Śāriputra's non-Buddhist teacher before Śāriputra converted to Buddhism.

28. Here I read *huai* 壞 for *rang* 壤 as a parallel to *luo* 落 in the following sentence, as suggested by Chen Jinhua (personal communication). Ochiai reads *rang* on the basis of a parallel passage in Sengrui's *Yuyi lun* 喻疑論 (Ochiai 1994, 16n4; Ochiai and Saitō 2000, 283n27). However, the Nanatsu-dera manuscript appears to have *huai*, as does the Saihō-ji manuscript, which Ochiai did not use for collating. The Kōshō-ji manuscript has insect damage at this point so is illegible. My thanks to Prof. Ochiai for giving me access to high-quality photographic reproductions of these manuscripts.

demise. He made the Way of the Greater Vehicle [flourish] once more throughout Jambu[dvīpa], again proclaiming the teaching of non-attachment during the Final Dharma [period]. Each time [Nāgārjuna] inked his quill and began composing treatises, he never failed to pay the utmost respect to Aśvaghoṣa. He composed verses for personally taking refuge and expressed his wish to rely on [Aśvaghoṣa's] profound illumination so as to become enlightened himself. It is said that now in India many kings and powerful gentlemen all build temples in homage to them and worship them like buddhas.

It is explained in this saying: "Nāgārjuna Bodhisattva is the light of the south, like a bright moon illuminating the deep night. Dharma-master Vīra (Weiluo 韋羅)[29] is the hero of the west, like Venus among the myriad stars. Dharma-master Kumāralāta (Jiumoluoluotuo 鳩摩羅羅陀)[30] is the beauty of the north, like Mercury amidst the constellations. Aśvaghoṣa Bodhisattva unifies the three directions, and in the Eastern Civilization [of India?][31] he is like the rays of light from the morning sun illuminating all in the six directions."

Some say that Kumāralāta dwelt in the north, like the light of the moon at night, and that Nāgārjuna Bodhisattva in the south succeeded him in being like the polestar encircled by constellations.[32] The two Dharma-masters Kumāralāta and Vīra performed the meritorious act of [contributing to] the Threefold Canon, but they did not believe in the Greater Vehi-

---

29. This Sanskrit reconstruction is from Ochiai 1994, 20. Cf. Akanuma 1967, 769–70 (which lists two Vīras, but both with different transliterations and both from eastern India). I have not found this transliteration in any lexicographic source, and it is nearly as absent from the extant Buddhist canon. Different editions of the biography offer Dharma-master Shiluo 事羅法師 and Dharma-master Jie 界法師, neither of whom is any more identifiable (Ochiai 1994, 20). Because Weiluo appears in the *Chu sanzang jiji* not far from Aśvaghoṣa in the first of Sengyou's Sarvāstivādin lineage lists (T no. 2145, 55:89a), Ochiai views this as the proper reading.

30. I follow Yamabe and Sueki (2009, xvi) for this Sanskrit reconstruction. As Lamotte (1944–1980, 3:ln1) notes, this figure was also known as Kumāralabdha, which Minowa (2003, 179) and Ochiai (1994, 21) favor. The only other source in which I have seen this transliteration is Sengrui's *Guanzhong chu chanjing xü* 關中出禪經序 (in *Chu sanzang jiji*, T no. 2145, 55:65a). Minowa and Ochiai identify this Jiumoluoluotuo with patriarch number twelve in the previously mentioned Sarvāstivādin lineage list, Jiumoluotuo 鳩摩羅馱 [*sic—tuo* 馱]. Cf. Mochizuki 1954–1963, 1:717a–c (s.v. "Kumarata 鳩摩羅多"). In the following paragraph of the present text, the transliterations given are Jiumoluotuo 鳩摩羅陀, lacking the second *luo* 羅, in all editions except Kōshō-ji and Saihō-ji.

31. *Dongxia* 東夏 was a conventional designation for China in medieval times, and is read as such by Ochiai and Saitō (2000, 294). However, as Chen Jinhua points out (personal communication), since the narrative here centers itself in India and radiates from there, *Dongxia* could also mean eastern India (*Xia* referring to the semi-mythical first Chinese dynasty of that name and thus being a general expression for "civilization"), which would fit with Aśvaghoṣa's placement in Sāketa at the beginning of the biography. On the juxtaposition of *Xixia* 西夏, *Dongxia*, and related terms, see Chen 2004, 237–246.

32. Perhaps adapted from the *Analects* 2.1: "The rule of virtue can be compared to the polestar that commands the homage of the multitude of stars without leaving its place." 為政以德，譬如北辰居其所而眾星共之. Translation adapted from Lau 1979, 63.

cle. Aśvaghoṣa and Nāgārjuna combined the Greater and Lesser [Vehicles] into one, and the commentaries that they composed only clarified the true aspect of the former Sage (the Buddha). They rescued the weak and dying from this dream world, thus they are praised by the bodhisattvas.[33]

馬鳴菩薩傳一卷
羅什譯

馬鳴菩薩, 佛滅後三百餘年, 出自東天竺, 桑岐多國婆羅門種也. 弱枝奇譽, 以文談見稱. 天竺俗法, 論師文士, 皆執勝相, 以表其德. 馬鳴用其俗法, 以利刀冠杖, 銘其下曰, "天下智士, 其有能以一理見屈, 一文見勝者, 當以此刀自刎其首."

常執此杖, 周遊諸國. 文論之士, 莫敢有抗一言而對一文者. 是時韻陀山中有六通三明阿羅漢, 名富樓那, 外道名理, 無不綰達. 馬鳴詣而候焉. 見其端坐林下, 志氣眇然, 若不可測. 神色謙退, 似如可屈. 遂與之言, "沙門, 說之. 敢有所明. 要必屈汝. 我若不勝, 便刎頸相謝."

沙門默然, 容无負色, 亦无勝顏. 加之數四, 曾无應情. 馬鳴退自思惟, "我負矣. 彼勝矣. 彼自無言, 故無可屈. 吾以言之, 雖知言者可屈. 自亦未免於言. 真可愧也."

進謝其屈, 便欲以刀自刎. 沙門止之 "汝以自刎謝我. 當隨我意, 剃汝周羅, 為我弟子. 進可問道洗心, 退可不負要言."

即以理伏, 落髮投簪, 受具足戒. 坐則文宣佛法, 遊則闡揚道化. 作莊嚴佛法諸論數百萬言, 大行於天竺.

是時雖近正法之末, 而人心猶得. 目擊之勢不足, 而文言之悟有餘. 馬鳴所以略煩文於理外, 簡華辭於意表. 敷婉旨以明宗, 述略本以盡美. 不其然乎? 其善屬文, 直爾言之, 便自妙絕. 於時舉世推崇, 以為造作之式. 雖復西河之亂孔父, 身子之疑聖師, 蔑以過也.

其後五百年, 龍樹菩薩出世. 宏才卓犖, 明鑒若神. 振般若大壞之綱, 紐無生已落之緒. 使大乘之道, 再一於閻浮, 無執之化, 重宣於末法. 及其染翰之初, 著論之始, 未嘗不稽首馬鳴, 作自歸之偈, 庶幾憑其冥照以自悟焉. 云今天竺諸王勢士, 皆為之立廟宗之若佛.

說訊有之曰, "龍樹菩薩南方之照, 若朗月之燭幽夜. 韋羅法師西方之桀, 若太白之在眾星. 鳩摩羅羅陀法師北方之美, 若辰星之在眾宿. 馬鳴菩薩兼三方, 於東夏, 其猶朝陽燈暉, 六合俱照."

或稱鳩摩羅(羅)[34] 陀處於北方, 若月照於夜, 龍樹菩薩南方繼之, 若眾宿之環極. 鳩摩羅(羅)*陀, 韋羅二法師, 善業三藏, 不信大乘. 馬鳴, 龍樹兼大小而一之. 其所著述, 但明實相於先賢. 拯弱喪於夢境, 故菩薩稱之焉.

---

33. The second half of the text is discussed and translated in Ochiai 1994 and Ochiai and Saitō 2000.

34. Only the Kōshō-ji and Saihō-ji editions have the character *luo* 羅 twice here and in the following instance; cf. Ochiai 1994, 22–23.

Appendix 2

The Canonical Tradition of Deva Bodhisattva

The Tradition of Deva Bodhisattva (*Tipo pusa zhuan* 提婆菩薩傳; hereafter *Tradition*) is an early and important testament to the most prominent medieval Chinese conceptions of the Indian patriarch Āryadeva. Although traditionally ascribed to Kumārajīva, this text probably appeared shortly after the compilation of the *Dharma-Treasury Transmission* (*Fu fazang yinyuan zhuan* 付法藏因緣傳), which includes a very similar narrative of Āryadeva's career. The *Dharma-Treasury Transmission* and *Tipo pusa zhuan* match one another scene for scene and often word for word; they both diverge considerably from the brief account of Āryadeva provided in Sengzhao's 僧肇 (ca. 374–414) preface to the *Hundred Treatise* (*Bai lun* 百論) (see chapter 1) and they emphasize different themes than those advanced in the patriarch tales written by Kumārajīva's associates. But while the *Tradition* appears to have arisen in the same milieu as the *Dharma-Treasury Transmission*, perhaps having been excerpted from this larger compilation,[1] the fact that it circulated independently made it a much different kind of biography. By placing Āryadeva in a series of Indian patriarchs who all played mostly the same role in propagating the Dharma, the *Dharma-Treasury Transmission* had a homogenizing effect. In this text each individual master was pressed into the same mold

1. Yamano (2010) raises the likely possibility that there was an older, no longer extant source for both the *Dharma-Treasury Transmission* account of Nāgārjuna and his independently circulating biography. This may be true for the *Tipo pusa zhuan* 提婆菩薩傳 as well. I maintain that neither the *Longshu pusa zhuan* 龍樹菩薩傳 nor *Tipo pusa zhuan* dates as far back as Kumārajīva's time, largely because they have little in common with the writings of his associates. The conceptual and linguistic similarities between these independent hagiographies and the *Dharma-Treasury Transmission* give the impression that they may have been drawn from it, at least in part, but this certainly does not preclude the possibility that Yamano raises. Further, I might add that one candidate for this missing source text is what Jizang 吉藏 (549–623) calls the "Khotanese tradition of Nāgārjuna" (Yutianguo Longshu zhuan 于闐國龍樹傳), which alone recounted Nāgārjuna's finding of the *Avataṃsakasūtra* in the dragon palace. See Yamano 2009, 93–96; and Yamano 2010, 54–55. Jizang also refers to this source as the "Transmission" (*xiangcheng* 相承), which recalls Sengyou's 僧祐 (445–518) *Record of the Masters and Disciples of the Sarvāstivādin Sect* (*Sapoduo bu shizi ji* 薩婆多部師資記), also titled *Sapoduo bu xiangcheng zhuan* 薩婆多部相承傳 and lost during the Tang period. I discuss this text in chapter 2.

and subordinated to the larger discursive aims of the Indian patriarchate as a whole. Āryadeva was given much more detailed treatment than most other patriarchs along the line, but his primary function was still the same as all the rest: to illustrate how, up to *bhikṣu* Siṃha, the Dharma had been maintained in perpetuity through master-disciple transmission. In contrast, as a separate biography removed from this broader context of patriarchal succession, the *Tradition* singled out Āryadeva as a foremost exemplar of the practices that rendered ordinary human beings into eminent Buddhist saints. The *Tradition* was one of a few such independently circulating biographies of the Indian patriarchs; the fact that it was composed, frequently cited, and reproduced in numerous editions of the Buddhist canon attests the unique and enduring importance of Āryadeva in medieval China.

Like the *Dharma-Treasury Transmission*, the *Tradition* includes four main episodes in which Āryadeva modeled a specific repertoire of saintly practices. First, after introducing Āryadeva as an eminent Brahman from southern India, both texts advanced their protagonist as an exemplar of self-immolation. According to the opening episode, Āryadeva visited a Maheśvara temple to investigate reports of the god's efficacy. Upon his arrival Āryadeva decried the ostentation of Maheśvara's golden statue and plucked out one of its crystal eyes. That night Maheśvara appeared in a bodily form that was missing the same eye that Āryadeva had removed from the statue. The god asked Āryadeva to pluck out his own eye to replace the one he had taken, and Āryadeva gladly obliged. In this way Āryadeva exemplified the bodhisattva's perfect renunciation, freely giving of his own flesh to illustrate the emptiness of all physical form—from the bodies of saints to the icons of gods (as discussed in chapter 2).

The next main episode of both the *Dharma-Treasury Transmission* and the *Tradition* illustrates how great Buddhist saints were made by securing the allegiance of kings. This episode appeared with few variations in the accounts of both Āryadeva and Nāgārjuna in the *Dharma-Treasury Transmission*, as well as in Nāgārjuna's independently circulating biography, with the name of its protagonist amended accordingly.[2] As per the Koryŏ recension of the *Tradition* (which will be discussed in greater detail),[3] the king of southern India supported non-Buddhist teachings, so Āryadeva set out to convert him to Buddhism. To this end Āryadeva enlisted to become the commander of the palace guards. The king was impressed with Āryadeva's work and so asked who he was. Āryadeva replied that he was an omniscient one, and the king tested this assertion by inquiring about the activities of the gods. Āryadeva reported that the gods were battling the *asuras*, whose body parts began falling from the sky to verify Āryadeva's claim. With this the king was converted to Buddhism, together with a host of Brahmans watching from the palace precincts.

---

2. See the discussion in Hasuzawa 1936, 465; Li 2002c, 18; Walleser (1923) 1979, 30–33; and Yamano 2010, 57–59.

3. *Koryŏ taejanggyŏng* 高麗大藏經 (*Tipo pusa zhuan*, K no. 1040, 30).

The account of Āryadeva in the *Dharma-Treasury Transmission* and other recensions of the *Tradition* omit the king's quizzing of Āryadeva about the gods and the *asuras*' falling body parts—an exchange identical to that between Nāgārjuna and a non-Buddhist in Sengzhao's *Vimalakīrti Commentary* (*Zhu weimojie jing* 注維摩詰經). Instead, according to these accounts, the king was won over not through Āryadeva's magnificent display of cosmic vision, but through a public debate in which Āryadeva soundly defeated the arguments of all non-Buddhists. In the Koryŏ edition of the *Tradition*, after securing the king's patronage, Āryadeva proceeded to convert everyone else in the kingdom by setting up a debate platform and proclaiming the superiority of the Three Jewels. Āryadeva offered to cut off his head if anyone could refute this proclamation—much like Aśvaghoṣa in his early biographies—but after defeating all opponents he claimed their allegiance to Buddhism rather than their severed heads. In this way Āryadeva exemplified both the wisdom and compassion of the great Buddhist saint, handily vanquishing everyone in the debate arena but only in order to liberate them from false views.

One non-Buddhist, however, did not look so kindly upon this effort to liberate his master, so he vowed to kill Āryadeva. In the fourth and final episode of the *Tradition*, this non-Buddhist followed through on his vow, thus giving Āryadeva the opportunity to demonstrate his perfection of forbearance. After Āryadeva defeated all the debate-masters in the kingdom, he retired to a forest hermitage to compose his *Hundred Treatise* and *Four-Hundred Treatise*.[4] The vengeful non-Buddhist found Āryadeva there and stabbed him with a knife. Pitying his deluded assailant, Āryadeva offered his robes and alms bowls and warned him to run for the hills before Āryadeva's disciples could find him. He then gave the non-Buddhist an in-depth lecture on the perils of attachment to name and form—longer and more complex than that found in the *Dharma-Treasury Transmission*—and awaited the return of his disciples. When they arrived and saw Āryadeva in a bloody heap, his disciples all screamed and cried, with some running off

4. While scholars agree that Kumārajīva's translation of the *Hundred Treatise* is in fact a portion of Āryadeva's original *Catuḥśataka* (*Four-Hundred Treatise*), medieval Chinese authors clearly thought these were two separate texts. The *Catuḥśataka* was never translated in full into Chinese (Sanskrit fragments and a complete Tibetan version remain), and in fact there seems never to have been a Chinese text bearing the title *Sibai lun* 四百論. Xuanzang translated roughly the second half of the *Catuḥśataka* in his *Guang bailun ben* 廣百論本 (T no. 1570). See Bhattacharya 1931; Lang 1986; Murti 1955, 93; Ren 2002; Robinson 1967, 242n11; and Vaidya 1923. In addition, by the early eighth century two more debate texts were attributed to Āryadeva: Bodhiruci's sixth-century translations titled *Po waidao sizong lun* 破外道四宗論 and *Po waidao neipan lun* 破外道涅槃論. The former was first ascribed to Āryadeva in the *Kaiyuan shijiao lu* 開元釋教錄 of 730 by Zhisheng 智昇 (fl. 700–786) (T no. 2154, 55:541a); Deva's name was first connected with the latter text in *Cheng weishi lun yanmi* 成唯識論演祕 by Zhizhou 智周 (678–733 or 688–723) (T no. 1833, 43:832a). These texts are now titled *Tipo pusa po Lengqie jing zhong waidao xiaosheng sizong lun* 提婆菩薩破楞伽經中外道小乘四宗論 (T no. 1639) and *Tipo pusa shi Lengqie jing zhong waidao xiaosheng niepan lun* 提婆菩薩釋楞伽經中外道小乘涅槃論 (T no. 1640; French trans. Tucci 1926), respectively.

to track down the perpetrator. Āryadeva then gave one last lecture on nonattachment before succumbing to his wounds and relinquishing his body like a cicada sheds its husk.

In sum, through these four main episodes the *Tradition* represents Āryadeva as a master of debate and converter of non-Buddhists, a keystone of state-sangha relations, and an exemplar of bodily renunciation. While these representations offer valuable testimony to how Āryadeva was conceived in medieval China—and how ideals of Buddhist sainthood were developed—equally significant are the elements absent from the *Tradition* as compared with other biographies of Āryadeva. These omissions provide important clues as to the provenance of the *Tradition*, which helps us understand its role in the history of the Indian patriarchs in China. First, as previously noted, although the *Tradition* and the *Dharma-Treasury Transmission* offer very similar accounts of Āryadeva's career, the former completely elides the theme of master-disciple succession. Only the *Dharma-Treasury Transmission* claims that Āryadeva followed Nāgārjuna in the patriarchal lineage and then bequeathed the teaching to his own disciple Rāhula (Luohouluo 羅睺羅).[5] According to the *Tradition*, Āryadeva was famous throughout the land, he converted non-Buddhists and kings, and he had many followers, but no specific disciple was singled out as his successor. Further, while the Koryŏ version of the *Tradition* twice asserts that Nāgārjuna was Āryadeva's master, other recensions of the text make no mention of this former patriarch. And even the Koryŏ edition omits the formal expression of master-disciple succession used in the *Dharma-Treasury Transmission*,[6] stating only in passing that Āryadeva received the Buddhist precepts from Nāgārjuna. As such, while the *Tradition* and the *Dharma-Treasury Transmission* are nearly identical in language and narrative structure, only the *Tradition* was composed (or excerpted) to promote Āryadeva above all others as a model of Buddhist sainthood.

Given that the *Tradition* appears born of different concerns than those animating the *Dharma-Treasury Transmission*, is it possible that the former was first conveyed by Kumārajīva, as traditionally claimed, and then reproduced in the latter text, as scholars often assume? As discussed in chapter 1, Kumārajīva's associates similarly promoted Āryadeva as a singular exemplar of Buddhist sainthood rather than an interchangeable member of a patriarchal lineage. And in fact, insofar as they often foregrounded notions of post-*parinirvāṇa* Dharma decline, the writings of Kumārajīva's associates were inimical to the model of patriarchal succession advanced in the *Dharma-*

---

5. I follow Maspero (1911, 142) for this Sanskrit reconstruction. See especially Akanuma (1967, 526–528) for a discussion of different individuals bearing this name. Yampolsky's (1967, 8) Rāhulata derives from the Luohoulouduo 羅睺羅多 of the *Baolin zhuan* 寶林傳, by Zhiju 智矩 (n. d.), ca. 801, 51. Cf. Mochizuki 1954–1963, 5:4953a–b, which follows the later Chan linage histories in reading this Luohouluo as Rāhulabhadra (Luohouluobatuoluo 羅睺羅跋陀羅).

6. See *Fu fazang yinyuan zhuan* 付法藏因緣傳, T no. 2058, 50:318c; Chinese trans. Li 1997a, 361.

Treasury Transmission, which instead emphasized the Dharma's continued efflorescence after nirvāṇa. Further, there is no evidence that Kumārajīva or his disciples saw Āryadeva as Nāgārjuna's direct disciple; this relationship seems to have been first forged in the *Dharma-Treasury Transmission*. Nevertheless, given the lack of any reference to the *Tradition* in the writings of Kumārajīva's disciples, the significant discrepancies between the former and the latter, and the fact that the *Tradition* is not listed in the oldest extant Buddhist catalogue, it is most likely that this text was composed not with Kumārajīva's coterie but in the decades following the compilation of the *Dharma-Treasury Transmission*.

As discussed in chapter 1, nearly every account of the Indian patriarchs produced by Kumārajīva's associates revolves around the themes of Dharmic history, the decline of the teaching over the generations after nirvāṇa, and the charge of Buddhist saints to revive a failing Buddhadharma through practices like public debate and doctrinal authorship. As a general rule, then, these themes can be taken as markers for how Kumārajīva's associates understood the Indian patriarchs, or at least of what they thought important to convey about the patriarchs' lives. It stands to reason that the patriarch accounts that lack these themes were most likely not produced by Kumārajīva's associates, barring evidence of other kinds that definitively links such accounts to this early-fifth-century group. In the case of the *Tradition* and the independently circulating biography of Nāgārjuna (*Longshu pusa zhuan* 龍樹菩薩傳), which have appeared in Chinese Buddhist catalogues since the late sixth century as Kumārajīva's translations,[7] there is no such evidence of a fifth-century Chang'an provenance. Both of these texts are conspicuously absent from the *Chu sanzang jiji* 出三藏記集 of ca. 515, neither is mentioned in any source from before the sixth century, and both are completely lacking in the aforementioned narrative themes: their protagonists are not given post-*parinirvāṇa* dates or situated in the True or Semblance Dharma periods; neither text evinces any concern with declining Dharma; and neither patriarch is depicted saving the teaching from the brink of oblivion. Given that Sengzhao, Sengrui 僧叡 (ca. 352–436), Huiyuan 慧遠 (ca. 334–416), and other associates of Kumārajīva almost always emphasize these issues in their accounts of the Indian patriarchs, these omissions strongly suggest that the separate biographies of Nāgārjuna and Āryadeva postdate Kumārajīva.[8]

One exception to this rule is Sengzhao's *Vimalakīrti Commentary*, which describes a debate between Nāgārjuna and an unnamed non-Buddhist in order to illustrate the concept of "spiritual penetration" (*shentong* 神通). In this account, the non-Buddhist inquired about the activities of the gods. Nāgārjuna replied that they were battling *asuras*. The non-Buddhist demanded proof, and Nāgārjuna made severed limbs fall from the sky in

7. *Zhongjing mulu* 眾經目錄, T no. 2146, 55:146a; *Lidai sanbao ji* 歷代三寶紀, T no. 2034, 49:79a.

8. A different opinion is given in Yamano 2009, 92.

order to verify his claim—thus manifesting his powers of *shentong*. The accounts of Nāgārjuna in the *Dharma-Treasury Transmission* and *Longshu pusa zhuan*, as well as Āryadeva's *Tradition*, all include a very similar encounter between their protagonist and a South Indian king. In all three cases the king asked about the activities of the gods; the patriarch said the gods were fighting *asuras*; proof was given in the form of falling weapons and limbs; and the king was converted to Buddhism. None of these versions promoted visions of Dharma decline and revival, but neither did this tale originally have anything to do with state-sangha relations. In the *Vimalakīrti Commentary*—and thus for Kumārajīva's associates—this episode was about *shentong* in the context of religious debate; it was not about converting royalty. In the separate biographies of Nāgārjuna and Āryadeva, and in the *Dharma-Treasury Transmission*, this episode was repurposed to illustrate the power of patriarchs over kings. This fact further indicates that the biographies of Nāgārjuna and Āryadeva are more closely affiliated with the *Dharma-Treasury Transmission*, which was principally concerned with state-sangha relations, than with the writings of Kumārajīva's associates—in this case the *Vimalakīrti Commentary*.[9]

Two more items of evidence bear on the provenance of the *Tipo pusa zhuan* and *Longshu pusa zhuan*. The first is Huiyuan's preface to his abridged version of the *Great Perfection of Wisdom Treatise*, discussed in chapter 1, which provides the fullest biography of Nāgārjuna that clearly dates to Kumārajīva's time. Richard Robinson claims that Huiyuan's account attests the *Longshu pusa zhuan*, given that the two texts agree with one another and "many of [Huiyuan's] allusions are intelligible only with a knowledge of" the latter (Robinson 1967, 22, 25). But this is simply not the case. Robinson points out numerous allusions in Huiyuan's Nāgārjuna biography to ancient Chinese classics like the *Shanhai jing* 山海經, *Yi jing* 已經, *Zhuangzi* 莊子, and *Daode jing* 道德經, but the only direct connection Robinson notes between Huiyuan's account and the separate biography is Nāgārjuna's famous journey to the undersea dragon palace (ibid., 285n7, 287n16, 287n18, 288n22, 288n24, 289n27). However, the story of this dragon-palace sojourn appeared earlier in two prefaces by Kumārajīva's disciples. These are far more likely sources for Huiyuan's account than a biography not attested until almost two centuries later. The only other point in common between the separate biography and Huiyuan's preface, which Robinson does not mention, is the focus on Nāgārjuna's solitary peregrinations—through the snowy moun-

9. Yamano (2009, 85) argues that, because Nāgārjuna's royal connections were known to the Chinese through the fifth-century translations of his *Suhṛllekha*, the "non-Buddhist" with whom he debated in the *Vimalakīrti Commentary* may have been this same south Indian king. This seems to me an improbable conjecture. The *Suhṛllekha* was not translated until after Kumārajīva's time, first by Guṇavarman (367–431) in 421 (T no. 1672) and then by Sanghavarman (fl. 420–445) in 434–442 (T no. 1673), and the writings of Kumārajīva's associates otherwise suggest no connections whatsoever between the Indian patriarchs and secular authority. Cf. Lamotte (1944–1980, 3:liii), who also doubts that the early fifth-century Chang'an community saw the *Suhṛllekha*.

tains and to the abode of a *śramaṇa* who expands Nāgārjuna's sūtra collection. However, given the affinity between this theme of otherworldly withdrawal and Huiyuan's own ideal of the *śramaṇic* "stranger," as discussed in chapter 1, Huiyuan's emphasis on this aspect of Nāgārjuna's career can be readily accounted for without recourse to the *Longshu pusa zhuan*, which Huiyuan nowhere mentions.

There are also significant discrepancies between Huiyuan's preface and the *Longshu pusa zhuan* that are difficult to explain if Huiyuan actually had the latter text before him. The most conspicuous of these discrepancies is the aforementioned king-conversion episode, which occurs in both the *Fu fazang zhuan* and *Longshu pusa zhuan* but is absent from Huiyuan's preface. This is an important discrepancy because, had he had the *Longshu pusa zhuan* to hand, Huiyuan certainly would have highlighted this episode of Nāgārjuna's triumph over secular authority. Around the beginning of the fifth century, Huiyuan himself had run-ins with the Eastern Jin official Huan Xuan 桓玄 (369–404), who usurped the throne in Jiankang and instituted measures to bring the Chinese sangha under state control. Huiyuan fought against these measures and eventually had them rescinded, but this experience left upon him an indelible impression of Buddhism's precarious position at the hands of unsympathetic secular rulers. Indeed, after these eventful years, Huiyuan maintained close ties with the leaders of the restored Jin regime in the south as well as the Later Qin in the north, though always from the confines of his Donglin monastery (東林寺) on Mt. Lu.[10] Therefore, and especially since he composed this preface some years after his experience with Huan Xuan, it is likely that if Huiyuan knew this king-conversion tale he would have used it to illustrate how great Buddhist saints were made by gaining the allegiance of kings, whose best interests were served by supporting the sangha.

While there are other conspicuous omissions from Huiyuan's Nāgārjuna biography, such as the description in the separate biography of Nāgārjuna's literary output, the point is that Huiyuan's preface is a completely different document than the *Longshu pusa zhuan*. Rather than being based on the latter, this preface is very much a product of Huiyuan's own immense learning and his religious milieu, and it carries many of the stylistic signatures of his other extant writings. In Robinson's thoroughly annotated translation of this preface, he highlights no less than thirty instances in which its language follows very closely that of Huiyuan's other works (1967, 285–295)—language that bears no resemblance to the *Longshu pusa zhuan*. If Huiyuan's account was a synopsis of the full-blown biography that has come down to us, it surely would have reproduced at least some of its phrasing. Summaries of the *Longshu pusa zhuan* produced by Jizang 吉藏 (549–623) and Daoshi 道世 (ca. 596–683), for example, read much like their source

10. See Zürcher (1959) 2007, 212–215.

text but with episodes abbreviated.[11] Huiyuan's preface, by contrast, reads most like Huiyuan's other writings. Given all these considerations, it is likely that Huiyuan composed his own brief biography of Nāgārjuna as part of his broader discussion of the *Great Perfection of Wisdom Treatise*, incorporating the few kernels of biographical information garnered by word of mouth or from earlier writings by Kumārajīva's disciples. The structure and content of Huiyuan's account later informed the independently circulating biography of Nāgārjuna, which, like the *Tradition*, probably appeared after the *Dharma-Treasury Transmission*.

The last piece of evidence bearing on the provenance of the *Tipo pusa zhuan* and *Longshu pusa zhuan* is a reference by Sengrui to a certain "Indian tradition" (*Tianzhu zhuan* 天竺傳) as his source of information about the Indian patriarchs. This reference is somewhat of a red herring, however, because we have no way of knowing what Sengrui meant. Was this a specific text bearing the title *Tianzhu zhuan*, which is otherwise unattested and is no longer extant? Was Sengrui just referring to oral tradition passed from India to China through Western missionaries like Kumārajīva? Scholars have speculated in both directions, even going so far as to claim that this "Indian tradition" attests the *Longshu pusa zhuan*. But there is no evidence for any of these speculations, which is why we cannot know what sources Sengrui, Sengzhao, and Huiyuan had for their Indian patriarch accounts. One thing that is clear, however, is that Sengrui's "Indian tradition" was not reproduced in the separate biographies that we have today. Sengrui quotes this source as saying, "At the end of the Semblance and True [Dharma periods], if not for Aśvaghoṣa and Nāgārjuna the teaching of the Way would have fallen into desuetude."[12] While this sentiment (if not phrasing) accords with the Nanatsu-dera 七寺 *Maming pusa zhuan* 馬鳴菩薩傳 and the brief patriarch accounts scattered throughout the writings of Kumārajīva's associates, neither the *Longshu pusa zhuan* nor *Tipo pusa zhuan* includes any statements about the decline of the teaching or the True and Semblance Dharma periods. So, while Sengrui's "*Tianzhu zhuan*" offers a tantalizing hint at the Indian sources circulating in early-fifth-century Chang'an, it does not attest the separate biographies of Nāgārjuna and Āryadeva, and in fact it further supports the presupposition that these texts were composed after Kumārajīva's time.

Below I provide a complete, annotated translation of the *Tradition*, following the Taishō edition of the text, which is a reprint of the recension in the second Koryŏ canon (completed in 1251). The Koryŏ text is representative

---

11. See *Dasheng xuan lun* 大乘玄論, by Jizang 吉藏 (549–623), T no. 1853, 45:77a–b; and *Fayuan zhulin* 法苑珠林, by Daoshi 道世 (ca. 596–683) in 668, T no. 2122, 53:681c–682c.

12. *Chu sanzang jiji* 出三藏記集, by Sengyou 僧祐 (445–518) ca. 515, T no. 2145, 55:75a; *Da zhidu lun* 大智度論, attributed to Nāgārjuna; trans. Kumārajīva (344–413 or 350–409) in 406, T no. 1509, 25:57b.

of that included in the Kaibao canon of 972 to 983.[13] The Taishō editors have included notes to variants in three editions: one of the Song dynasty (the Zifu canon 資福藏 or Later Sixi 後思溪 edition, compiled ca. 1241–1252); one of the Yuan dynasty (the Puning temple 普寧寺 edition, completed in 1290); and one of the Ming dynasty (the Jiaxing canon 嘉興藏 or Jingshan canon 徑山藏, compiled ca. 1589–1712). They also included notes to the "Palace edition" belonging to the Japanese imperial library—a copy of the Pilu canon 毗盧藏 (a.k.a. Fuzhou 福州 edition) completed by 1176. I further consulted the Qisha 磧砂 edition of the Song canon (completed in 1322), which was lost until 1929 and not used for Taishō collating; the Qing dynasty Qianlong 乾隆 edition (compiled 1735–1738); and the manuscripts of the *Tradition* preserved at Dunhuang 敦煌 and at Kōshō-ji 興聖寺 in Kyoto.[14] Finally, I have included references to Yanshou's 延壽 (904–975) *Record of the Principle That Mirrors* [*the Ten Thousand Dharmas*] (*Zongjing lu* 宗鏡錄), which reproduces roughly the first half of the *Tradition* nearly verbatim.[15] There are also manuscripts of the *Tradition* housed in Japan at Ishiyama-dera 石山寺, Myōren-ji 妙蓮寺 (Matsuo-sha 松尾社), and Nanatsu-dera, but I have not yet been able to consult these.[16]

The *Tradition* has been translated into English by Saroj Kumar Chaudhuri and into Japanese by Hasuzawa Shōjūn 蓮澤成淳; its opening and closing episodes have been paraphrased by Yamakami Sōgen; and E. Lyall made an English translation of Vasilief's brief Russian summary of the text.[17] Li Yuxi's 黎玉璽 modern Chinese translation of the *Dharma-Treasury Transmission* is also worth consulting.[18]

---

13. The Kaibao edition was brought from the Northern Song court to Korea in 991 and subsequently used for carving the wood-blocks of the first Koryŏ canon in 1011. The Mongols burned these xylographs in 1232, but rubbings of them had been made and were not all lost. The first 1,087 texts in the second Koryŏ canon were reportedly reproduced from these rubbings, and the *Tipo pusa zhuan* is of this group. See Lancaster 1979, introduction; cf. Deleanu 2007, 12, 38–39n76.

14. *Yingyin Song qisha zangjing* 影印宋磧砂藏經 (*Tipo pusa zhuan*, Qisha no. 1058, 28); *Qianlong dazangjing* 乾隆大藏經 (*Tipo pusa zhuan*, Qianlong no. 1455, 110). See Deleanu (2007, 7–9) for the dates of these printed editions of the canon. Roughly the first half of the *Tipo pusa zhuan* is copied on the verso side of Dunhuang manuscript *Zhong lun juan di yi* 中論卷第一 (S 3286; *Dunhuang baozang* 敦煌寶藏, 27:338–339). According to Giles (1957, 124), the handwriting in this manuscript is of the fifth century. A postscript on the Kōshō-ji manuscript dates it to the twentieth day of the eleventh month of the third year Jōō 貞応, or 1224 (Ochiai 1992b, 295). It is a fickle witness to the various extant printed editions of the *Tradition*, sometimes agreeing only with the Koryŏ text and sometimes only with all others.

15. *Zongjing lu* 宗鏡錄, T no. 2016, 48:950c–951b. I follow Benn (2007, 110) for the English translation of this text's title.

16. See Kokusai Bukkyōgaku Daigakuin Daigaku Gakujutsu Furontia Jikkō Iinkai 2007, 325.

17. See Chaudhuri 2008, 25–31; Hasuzawa 1936; Sōgen 1912, 187–194; and Vasilief 1875.

18. Li 1997a, 360–376, for the section on Āryadeva.

Tradition of Deva Bodhisattva Translated by Threefold Canon [Master] Kumārajīva of the Yao Qin dynasty.[19]

Deva Bodhisattva, a Brahman from south India, was the disciple of the bodhisattva Nāgārjuna.[20] He had extensive knowledge, grasped the profound, and was matchless as a debater. He was famed and praised throughout all of the states of India. After examining his innermost heart, he felt that he had nothing to be ashamed of.[21] The only deficiency that troubled him was that people did not believe and apply his word.

In [Deva's] country there was a golden image cast of a great heavenly god; its body was in a seated position and measured two zhang [tall].[22] It was styled Maheśvara,[23] and whenever people prayed to it, it could cause their wishes to be fulfilled in their present life. Deva went to the temple [where the image was housed] and asked to enter and pay homage.

The temple caretaker said, "The image of this god is most numinous. People who come to see it dare not look directly upon it; it has even caused them to fall back and lose control of themselves in a frightful panic for many days. You just say your prayers from the [outer] gate;[24] why do you need to see it?"

Deva said, "If this [image of the] god can really do as you say, let me see it. If it were not [truly numinous], why should I wish to see?"

At that time the people [who heard this] were surprised at [Deva's] determination and admired his cleverness and integrity, so many thousands of people followed him into the temple. After Deva entered the temple, the image of the god moved its eyes and glared angrily at him.

Deva asked, "This heavenly god is numinous indeed, but why the mere trifles? [A god] should move people with his divine power, and subdue beings with his wisdom and virtue. But here gold stands for self-importance[25]

---

19. *Tipo pusa zhuan*, T no. 2048, 50:186c.

20. Only the Koryŏ and Kōshō-ji editions of the text state here that Deva was Nāgārjuna's disciple. The Palace edition, the three editions of the Song, Yuan, and Ming dyanasties, the Qisha and Qianlong editions, and Yanshou's *Zongjing lu* (T no. 2016, 48:950c–951a) all omit mention of Nāgārjuna at this point in the text. See T no. 2048, 50:186n23.

21. In the Koryŏ text: *Zetan xionghuai ji wusuo kui* 賾探胸懷既無所愧. The three editions of the Song, Yuan, and Ming dyansties, the Qisha edition, and the Qianlong edition all have *tanze* 探賾 in place of *zetan* 賾探; the Palace edition has only *tan* 探. See T no. 2048, 50:186n26. The Kōshō-ji manuscript retains *zetan* but concludes the previous sentence with *zong* 宗 and replaces *xiong* 胸 with *zi* 自.

22. One *zhang* 丈 equaled 296 centimeters in the Six Dynasties period and the Sui dynasty (Luo 1987–1995, 7763).

23. Maheśvara is here translated as Da zizai tian 大自在天, literally "Great God of Omniscience." Maheśvara is an ancient Brahmanical god, also known as Rudra, Śaṃkara, Īśāna, or Śiva.

24. Reading *men* 門 for *wen* 問, as in all editions except the Koryŏ; see T no. 2048, 50:186n29.

25. Following the Koryŏ, Dunhuang, and Kōshō-ji reading of *zi* 自 rather than *mu* 目, as in all other editions. *Ziduo* 自多 ("self-importance") makes more sense here than *muduo* 目多

and crystal (*sphaṭika*)[26] [eyes] move to confuse [the people]. This is not what I expected [of a god]."

He then climbed up a ladder and bored out the eye [of the image].

All of the spectators were troubled with doubt as they thought, "How could Maheśvara suffer at the hands of a meager Brahman? Could it be that his renown transcends his actual capacity and his eloquence is defeated by the truth [put forth by Deva]?"

At this Deva explained to the people, saying "[Maheśvara's] divine radiance is boundless, so he used these superficial means to test me. I discerned his mind, so I mounted his golden [image] and removed his *sphaṭika* to allow you to see that his spirit does not depend on substance, nor does his essence rely upon appearance.[27] I am not an arrogant man, and the god has not been dishonored." With these words he left, and that night sought offerings to prepare for a divine sacrifice the following morning.

With Deva's eminent reputation and divine intelligence, his word echoed in support as far as it reached. In one night he managed to get all the offerings ready; the necessary things were all prepared. Maheśvara [then appeared] clad in a bodily form that was four *zhang* tall, but was missing its left eye. He came and sat down, looked over the offerings and praised them as the best he ever had. He extolled [Deva's] merit in being able to accomplish such [a presentation of offerings] and told him, "You have understood my heart, while the people have only grasped at my form. You offer with your heart, and the people offer only things. You understand and respect me, while the people fear and accuse me. Your offerings are foremost in goodness and beauty, but they are not what I need. If you can give what I need, that would truly be the greatest gift."

Deva declared, "You, o god, have perceived my mind. Only command and I shall obey."

The god said, "What I lack is my left eye. If you are able to give me this, then it will reappear."

Deva responded, "I honor this divine command," as he took out his eye with his left hand and presented it [to Maheśvara].

Because of the god's divine power, [when Deva] pulled out [his eye] another grew in its place, which [Maheśvara] then asked for. This did not cease from morning to night, as some ten thousand eyes were plucked out.

At this the heavenly god commended [Deva], saying "Well done, *māṇava* (young man)![28] This is truly the greatest gift! What would you like to ask for? I will provide anything you desire."

("many eyes"). See T no. 2048, 50:186n34. Also, the Kōshō-ji text is unique in putting *shen* 身 between *zi* and *duo*.

26. *Poli* 頗梨 is the transliteration used here for the Sanskrit *sphaṭika*. It is one of the seven precious jewels. See Muller 1995– (s.v. "*poli*").

27. *Tipo pusa zhuan*, T no. 2048, 50:187a.

28. *Mona* 摩納 is the Chinese transliteration used here for *māṇava* (or *māṇavaka*); see Muller 1995– (s.v. "*mona*").

Deva said, "I uphold the wisdom in my heart and rely upon nothing external. My only regret is that those who are childish and ignorant do not understand and accept my word. O god, grant my wish: do not let my words be in vain. I ask only this; nothing else do I require."

The god replied, "It shall be as you wish."

Thereupon, [Deva] withdrew and visited Nāgārjuna Bodhisattva,[29] from whom he received the rites of leaving the household life. After shaving his head and donning the monastic garb, he traveled around to spread the teaching.

The king of southern India, who controlled many countries, believed in and followed false teachings.[30] He refused to grant audience to even a single *śramaṇa* who was a disciple of Śākyamuni. The people from lands far and near were all converted to his teachings.[31] Deva thought to himself, "If a tree is not cut down at its roots, then its branches will not wilt. If this ruler of men is not converted, then the Way will never be spread."

This country had a regulation according to which the household of the king would pay out money to hire men as palace guards. Deva thus responded by enlisting to be their commander. With a halberd slung over his shoulder he led their forward march. Every column was perfectly ordered and each division was well controlled. Although he was not severe, his orders were followed; although he did not make a display of virtue, people enjoyed following him. The king was greatly pleased at this and asked who this man was.

An attendant replied, "This man answered [the call] to enlist [as the guard commander]. He takes no rations and accepts no payment. Despite this, he performs his duties with reverence and in an expert manner. I know not his intentions, what he seeks or what he desires."

The king summoned [Deva] and asked him, "Who are you?"

---

29. Only the Koryŏ and Kōshō-ji editions of the text here read Nāgārjuna Bodhisattva. The Palace edition and Yanshou's *Zongjing lu* (T no. 2016, 48:951b) state that Deva withdrew to a temple; the Dunhuang text simply says that he withdrew; and all other editions say that Deva withdrew to Nāgārjuna's temple. See T no. 2048, 50:187n8, n9. Jizang 吉藏 (549–623), in his *Bailun shu* (T no. 1827, 42:233a), agrees with the Koryŏ and Kōshō-ji editions.

30. This sentence begins the king-conversion episode (T no. 2048, 50:187a19-b14) that is nearly identical to that found in the biography of Nāgārjuna (T no. 2047, 50:185a4–28, 186a16-b7), and which appears in abbreviated form with some variations in the sections on Āryadeva (T no. 2058, 50:319b5–14) and Nāgārjuna (T no. 2058, 50:318a19–b9) in the *Dharma-Treasury Transmission*. This entire episode is missing from the Palace edition, where it is replaced with the sentence 於天竺大國之都，四衢道中敷 ("He propagated the true teaching of the Four Noble Truths throughout the cities of the great kingdom of India") (T no. 2048, 50:187n11). The Dunhuang and Kōshō-ji texts, as well as Yanshou's *Zongjing lu* (T no. 2016, 48:951b), all differ from the Koryŏ edition in the same way. For translations of this episode in Nāgārjuna's separate biography, see Chaudhuri 2008, 22–24; Corless 1995, 530–531; Li 2002c, 25–27; and Walleser (1923) 1979, 31–32.

31. The four-character phrase appearing here, *jiehua qidao* 皆化其道, reads *ganshou qihua* 感受其化 ("gratefully accepted his teaching") in the three editions of the Song, Yuan, and Ming dyanasties, as well as in the Palace edition of the text, which is puzzling because according to the preceding note in the Taishō, this entire section should be missing from the Palace edition. See T no. 2048, 50:187n12.

"I am an omniscient one," he answered.

The king[32] was amazed at this, and asked him, "It is said that there is but one omniscient through many ages. How can you prove what you say of yourself?"[33]

[Deva] replied, "If the king wishes to know the wisdom of my words, he should question me."

The king then thought to himself, "I am a lord of wisdom, a great master of debate. Even if I subdue him through inquisition, it would not add to my renown. But if only once [I appear] inferior, it would be no small matter. Yet, if I do not question him, it would indicate submission."

[The king] troubled over this for awhile [before deciding that] he had no choice but to question [Deva]: "What are the gods doing at this moment?"

Deva said, "The gods are now at war with the *asuras.*"

As the king heard these words he was like a man choking who could neither spit up nor swallow. There was no evidence with which to refute [Deva's] assertion, nor was there anything to affirm it. Before [the king] could reply, Deva again said, "This is no empty assertion made to win a debate. If the king will but wait a moment, soon there will be proof [of what I say]."

As soon as [Deva] finished speaking, shields, lances, halberds, and all sorts of weapons fell from the sky, one after another. The king remarked, "Although shields, lances, spears, and halberds are instruments of war, how can you be sure that the gods and *asuras* are battling?"

Deva said, "Putting forth empty words does not match verifying with real things."

After he spoke, the hands, feet, fingers, ears, and noses of *asuras* fell from the sky. The king then bowed his head in submission and converted to the Dharma. At the palace there were ten thousand Brahmans who all shaved off their tufts of hair and received the full precepts [to become Buddhist monks].

At that time Deva set up an elevated platform within the capital of the kingdom from which he proclaimed three points, saying:

"Of all the various saints, the Buddha is greatest.

"Of all the various teachings, the Buddhadharma is truest.

"Of all the various saviors, the Buddhist sangha is foremost.

"If there are any debate masters in the eight directions who can refute my words, I will cut off my head as admission of defeat. On what grounds do I propose this? If the principles that I establish are incorrect, then I am but a fool. The head of a fool is of no use to me; I would have no regret severing it in admission of defeat."

---

32. In the three editions of the Song, Yuan, and Ming dynasties, the next sixteen lines of the Koryŏ text (T no. 2048, 50:187a28–b14) are replaced by: "欲於王前, 而求驗試." 王即許之, 於天竺大國之都, 四衢道中敷 ("'I seek an audience with the king so that he may verify [my omniscience].' The king immediately assented and [Deva] propagated the true teaching of the Four Noble Truths throughout the cities of the great kingdom of India.") See T no. 2048, 50:187n17. The Qisha and Qianlong editions differ from the Koryŏ text in the same way.

33. *Tipo pusa zhuan*, T no. 2048, 50:187b.

When the debate masters of the eight directions heard these words, each of them came and gathered together. They made an oath, saying "If we fail then we too shall cut off our heads. We have no regrets over the heads of fools."

At this Deva said, "The Dharma that I practice is giving life by means of benevolence to all beings. Whoever is not my equal [in debate] should shave his hair and beard and become a disciple [of the Buddha]. You need not cut off your heads."

After setting this stipulation, each [debater] determined [his own] definitions and principles, and put forth his argument in any manner he wished. [Deva] responded to each in turn.[34] Those of shallow wisdom and superficial bearing were defeated with a single word. Those of deep wisdom and expansive bearing took up to two days before the logic of their arguments was [finally proven] deficient,[35] and they all submitted to cutting their hair. [The debate] went on like this day after day, as the king's household donated ten cartloads of robes and bowls per day. After three months, millions of people were converted.[36]

There was one follower of false teachings who was stubborn in his evil ways and lacked wisdom. He was ashamed at the defeat of his master, and although he apparently followed the group [of recent converts] his heart was knotted up with bitterness. With a knife clenched between his teeth, he vowed to himself, "As you have defeated me with your words, so shall I defeat you with my knife! As you have subdued me with the blade of emptiness,[37] so shall I subdue you with a real blade!"

Upon making this vow, he concealed his sharp blade and sought his chance.

[At that time,] the great men and masters of debate from all the lands had completely succumbed. Deva thereupon left [the city] and secluded himself in a forest [hermitage] where he composed the *Hundred Treatise* in twenty chapters. He also composed the *Four Hundred Treatise* in order to eliminate false views.

[Deva's] disciples were scattered about [the forest] engaged in seated *dhyāna* meditation under the trees. As Deva arose from *dhyāna* to take a walk,[38] the Brahman disciple came to him brandishing a knife. He blocked

---

34. This interpretation of *chouzuo* 酬酢 is based on Luo 1987–1995, 5897, which provides a reference to the *Yi jing* in which it means "to answer questions" or "to deal with," as opposed to its modern meaning of "social intercourse."

35. The Dunhuang text ends here.

36. Here Yanshou ends his retelling of the Deva biography and begins his brief commentary in which he extols the virtue of Deva's forthright character, with which he was able move the gods—as exemplified by the episode in which he removed the eye of Maheśvara (T no. 2016, 48:951b).

37. *Tipo pusa zhuan*, T no. 2048, 50:187c.

38. Reading *qi* 起 for *jue* 覺, as in all editions except the Koryŏ; see T no. 2048, 50:187n27. *Jingxing* 經行 refers to breaks taken during periods of seated meditation in which the practitioner takes a walk to eliminate drowsiness. It could also mean walking meditation. See Muller 1995– (s.v. "*jingxing*").

[Deva's] path, saying, "Since you cut my master with your words, how would you feel if I cut your belly with my blade?!"

With that he stabbed [Deva] with his knife, spilling his five viscera out onto the ground. As his life was coming to an end, he felt pity for this foolish murderer and told him, "I have three robes and bowls near my seat. You may take them. Make haste up the mountain and go with caution. Do not come down to the well-traveled paths. Those of my disciples who have not yet attained the forbearance of [non-arising] dharmas[39] will surely seize you or hand you over to the magistrate. The king will have you immediately imprisoned. You have not yet attained the benefit of the Dharma, so you cherish your bodily form most passionately and value your name second only to this. From bodily form and name arise the aggregate of calamities, and the conflicts among the masses are born. Body[40] and name are the roots of great evil. Foolish men do not listen [to this truth] and are corrupted by baseless views. They value what is of no value, and do not value what should be valued. Is this not pitiable? Having received the Dharma bequeathed by the Buddha, I will never again be like this. I reflect upon those such as yourself, who are deceived by their frenzied minds and burned by the poison of malice. There will be no end to the retribution for their misdeeds, and they weep and wail as they suffer this. One who suffers such [retribution] is truly not a master of himself; one who commits such [evil deeds] is truly without humanity.[41] For those miserable ones who lack humanity and self-mastery, whoever beseeches them with the truth can never finally reach them. Those who are not awakened to this are thrown into confusion by their frenzied minds, spun around by perverted views. With the mind being thus attached, there is a self and there are persons, there is suffering and there is joy. The origination of suffering and joy depends on attachment [stemming from] contact [between consciousness and external objects]. Once liberated from attachment, then there is no dependence. Without dependence there is no suffering, and without suffering there is no joy. When both suffering and joy are absent, this is tranquility (i.e., nirvāṇa)."

After he finished speaking, the first of his disciples to arrive sobbed loudly until he lost his voice. The other disciples [came running] one by one from out of the forest and gathered around [where Deva lay]. Those who had not yet attained the forbearance of [non-arising] dharmas wept

39. *Faren* 法忍, as the text has here, is an abbreviation of *wusheng faren* 無生法忍 (as explained, e.g., in the *Da zhidu lun* 大智度論 [*Mahāprajñāpāramitāśāstra*], T no. 1509, 25:676a). *Faren* is the counterpart of *shengren* 生忍 (forbearance for sentient beings), which are together termed the "two endurances" or "two forbearances" (*erren* 二忍); cf. Ciyi 1988–1989, 1:196b–c. As *faren* is insight into the nature of dharmas and *shengren* is empathy toward all living things, these "endurances" represent the standard Buddhist dichotomy of wisdom and compassion, *prajñā* and *upāya*.

40. Twelve characters (之與名患累出焉眾釁生焉身) are missing here from the Palace edition of the text; see T no. 2048, 50:187n32. The Kōshō-ji manuscript differs in the same way.

41. The remainder of this paragraph is missing from Chaudhuri's translation.

with shock and fright, as they beat their chests and knocked their heads upon the ground.[42] "What calamity! What atrocity! Who has taken our master like this?!" Some of them rushed away in a frenzy to hunt down [the murderer] and cut him off along the main roads. They all split up into groups and yelled out in pursuit of him, their cries clamoring into the deep, dark valleys.

At this Deva admonished them, saying, "[According to] the truth of all dharmas, for whom is there calamity and atrocity? Who is sliced and severed? [According to] the truth of all dharmas, there is no one who suffers and no one who harms. Who is friend and who is foe? Who despoils and who injures? You are deluded by the poison of ignorance. With this error clouding your perception, and with your weeping and wailing, you sow the seeds of bad karma. This [murderer has only] damaged [his own] karmic lot; he has not injured me. You should reflect upon this, and take care not[43] to hunt the mad with madness, nor grieve over the miserable in misery."

Thereupon, without any worries or regrets [Deva] discarded his bodily form—like the husk of a cicada—and departed.

Because he took out his eye and gave it to the god, he was missing one eye. At that time people called him Kāṇadeva [meaning "one-eyed god"].

提婆菩薩傳

姚秦三藏鳩摩羅什譯

提婆菩薩者, 南天竺人, 龍樹菩薩弟子, 婆羅門種也. 博識淵攬, 才辯絕倫. 擅名天竺, 為諸國所推. 賾探胸懷, 既無所愧, 以為所不盡者, 唯以人不信用其言為憂.

其國中有大天神, 鑄黃金像之座, 身長二丈, 號曰大自在天. 人有求願, 能令現世如意. 提婆詣廟, 求入拜見. 主廟者言, "天像至神, 人有見者, 既不敢正視, 又令人退後失守百日. 汝但詣問求願, 何須見耶?" 提婆言, "若神必能, 如汝所說, 乃但令我見之. 若不如是, 豈是吾之所欲見耶?" 時人奇其志氣, 伏其明正. 追入廟者, 數千萬人. 提婆既入於廟, 天像搖動其眼, 怒目視之. 提婆問, "天神則神矣, 何其小也? 當以威靈感人, 智德伏物, 而假黃金以自多, 動頗梨以熒惑. 非所望也."

即便登梯, 鑿出其眼. 時諸觀者, 咸有疑意, "大自在天, 何為一小婆羅門所困? 將無名過其實, 理屈其辭也?" 提婆曉眾人言, "神明遠大, 故以近事試我. 我得其心, 故登金聚, 出頗梨, 令汝等知, 神不假質, 精不託[44]形. 吾既不慢, 神亦不辱也." 言已而出. 即以其夜, 求諸供備. 明日清旦, 敬祠天神.

提婆先名既重, 加以智參神契, 其所發言, 聲之所及, 無不響應. 一夜之中, 供具精饌, 有物必備. 大自在天, 貫一肉形, 高數四丈, 左眼枯涸, 而來在坐. 遍觀供饌, 歎未曾

---

42. The four-character phrase appearing here in the Koryŏ and Kōshō-ji editions is *fuxiong koudi* 拊[曷-日]扣地. In all other editions, *fuxiong* 撫胸 replaces *fuxiong* 拊[曷-日] (T no. 2048, 50:187n37), and *koudi* 叩地 was the form of the latter compound in the manuscript that Huilin 慧琳 (737–820) had before him when compiling his *Yiqiejing yinyi* 一切經音義 (783–807). Huilin wrote that *kou* 叩 often appeared written as *kou* 扣, and *fuxiong* 撫胸 (cf. Luo 1987–1995, 3752) had roughly the same meaning as *fuxiong* 拊[曷-日], according to Huilin's gloss of the latter term (T no. 2128, 54:805a).

43. *Tipo pusa zhuan*, T no. 2048, 50:188a.

44. *Tipo pusa zhuan*, T no. 2048, 50:187a.

有. 嘉其德力, 能有所致. 而告之言, "汝得我心, 人得我形. 汝以心供, 人以質饋. 知而敬我者汝, 畏而誣我者人. 汝所供饌, 盡善盡美矣. 唯無我之所須. 能以見與者, 真上施也. 提婆言, "神鑑我心, 唯命是從." 神言, "我所乏者, 左眼. 能施我者, 便可出之" 提婆言, "敬如天命!" 即以左手, 出眼與之. 天神力故, 出而隨生. 索之不已, 從旦終朝, 出眼數萬. 天神讚曰, "善哉摩納, 真上施也! 欲求何願, 必如汝意." 提婆言, "我稟明於心, 不假外也. 唯恨悠悠童矇, 不知信受我言. 神賜我願, 必當令我言不虛設. 唯此為請, 他無所須." 神言, "必如所願."

於是而退, 詣龍樹菩薩, 受出家法. 剃頭法服, 周遊揚化.

南天竺王, 總御諸國, 信用邪道. 沙門釋子, 一不得見. 國人遠近, 皆化其道. 提婆念曰, "樹不伐本, 則條不傾; 人主不化, 則道不行." 其國政法: 王家出錢, 雇人宿衛. 提婆乃應募為其將. 荷戟前驅, 整行伍, 勒部曲. 威不嚴而令行, 德不彰而物樂隨. 王甚喜之, 而問是何人. 侍者答言, "此人應募, 既不食廩, 又不取錢. 而其在事, 恭謹閑習如此. 不知其意, 何求何欲." 王召而問之, "汝是何人?" 答言, "我是一切智人." 王大驚愕, 而問之言, "一切智人, 曠代一有. 汝自言是, 何以[45] 驗之?" 答言, "欲知智在說, 王當見問." 王即自念, "我為智主, 大論議師, 問之能屈, 猶不足名. 一旦不如, 此非小事. 若其不問, 便是一屈." 持疑良久, 不得已而問, "天今何為耶?" 提婆言, "天今與阿修羅戰." 王得此言, 譬如人噎, 既不得吐, 又不得咽. 欲非其言, 復無以證之. 欲是其事, 無事可明. 未言之間, 提婆復言, "此非虛論, 求勝之言. 王小待, 須臾有驗." 言訖, 空中便有干戈來下, 長戟短兵, 相係而落. 王言, "干戈矛戟, 雖是戰器, 汝何必知, 是天與阿修羅戰?" 提婆言, "構之虛言, 不如校以實事." 言已, 阿修羅手足指及其耳鼻, 從空而下. 王乃稽首, 伏其法化. 殿上有萬婆羅門, 皆棄其束髮, 受成就戒.

是時提婆, 於王都中建高座, 立三論. 言, "一切諸聖中, 佛聖最第一; 一切諸法中, 佛法正第一; 一切救世中, 佛僧為第一. 八方諸論士, 有能壞此語者, 我當斬首, 以謝其屈. 所以者何? 立理不明, 是為愚癡. 愚癡之頭, 非我所須. 斬以謝屈, 甚不惜也." 八方論士, 既聞此言亦各來集. 而立誓言, "我等不如, 亦當斬首. 愚癡之頭, 亦所不惜." 提婆言, "我所修法, 仁活萬物. 要不如者, 當剃汝鬚髮, 以為弟子, 不須斬首也." 立此要已, 各撰名理, 建無方論, 而與酬酢. 智淺情短者, 一言便屈; 智深情長者, 遠至二日. 則辭理俱匱, 即皆下髮. 如是日日, 王家日送, 十車衣鉢. 終竟三月, 度百餘萬人.

有一邪道弟子, 凶頑無智. 恥其師屈形, 雖隨眾, 心結怨忿, 嚙刀自誓, "汝以口勝伏我, 我當以刀勝伏汝! 汝以空刀困[46] 我, 我以實刀困汝!" 作是誓已, 挾一利刀, 伺求其便.

諸方論士, 英傑都盡. 提婆於是, 出就閑林, 造百論二十品, 又造四百論, 以破邪見. 其諸弟子, 各各散諸樹下, 坐禪思惟. 提婆從禪覺經行, 婆羅門弟子來到其邊, 執刀窮之曰, "汝以口破我師, 何如我以刀破汝腹?" 即以刀決之, 五藏委地. 命未絕間, 愍此愚賊, 而告之曰, "吾有三衣鉢釪, 在吾坐處, 汝可取之. 急上山去, 慎勿下就平道. 我諸弟子, 未得法忍者, 必當捉汝. 或當相得, 送汝於官. 王便困汝, 汝未得法利. 惜身情重, 惜名次之. 身之與名, 患累出焉, 眾釁生焉. 身名者, 乃是大患之本也. 愚人無聞, 為妄見所侵. 惜其所不惜, 而不惜所應惜. 不亦哀哉? 吾蒙佛之遺法, 不復爾也. 但念汝等, 為狂心所欺, 忿毒所燒, 罪報未已, 號泣受之. 受之者實自無主, 為之者實自無人. 無人無主哀酷者, 誰以實求之, 實不可得. 未悟此者, 為狂心所惑, 顛倒所迴. 見得心著, 而有我有人, 有苦有樂. 苦樂之來, 但依觸著. 解著則無依, 無依則無苦, 無苦則無樂, 苦樂既無, 則幾乎息矣."

說此語已, 弟子先來者, 失聲大喚. 門人各各, 從林樹間集, 未得法忍者, 驚怖號咷, 拊丐扣地, "冤哉酷哉! 誰取我師乃如是者?!" 或有狂突奔走, 追截要路. 共相分部, 號

45. *Tipo pusa zhuan*, T no. 2048, 50:187b.
46. *Tipo pusa zhuan*, T no. 2048, 50:187c.

叫追之, 聲聒幽谷. 提婆誨諸人言, "諸法之實, 誰冤誰酷, 誰割誰截? 諸法之實, 實無受者, 亦無害者. 誰親誰怨, 誰賊誰害? 汝為癡毒所欺, 妄生著見而大號咷, 種不善業. 彼人所害, 害諸業報, 非害我也. 汝等思之, 慎無[47] 以狂追狂, 以哀悲哀也." 於是放身, 脫然無矜, 遂蟬蛻而去.

初出眼與神故, 遂無一眼. 時人號曰, 迦那提婆也.

47. *Tipo pusa zhuan*, T no. 2048, 50:188a.

Appendix 3

The Ritual Manuals of Aśvaghoṣa Bodhisattva

1. Aśvaghoṣa's *Ritual Instructions*

The following translation of the *Maming pusa dashenli wubiyanfa niansong guiyi* 馬鳴菩薩大神力無比驗法念誦儀軌 is based upon the Taishō edition of the text, number 1166, volume 20. I further consulted the editions in the *Dainippon kōtei shukusatsu daizōkyō* 大日本校訂縮刷大藏經 (Great Japanese Revised Small-Print Edition of the Buddhist Canon, Himitsu bu 祕密部 [Esoteric section], 2:58), and the *Dainippon zokuzōkyō* 大日本續藏經 (Great Japanese Edition of the Buddhist Canon, Continued, Z 1:3:2:141c–d), which aside from a few typographical variants are identical to the Taishō text. I have found no complete translation of this text in any language. Iyanaga Nobumi 彌永信美 and Mochizuki Shinkō 望月信亨 translate excerpts of it into Japanese, and brief content summaries are provided by Endo Yujun 遠藤純祐, Ono Gemmyō 小野玄妙, and Xiao Dengfu 蕭登福, and in the *Mikkyō daijiten* 密教大辭典.[1] The only English discussion I have seen of this text is Raoul Birnbaum's (1983, 112–114), where he offers a few preliminary observations in connection with a Japanese iconographic drawing of Aśvaghoṣa dating to the thirteenth or fourteenth century.

Ritual Instructions for the Recitation of the Incomparably Efficacious Method of the Divine Power of Aśvaghoṣa Bodhisattva

A translation respectfully presented by Vajrabodhi by imperial decree.[2]

Once upon a time, Śākyamuni the Thus-Come One sat beneath the Bodhi tree amidst a great assembly. At that time Aśvaghoṣa Bodhisattva came before the Buddha and said, "I wish to speak my sublime Buddhadharma so that come the Semblance and Final [Dharma periods], the masses of the low and destitute and the myriad sentient beings who are naked will be clothed. Having passed countless *kalpas* treading the path of the bodhisattva,

1. See Iyanaga 2002, 524; Mochizuki 1954–1963, 5:4863; Endo 2001; Ono 1933–1936, 11:2b; Xiao 1994, 201; and Mikkyō Daijiten Saikan Iinkai 1979, 3:2153–2154.

2. *Maming pusa dashenli wubiyanfa niansong guiyi*, T no. 1166, 20:674c.

the great spirit-spell that I have obtained is of surpassing power and virtue. Its power within [the realm of] form[3] is beyond compare, and it is capable of accomplishing the most excellent deeds in the world. It cannot be hindered."

The Buddha then smiled and said to Aśvaghoṣa Bodhisattva, "Excellent, brave sir! Quickly, speak, speak!"

"Yes, the World-Honored One has such thoughts of pity," [replied Aśvaghoṣa,] "I will follow his words."

He joined his palms together joyously and from his mouth issued forth a great ray of light. Spoken from within the light was this spirit-spell:

"*Nang-mo-san-man-duo-mei-ta-na-jia-jia-ma-ming-chi-li-zha-luo-qu-zha-luo-qu-sha-fu-he.*"

If one wishes to receive and maintain this method, one must first follow a master, exhaust one's wealth making generous offerings, and receive and practice the *mudrā* [later described] and mantra [just recited]. Then paint an image of the bodhisattva. His body appears in the color of white flesh. His palms are joined together as he sits upon a white lotus flower, which is mounted upon a white horse. He is wearing white clothing, and a necklace of precious stones adorns his body. Upon his head he wears a floral crown, and his right leg is pendent.

After painting the image, smear the altar [with ox dung?] and begin [the following rite] from the third day of the third month. Face east toward the image, which is to face west, and make offerings of butter lamps and all other sorts of excellent offerings for twenty-eight days. Up until the one-hundredth day, one must cleanse and purify oneself. For a *bhikṣu* [monk], when it comes to the kindness of the master who has transmitted this method for the benefit of the living, he must not be delinquent in this timing.

[In this way,] I will always shine great rays of light upon the household and kingdom of the *dāna*[*pati*] [donor].[4] He or she will obtain all kinds of rich brocades, patterned silks, money, firm silks, and fine woven silks. Treasures of gold will pile up like a mountain for all the world to enjoy!

If there is but one person in a kingdom who puts into practice my original vow, all the people of the entire kingdom will be as said before. Completely perfecting wealth and adornments, not a single person will be poor or have sickness. My original vow is that all will be adorned with riches.

If this method attains to a mind of doubt, which gives rise to thoughts of disbelief, and the vows of one generation are not realized, then the fruits of future generations will be uncertain. It is best to take refuge in this method with a feeling of resolution, and not shun the virtue that has been trans-

3. *Seli* 色力 is one of the sixteen great powers of the bodhisattva. It is his ability to eclipse the elegance of gods and kings with the august bearing of his physical appearance. See Ciyi 1988–1989, 1:379b–c; and Muller 1995– (s.v. "*shiliu dali* 十六大力"). However, since *seli* is here used to describe a spirit-spell, it would appear to carry less emphasis on physical appearance and more on efficacy in the phenomenal realm.

4. *Maming pusa dashenli wubiyanfa niansong guiyi*, T no. 1166, 20:675a.

mitted. [Thus] I shall, continuously day after day, hold to this thought of divine protection:[5] I will fill the entire world with the profit and riches of the utmost sublime bliss.

If one seeks that of which I have spoken, one must fix one's mind upon this original vow. Standing before and facing the precious platform, form [the following] *mudrā* and recite [the above mantra]. Bend the middle finger and ring finger of the left hand, and with the thumb press these two fingernails [against the palm]. Extend the forefinger and pinky finger and place [the hand] upon the heart. With the right hand [count] the recitations of the mantra with a rosary.[6] This is called the Jade-Bracelet-All-Vow-Fulfilling *mudrā*.

In the age of the Final [Dharma], ignorant [people] of shallow learning will be unable to record this *mudrā* in written words. Among ten thousand people ten will be chosen, and among ten people one will be chosen and permitted [to receive the transmission of this teaching].

Instructions for the Rites for Perfect Silkworm Cultivation[7]

馬鳴菩薩大神力無比驗法念誦軌儀[8]
金剛智奉　詔譯

曩日釋迦如來, 菩提樹下, 坐大眾集會中. 時馬鳴菩薩, 前白佛言, "欲說我莊嚴佛法, 及為成, 像末貧窮下賤, 裸形眾生有情, 衣服. 歷無數劫, 行菩薩行. 所得大神咒, 有大威德. 色力無比, 能於世間, 行殊勝事. 無能礙罣."

時即佛微笑, 告馬鳴菩薩言, "善哉, 大丈夫! 汝速可說可說."

"唯然世尊愍念, 我聽說."

合掌歡喜, 從口中放大光明, 說光中神咒曰:

"曩謨三曼多沒他那迦迦馬鳴吃哩吒囉佉吒囉佉莎縛訶"

若欲受持此法, 先從師, 盡財利布施供給, 受習印契真言. 則畫作菩薩像. 色相白肉色, 而合掌, 坐白蓮華, 乘白馬, 著白色衣, 以瓔珞莊嚴身, 首戴花冠, 垂右足.

畫像了泥壇. 始自三月三日. 東面像向西, 以種種廣大供具, 蘇乳蘇燈供養, 二十八日. 乃至百日, 須清淨潔淨. 比丘, 及傳法利生之師恩, 不已失時.

我常檀[9] 那家及國土, 放大光明. 成就錦繡羅綿財絹縺緻之類. 金寶積如山岳, 世間受用咨(矣).

5. *Jiahu* 加護 indicates the power of buddhas and bodhisattvas to aid and protect sentient beings. See Mochizuki 1954–1963, 1:457b–c; and Nakamura 1981, 146a.

6. *Shuzhu* 數珠, literally "counting beads," were and are often used to keep track of the number of scripture, mantra, or Buddha-name recitations. The beads, often numbering 108, were placed along a string and worn as a necklace or wrapped around the wrist, and passed between the thumb and forefinger, bead by bead, with each completed recitation. For a useful discussion of the use of these "rosaries" in India and China, see Kieschnick 2003, 116–138.

7. This last line is separated from the rest of the text in the *Zokuzōkyō* and *Shukusatsu* editions, and so, following Birnbaum (1983, 112), I treat it as an alternate title for the text.

8. *Maming pusa dashenli wubiyanfa niansong guiyi*, T no. 1166, 20:674c.

9. *Maming pusa dashenli wubiyanfa niansong guiyi*, T no. 1166, 20:675a.

若有一國一人，修行我本誓故，普天率土，民家皆悉如前所說．財利莊嚴具成就，一人莫乏有患．我本願，皆悉為莊嚴財寶．

於若法至疑惑之心，發起不信之念，不成就一世之願故，後世之果不定．好好以堅固之情歸於法，非忌傳授之德．我必日日時時，加護念：圓滿世間，第一妙樂之財利．

如向所說，係念本誓．向寶壇前，作契印念誦．屈左中指無名指，以大母指押彼二指甲．舒頭指及小指，安心上．右手把數珠念真言．此名玉環成就一切所願印．此契印，末代愚學之妄，不可記於文字．萬人中撰十人，十人之中撰一人，許可(矣)."

成就蠶養儀軌

2. Aśvaghoṣa's *Siddhī Recitation*

The following translation of the *Maming pusa chengjiu xidi niansong* 馬鳴菩薩成就悉地念誦 is based upon the *Dainippon zokuzōkyō* edition of the text (Z 1:3:5:416b–d). I have not found this text reprinted in any other collection, nor seen it translated into any language. It receives only the briefest of content summaries in a few Chinese and Japanese scholarly works.[10] Birnbaum notes in passing that the *Byakuhōkushō* 白寶口抄 refers to a ritual manual attributed to Amoghavajra that was said to have been brought to Japan by Kibi no Makibi.[11] The *Siddhī Recitation* is undoubtedly this text, although its current contents do not always match its citations in the *Byakuhōkushō*.

The Perfect Siddhī Recitation of Aśvaghoṣa Bodhisattva, in one scroll (Brought [to Japan] by Grand Minister Kibi [no Makibi])

Translated by imperial decree, respectfully submitted by the Śramaṇa of the Threefold-Canon, Da Guangzhi (Great Broad Wisdom) Amoghavajra of Daxingshan si (Great Arising of Goodness Monastery).

At one time the bodhisattva addressed the Buddha saying, "I have the most profound *dhāraṇī* of great divine power. In order to liberate the various sentient beings in the defiled world of the coming Final Dharma [period], I wish to speak this spirit-spell, with the Buddha's approval."

At that time the world-honored Buddha praised the bodhisattva saying, "Excellent! Excellent! All the buddhas approve, all the bodhisattvas and all the gods are greatly pleased—quickly, speak!"

10. See Mikkyō Daijiten Saikan Iinkai 1979, 3:2154a; Mochizuki 1954–1963, 5:4863; Ono 1933–1936, 11:2a; and Xiao 1994, 416–417.

11. The *Byakuhōkushō* presents a list of sources on Aśvaghoṣa, beginning with the *Ritual Instructions* attributed to Vajrabodhi. It then lists "a separate text of ritual instructions, some say that Amoghavajra translated it and Grand Minister Kibi [no Makibi] brought it [to Japan]; the *Mahāmāyā sūtra*, etc." *Byakuhōkushō* 白寶口抄, T no. 3119, 92 (*Zuzō* supplement vol. 7): 255a: 別本儀軌，或云不空譯，吉備大臣比來本也；摩訶摩耶經，等. Birnbaum (1983, 112) takes the string of characters from Kibi 吉備 to *kyō* 經 to be one long title for the "separate text of ritual instructions" attributed to Amoghavajra.

The bodhisattva then arose from his seat, clasped his palms together and bowed his head. He jumped up joyously and circumambulated the Buddha three times before withdrawing to seat himself in front of and facing the Buddha. He then spoke this great spirit-spell:

"*Nang-mo-san-man-tuo-mei-tuo-nan-jia-fu-ri-luo* (combine [these last] two [phonemes]) *fu-duo-nang-ou-du-ming*(?)*-qi-li* (combine [these last] two [phonemes]) *po-he*."

At that time, after this sublime mantra was spoken, one billion worlds shook in six ways, the heavens rained down *māndārava* [red heavenly] flowers, and the seven jewels sprung forth from the earth. All the myriad sentient beings obtained the *siddhīs*, money and silks, rich brocades, and treasures of gold piled up like mountain peaks. [People of] the world regard these as the most wondrous [treasures].

If there is a good man or good woman who is either a householder or a renunciant, who receives and upholds but one word of this sublime mantra, and my name passes his or her ear but once, then the retribution of utmost destitution [accumulated] through rebirth after rebirth will be eliminated. In an instant this world and the world beyond will be endowed with glorious joyousness and perfectly fulfilled.

[Also] make offerings to the Three Jewels and the six relations[12] for nine generations, and perform charity even to all the beggars, then everything will be as you wish.

If you wish to receive and uphold this method, first paint an image of the bodhisattva. His body has six arms and two protuberances (?),[13] and is red in color. He sits upon a lotus flower and white horse, and surrounding him are six great attendants.

After painting the bodhisattva, receive transmission of this mantra from a master. First, donate to this master your rich brocades, your immaculate clothes, and even the riches held by your wives, children, and retinue. I will thereupon display my pleasure in the form of all the myriad treasures, and bestow kindness in the form of the seven jewels.

As for people who do not believe in this vow, do not allow them to hear it and do not speak of it to them, lest the path of practice taken be rendered inefficacious. This sublime mantra is worth countless Buddha-merits.

---

12. There are various definitions of the six relations (*liuqin* 六親). Often included are father, mother, older siblings, younger siblings, husband, wife, and children. See Muller 1995– (s.v. "*liuqin*").

13. Here reading *shen* 腎 with the *rou* 肉 radical rather than with the more common *yue* 月 radical (following the *Hanyu da cidian* radical classification of these characters), since *yue*, meaning "kidney(s)" or "testicle(s)," makes no sense here. The *Asabashō* 阿娑縛抄 (T no. 3190, 94 [*Zuzō* supplement vol. 9]: 297a); *Bessonzakki* 別尊雜記 (T no. 3007, 88 [*Zuzō* supplement vol. 3]: 310c); and *Byakuhōkushō* (T no. 3119, 92 [*Zuzō* supplement vol. 7]: 256c) all quote the *Siddhī Recitation* as having *bi* 臂 (arm) here rather than *shen*, in which case it would read something like, "his body has six-armed and also two-armed [forms]."

If a person is sincere, making offerings to and revering the yogi like a Buddha, receiving and upholding this venerable and sublime verse, he or she will obtain great merit, as said before.

If kings, great ministers, and the various rulers, at times when the living things upon their lands are completely withered, the harvest of the five grains is meager, the silkworms do not produce rich brocades, and money and silks are lacking, put this method into practice for three months out of the year—the third day of the third month, the fifth day of the fifth month, and the ninth day of the ninth month—scattering about the myriad varieties of sublime flowers and making offerings of all sorts of food and drink, the five grains will achieve a rich harvest of ten thousand fruits, and all the people of their kingdoms will be completely fulfilled with the joy of heavenly beings.

The method of [setting up the ritual] altar [is thus]:

It measures two-and-a-half cubits.[14] Use ox dung to smear [around the altar]; mix various kinds of choice incense together with mud and smear [the mixture] upon the four corners of auspicious vessels. Place these at each of the ten directions and in them burn *pidiluo* 毗底羅[15] incense. If this incense is not burned, the [ritual] method will not be complete. [If] the offerings that have been set up are used in accordance with a sincere mind, the bodhisattva will come himself without being summoned to receive them and verify the sincerity of the donor. [The bodhisattva] will cause his or her prayers to be fulfilled.

If there is a man or a woman of faith, no matter whether he or she is pure or impure, who every day in the early morning receives and upholds this sublime mantra 108 times, and eulogizes the bodhisattva seven times, recitation never being far from his or her person, then the manifestations of recompense for the myriad actions in this world, government office, fortune, and longevity will be attained as he or she wishes.

Also, [the accompanying] *mudrā* is said [to be formed by] clasping the ten fingers [of both hands], with the right pushing the left wrist. Separate them from one another and with this *mudrā* seal the five parts of the body.[16] Because of this binding seal and the power of reciting the mantra, the retribution for immeasurable crimes, the grave injury caused by curses of loathing, evil demons and *rākśasas* [malignant spirits], spirits of the dead and goblins, and all of the various calamities will be completely expurgated. You will obtain countless fortunes, your present life will be immeasurably happy, and in a later life you will be reborn in [the land of] utmost bliss.

---

14. *Zhou* 肘 is a translation of the Sanskrit *hasta* or *hastaka*, which is an ancient Indian unit of length. It is roughly equivalent to an arm's length from the elbow to the tip of the middle finger. See Ciyi 1988–1989, 3:2988c–2989a; Luo 1987–1995, 3877; Mochizuki 1954–1963, 1:153a–b; and Nakamura 1981, 961c.

15. I have been unable to locate this transliteration (or logical variants) in any lexicon or other primary text.

16. *Wuchu* 五處 often indicates the forehead, left and right shoulders, heart, and throat. See Muller 1995– (s.v. "*wuchu jiachi* 五處加持"); and Strickmann 2002, 319n58.

With careful attention to sequence, one can know, receive and practice the great numinous efficacy and expeditious magic of this talisman.[17]

One proofreading completed.

The colophon bears the Kōwa (1099–1103), Tennin (1108–1109), Daiji (1126–1130), and Hoen (1135–1140) reign titles. Because of bookworm damage, some characters were not clearly discernable, so they have been omitted.

Copied from the text of the Kōzan-ji (Lofty Mountain Monastery) canon.

27th day of the seventh month of the *kōshi* year of the Bunka reign period (1804).

One proofreading completed.

Jijun

馬鳴菩薩成就悉地念誦一卷

(吉備大臣持來)

大興善寺三藏沙門大廣智不空奉 詔譯

爾時, 菩薩白佛言, "我有大神力極祕密陀羅尼, 為度脫當來末法, 雜染世界眾生, 欲說是神咒, 佛聽許."

爾時, 佛世尊讚菩薩言, "善哉! 善哉! 汝諸佛聽許, 諸菩薩, 諸天皆悉以隨喜. 速疾可說."

即菩薩從座而起, 合掌低頭, 踊躍歡喜, 右遶佛三匝, 退坐一面佛前, 即說大神咒曰:

"曩莫三曼馱沒馱喃迦縛日羅 (二合) 縛多曩吽篤[艸/鳴]訖哩 (二合) 婆呵"

爾時, 說妙真言已, 三千大千世界, 六種震動, 天雨曼荼羅華, 地涌出七寶. 一切眾生獲得悉地, 財綿[18] 錦繡金寶, 種[19] 如山岳. 世間甚以為希有.

若有在家出家, 善男善女, 受持是妙真言之中一字, 及我名一經於耳, 消滅生生世世極貧窮果報. 速疾世間出世間, 榮華樂具, 滿足成就.

供養三寶, 及六親九族, 乃至一切乞[曷-曰]給施, 莫不如意.

若欲受持此法, 先畫菩薩像. 其形六臂, 又二臂色紅, 蓮華白馬為座, 圍遶六大使者.

菩薩畫已, 從師傳授真言. 先錦繡淨潔衣服, 乃至妻子眷屬, 所持財寶, 用施與師. 我即歡喜以一切寶, 施恩以七寶.

若是誓願, 不信為人, 不可令聞, 不可說假, 令受習修道, 不感應.

斯妙真言價值無央數佛功德.

若發信心, 供養恭敬, 瑜伽者如佛, 敬妙句受持之人, 得大功德, 如前所說.

若有國王大臣及諸小國王, 國土萬物枯盡, 五穀不豐登, 又蠶子不生錦繡, 財綿乏少時, 年中三箇月, 修行是法所謂, 三月三日, 五日[20] 五日, 九月九日, 種種妙華散, 種種餚[食+善]飲食用供養, 五穀成就萬[艸/果]豐登, 國民皆悉天上人中所有樂具滿足.

其壇法, 量二肘半, 用牛糞塗, 種種名香, 和泥塗賢瓶四角, 置十方, 毗底羅香燒. 不燒是香, 不成就法. 所設供具, 用至其信心, 不喚菩薩, 自來至納受證誠, 令滿足施主所求願.

---

17. Xiao (1994, 417) takes this statement to indicate that a separate diagram of a talisman was originally appended to the text, although it has gone missing from the extant manuscript. Another possible interpretation is that the text itself was considered talismanic.

18. *Zoku zōkyō* editors amend to *bo* 帛.

19. *Zoku zōkyō* editors amend to *ji* 積, which I have followed in translation.

20. Read *yue* 月.

若有信男信女, 不論淨不淨, 日日晨朝時, 受持妙真言一百八遍, 并菩薩讚歎七遍, 稱誦不離身體, 世間諸事報示, 又官位福壽, 如意成就.

又印相說, 十指交絞, 右押左腕, 相離以印, 印五處. 由結印誦, 真言力故, 滅除無量罪報, 厭眉咒咀, 惡鬼羅刹, 亡靈魑魅之毒害, 一切災難. 得無量福, 現世有無量快樂, 後生往生極樂.

子細次第, 可見又可受習, 符書大靈, 驗速疾術.

一校了

奥書有康和天仁大治保延年號. 蠹損文字不分明, 故略之

以高山寺藏本寫得畢

文化甲子七月二十七日　　一校了　　慈順

Bibliography

A list of abbreviations used in the bibliography and citations appears at the beginning of this book.

Primary Sources

Chinese Texts Attributed to Aśvaghoṣa, Nāgārjuna, and Āryadeva (Deva)

Bai lun 百論 (*Śata[ka]śāstra*). Verse attributed to Deva, commentary by a certain Vasu Bodhisattva; trans. Kumārajīva (344–413 or 350–409) in 402, revised in 404. T no. 1569, 30.

Baizi lun 百字論 (*Akṣaraśataka[vṛtti]*). Attributed to Deva; trans. Bodhiruci (fl. 508–535). T no. 1572, 30.

Baoxing wang zheng lun 寶行王正論 (*Ratnāvalī*). Attributed to Nāgārjuna; trans. Paramārtha (499–569). T no. 1656, 32.

Bore deng lun shi 般若燈論釋 (*Prajñāpradīpa*). Attributed to Nāgārjuna; trans. Prabhākaramitra (564–633). T no. 1566, 30.

Chimingzang yuqie dajiao Zunna pusa daming chengjiu yigui jing 持明藏瑜伽大教尊那菩薩大明成就儀軌經. Attributed to Nāgārjuna; trans. Dharmabhadra (d. 1001) ca. 989–999. T no. 1169, 20.

Dasheng ershisong lun 大乘二十頌論 (*Mahāyānaviṁśikā*). Attributed to Nāgārjuna; trans. Dānapāla (fl. 980–1017). T no. 1576, 30.

Dasheng guang bailun shi lun 大乘廣百論釋論 (Commentary by Dharmapāla on Deva's *Catuḥśatikā*). Trans. Xuanzang 玄奘 (602–664) in 650. T no. 1571, 30.

Dasheng poyou lun 大乘破有論 (*Mahāyānabhavabhedaśāstra*). Attributed to Nāgārjuna; trans. Dānapāla (fl. 980–1017). T no. 1574, 30.

Dasheng qixin lun 大乘起信論. Attributed to Aśvaghoṣa; translation attributed to Paramārtha (499–569) in ca. 550. T no. 1666, 32.

Dasheng qixin lun 大乘起信論. Attributed to Aśvaghoṣa; translation attributed to Śikṣānanda (652–710) ca. 700. T no. 1667, 32.

Da zhangfu lun 大丈夫論 (*Mahāpurusaśāstra*). Attributed to Deva; trans. Daotai 道泰 (fl. ca. 437–439). T no. 1577, 30.

Da zhidu lun 大智度論 (*Mahāprajñāpāramitāśāstra*). Attributed to Nāgārjuna; trans. Kumārajīva (344–413 or 350–409) in 406. T no. 1509, 25.

Da zhuangyan jing lun 大莊嚴經論 (*Kalpanāmaṇḍitikā* or *Sūtrālaṃkāraśāstra*). Attributed to Aśvaghoṣa; translation attributed to Kumārajīva (344–413 or 350–409). T no. 201, 4.

Dazong di xuanwen benlun 大宗地玄文本論. Attributed to Aśvaghoṣa; translation attributed to Paramārtha (599–569). T no. 1669, 32.

Fo suo xing zan 佛所行讚 (*Buddhacarita*). Attributed to Aśvaghoṣa; translation attributed to Dharmakṣema (385–433) ca. 414–421. T no. 192, 4.

Fu gai zhengxing suo ji jing 福蓋正行所集經. Attributed to Nāgārjuna; trans. Richeng 日稱 (1017–after 1073) after 1064. T no. 1671, 32.

Guang bailun ben 廣百論本 (*Catuḥśatikāśāstrakārikā*). Attributed to Deva; trans. Xuanzang 玄奘 (602–664) in 647 or 650. T no. 1570, 30.

Guangda fayuan song 廣大發願頌 (*Mahāpraṇidhānotpādagāthā*). Attributed to Nāgārjuna; trans. Dānapāla (fl. 980–1017). T no. 1676, 32.

Hui zheng lun 迴諍論 (*Vigrahavyāvartanī*). Attributed to Nāgārjuna; trans. Vimokṣapra (fl. early 6th century) and Gautama Prajñāruci (arrived in China 516). T no. 1631, 32.

Liuqu lunhui jing 六趣輪迴經 (*Ṣaḍgatikārikā*). Attributed to Aśvaghoṣa; trans. Richeng 日稱 (1017–after 1073). T no. 726, 17.

Liushi song ruli lun 六十頌如理論 (*Yuktiṣaṣṭikā*). Attributed to Nāgārjuna; trans. Dānapāla (fl. 980–1017). T no. 1575, 30.

Longshu pusa li Emituo fo wen 龍樹菩薩禮阿彌陀佛文. BJ 8503 (果 088).

Longshu pusa quanjie wang jing 龍樹菩薩勸誡王經 (*Suhṛllekha*). Attributed to Nāgārjuna; trans. Yijing 義淨 (635–713). T no. 1674, 32.

Longshu pusa tuoluoni 龍樹菩薩陀羅尼. Attributed to Nāgārjuna. P 2322a.

Longshu pusa wei chantuojia wang shuo fayao jie 龍樹菩薩為禪陀迦王說法要偈 (*Suhṛllekha*). Attributed to Nāgārjuna; trans. Guṇavarman (367–431) in 421. T no. 1672, 32.

Longshu pusa yan lun 龍樹菩薩眼論. Attributed to Nāgārjuna. In *Yifang leiju* 醫方類聚. Taipei: Zhonghua shijie ziliao gongying chubanshe, 1978.

Longshu wuming lun 龍樹五明論. Attributed to Nāgārjuna and Aśvaghoṣa. T no. 1420, 21.

Maming pusa chengjiu xidi niansong 馬鳴菩薩成就悉地念誦. Attributed to Aśvaghoṣa; translation attributed to Amoghavajra (705–774). Z 1:3:5:416b–d

Maming pusa dashenli wubiyanfa niansong guiyi 馬鳴菩薩大神力無比驗法念誦軌儀. Attributed to Aśvaghoṣa; translation attributed to Vajrabodhi (662–732). T no. 1166, 20.

Miaofa lianhua jing Maming pusa pin di sanshi 妙法蓮華經馬明菩薩品第三十. Attributed to Aśvaghoṣa. T no. 2899, 85; S 2734.

Niganzi wen wuwo yi jing 尼乾子問無我義經 (*Nairātmyaparipṛcchā*). Attributed to Aśvaghoṣa; trans. Richeng 日稱 (1017–after 1073). T no. 1643, 32.

Puti xing lun 菩提行論 (*Bodhicaryāvatāra*). Attributed to Nāgārjuna; trans. Tianxizai 天息災 (perhaps Devaśānti; d. 1000). T no. 1662, 32.

Puti xin lixiang lun 菩提心離相論 (*Lakṣaṇavimuktabodhihrdaya*[*citta*]*śāstra*). Attributed to Nāgārjuna; trans. Dānapāla (fl. 980–1017). T no. 1661, 32.

Puti ziliang lun 菩提資糧論 (*Bodhisambhāraśāstra*). Attributed to Nāgārjuna; trans. Dharmagupta (d. 619). T no. 1660, 32.

Quan fa zhuwang yao jie 勸發諸王要偈 (*Suhṛllekha*). Attributed to Nāgārjuna; trans. Sanghavarman (fl. 420–445) in 434–442. T no. 1673, 32.

Shibakong lun 十八空論 (*Aṣṭādaśaśūnyatāśāstra*). Attributed to Nāgārjuna; trans. Paramārtha (499–569). T no. 1616, 31.

Shibushan yedao jing 十不善業道經 (*Daśākuśalakarmapathanirdeśa*). Attributed to Aśvaghoṣa; trans. Richeng 日稱 (1017–after 1073). T no. 727, 17.

Shi'er li 十二禮 (*Zan Emitofo wen* 讚阿彌陀佛文). Attributed to Nāgārjuna; translation attributed to Jñānagupta (523–600). Z 1:2:2:195a–c; BJ 8503 (果 088).

Shi'ermen lun 十二門論 (*Dvādaśamukhaśāstra* or *Dvādaśanikāyaśāstra*). Attributed to Nāgārjuna; trans. Kumārajīva (344–413 or 350–409) in 409. T no. 1568, 30.

Shi moheyan lun 釋摩訶衍論. Attributed to Nāgārjuna; translation attributed to Vṛddhimata (n.d.) ca. 401, but likely written in Korea ca. 720–779 by the monk Wŏlch'ung 月忠 (n.d.). T no. 1668, 32.

Shishi fa wushisong 事師法五十頌 (*Gurupañcāśikā*). Attributed to Aśvaghoṣa; trans. Richeng 日稱 (1017–after 1073). T no. 1687, 32.

Shizhu piposha lun 十住毘婆沙論 (*Daśabhūmikavibhāṣāśāstra*). Attributed to Nāgārjuna; trans. Kumārajīva (344–413 or 350–409) in 408. T no. 1521, 26.

Shun zhonglun yi ru da bore boluomi jing chupin famen 順中論義入大般若波羅蜜經初品法門 (*Madhyamakānugamaśāstra*). Attributed to Nāgārjuna; trans. Gautama Prajñāruci (arrived in China 516). T no. 1565, 30.

Tipo pusa po Lengqie jing zhong waidao xiaosheng sizong lun 提婆菩薩破楞伽經中外道小乘四宗論. Attributed to Deva; trans. Bodhiruci (fl. 508–535). T no. 1639, 32.

Tipo pusa shi Lengqie jing zhong waidao xiaosheng niepan lun 提婆菩薩釋楞伽經中外道小乘涅槃論. Attributed to Deva; trans. Bodhiruci (fl. 508–535). T no. 1640, 32.

Wuchang jing 無常經 (*Anityatāsūtra*). Attributed to Aśvaghoṣa; trans. Yijing 義淨 (635–713) in 701. T no. 801, 17.

Yinyuan xin lun song 因緣心論頌; or *Yin yuan xin lun shi* 因緣心論釋 (*Pratītyasamutpād ahṛdayaśāstra*). Attributed to Nāgārjuna (Longmeng 龍猛). T no. 1654, 32.

Yishu lujia lun 壹輸盧迦論 (*Ekaślokaśāstra*). Attributed to Nāgārjuna; trans. Gautama Prajñāruci (arrived in China 516). T no. 1573, 30.

Zan fajie song 讚法界頌 (*Dharmadhātustava*). Attributed to Nāgārjuna; trans. Dānapāla (fl. 980–1017). T no. 1675, 32.

Zhong lun 中論 (*Madhyamakaśāstra*). Verse attributed to Nāgārjuna, commentary by Qingmu 青目; trans. Kumārajīva (344–413 or 350–409) in 409. T no. 1564, 30.

Zuochan sanmei jing 坐禪三昧經. Attributed in part to Aśvaghoṣa; trans. Kumārajīva (344–413 or 350–409) in 402. T no. 614, 15.

Other Primary Sources

Anle ji 安樂集. By Daochuo 道綽 (562–645). T no. 1958, 47.

Apidamo jushe lun 阿毘達磨俱舍論 (*Abhidharmakośabhyāṣa*). By Vasubandhu (4th century). T nos. 1558–1559, 29.

Asabashō 阿娑縛抄. By Shōchō 承澄 (1205–1281). T no. 3190, 94 (*Zuzō* supplement, vol. 9).

Ayuwang jing 阿育王經 (*Aśokarājasūtra*). Trans. Sanghapāla (460–524) in 512. T no. 2043, 50.

Ayuwang zhuan 阿育王傳 (*Aśokāvadāna*). Trans. An Faqin 安法欽 (fl. 281–306) ca. 306. T no. 2042, 50.

Bailun shu 百論疏. By Jizang 吉藏 (549–623); presented as a lecture in 608. T no. 1827, 42.

Baolin zhuan 寶林傳. By Zhiju 智炬 (n. d.) ca. 801; ed. Yanagida Seizan 柳田聖山 1983. *Sōzō ichin: Hōrinden, Dentō gyokuei shū* 宋藏遺珍: 寶林傳, 傳燈玉英集. Kyoto: Chūbun shuppansha.

Ba yiqie yezhang genben desheng jingtu shenzhou 拔一切業障根本得生淨土神咒. Trans. Guṇabhadra (392–468). T no. 368, 12.

Beishan lu 北山錄. By Shenqing 神清 (d. ca. 814). T no. 2113, 52.

Bessonzakki 別尊雜記. By Shinkaku 心覺 (1117–1180). T no. 3007, 88 (*Zuzō* supplement, vol. 3).

Bianzheng lun 辯正論. By Falin 法琳 (572–640). T no. 2110, 52.

Bukong xingzhuang 不空行狀. By Zhao Qian 趙遷 (d. after 775) in 774. T no. 2056, 50.

Byakuhōkushō 白寶口抄. By Ryōson 亮尊 (fl. 1300). T no. 3119, 92 (*Zuzō* supplement, vol. 7).

Chanfa yaojie 禪法要解. Trans. attributed to Kumārajīva (344–413 or 350–409). T no. 616, 15.

Chang ahan jing 長阿含經 (*Dīrghāgama*). Trans. Buddhayaśas (fl. 384–417) and Zhu Fonian 竺佛念 (n. d.) in 412–413. T no. 1, 1.

Chengshi lun 成實論 (*Satyasiddhiśāstra*). Trans. Kumārajīva (344–413 or 350–409). T no. 1646, 32.

Cheng weishi lun yanmi 成唯識論演祕. By Zhizhou 智周 (678–733 or 688–723). T no. 1833, 43.

Chen shu 陳書. By Yao Silian 姚思廉 (d. 637); completed in 636. 2 vols. Beijing: Zhonghua shuju, 1972.

Chishi jing 持世經 (*Vasudharasūtra*). Trans. attributed to Kumārajīva (344–413 or 350–409). T no. 482, 14.

Chuanfa zhengzong dingzu tu 傳法正宗定祖圖. By Qisong 契嵩 (1007–1072). T no. 2079, 51.

Chuanfa zhengzong ji 傳法正宗記. By Qisong 契嵩 (1007–1072) in 1061. T no. 2078, 51.

Chu sanzang jiji 出三藏記集. By Sengyou 僧祐 (445–518) ca. 515. T no. 2145, 55.

Da aluohan Nantimiduoluo suoshuo fazhu ji 大阿羅漢難提蜜多羅所說法住記 (*Nandimitrāvadāna*). Trans. Xuanzang 玄奘 (602–664). T no. 2030, 49.

Da fangdeng tuoluoni jing 大方等陀羅尼經 (*Pratyutpannabuddhasaṃmukhāvasthitasamādhisūtra*). Trans. Fazhong 法眾 (n.d.) 402–413. T no. 1339, 21.

Da fangguang fo huayan jing 大方廣佛華嚴經 (*Avataṃsakasūtra*). Trans. Buddhabhadra (ca. 360–429) ca. 420. T no. 278, 9. Trans. Śikṣānanda (652–710) ca. 699. T no. 279, 10. Trans. Prajñā (ca. 734–810) ca. 800. T no. 293, 10.

Da fangguang fo huayan jing suishu yanyi chao 大方廣佛華嚴經隨疏演義鈔. By Chengguan 澄觀 (738–839). T no. 1736, 36.

Da fangguang pusa zang wenshushili genben yigui jing 大方廣菩薩藏文殊師利根本儀軌經 (*Āryamañjuśrīmūlakalpa*). Trans. Tianxizai 天息災 (perhaps Devaśānti; d. 1000) ca. 980. T no. 1191, 20.

Da fangguang yuanjue xiuduoluo liaoyi jing lüeshu 大方廣圓覺修多羅了義經略疏. By Zongmi 宗密 (780–841). T no. 1795, 39.

Dainippon kōtei shukusatsu daizōkyō 大日本校訂縮刷大藏經. 419 vols. Ed. Fukuda Gyōkai 福田行誡, Shimada Bankon 島田蕃根, and Shikikawa Seiichi 色川誠一, 1880–1885. Tokyo: Kōkyō Shoin.

Daji jing xukong mu fen 大集經虛空目分. Trans. Dharmakṣema (385–433) 414–426. T no. 397.10, 13.

Daji jing Yuezang fen 大集經月藏分 (*Candragarbhasūtra*). Trans. Narendrayaśas (ca. 490–589). T no. 397.15, 13.

Damoduoluo chan jing 達摩多羅禪經. Trans. Buddhabhadra (359/60–429) ca. 410. T no. 618, 15.

Dasheng baifa mingmen lun kaizong yijue 大乘百法明門論開宗義決. By Tankuang 曇曠 (ca. 700–before 788). T no. 2812, 85.

Dasheng qixin lun bieji 大乘起信論別記. By Wŏnhyo 元曉 (617–686). T no. 1845, 44.

Dasheng qixin lun neiyi luetan ji 大乘起信論內義略探記. By Daehyeon 大賢 (fl. ca. 753). T no. 1849, 44.

Dasheng qixin lun yiji 大乘起信論義記. By Fazang 法藏 (643–712). T no. 1846, 44.

Dasheng qixin lun yiji bieji 大乘起信論義記別記. By Fazang 法藏 (643–712). T no. 1847, 44.

Dasheng qixin lun yishu 大乘起信論義疏. Attributed to Huiyuan 慧遠 (523–592). T no. 1843, 44.

Dasheng ru lengqie jing 大乘入楞伽經 (*Laṅkāvatārasūtra*). Trans. Śikṣānanda (652–710) 700–704. T no. 672, 16.

Dasheng xuan lun 大乘玄論. By Jizang 吉藏 (549–623). T no. 1853, 45.

Dasheng yizhang 大乘義章. By Huiyuan 慧遠 (523–592) ca. 590. T no. 1851, 44.

Da Tang Da Ci'ensi Sanzang fashi zhuan 大唐大慈恩寺三藏法師傳. By Huili 慧立 (b. 615) and Yancong 彥悰 (fl. 627–649). T no. 2053, 50.

Da Tang neidian lu 大唐內典錄. By Daoxuan 道宣 (596–667) in 664. T no. 2149, 55.

Da Tang xiyu ji 大唐西域記. By Xuanzang 玄奘 (602–664) in 646. T no. 2087, 51.

Da Tang xiyu qiufa gaoseng zhuan 大唐西域求法高僧傳. By Yijing 義淨 (635–713) in 691. T no. 2066, 51.

Da Zhou kanding zhongjing mulu 大周刊定眾經目錄. By Mingquan 明佺 (d. after 695) in 695. T no. 2153, 55.

Dunhuang baozang 敦煌寶藏. 140 vols. Ed. Huang Yongwu 黃永武 1981–1986. Taipei: Xinwenfeng chuban gongsi.

Emituo jing yishu 阿彌陀經義述. By Huijing 慧淨 (578–645). T no. 1756, 37.

Fahua yi shu 法華義疏. By Jizang 吉藏 (549–623). T no. 1721, 34.

Fahua zhuanji 法華傳記. By Sengxiang 僧詳 (var. Huixiang 慧/惠詳; fl. 667). T no. 2068, 51.

Fajing jing 法鏡經 (*Ugra[data]paripṛcchā*). Trans. Anxuan 安玄 (fl. 181). T no. 322, 12.

Fangbian xin lun 方便心論. Trans. Kiṅkara (fl. ca. 460–472) and Tanyao 曇曜 (ca. 410–485) in 472. T no. 1632, 32.

Fantian huoluo jiuyao 梵天火羅九曜. By Yixing 一行 (683–727). T no. 1311, 21.

Fanyi ming yi ji 翻譯名義集. By Fayun 法雲 (1088–1158) in 1151. T no. 2131, 54.

Fayuan zhulin 法苑珠林. By Daoshi 道世 (ca. 596–683) in 668. T no. 2122, 53.

Fo benxing jing 佛本行經. Trans. Baoyun 寶雲 (376–449) ca. 424–449. T no. 193, 4.

Foshuo beidou qixing yanming jing 佛說北斗七星延命經. T no. 1307, 21.

Foshuo dasheng wuliangshou zhuangyan jing 佛說大乘無量壽莊嚴經 (*Sukhāvatīvyūhasūtra*). Trans. Dharmabhadra (d. 1001) in 991. T no. 363, 12.

Foshuo Emituo jing 佛說阿彌陀經. Translation attributed to Kumārajīva (344–413 or 350–409). T no. 366, 12.

Foshuo hailongwang jing 佛說海龍王經. Trans. Dharmarakṣa (fl. 266–313) in 285. T no. 598, 15.

Foshuo jinpiluo tongzi weide jing 佛說金毘羅童子威德經. Trans. Amoghavajra (705–774). T no. 1289, 21.

Foshuo jueding pini jing 佛說決定毘尼經 (*Vinayaviniścaya* or *Upālipariprccha*). Trans. Dharmarakṣa (fl. 266–313). T no. 325, 12.

Foshuo renwang boreboluomi jing 佛說仁王般若波羅蜜經. Translation attributed to Kumārajīva (344–413 or 350–409). T no. 245, 8.

Fozu tongji 佛祖統紀. By Zhipan 志磐 (1220–1275), completed 1269. T no. 2035, 49.

Fu fazang yinyuan zhuan 付法藏因緣傳. Trans. attributed to Kiṅkara (fl. ca. 460–472) and Tanyao 曇曜 (ca. 410–485) in 472. T no. 2058, 50.

Gaoseng Faxian zhuan 高僧法顯傳. By Faxian 法顯 (ca. 337–422) in 416. T no. 2085, 51.

Gaoseng zhuan 高僧傳. By Huijiao 慧皎 (497–554) ca. 531. T no. 2059, 50.

Guan fo sanmei hai jing 觀佛三昧海經 (*Buddhānusmṛtisamādhisāgarasūtra*). Trans. attributed to Buddhabhadra (ca. 360–429). T no. 643, 15.

Guang bailun shu 廣百論疏. By Wengui 文軌 (n.d.) in 707. T no. 2800, 85.

Guang hongming ji 廣弘明集. By Daoxuan 道宣 (596–667). T no. 2103, 52.

Guang qingliang zhuan 廣清涼傳. By Yanyi 延一 (fl. ca. 1060). T no. 2099, 51.

Guan wuliangshou jing 觀無量壽經. Trans. Kālayaśas (fl. early 5th century). T no. 365, 12.

Guan wuliangshou jing yishu 觀無量壽經義疏. By Huiyuan 慧遠 (523–592). T no. 1749, 37.

Guan wuliangshou jing yishu 觀無量壽經義疏. By Jizang 吉藏 (549–623). T no 1752, 37.

Guanxin lun 觀心論. Presented as a lecture by Zhiyi 智顗 (538–97) in 597. T no. 1920, 46.

Gujin yijing tuji 古今譯經圖紀. By Jingmai 靜邁 (fl. ca. 665) in 664–665. T no. 2151, 55.

Guoqing bailu 國清百錄. Compiled by Guanding 灌頂 (561–632) ca. 601–607. T no. 1934, 46.

Huandan zhongxian lun 還丹眾仙論. By Yang Zai 楊在 in 1052. DZ 233.

Huayan jing chuan ji 華嚴經傳記. By Fazang 法藏 (643–712). T no. 2073, 51.

Huayan jing tanxuan ji 華嚴經探玄記. By Fazang 法藏 (643–712). T no. 1733, 35.

Jianlao ditian yigui 堅牢地天儀軌. Trans. Śubhakarasiṃha (637–735) ca. 717–734. T no. 1286, 21.

Jin'gang boreboluomi jing 金剛般若波羅蜜經 (*Vajracchedikāprajñāpāramitāsūtra*). Trans. Kumārajīva (344–413 or 350–409) in 403. T no. 235, 8.

Jin'gang bore jing po quzhao buhuai jiaming lun deng sizhong 金剛波若經破取著不壞假名論等四種. Ed. Liu Xiuqiao 劉修橋. Taipei: Xinwenfeng, 1977.

Jingang ding jing da yujia mimi xin di famen yijue 金剛頂經大瑜伽祕密心地法門義訣. By Amoghavajra (705–774). T no. 1798, 39.

Jingde chuandeng lu 景德傳燈錄. By Daoyuan 道原 (fl. ca. 1004) in 1004. T no. 2076, 51.

Jingming xuan lun 淨名玄論. By Jizang 吉藏 (549–623). T no. 1780, 38.

Jingtu lun 淨土論. By Jiacai 迦才 (fl. ca. 627–649). T no. 1963, 47.

Jingtu shiyi lun 淨土十疑論. By Zhiyi 智顗 (538–97). T no. 1961, 47.
Jingtu wangsheng zhuan 淨土往生傳. By Jiezhu 戒珠 (985–1077). T no. 2071, 51.
Ji zhujing lichan yi 集諸經禮懺儀. By Zhisheng 智昇 (fl. 700–786). T no. 1982, 47.
Jōgyō kasho shōrai mokuroku 常曉和尚請來目錄. By Jōgyō 常曉 (d. 865). T no. 2163, 55.
Jueding pini jing 決定毘尼經 (*Vinayaviniścaya*). Translation attributed to Dharmarakṣa (fl. 266–313). T no. 325, 12.
Kaiyuan shijiao lu 開元釋教錄. By Zhisheng 智昇 (fl. 700–786) in 730. T no. 2154, 55.
Koryŏ taejanggyŏng 高麗大藏經. 47 vols. 1976. Seoul: Tongguk University Press.
Lengqie abaduoluo bao jing 楞伽阿跋多羅寶經 (*Laṅkāvatārasūtra*). Trans. Guṇabhadra (392–468) in 443. T no. 670, 16.
Lengqie shizi ji 楞伽師資記. By Jingjue 淨覺 (683–ca. 750) ca. 710–720. T no. 2837, 85.
Lidai fabao ji 曆代法寶記. By disciples of the monk Wuzhu 無住 (714–774) ca. 780. T no. 2075, 51.
Lidai sanbao ji 歷代三寶紀. By Fei Zhangfang 費長房 (d. after 598); completed in 598. T no. 2034, 49.
Lingbao tianzun shuo yangcan yingzhong jing 靈寶天尊說養蠶營種經. DZ 360.
Lingjian zi yindao ziwu ji 靈劍子引導子午記. Northern Song dynasty (960–1127). DZ 571.
Liudu jijing 六度集經. Trans. Kang Senghui 康僧會 (d. ca. 280). T no. 152, 3.
Longshu pusa zhuan 龍樹菩薩傳. Translation attributed to Kumārajīva (344–413 or 350–409). T no. 2047, 50.
Longshu zengguang jingtu wen 龍舒增廣淨土文. By Wang Rixiu 王日休 (d. 1173) in 1161–1162 or 1173. T no. 1970, 47.
Maming pusa zhuan 馬鳴菩薩傳. Translation attributed to Kumārajīva (344–413 or 350–409). T no. 2046, 50. Nanatsu-dera 七寺 edition in Ochiai and Saitō 2000.
Miaofa lianhua jing 妙法蓮華經. Trans. Kumārajīva (344–413 or 350–409). T no. 262, 9.
Mohemoye jing 摩訶摩耶經 (*Mahāmāyāsūtra*). Trans. Tanjing 曇景 (fl. 479–502). T no. 383, 12.
Mohe sengqi lü 摩訶僧祇律 (*Mahāsāṃghikavinaya*). Trans. Buddhabhadra (ca. 360–429) and Faxian 法顯 (ca. 337–422). T no. 1425, 22.
Mohe zhiguan 摩訶止觀. Presented as a lecture by Zhiyi 智顗 (538–97) and recorded by Guanding 灌頂 (561–632) ca. 607–632. T no. 1911, 46.
Poshupandou fashi zhuan 婆藪槃豆法師傳. Trans. Paramārtha (499–569). T no. 2049, 50.
Pusa chutai jing 菩薩處胎經. Trans. Zhu Fonian 竺佛念 (fl. ca. 365–416). T no. 384, 12.
Pusa he seyu fa jing 菩薩訶色欲法經. Trans. Kumārajīva (344–413 or 350–409). T no. 615, 15.
Pusa shizhu xingdao pin 菩薩十住行道品 (*Daśabhūmikasūtra*). Trans. Dharmarakṣa (fl. 266–313). T no. 283, 10.
Qianlong dazangjing 乾隆大藏經. 168 vols. Ed. Chuanzheng Youxian Gongsi Bianjibu 傳正有限公司編輯部, 1997. Zhanghua, Taipei County, Taiwan: Chuanzheng youxian gongsi.
Qixin lun shu 起信論疏. By Wŏnhyo 元曉 (617–686). T no. 1844, 44.
Qixin lun shu bixue ji 起信論疏筆削記. By Zixuan 子璿 (965–1038). T no. 1848, 44.
Qixin lun yishu 起信論義疏. Attributed to Tanyan 曇延 (516–588). Z 1:71:3.
Quan Tang shi 全唐詩. 900 *juan*. Compiled by Peng Dingqiu 彭定求 (1645–1719) et al.; printed by Cao Yin 曹寅 (1658–1712), imperial preface of 1707. Modern edition published in 1960, 25 vol. (Beijing: Zhonghua shuju).

Renwang bore jing shu 仁王般若經疏. By Jizang 吉藏 (549–623). T no. 1707, 33.

Renwang huguo bore jing shu 仁王護國般若經疏. Attributed to Zhiyi 智顗 (538–97) and Guanding 灌頂 (561–632). T no. 1705, 33.

Ru lengqie jing 入楞伽經 (*Laṅkāvatārasūtra*). Trans. Bodhiruci (fl. 508–35) in 513. T no. 671, 16.

Ru lengqie xin xuanyi 入楞伽心玄義. By Fazang 法藏 (643–712). T no. 1790, 39.

Sanbao ganying yaolüe lu 三寶感應要略錄. By Feizhuo 非濁 (d. 1063). T no. 2084, 51.

Sanguo zhi 三國志. By Chen Shou 陳壽 (233–397); completed in 297. Modern edition published in 1982, 5 vols. (Beijing: Zhonghua shuju).

Sanlun xuanyi 三論玄義. By Jizang 吉藏 (549–623). T no. 1852, 45.

Sanlun youyi yi 三論遊意義. By Dharma-master Qi 磧法師 (fl. 590–618). T no. 1855, 45.

Shanjian lü piposha 善見律毘婆沙 (*Samantapāsādikā*). Trans. Sanghabhadra (fl. ca. 488–489) in 488. T no. 1462, 24.

Shelifu wen jing 舍利弗問經 (*Śāriputraparipṛcchāsūtra*). Trans. ca. 317–420. T no. 1465, 24.

Shenxian zhuan 神仙傳. By Ge Hong 葛洪 (283–343) ca. 317. Taipei: Sanmin shuju, 2004.

Shidi jing lun 十地經論 (*Daśabhūmikasūtraśāstra*). By Vasubandhu (4th century); trans. Bodhiruci (fl. 508–535) et al. T no. 1522, 26.

Shi'ermen lun shu 十二門論疏. By Jizang 吉藏 (549–623); presented as a lecture in 608. T no. 1825, 42.

Shi'ermen lun zongzhi yi ji 十二門論宗致義記. By Fazang 法藏 (643–712). T no. 1826, 42.

Shijia fangzhi 釋迦方志. By Daoxuan 道宣 (596–667). T no. 2088, 51.

Shijia pu 釋迦譜. By Sengyou 僧祐 (445–518). T no. 2040, 50.

Shijia shipu 釋迦氏譜. By Daoxuan 道宣 (596–667). T no. 2041, 50.

Shimen yingyong wen(fan) 釋門應用文(範). See *Yinyuan lun* 因緣論.

Shisong lü 十誦律 (*Sarvāstivādavinaya* or *Daśādhyāyavinaya*). Trans. Puṇyatara (active in Chang'an ca. 399–415); Kumārajīva (344–413 or 350–409); and Dharmaruci (fl. early 5th century) 404–409. T no. 1435, 23.

Shizhu jing 十住經 (*Daśabhūmikasūtra*). Trans. Kumārajīva (344–413 or 350–409). T no. 286, 10.

Sho ajari shingon mikkyō burui sōroku 諸阿闍梨真言密教部類總錄. By Annen 安然 (841–ca. 889). T no. 2176, 55.

Shu pu 鼠璞. By Daizhi 戴植 (or 埴) (fl. 1241); "styled" (*zi* 字) Zhongpei 仲培. Modern edition ed. Zhou Guangpei 周光培 1995. *Songdai biji xiaoshuo* 宋代筆記小說 (Notebook Fictions of the Song Dynasty). Vol. 23 of *Lidai biji xiaoshuo jicheng* 歷代筆記小說集成 (Collection of Notebook Fictions through the Ages) (Shijiazhuang: Hebei jiaoyu chubanshe).

Sifen lü 四分律 (*Dharmaguptakavinaya*). Trans. Buddhayaśas (fl. 384–417) and Zhu Fonian 竺佛念 (n.d.). T no. 1428, 22.

Sishi'erzhang jing 四十二章經. Trans. Jiayemoteng 迦葉摩騰 (d. ca. 73 CE) and Zhu Falan 竺法蘭 (arrived in China 67 or 75 CE). T no. 784, 17.

Songdai biji xiaoshuo 宋代筆記小說. Ed. Zhong Guangpei 周光培, 1995 (Shijiazhuang: Hebei jiaoyu chubanshe).

Song gaoseng zhuan 宋高僧傳. By Zanning 賛寧 (919–1001). T no. 2061, 50.

Soushen ji 搜神記. By Gan Bao 干寶 (fl. 317–322). Ed. Yang Jialuo 楊家駱, 1962. *Xinjiao Soushen ji* 新校搜神記 (Taipei: Shijie shuju).

Sui shu 隋書. By Wei Zheng 魏徵 (580–643); completed in 636. Modern edition published 1973 (Beijing: Zhonghua shuju).

Sui Tiantai Zhizhe dashi biezhuan 隋天台智者大師別傳. Compiled by Guanding 灌頂 (561–632) ca. 601–605. T no. 2050, 50.

Taishang ganying pian 太上感應篇. By Li Changling 李昌齡 (937–1008). DZ 1167.

Taishang shuo liyi canwang miaojing 太上說利益蠶王妙經. DZ 365.

Tan jing 壇經. Composed ca. 820. T no. 2007, 48.

Tipo pusa zhuan 提婆菩薩傳. Trans. attributed to Kumārajīva (344–413 or 350–409). T no. 2048, 50.

Wangsheng lizan jie 往生禮讚偈. By Shandao 善導 (613–681). T no. 1980, 47.

Wangsheng xifang jingtu ruiying zhuan 往生西方淨土瑞應傳. Compiled by Shaotang 少唐 (d. 805) and Wenshen 文諗 (n.d.). T no. 2070, 51.

Weimojie suoshuo jing 維摩詰所說經 (*Vimalakīrtinirdeśa*). Trans. Kumārajīva (344–413 or 350–409) in 406. T no. 475, 14.

Weimo jing yi shu 維摩經義疏. By Jizang 吉藏 (549–623). T no. 1781, 38.

Weishi sanshi lun song 唯識三十論頌 (*Triṃśikāvijñaptikārikā*), T no. 1586, 31. By Vasubandhu (4th century); trans. Xuanzang 玄奘 (602–664).

Wuliangshou jing youpotishe 無量壽經優波提舍 (*Sukhāvativyūhopadeśa*). By Vasubandhu (4th century); trans. Bodhiruci (fl. 508–535) in 529. T no. 1524, 26.

Wuliangshou jing youpotishe yuansheng jie zhu 無量壽經優婆提舍願生偈註. By Tanluan 曇鸞 (476–542). T no. 1819, 40.

Xin huayan jing lun 新華嚴經論. By Li Tongxuan 李通玄 (ca. 635–730). T no. 1739, 36.

Xu gaoseng zhuan 續高僧傳. By Daoxuan 道宣 (596–667); initially completed in 645, supplemented until 667. T no. 2060, 50.

Yingyin Song qisha zangjing 影印宋磧砂藏經. 591 vols. Ed. Yingyin Songban Zangjinghui 影印宋版藏經會, 1935. Shanghai: Songban zangjinghui.

Yinyuan lun 因緣論(a.k.a. *Shimen yingyong wen[fan]* 釋門應用文[範]). S 5639.

Yiqie jing yinyi 一切經音義. By Huilin 慧琳 (737–820) 783–807. T no. 2128, 54.

Youposai jie jing 優婆塞戒經 (*Upāsakaśīlasūtra*). Trans. Dharmakṣema (385–433). T no. 1488, 24.

Za ahan jing 雜阿含經 (*Saṃyuktāgama*). Trans. Guṇabhadra (392–468) 435–443. T no. 99, 2.

Za baozang jing 雜寶藏經. Trans. Kiṅkara (Jijiaye 吉迦夜) (fl. ca. 460–472) and Tanyao 曇曜 (ca. 410–485) in 472. T no. 203, 4.

Zan Emituofo jie 讚阿彌陀佛偈. By Tanluan 曇鸞 (476–542). T no. 1978, 47.

Zhao lun 肇論. By Sengzhao 僧肇 (ca. 374–414). T no. 1858, 45.

Zheng fahua jing 正法華經 (*Saddharmapuṇḍrīka*). Trans. Dharmarakṣa (fl. 266–313). T no. 263, 9.

Zhenyuan xinding shijiao mulu 貞元新定釋教目錄. By Yuanzhao 圓照 (fl. ca. 778–800) in 800. T no. 2157, 55.

Zhiguan fuxing chuanhong jue 止觀輔行傳弘決. By Zhanran 湛然 (711–782). T no. 1912, 46.

Zhong ahan jing 中阿含經 (*Mādhyamāgama*). Trans. Gautama Sanghadeva (fl. ca. 383–398) in 397–398. T no. 26, 1.

Zhongguan lun shu 中觀論疏. By Jizang 吉藏 (549–623); presented as a lecture in 608. T no. 1824, 42.

Zhongjing mulu 眾經目錄. By Fajing 法經 (n.d.); completed ca. 594. T no. 2146, 55.
Zhongjing mulu 眾經目錄. By Yancong 彥琮 (557–610) in 602. T no. 2147, 55.
Zhongjing mulu 眾經目錄. By Jingtai 靜泰 (n.d.); completed ca. 665. T no. 2148, 55.
Zhong lun juan di yi 中論卷第一. S 3286.
Zhuangzi jinzhu jinyi 莊子今注今譯. Modern Chinese trans. Chen Guying 陳鼓應, 1990 (Xianggang: Zhonghua shuju).
Zhujing yao lüewen 諸經要略文. Early ninth century. T no. 2821, 85; S. 779.
Zhu weimojie jing 注維摩詰經. By Sengzhao 僧肇 (384–414) ca. 406–410. T no. 1775, 38.
Zongjing lu 宗鏡錄. By Yanshou 延壽 (904–975) in 961. T no. 2016, 48.
Zuochan sanmei jing 坐禪三昧經. Attributed in part to Aśvaghoṣa; trans. Kumārajīva (344–413 or 350–409) in 402. T no. 614, 15.

Secondary Sources

Concordances, Dictionaries, and Encyclopedias

Akanuma Chizen 赤沼智善. 1967. *Indo Bukkyō koyū meishi jiten* 印度仏教固有名詞辞典 (Dictionary of Indian Buddhist Proper Nouns). Kyoto: Hōzōkan.
Cai Yunchen 蔡運辰. 1983. *Ershiwu zhong zangjing mulu duizhao kaoshi* 二十五種藏經目錄對照考釋 (Comparative Study of Twenty-Five Catalogues of the [Chinese Buddhist] Canon). Taipei: Xinwenfeng chuban gongsi.
Ciyi 慈怡, ed. 1988–1989. *Foguang da cidian* 佛光大辭典 (Encyclopedia of the Buddha's Light). 8 vols. Taipei: Foguang wenhua shiye youxian gongsi.
Demiéville, Paul, Hubert Durt, and Anna Seidel, eds. 1978. *Répertoire du canon bouddhique sino-japonais, fascicule annexe du Hōbōgirin* (Catalogue of the Sino-Japanese Buddhist Canon, Hōbōgirin Appendix Volume). Tokyo: Maison Franco-Japonaise.
Dunhuang Yanjiu Yuan 敦煌研究院, ed. 2000. *Dunhuang yishu zongmu suoyin xinbian* 敦煌遺書總目索引新編 (Catalogue and Index of Texts Preserved at Dunhuang, Newly Compiled). Beijing: Zhonghua shuju.
Giles, Lionel. 1957. *Descriptive Catalogue of the Chinese Manuscripts from Tunhuang in the British Museum.* London: Trustees of the British Museum.
Kokusai Bukkyōgaku Daigakuin Daigaku Gakujutsu Furontia Jikkō Iinkai 国際仏教学大学院大学学術フロンチイア実行委員会, ed. 2007. *Nihon genzon hasshu Issaikyō taishō mokuroku, zantei dainihan* 日本現存八種一切経対照目録, 暫定第二版 (Concordance of Eight Buddhist Manuscript Canons Extant in Japan). 2nd edition. Tokyo: Kokusai Bukkyōgaku daigakuin daigaku. http://www.icabs.ac.jp/frontia/Hachishu.pdf.
Luo Zhufeng 羅竹風, ed. 1987–1995. *Hanyu da cidian* 漢語大詞典 (Dictionary of the Chinese Language). Shanghai: Shanghai cishu chubanshe.
Mikkyō Daijiten Saikan Iinkai 密教大辭典再刊委員會, ed. 1979. *Mikkyō daijiten* 密教大辭典 (Encyclopedia of Esoteric Buddhism). 3 vols. Kyoto: Hōzōkan.
Mochizuki Shinkō 望月信亨, ed. 1954–1963. *Bukkyō daijiten* 佛教大辭典 (Encyclopedia of Buddhism). Rev. ed. 10 vols. Kyoto: Seikai seiten kankō kyōkai.
Muller, A. Charles, ed. 1995–. *Digital Dictionary of Buddhism.* http://buddhism-dict.net/ddb.

Nakamura Hajime 中村元, ed. 1981. *Bukkyōgo daijiten* 佛教語大辭典 (Encyclopedia of Buddhist Terminology). Tokyo: Tokyo shoseki.

Ono Gemmyō 小野玄妙, ed. 1933–1936. *Bussho kaisetsu daijiten* 佛書解說大辭典 (Encyclopedia of Buddhist Texts). 13 vols. Tokyo: Daitō shuppansha.

Ren Jiyu 任繼愈. 1995. *Daozang tiyao* 道藏提要 (Synopsis of the Daoist Canon). Beijing: Zhongguo shehui kexue chubanshe.

Sawa Ryūken 佐和隆研. 1975. *Mikkyō jiten* 密教辞典 (Dictionary of Esoteric Buddhism). Kyoto: Hōzōkan.

———. 1990. *Butsuzō zuten* 仏像図典 (Illustrated Dictionary of Buddhist Images). Tokyo: Yoshikawa kōbunkan.

Schipper, Kristofer, and Franciscus Verellen, eds. 2005. *The Taoist Canon: A Historical Companion to the Daozang.* 3 vols. Chicago: University of Chicago Press.

Werner, E. T. C. 1932. *A Dictionary of Chinese Mythology.* Shanghai: Kelley and Walsh.

Other Secondary Sources

Abé Ryūichi. 1999. *The Weaving of Mantra: Kūkai and the Construction of Esoteric Buddhist Discourse.* New York: Columbia University Press.

Adamek, Wendi Leigh. 2007. *The Mystique of Transmission: On an Early Chan History and Its Contexts.* New York: Columbia University Press.

———. 2009. "A Niche of Their Own: The Power of Convention in Two Inscriptions for Medieval Chinese Buddhist Nuns." *History of Religions* 49 (1): 1–26.

Aramaki Noritoshi 荒牧典俊. 2000. "Hokuchō kōhanki bukkyō shisō-shi josetsu" 北朝後半期佛教思想史序說 (An Introduction to the History of Buddhist Thought in the Latter Part of the Northern Dynasties). In *Hokuchō Zui-Tō chūgoku bukkyōshi* 北朝隋唐中國仏教思想史 (History of Buddhist Thought during the Northern Dynasties, Sui and Tang), ed. Aramaki Noritoshi, 13–85. Kyoto: Hōzōkan.

Barrett, Timothy H. 1990. "Kill the Patriarchs!" In *The Buddhist Forum,* ed. Tadeusz Skorupski, 1:87–97. London: School of Oriental and African Studies, University of London.

Beal, Samuel, trans. 1883. *"The Fo-sho-hing-tsan-king, a Life of Buddha," by Asvaghosa, Bodhisattva; Translated from Sanskrit into Chinese by Dharmaraksha, A.D. 420, and from Chinese into English.* Vol. 19 of *Sacred Books of the East.* Oxford: Clarendon Press.

———, trans. 1884. *Si-yu-ki: Buddhist Records of the Western World.* 2 vols. London: Trubner and Co.

———. 1886. "The Age and Writing of Nāgārjuna Bodhisattva." *Indian Antiquary,* 353–356.

Bechert, Heinz, ed. 1991. *The Dating of the Historical Buddha / Die Datierung des historischen Buddha: Part 1.* Göttingen, Germany: Vandenhoeck and Ruprecht.

Benn, James A. 2007. *Burning for the Buddha: Self-Immolation in Chinese Buddhism.* Honolulu: University of Hawai'i Press.

———. 2009. "The Silent Sangha: Some Observations on Mute Sheep Monks." *JIABS* 32 (1–2): 11–38.

Berkowitz, Alan J. 2000. *Patterns of Disengagement: The Practice and Portrayal of Reclusion in Early Medieval China.* Stanford, Calif.: Stanford University Press.

———. 2010. "Social and Cultural Dimensions of Reclusion in Early Medieval China." In *Philosophy and Religion in Early Medieval China*, ed. Alan K. L. Chan and Yuet-Keung Lo, 291–318. Albany: State University of New York Press.

Bhattacharya, Vidhushekhara. 1931. *The Catuhśataka of Āryadeva: Sanskrit and Tibetan Texts with Extracts from the Commentary of Candrakīrti*. Calcutta: Visva-Bharati Book Shop.

Bielefeldt, Carl. 1985. "Recarving the Dragon: History and Dogma in the Study of Dōgen." In *Dōgen Studies*, ed. William R. LaFleur, 21–53. Honolulu: University of Hawai'i Press.

Birnbaum, Raoul. 1983. *Studies on the Mysteries of Mañjuśrī: A Group of East Asian Maṇḍalas and Their Traditional Symbolism*. Boulder, Colo.: Society for the Study of Chinese Religions.

Birrell, Anne. 1993. *Chinese Mythology: An Introduction*. Baltimore: Johns Hopkins University Press.

Bocking, Brian. 1995. *Nāgārjuna in China: A Translation of the Middle Treatise*. Lewiston, N.Y.: Edwin Mellen Press.

Bodde, Derk. 1975. *Festivals in Classical China: New Year and Other Annual Observances during the Han Dynasty, 206 B.C.–A.D. 220*. Princeton, N.J.: Princeton University Press.

Bokenkamp, Stephen R. 1994. "Time after Time: Taoist Apocalyptic History and the Founding of the T'ang Dynasty." *Asia Major*, 3rd series, 7 (1): 59–88.

———. 1997. *Early Daoist Scriptures*. Berkeley: University of California Press.

Boltz, William G. 1980. "Cicada Sinica Quotidiana, the Vocabulary of Common and Classical Chinese." *Journal of the American Oriental Society* 100 (4): 495–502.

Bray, Francesca. 1997. *Technology and Gender: Fabrics of Power in Late Imperial China*. Berkeley: University of California Press.

Broadwin, Julie. 1999. "Intertwining Threads: Silkworm Goddesses, Sericulture Workers and Reformers in Jiangnan, 1880s–1930s." Ph.D. diss., University of California, San Diego.

Brown, Peter. 1971. "The Rise and Function of the Holy Man in Late Antiquity." *Journal of Roman Studies* 61: 81–101.

———. 1981. *The Cult of the Saints: Its Rise and Function in Latin Christianity*. Chicago: University of Chicago Press.

———. 1983. "The Saint as Exemplar in Late Antiquity." *Representations* 1: 1–25.

———. 2000. "Enjoying the Saints in Late Antiquity." *Early Medieval Europe* 9 (1): 1–24.

Buswell, Robert E., Jr. 1989. *The Formation of Ch'an Ideology in China and Korea: The Vajrasamādhi-Sūtra, a Buddhist Apocryphon*. Princeton, N.J.: Princeton University Press.

Campany, Robert. 1991. "Notes on the Devotional Uses and Symbolic Functions of Sūtra Texts as Depicted in Early Chinese Buddhist Miracle Tales and Hagiographies." *JIABS* 14 (1): 28–72.

———. 1993. "The Real Presence." *History of Religions* 32 (3): 233–272.

———. 2002. *To Live as Long as Heaven and Earth: A Translation and Study of Ge Hong's Traditions of Divine Transcendents*. Berkeley: University of California Press.

———. 2003. "On the Very Idea of Religions (in the Modern West and in Early Medieval China)." *History of Religions* 42 (2): 287–319.

———. 2005. "Living off the Books: Fifty Ways to Dodge *Ming* in Early Medieval China." In *The Magnitude of* Ming*: Command, Allotment, and Fate in Chinese Culture*, ed. Christopher Lupke, 129–150. Honolulu: University of Hawai'i Press.

———. 2009. *Making Transcendents: Ascetics and Social Memory in Early Medieval China*. Honolulu: University of Hawai'i Press.

———. 2012a. "Religious Repertoires and Contestation: A Case Study Based on Buddhist Miracle Tales." *History of Religions* 52 (2): 99–141.

———. 2012b. *Signs from the Unseen Realm: Buddhist Miracle Tales from Early Medieval China*. Honolulu: University of Hawai'i Press.

Cao Shibang 曹仕邦. 1994. *Zhongguo shamen waixue de yanjiu: Hanmo zhi wudai* 中國沙門外學的研究: 漢末至五代 (Studies of the Non-Buddhist Scholarship of Chinese Śramaṇas: From the End of the Han to the Five Dynasties Period). Taipei: Dongchu chubanshe.

———. 1999. *Zhongguo Fojiao shixue shi—Dongjin zhi Wudai* 中國佛教史學史—東晉至五代 (A History of Chinese Buddhist Historiography—from the Eastern Jin to the Five Dynasties). Taipei: Fagu wenhua.

Cedzich, Ursula-Angelica. 2001. "Corpse Deliverance, Substitute Bodies, Name Change, and Feigned Death: Aspects of Metamorphosis and Immortality in Early Medieval China." *Journal of Chinese Religions* 29: 1–68.

Chappell, David W. 1976. "Tao-ch'o (562–645): A Pioneer of Chinese Pure Land Buddhism." Ph.D. diss., Yale University.

Chaudhuri, Saroj Kumar. 2008. *Lives of Early Buddhist Monks: The Oldest Extant Biographies of Indian and Central Asian Monks*. New Delhi: Abha Prakashan.

Chavannes, Édouard, trans. 1910–1934. *Cinq cents contes et apologues*. 4 vols. Paris: Ernest Leroux.

Chen Jinhua. 1999. *Making and Remaking History: A Study of Tiantai Sectarian Historiography*. Studia Philologica Buddhica Monograph Series 14. Tokyo: The International Institute for Buddhist Studies.

———. 2002. *Monks and Monarchs, Kinship and Kingship: Tanqian in Sui Buddhism and Politics*. Kyoto: Scuola Italiana di Studi sull' Asia Orientale.

———. 2004. "The Indian Buddhist Missionary Dharmakṣema (385–433): A New Dating of His Arrival in Guzang and of His Translations." *T'oung Pao* 90: 215–263.

———. 2010. *Crossfire: Shingon-Tendai Strife as Seen in Two Twelfth-Century Polemics, with Special References to Their Background in Tang China*. Tokyo: International Institute for Buddhist Studies.

Ch'en, Kenneth. 1964. *Buddhism in China: A Historical Survey*. Princeton, N.J.: Princeton University Press.

Chen Mingda 陳明達 and Ding Mingyi 丁明夷, eds. 1989. *Gongxian, Tianlongshan, Xiangtangshan, Anyang shiku diaoke* 鞏縣天龍山響堂山安陽石窟雕刻 (The Grotto Sculptures of Gong County, Mount Tianlong, Mount Xiangtang, and Anyang). Vol. 13 of *Zhongguo meishu quanji* 中國美術全集 (Complete Collection of Chinese Arts). Beijing: Wenwu chubanshe.

Chen Zuolong 陳祚龍. 1979. "Shi Feizhuo xinzhuan" 釋非濁新傳 (A New Account of Shi Feizhuo). In *Zhonghua fojiao wenhua shi sance* 中華佛教文化史散策 (Essays on the History of Chinese Buddhist Culture), 2: 123–124. Taipei: Xinwenfeng chuban gongsi.

Cheng Hsueh-li. 1982. *Nāgārjuna's Twelve Gate Treatise.* Dordrecht: D. Reidel.

Chou Po-kan. 2000. "The Translation of the Dazhidulun: Buddhist Evolution in China in the Early Fifth Century." Ph.D. diss., Committee on History of Culture, University of Chicago.

———. 2004. "The Problem of the Authorship of the *Mahāprajñāpāramitopadeśa:* A Re-examination." *Taida lishi xuebao* 臺大歷史學報 (National Taiwan University Journal of Historical Inquiry) 34: 281–327.

Cohn, Robert L. 1987. "Sainthood." In *Encyclopedia of Religion*, ed. M. Eliade, 13: 1–6. New York: MacMillan and Free Press.

Cole, Alan. 2005. "A Plan for the Past: The Role of Innate Perfection in the *Awakening of Faith*'s Sinification of Buddhism." Unpublished manuscript of a paper presented at the Annual Meeting of the American Academy of Religion, Philadelphia.

———. 2009. *Fathering Your Father: The Zen of Fabrication in Tang Buddhism.* Berkeley: University of California Press.

Como, Michael. 2009. *Weaving and Binding: Immigrant Gods and Female Immortals in Ancient Japan.* Honolulu: University of Hawai'i Press.

Copp, Paul F. 2008. "Notes on the Term '*Dhāraṇī*' in Medieval Chinese Buddhist Thought." *Bulletin of the School of Oriental and African Studies* 71 (3): 493–508.

———. 2011. "Manuscript Culture as Ritual Culture in Late Medieval Dunhuang: Buddhist Talisman-Seals and Their Manuals." *Cahiers d'Extrême-Asie* 20: 193–226.

———. 2014. *The Body Incantatory: Spells and the Ritual Imagination in Medieval Chinese Buddhism.* New York: Columbia University Press.

Corless, Roger. 1973. "T'an-luan's Commentary on the Pure Land Discourse: An Annotated Translation and Soteriological Analysis of the *Wang-sheng-lun chu* (T.1819)." Ph.D. diss., University of Wisconsin, Madison.

———. 1987. "T'an-luan: Taoist Sage and Buddhist Bodhisattva." In *Buddhist and Taoist Practice in Medieval Chinese Society*, ed. David W. Chappell, 36–45. Honolulu: University of Hawai'i Press.

———. 1989. "T'an-luan's Canticles to Amita Buddha." *Pure Land*, new series, 6: 262–278.

———. 1990. "Tsan A-mi-t'o fo chi (2): Canticles to Amita Buddha." *Pure Land*, new series, 7: 124–137.

———. 1995. "The Chinese Life of Nāgārjuna." In *Buddhism in Practice*, ed. Donald S. Lopez, Jr., 525–531. Princeton, N.J.: Princeton University Press.

Cowell, E. B. 1893. *The Buddha-Karita of Asvaghosha Edited from Three Mss.* Oxford: Anecdota Oxoniensia.

———, trans. 1894. *The Buddha-karita of Asvahgosha, Translated from the Sanskrit.* Part 1 of *Buddhist Mahāyāna Texts.* Sacred Books of the East 49. Oxford: Clarendon Press.

Dalia, Albert A., trans. 2002. "Biography of Dharma Master Vasubandhu." In *Lives of Great Monks and Nuns*, trans. Albert A. Dalia and Li Rongxi, 31–53. Berkeley, Calif.: Numata Center for Buddhist Translation and Research.

Daoan 道安. 1978. "Sanlun zong shi lun" 三論宗史論 (On the History of the Sanlun School). In *Xiandai fojiao xueshu congkan* 現代佛教學術叢刊 (Modern Buddhism Research Series), ed. Zhang Mantao 張曼濤, 47: 53–75. Taipei: Dasheng wenhua chubanshe yinxing.

Das, S. C. 1882. "Life and Legend of Nāgārjuna." *Journal of the Asiatic Society of Bengal* 5: 115–121.

Davis, Edward L. 2001. *Society and the Supernatural in Song China*. Honolulu: University of Hawai'i Press.

Deeg, Max. 2005. *Das Gaoseng-Faxian-Zhuan als religionsgeschichtliche Quelle* (The *Tradition of the Eminent Monk Faxian* as Religious-Historical Source). Weisbaden: Harrassowitz.

de Jong, J. W. 1971. Review of *Le traité de la grande vertu de sagesse de Nāgārjuna* (The Treatise on the Great Perfection of Wisdom by Nāgārjuna), vol. 3, by E. Lamotte. *Asia Major* 17: 105–112.

———. 1978. Review of *Aśvaghoṣa*, by Biswanath Bhattacharya. *Indo-Iranian Journal* 20 (1–2): 124–127.

Deleanu, Florin. 2007. "The Transmission of Xuanzang's Translation of the *Yogācārabhūmi* in East Asia." In *Kongōji issaikyō no sōgōteki kenkyū to kongōji seikyō no kisoteki kenkyū: kenkyū seika hōkokusho* 金剛寺一切経の総合的研究と金剛寺聖教の基 礎的研究: 研究成果報告書 (General Research on the Kongō-ji Manuscript Canon and a Basic Survey of the Kongō-ji Sacred Texts: Report of Research Results), ed. Ochiai Toshinori 落合俊典, 2: 1–44. Tokyo: Kokusai Bukkyōgaku Daigakuin Daigaku.

Delehaye, Hippolyte. 1962. *The Legends of the Saints*. New York: Fordham University Press.

Demiéville, Paul. 1929. "Sur l'authenticité du Ta Tch'eng K'i Sin Louen" (On the Authenticity of the *Treatise on the Mahāyāna Awakening of Faith*). *Bulletin de la Maison Franco-Japonaise* 2 (2): 1–79.

Deshpande, Vijaya. 2000. "Ophthalmic Surgery: A Chapter in the History of Sino-Indian Medical Contacts." *Bulletin of the School of Oriental and African Studies* 63 (3): 370–388.

De Visser, Martinus Willem. 1923. *The Arhats in China and Japan*. Berlin: Oesterheld and Co.

DeWoskin, Kenneth. 1983. *Doctors, Diviners, and Magicians of Ancient China: Biographies of Fang-shih*. New York: Columbia University Press.

DeWoskin, Kenneth, and J. I. Crump, Jr., trans. 1996. *In Search of the Supernatural: The Written Record*. Stanford, Calif.: Stanford University Press.

Di Cosmo, Nicola, and Don J. Wyatt, ed. 2003. *Political Frontiers, Ethnic Boundaries, and Human Geographies in Chinese History*. London and New York: RoutledgeCurzon.

Ding Mingyi 丁明夷, trans. 1998. *Fojiao xinchu beizhi jicui* 佛教新出碑志集粹 (Selection of Newly Discovered Buddhist Inscriptions). Taipei: Foguangshan zongwu weiyuanhui yinhang.

Dobbins, James. 1989. *Jōdo Shinshū: Shin Buddhism in Medieval Japan*. Bloomington: Indiana University Press.

———. 1990. "The Biography of Shinran: Apotheosis of a Japanese Buddhist Visionary." *History of Religions* 30 (2): 179–194.

Donner, Neal, and Daniel B. Stevenson. 1993. *The Great Calming and Contemplation: A Study and Annotated Translation of the First Chapter of Chih-I's "Mo-ho chih-kuan."* Honolulu: University of Hawai'i Press.

Dreyfus, Georges B. J. 2003. *The Sound of Two Hands Clapping: The Education of a Tibetan Buddhist Monk*. Berkeley: University of California Press.

Duara, Prasenjit. 1988. "Superscribing Symbols: The Myth of Guandi, Chinese God of War." *Journal of Asian Studies* 47 (4): 778–795.

Durt, Hubert. 1991. "La Date du Buddha en Corée et au Japon" (The Date of the Buddha in Korea and Japan). In *The Dating of the Historical Buddha / Die Datierung des historischen Buddha*, ed. Heinz Bechert, 1: 458–489. Göttingen, Germany: Vandenhoeck and Ruprecht.

———. 1994. *Problems of Chronology and Eschatology: Four Lectures on the "Essay on Buddhism," by Tominaga Nakamoto (1715–1746)*. Kyoto: Istituto Italiano di Cultura Scuola di Studi sull'Asia Orientale.

———. 2006. "The *Shijiapu* of Sengyou: The First Chinese Attempt to Produce a Critical Biography of the Buddha." *Kokusai Bukkyōgaku daigakuin daigaku kenkyū kiyō* 国際仏教学大学院大学研究紀要 (*Journal of the International College for Postgraduate Buddhist Studies*) 10: 51–86.

———. 2007. "The Meeting of the Buddha with Māyā in the Trāyastriṃśa Heaven: Examination of the *Mahāmāyā Sūtra* and Its Quotations in the *Shijiapu*—Part I." *Kokusai Bukkyōgaku daigakuin daigaku kenkyū kiyō* 国際仏教学大学院大学研究紀要 (*Journal of the International College for Postgraduate Buddhist Studies*) 11: 45–66.

———. 2008. "The Post-Nirvāṇa Meeting of the Buddha with Māyā: Examination of the *Mahāmāyā Sūtra* and Its Quotations in the *Shijiapu*—Part II." *Kokusai Bukkyōgaku daigakuin daigaku kenkyū kiyō* 国際仏教学大学院大学研究紀要 (*Journal of the International College for Postgraduate Buddhist Studies*) 12: 1–35.

Dutt, Nalinaksha. 1931. "Nāgārjunikoṇḍa and Nāgārjuna." *Indian Historical Quarterly* 7: 633–650.

———. 1934. "Home of Āryadeva." *Indian Historical Quarterly* 10: 137–142.

Endo Yujun 遠藤純祐. 2001. "Memyō mandara seiritsu no haikei ni tsuite" 馬鳴曼荼羅成立の背景について (On the Background of the Formation of Aśvaghoṣa's *Maṇḍala*). *Gendai mikkyō* 現代密教 (*Modern Esoteric Buddhism*) 14: 193–210.

Fan Jinmin 范金民. 1993. *Jiangnan sichou shi yanjiu* 江南絲綢史研究 (Research on the History of Silk in the Jiangnan Region). Beijing: Yiye chubanshe.

Fan Lizhu. 2003. "The Cult of the Silkworm Mother as a Core of Local Community Religion in a North China Village: Field Study in Zhiwuying, Boading, Hebei." *China Quarterly* 174: 373–394.

Faure, Bernard. 1991. *The Rhetoric of Immediacy*. Princeton, N.J.: Princeton University Press.

Forte, Antonino. 1976. *Political Propaganda and Ideology in China at the End of the Seventh Century: Inquiry into the Nature, Author, and Function of the Tunhuang Docu-

ment S. 6052, Followed by an Annotated Translation. Naples: Istituto Universitario Orientale.

Foulk, T. Griffith. 1999. "Sung Controversies Concerning the 'Separate Transmission' of Ch'an." In *Buddhism in the Sung*, ed. Peter N. Gregory and Daniel A. Getz. Jr., 220–294. Honolulu: University of Hawai'i Press.

Foulk, T. Griffith, and Robert H. Sharf. 1993–1994. "On the Ritual Use of Ch'an Portraiture in Medieval China." *Cahiers d'Extrême-Asie* 7: 149–219.

Franke, Herbert. 1991. "On Chinese Traditions Concerning the Dates of the Buddha." In *The Dating of the Historical Buddha/Die Datierung des historischen Buddha*, ed. Heinz Bechert, 1: 441–448. Göttingen, Germany: Vandenhoeck and Ruprecht.

Funayama Toru 船山徹. 2000. "Ryō no Sōyū sen *Satsubata shi shiden* to Tōdai bukkyō" 梁の僧祐撰『薩婆多師資伝』と唐代佛教 (Liang Sengyou's *Biographies of the Sarvāstivādin Masters and Disciples* and Tang Dynasty Buddhism). In *Tōdai no shūkyō* 唐代の宗教 (Tang Dynasty Religion), ed. Yoshikawa Tadao 吉川忠夫, 325–353. Kyoto: Hoyu shoten.

———. 2008. "The Work of Paramārtha: An Example of Sino-Indian Cross-Cultural Exchange." *JIABS* 31 (1–2): 141–183.

Garrett, Mary M. 1997. "Chinese Buddhist Religious Disputation." *Argumentation* 11: 195–209.

Gernet, Jacques. 1995. *Buddhism in Chinese Society: An Economic History from the Fifth to the Tenth Centuries*, trans. Franciscus Verellen. New York: Columbia University Press.

Gethin, Rupert. 1998. *The Foundations of Buddhism*. Oxford: Oxford University Press.

Gimello, Robert M. 2004. "Icon and Incantation: The Goddess Zhunti and the Role of Images on the Occult Buddhism of China." In *Images in Asian Religions: Texts and Contexts*, ed. Phyllis Granoff and Koichi Shinohara, 225–256. Vancouver: University of British Columbia Press.

Girard, Frédéric, trans. 2004. *Traité sur l'acte de foi dans le Grand Véhicule, Traduction commentée et Introduction par Frédéric Girard* (*Treatise on the Awakening of Faith in the Great Vehicle*, Annotated Translation and Introduction by Frédéric Girard). Tokyo: Keio University Press.

Gokhale, Vasudev, trans. 1930. *Akṣara-śatakam, The Hundred Letters*. Heidelberg: O. Harrassowitz.

Gombrich, Richard F. 1966. "The Consecration of a Buddhist Image." *Journal of Asian Studies* 26 (1): 23–36.

———. 1978. "The Buddha's Eye, the Evil Eye, and Dr. Ruelius." In *Buddhism in Ceylon and Studies on Religious Syncretism in Buddhist Countries*, ed. Heinz Bechert, 335–338. Göttingen, Germany: Vandenhoeck and Ruprecht.

Gómez, Luis O. 1996. *The Land of Bliss: The Paradise of the Buddha of Measureless Light*. Honolulu: University of Hawai'i Press.

Gong Dazhong 宫大中. 2002. *Longmen shiku yishu* 龍門石窟藝術 (The Art of the Longmen Grottoes). Beijing: Renmin meishu chubanshe.

Granoff, Phyllis. 1988. "Jain Biographies of Nagarjuna: Notes on the Composing of a Biography in Medieval India." In *Monks and Magicians: Religious Biographies in Asia*, ed. Phyllis Granoff and Koichi Shinohara, 45–66. Oakville, Ontario: Mosaic Press.

Granoff, Phyllis, and Koichi Shinohara, ed. 1988. *Monks and Magicians: Religious Biographies in Asia*. Oakville, Ontario: Mosaic Press.

———. 1992. *Speaking of Monks: Religious Biography in India and China*. Oakville, Ontario: Mosaic Press.

———, ed. 1994. *Other Selves: Autobiography and Biography in Cross-Cultural Perspective*. Oakville, Ontario: Mosaic Press.

Gregory, Peter N. 1986. "The Problem of Theodicy in the *Awakening of Faith*." *Religious Studies* 22: 63–78.

———. 1991. *Tsung-mi and the Sinification of Buddhism*. Princeton, N.J.: Princeton University Press.

Grosnick, William H. 1989. "The Categories of *T'i, Hsiang* and *Yung*: Evidence that Paramārtha Composed the *Awakening of Faith*." *JIABS* 12 (1): 65–92.

Hahn, Thomas H. 2000. "Daoist Sacred Sites." In *Daoism Handbook*, ed. Livia Kohn, 683–708. Leiden: Brill.

Hakeda, Yoshito S., trans. 1967. *Awakening of Faith Attributed to Aśvaghoṣa*. New York: Columbia University Press.

Haraprasad, Shastri. 1911. "Notes on the Newly-Found Manuscript of Chatuḥśatika by Āryadeva." *Journal of the Asiatic Society of Bengal* 7: 431–436.

Hardacre, Helen. 2002. *Religion and Society in Nineteenth-Century Japan*. Ann Arbor: University of Michigan.

Harrison, Paul M. 2000. "Mañjuśrī and the Cult of the Celestial Bodhisattvas." *Zhonghua foxue xuebao* 中華佛學學報 (*Chung-Hwa Buddhist Journal*) 13: 157–193.

Hasuzawa Shōjūn 蓮澤成淳. 1936. "Daiba bosatsu den gedai" 提婆菩薩傳解題 (Synopsis of the Biography of Deva Bodhisattva). In *Kokuyaku issaikyō: Indo senjutsubu* 國譯一切經: 印度撰述部 (National Translation of the Complete Buddhist Canon, Indian Commentaries Section), ed. Iwano Shin'yū 岩野眞雄, 465–466. Tokyo: Daitō Shuppansha.

Henan Sheng Gudai Jianzhu Baohu Yanjiusuo 河南省古代建筑保护研究所 (Henan Province Research Institute for the Preservation of Antiquities), ed. 1992. *Baoshan lingquansi* 寶山靈泉寺 (Lingquan Monastery at Mt. Bao). Zhengzhou: Henan renmin chubanshe.

Hendrichke, Barbara. 2000. "Early Daoist Movements." In *Daoism Handbook*, ed. Livia Kohn, 134–164. Leiden: Brill.

———. 2002. "The Virtue of Conformity: The Religious Re-Writing of Political Biography." In *Religion and Biography in China and Tibet*, ed. Benjamin Penny, 30–48. Richmond, UK: Curzon Press.

Henricks, Robert G., trans. 1989. *Lao-Tzu Te-Tao Ching*. New York: Ballantine Books.

Hill, John E. 2003. *The Western Regions According to the "Hou Hanshu": The "Xiyu juan" "Chapter on the Western Regions" from "Hou Hanshu" 88*. 2nd ed. Walter Chapin Simpson Center for the Humanities at the University of Washington. Accessed April 21, 2014. http://depts.washington.edu/silkroad/texts/hhshu/hou_han_shu.html#index.

Hirosato Iwai 岩井大慧. 1951. "The Compilers of *Ching-t'u pao-chu chi*." *Memoirs of the Research Department of the Toyo Bunko* 13: 47–86.

Hopkins, L. C., and R. L. Hobson. 1912. "A Royal Relic of Ancient China." *Man* 12: 49–52.

Hou Chuanwen 侯傳文. 1999. *Maming dashi zhuan* 馬鳴大師傳 (Biography of the Great Master Aśvaghoṣa). Sanchong, Taiwan: Foguang shizhuan congshu.

Howard, Angela F. 1996. "Buddhist Cave Sculpture of the Northern Qi Dynasty: Shaping a New Style, Formulating New Iconographies." *Archives of Asian Art* 49: 6–25.

———. 1999. "The Eight Brilliant Kings of Wisdom of Southwest China." *RES* 35: 92–107.

Huang Diming 黃滌明, trans. 1991. *Soushen ji quanyi* 搜神記全譯 (Complete Translation of the *Record of the Search for the Supernormal*). Guiyang, China: Guozhou renmin chubanshe.

Huang Zheng 黃徵 and Wu Wei 吳偉, eds. 1995. *Dunhuang yuanwen ji* 敦煌願文集 (Collected Dunhuang Prayer Texts). Changsha, China: Yuelu shushe.

Hubbard, Jamie. 2001. *Absolute Delusion, Perfect Buddhahood: The Rise and Fall of a Chinese Heresy*. Honolulu: University of Hawai'i Press.

Huber, Édouard, trans. 1908. *Açvaghoṣa, Sūtrālaṃkāra, traduit en français sur la version chinoise de Kumārajīva* (Aśvaghoṣa's *Sūtrālaṃkāra* Translated into French from the Chinese Version of Kumārajīva). Paris: Ernest Leroux.

Huber, Toni. 2008. *The Holy Land Reborn: Pilgrimage and the Tibetan Reinvention of Buddhist India*. Chicago: University of Chicago Press.

Hulsewé, A. F. P., and M. Loewe. 1979. *China in Central Asia: The Early Stage, 125 BC–AD 23: An Annotated Translation of Chapters 61 and 96 of "The History of the Former Han Dynasty."* Leiden: E. J. Brill.

Hurvitz, Leon. 1957. "'Render unto Ceasar' in Early Chinese Buddhism: Hui-Yüan's Treatise on the Exemption of the Buddhist Clergy from the Requirements of Civil Etiquette." In *Liebenthal Festschrift*, ed. Kshitis Roy, 80–114. West Bengal: Santiniketan.

———, trans. 1976. *Scripture of the Lotus Blossom of the Fine Dharma*. New York: Columbia University Press.

Hu-von Hinüber, Haiyan. 2011. "Faxian's (法顯 342–423) Perception of India: Some New Interpretation of his *Foguoji* 佛國記." *Annual Report of the International Research Institute for Advanced Buddhology at Soka University* 14: 223–247.

Hymes, Robert. 2002. *Way and Byway: Taoism, Local Religion, and Models of Divinity in Sung and Modern China*. Berkeley: University of California Press.

Inada, Kenneth K. 1970. *Nāgārjuna: A Translation of his Mūlamadhyamakakārikā with an Introductory Essay*. Tokyo: Hokuseido Press.

Inagaki Hisao, trans. 1998. *Nāgārjuna's Discourse on the Ten Stages (Daśabhūmika-vibhāṣā)*. Kyoto: Ryukoku University.

Inui Katsumi 乾克己. 1990. "Memyō chōkoto setsuwa to sono tenkai" 馬鳴調琴説話とその展開 (The Development of the Legend of Aśvaghoṣa's Music). *Wayō joshi daigaku kiyō* 和洋女子大学紀要 (Journal of Wayō Women's University), 30: 19–34.

Iyanaga Nobumi 彌永信美. 2002. *Kannon henyō tan* 觀音變容譚 (Tales of the Transformations of Kannon). Kyoto: Hōzōkan.

Jan Yün-Hua. 1966a. "Buddhist Relations between India and Sung China." *History of Religions* 6 (1): 24–42.

———. 1966b. "Buddhist Relations between India and Sung China, Part II." *History of Religions* 6 (2): 135–168.

———. 1970. "Nāgārjuna, One or More? A New Interpretation of Buddhist Hagiography." *History of Religions* 10 (2): 139–155.

Jeon Hae-ju. 2003. "Nagarjuna as Viewed in Korean Buddhist Prayer Books." *International Journal of Buddhist Thought and Culture* 2: 277–289.

Jia Jinhua. 2006. *The Hongzhou School of Chan Buddhism in Eighth- through Tenth-Century China*. Albany: State University of New York Press.

Johnson, E. H, trans. 1932. *The Saundarananda, or Nanda the Fair.* Oxford: Oxford University Press.

———, trans. (1936) 1984. *The Buddhacarita: Or, Acts of the Buddha*. Delhi: Motilal Banarsidass.

Joo, Ryan Bongseok. 2007. "The Ritual of Arhat Invitation during the Song Dynasty: Why Did Mahāyānists Venerate the Arhat?" *JIABS* 30 (1–2): 81–116.

Jorgensen, John. 1987. "The 'Imperial' Lineage of Ch'an Buddhism: The Role of Confucian Ritual and Ancestor Worship in Ch'an's Search for Legitimation in the Mid-T'ang Dynasty." *Papers on Far Eastern History* 35: 89–133.

———. 2005. *Inventing Hui-neng, the Sixth Patriarch: Hagiography and Biography in Early Ch'an*. Leiden: Brill.

Joshi, L. M. 1965. "Life and Times of the Mādhyamika Philosopher Nāgārjuna." *Mahabodhi* 73 (1–2).

———. 1977. "The Legend of Nāgārjuna's Murder." In *Madhyamika Dialectic and the Philosophy of Nāgārjuna*, ed. Samdhong Rinpoche, 166–168. Sarnath: Tibetan Institute.

Juan Chung-jen 阮忠仁. 1990. "Cong *Lidai sanbao ji* lun Fei Zhangfang de shixue tezhi ji yiyi" 從《歷代三寶記》論費長房的史學特質及意義 (A Discussion of the Historical Significance and Special Historiographic Qualities of the *Record of the Three Jewels in History*, by Fei Ch'ang-fang). *Dongfang zongjiao yanjiu* 東方宗教研究 (Studies in Eastern Religions), new series, 1: 93–129.

Kalupahana, David J. 1986. *Nāgārjuna: The Philosophy of the Middle Way*. Albany: State University of New York Press.

Kanakura Yensho. 1959. "A Bibliographical Study of Aśvaghoṣa's Works." In *Religious Studies in Japan*, ed. Nihon Shūkyō Gakkai, 300–307. Tokyo: Maruzen.

Karambelkar, V. W. 1952. "The Problem of Nāgārjuna." *Journal of Indian History* 30 (1): 21–33.

Kashiwagi Hiroo 柏木弘雄. 1981. *Daijō kishinron no kenkyū: Daijō kishinron no seiritsu ni kansuru shiryōronteki kenkyū* 大乗起信論の研究: 大乗起信論の成立に関する資料論的研究 (A Study of the *Mahāyāna Awakening of Faith*: Critical Research on the Materials Concerning the Composition of the *Mahāyāna Awakening of Faith*). Tokyo: Shunjūsha.

Keyes, Charles F. 1982. "Death of Two Buddhist Saints in Thailand." In *Charisma and Sacred Biography*, ed. Michael A. Williams. Chambersburg, Pa.: American Academy of Religion.

Khosla, Sarla. 1986. *Aśvaghoṣa and His Times*. New Delhi: Intellectual Publishing House.

Kieschnick, John. 1997. *The Eminent Monk: Buddhist Ideals in Medieval Chinese Hagiography*. Honolulu: University of Hawai'i Press.

———. 2003. *The Impact of Buddhism on Chinese Material Culture*. Princeton, N.J.: Princeton University Press.

Kieschnick, John, and Meir Shahar, eds. 2013. *India in the Chinese Imagination: Myth, Religion, and Thought*. Philadelphia: University of Pennsylvania Press.

Kim, Sunkyung. 2011. "Seeing Buddhas in Cave Sanctuaries." *Asia Major*, 3rd series, 24 (1): 87–126.

Kleine, Christoph. 1996. "The *Separate Biography* of Hōnen: A Translation and Critical Analysis of the *Betsu-Denki*." *Japanese Religions* 21 (1): 70–99.

———. 1998. "Portraits of Pious Women in East Asian Buddhist Hagiography: A Study of Accounts of Women Who Attained Birth in Amida's Pure Land." *Bulletin de l'École Française d'Extrême-Orient* 85: 325–361.

Knoblock, John. 1988. *Xunzi: A Translation and Study of the Complete Works*. 3 vols. Stanford: Stanford University Press.

Kohn, Livia. 1995. *Laughing at the Tao: Debates among Buddhists and Taoists in Medieval China*. Princeton, N.J.: Princeton University Press.

———. 1998. "The Lao-tzu Myth." In *Lao-tzu and the Tao-te-ching*, ed. Livia Kohn and Michael LaFargue, 41–62. Albany: State University of New York Press.

Koseki, Aaron Ken. 1977. "Chi-tsang's *Ta-ch'eng-hsuan-lun*: The Two Truths and the Buddha Nature." Ph.D. diss., University of Wisconsin, Madison.

Kroll, J. R. 1985. "Disputation in Ancient Chinese Culture." *Early China* 11–12: 118–145.

Ku, Kathy Cheng-Mei. 2010. "The *Buddharāja* Image of Emperor Wu of Liang." In *Philosophy and Religion in Early Medieval China*, ed. Alan K. L. Chan and Yuet-Keung Lo, 265–290. Albany: State University of New York Press.

Kucera, Karil. 2006. "Recontextualizing Kanjingsi: Finding Meaning in the Emptiness at Longmen." *Archives of Asian Art* 56: 61–80.

Kuhn, Dieter. 1984. "Tracing a Chinese Legend: In Search of the Identity of the 'First Sericulturalist.'" *T'oung Pao* 70: 213–245.

Lahiri, Latika, trans. 1986. *Chinese Monks in India: Biography of Eminent Monks Who Went to the Western World in Search of the Law during the Great T'ang Dynasty*. Delhi: Motilal Banarsidass.

Lai, Whalen. 1975. "The Awakening of Faith in Mahayana (Ta-ch'eng ch'i-hsin lun)—A Study of the Unfolding of Sinitic Mahayana Motifs." Ph.D. diss., Harvard University.

———. 1980. "A Clue to the Authorship of the *Awakening of Faith*: 'Śikṣānanda's' Redaction of the word '*Nien*.'" *JIABS* 3 (1): 34–53.

———. 1990. "The *Chan-ch'a ching*: Religion and Magic in Medieval China." In *Chinese Buddhist Apocrypha*, ed. Robert E. Buswell, Jr., 175–206. Honolulu: University of Hawai'i Press.

Lamotte, Étienne. 1944–1980. *Le traité de la grande vertu de sagesse de Nāgārjuna (Mahāprajñāpāramitāśāstra)* (The Treatise on the Great Perfection of Wisdom by Nāgārjuna). 5 vols. Louvain-La-Neuve, Belgium: Institut Orientaliste, Université de Louvain.

———. 1988. *History of Indian Buddhism*, trans. Sara Webb-Boin. Louvain-La-Neuve, Belgium: Institut Orientaliste, Université de Louvain.

Lancaster, Lewis R. 1979. *The Korean Buddhist Canon: A Descriptive Catalogue*. Berkeley: University of California Press.

———. 1981. "The Bodhisattva Concept: A Study of the Chinese Buddhist Canon." In *The Bodhisattva Doctrine in Buddhism*, ed. L. S. Kawamura, 153–163. Ontario: Wilfrid Laurier University.

———. 1991. "The Dating of the Buddha in Chinese Buddhism." In *The Dating of the Historical Buddha / Die Datierung des historischen Buddha*, ed. Heinz Bechert, 1: 449–457. Göttingen, Germany: Vandenhoeck and Ruprecht.

Lang, Karen. 1986. *Āryadeva's Catuḥśataka: On the Bodhisattva's Cultivation of Merit and Knowledge*. Copenhagen: Akademisk Forlag.

Lau, D. C., trans. 1979. *Confucius: The Analects*. London: Penguin Books.

La Vallée Poussin, Louis de. 1913. *Mūlamadhyamakakārikās de Nāgārjuna avec la Prasannapadā de Candrakīrti* (Nāgārjuna's *Middle Stanzas* and Candrakīrti's *Clear Worded* Commentary). Bibliotheca Buddhica 4. St. Petersberg: Imperial Academy of Sciences.

Lee Yu-min 李玉珉. 1999. "Baoshan Dazhusheng ku chutan 寶山大住聖窟初探" (A Preliminary Study of the Cave of Great Perduring Saints at Mt. Bao). *Gugong xueshu jikan* 故宮學術季刊 (*The National Palace Museum Research Quarterly*) 16 (2): 1–52.

Legge, James, trans. (1885) 1967. *Li Chi: Book of Rites*. 2 vols. New York: University Books.

———. (1895) 1970. *The Works of Mencius*. New York: Dover Publications, Inc.

Lévi, Sylvain. 1896. "Notes sur les Indo-Scythes." *Journal Asiatique*, 9th series, 8: 444–484.

———. 1908. "Açvaghoṣa: Le Sūtrālaṃkāra et ses sources." *Journal Asiatique*, 10th series, 12: 57–184.

———. 1928. "Encore Aśvaghoṣa." *Journal Asiatique* 213: 193–216.

———. 1929. "Autour d'Aśvaghoṣa." *Journal Asiatique* 215: 255–285.

Lévi, Sylvain, and Édouard Chavannes. 1916. "Les seize *arhat* protecteurs de la loi" (The Sixteen Arhat Protectors of the Dharma). *Journal Asiatique* 8: 1–166.

Li Fuhua 李富華 and He Mei 何梅. 2003. *Hanwen fojiao dazangjing yanjiu* 漢文佛教大藏經研究 (A Study of the Chinese Buddhist Canon). Beijing: Zongjiao wenhua chubanshe.

Li Qiao 李乔. 1999. *Hangye shen chongbai: Zhongguo minzhong zaoshen yundong yanjiu* 行业神崇拜: 中国民众造神运动研究 (Worshipping the Gods of Industry: Studies in the Creation of Gods by the Chinese People). Beijing: Zhongguo wenlian chubanshe.

Li Rongxi, trans. 1993. *The Biographical Scripture of King Aśoka*. Berkeley, Calif.: Numata Center for Buddhist Translation and Research.

———. 1995. *A Biography of the Tripiṭaka Master of the Great Ci'en Monastery of the Great Tang Dynasty*. Berkeley, Calif.: Numata Center for Buddhist Translation and Research.

———. 1996. *The Great Tang Dynasty Record of the Western Regions*. Berkeley, Calif.: Numata Center for Buddhist Translation and Research.

———. 2002a. "The Journey of the Eminent Monk Faxian." In *Lives of Great Monks and Nuns*, trans. Albert A. Dalia and Li Rongxi, 155–214. Berkeley, Calif.: Numata Center for Buddhist Translation and Research.

———. 2002b. "The Life of Aśvaghoṣa Bodhisattva." In *Lives of Great Monks and Nuns*, trans. Albert A. Dalia and Li Rongxi, 5–16. Berkeley, Calif.: Numata Center for Buddhist Translation and Research.

———. 2002c. "The Life of Nāgārjuna Bodhisattva." In *Lives of Great Monks and Nuns*, trans. Albert A. Dalia and Li Rongxi, 17–30. Berkeley, Calif.: Numata Center for Buddhist Translation and Research.

Li Yuxi 黎玉璽, trans. 1997a. *Fu fazang yinyuan zhuan* 付法藏因緣傳 (Tradition of the Causes and Conditions of the Dharma-Treasury Transmission). Taipei: Daqian chubanshe.

———, trans. 1997b. "Maming pusa zhuan 馬鳴菩薩傳" (The Biography of Aśvaghoṣa Bodhisattva). In *Fu fazang yinyuan zhuan* 付法藏因緣傳 (Tradition of the Causes and Conditions of the Dharma-Treasury Transmission). Taipei: Daqian chubanshe.

Liebenthal, Walter. 1950. "Shih Hui-Yuan's Buddhism as Set Forth in His Writings." *Journal of the American Oriental Society* 70 (4): 243–259.

———. 1955. "A Biography of Chu Tao-sheng." *Monumenta Nipponica* 11 (3): 64–96.

———. 1958. "The Oldest Commentary of the Mahāyānaśraddhotpāda śāstra." *Bukkyō bunka kenkyū* 6–7: 1–7.

———. 1959. "New Light on the Mahāyāna-śraddhotpāda śāstra." *T'oung Pao* 46: 155–216.

———. 1968. *Chao Lun: The Treatises of Seng-chao*. Hong Kong: Hong Kong University Press.

Lin Xin 林鑫. 2000. *Zhongguan diyi ren: Longshu Pusa* 中觀第一人：龍樹菩薩 (Founder of the Middle View: Nāgārjuna Bodhisattva). Sanchong: Foguang manhua congshu.

Lindtner, Christian. 1982. *Nagarjuniana: Studies in the Writings and Philosophy of Nāgārjuna*. Delhi: Motilal Banarsidass Publishers.

———. 1986. *Master of Wisdom: Writings of the Buddhist Master Nāgārjuna*. Oakland, Calif.: Dharma Press.

Liu, Gaines Kan-Chih. 1950. "Cicadas in Chinese Culture (Including the Silver-Fish)." *Osiris* 9: 275–396.

Liu Ming-Wood. 1994. *Madhyamaka Thought in China*. Leiden: E. J. Brill.

Liu Xinru. 1996. *Silk and Religion: An Exploration of Material Life and the Thought of People, AD 600–1200*. Delhi: Oxford University Press.

Lo, Yuet-Keung. 2002. "Persuasion and Entertainment at Once: Kumārajīva's Buddhist Storytelling in His Commentary on the *Vimalakīrti-sūtra*." *Zhongguo wenzhe yanjiu jikan* 中國文哲研究集刊 (Bulletin of the Institute of Chinese Literature and Philosophy) 21: 89–116.

———. 2010. "Destiny and Retribution in Early Medieval China." In *Philosophy and Religion in Early Medieval China*, ed. Alan K. L. Chan and Yuet-Keung Lo, 319–356. Albany: State University of New York Press.

Lu Yang. 2004. "Narrative and Historicity in the Buddhist Biographies of Early Medieval China: The Case of Kumārajīva." *Asia Major* 17 (2): 1–43.

Lü Youxiang 呂有祥, trans. 1996. *Chu sanzang jiji* 出三藏記集 (Collected Records on the Production of the Threefold Canon). Gaoxiong: Foguang.

Lusthaus, Dan. 2002. *Buddhist Phenomenology: A Philosophical Investigation of Yogācāra Buddhism and the "Ch'eng Wei-shih lun."* London: RoutledgeCurzon.

Lyons, John D. 1989. *Exemplum: The Rhetoric of Example in Early Modern France and Italy.* Princeton, N.J.: Princeton University Press.

Mabbett, Ian. 1998. "The Problem of the Historical Nāgārjuna Revisited." *Journal of the American Oriental Society* 118 (3): 332–346.

Makita Tairyō 牧田諦亮. 1964. "Hōzanji Reiyū ni tsuite" 寶山寺靈裕について (On Lingyu of Baoshan Monastery). *Tōhō gakuhō* 東方學報 (Journal of Oriental Studies) 36: 261–286.

———. 1981. *Chūgoku bukkyō-shi kenkyū* 中國仏教史研究 (Studies in Chinese Buddhist History), Vol 1. Tokyo: Daitō Shupansha.

Maspero, Henri. 1911. "Sur la date et l'authenticité du *Fou fa tsang yin yüan tchouan*" (On the Date and Authenticity of the *Fu fazang yinyuan zhuan*). In *Mélanges d'Indianisme offerts par ses élèves à M. Sylvain Lévi* (Studies in Indology Offered to Sylvain Lévi by His Students), 129–149. Paris: E. Leroux.

Mather, Richard B. 1963. "Wang Chin's 'Dhūta Temple Stele Inscription' as an Example of Buddhist Parallel Prose." *Journal of the American Oriental Society* 83 (3): 338–359.

———. 1968. "Vimalakīrti and Gentry Buddhism." *History of Religions* 8 (1): 60–73.

———. 1979. "K'ou Ch'ien-chih and the Taoist Theocracy at the Northern Wei Court, 425–451." In *Facets of Taoism: Essays in Chinese Religion*, ed. Holmes Welch and Anna Seidel, 103–122. New Haven, Conn.: Yale University Press.

———. 1992. "Chinese and Indian Perceptions of Each Other between the First and Seventh Centuries." *Journal of the American Oriental Society* 112 (1): 1–8.

———, trans. 2002. *Shih-shuo Hsin-yu: A New Account of Tales of the World.* 2nd ed. Ann Arbor: Center for Chinese Studies, University of Michigan.

Matsuyama Sadayoshi 松山貞好. 2009a. "Chūgoku Bukkyō ni okeru *Fu hōzō innen den* no ichi" 中国仏教に於ける「付法蔵因縁伝」の位置 (The Place of the *Tradition of the Causes and Conditions of the Dharma-Treasury Transmission* in Chinese Buddhism). *Ōtani Daigaku Daigakuin kenkyū kiyō* 大谷大学大学院研究紀要 (Research Journal of the Graduate School of Ōtani University) 26: 197–217.

———. 2009b. "Donyō to Hokugi haibutsu—*Fu hōzō innen den* o chūshin ni" 曇曜と北魏廃仏–「付法蔵因縁伝」を中心に (Tanyao and the Northern Wei Abolition of Buddhism, Focusing on the *Tradition of the Causes and Conditions of the Dharma-Treasury Transmission*). *Indogaku Bukkyōgaku kenkyū* 印度學佛教學研究 (Journal of Indian and Buddhist Studies) 57 (2): 805–808.

McBride, Richard D. 2005. "Dhāraṇī and Spells in Medieval Sinitic Buddhism." *JIABS* 28 (1): 85–114.

McDaniel, Justin Thomas. 2011. *The Lovelorn Ghost and the Magical Monk: Practicing Buddhism in Modern Thailand.* New York: Columbia University Press.

McNair, Amy. 2007. *Donors of Longmen: Faith, Politics, and Patronage in Medieval Chinese Buddhist Sculpture.* Honolulu: University of Hawai'i Press.

McRae, John R. 1986. *The Northern School and the Formation of Early Ch'an Buddhism.* Honolulu: University of Hawai'i Press.

Middendorf, Ulrike. 2010. "The Sage without Emotion: Music, Mind, and Politics in Xi Kang." In *Philosophy and Religion in Early Medieval China*, ed. Alan K. L. Chan and Yuet-Keung Lo, 135–171. Albany: State University of New York Press.

Miller, Alan. 1995. "The Woman Who Married a Horse: Five Ways of Looking at a Chinese Folktale." *Asian Folklore Studies* 54: 275–305.

Mimaki Katsumi. 1987. "Āryadeva." In *Encyclopedia of Religion*, 1: 431–432. New York: Macmillan.

Mino, Katherine R. Tsiang. 1996. "Bodies of Buddhas and Princes at the Xiangtangshan Caves: Image, Text, and *Stūpa* in Buddhist Art of the Northern Qi Dynasty (550–577)." Ph.D. diss., University of Chicago.

Minowa Kenryō 蓑輪顕量. 2003. "*Zazen sammai kyō* niokeru shugyō michi" 『坐禅三昧経』における修行道 (The Path of Practice in the *Sūtra on Seated Dhyāna Samādhi*). In *Bukkyō no shugyōhō: Abe Jion Hakushi tsuitō ronshū* 仏教の修行法: 阿部慈園博士追悼論集 (Methods of Buddhist Practice: Festschrift for Dr. Abe Jion), ed. Kimura Kiyotaka 木村清孝, 177–196. Tokyo: Shunjūsha.

Miyake Tetsujo 三宅徹誠. 2008. "Kongōji zō Hōen shitoshi utsu *Muryōjukyō ronchū* ni tsuite" 金剛寺蔵保延四年写『無量寿経論註』について (On the *Wuliangshoujing lunzhu* Manuscript Written in the Fourth Year Hōen Preserved at Kongōji). *Indōgaku bukkyōgaku kenkyū* 印度學佛教學研究 (Journal of Indian and Buddhist Studies) 56 (2): 577–583.

Mizuno Seiichi 水野清一. 1968. "*Fu hōzō den* to Unkō sekkutsu" 付法蔵伝と雲岡石窟 (The *Tradition of the Dharma-Treasury Transmission* and the Yungang Caves). In *Chūgoku no Bukkyō bijutsu* 中國の佛教美術 (Chinese Buddhist Art), 332–335. Tokyo: Heibonsha.

Mo Yan 默言. 1999. *Dasheng chuanfa ren: Longshu Pusa* 大乘傳法人：龍樹菩薩 (Mahāyāna Transmitter of the Dharma: Nāgārjuna Bodhisattva). Taipei: Fagu wenhua shiye.

Mochizuki Shinkō 望月信亨. 1922. *Daijō kishinron no kenkyū* 大乘起信論之研究 (A Study of the *Mahāyāna Awakening of Faith*). Tokyo: Kanao Bun'endō.

———. 1938. *Kōjutsu Daijō kishinron* 講述大乘起信論 (Lectures on the *Mahāyāna Awakening of Faith*). Tokyo: Huzanbō hyakkabunko.

Mollier, Christine. 2008. *Buddhism and Taoism Face to Face: Scripture, Ritual, and Iconographic Exchange in Medieval China*. Honolulu: University of Hawai'i Press.

Morrison, Elizabeth. 1996. "Contested Visions of the Buddhist Past and the Curious Fate of an Early Medieval Buddhist Text." Unpublished manuscript.

———. 2010. *The Power of Patriarchs: Qisong and Lineage in Chinese Buddhism*. Leiden: Brill.

Mun, Chanju. 2006. *The History of Doctrinal Classification in Chinese Buddhism: A Study of the Panjiao Systems*. Lanham, Md.: University Press of America.

Murti, T. R. V. 1955. *The Central Philosophy of Buddhism: A Study of the Mādhyamika System*. New Delhi: Munshiram Manoharlal Publishers.

Murty, K. Satchidananda. 1971. *Nāgārjuna*. New Delhi: National Book Trust.

Nagahiro Toshio 長廣敏雄. 1994. "Yungang shiku di jiu, shi shuangku de tezheng" 雲岡石窟第九, 一〇雙窟的特徵 (The Characteristics of Twin Caves Nine and Ten at the Yungang Grottoes). In *Yungang shiku* 云冈石窟 (The Yungang Grottoes), ed. Yungang shiku wenwu baoguan 云冈石窟文物保管, 193–207. Beijing: Wenwu chubanshe.

Nattier, Jan. 1988. "The 'Candragarbha-sūtra' in Central and East Asia: Studies in a Buddhist Prophecy of Decline." Ph.D. diss., Harvard University.

———. 1991. *Once upon a Future Time: Studies in a Buddhist Prophecy of Decline.* Berkeley, Calif.: Asian Humanities Press.

———. 2003. *A Few Good Men: The Bodhisattva Path According to "The Inquiry of Ugra" (Ugraparipṛcchā).* Honolulu: University of Hawai'i Press.

———. 2008. *A Guide to the Earliest Chinese Buddhist Translations: Texts from the Eastern Han* 東漢 *and Three Kingdoms* 三國 *Periods.* Tokyo: International Research Institute for Advanced Buddhology, Soka University.

Needham, Joseph, with Lu Gwei-Djen. 1974. *Chemistry and Chemical Technology*; pt. 2, *Spagyrical Discovery and Invention: Magisteries of Gold and Immortality.* Vol. 5 of *Science and Civilisation in China.* Cambridge: Cambridge University Press.

Needham, Joseph, with Deiter Kuhn. 1988. *Chemistry and Chemical Technology*; pt. 9, *Textile Technology: Spinning and Reeling.* Vol. 5 of *Science and Civilisation in China.* Cambridge: Cambridge University Press.

Ng, Zhiru. 2007. *The Making of a Savior Bodhisattva: Dizang in Medieval China.* Honolulu: University of Hawai'i Press.

Niu Tianwei 牛天伟. 2004. "Hanjin huaxiang shi, zhuan zhong de 'Canma shenxiang' kao" 汉晋画像石, 砖中的'蚕马神像'考 (A Study of the Han and Jin [Period] Portrayals in Stone and Brick of the "Image of the Silkworm-Horse God"). *Zhongguo hanhua yanjiu* 中国汉画研究 (Studies of Han-Era Chinese Art) 1: 89–101.

Obeyesekere, Gananath. 1976. "Personal Identity and Cultural Crisis: The Case of Angārika Dharmapala of Sri Lanka." In *The Biographical Process: Studies in the History and Psychology of Religion*, ed. Frank E. Reynolds and Donald Capps. The Hague: Mouton.

Ochiai Toshinori 落合俊典. 1991. *The Manuscripts of Nanatsu-dera.* With remarks by Makita Tairyō and Antonino Forte. Ed. and trans. Silvio Vita. Kyoto: Italian School of East Asian Studies.

———. 1992a. "Heisei shinshutsu *Memyō bosatsu den* no bunkengakuteki kōsatsu" 平成新出馬鳴菩薩伝の文献学的考察 (Philological Investigation of the *Tradition of Aśvaghoṣa Bodhisattva* Discovered in the Heisei Period [part 1]). *Kachō tanki daigaku kenkyū kiyō* 華頂短期大学研究紀要 (Research Journal of Kacho College) 37: 1–14.

———. 1992b. "Kōshōji hon *Memyō bosatsu den* ni tsuite" 興聖寺本馬鳴菩薩伝について (On the Kōshōji Manuscript of the *Tradition of Aśvaghoṣa Bodhisattva*). *Indōgaku bukkyōgaku kenkyū* 印度學佛教學研究 (Journal of Indian and Buddhist Studies) 81 (41-1): 293–299.

———. 1993. "Heisei shinshutsu *Memyō bosatsu den* no bunkengakuteki kōsatsu" 平成新出馬鳴菩薩伝の文献学的考察 (Philological Investigation of the *Tradition of Aśvaghoṣa Bodhisattva* Discovered in the Heisei Period [part 2]). *Kachō tanki daigaku kenkyū kiyō* 華頂短期大学研究紀要 (Research Journal of Kacho College) 38: 31–47.

———. 1994. "Heisei shinshutsu *Memyō bosatsu den* no bunkengakuteki kōsatsu" 平成新出馬鳴菩薩伝の文献学的考察 (Philological Investigation of the *Tradition of*

Aśvaghoṣa Bodhisattva Discovered in the Heisei Period [part 3]). *Kachō tanki daigaku kenkyū kiyō* 華頂短期大学研究紀要 (Research Journal of Kacho College) 39: 11–27.

———. 1996. "Sōei to *Memyō bosatsu den*" 僧叡と馬鳴菩薩伝 (Sengrui and the *Tradition of Aśvaghoṣa Bodhisattva*). *Indōgaku bukkyōgaku kenkyū* 印度學佛教學研究 (Journal of Indian and Buddhist Studies) 44 (2): 562–567.

———. 2000. "Nishu no *Memyō bosatsu den*—sono seiritsu to ryūden" 二種の『馬鳴菩薩傳』—その成立と流傳 (The Origins and Development of the Two Textual Traditions of the *Tradition of Aśvaghoṣa Bodhisattva*). In *Chūgoku Nihon senjutsu kyōten (senjutsusho)* 中國日本撰述經典（撰述書）(Scriptures and Commentaries Composed in China and Japan), 619–646. *Nanatsu-dera koitsu kyōten kenkyū sōsho* 七寺古逸經典研究叢書 (The Long Hidden Scriptures of Nanatsu-dera Research Series) 5, ed. Makita Tairyō 牧田諦亮 and Ochiai Toshinori 落合俊典. Tokyo: Daitō shuppansha.

Ochiai Toshinori 落合俊典 and Saitō Takanobu 齊藤隆信. 2000. "Memyō bosatsu den" 馬鳴菩薩傳 (Tradition of Aśvaghoṣa Bodhisattva). In *Chūgoku Nihon senjutsu kyōten (senjutsusho)* 中國日本撰述經典（撰述書）(Scriptures and Commentaries Composed in China and Japan), 265–295. *Nanatsu-dera koitsu kyōten kenkyū sōsho* 七寺古逸經典研究叢書 (The Long Hidden Scriptures of Nanatsu-dera Research Series) 5, ed. Makita Tairyō 牧田諦亮 and Ochiai Toshinori 落合俊典. Tokyo: Daitō shuppansha.

Ōfuchi, Ninji. 1979. "The Formation of the Taoist Canon." In *Facets of Taoism: Essays in Chinese Religion*, ed. Holmes Welch and Anna Seidel, 253–267. New Haven, Conn.: Yale University Press.

Ohnuma Reiko. 2007. *Head, Eyes, Flesh, and Blood: Giving Away the Body in Indian Buddhist Literature.* New York: Columbia University Press.

Ōmura Seigai 大村西崖. 1918. *Mikkyō hattatsushi* 密教發達志 (The Development of Esoteric Buddhism). Vol. 5. Tokyo: Bussho kankōkai zuzobu.

Orzech, Charles D. 1998. *Politics and Transcendent Wisdom: The "Scripture for Humane Kings" in the Creation of Chinese Buddhism.* University Park: Pennsylvania State University Press.

Orzech, Charles D., and James H. Sanford. 2000. "Worship of the Ladies of the Dipper." In *Tantra in Practice*, ed. David Gordon White, 383–395. Princeton, N.J.: Princeton University Press.

Osabe Kazuo 長部和雄. 1982. *Tō-Sō mikkyōshi ronkō* 唐宋密教史論考 (Studies on Esoteric Buddhism in the Tang and Song). Kyoto: Nagada bunshōdō.

Ōuchi Humio 大內文雄. 1997. "Hōzan Reisenji sekkutsu tōmei no kenkyū—Zui-Tō jidai no Hōzan Reisenji" 寶山靈泉寺石窟塔銘の研究—隋唐時代の寶山靈泉寺 (Baoshan Lingquansi of the Sui-Tang Period—A Study of the Buddhist Pagoda Inscriptions in the Baoshan Lingquansi Grottoes). *Tōhō gakuhō* 東方學報 (Journal of Oriental Studies) 69: 287–355.

Pan Lusheng 潘魯生, ed. 1993. *Shenxiang juan* 神像卷 (Images of Deities). Vol. 1 of *Zhongguo minjian meishu quanji* 中國民間美術全集 (Complete Collection of Chinese Folk Art). Ji'nan, China: Shandong jiaoyu chubanshe.

Pas, Julian F. 1995. *Visions of Sukhāvatī: Shan-Tao's Commentary on the "Kuan Wu-Liang-Shou-Fo Ching."* Albany: State University of New York Press.

Pearce, Scott. 2012. "A King's Two Bodies: The Northern Wei Emperor Wencheng and Representations of the Power of His Monarchy." *Frontiers of History in China* 7 (1): 90–105.

Pelliot, Paul. 2002. "Notes sur Kumārajīva." In *A Life Journey to the East: Sinological Studies in Memory of Giuliano Bertuccioli*, ed. Antonino Forte and Federico Masini, 1–19. Kyoto: Scuola Italiana di Studia sull'Asia Orientale.

Penkower, Linda. 1993. "T'ien T'ai during the T'ang dynasty: Chan-jan and the Sinification of Buddhism." Ph.D. diss., Columbia University.

———. 2000. "In the Beginning . . . : Guanding 灌頂 (561–632) and the Creation of Early Tiantai." *JIABS* 23 (2): 245–296.

Penny, Benjamin. 2002. "Jiao Xian's Three Lives." In *Religion and Biography in China and Tibet*, ed. Benjamin Penny, 13–29. Richmond, UK: Curzon Press.

Potter, Karl H. 1982. "Śaṃkarācārya: The Myth and the Man." In *Charisma and Sacred Biography*, ed. Michael A. Williams. Chambersburg, Pa.: American Academy of Religion.

Przyluski, Jean. 1923. *La légende de l'empereur Açoka (Açoka-Avadāna): Dans les Textes Indiens et Chinois* (*The Legend of King Aśoka*: In Indian and Chinese Texts). Paris: Paul Geuthner.

Puett, Michael. 2001. *The Ambivalence of Creation: Debates Concerning Innovation and Artifice in Early China*. Stanford, Calif.: Stanford University Press.

———. 2010. "Becoming Laozi: Cultivating and Visualizing Spirits in Early-Medieval China." *Asia Major*, 3rd series, 23 (1): 223–252.

Pulleyblank, Edwin G. 1991. *Lexicon of Reconstructed Pronunciation in Early Middle Chinese, Late Middle Chinese, and Early Mandarin*. Vancouver: University of British Columbia Press.

Qiang Yu 强昱, trans. 1997. *Bai lun* 百論 (Hundred Treatise). Gaoxiong: Foguangshan zong wuweiyuanhui yinhang.

Radich, Michael. 2011. *How Ajātaśatru Was Reformed: The Domesticaiton of "Ajase" and Stories in Buddhist History*. Tokyo: International Institute for Buddhist Studies.

Ramanan, K. Venkata. 1966. *Nāgārjuna's Philosophy as Presented in the Mahā-Prajñāpāramitā-Śāstra*. Rutland, Vt.: Charles E. Tuttle Company.

Ray, Reginald. 1994. *Buddhist Saints in India*. Oxford: Oxford University Press.

———. 1997. "Nāgārjuna's Longevity." In *Sacred Biography in the Buddhist Traditions of South and Southeast Asia*, ed. Juliane Schober, 129–159. Honolulu: University of Hawai'i Press.

Raz, Gil. 2012. *The Emergence of Daoism: Creation of Tradition*. London: Routledge.

Reis-Habito, Maria. 1994. "The Great Compassion *Dhāraṇī*." In *The Esoteric Buddhist Tradition*, ed. Henrik H. Sørensen, 31–49. Copenhagen: Seminar for Buddhist Studies.

Ren Jie 任杰, trans. (from Tibetan). 2002. *Sibai lun shi* 四百論釋 (Commentary on the *Four Hundred Treatise*). Hong Kong: Zhongguo fojiao wenhua chuban youxian gongsi.

Richard, Timothy, trans. (1894) 1918. *The Awakening of Faith in the Mahayana Doctrine: The New Buddhism*. Shanghai: Methodist Publishing House.

Robinson, Richard H., trans. 1954. *Chinese Buddhist Verse*. London: John Murray.

———. 1967. *Early Mādhyamika in India and China.* Madison: University of Wisconsin Press.

Ruegg, David S. 1981. *The Literature of the Madhyamaka School of Philosophy in India.* Wiesbaden, Germany: O. Harrassowitz.

Salguero, C. Pierce. 2009. "The Buddhist Medicine King in Literary Context: Reconsidering an Early Medieval Example of Indian Influence on Chinese Medicine and Surgery." *History of Religions* 48 (3): 183–210.

Salomon, Richard. 1999. "Aśvaghoṣa in Central Asia: Some Comments on the Recensional History of His Works in Light of Recent Manuscript Discoveries." In *Collection of Essays 1993: Buddhism across Boundaries—Chinese Buddhism and the Western Regions,* ed. Erik Zürcher and Lore Sander, 219–263. Sanchung, Taiwan: Foguang Shan Foundation for Buddhist and Culture Education.

Sastri, P. S. 1955. "Nāgārjuna and Āryadeva." *Indian Historical Quarterly* 31 (3): 193–202.

Satō Tetsuei 佐藤哲英. (1961) 2005. *Tendai Daishi no kenkyū: Chigi o no chosaku ni kansuru kisoteki kenkyū* 天台大師の研究: 智顗の著作に關する基礎的研究 (Studies of the Great Tiantai Master: Preliminary Research into the Writings of Zhiyi), Chinese trans. Shi Yiguan 釋依觀. Taipei: Zhonghua fojiao wenxian bianzhuanshe.

Saunders, Rebecca, ed. 2003. *The Concept of the Foreign: An Interdisciplinary Dialogue.* Lanham, Md.: Lexington Books.

Schipper, Kristofer. 1995. "An Outline of Daoist Ritual." In *Essais sur le rituel,* ed. Anne-Marie Blondeau and Kristofer Schipper, 97–126. Leuven, Belgium, and Paris: Peeters.

Schober, Juliane, ed. 1997. *Sacred Biography in the Buddhist Traditions of South and Southeast Asia.* Honolulu: University of Hawai'i Press.

Seidel, Anna. 1969–1970. "The Image of the Perfect Ruler in Early Taoist Messianism: Lao-tzu and Li Hung." *History of Religions* 9: 216–247.

———. 1987. "Post-mortem Immortality; or, the Taoist Resurrection of the Body." In *Gilgul: Essays on Transformation, Revolution, and Permanence in the History of Religions,* ed. S. Shaked, D. Shulman, and G. G. Stroumsa, 223–237. Leiden: E. J. Brill.

Sen, Tansen. 2003. *Buddhism, Diplomacy, and Trade: The Realignment of Sino-Indian Relations, 600–1400.* Honolulu: University of Hawai'i Press.

Seok, Gilam. 2010. "*Daijō kishin ron* no Jironshū senjutsu setsu ni tai suru iken" 『大乗起信論』の地論宗撰述説に対する異見 (An Objection to the Argument that the *Mahāyāna Awakening of Faith* Was Composed within the Dilun School). In *Jiron shisō no keisei to henyō* 地論思想の形成と変容 (The Formation and Transformation of Dilun Thought), ed. Kongō Daigakkō Bukkyō Bunka Kenkyūjo 金剛大学校仏教文化研究所, 247–267. Tokyo: Kokusho Kankōkai.

Shahar, Meir, and Robert P. Weller, eds. 1996. *Unruly Gods: Divinity and Society in China.* Honolulu: University of Hawai'i Press.

Shanhui 善慧. 1979. "Longshu longgong qujing kao" 龍樹龍宮取經考 (A Study of Nāgārjuna Obtaining Scriptures from the Dragon Palace). In *Xiandai fojiao xueshu congkan* 現代佛教學術叢刊 (Modern Buddhism Research Series), ed. Zhang Mantao 張曼濤, 100: 135–142. Taipei: Dasheng wenhua chubanshe yinxing.

Sharf, Robert H. 1992. "The Idolization of Enlightenment: On the Mummification of Ch'an Masters in Medieval China." *History of Religions* 32: 1–31.

———. 2001. "Introduction." In *Living Images: Japanese Buddhist Icons in Context*, ed. Robert H. Sharf and Elizabeth Horton Sharf, 1–18. Stanford, Calif.: Stanford University Press.

———. 2002. *Coming to Terms with Chinese Buddhism: A Reading of the "Treasure Store Treatise."* Honolulu: University of Hawai'i Press.

Shih Heng-ching, trans. 1994. *The Sutra on Upāsaka Precepts*. Berkeley, Calif.: Numata Center for Buddhist Translation and Research.

Shih Jen Lang. 2002. "The Perpetuity of the Dharma: A Study and Translation of *Da Aluohan Nantimiduoluo Suoshuo Fazhu Ji* 大阿"羅漢難提蜜多羅所說法住記 (A Record of the Perpetuity of the Dharma, Narrated by the Great Arhat Nandimitra, *Nandimitrāvadāna*). Ph.D. diss., University of California, Berkeley.

Shih, Robert. 1981. "The Preface to the *Ta Chih Tu Lun*." In *Zhongyang yanjiu yuan guoji Hanxue huiyi lunwen ji* 中央研究院國際漢學會議論文集 (Proceedings of the Academia Sinica International Conference on Han Studies), 4: 735–750. Taipei: Zhongyang yanjiuyuan.

Shimizu Ryōshō 清水亮昇. 1937. "Sanshin Memyō bosatsu narabini sono kigen ni tsuite" 蠶神馬鳴菩薩並にその起原について (On the Origins of the Silkworm God Aśvaghoṣa Bodhisattva). *Mikkyō ronsō* 密教論叢 (Journal of Buddhist Esoteric Teachings) 11: 73–86.

Shinohara, Koichi. 1988. "Two Sources of Chinese Buddhist Biographies: Stupa Inscriptions and Miracle Stories." In *Monks and Magicians: Religious Biographies in Asia*, ed. Phylis Granoff and Koichi Shinohara, 119–228. Oakville, Ontario: Mosaic Press.

———. 1992. "Guanding's Biography of Zhiyi, the Fourth Chinese Patriarch of the Tiantai Tradition." In *Speaking of Monks: Religious Biography in India and China*, ed. Phyllis Granoff and Koichi Shinohara, 97–218. Oakville, Ontario: Mosaic Press.

———. 1994. "Biographies of Eminent Monks in a Comparative Perspective: The Function of the Holy in Medieval Chinese Buddhism." *Zhonghua foxue xuebao* 中華佛學學報 (Chung-Hwa Buddhist Journal) 7: 479–498.

Sivin, Nathan. 1978. "On the Word 'Taoist' as a Source of Perplexity." *History of Religions* 17: 303–330.

Smith, Jonathan Z. 2004. *Relating Religion: Essays in the Study of Religion*. Chicago: University of Chicago Press.

Snellgrove, David L. 1987. "Celestial Buddhas and Bodhisattvas." In *Encyclopedia of Religion*, ed. M. Eliade, 3: 133–144. New York: MacMillan and Free Press.

Sofukawa Hiroshi 曽布川寛. 1992. "Tangdai Longmen shiku zaoxiang de yanjiu (xiapian)" 唐代龍門石窟造像的研究 (下篇) (A Study of the Construction of Images at the Longmen Caves in the Tang Period [Part Two]), trans. Yan Juanying 顏娟英. *Yishuxue* 藝術學 (Art Studies) 8: 99–166.

Sōgen Yamakami. 1912. *Systems of Buddhistic Thought*. Calcutta: Calcutta University Press.

Sowa Yoshihiro 曽和義宏. 2006. "Dainembutsuji zō, Kazai *Jōdo ron* ni tsuite" 大念佛寺蔵、迦才『浄土論』について (On Jiacai's *Jingtu lun* in the Dainembutsuji Canon).

Indōgaku bukkyōgaku kenkyū 印度學佛教學研究 (Journal of Indian and Buddhist Studies) 55 (1): 101–105.
Stcherbatsky, Theodore. 1923. *The Central Conception of Buddhism.* London: Royal Asiatic Society.
Sterckx, Roel. 2002. *The Animal and the Daemon in Early China.* Albany: State University of New York Press.
Strickmann, Michel. 1979. "On the Alchemy of T'ao Hung-ching." In *Facets of Taoism: Essays in Chinese Religion,* ed. Holmes Welch and Anna Seidel, 123–192. New Haven, Conn.: Yale University Press.
———. 1990. "The *Consecration Sūtra*: A Buddhist Book of Spells." In *Chinese Buddhist Apocrypha,* ed. Robert E. Buswell, Jr., 75–118. Honolulu: University of Hawai'i Press.
———. 1996. *Mantras et mandarins: Le bouddhisme tantrique en Chine.* Paris: Gallimard.
———. 2002. *Chinese Magical Medicine.* Stanford, Calif.: Stanford University Press.
Strong, John S. 1979. "The Legend of the Lion-Roarer: A Study of the Buddhist Arhat Piṇḍola Bhāradvāja." *Numen* 26 (1): 50–88.
———. 1983. *The Legend of King Aśoka: A Study and Translation of the Aśokavadāna.* Princeton, N.J.: Princeton University Press.
Suwa Gijun 諏訪義純. 1988. *Chūgoku chūsei bukkyōshi kenkyū* 中国中世仏教史研究 (Studies in the History of Medieval Chinese Buddhism). Tokyo: Daitō Shuppansha.
Suzhou Shi Wenguan Hui 蘇州市文官會 and Suzhou Bowuguan 蘇州博物館. 1979. "Suzhou shi Ruiguangsi ta faxian yipi Wudai Bei Song wenwu" 蘇州市瑞光寺塔發現一批五代北宋文物 (Five Dynasties and Northern Song Cultural Relics Discovered in the Pagoda of Ruiguang Monastery, Suzhou City). *Wenwu* 文物 (Cultural Relics) 11: 21–31.
Suzuki Daisetz Teitaro, trans. 1900. *Açvaghosha's Discourse on the Awakening of Faith in the Mahāyāna.* Chicago: Open Court Publishing Co.
———, trans. 1932. *The Laṅkāvatāra Sūtra: A Mahāyāna Text.* London: G. Routledge and Sons.
Swanson, Paul L. 1989. *Foundations of T'ien-T'ai Philosophy: The Flowering of the Two-Truth Theory in Chinese Buddhism.* Berkeley, Calif.: Asian Humanities Press.
Swearer, Donald K. 2004. *Becoming the Buddha: The Ritual of Image Consecration in Thailand.* Princeton, N.J.: Princeton University Press.
Tambiah, Stanley Jeyaraja. 1984. *The Buddhist Saints of the Forest and the Cult of Amulets: A Study in Charisma, Hagiography, Sectarianism, and Millennial Buddhism.* New York: Cambridge University Press.
Tanaka, Kenneth K. 1990. *The Dawn of Chinese Pure Land Buddhist Doctrine: Ching-ying Hui-yüan's Commentary on the "Visualization Sutra."* Albany: State University of New York Press.
Tanaka Ryōshō 田中良昭. 1962. "*Fu hōzō innen den* to Zen no dentō—Tonkō shiryō sūshu o chūshin to shite" 付法藏因縁伝と禅の伝灯—敦煌資料数種を中心として (The *Fu fazang yinyuan zhuan* and Zen Transmission of the Lamp—Focusing on Various Dunhuang Materials). *Indogaku bukkyōgaku kenkyū* 印度學佛教學研究 (Journal of Indian and Buddhist Studies) 10 (1): 243–246.

———. 1981a. "*Fu hōzō innen den* no seiten sotō setsu" 付法藏因縁伝の西天祖統説 (The Indian Patriarchate of the *Fu fazang yinyuan zhuan*). *Shūgaku kenkyū* 宗学研究 (Journal of Sect Studies) 23: 182–188.

———. 1981b. "*Fu hōzō innen den* to sono hatten—P ni nana nana roku shahon to sono ihon" 付法藏因縁伝とその発展—P二七七六写本とその異本 (The Development of the *Fu fazang yinyuan zhuan*—The Manuscript P2776 and Other Editions). *Komazawa daigaku bukkyō gakubu kenkyū kiyō* 駒沢大学仏教学部研究紀要 (Research Journal of the Buddhist Studies Department of Komazawa University) 39: 67–90.

———. 1983. *Tonkō Zenshū bunken no kenkyū* 敦煌禅宗文献の研究 (A Study of Dunhuang Zen Manuscripts). Tokyo: Daitō Shuppansha.

———. 2003. *Hōrinden yakuchū* 寶林傳訳注 (Annotated Translation of the *Baolin zhuan*). Tokyo: Naiyama shoten.

Tang Yiming. 1991. "The Voices of Wei-Jin Scholars: A Study of 'Qingtan.'" Ph.D. diss., Columbia University.

Tang Yongtong 湯用彤. 1938. *Han Wei Liangjin Nanbeichao Fojiao shi* 漢魏兩晉南北朝佛教史 (History of Buddhism in the Han, Wei, Two Jins, and Northern and Southern Dynasties). Shanghai: Commercial Press.

Tarocco, Francesca. 2008. "Lost in Translation? The *Treatise on the Mahāyāna Awakening of Faith* (*Dasheng qixin lun*) and Its Modern Readings." *Bulletin of the School of Oriental and African Studies* 71 (2): 323–343.

Taussig, Michael. 1993. *Mimesis and Alterity: A Particular History of the Senses.* New York: Routledge.

Teiser, Stephen. 1988. *The Ghost Festival in Medieval China.* Princeton, N.J.: Princeton University Press.

———. 1994. *The Scripture on the Ten Kings and the Making of Purgatory in Medieval Chinese Buddhism.* Honolulu: University of Hawai'i Press.

———. 2004. "Prayers for the Dead: A Preliminary Definition of a Liturgical Genre from Dunhuang." Paper presented at the conference "Hagiography and Zen Poetry: An International Conference on Chinese Literature and Religion." Academia Sinica, Taipei.

Thurman, Robert A. F., trans. 1976. *The Holy Teaching of Vimalakīrti: A Mahāyāna Scripture.* University Park: Pennsylvania State Universtity Press.

Tokiwa Daijō 常盤大定. 1905. *Memyō bosatsu ron: Kyōkai bungō* 馬鳴菩薩論: 教界文豪 (The Writings of Aśvaghoṣa Bodhisattva). Tokyo: Kinkōdō shoseki kabushiki gaisha.

———. 1943–1944. *Shina Bukkyō no kenkyū* 支那佛教の研究 (Studies in Chinese Buddhism). 3 vols. Tokyo: Shunjūsha Shōhakukan.

Tokuno Kyoko. 1990. "The Evaluation of Indigenous Scriptures in Chinese Buddhist Bibliographical Catalogues." In *Chinese Buddhist Apocrypha,* ed. Robert E. Buswell, Jr., 31–74. Honolulu: University of Hawai'i Press.

Tomomatsu Entai. 1931. "Sūtrālaṃkāra et Kalpanāmaṇḍitikā." *Journal Asiatique* 219: 135–174.

Tsukamoto Zenryū 塚本善隆. (1942) 1957. "The Śramaṇa Superintendent T'an-yao 曇曜 and His Times." Trans. Galen Eugene Sargent. *Monumenta Serica* 16: 363–96.

Tucci, Guiseppe, trans. 1926. "Un traité d'Āryadeva sur le 'Nirvāṇa' des hérétiques." *T'oung Pao* 24: 16–31.

———, trans. (1929) 1976. *Pre-Dinnaga Buddhist Texts on Logic from Chinese Sources.* Baroda, India: Oriental Institute.

———. 1930. "A Sanskrit Biography of the Siddhas and Some Questions Connected with Nāgārjuna." *Journal and Proceedings of the Asiatic Society of Bengal* 26: 138–155.

Tucker, John Allen. 1984. "Nāgārjuna's Influence on Early *Hua-yen* and *Ch'an* Thought." *Chinese Culture* 25 (2): 43–61.

Twitchett, Denis. 1961. "Chinese Biographical Writing." In *Historians of China and Japan*, ed. W. G. Beasley and E. G. Pulleyblank, 95–114. London: Oxford University Press.

———. 1962. "Problems of Chinese Biography." In *Confucian Personalities*, ed. Arthur F. Wright and Denis Twitchett. Stanford, Calif.: Stanford University Press.

———. 1970. *Financial Administration under the T'ang Dynasty.* London: Cambridge University Press.

Vaidya, P. L. 1923. *Études sur Āryadeva et son Catuḥśataka* (A Study of Āryadeva and His Catuḥśataka). Paris: Geuthner.

van Gulik, R. H. 1935. *Hayagrīva: The Mantrayānic Aspect of Horse-Cult in China and Japan.* Leiden: E. J. Brill.

Vasilief. 1875. "Biographies of Aśvaghoṣa, Nāgārjuna, Āryadeva, Vasubandhu." Trans. (from Russian) E. Lyall. *Indian Antiquary* 4: 141–144.

Verellen, Franciscus. 2004. "The Heavenly Master Liturgical Agenda According to Chisong Zi's Petition Almanac." *Cahiers d'Extrême-Asie* 14: 291–343.

Vervoorn, Aat. 1990. *Men of the Cliffs and Caves: The Development of the Chinese Eremitic Tradition to the End of the Han Dynasty.* Hong Kong: Chinese University Press.

Vorenkamp, Dirck, trans. 2004. *An English Translation of Fa-Tsang's Commentary on the Awakening of Faith.* Lewiston, N.Y.: Edwin Mellen Press.

Walleser, M. (1923) 1979. *The Life of Nāgārjuna from Tibetan and Chinese Sources.* Delhi: Nag Publishers.

Walser, Joseph. 2002. "Nāgārjuna and the *Ratnāvalī*: New Ways to Date an Old Philosopher." *JIABS* 25 (1–2): 209–262.

———. 2005. *Nāgārjuna in Context: Mahāyāna Buddhism and Early Indian Culture.* New York: Columbia University Press.

Walsh, Michael J. 2010. *Sacred Economies: Buddhist Monasticism and Territoriality in Medieval China.* New York: Columbia University Press.

Wang Bangwei. 1994. "Buddhist Nikāyas through Ancient Chinese Eyes." In *Sanskrit-Wörterbuch der buddhistischen Texte aus den Turfan-Funden*, ed. Heinz Bechert, 165–203. Göttingen, Germany: Vandenhoeck and Ruprecht.

———. 1997. "The Indian Origin of the Chinese Buddhist Chan School's Patriarch Tradition." In *Dharmaduta: Mélanges offerts au Vénérable Thich Huyên-Vi à l'óccasion de son soixante-dixième anniversaire* (Festschrift for Venerable Thich Huyên-Vi on the Occasion of His Seventieth Birthday), ed. Bhikkhu Tampalawela Dhammaratna and Bhikkhu Pāsādika, 261–270. Paris: Editions You-Feng.

Wang Shaoying 汪紹楹, ed. 1979. *Soushen ji Wang Shaoying jiaozhu* 搜神記汪紹楹校注 (*Record of the Search for the Supernormal*, Wang Shaoying Edited Edition). Beijing: Zhonghua shuju.

Watson, Burton, trans. 1968. *The Complete Works of Chuang Tzu*. New York: Columbia University Press.

———, trans. 1969. *Records of the Historian: Chapters from the Shih Chi of Ssu-ma Ch'ien*. New York: Columbia University Press.

———, trans. 1997. *The Vimalakīrti Sūtra*. New York: Columbia University Press.

Wedemeyer, Christian. 2007. *Āryadeva's Lamp that Integrates the Practices (Caryāmelāpakapradīpa): The Gradual Path of Vajrayāna Buddhism According to the Esoteric Community Noble Tradition*. New York: American Institute of Buddhist Studies at Columbia University.

Weinstein, Stanley. 1987. *Buddhism under the T'ang*. Cambridge: Cambridge University Press.

Westerhoff, Jan. 2009. *Nāgārjuna's Madhyamaka: A Philosophical Introduction*. Oxford: Oxford University Press.

White, David Gordon. 1996. *The Alchemical Body: Siddhi Traditions in Medieval India*. Chicago: University of Chicago Press.

Wilkinson, Endymion. 2000. *Chinese History: A Manual*, Rev. ed. Cambridge, Mass.: Harvard University Press.

Willemen, Charles, trans. 1994. *The Storehouse of Sundry Valuables*. Berkeley, Calif.: Numata Center for Buddhist Translation and Research.

Williams, Bruce C. 2005. "Seeing through Images: Reconstructing Buddhist Meditative Visualization Practice in Sixth-Century Northeastern China." *Pacific World*, 3rd series, 7: 33–89.

Williams, Michael A, ed. 1982. *Charisma and Sacred Biography*. Chambersburg, Pa.: American Academy of Religion.

Wright, Arthur F. (1948) 1990. "Fo-t'u-teng: A Biography." In *Studies in Chinese Buddhism*, ed. Robert M. Somers, 34–68. New Haven, Conn.: Yale University Press.

———. (1954) 1990. "Biography and Hagiography: Hui-chiao's *Lives of Eminent Monks*." In *Studies in Chinese Buddhism*, ed. Robert M. Somers, 73–111. New Haven, Conn.: Yale University Press.

———. 1957a. "The Formation of Sui Ideology." In *Chinese Thought and Institutions*, ed. John Fairbank, 71–104. Chicago: University of Chicago Press.

———. 1957b. "Seng-jui Alias Hui-jui: A Biographical Bisection in the Kao-Seng Chuan." In *Liebenthal Festschrift*, ed. Kshitis Roy, 272–294. West Bengal: Santiniketan.

Wu Yankang. 2006. "Yang Renshan and the Jinling Buddhist Press." *East Asian Library Journal* 12 (2): 49–98.

Xiao Dengfu 蕭登福. 1994. *Daojiao shuyi yu mijiao dianji* 道教術儀與密教典籍 (Daoist Rites and Esoteric Buddhist Texts). Taipei: Xinwenfeng chuban gongsi.

Xiong, Victor Cunrui. 2006. *Emperor Yang of the Sui Dynasty: His Life, Times, and Legacy*. Albany: State University of New York Press.

Yagi Sentei 八木宣諦. 1979. "Memyōji Konhōshi hi ni tsuite" 馬鳴寺根法師碑について (On the Memorial Tablet of Dharma-Master Gen of the Aśvaghoṣa Temple). In *Bukkyō ronsō* 佛教論叢 (Journal of Buddhist Studies) 23: 124–38.

Yamabe, Nobuyoshi. 1999. "The *Sūtra on the Ocean-Like Samādhi of the Visualization of the Buddha*: The Interfusion of the Chinese and Indian Cultures in Central Asia as Reflected in a Fifth Century Apocryphal Sūtra." Ph.D. diss., Yale University.

———. 2003. "On the School Affiliation of Aśvaghoṣa: 'Sautrāntika' or 'Yogācāra'?" *JIABS* 26 (2): 225–254.

———. 2005. "Visionary Repentance and Visionary Ordination in the *Brahmā Net Sūtra*." In *Going Forth: Visions of Buddhist Vinaya*, edited by William M. Bodiford, 17–39. Honolulu: University of Hawai'i Press.

Yamabe, Nobuyoshi, and Fumihiko Sueki, trans. 2009. *The Sutra on the Concentration of Sitting Meditation*. Berkeley, Calif.: Numata Center for Buddhist Translation and Research.

Yamano Chieko 山野智恵. 2009. "Shoki no Ryūju den" 初期の龍樹伝 (The Earliest Biographies of Nāgārjuna). *Rengeji Bukkyō kenkyūsho kiyō* 蓮花寺佛教研究所紀要 (Journal of the Rengeji Institute of Buddhist Studies) 2: 59–109.

———. 2010. "*Ryūju bosatsu den* no seiritsu mondai" 龍樹菩薩伝の成立問題 (On the Development of the *Tradition of Nāgārjuna Bodhisattva*). *Sengokuyama Bukkyōgaku ronshū* 仙石山仏教学論集 (Sengokuyama Journal of Buddhist Studies) 5: 49–70.

———. 2011. "Nāgārjuna to ijyutsu—*Ryūju ganron* no seiritsu to tenkai" ナーガールジュナと医術 – 『龍樹眼論』の成立と展開 (Nāgārjuna's *Discourse on Opthalmopathy*: Its Origin and Development). *Rengeji Bukkyō kenkyūsho kiyō* 蓮花寺佛教研究所紀要 (Journal of the Rengeji Institute of Buddhist Studies) 4: 20–44.

Yampolsky, Philip. 1967. *The Platform Sutra of the Sixth Patriarch*. New York: Columbia University Press.

Yanagida Seizan 柳田聖山, ed. 1983. *Sōzō ichin: Hōrinden, Dentō gyokuei shū* 宋藏遺珍: 寶林傳, 傳燈玉英集 (The *Tradition of the Baolin* [*Temple*] and the *Collection of Jade Heroes Who Transmitted the Lamp* of the Yizhen Song [-Dynasty Chinese Buddhist] Canon). Kyoto: Chūbun shuppansha.

Yang Jialuo 楊家駱, ed. 1962. *Xinjiao Soushen ji* 新校搜神記 (Newly Revised *Record of the Search for the Supernormal*). Taipei: Shijie shuju.

Yin Wei 殷偉 and Yin Feiran 殷斐然. 2002. *Zhongguo minjian sushen* 中國民間俗神 (Popular Chinese Gods). Kunming, China: Yunnan renmin chubanshe.

Young, Stuart H., trans. 2002. "Biography of the Bodhisattva Aśvaghoṣa." National Taiwan University, Digital Buddhist Library and Museum. Accessed April 21, 2014. http://ccbs.ntu.edu.tw/FULLTEXT/JR-AN/103180.htm.

———. 2013. "For a Compassionate Killing: Chinese Buddhism, Sericulture, and the Silkworm God Aśvaghoṣa." *Journal of Chinese Religions* 41 (1): 25–58. http://www.maneyonline.com/loi/jcr.

Yu, Anthony C. 2005. *State and Religion in China: Historical and Textual Perspectives*. Chicago: Open Court.

Yü, Chün-Fang. 2001. *Kuan-yin: The Chinese Transformation of Avalokiteśvara*. New York: Columbia University Press.

Zürcher, Erik. (1959) 2007. *The Buddhist Conquest of China: The Spread and Adaptation of Buddhism in Early Medieval China*. Leiden: E. J. Brill.

———. 1968. "The Yuezhi and Kaniṣka in Chinese Sources." In *Papers on the Date of Kaniṣka: Submitted to the Conference on the Date of Kaniṣka, London, 20–22 April, 1960*, ed. A. L. Basham, 346–390. Australian National University Centre of Oriental Studies, Oriental Monograph Series 4. Leiden: E. J. Brill.

———. 1982. "Prince Moonlight: Messianism and Eschatology in Early Chinese Buddhism." *T'oung Pao* 68 (1–3): 1–75.

Index

Page numbers in **boldface** type refer to illustrations.

Kuroda Institute
Studies in East Asian Buddhism

Studies in Ch'an and Hua-yen
Robert M. Gimello and Peter N. Gregory, editors

Dōgen Studies
William R. LaFleur, editor

The Northern School and the Formation of Early Ch'an Buddhism
John R. McRae

Traditions of Meditation in Chinese Buddhism
Peter N. Gregory, editor

Sudden and Gradual: Approaches to Enlightenment in Chinese Thought
Peter N. Gregory, editor

Buddhist Hermeneutics
Donald S. Lopez, Jr., editor

Paths to Liberation: The Margā and Its Transformations in Buddhist Thought
Robert E. Buswell, Jr., and Robert M. Gimello, editors

Sōtō Zen in Medieval Japan
William M. Bodiford

The Scripture on the Ten Kings and the Making of Purgatory in Medieval Chinese Buddhism
Stephen F. Teiser

The Eminent Monk: Buddhist Ideals in Medieval Chinese Hagiography
John Kieschnick

Re-Visioning "Kamakura" Buddhism
Richard K. Payne, editor

Original Enlightenment and the Transformation of Medieval Japanese Buddhism
Jacqueline I. Stone

Buddhism in the Sung
Peter N. Gregory and Daniel A. Getz, Jr., editors

Coming to Terms with Chinese Buddhism: A Reading of The Treasure Store Treatise
Robert H. Sharf

Ryōgen and Mount Hiei: Japanese Tendai in the Tenth Century
Paul Groner

Tsung-mi and the Sinification of Buddhism
Peter N. Gregory

Approaching the Land of Bliss: Religious Praxis in the Cult of Amitābha
Richard K. Payne and Kenneth K. Tanaka, editors

Going Forth: Visions of Buddhist Vinaya
William M. Bodiford, editor

Burning for the Buddha: Self-Immolation in Chinese Buddhism
James A. Benn

The Buddhist Dead: Practices, Discourses, Representations
Bryan J. Cuevas and Jacqueline I. Stone, editors

The Making of a Savior Bodhisattva: Dizang in Medieval China
Zhiru

How Zen Became Zen: The Dispute over Enlightenment and the Formation of Chan Buddhism in Song-Dynasty China
Morten Schlütter

Hokkeji and the Reemergence of Female Monasticism in Premodern Japan
Lori Meeks

Conceiving the Indian Buddhist Patriarchs in China
Stuart H. Young

About the Author

Stuart H. Young (Ph.D., Princeton University) is assistant professor of East Asian religions in the Department of Religious Studies at Bucknell University.

Production Notes for Young | *Conceiving the Indian Buddhist Patriarchs in China*

Jacket design by Wanda China

Display type and text type
in New Baskerville Hawn TT

Composition by Westchester Publishing Services

Printing and binding by Sheridan Books, Inc.

Printed on 60 lb. House White, 444 ppi.